Digital Transformation, Sustainability, and Ethical Globalization in Halal Ecosystems

Ahmad Rafiki
https://orcid.org/0000-0002-6360-8131
Universitas Medan Area, Indonesia

Hidayatul Ihsan
Politeknik Negeri Padang, Indonesia

Azman Ab Rahman
Universiti Sains Islam Malaysia, Malaysia

IGI Global
Scientific Publishing
Publishing Tomorrow's Research Today

Published in the United States of America by
IGI Global Scientific Publishing
701 East Chocolate Avenue
Hershey, PA, 17033, USA
Tel: 717-533-8845 | Fax: 717-533-7115
Website: https://www.igi-global.com E-mail: cust@igi-global.com

Library of Congress Cataloging-in-Publication Data

Names: Rafiki, Ahmad, 1981- editor | Ihsan, Hidayatul, 1977- editor | Azman Ab. Rahman editor
Title: Digital transformation, sustainability, and ethical globalization in halal ecosystems / [edited by] Ahmad Rafiki, Hidayatul Ihsan, Azman ab Rahman.
Description: Hershey, PA : IGI Global Scientific Publishing, [2027] | Includes bibliographical references and index. | Summary: "This book aims to contribute both the practical solutions and knowledge production in Muslim countries by adopting Islamic approaches to contemporary socio-economic"-- Provided by publisher.
Identifiers: LCCN 2025021028 (print) | LCCN 2025021029 (ebook) | ISBN 9798337327921 hardcover | ISBN 9798337327938 paperback | ISBN 9798337327945 ebook
Subjects: LCSH: Halal food industry--Environmental aspects
Classification: LCC HD9334.A2 E36 2026 (print) | LCC HD9334.A2 (ebook) | DDC 381/.41091767--dc23/eng/20250724
LC record available at https://lccn.loc.gov/2025021028
LC ebook record available at https://lccn.loc.gov/2025021029

British Cataloguing in Publication Data
A Cataloguing in Publication record for this book is available from the British Library.

Table of Contents

Preface... xvi

Chapter 1
Digital Transformation in the Halal Industry: Enhancing Integrity, Efficiency, and Reach... 1
Yuslina binti Yusoff, Universiti Teknologi MARA, Malaysia
Zuhaira Muhammad Zain, Princess Nourah University, Saudi Arabia
Syarifah Bahiyah Rahayu Syed Mansoor, National Defence University of Malaysia, Malaysia
Hafizah Mat Nawi, National Defence University of Malaysia, Malaysia
Nur Shaliza Sapiai, Universiti Teknologi MARA, Malaysia
Norazmila Yusuf, Universiti Teknologi MARA, Malaysia

Chapter 2
Halal Information Systems: Bridging Islamic and Western Theories 35
Norlaila Mazura Hj. Mohaiyadin, National Defence University of Malaysia, Malaysia
Hafizah Mat Nawi, National Defence University of Malaysia, Malaysia
Hasan Al-Banna Mohamed, National Defence University of Malaysia, Malaysia
Khairnunnisa Mardzuki, National Defence University of Malaysia, Malaysia
Mohd Abdullah Jusoh, National Defence University of Malaysia, Malaysia

Chapter 3
Analysis of Halal Policy Based on Sustainability Principles to Realize Green Halal in Indonesia 65
Zulfia Hanum Alfi Syahr, National Research and Innovation Agency, Indonesia
Buyamin Buyamin, National Research and Innovation Agency, Indonesia
Dian Hafit Syaifullah, National Research and Innovation Agency, Indonesia
Zaenal Abidin, National Research and Innovation Agency, Indonesia
Nurhuda Firmansyah, National Research and Innovation Agency, Indonesia

Chapter 4
Eco-Innovation by Islamic Boarding Schools (Pesantren) to Enhance the Sustainable Halal Industry Evidence From Indonesia 89
Ridan Muhtadi, IAI Miftahul Ulum Pamekasan, Indonesia & Kiai Haji Achmad Siddiq State Islamic University, Indonesia
Zaenol Hasan, Kiai Haji Achmad Siddiq State Islamic University, Indonesia & STIS Nurul Qarnain, Indonesia
Halili Halili, Kiai Haji Achmad Siddiq State Islamic University, Indonesia & STIS Nurul Qarnain, Indonesia
Khairunnisa Musari, Kiai Haji Achmad Siddiq State Islamic University, Indonesia

Chapter 5
Halal Business and Food Waste: Examining Factors and Consumer Intentions in Brunei Darussalam 127
Zahidah Borhan, Universiti Brunei Darussalam, Brunei
Mohamed Syazwan Ab Talib, Universiti Brunei Darussalam, Brunei

Chapter 6
Halal Entrepreneurship a Catalyst for Sustainable and Ethical Global Business Ecosystem 151
Sevdie Alshiqi, University of Prishtina, Kosovo
Shujahat Ali, University of Kotli AJK, Pakistan
Wajahat Ali Ghulam, University of Science and Technology of China, China

Chapter 7
Halal Entrepreneurship Beyond Compliance 177
Jisu Kim, Institute for Mediterranean Studies, Busan University of Foreign Studies, South Korea

Chapter 8
Halal Innovation in Sustainable Nutrition: Shariah-Compliant Insect Protein as a Future Food Source 193
Nazariyah Yahaya, Universiti Sains Islam Malaysia, Malaysia
Mohd Mahyeddin Mohd Salleh, Institute of Fatwa and Halal (IFFAH), Malaysia
Syamila Mansor, Independent Researcher, Malaysia
Syaza Azhari, Independent Researcher, Malaysia
A'wani Aziz Nurdalila, Institut Fatwa dan Halal (IFFAH), Malaysia
Hussein 'Azeemi Abdullah Thaidi, Independent Researcher, Malaysia

Chapter 9
A Shariah-Compliant Marketing Control Framework in Halal E-Commerce: A Thematic Analysis of Prophetic Principles 225
Mohd Zohdi Mohd Amin, Universiti Sains Islam Malaysia, Malaysia
Mohd Sobri Ellias, Universiti Sains Islam Malaysia, Malaysia
Ahmad Obeid Jassim Hammadi, University of Anbar, Iraq
Abdulrahman Obeid Hussein, Universiti Sains Islam Malaysia, Malaysia

Chapter 10
How Brand Experience and Emotional Attachment Build Trust, Satisfaction, and Loyalty to Drive Behavioural Intentions in the Halal Fast Food Sector 249
Syed Ahamed Suban, Alliance School of Business, Alliance University, Bangalore, India

Chapter 11
Leveraging AI in Halal Business Customer Relationship Management to Enhance Consumer Loyalty 277
Riza Fanny Meutia, Universitas Medan Area, Indonesia
Andre Hasudungan Lubis, Universitas Medan Area, Indonesia

Chapter 12
Operational Challenges in Maintaining Halal Integrity in Cold Chain Logistics: A Study Based on Practitioner Interviews 321
Mohd Asyran Safwan Kamaruzaman, Universiti Teknologi MARA, Malaysia
Adli Iskandar Md Fauzi, Universiti Teknologi MARA, Malaysia
Mohamad Hasif Jaafar, Universiti Teknologi MARA, Malaysia
Nasif Sidquee Pauzi, Universiti Teknologi MARA, Malaysia

Chapter 13
The Role of Maqasid al-Shari'ah in Influencing Halal Travel Intentions: Evidence From Muslim-Friendly Tourism in Yogyakarta, Indonesia 337
Wahyu Wibowo, Sunan Kalijaga State Islamic University, Yogyakarta, Indonesia
Siti Nur Azizah, Sunan Kalijaga State Islamic University, Yogyakarta, Indonesia

Chapter 14
Halal as a Means of Kalimatun Sawa': A Unifying Element among Religious Communities in Malaysia 369
Nur Farhana Abdul Rahman, National University of Malaysia, Malaysia
Jaffary Awang, National University of Malaysia, Malaysia

Compilation of References 393

About the Contributors 473

Index 481

Detailed Table of Contents

Preface xvi

Chapter 1
Digital Transformation in the Halal Industry: Enhancing Integrity, Efficiency, and Reach 1
Yuslina binti Yusoff, Universiti Teknologi MARA, Malaysia
Zuhaira Muhammad Zain, Princess Nourah University, Saudi Arabia
Syarifah Bahiyah Rahayu Syed Mansoor, National Defence University of Malaysia, Malaysia
Hafizah Mat Nawi, National Defence University of Malaysia, Malaysia
Nur Shaliza Sapiai, Universiti Teknologi MARA, Malaysia
Norazmila Yusuf, Universiti Teknologi MARA, Malaysia

The halal industry has emerged as one of the fastest-growing global markets, expanding beyond food and beverages into pharmaceuticals, cosmetics, tourism, logistics, and finance. This growth is driven by rising Muslim populations, increasing consumer awareness, and global demand for ethical and high-quality products. However, the complexity of halal supply chains presents challenges in maintaining transparency, traceability, and compliance. Digital transformation offers strategic solutions to these challenges by integrating technologies such as blockchain, artificial intelligence (AI), the Internet of Things (IoT), and big data analytics. These innovations strengthen halal assurance through real-time monitoring, fraud prevention, and efficient certification processes, while also supporting e-commerce platforms and digital marketing to expand market reach. Importantly, digitalization aligns with Islamic ethical principles, particularly the Maqasid al-Shariah, by safeguarding faith, health, intellect, lineage, and wealth.

Chapter 2
Halal Information Systems: Bridging Islamic and Western Theories 35
Norlaila Mazura Hj. Mohaiyadin, National Defence University of Malaysia, Malaysia
Hafizah Mat Nawi, National Defence University of Malaysia, Malaysia
Hasan Al-Banna Mohamed, National Defence University of Malaysia, Malaysia
Khairnunnisa Mardzuki, National Defence University of Malaysia, Malaysia
Mohd Abdullah Jusoh, National Defence University of Malaysia, Malaysia

This study aims to develop a conceptual framework regarding the use of the coalescence of Islamic and Western theories in halal information systems. A qualitative method was employed in this study, specifically content analysis from journal articles and other publications, which are considered substantial for developing its conceptual framework. This study anticipates the coalescence of Islamic and Western theories in the halal information systems. From the people's perspective, shariah compliance and Deontological Theory can serve as a bridge between supplier integrity and consumer trust. Shariah compliance may also be aligned with Stakeholder Theory, as it clarifies to stakeholders that shariah governance ensures the accountability of the board of directors and contributes significantly to sustainability performance. In the process perspective, shariah compliance can be bridged with Stakeholder Theory in ensuring fairness, transparency and accountability to all stakeholders. Moreover, Shariah compliance can also be associated with Institutional Theory in the design of the shariah governance framework. From a technological perspective, maslahah can be bridged with the Diffusion of Innovation Theory in terms of maslahah radical halal innovation. Finally, shariah compliance can be bridged with Task Technology Fit Theory in terms of Islamic microfinance. The contribution of this study is directed towards halal industry players, academicians, researchers and students researching the halal information system, and the development of the theory integration between Islam and the West. Future research can be extended to empirical evidence and quantitative research.

Chapter 3
Analysis of Halal Policy Based on Sustainability Principles to Realize Green Halal in Indonesia 65
Zulfia Hanum Alfi Syahr, National Research and Innovation Agency, Indonesia
Buyamin Buyamin, National Research and Innovation Agency, Indonesia
Dian Hafit Syaifullah, National Research and Innovation Agency, Indonesia
Zaenal Abidin, National Research and Innovation Agency, Indonesia
Nurhuda Firmansyah, National Research and Innovation Agency, Indonesia

As a country with a Muslim majority, the Indonesian government has regulations and policies to provide halal product guarantees to the public. However, regulations related to halal products are not only based on Islamic law but also need to follow the principles of the Sustainable Development Goals (SDGs) globally. Therefore, the problem that will be studied in this paper is how to structure halal regulations and policies based on the principles of a sustainable environment in Indonesia. To achieve this, the study will develop a comprehensive policy framework grounded in sustainability principles and environmental stewardship. Based on an analysis of study documents, it was found that in halal regulations, both from the government and nongovernment agencies, no one explicitly explains the importance of implementing environmentally friendly, sustainable principles from manufacturing to production.

Chapter 4
Eco-Innovation by Islamic Boarding Schools (Pesantren) to Enhance the Sustainable Halal Industry Evidence From Indonesia 89
Ridan Muhtadi, IAI Miftahul Ulum Pamekasan, Indonesia & Kiai Haji Achmad Siddiq State Islamic University, Indonesia
Zaenol Hasan, Kiai Haji Achmad Siddiq State Islamic University, Indonesia & STIS Nurul Qarnain, Indonesia
Halili Halili, Kiai Haji Achmad Siddiq State Islamic University, Indonesia & STIS Nurul Qarnain, Indonesia
Khairunnisa Musari, Kiai Haji Achmad Siddiq State Islamic University, Indonesia

This chapter explores the strategic role of Islamic boarding schools (pesantren) in promoting eco-innovation within the halal industry. Focusing on the "One Pesantren One Product" (OPOP) initiative, the chapter highlights how pesantren-based business units integrate environmentally friendly practices to enhance the sustainability of halal production. Drawing on qualitative case studies from East Java Indonesia, the chapter presents a structured analysis across three dimensions: the implementation of eco-innovation by pesantren business units, their contribution to sustainable development, and the challenges and opportunities in embedding sustainability within pesantren-based enterprises. Findings show that pesantren possess inherent local wisdom and organizational capacity to act as agents of green transformation, supporting both the halal value chain and broader sustainable development goals. The chapter offers practical insights and policy recommendations to strengthen eco-friendly practices in Islamic educational institutions and align them with Indonesia's green economy agenda.

Chapter 5
Halal Business and Food Waste: Examining Factors and Consumer Intentions in Brunei Darussalam 127
Zahidah Borhan, Universiti Brunei Darussalam, Brunei
Mohamed Syazwan Ab Talib, Universiti Brunei Darussalam, Brunei

Food waste is a growing environmental and economic concern, particularly within the halal food industry, where ethical consumption and sustainability are key principles. This study examines the factors influencing halal food waste prevention intentions in Brunei, applying the Theory of Planned Behaviour to assess the roles of subjective norms, perceived behavioural control, and attitudes. A survey of 105 respondents, analyzed using correlation and regression, found that attitudes and perceived behavioural control significantly influence food waste prevention, while subjective norms have minimal impact. These findings suggest that effective waste reduction strategies should focus on self-efficacy and positive attitudes. From a halal business perspective, this study highlights the role of Islamic values in promoting sustainability. Insights from this research can guide halal food producers, policymakers, and consumers in developing effective waste management strategies aligned with Brunei's Vision 2035 and the United Nations' Sustainable Development Goals.

Chapter 6
Halal Entrepreneurship a Catalyst for Sustainable and Ethical Global Business Ecosystem 151
Sevdie Alshiqi, University of Prishtina, Kosovo
Shujahat Ali, University of Kotli AJK, Pakistan
Wajahat Ali Ghulam, University of Science and Technology of China, China

Halal entrepreneurship is a business model rooted in Islamic principles, emphasizing ethical, socially responsible, and halal economic practices. Originating from the time of Prophet Muhammad (SAW), it is viewed as an honorable livelihood. The term "Halalpreneur" distinguishes entrepreneurs who offer shariah-compliant products and services from conventional counterparts. Despite its growth, the halal entrepreneurship ecosystem remains underexplored. This chapter conceptualizes halal entrepreneurship and investigates its key ecosystem components. Using a qualitative approach, it combines a structured literature review and global case studies to examine theoretical foundations, ecosystem actors, enabling factors, and sectoral implementation. The findings reveal challenges, research gaps, and offer policy suggestions to foster halal entrepreneurship. This study contributes by integrating theory and practice, offering a framework to guide scholars, practitioners, and policymakers in developing global halal entrepreneurial ecosystems.

Chapter 7
Halal Entrepreneurship Beyond Compliance 177
Jisu Kim, Institute for Mediterranean Studies, Busan University of Foreign Studies, South Korea

The paper utilizes qualitative research and relies much on previous literatures supported by examples of local cases. The research introduces 'theory and case' as a unit and drives conclusion from two cases and conclusively expects to foster subsequent research be expanded in sociological field. Ultimate goal of this research is to introduce conceptualized Halal entrepreneurship within non-Islamic context and examine the substance of Halal entrepreneurship in contemporary perspective. This chapter first provides concise overview of academic history regarding to entrepreneurship and elaborate the concept on Halal industry, discussing Halal entrepreneurship by re-evaluating the concept. Then, it introduces studies of locality which the author intends to integrate Halal studies with. The author claims that research of locality takes significant position in entrepreneurship, distinguishing the concept from entrepreneurial skills. Following part of the paper seeks cases that Halal entrepreneurship contributes in locality context especially in non-Islamic circumstances.

Chapter 8
Halal Innovation in Sustainable Nutrition: Shariah-Compliant Insect Protein as a Future Food Source... 193
Nazariyah Yahaya, Universiti Sains Islam Malaysia, Malaysia
Mohd Mahyeddin Mohd Salleh, Institute of Fatwa and Halal (IFFAH), Malaysia
Syamila Mansor, Independent Researcher, Malaysia
Syaza Azhari, Independent Researcher, Malaysia
A'wani Aziz Nurdalila, Institut Fatwa dan Halal (IFFAH), Malaysia
Hussein 'Azeemi Abdullah Thaidi, Independent Researcher, Malaysia

The chapter explores the potential of insect protein as a sustainable and halal-compliant food source. The aim of this study is to examine Shariah rulings (hukm) and address insect protein processing techniques to ensure food safety and enhance their nutritional value, with the ultimate goal of formulating halal guidelines tailored to insect protein enterprises. This guideline offers significant opportunities for economic growth and food security. In this study, we employ documentation, data analysis, and literature search.

Chapter 9
A Shariah-Compliant Marketing Control Framework in Halal E-Commerce: A Thematic Analysis of Prophetic Principles 225
Mohd Zohdi Mohd Amin, Universiti Sains Islam Malaysia, Malaysia
Mohd Sobri Ellias, Universiti Sains Islam Malaysia, Malaysia
Ahmad Obeid Jassim Hammadi, University of Anbar, Iraq
Abdulrahman Obeid Hussein, Universiti Sains Islam Malaysia, Malaysia

The halal online retail sector is growing rapidly, yet ethical challenges in digital marketing remain unresolved, including fake ads, misleading halal claims, and dishonest pricing that weaken consumer trust. This chapter proposes the Shariah-Compliant Online Marketing Control Framework (KKK-PEMASTI), developed through thematic analysis of prophetic adīths on trade and ethics. It highlights four principles— idq (honesty), amānah (trustworthiness), the prohibition of tadlīs (fraud), and ʿadālah (justice)—to guide pricing, advertising, product information, and customer relations. Findings show that Sunnah-based ethics provide flexible yet prescriptive guidance aligned with maqā id al-sharīʿah, particularly in protecting wealth and life, thereby restoring trust and supporting sustainable growth in the halal ecosystem.

Chapter 10
How Brand Experience and Emotional Attachment Build Trust, Satisfaction, and Loyalty to Drive Behavioural Intentions in the Halal Fast Food Sector 249
Syed Ahamed Suban, Alliance School of Business, Alliance University, Bangalore, India

The study intends to analyse the impact of brand experience on the dimensions of brand love and its subsequent effect on satisfaction, trust, and loyalty through a conceptual model. Moreover, it even investigates the impact of behavioural intention towards halal fast food.The study was conducted among Indian Muslim consumers of halal-certified fast-food chains via online surveys, employing a snowball sampling technique. .The study demonstrates that brand experience fosters significant brand affection by influencing intimacy and passion, highlighting how multisensory and emotionally engaging interactions cultivate profound consumer-brand connections. The two dimensions of brand love serve as crucial links between brand experience and crucial consumer outcomes. The correlation between intimacy and passion enhances customer trust and satisfaction, thereby fostering greater brand loyalty. The model results imply that brand experience influences purchase intention through a sequential relationship involving brand love, trust, satisfaction, and ultimately, loyalty.

Chapter 11
Leveraging AI in Halal Business Customer Relationship Management to Enhance Consumer Loyalty 277
Riza Fanny Meutia, Universitas Medan Area, Indonesia
Andre Hasudungan Lubis, Universitas Medan Area, Indonesia

This chapter investigates the impact of AI-based personalization in Customer Relationship Management (CRM) on consumer loyalty within the halal business sector, addressing the growing reliance on AI-driven marketing while balancing ethical, religious, and trust-related concerns. Despite the increasing adoption of AI in business, limited research has explored its effects in faith-driven markets. Through the Stimulus-Organism-Response framework, integrated with Expectation-Confirmation Theory and the Technology Acceptance Model, we conduct a quantitative approach with 700 respondents to examine how trust, satisfaction, and perceived value mediate AI-driven CRM effects, while religiosity and digital literacy moderate consumer responses. This study aims to provide fresh insights into how businesses can integrate AI-driven CRM strategies while maintaining consumer trust and ethical compliance. The findings are expected to contribute to both academic literature and industry practices, particularly in understanding how AI can enhance customer engagement in value-driven consumer segments.

Chapter 12
Operational Challenges in Maintaining Halal Integrity in Cold Chain Logistics: A Study Based on Practitioner Interviews 321
Mohd Asyran Safwan Kamaruzaman, Universiti Teknologi MARA, Malaysia
Adli Iskandar Md Fauzi, Universiti Teknologi MARA, Malaysia
Mohamad Hasif Jaafar, Universiti Teknologi MARA, Malaysia
Nasif Sidquee Pauzi, Universiti Teknologi MARA, Malaysia

Maintaining halal integrity is becoming more important in cold chain logistics due to increasing global demand for halal-certified products. However, this integrity can be compromised if key operational issues are not properly managed, particularly in handling, temperature control, and storage. This study looks at the challenges faced by Bismi Cergas Sdn Bhd, a logistics company, in keeping its operations halal-compliant. A qualitative method was used, involving semi-structured interviews with four company staff members. The interview data were analyzed using thematic analysis. The results identified several major challenges: unclear halal guidelines, issues with product thawing and refreezing, limited halal awareness among non-Muslim employees, and problems with animals or pests entering the premises. The study highlights that maintaining halal integrity in cold chain logistics depends on having proper standard operating procedures (SOPs), staff awareness, good infrastructure, and clear guidance from halal authorities.

Chapter 13
The Role of Maqasid al-Shari'ah in Influencing Halal Travel Intentions: Evidence From Muslim-Friendly Tourism in Yogyakarta, Indonesia 337
Wahyu Wibowo, Sunan Kalijaga State Islamic University, Yogyakarta, Indonesia
Siti Nur Azizah, Sunan Kalijaga State Islamic University, Yogyakarta, Indonesia

This study examines the impact of religious experience, visitor satisfaction, service quality, destination image, and affordability on Muslim tourists' intentions to visit Muslim-friendly destinations in Yogyakarta, Indonesia. Using the Maqā id al-Sharīʿah framework, the research applies a Shariah-oriented lens to understand travel behavior. A structured survey was conducted with 300 Muslim tourists, and data were analyzed using SPSS version 30, including validity, reliability, and regression tests. Results indicate that religious experience, satisfaction, service quality, and destination image significantly influence travel intention, with religious experience being the strongest predictor. Affordability, however, showed no significant effect. The findings validate the relevance of Maqā id al-Sharīʿah in explaining Muslim travel behavior. The study is limited to one location and does not account for variables such as religiosity or cultural background. Future research is encouraged to use broader, comparative, or longitudinal designs.

Chapter 14
Halal as a Means of Kalimatun Sawa': A Unifying Element among Religious Communities in Malaysia 369
Nur Farhana Abdul Rahman, National University of Malaysia, Malaysia
Jaffary Awang, National University of Malaysia, Malaysia

This chapter explores halal elements in Islam as a medium for Kalimatun Sawa, highlighting its role in fostering interfaith harmony in Malaysia. Within Malaysia's diverse society, certain non-Muslim groups perceive halal in a negative light, mainly associating it with religious sensitivity. However, various other religious traditions also highlight values that align with halal principles, such as cleanliness, safety, and the prevention of harm. Through qualitative analysis of Muslim and non-Muslim perspectives, it reveals shared values of cleanliness and safety, positioning halal as a unifying principle promoting tolerance and cooperative coexistence.The results indicate that while some non-Muslims regard halal solely as an Islamic requirement, most acknowledge cleanliness and safety as universal principles shared across all religions. These results illustrate that halal can become a point of strengthening harmonious coexistence (ta'ayush) and fostering positive interactions among the diverse religious communities in Malaysia.

Compilation of References 393

About the Contributors 473

Index 481

Preface

INTRODUCTION

The rapid transformation of the global economy has created new opportunities and challenges for the halal industry. In recent years, halal products and services have emerged as important drivers of economic growth, innovation, sustainability, and ethical business practices across many countries. The increasing awareness and demand for halal products among Muslim and non-Muslim consumers alike have encouraged governments, industries, researchers, and entrepreneurs to strengthen the halal ecosystem through policies, certifications, technological integration, and global collaboration.

Islam pays great attention to the ultimate purpose of business and economic activities. While worldly success and material prosperity are encouraged, Islamic teachings emphasize that all human endeavors must ultimately contribute to achieving success in the hereafter. Business practices in Islam are therefore not merely profit-oriented, but are guided by ethical values, social responsibility, justice, and the principles of *maqasid shariah*, which aim to preserve and promote the well-being of individuals and society. In this context, Islamic business values provide a strong moral foundation for sustainable and responsible economic development.

The transformation of halal products and industries today encompasses various interconnected dimensions. These include innovation in product development and ingredient sourcing, enhancement of halal supply chain systems through traceability and strategic partnerships, strengthening of regulatory frameworks and certification standards, expansion into global markets, consumer education, technological integration such as blockchain, Internet of Things (IoT), and e-commerce, as well as sustainability initiatives that address environmental protection and animal welfare. At the same time, culinary and cultural transformations continue to enrich the global appreciation of halal lifestyles and values.

This edited reference book, *Digital Transformation, Sustainability, and Ethical Globalization in Halal Ecosystems*, brings together scholarly perspectives and empirical studies that critically examine the contemporary development of Islamic business and halal industries. The contributors explore how innovation, digitalization, ethical values, and sustainability can be integrated into Islamic business strategies to address current socio-economic challenges faced by Muslim communities and the broader global society.

The editors believe that the advancement of halal ecosystems requires not only theoretical discussions but also practical and impactful strategies that support long-term sustainability. Through interdisciplinary approaches and diverse case studies, this book seeks to contribute to knowledge production, policy development, and practical solutions grounded in Islamic principles and cultural contexts. It also aims to stimulate further academic discourse on the role of halal industries in promoting inclusive economic growth and ethical globalization.

We hope that this volume will serve as a valuable resource for entrepreneurs, practitioners, policymakers, academicians, researchers, and students who are interested in Islamic business and halal industry development. We also hope that the insights presented in this book will inspire future initiatives that strengthen ethical business practices, foster innovation, and contribute positively to society and the environment.

Finally, we would like to express our sincere appreciation to all chapter contributors, reviewers, and publishing teams whose dedication and support have made this publication possible. May this book provide beneficial knowledge and contribute meaningfully to the advancement of halal ecosystems worldwide.

ORGANIZATION OF THE BOOK

This edited volume presents a diverse collection of scholarly works that critically explore the evolving landscape of halal ecosystems through the lenses of digital transformation, sustainability, ethical governance, innovation, entrepreneurship, and socio-economic development. Collectively, the chapters demonstrate how Islamic principles can guide contemporary business practices while responding to global challenges and technological advancement.

Chapter 1 discusses the growing significance of digital transformation in strengthening the halal industry across sectors such as food, pharmaceuticals, cosmetics, tourism, logistics, and finance. The chapter highlights how technologies including blockchain, artificial intelligence (AI), Internet of Things (IoT), and big data analytics enhance transparency, traceability, operational efficiency, and halal compliance. It further emphasizes that digitalization within halal ecosystems aligns closely with the objectives of Maqasid al-Shariah by safeguarding consumer welfare, trust, and ethical business conduct.

Chapter 2 examines the conceptual integration of Islamic and Western theories in halal information systems. Through qualitative content analysis, the chapter proposes a framework that bridges shariah compliance with theories such as Deontological Theory and Stakeholder Theory. The discussion highlights how ethical accountability, transparency, governance, and supplier integrity contribute to consumer trust and sustainability performance within halal organizational systems.

Chapter 3 focuses on halal policy development in Indonesia from the perspective of sustainability principles and environmental stewardship. The chapter critically evaluates existing halal regulations and identifies gaps in incorporating environmentally sustainable practices into halal manufacturing and production processes. It proposes a more comprehensive policy framework that aligns halal governance with Sustainable Development Goals (SDGs) and the broader green halal agenda.

Chapter 4 explores the strategic role of Islamic boarding schools (pesantren) in promoting eco-innovation and sustainable halal industries in Indonesia. Through case studies related to the "One Pesantren One Product" initiative, the chapter demonstrates how pesantren-based enterprises integrate environmentally friendly practices into halal production. The findings position pesantren as important agents of green transformation capable of contributing to sustainable development and Indonesia's green economy aspirations.

Chapter 5 addresses the issue of food waste within the halal food industry in Brunei Darussalam. Applying the Theory of Planned Behaviour, the chapter investigates consumer intentions toward halal food waste prevention and identifies attitudes and perceived behavioural control as significant influencing factors. The discussion underscores the importance of Islamic ethical values in encouraging responsible consumption and sustainability practices consistent with national development goals and global sustainability agendas.

Chapter 6 presents halal entrepreneurship as a catalyst for sustainable and ethical global business ecosystems. The chapter conceptualizes halal entrepreneurship as a business model rooted in Islamic values, ethical responsibility, and shariah compliance. Through literature review and international case studies, it explores ecosystem actors, enabling factors, challenges, and policy implications for developing stronger halal entrepreneurial ecosystems globally.

Chapter 7 extends the discussion on halal entrepreneurship beyond conventional compliance by examining its conceptual and sociological dimensions within non-Islamic contexts. The chapter integrates entrepreneurship studies with locality-based perspectives and demonstrates how halal entrepreneurship can contribute meaningfully to local communities and socio-economic development, particularly in multicultural and non-Muslim environments.

Chapter 8 investigates halal innovation in sustainable nutrition through the exploration of insect protein as a future halal food source. The chapter examines shariah rulings, food safety considerations, and processing techniques related to insect-based protein products. It further discusses the potential of halal-compliant insect protein industries in addressing food security challenges while supporting sustainable economic growth.

Chapter 9 proposes a Shariah-Compliant Online Marketing Control Framework for halal e-commerce grounded in prophetic principles and thematic analysis of hadith literature. Addressing ethical challenges such as misleading advertisements, dishonest pricing, and false halal claims, the chapter emphasizes principles including honesty, trustworthiness, justice, and the prohibition of fraud as foundational elements for sustainable and ethical digital marketing practices.

Chapter 10 examines how brand experience and emotional attachment influence trust, satisfaction, loyalty, and behavioural intentions within the halal fast-food sector. Focusing on Muslim consumers, the chapter demonstrates how emotionally engaging brand experiences cultivate brand love and strengthen consumer loyalty. The findings contribute to understanding consumer behaviour and strategic branding within halal food industries.

Chapter 11 explores the role of artificial intelligence (AI) in enhancing customer relationship management (CRM) and consumer loyalty within halal businesses. By integrating technological acceptance models with ethical and religious considerations, the chapter examines how AI-driven personalization, trust, satisfaction, and perceived value shape consumer engagement. It also highlights the importance of balancing technological innovation with ethical compliance and consumer trust in faith-driven markets.

Chapter 12 investigates operational challenges in maintaining halal integrity within cold chain logistics. Based on practitioner interviews, the chapter identifies key issues including unclear halal guidelines, improper product handling, limited halal awareness among employees, and infrastructure-related challenges. The findings emphasize the importance of standard operating procedures, employee awareness, and effective governance in safeguarding halal compliance throughout logistics operations.

Chapter 13 examines the influence of Maqasid al-Shariah on Muslim-friendly travel intentions in Yogyakarta, Indonesia. The chapter analyzes how factors such as religious experience, service quality, destination image, and visitor satisfaction shape Muslim tourist behaviour. The findings validate the relevance of Maqasid al-Shariah as an important framework for understanding halal tourism and developing Muslim-friendly destinations.

Chapter 14 concludes the volume by discussing halal as a medium for promoting interfaith harmony and social cohesion in Malaysia. Through qualitative analysis of

Muslim and non-Muslim perspectives, the chapter highlights shared universal values such as cleanliness, safety, and prevention of harm. It demonstrates how halal principles can function as a unifying element that strengthens tolerance, mutual understanding, and harmonious coexistence within multicultural societies.

Taken together, the chapters in this volume offer important theoretical insights, empirical evidence, and practical recommendations for advancing halal ecosystems in an increasingly interconnected and digitalized world. The editors hope that this collection will contribute meaningfully to academic discourse, policymaking, industry practices, and the sustainable development of ethical and inclusive halal economies worldwide.

CONCLUSION

The chapters presented in this edited volume collectively demonstrate that the future of halal ecosystems lies not only in compliance and certification, but also in the integration of ethical values, technological innovation, sustainability, and inclusive global engagement. As the halal industry continues to expand across sectors and geographical boundaries, it becomes increasingly important to ensure that its development remains grounded in the principles of Maqasid al-Shariah, promoting justice, transparency, human well-being, environmental stewardship, and socio-economic prosperity.

This book highlights how digital transformation, artificial intelligence, blockchain technology, sustainable production, ethical marketing, halal entrepreneurship, and Muslim-friendly services are reshaping contemporary Islamic business landscapes. At the same time, the contributors emphasize that the advancement of halal industries must remain people-centered and values-driven, balancing innovation with integrity and commercial growth with social responsibility. The discussions throughout this volume also reveal the growing importance of interdisciplinary approaches that connect Islamic teachings with modern management practices, sustainability frameworks, and global economic systems.

The editors believe that the halal ecosystem possesses significant potential to contribute to sustainable development, ethical globalization, and intercultural understanding. Beyond serving Muslim consumers, halal principles increasingly resonate with universal concerns related to food safety, environmental responsibility, fairness, trust, and ethical consumption. In this regard, halal industries can play an important role in fostering responsible business ecosystems that benefit humanity as a whole.

We hope that this volume will inspire further research, policy development, industry collaboration, and innovative practices within the field of Islamic business and halal studies. The insights offered by the contributors are intended to encourage critical reflection and constructive action among scholars, practitioners, entrepreneurs, regulators, and students seeking to strengthen halal ecosystems in both Muslim and non-Muslim contexts.

Finally, the editors express their sincere appreciation to all contributors, reviewers, academic institutions, and publishing teams whose commitment and scholarly efforts have made this publication possible. It is our aspiration that this book will serve as a valuable reference and a catalyst for future advancements in digital transformation, sustainability, and ethical globalization within halal ecosystems.

Chapter 1
Digital Transformation in the Halal Industry: Enhancing Integrity, Efficiency, and Reach

Yuslina binti Yusoff
http://orcid.org/0009-0001-2261-3065
Universiti Teknologi MARA, Malaysia

Zuhaira Muhammad Zain
http://orcid.org/0000-0002-5973-387X
Princess Nourah University, Saudi Arabia

Syarifah Bahiyah Rahayu Syed Mansoor
National Defence University of Malaysia, Malaysia

Hafizah Mat Nawi
http://orcid.org/0000-0003-2232-9547
National Defence University of Malaysia, Malaysia

Nur Shaliza Sapiai
http://orcid.org/0000-0003-1109-2230
Universiti Teknologi MARA, Malaysia

Norazmila Yusuf
Universiti Teknologi MARA, Malaysia

ABSTRACT

The halal industry has emerged as one of the fastest-growing global markets, expanding beyond food and beverages into pharmaceuticals, cosmetics, tourism, logistics, and finance. This growth is driven by rising Muslim populations, increasing consumer awareness, and global demand for ethical and high-quality products. However, the complexity of halal supply chains presents challenges in maintaining transparency, traceability, and compliance. Digital transformation offers strategic solutions to these challenges by integrating technologies such as blockchain, artificial intelligence (AI), the Internet of Things (IoT), and big data analytics. These innovations strengthen halal assurance through real-time monitoring, fraud prevention, and efficient certification processes, while also supporting e-commerce platforms and

DOI: 10.4018/979-8-3373-2792-1.ch001

digital marketing to expand market reach. Importantly, digitalization aligns with Islamic ethical principles, particularly the Maqasid al-Shariah, by safeguarding faith, health, intellect, lineage, and wealth.

1. INTRODUCTION

The global halal industry is swiftly growing beyond food and beverages to include pharmaceuticals, cosmetics, tourism, logistics, and finance. Valued in the trillions within the coming decade, growth is fueled by a rising Muslim population, greater awareness of halal standards, and non-Muslim demand for ethical, safe, and high-quality products. Countries across Asia, the Middle East, Europe, and the Americas are embedding halal compliance into manufacturing and supply chains. This expansion reflects not only religious obligations but also alignment with modern consumer preferences for sustainability, traceability, and ethical responsibility, positioning halal as a significant driver of global economic development.

In the environment of rushing globalization, transforming consumer behavior, and intensified market rivalry, the halal sector is encountering mounting pressure to modernize its operational paradigms. The phenomenon of digital transformation has surfaced as a pivotal facilitator in addressing these challenges, empowering industry stakeholders to enhance transparency, optimize certification procedures, and uphold integrity throughout intricate supply chains. Technologies such as blockchain, artificial intelligence (AI), the Internet of Things (IoT), and big data analytics are being assimilated to authenticate halal compliance in real-time, oversee product trajectories from origin to consumer, and mitigate fraud or mislabeling. Furthermore, the transition toward e-commerce and digital marketing frameworks has broadened the accessibility of halal products to international markets, thereby promoting cross-border commerce and augmenting brand competitiveness. Consequently, the embrace of digital solutions is no longer a mere option; it has become a strategic imperative to ensure market relevance, operational efficacy, and consumer confidence in an increasingly interconnected global landscape.

Digital transformation within the halal sector should not be perceived just as a technological improvement but rather as a moral and spiritual obligation that is consistent with Islamic business tenets, particularly the aims delineated in Maqasid al-Shariah. These aims—safeguarding faith (hifz al-din), human life (hifz al-nafs), intellect (hifz al-‘aql), lineage (hifz al-nasl), and financial well-being (hifz al-mal)- can be encouraged through the addition of digital innovations. For instance, blockchain-enabled traceability guarantees that products adhere to halal standards, thus protecting religious duties (hifz al-din). The implementation of Internet of Things (IoT) technologies for monitoring hygiene and quality ensures the preservation of human health and life (hifz al-nafs), while digital platforms that facilitate knowledge-sharing and enhance consumer awareness play a significant role in the conservation of intelligence (hifz al-'aql). Furthermore, robust digital record-keeping and transparent supply chain operations defend economic interests (hifz al-mal) and promote responsible management of resources for subsequent generations (hifz al-nasl). By incorporating these ethical principles into their digital strategies, the halal industry can concurrently attain operational superiority and maintain its core ethical values, thereby establishing itself as a paragon of integrity and sustainability within the international market.

2. CONCEPTUAL FOUNDATIONS: DIGITALIZATION MEETS HALAL

2.1 Defining Digitalization in the Halal Context: Beyond mere digitization to fundamental process transformation.

Digitalization in the halal industry spreads outside simple digitization; it represents a comprehensive transformation of supply chain processes through technological innovation. This modification aligns with the Fourth Industrial Revolution, emphasizing automation, artificial intelligence (AI), big data, and the Internet of Things (IoT) (Ab Talib et al., 2022). An essential pillar of this transformation is endwise traceability, qualified by global standards such as GS1 EPCIS 2.0, which records critical tracking events and key data elements to ensure interoperability and supportable halal integrity (GS1, 2022).

Malaysia is pioneering digital halal certification through the MYeHALAL system, with all certificates to be issued electronically from May 2025, enhancing efficiency and minimizing forgery (BERNAMA, 2025). Developing technologies further strengthens halal assurance: blockchain ensures absolute records, IoT supports real-time monitoring, and AI enables difference detection (Khan, Rahman, and Yusoff 2024). Significantly, digitalization complements rather than replaces Shariah requirements, reinforcing compliance with standards such as MS 1500:2019, OIC/SMIIC, and ISO 22005 (Department of Standards Malaysia, 2019; Standards and Metrology Institute for Islamic Countries, 2021).

Malaysia is pioneering digital halal certification through the MYeHALAL system, with all certificates to be issued electronically from May 2025, enhancing efficiency and minimizing forgery (BERNAMA, 2025). Developing technologies further strengthens halal assurance: blockchain ensures absolute records, IoT supports real-time monitoring, and AI enables difference detection (Khan, Rahman, and Yusoff 2024). Significantly, digitalization complements rather than replaces Shariah requirements, reinforcing compliance with standards such as **MS** 1500:2019, OIC/SMIIC, and ISO 22005 (Department of Standards Malaysia, 2019; Standards and Metrology Institute for Islamic Countries, 2021).

2.2 Core Islamic Business Values & Ethics Relevant to Digitalization: Transparency (*Shaffafiyah*), Trust (*Amanah*), Accountability (*Muhasabah*), Avoidance of Uncertainty (*Gharar*), and Social Responsibility.

Transparency (shafāfiyyah) occupies a pivotal role in the realm of halal digitalization. In practical terms, this involves the provision of accessible information regarding product ingredients, slaughtering methodologies, handling procedures, and logistical operations. The utilization of advanced technologies such as smart labeling and digital traceability platforms significantly enhances consumer confidence by guaranteeing that essential halal information is readily accessible (Amin & Isa 2021).

Trust (amānah) emphasizes the imperative to manage digital information with due diligence. In a contemporary context characterized by data-centric halal governance, the dependability of information systems becomes integrally associated with the ethical quality of trustworthiness. Organizations are obligated to implement safeguards against data manipulation, falsification, or negligence in the stewardship of halal-related information, thereby upholding stakeholder trust (Dusuki & Abozaid 2021).

Accountability (muḥāsabah) is further bolstered through the mechanisms of digitalization. Technologies that meticulously document and audit each phase of the supply chain generate comprehensive digital records that can be scrutinized by certifying authorities, regulatory bodies, and even consumers. This ensures that businesses retain liability for their conduct, in alignment with the Islamic focus on ethical and operational accountability (Kamali, 2022).

The principle of evading gharar (uncertainty) holds particular significance in the context of halal assurance. Ambiguity regarding the status of raw materials, slaughtering techniques, or handling protocols can severely compromise consumer confidence. The standardization of data through digital traceability systems—such as ISO 22005 or GS1 EPCIS—effectively diminishes uncertainty and ensures unequivocal clarity regarding halal status (Ab Talib et al., 2022).

Ultimately, social responsibility (maṣlaḥah/muqāṣid) mandates that halal digitalization should enhance societal well-being. This encompasses the safeguarding of food safety, the promotion of environmental sustainability, and the facilitation of equitable access to halal-certified goods. Recent scholarly investigations indicate that digital transformation can be harmonized with the objectives of maqā id al-sharī'ah alongside global sustainability frameworks, such as the Sustainable Development Goals established by the United Nations (Ali & Suleiman, 2023).

2.3 The Unique Requirements of Halal Assurance: Traceability, Verification, Segregation, and Compliance.

Halal assurance has unique requirements—traceability, verification, segregation, and compliance—well supported by digitalization. Traceability documents every stage of the halal product lifecycle, including religiously significant processes, supported by ISO 22005 and GS1 EPCIS frameworks (GS1, 2022). Verification is enhanced through blockchain, IoT, and AI, which secure certificates and minimize errors (Khan et al., 2024). Segregation, mandated by MS 1500:2019 and OIC/SMIIC, can be digitally monitored using IoT sensors and geofencing (Department of Standards Malaysia, 2019; Standards and Metrology Institute for Islamic Countries, 2021). Finally, compliance is strengthened by platforms like MYeHALAL, with Malaysia set to issue fully electronic halal certificates by May 2025 (BERNAMA, 2025).

3. KEY DIGITAL TECHNOLOGIES TRANSFORMING THE HALAL ECOSYSTEM

The Halal ecosystem is essential in recognizing, improving, and certifying halal products. The Halal ecosystem needs a robust Halal supply chain to verify and preserve the Halal status of products, hence reducing the risk of contamination (Kurniawati & Cakravastia, 2023), and safeguarding Halal authenticity (Ab Rashid & Bojei, 2020; Ali & Suleiman, 2018; Kurniawati & Rochman, 2023). This section describes three key digital technologies, as shown in Figure 1—blockchain, Internet of Things (IoT), and artificial intelligence (AI)—which may help in transforming the Halal ecosystem that is more traceable, transparent, efficient, and trustworthy, aligning with Islamic ethical principles and minimizing *Gharar* (ambiguity).

Figure 1. Key digital technologies in transforming Halal ecosystem

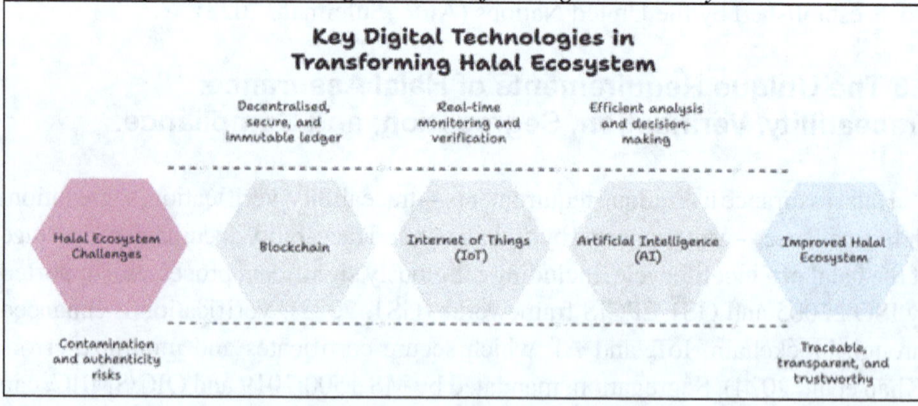

3.1 Blockchain - Immutable Ledger for Halal Certification and Supply Chain Integrity

Blockchain technology can help in developing a decentralized, consensus-driven, and immutable ledger system for recording transactions across the Halal supply chain, from raw material sourcing to final product delivery. The system can store every verification process, such as slaughter compliance, ingredient validation, or transportation logs, as a timestamped record accessible to authorized stakeholders. This transparency directly addresses *Gharar* by ensuring origins, handling processes, and certifications are verifiable, thereby reinforcing *Amanah* (trust) among producers, certifiers, and consumers.

Blockchain-powered traceability systems support real-time monitoring and faster decision-making, which can improve supply chain visibility and meet consumer expectations for transparency and quality assurance (Wahyuni et al., 2025). There are three key components of a blockchain-powered traceability systems; distributed ledger, smart contracts, and public key cryptography. The distributed ledger enables secure, efficient data sharing between organizations. The smart contracts automate compliance checks, reduce dependence on intermediaries, lower overall costs, and facilitate faster transactions. In the Halal meat industry, smart contracts are used to streamline collaboration between stakeholders and enhance transparency across operations within the industry. Public key cryptography protects sensitive information from breaches or unauthorized access. These capabilities promote trust and integrity in Halal supply chains (Wahyuni et al., 2025). Moreover, blockchain assists in reducing waste, preventing fraud, and improving productivity (Bhatt et al., 2013), making it a highly suitable platform for maintaining Halal integrity in today's competitive and globalized market (Hu & Ghadimi, 2022).

3.2 Internet of Things (IoT) - Real-Time Monitoring and Verification of the Critical Halal Conditions

The Internet of Things (IoT) is defined as follows:

"A network of infrastructures that interconnects objects, enabling their management, data processing, and access to generated data (Dorsemaine et al., 2016)."

It consists of wireless connected devices such as Radio-Frequency Identification (RFID) tags, sensors, actuators, and mobile devices, which typically transmit data to cloud storage via the internet (Atzori et al., 2010).

To ensure ongoing monitoring and promptly alert stakeholders of any issues that may affect Halal compliance in the Halal supply chain, IoT devices such as temperature, humidity, and motion sensors are integrated into logistics, storage, and processing operations. For example, IoT supports cold-chain management for meat, dairy, and processed products, ensuring contamination prevention in food logistics (Mohammed et al., 2017). Furthermore, IoT systems play an important role in authenticating Halal status, which allows consumers to verify certification logos and trace product origins (Rejeb et al., 2021).

The hybrid of IoT with blockchain enables storing the IoT sensor data in immutable ledgers to produce tamper-proof compliance records. The integration promotes openness and trust by ensuring verifiable Halal compliance at every phase. In addition, IoT analytics can identify inefficiencies, optimize delivery routes, and minimize waste that supports sustainability objectives in line with *Maqasid al-Shariah* (Rejeb et al., 2021).

3.3 Artificial Intelligence (AI) - Efficient Analysis and Decision Making of Halal Compliance

Artificial intelligence (AI) is technology that allows the simulation of human learning, comprehension, problem-solving, decision-making, creativity, and autonomy by computers and machines. It provides significant advantages to the whole process of Halal compliance. Figure 2 illustrates the role of AI in three phases of Halal compliance.

Figure 2. AI's roles in Halal compliance

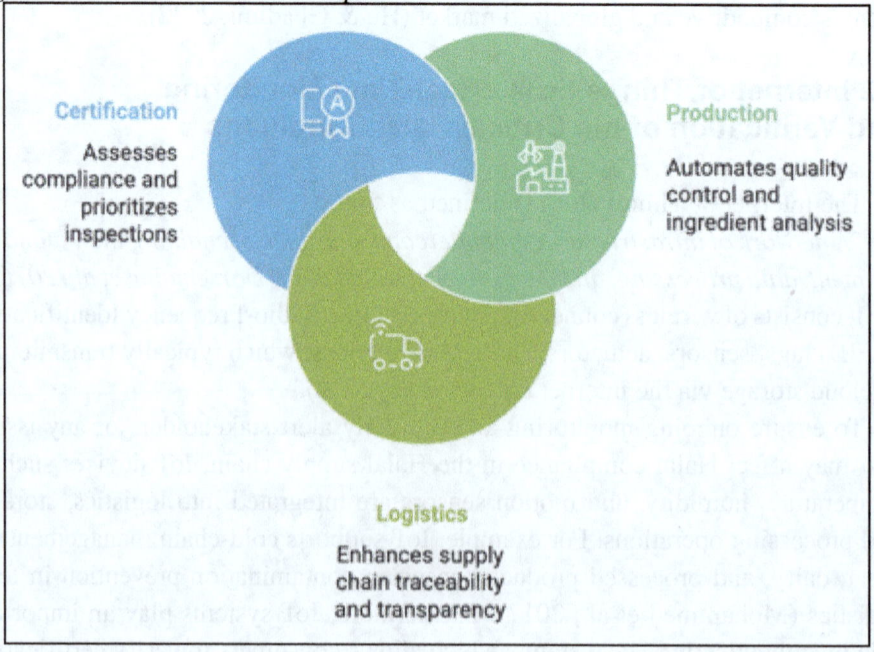

In the production phase, AI can be utilized to automate quality control and analyze non-Halal ingredients in order to ensure compliance with Halal standards (Ridho, 2025). While in the logistics phase, AI can be used to strengthen supply chain traceability, ensure transparency, and reinforce consumer confidence in certification outcomes. As for the certification phase, AI can be adopted to assist in assessing compliance by analyzing product labels, ingredient lists, and supplier records, regardless of whether it is multilingual and unstructured (Alourani & Khan, 2024). Certification bodies can prioritize inspection based on dynamic risk profiles created by the AI predictive analytics, which aligns with the Islamic principle of *Maslahah* (public interest) to safeguard consumer welfare.

To further explore significant potential for advancing Halal compliance, AI can be integrated with blockchain to perform pattern recognition and data analysis while maintaining an immutable ledger that tracks the supply chain from raw material sourcing to final distribution (Alourani & Khan, 2024). This will ensure the integrity of Halal products, prevent fraud, and enable real-time verification. While AI automates error detection and improves analytical precision, blockchain will guarantee the immutability of data, which will promote greater public trust and satisfaction in certification processes (Ridho, 2025).

In summary, these technologies, blockchain, IoT, and AI, can be used to transform the Halal ecosystem from risk-prone manual processes to reliable automated systems. They are essential in developing Digital Halal certification platforms for managing certification applications, storing compliance records, and verifying product status in a centralized hub/ one-stop centre. This empowers consumers and business partners to make informed decisions, facilitate cross-border recognition, and reduce bureaucratic hurdles. By using these integrated technologies, the Halal ecosystem can achieve greater transparency, operational efficiency, and global interoperability.

4. REVOLUTIONIZING MARKET ACCESS & CONSUMER ENGAGEMENT

The Halal industry has been significantly transformed by the rapid development of digital technologies, which have provided extraordinary opportunities to recover operational efficiency, integrity, and market influence. The industry can balance religious compliance with global sustainability goals, and digital transformation is enhancing the pace and precision of business operations. In this context, it is crucial to implement innovations in market entry, consumer engagement, and supply chain management to ensure that Halal products meet the demands of a global market that is gradually becoming environmentally conscious.

4.1 Shifting Consumer Engagement and Market Access

The global market access for producers and consumers has been transformed by the emergence of devoted Halal e-commerce platforms(Imani et al., 2022). These niche markets offer a carefully chosen range of goods that follow strict Shariah compliance and increasingly contain environmental principles, going beyond traditional internet retail. Such platforms enhance supply chain transparency and lessen the risk of counterfeit claims by concentrating Halal-certified products. Digital marketplaces offer unparalleled opportunities for small and medium-sized enterprises (SMEs) to connect with global consumers without the need for expensive intermediaries, particularly in developing countries. This disintermediation enhances profit margins and mitigates the environmental consequences of multiple distribution layers. By integrating blockchain technology into these platforms, consumer trust is further stimulated by the creation of immutable, tamper-proof recordings of product origins and accreditation details. Furthermore, the integration of artificial intelligence into e-commerce operations permits businesses to freely align products with a variety of Halal standards across various authorities, thereby reducing rejection and preventing waste (Rasyidah et al., 2025). By refining logistics, expediting supply chains, and nurturing consumption on a global scale, this digitalization of Halal trade underwrites to both commercial growth and environmental responsibility.

Figure 3. Halal E-commerce revolutionizes market access

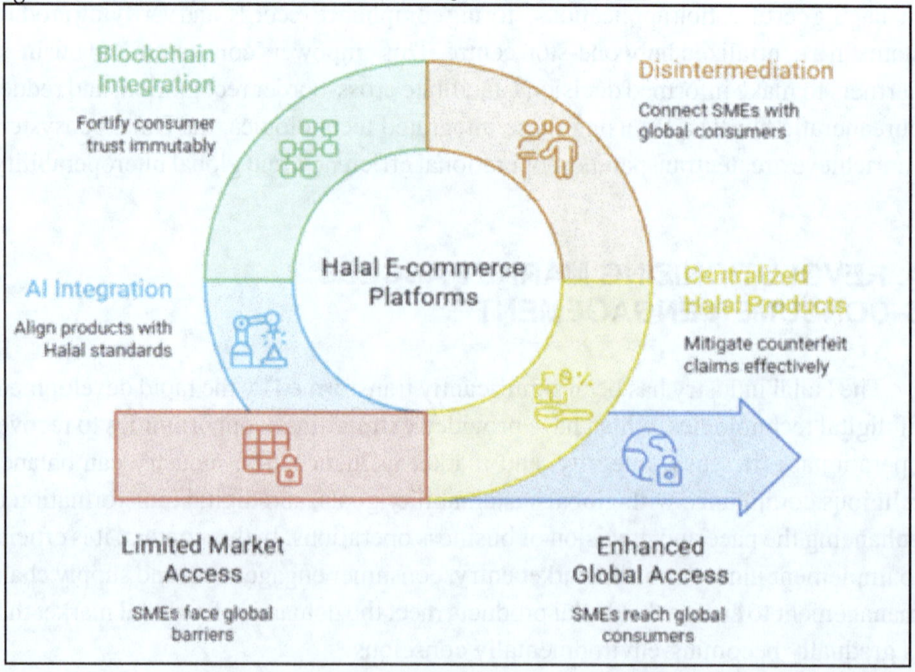

Consumer access to Halal products and services has been further revolutionized by mobile applications. By utilizing barcode or QR code scanning capabilities, users can instantaneously confirm the Halal status of a product by accessing live certification databases, thereby reducing the likelihood of misinformation. GPS-enabled restaurant locator applications direct consumers to the nearest Halal-certified food establishments, thereby reducing superfluous travel and supporting local Halal businesses, both of which contribute to environmental sustainability. The validity and expiration dates of Halal certifications can be verified by users through the certification verification tools that are integrated into these applications, thereby protecting against fraudulent or obsolete claims (Ridho, 2025). In addition to transactional functions, mobile applications function as educational platforms, offering resources on sustainable Halal practices, such as ethical sourcing, waste minimization, and animal welfare. Some even integrate gamification elements to promote eco-conscious consumer behavior by rewarding users for selecting Halal products that are environmentally friendly. This transforms ethical consumption into a socially appealing activity.

Figure 4. Exploring the multifaceted impact of Halal mobile apps

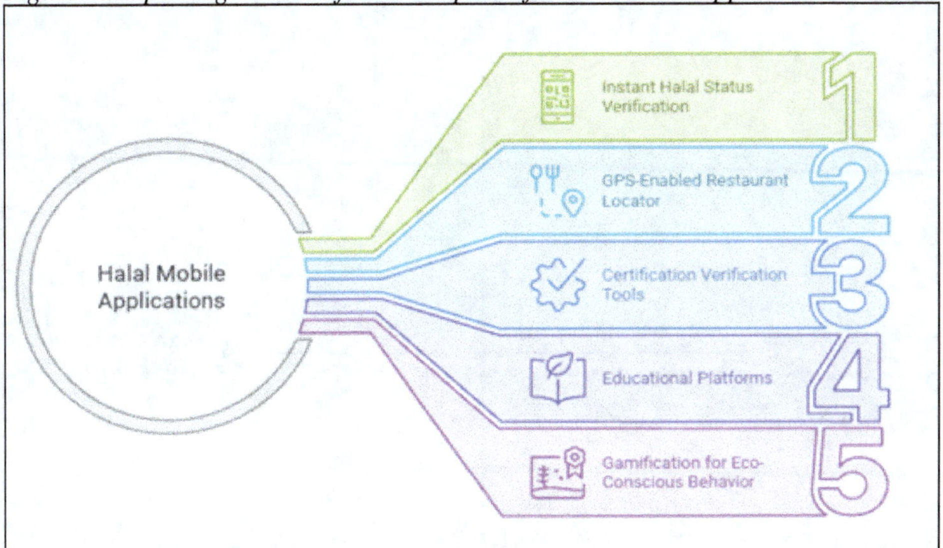

Social media and digital marketing have become evolutionary forces in the shaping of consumer engagement with Halal products and services. These platforms enable the specific communication of Halal businesses' brand values, sustainability commitments, and certification integrity to their targeted audiences. Through the application of data analytics and AI-driven segmentation, businesses can customize campaigns to appeal to consumers who emphasize both religious compliance and eco-friendly practices. Social media generates collaborative places that empower producers, certifiers, and consumers to exchange ideas, share feedback, and discuss developments in sustainable Halal innovations, in addition to facilitating promotional activity. This nurtures community building. In particular, storytelling has established its efficiency as a potent tool, as brands share genuine explanations about their procurement procedures, certification journeys, and environmentally mindful production methods. Brands are refined and their emotional connections with consumers are stimulated by this transparency. Real-time perceptions that can be leveraged to improve sustainability performance and compliance are provided by feedback cycles helped by social platforms, such as polls, remark threads, and reviews (Oye & Emma, 2024). Furthermore, the implementation of sustainable Halal products is encouraged, and awareness is enlarged through partnerships with influencers in the Halal lifestyle, ethical consumerism, and environmental advocacy divisions. Social media and digital marketing not only extend the reach of Halal businesses but also strengthen the resemblance of religious principles with global sustainability goals by integrating authenticity, transparency, and interactivity.

Figure 5. Digital marketing strategies in Halal industry

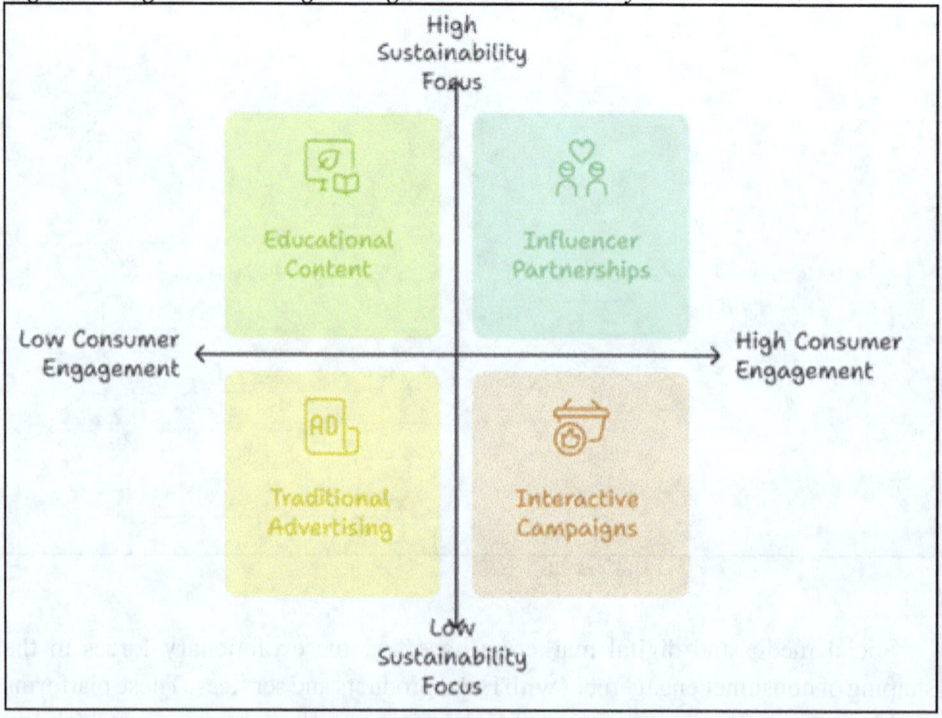

4.2 Optimization of Operations and Supply Chain

Operational and supply chain processes are also transformed by digital transformation in the Halal industry, in addition to consumer-facing innovations. The application of cloud computing and Enterprise Resource Planning (ERP) systems, for example, has been developed as a transformative method to improve operations in Halal-compliant enterprises. These digital resolutions enable the seamless administration of a variety of business functions within an incorporated platform, such as procurement, inventory control, production planning, and quality assurance. ERP systems can be modified to include isolation controls that guarantee the firm separation of Halal and non-Halal resources during production for Halal-certified enterprises. This eases the risk of contamination and preserves religious compliance, which could otherwise cause financial losses and wasteful recalls. Decision-makers may display supply chain activity from any place and react quickly to disruptions. This is the impact of the added benefit of real-time data access and analytics offered by cloud-based technologies. The scalability of cloud computing enables businesses to expand their operations without the requirement for a significant physical infrastructure, thereby dropping their carbon footprint.

Moreover, the incorporation of reporting tools within ERP systems can harvest sustainability performance metrics, including energy consumption, refuse generation, and transportation emissions, which enable the arrangement of Halal operations with environmentally promising business objectives (Russo et al., 2025). Cloud computing and ERP solutions improve transparency and streamline developments, thereby encouraging operational efficiency and environmental stewardship and firming Halal integrity.

Figure 6. Enhancing Halal integrity and efficiency

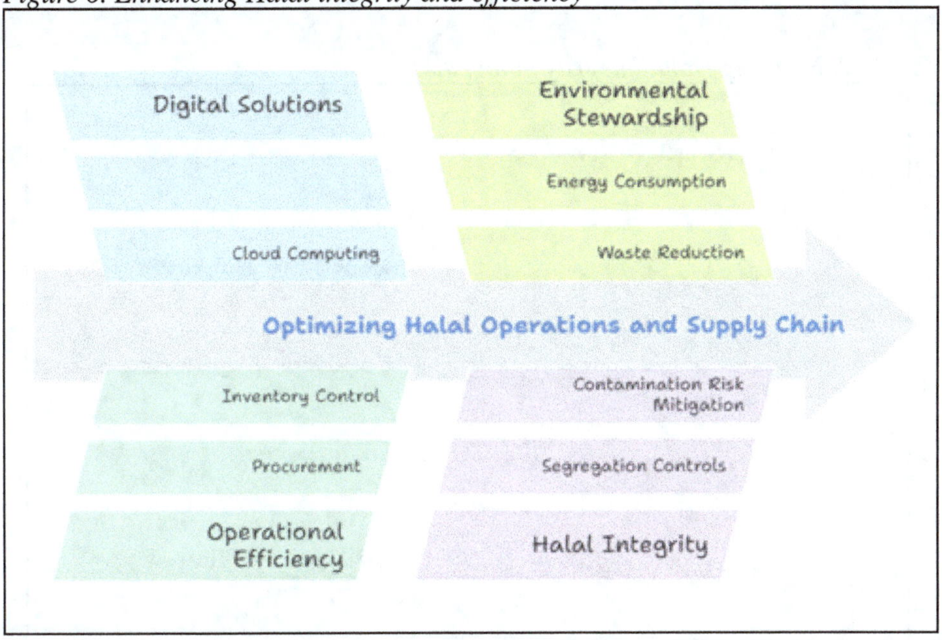

The fortification of Halal integrity during the physical distribution of products from the point of origin to the end consumer depends upon the employment of intelligent logistics and warehouse management technologies. Advanced tracking systems, which are driven by Radio-Frequency Identification (RFID) markers and Internet of Things (IoT) devices, facilitate real-time monitoring of product movement, storage conditions, and handling procedures (Yushaniza et al., 2021). These assurances that separation protocols are meticulously followed and that no cross-contamination with non-Halal items happens at any point in Halal supply chains. Temperature and humidity sensors can be integrated into transportation and storage facilities to ensure that fragile Halal products are preserved in ideal settings, thereby reducing food waste and corrosion. Route optimization software further alters sustainability by optimizing delivery scheduling to reduce greenhouse gas emissions and minimize fuel consumption. Automation technologies, including AI-driven inventory management and autonomous sorting systems, simplify the fulfillment of orders more competently and minimize energy consumption in warehouse operations. Besides, the digital audit traces produced by these systems offer verifiable records of adherence to Halal standards that are easily available to regulators and certifying bodies. Smart logistics and warehouse management systems defend the purity of Halal products and encourage larger eco-friendly objectives within the global supply chain by blending environmental responsibility, efficiency, and precision (Ghalih & Chang, n.d.).

Figure 7. Ensuring Halal integrity in logistics

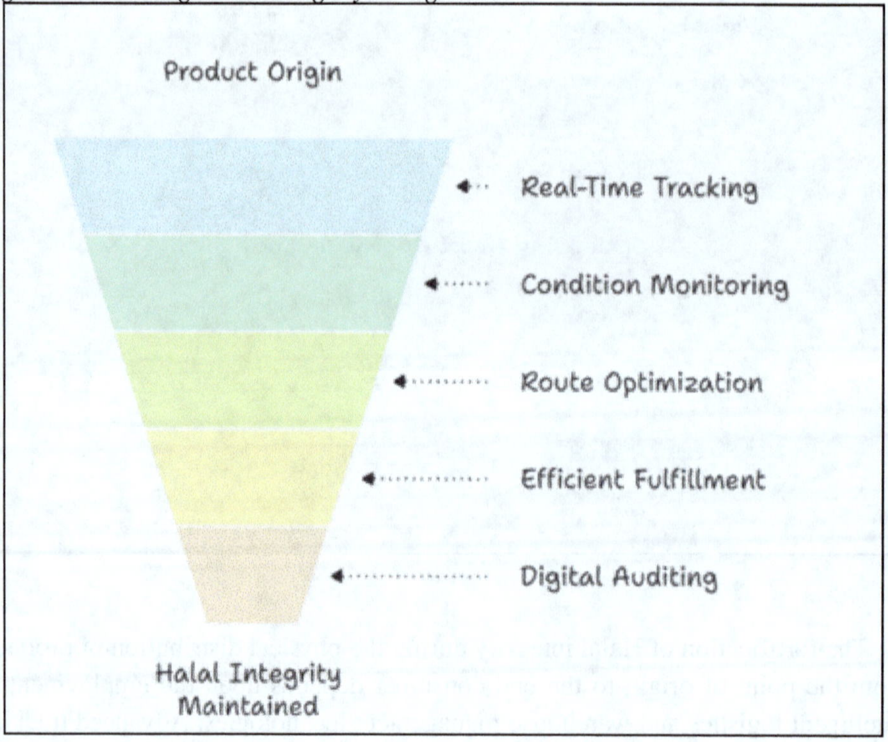

The Halal industry's ability to grow efficiency, maintain integrity, and increase its market influence is redefined by the combination of digital technologies across consumer engagement, operations, and supply chain management. As a result of these innovations, Shariah-compliant practices and global environmental goals are changing into more closely linked (Asif & Akhlaq, 2024). For example, e-commerce platforms and mobile apps give customers permission to authorized information, and ERP systems and smart logistics ensure that operations are carefully parted and sustained. The outcome is a Halal ecosystem that is more receptive to the ethical and ecological apprehensions of modern consumers, as well as more transparent and efficient. The challenge for industry stakeholders as digital transformation remains to grow is to guarantee that these tools are executed in a means that conserves religious principles and increases their potential to contribute to a more inclusive, sustainable global marketplace.

5. ADDRESSING CHALLENGES AND ENSURING ETHICAL DIGITALIZATION

5.1 Standardization and Interoperability

One of the most pressing challenges in halal digitalization is the lack of unified global standards. Certification bodies across different countries use varied formats and protocols, which hinders mutual recognition and complicates cross-border trade. This fragmentation undermines consumer confidence and creates inefficiencies in the halal supply chain. Efforts by organizations like the Organisation of Islamic Cooperation (OIC) and the Standards and Metrology Institute for Islamic Countries (SMIIC) aim to harmonize standards, but adoption remains uneven (Salaam Gateway, 2019).

5.2 Cybersecurity and Data Privacy (Amanah)

Digital halal systems handle sensitive data, including certification records and consumer information. Breaches in these systems can violate the Islamic principle of Amanah, which emphasizes trust and responsibility. Ensuring robust cybersecurity and transparent data governance is critical to maintaining consumer confidence. Islamic data ethics require the secure handling of information, aligning with both religious values and international regulations, such as the GDPR (Susanty et al., 2025).

5.3 Digital Divide and Accessibility

Many SMEs in developing Muslim-majority countries face barriers to digital adoption due to limited infrastructure, financial constraints, and lack of technical expertise. This digital divide restricts their access to global halal markets and hampers their competitiveness. Addressing these disparities requires targeted capacity-building programs and inclusive investments in digital infrastructure (Halal Times, 2025).

5.4 Cost of Implementation

Implementing advanced technologies such as blockchain and AI involves significant upfront costs, including infrastructure development, software licensing, and staff training. For SMEs, these financial barriers can be prohibitive, especially when the return on investment is uncertain. Long-term sustainability of digital systems also demands ongoing maintenance and updates, adding to the financial burden (Sunmola et al., 2025).

5.5 Regulatory Adaptation

While some halal authorities have embraced digital certification, others continue to rely on paper-based systems. This inconsistency creates compliance challenges for multinational companies operating across different jurisdictions. To facilitate seamless halal trade, regulatory bodies must evolve their frameworks to accommodate digital processes and promote mutual recognition of digital certificates (Malay Mail, 2024).

5.6 Combating Digital Gharar (Fraud and Misrepresentation)

Digital platforms can be exploited to issue fake halal certificates or make misleading claims about product compliance. This form of digital Gharar undermines the integrity of the halal ecosystem and erodes consumer trust. Robust verification systems, including blockchain-based traceability, are essential to combat fraud and ensure authenticity (Susanty et al., 2025).

6. ETHICAL CONSIDERATIONS IN DIGITAL HALAL

6.1 Algorithmic Fairness

AI systems used in halal certification must be designed to avoid bias against specific regions, producers, or practices. Upholding Adl (justice) requires transparency in algorithmic decision-making and continuous monitoring to detect and correct biases. Ethical AI frameworks should incorporate diverse datasets and ensure fairness in automated processes (Sunmola et al., 2025).

6.2 Data Usage Ethics

Islamic principles emphasize the importance of minimal and purposeful data collection. Practices such as informed consent, data minimization, and the right to erase personal data align with values of dignity and individual rights. Digital halal systems must be designed to respect privacy and avoid excessive surveillance, following Islamic ethics (Susanty et al., 2025).

6.3 Maintaining Human Oversight

While AI and blockchain can streamline halal certification, they should not replace the role of qualified Shariah scholars. Complex religious determinations require human judgment and spiritual insight. Technology should serve as a support tool, enhancing the efficiency of halal audits while preserving religious authority (Malay Mail, 2024).

7. CASE STUDIES / EXAMPLES OF DIGITAL INNOVATION IN HALAL

7.1 PT Sreeya Sewu Indonesia – Blockchain Halal Traceability

In response to concerns over transparency and fraud in halal poultry products, PT Sreeya Sewu Indonesia implemented a blockchain-based traceability system. This system records every stage of the production process on an immutable ledger, allowing consumers to verify product origins through QR codes. The integration with regulatory bodies ensures that certification data is accurate and tamper-proof. The impact has been significant: audit times for authorities have decreased, consumer trust has improved, and the company has enhanced its export potential. This case illustrates how blockchain can address both operational inefficiencies and ethical concerns in halal supply chains (HARA AgriTech, 2019).

7.2 JAKIM – AI Certification via MYeHALAL

The Department of Islamic Development Malaysia (JAKIM) has taken a pioneering step by integrating AI into its halal certification process through the MYeHALAL platform. The system automates ingredient compliance checks and supports auditors with digital tools, enabling faster and more consistent evaluations. This digital transformation has reduced processing times while maintaining religious oversight. It has also made certification more accessible for SMEs, demonstrating how AI can enhance both efficiency and inclusivity in halal governance (Halal Times, 2025; Malay Mail, 2024).

7.3 DagangHalal – Global Halal B2B Marketplace

DagangHalal addresses the challenge of global market access for halal-certified SMEs by offering a dedicated B2B e-commerce platform. The platform includes a Halal Verified Engine for product validation, digital certification management, and a mobile app (Meembar) tailored for small businesses. With partnerships involving 42 certification bodies, DagangHalal has expanded international buyer confidence and maintained halal integrity across borders. It exemplifies how digital platforms can democratize access to global halal markets (Salaam Gateway, 2019).

8. HALALCHAIN – DECENTRALIZED BLOCKCHAIN MODEL

HalalChain offers a decentralized blockchain solution for halal food supply chains, enabling producers, regulators, and consumers to access and verify data in real time. The system ensures compliance with Islamic jurisprudence by maintaining a transparent and immutable record of product origins and processing steps. This model strengthens supply chain transparency, reduces the risk of fraud, and increases consumer trust. It highlights the potential of decentralized technologies to uphold halal standards in complex, multi-stakeholder environments (Susanty et al., 2025).

8.1 AI and Blockchain Integration

A holistic framework that integrates AI and blockchain has been developed to streamline halal certification. AI automates compliance checks and ingredient analysis, while blockchain ensures traceability and data security. This dual approach aligns with Islamic ethical principles by enhancing both accuracy and accountability. The result is a more efficient certification workflow with reduced human error and improved reliability. This integration represents a forward-looking model for halal compliance in the digital age (Sunmola et al., 2025).

8.2 Consumer Acceptance of Digital Halal Traceability

Consumer trust is a critical factor in the success of digital halal systems. A study by Susanty et al. (2025) analyzed the factors influencing consumer acceptance of halal traceability technologies. The research found that transparency, ease of use, and perceived credibility significantly affect adoption rates. These insights help businesses design user-friendly systems and develop strategies to build consumer confidence. The study underscores the importance of aligning technological innovation with user expectations and ethical transparency.

Digital transformation in the halal industry offers immense potential to enhance integrity, efficiency, and global reach. However, realizing these benefits requires addressing key challenges such as standardization, cybersecurity, accessibility, and ethical governance. By aligning digital tools with Islamic principles like Amanah and Adl, stakeholders can ensure that innovation supports—not compromises—halal authenticity. The case studies presented demonstrate that responsible and inclusive digitalization can strengthen consumer trust and operational resilience. Moving forward, collaboration among businesses, certification bodies, regulators, and scholars will be essential to navigate the evolving digital halal landscape and fulfill the objectives of Maqasid al-Shariah.

9. THE FUTURE LANDSCAPE: EMERGING TRENDS AND OPPORTUNITIES

Despite notable progress in the Halal industries through digital transformation, several constraints persist:

- Ethical implications – including risks of data misuse and algorithmic bias (Latif et al., 2021; Ogbuke et al., 2022).
- Cybersecurity vulnerabilities – exposing businesses to threats of fraud, hacking, and breaches of consumer trust.
- Misinformation (*gharar*) – the spread of false or misleading claims regarding Halal status.
- Fragmented international standards – inconsistencies in certification processes across regions.
- High compliance costs – disproportionately affecting small and medium-sized enterprises (SMEs).

Looking forward, these challenges may be reframed as opportunities through the strategic adoption of emerging technologies. A key requirement is to integrate Islamic ethical values into digital innovation to strengthen inclusivity, resilience, and sustainability in the Halal ecosystem.

- *Shaffafiyah*[1] (Transparency): Upholding openness in data use, certification, and supply chain processes.

- *Amanah* (Trust): Safeguarding consumer confidence by ensuring accuracy, security, and authenticity.
- *Mas'uliyyah*[2] (Responsibility): Promoting accountability in technological applications and decision-making.

Together, these values serve as a moral compass, guiding the adoption of digital transformation while maintaining fidelity to Shariah principles within the Halal industry.

9.1 Integration of AI for Predictive Halal Compliance and Consumer Insights

Traditional Halal certification relied on manual audits and reactive assessments. Naturally, these procedures lack real-time capabilities and overlook numerous occurrences of both fraud and compliance violations. AI has facilitated the development of a more proactive prediction model. Through the analysis of supply chain data, AI systems may anticipate contamination or certification failures before they happen (Fauzi et al., 2024). They can detect irregular trends across numerous vendors and propose swift corrective actions to prevent infringement.

AI-driven analytical instruments can be utilised for the creation and provision of Shariah-compliant products or services (Tobing et al., 2024). Such insights enable organisations to get a more detailed comprehension of consumer behaviour and preferences, enhancing their capacity to align their values with the markets they serve. Similarly, removing AI from Halal ecosystems will enhance governance, trust and loyalty when carried out with the right principles such as *Shaffafiyah, Amanah,* and *Mas'uliyyah*.

9.2 Rise of the Metaverse and Virtual Halal Experiences

In the metaverse, new technologies also create new opportunities to bridge this gap through communication and interaction with virtual Halal trade fairs, immersive tourist exhibitions, educational interactive spaces (Dwivedi et al., 2023). SMEs frequently lack the resources necessary to compete globally, perpetuating the digital disparity within the Halal industry. By holding Shariah-compliant rules in check, these tools can serve as feasible entry points that will better position SMEs in the world marketplace.

Virtual Halal learning centers can also counter misinformation by offering immersive consumer education about Halal certification processes. For instance, consumers could tour a virtual Halal slaughterhouse to understand standards and safeguards. Such initiatives support *Maqasid al-Shariah*'s protection of intellect (*'aql*) by promoting education and transparency.

9.3 Advanced Biotech and Halal Verification: Lab-Grown Meat Authentication

Biotechnology, especially lab-cultivated or cell-based meat, presents intricate issues with Halal authenticity. In the absence of explicit proof, consumer confidence may be undermined. Advanced digital tools—such as DNA analysis, blockchain-integrated laboratory records, and IoT-enabled monitoring—can authenticate production methods and ensure compliance with Shariah standards (Rahman & Razimi, 2023).

Halal authorities in Malaysia, Indonesia, and Singapore have already begun exploring frameworks for biotechnology-based food authentication (Tieman & Van Nistelrooy, 2014; Irfany et al., 2025). These developments address the challenge of fragmented standards by offering scientifically validated methods of global Halal verification.

9.4 Smart Contracts for Automated Halal Compliance and Transactions

Halal certification and compliance processes remain heavily bureaucratic, creating inefficiencies for businesses and certification bodies alike. Smart contracts, built on blockchain platforms, offer a solution by automating certification renewals, supplier agreements, and payments (Fauzan, 2025).

For example, a logistics contract for Halal meat transport could be encoded to release payment only if IoT data confirms compliance with temperature and segregation requirements (Ellahi et al., 2025). This innovation not only reduces costs and delays but also minimizes the risk of fraud, directly addressing weaknesses in manual certification systems.

9.5 Enhanced Personalization through Big Data While Respecting Privacy

The rise of big data analytics allows businesses to personalize consumer experiences, such as dietary recommendations, Halal skincare tailored to demographics, or region-specific product offerings. However, personalization raises risks of privacy violations and algorithmic bias.

To ensure Shariah compliance, big data systems must incorporate transparent consent protocols, non-exploitative practices, and respect for privacy (*sitr*). When ethically governed, personalization becomes a powerful way to strengthen consumer trust and counter misinformation while upholding Amanah in handling sensitive data (Ogbuke et al., 2022).

9.6 Convergence of Digital Halal with ESG (Environmental, Social, Governance) Tracking

Current Halal certification systems focus primarily on religious compliance, often overlooking broader sustainability and governance concerns. Yet, global consumers and investors increasingly demand that businesses demonstrate environmental and social responsibility.

By converging Halal assurance with ESG tracking tools, businesses can simultaneously prove Shariah compliance and sustainable practices (DinarStandard, 2023). Blockchain and IoT, for example, can ensure that Halal-certified palm oil or meat products are sourced without deforestation or labor exploitation. This elevates Halal from a religious marker to a holistic ethical standard that resonates with global sustainability movements.

9.7 Bridging Challenges and Opportunities

The future of digital Halal transformation lies in turning today's vulnerabilities into strengths. AI addresses inefficiencies in compliance, the metaverse bridges market access gaps, biotech verification tackles global standardization issues, smart contracts cut bureaucracy, big data strengthens consumer trust when managed ethically, and ESG convergence repositions Halal as a global ethical benchmark.

The digital future of Halal industry is not just about embracing technology rather it ought to be the Islamic ramifications imbued in the blood and bones of a digital governance. The aims are to maintain the competitiveness, transparency and integrity of the industry, as well as to serve the *Maqasid al-Shariah*.

10. IMPLICATIONS FOR STAKEHOLDERS: RECOMMENDATIONS

Digitalization is revolutionizing this traditional sector by disrupting processes, redefining stakeholders, and changing the global value chain that characterizes the halal industry. Artificial intelligence, blockchain, the Internet of Things (IoT), and digital platforms are reshaping halal production, certification process, supply chain traceability, and consumer engagement. Digital transformation, more than just digitization, represents a shift in the method to secure halal integrity, efficiency, and accessibility globally. This shift has a broad implication that pertains to five main stakeholder groups: businesses (Small and Medium Enterprise (SMEs) & Multi-National Corporations (MNCs) halal certification bodies (HCBs), governments/ regulators, consumers, and academia.

10.1 Effect on Small and Medium Enterprise (SMEs) & Multi-National Corporations (MNCs)

10.1.1 Adoption of Scalable Digital Solutions

Halal certification is surrounded by a variety of substantial barriers that make it almost impossible for Small and Medium Enterprises (SMEs) to access such certification, mainly as a result of manual verification processes, compliance obligations to complex laws and high related costs. Artificial Intelligence (AI) uses a prime example that AI can be employed to automate ingredient validation and predictive compliance, which reduces, potentially eliminating human error and drastically increasing speed to market. Halal SMEs may benefit from using AI-based halal compliance tools and blockchain-based traceability systems to expedite procedural hurdles, as it helps them respond quickly to regulatory demands, and at the same time enhance transparency and consumer trust.(Ellahi et al., 2025; Rangkuti, 2023) . MNCs also enjoy a halo of sincerity by the seamless implementation of blockchain and IoT technology for end-to-end supply chain traceability where halal integrity had been well-preserved from sourcing to production and distribution. Such technologies offer an indemnifiable audit log of compliance, thereby strengthening trust in the brand both in Muslim-majority and minority markets.

10.1.2 Investment in Digital Literacy

It means that organizational culture must change too, for a real digital transformation to occur (Ologeanu-Taddei et al., 2025). Businesses are building human capacity by improving digital literacy, training in use of halal-compliant tech applications and refining internal governance to meet emerging digital standards. This builds the capacity among SMEs to engage more effectively in the digital halal ecosystem and less reliant on intermediaries.

10.1.3 Ethical Use of Technology and Data Protection

This also means all the digital systems need to have high-end cybersecurity in place and should have ethical data management protocols. The more data about halal certification that companies collect and process, including consumer preference information, the greater responsibility they have to comply with global privacy standards as well as Shariah principles on transparency and trust. Platforms that are adaptive and which strategically integrate halal-compliant fintech can enable SMEs and MNCs to maintain as well as expand market access, leveraging digital resilience whilst upholding Shariah values (Asadullah et al., 2018)

10.2 Effect on Halal Certification Bodies (HCBs)

10.2.1 Development of Digital Standards

In efforts to modernize legacy systems, Halal Certification Bodies are under pressure (Nusran et al., 2023). This is how AI and big data lead to reduce processing time, lower audit expenses and eradicating fraud. But it needs to create accepted and compliant digital halal certification standards which are universally recognised as interoperable from one jurisdiction to another. AI and IoT based digitization of workflows for halal certification provides for real-time verification and predictive analytics, which will further more efficiencies in aiding to develop trust along the whole halal supply chain nod amongst stakeholders.

10.2.2 Enhancing Trust and Efficiency through Tech Adoption

This translates to a quicker and easier verification process and therefore improves the confidence level of consumers to trust the halal logo. Digitalising HCBs' operations using, say, smart contracts for certification or biometric solutions for monitoring slaughter processes or advanced AI models for verifying documents are digitalisation means that increase efficiency and trust in halal logos as well as ensure compliance with relevant regulations. In order to curb illegal certification fraud, it was proposed that blockchain technology could be deployed, particularly in verifying halal proof for meat and pharmaceutical products, where halal authenticity is almost impossible to verify manually(León-Ecay et al., 2025).

10.3.2 Collaboration with Industry and Academia

HCBs must foster deeper collaboration with academic and tech companies to co-create certifiable digital frameworks (Bakar et al., 2025). Pilot studies on AI-based halal audits or cloud-based compliance platforms are examples where multi-stakeholder partnerships yield practical innovations. New technology layers require HCBs to create integral digital-friendly ways of governance, always in line with common international halal standards and technological scaling.

10.4 Impact on Governments and Regulators

10.4.1 Digital Halal Ecosystems Policy Framework

In crafting national and transnational digital halal ecosystems, Governments have a significant responsibility (Rasyidah et al., 2025). The public sector can play a vital role in digital halal transformation through infrastructure investment, regulatory harmonization, and tech incubators, which enhance the competitiveness of the halal industry as well as traceability systems overall (Noman et al., 2025). Developing regulatory sandboxes for halal startups, releasing some halal tech grants, and rolling out fiscal incentives for digital improvements inside halal zones are strategic initiatives.

10.4.2 Investment in Digital Infrastructure

Any high-tech digital transformation requires good infrastructure: fiber optic networks, cloud computing environments, and data centers. Infrastructure, particularly for any halal-dedicated infrastructure, such as blockchain nodes specifically for national halal registries or traceability hubs for exports, should be built by the governments (Noman et al., 2025). In addition, with the burgeoning of 5G and IoT, real-time halal logistics monitoring is also made possible – a key feature especially for temperature-sensitive halal pharmaceuticals as well as perishable goods.

10.5 Impact on Consumers

10.5.1 Empowered and Informed Decision-Making

When they go digital, consumers are always connected to the necessary information on halal products, such as product information itself, its certification status and even traceability of origin. These apps might use QR codes or NFC (Near Field Communication) that could be used at the point of sale, consequently boosting informed consumption and trust. Through the use of mobile halal verification tools and an AR-product-tracing system, real-time integrity assurance benefiting participatory halal audits will be offered to the consumers, where it will result in more ethical and balanced consumption (Ellahi et al., 2025). This is especially important for Muslim consumers living in non-Muslim majority countries where the availability of halal food may be limited and/or the legitimacy of certification questionable.

10.5.2 Participatory Feedback and Ratings

The bottom line is that this type of consumer has changed. By using digital feedback loops in the form of product reviews, halal audit transparency reports, or crowd-verification systems, and designing a participatory Halal economy (Nusran et al., 2023). This allows consumers to report up-to-the-minute evidence of fraud in the halal supply chain, resulting in quicker regulatory or business action.

10.5.3 Shifts in Behavioral Patterns

Digital technologies are reshaping halal consumer behavior. Ethical consumption, eco-halal preferences, and demand for traceability are gaining prominence. These changes require businesses to adapt rapidly to align with evolving consumer expectations in the digital age. The digital consumer journey in the halal economy is increasingly shaped by platform-based transparency, e-commerce halalization, and feedback loops embedded in decentralized apps (Asadullah et al., 2018).

10.6 Impact on Academia

10.6.1 Advancing Halal Tech Research

Academia is crucial in evaluating the ethical, technical, and social issues of digital halal transformation. Pioneering the shariah-digital innovation frontier, nevertheless, cutting-edge areas where scientific research has gone to meld between shariah crises and digital technology include thoughtful AI in halal decision making, size ability of halal blockchains, etc., aeronautics/ machine learning(Noman et al., 2025). Curricula must evolve to accommodate the realities of digital halal ecosystems(Syed Hamzah et al., 2024). A multidisciplinary approach should be utilized, incorporating Islamic jurisprudence, computer science, supply chain management, and digital ethics curricula in imperatives as the must-haves of training for future halal professionals. Universities are key in setting halal tech ethics, blockchain compliance, scalable innovation, and producing research AI that has a halal socio-economic impact(Ahmad et al., 2011).

11. CONCLUSION

The digital transformation has immense potential to disrupt the Halal industry by reinforcing supply chain integrity with traceability, improving operational efficiency through better demand planning, and expanding market reach through e-commerce platforms. Let AI and big data analytics drive processes to improve decision-making, while blockchain and IOT technologies ensure transparent, trustworthy traceability. Mobile applications and e-commerce platforms have radically changed the way producers globally connect to consumers, increasing accessibility and engagement. On the other hand, it still deals with difficulties in standardizing, securing cybersecurity and data protection, crossing digital gaps, especially by supporting SMEs and solving ethical problems such as algorithm discrimination and misinformation. The synthesis of the previous solutions leads to practical frameworks; however, it also shows gaps where more research is required. Moving forward, the focus should be on having robust digital standards that are based on principles of Maqasid al-Shariah, inclusive policies for a multitude of stakeholders, and ethical usage by all parties by Sharia. With these policies, we hope to create a stronger, more transparent, and efficient Halal ecosystem that not only satisfies market requirements but also ethical imperatives.

REFERENCES

Ab Rashid, N., & Bojei, J. (2020). The relationship between halal traceability system adoption and environmental factors on halal food supply chain integrity in Malaysia. *Journal of Islamic Marketing*, *11*(1), 117–142. Advance online publication. DOI: 10.1108/JIMA-01-2018-0016

Ab Talib, M. S., Mohd. Riaz, M., & Johan, M. R. M. (2022). Halal Supply Chain Digitalisation: Enhancing Traceability and Consumer Trust. *Journal of Islamic Marketing*, *13*(7), 1423–1440. DOI: 10.1108/JIMA-10-2020-0316

Ahmad, H., Fazullah, A., Borham, A. J., & Hashim, H. (2011). Halal Studies In Universities : A Way Forward To Manage Halal Introduction to Fundamental Halal Halal Industry and Awareness. *International Jornal of Arts and Sciences Conference, 4*(09), 1–9.

Ali, A., & Suleiman, N. (2023). Digital Transformation and Sustainability in the Halal Industry: A Maqasid al-Shariah Perspective. *International Journal of Islamic Business and Management*, *7*(1), 55–68. DOI: 10.46281/ijibm.v7i1.1909

Ali, M. H., & Suleiman, N. (2018). Eleven shades of food integrity: A halal supply chain perspective. In *Trends in Food Science and Technology* (Vol. 71). DOI: 10.1016/j.tifs.2017.11.016

Alourani, A., & Khan, S. (2024). A blockchain and artificial intelligence based system for halal food traceability [Preprint]. arXiv. https://doi.org//arXiv.2410.07305DOI: 10.48550

Amin, H., & Isa, M. S. (2021). Transparency and Accountability in Halal Certification: The Role of Digital Technologies. *Journal of Halal Studies*, *3*(2), 45–59.

Asadullah, A., Faik, I., & Kankanhalli, A. (2018). Digital platforms: A review and future directions. *Proceedings of the 22nd Pacific Asia Conference on Information Systems - Opportunities and Challenges for the Digitized Society: Are We Ready? PACIS 2018.*

Asif, M., & Akhlaq, M. (2024). Sharia Compliance in Modern Business Practices. *Tanazur, 5*(2), 285–301. https://tanazur.com.pk/index.php/tanazur/article/view/305

Atzori, L., Iera, A., & Morabito, G. (2010). The Internet of Things: A survey. *Computer Networks*, *54*(15), 2787–2805. Advance online publication. DOI: 10.1016/j.comnet.2010.05.010

Bakar, M. A., Noor, A. M., Ismail, S., & Yusoff, M.Marina Abu BakarAfiffudin Mohammed NoorSyaimak Ismail @ Mat Yusoff. (2025). Halal Meets Biotech: Exploring Integration Opportunities and Challenges in Malaysian Universities: Halal Bertemu Bioteknologi: Meneroka Peluang dan Cabaran Integrasi di Universiti-Universiti Malaysia. *Sains Insani*, *10*(1), 62–74. DOI: 10.33102/sainsinsani.vol10no1.721

BERNAMA. (2025). "Malaysia to Issue Halal Certificates Electronically from May 5." *BERNAMA News Agency*, January 15, 2025. https://www.bernama.com

Bhatt, T., Hickey, C., & McEntire, J. C. (2013). Pilot projects for improving product tracing along the food supply system. *Journal of Food Science*, *78*(s2, Suppl 2.). Advance online publication. DOI: 10.1111/1750-3841.12298 PMID: 24171802

Department of Standards Malaysia. (2019). [*– Halal Food – General Requirements] [Third Revision] [*. Putrajaya: Standards Malaysia.]. *Ms*, *1500*, 2019.

DinarStandard. (2023). *State of the Global Islamic Economy Report 2023*. Dubai: DinarStandard. Retrieved from: https://www.dinarstandard.com/post/state-of-the -global-islamic-economy-report-2023

Dorsemaine, B., Gaulier, J. P., Wary, J. P., Kheir, N., & Urien, P. (2016). Internet of Things: A Definition and Taxonomy. *Proceedings - NGMAST 2015: The 9th International Conference on Next Generation Mobile Applications, Services and Technologies*. DOI: 10.1109/NGMAST.2015.71

Dusuki, A. W., & Abozaid, A. (2021). Trust and Responsibility in Islamic Business Ethics. *International Journal of Islamic and Middle Eastern Finance and Management*, *14*(6), 1004–1020. DOI: 10.1108/IMEFM-05-2020-0223

Dwivedi, Y. K., Hughes, L., Wang, Y., Alalwan, A. A., Ahn, S. J., Balakrishnan, J., Barta, S., Belk, R., Buhalis, D., Dutot, V., Felix, R., Filieri, R., Flavián, C., Gustafsson, A., Hinsch, C., Hollensen, S., Jain, V., Kim, J., Krishen, A. S., & Wirtz, J. (2023). Metaverse marketing: How the metaverse will shape the future of consumer research and practice. *Psychology and Marketing*, *40*(4), 750–776. DOI: 10.1002/mar.21767

Ellahi, R. M., Wood, L. C., Khan, M., & Bekhit, A. E. D. A. (2025). Integrity challenges in halal meat supply chain: Potential industry 4.0 technologies as catalysts for resolution. *Foods*, *14*(7), 1135. DOI: 10.3390/foods14071135 PMID: 40238310

Fauzan, A.Rezki Akbar Norrahman. (2025). Smart Contracts in Increasing Sharia Compliance on Peer To Peer Lending Platforms in Sharia Fintech. *Journal of Society and Scientific Studies*, *1*(1), 45–55. DOI: 10.62504/scientiva1

Fauzi, M. A., Mohd Ali, N. S., Mat Russ, N., Mohamad, F., Battour, M., & Mohd Zaki, N. N. (2024). Halal certification in food products: Science mapping of present and future trends. *Journal of Islamic Marketing*, *15*(12), 3564–3580. DOI: 10.1108/JIMA-12-2023-0407

GS1. 2022. *EPCIS and Core Business Vocabulary Standard, Version 2.0.* Brussels: GS1 AISBL. https://www.gs1.org/standards/epcis

Ghalih, M., & Chang, C.-H. (n.d.). *Aligning Halal Supply Chain Management Improvements with Global Sustainability Standards: A DEMATEL-Based Analysis.* DOI: 10.2478/mdke-2025-0012

Halal Times. (2025). Malaysia's halal certification goes fully digital via MYeHALAL platform.

HARA AgriTech. (2019). *HARA and Sreeya collaborate to invent halal traceability with the first blockchain technology in Indonesia.* Medium.

Hu, Y., & Ghadimi, P. (2022). A review of blockchain technology application on supply chain risk management. *IFAC-PapersOnLine*, *55*(10), 958–963. Advance online publication. DOI: 10.1016/j.ifacol.2022.09.472

Imani, S., Mi'raj, D. A., Bawana, T. A., & Malik, A. R. (2022). E-Commerce Platform As a Halal Life Style Ecosystem Innovation of The Maqashid Shariah Approach. *Journal of Digital Business and Innovation Management*, *1*(2), 101–118. DOI: 10.26740/jdbim.v1i2.50498

Irfany, M. I., Nekha, A., Tieman, M., & Haq, D. A. (2025). Halal procurement strategy for the halal pharmaceutical industry in Indonesia. *Journal of Islamic Marketing*, *16*(4), 1073–1094. DOI: 10.1108/JIMA-09-2023-0274

Kamali, M. H. (2022). *Maqasid al-Shariah, Ijtihad and Civilisational Renewal: A Reformist Approach to Shariah Governance*. IAIS Malaysia.

Khan, S., Rahman, N. A., & Yusoff, R. (2024). Blockchain and AI Integration for Halal Traceability: A Systematic Review. *Food Control*, *156*, 110123. DOI: 10.1016/j.foodcont.2023.110123

Kurniawati, D. A., & Cakravastia, A. (2023). A review of halal supply chain research: Sustainability and operations research perspective. *Cleaner Logistics and Supply Chain*, *6*, 100096. Advance online publication. DOI: 10.1016/j.clscn.2023.100096

Kurniawati, D. A., & Rochman, M. A. (2023). Two stages of halal food distribution model for perishable food products. *International Journal of Production Management and Engineering*, *11*(2), 147–166. Advance online publication. DOI: 10.4995/ijpme.2023.18233

Latif, M. N. A., Aziz, N. A. A., Hussin, N. S. N., & Aziz, Z. A. (2021). Cyber security in supply chain management: A systematic review. *LogForum*, *17*(1), 49–57. DOI: 10.17270/J.LOG.2021555

León-Ecay, S., Insausti, K., López-Maestresalas, A., & Prieto, N. (2025). Non-destructive spectroscopy-based technologies for meat and meat product discrimination - A review. *Meat Science*, *228*, 109893. https://doi.org/https://doi.org/10.1016/j.meatsci.2025.109893. DOI: 10.1016/j.meatsci.2025.109893 PMID: 40570613

Malay Mail. (2024). Jakim developing AI system to simplify halal certification approval.

Mohammed, A., Wang, Q., & Li, X. (2017). A cost-effective decision-making algorithm for an RFID-enabled HMSC network design A multi-objective approach. *Industrial Management & Data Systems*, *117*(9), 1782–1799. Advance online publication. DOI: 10.1108/IMDS-02-2016-0074

Noman, A., Al, , Afif, M. M., Huq, A. M. R., Rahman, A. F. F., & Islam, M. (2025). Blockchain-Driven Halal Supply Chains: Enhancing Transparency and Efficiency While Ensuring Shariah Adherence. *International Journal of Innovative Science and Research Technology*, (April), 1992–1997. DOI: 10.38124/ijisrt/25apr1001

Nusran, M., Nasution, E. N., Prayitno, M. A., & Sudarmanto, E. (2023). Halal Certification in The Digital Age: Leveraging Online Platforms for Enhanced Transparency and Accessibility. *Jurnal Ekonomi. Akuntansi Dan Manajemen Indonesia*, *2*(01), 105–115. DOI: 10.58471/jeami.v2i01.379

Ogbuke, N. J., Yusuf, Y. Y., Dharma, K., & Mercangoz, B. A. (2022). Big data supply chain analytics: Ethical, privacy and security challenges posed to business, industries and society. *Production Planning and Control*, *33*(2-3), 123–137. DOI: 10.1080/09537287.2020.1810764

Ologeanu-Taddei, R., Hönigsberg, S., Weritz, P., Wache, H., Mittermeier, F., Tana, S., Dang, D., Hautala-Kankaanpää, T., & Pekkola, S. (2025). The relationship of digital transformation and corporate sustainability: Synergies and tensions. *Technological Forecasting and Social Change*, *210*, 123809. https://doi.org/https://doi.org/10.1016/j.techfore.2024.123809. DOI: 10.1016/j.techfore.2024.123809

Oye, E., & Emma, O. (2024). *The Role of Big Data Analytics in Enhancing Corporate Social Responsibility (CSR) Initiatives in American Firms*. https://www.researchgate.net/publication/388005010

Rahman, M. M., & Razimi, M. S. A. (2023). Halal biotechnology product: halal supply chain compliance and integrity risk. In *Innovation of food products in Halal supply chain worldwide* (pp. 195–204). Academic Press. DOI: 10.1016/B978-0-323-91662-2.00016-8

Rangkuti, M. Y. (2023). Toward a Holistic Framework of Islamic Business Ethics: Insights from Leadership, Halal Practices, and Finance in a Digital Age. *Sinergi International Journal of Islamic Studies*, *1*(3), 114–127. DOI: 10.61194/ijis.v1i3.593

Rasyidah, A. N., Azizi, A. Q., & Kholis, N. (2025). Digital Ecosystems in Supporting Global Trade of Halal Products: Innovation and Challenges. *ADPEBI International Journal of Business and Social Science*, *5*(2), 1–11.

Rejeb, A., Rejeb, K., Zailani, S., Treiblmaier, H., & Hand, K. J. (2021). Integrating the Internet of Things in the halal food supply chain: A systematic literature review and research agenda. In *Internet of Things (Netherlands)* (Vol. 13). DOI: 10.1016/j.iot.2021.100361

Ridho, A. (2025). Integrating artificial intelligence and blockchain to improve the accuracy of halal certification. *Journal of Halal Review*, *1*(1), 12–22. Advance online publication. DOI: 10.70764/gdpu-jhr.2025.1(1)-02

Ridho, A. (2025). Integrating Artificial Intelligence and Blockchain to Improve the Accuracy of Halal Certification. *Journal of Halal Review*, *1*(1), 12–22. DOI: 10.70764/gdpu-jhr.2025.1(1)-02

Russo, I., Patrucco, A. S., Klumpp, M., & Stanton, D. (2025). Leveraging social media to bridge academia and industry in supply chain management research: A framework for integrated strategies. *International Journal of Physical Distribution & Logistics Management*, *55*(11), 144–162. DOI: 10.1108/IJPDLM-10-2024-0387

Salaam Gateway. (2019). *Malaysia's B2B halal e-commerce platforms DagangHalal, Zilzar, AladdinStreet: Where are they now? Standards and Metrology Institute for Islamic Countries. (2021). OIC/SMIIC Standards on Halal Food and Certification.* SMIIC.

Sunmola, F., Baryannis, G., Tan, A., Co, K., & Papadakis, E. (2025). Holistic framework for blockchain-based halal compliance in supply chains enabled by artificial intelligence. *Systems*, *13*(1), 21. DOI: 10.3390/systems13010021

Susanty, A., et al. (2025). Consumer acceptance of halal food traceability systems. Cleaner Logistics and Supply Chain.

Syed Hamzah, S. A., Johari, S., Yusof, Y. A., Ramlan, M. A., & Mohd Azmi, P. U. B. (2024). a Research Trend: Talent Management Practice in Halal Management. *International Journal of Entrepreneurship and Management Practices*, *7*(28), 559–584. DOI: 10.35631/IJEMP.728040

Tieman, M., & Van Nistelrooy, M. (2014). Perception of Malaysian food manufacturers toward halal logistics. *Journal of International Food & Agribusiness Marketing*, *26*(3), 218–233. DOI: 10.1080/08974438.2013.833572

Tobing, F., Fauzan, H., Simatupang, K., & Aulia, R. (2024). The Role of Artificial Intelligence in the Halal Industry. *Information Management and Business Review*, *16*(3), 159–166. DOI: 10.22610/imbr.v16i3(I)S.4050

Wahyuni, H. C., Rosid, M. A., Azara, R., & Voak, A. (2025). Blockchain technology design based on food safety and halal risk analysis in the beef supply chain with FMEA-FTA. *Journal of Engineering Research (Kuwait)*, *13*(2), 590–595. Advance online publication. DOI: 10.1016/j.jer.2024.02.002

Yushaniza, Z., Yusoff, M., Ishak, M. K., & Alezabi, K. A. (2021). The Role of RFID in Green IoT: A Survey on Technologies, Challenges and A Way Forward. *Technology and Engineering Systems Journal*, *6*(1), 17–35.

ENDNOTES

1. *"Indeed, Allah commands you to render trusts to whom they are due and when you judge between people to judge with justice. Excellent is that which Allah instructs you. Indeed, Allah is ever Hearing and Seeing."(Surah An-Nisa' 4:58)*

2. *"And establish weight in justice and do not make deficient the balance."(Surah Ar-Rahman 55:9)*

Chapter 2
Halal Information Systems: Bridging Islamic and Western Theories

Norlaila Mazura Hj. Mohaiyadin
http://orcid.org/0000-0003-2024-7644
National Defence University of Malaysia, Malaysia

Hafizah Mat Nawi
http://orcid.org/0000-0003-2232-9547
National Defence University of Malaysia, Malaysia

Hasan Al-Banna Mohamed
http://orcid.org/0000-0001-6096-0052
National Defence University of Malaysia, Malaysia

Khairnunnisa Mardzuki
http://orcid.org/0009-0002-3900-9208
National Defence University of Malaysia, Malaysia

Mohd Abdullah Jusoh
http://orcid.org/0009-0000-9656-6583
National Defence University of Malaysia, Malaysia

ABSTRACT

This study aims to develop a conceptual framework regarding the use of the coalescence of Islamic and Western theories in halal information systems. A qualitative method was employed in this study, specifically content analysis from journal articles and other publications, which are considered substantial for developing its conceptual

DOI: 10.4018/979-8-3373-2792-1.ch002

framework. This study anticipates the coalescence of Islamic and Western theories in the halal information systems. From the people's perspective, shariah compliance and Deontological Theory can serve as a bridge between supplier integrity and consumer trust. Shariah compliance may also be aligned with Stakeholder Theory, as it clarifies to stakeholders that shariah governance ensures the accountability of the board of directors and contributes significantly to sustainability performance. In the process perspective, shariah compliance can be bridged with Stakeholder Theory in ensuring fairness, transparency and accountability to all stakeholders. Moreover, Shariah compliance can also be associated with Institutional Theory in the design of the shariah governance framework. From a technological perspective, maslahah can be bridged with the Diffusion of Innovation Theory in terms of maslahah radical halal innovation. Finally, shariah compliance can be bridged with Task Technology Fit Theory in terms of Islamic microfinance. The contribution of this study is directed towards halal industry players, academicians, researchers and students researching the halal information system, and the development of the theory integration between Islam and the West. Future research can be extended to empirical evidence and quantitative research.

INTRODUCTION

While a clear-cut definition of halal information systems remains scarce in existing literature, the authors have identified two key studies that offer valuable insights into the definition, namely Hidayah et al. (2024) and Ibrahim et al. (2024). In the study by Hidayah et al. (2024), the web-based information system was referred to as halal certification processes. Meanwhile, Ibrahim et al. (2024) stated that Halal Traceability System for halal chicken meat supply chain integrates with the Internet of Things. Thus, from both discussions, the halal information system is defined in this study as a technology-driven solution that ensures halal integrity by enabling end-to-end traceability, ensuring transparency across the supply chain and supporting full compliance with regulatory compliance. Integrating digital tools such as blockchain and empowering stakeholders to verify the authenticity of halal products at every stage not only builds trust in the halal ecosystem but also enhances operational efficiency and accountability.

Roles of halal information systems include ensuring compliance with halal standards, meaning that these systems can track, manage and ensure products or services are halal-compliant (Ibrahim et al., 2024). However, there are inadequate research theories in the field of halal information systems. Based on the existing literature review, studies emphasising the bridging of Islamic and Western theories in Halal Information Systems remain very limited and have primarily focused on other contexts, such as Islamic banking, finance, and e-commerce, rather than on Halal Information Systems. Moreover, some studies only proposed Western theories, such as Diffusion of Innovations (Rogers, 2003) or Institutional Theory (DiMaggio & Powell, 1983) to explain adoption and governance behaviours in Halal studies (Gunsun & Chirapanda, 2024; Talib et al., 2019). While others suggested Islamic theories, such as shariah compliance and *maslahah* (public benefit), insufficiently capture the technological diffusion and organisational legitimacy. Indeed, there is a need for contributions to the development of Islamic theories. This dichotomy underscores a critical research opportunity to either adapt existing Western theories to Islamic contexts or develop hybrid theories and remains limited.

The lack of a unified theoretical foundation presents a major limitation in the development of halal information systems studies. This is also consistent with Moniruzzaan and Hamid Aziz (2022), who mentioned that the existing halal certification system can ease difficulties in distinguishing between halal and haram and enhance the explanatory power of Halal information system research. Thus, this study identified a research gap regarding the use of a coalescence of Western and Islamic theories in the halal information systems study. Moreover, this gap highlights the importance of building a distinct theoretical lens that is religiously relevant, especially as halal industries grow globally, intersecting with diverse regulatory and technological environments.

Therefore, this study attempts to develop a conceptual framework on the use of the coalescence of Western and Islamic theories that can be effectively applied within Halal Information Systems. This framework seeks to bridge the gap between conventional information system models, which often stem from secular or Western theories, and Islamic theories governing halal compliance. By combining theories from both perspectives, such as shariah compliance from Islamic theories and Institutional Theory and Stakeholder Theory from the Western perspectives, this study seeks to provide a more holistic conceptual framework for managing and improving halal information systems that is not only theoretically sound but also contextually appropriate. Such a conceptual framework can ensure that technological solutions align with operational efficiency and religious obligations. It also opens new avenues for theoretical and practical research in aligning digital transformation with faith-based values in an increasingly globalised halal industry.

This study uses a qualitative method, with content analysis as the primary method. This method was used to systematically analyse textual data from multiple sources, including the journal articles and other publications, which are considered substantial to developing this study's conceptual framework. Articles were retrieved from Google Scholar and Scopus using the keywords 'Halal information systems', 'system perspectives', 'western theories perspective', and 'Islamic theories perspective', covering publications from 2019 to present. Inclusion criteria comprised reviewed journal articles focusing on Halal information systems, published in English, and containing empirical or conceptual discussion.

A qualitative method allows researchers to explore phenomena within their natural settings, focusing on how researchers interpret (Creswell & Poth, 2018) based on their understandings, meanings, experiences, perspectives and underlying patterns within the social context. This method involves coding and categorising themes or patterns that emerge from the text based on Creswell and Creswell (2018). Through this process, this study was able to construct meaningful interpretations of its objectives. To ensure the rigour and trustworthiness of the findings, this study used a structured coding process by Creswell and Creswell (2018). Employing this methodology allowed this study not only to contribute to the conceptual understanding of bridging theories, Islamic and Western theories on halal information systems, but also to the development of a theoretically grounded framework for future study and practical application.

This study encompasses three perspectives of halal information systems, Islamic theories in halal information systems, Western theories in halal information systems, bridging Islamic and Western theories in halal information systems and conclusion. Three perspectives of halal information systems unveiled three essential perspectives widely examined in system research, namely people, process and technology. The authors spotlighted two central Islamic theories in this study, namely shariah compliance and *maslahah.* The authors further explored five foundational Western theories, namely Deontological Theory, Institutional Theory, Stakeholder Theory, Diffusion of Innovation Theory and Task-Technology Fit Theory. This study aims to fulfil its objectives through the bridging Islamic and Western theories in the halal information system section and ends with the conclusion. The upcoming section unpacks the three perspectives of halal information systems.

THREE PERSPECTIVES OF HALAL INFORMATION SYSTEMS

System studies often revolve around three core perspectives, namely people, process and technology, according to Mohaiyadin (2024), Schneier (2015), Zhang et al. (2013), Haron et al. (2013) and Barney et al. (2008). These three perspectives become a widely adopted approach in system studies owing to their holistic view of how organisations and systems function, as demonstrated in Table 1. Many studies alike appreciate its simplicity and adaptability across various contexts such as waqf, zakat, endowment and importantly, halal information systems. All three perspectives must work together in harmony to create robust and reliable halal information systems that enhance consumer trust, ensure compliance and facilitate growth in halal industries globally. Therefore, to develop a conceptual framework regarding the use of coalescence of Western and Islamic theories in halal information systems, all three perspectives were considered in developing a conceptual framework for this study. Moving further, the following section explores the people perspective on halal information systems.

Table 1. Interpretation of three perspectives in Halal information systems

Perspective	Interpretation
People	• Consumers (Mahmud Zuhudi & Dolah, 2020; Ramli et al., 2023). • Regulatory bodies, producers, or certification agencies (Ridwan et al., 2020). • Local government (Naznii, 2023).
Process	• Halal certification (Mohaiyadin et al., 2024; Novianti et al., 2022). • Halal production, business process (from purchase of materials to selling to the end user), and material storage (Novianti et al. 2022).
Technology	• Use of blockchain can ensure traceability of halal products (Mohaiyadin et al., 2024). • Use of artificial intelligence helps in halal compliance monitoring and detecting non-halal elements in supply chains (Ahmad, 2024).

People Perspective

People perspective focuses on the human element involved in the halal information system, which emphasises the role, responsibility and capability of individuals and teams who design, manage and use the system. This includes stakeholders and the external parties such as halal certifiers (JAKIM, MUIS, IFANCA), employees, consumers, producers, Islamic scholars, fiqh experts, regulators and authorities. Zhang et al. (2013) mentioned that the manager, user, system developer and senior executive influence information system project management. People perspective includes stakeholders, managers and system developers (Haron et al., 2013). Mohaiyadin (2024) highlighted that people perspective refers to stakeholders. In the waqf management information system, stakeholders include administrator, agent, giver (community), government (*sultan, fatwa council*, court, authority and auditor), beneficiary and academician (Mohaiyadin, 2024). This information can also be used for halal information systems. Table 1 illustrates the interpretation of people perspectives in halal information systems.

Interestingly, over the past five years, only a few studies, namely those by Mahmud Zuhudi and Dolah (2020) and Ramli et al. (2023), have specifically highlighted consumers as key stakeholders in the Halal industry. Despite consumers being the end recipients and decision makers in halal products and service acceptance, much of the existing literature tends to focus more on regulatory bodies, producers, or certification agencies, such as Ridwan et al. (2020) on the authorisation of halal certification in Indonesia, Malaysia and Singapore. Similarly, Naznii (2023) investigated the role of local government in Australia in regulating halal certification, again centring the discussion around governance structure. Thus, there is a lack of comprehensive investigation into how consumers perceive, influence and interact with halal assurance systems, as well as how their trust, knowledge and behaviour shape the development and sustainability of the halal industry. Addressing this gap is crucial for creating a more inclusive, demand-driven understanding of Halal governance and industry practices. Consumer engagement directly influences the effectiveness of traceability and transparency mechanisms; for instance, authorities affect the integrity of certification workflows. Thus, it is important to connect the people with the process perspective as follows.

Process Perspective

Haron et al. (2013) stated that the process perspective relates to circulars, strategic frameworks, and service delivery models in the system. Mohaiyadin (2024) mentioned that waqf management systems operate through a simple flow: Input, process and output, starting with waqf giver (input), followed by issuing receipts, BS distributing of funds (process) and ending with beneficiaries (output). However, the process perspective in halal information systems is concerned with how the business processes and workflows are structured and integrated within the halal information system, such as halal certification process, traceability, raw material sourcing, logistics and supply chain, quality control, audit monitoring, as well as retail and consumer assurance. According to Mohaiyadin et al. (2024) and Novianti et al. (2022), process in the halal industry refers to halal certification. Moreover, Novianti et al. (2022) also mentioned that the process in the halal industry includes halal production, business process (from purchase of materials to selling to the end user) and material storage, as shown in Table 1. It suggests a pressing need to map and analyse the end-to-end integration of halal business processes, especially how blockchain and artificial intelligence can enhance traceability, transparency and compliance across the halal value chain. Concerning technology, the following outlines the key aspects.

Technology Perspective

In terms of technology perspective, the underlying technology developed must comply with Islamic principles in supporting halal activities, avoid *haram* (forbidden) practices, ensure halal operation, security and data handling. Technology perspective refers to the tools, systems and infrastructure that enable the halal information system to function efficiently, such as blockchain and artificial intelligence. Technology helps save time, reduce implementation costs and streamlines processes for greater efficiency (Zhang et al., 2013). The use of blockchain can ensure traceability of halal products (Mohaiyadin et al., 2024). The use of artificial intelligence aids in halal compliance monitoring and detecting non-halal elements in supply chains (Ahmad, 2024), as shown in Table 1. Ethical artificial intelligence should be designed to avoid bias, ensure fairness and promote social justice, which aligns with Islamic values. The next section explores the Islamic theories in halal information systems.

ISLAMIC THEORIES IN HALAL INFORMATION SYSTEMS

This section delves into key Islamic theories underpinning the foundation of this study. Two central concepts are brought to the forefront, namely shariah compliance and *maslahah,* as guiding theories. By grounding this study in shariah compliance and *maslahah,* the research not only aligns with Islamic epistemology but also offers a holistic framework that considers legal obligations and social welfare. Table 2 presents the Islamic theories underpinning halal information systems. The following discussion explores these frameworks in detail, highlighting their relevance and application to this study.

Table 2. Islamic theories underpinning halal information systems

Islamic theories	Halal Information Systems
Shariah Compliance	• To ensure that the livestock they supply is shariah-compliant (Ab Rashid & N. Bojei, 2019). • Ensures that Islamic banks or other financial institutions are conducting themselves following prescribed rules, regulations and processes (AbdulKareem et al., 2022). • Shariah Compliance was the underpinning theory in addressing challenges in halal certification using blockchain technology (Mohaiyadin et al., 2024).
Maslahah (Social Welfare)	• Halal certification programme for macro and small entrepreneurs (Suhartini et al., 2024). • *Maslahah Mursalah* is used in the halal certification (Mas'ud et al., 2025).

Shariah Compliance

It was discovered that the phrase "shariah compliance" is not exactly stated in the Quran, but the word "shariah" can be found in Surah Al-Jathiyah (45:18) as follows:

ثُمَّ جَعَلْنَٰكَ عَلَىٰ شَرِيعَةٍ مِّنَ ٱلْأَمْرِ فَٱتَّبِعْهَا وَلَا تَتَّبِعْ أَهْوَآءَ ٱلَّذِينَ
لَا يَعْلَمُونَ ١٨

"Then We put you, [O Muhammad], on an ordained way concerning the matter [of religion]; so, follow it and do not follow the inclinations of those who do not know" Source: https://legacy.quran.com/45/18 (n.d.)

It shows that shariah is related to Islam and must be practised in all aspects of life, including halal goods and services, avoiding *riba* (interest-based transactions), *gharar* (uncertainty or speculation) and *maysir* (gambling). This verse reminds Muslims to anchor their beliefs and actions in authentic Islamic teachings, especially when facing pressure to conform to Western theories that contradict Islam. It calls for discernment and firmness in faith, following what Allah SWT has revealed rather than what is popular or convenient. In addition, shariah compliance refers to the adherence to Islamic legal and ethical principles, as derived from the Quran, sunnah, *Ijma'* (consensus) and *Qiyas* (analogical reasoning). Various studies embraced shariah compliance as the foundation of halal studies. For example, a study by Aizat Jamaludin et al. (2019) stated that the shariah compliance healthcare system is an urgent demand for Muslim consumers and guarantees the pipeline of shariah compliance and *halalan tayyiban* chain from farm to hospital bedside. It shows a greater inclination for growth in medical tourism and halal industry in Malaysia (Aizat Jamaludin et al., 2019). This is also confirmed by Che Jamaludin et al. (2025), stating that the target population for shariah compliance healthcare services in Malaysia includes local Muslim patients within the public healthcare system and international Muslim medical tourists who often opt for private hospitals' specialised services.

Ab Rashid and N Bojei (2019) mentioned that the concern of the suppliers in the halal industry is to ensure that the livestock they supply is shariah-compliant, such as being fed with good, clean, permitted and legal nutritious food. This means that the halal information system must be created with a transparent, honest and sustainable architecture that promotes welfare and avoids harm. In the waqf matters, Abu Talib et al. (2020) mentioned that shariah compliance is considered as the interplay of coercive isomorphism, one of the elements of institutional theory, which becomes the potent forces (rules and regulations) by the State Islamic Religious Council and Fatwa Council inducing the intention to adopt a standardised waqf accounting and reporting. According to Awang et al. (2023), the Fatwa Council can explain any legal issues arising out of the halal consumerism of the Muslim community, especially in ensuring clarity and compliance in food-related matters for the Muslim community.

Mohaiyadin et al. (2022) stated that shariah compliance poses a challenge for waqf administrators when dealing with stakeholders concerned with waqf distribution decisions, specifically the State Islamic Religious Council and Fatwa Council. AbdulKareem et al. (2022) mentioned that shariah compliance is a process that assures that Islamic banks or other financial institutions are conducting themselves following prescribed rules, regulations and processes. Additionally, Mohaiyadin et al. (2024) also emphasised that shariah compliance was the underpinning theory in addressing challenges in halal certification using blockchain technology. Blockchain is increasingly viewed as a disruptive technology with applications in shariah-compliant digital contracts, including smart contracts that are transparent, traceable, immutable and free from speculative trading or support activities prohibited in Islam. Related to halal information systems, shariah compliance refers to the adherence to Islamic principles on the use, processing and sharing of data without manipulation in financial transactions and the halal logo. Developers and administrators need to ensure that halal information systems are not only technologically functional but are also fully compliant with Islamic law, which refers to shariah compliance.

Maslahah (Social Welfare)

Arifin and Hatoli (2021) introduced *maslahah* perspective in halal certificate application in Indonesia. Sulistyawati et al. (2024) stated that *maslahah* indicates the understanding of something with many benefits. These benefits refer to the public interest or social welfare in promoting well-being and the common good of the broader community, and prevent harm, not only for the individual but also to society. The concept of maslahah, while not explicitly mentioned, is reflected in the Quran, particularly in Surah Al-Baqarah (2:185), as follows:

يُرِيدُ ٱللَّهُ بِكُمُ ٱلْيُسْرَ وَلَا يُرِيدُ بِكُمُ ٱلْعُسْرَ

"Allah intends for you ease and does not intend for you hardship" Source: https://legacy.quran.com/2/185 (n.d.)

The above phrase reflects Islam's emphasis on ease and practicality, not hardship. *Maslahah* is also closely associated with halal information systems, which should prioritise community benefit over profit maximisation. These systems ought to serve the public good by promoting social equity, implying that developers are not merely builders of technology but enablers of community empowerment and shared accountability. This mindset should guide the design and implementation of such systems. Suhartini et al. (2024) stated that *maslahah* is related to the halal certification programme for macro and small entrepreneurs, as well as the benefits of the programme. Al Farisi et al. (2025) stated that halal cosmetics products fall under *maslahah tahsiniyat* or tertiary needs for comfort and beauty. A halal information system ensures that only certified halal products, including cosmetics, are available to consumers. In addition, Mas'ud et al. (2025) and Abdul Jafar (2022) stated that *maslahah mursalah is* used in the halal certification. Thus, using the *maslahah* perspective in halal information systems would promote transparency and trust in societal dealings and would not lead to negative consequences such as the spread of misinformation. Additionally, Abdul Jafar (2022) mentioned that *maslahah mursalah* is considered more appropriate in the halal food certification context. It shows that the *maslahah* perspective can be used to support technological advancements such as blockchain and artificial intelligence with clear, accessible and traceable information that benefits society in online halal certification systems, to ensure technological progress while maintaining halal authenticity.

WESTERN THEORIES IN HALAL INFORMATION SYSTEMS

This section explores key Western theories that offer valuable insight into the development of halal information systems. Five prominent theories have been identified: Deontological Theory, Stakeholder Theory, Institutional Theory, Diffusion of Innovation Theory, and Task-Technology Fit Theory. These theories provide a multidimensional framework for analysing halal information systems study, balancing technical performance, ethical duty, organisational pressures and stakeholder dynamics. While each theory has its strengths, their combined application offers a holistic approach to understanding how halal information systems can be effectively designed, adopted and sustained in real-world contexts. Table 3 shows the Western theories underpinning halal information systems. The following discussion unpacks each framework and its relevance to the halal information systems context.

Deontological Theory

The founder of the Deontological Theory was Immanuel Kant. According to Kant (1997), Deontological Theory is defined as a moral framework that judges the morality of an action based on whether it adheres to a set of rules or duties, rather than on its consequences. Deontology focuses on righteousness in the process of action rather than the result of the action (Vasudevan & Aslan, 2021). It shows that Deontological Theory focuses on duty and obligation. To relate it to halal information systems, system developers must ensure that the system upholds moral rights and respects user autonomy, privacy and fairness. Puspitasari et al. (2023) used Deontological Theory with Al-Ghazali's insights, such as being responsible, honest and fair in fashion sales and purchase transactions. Thus, it seems that Puspitasari et al. (2023) aimed to bridge between Islamic and Western theories. On the other hand, Raimi (2024) stated that the Deontological Theory enrich application of Islamic ethical foundations in the context of sustainable development to ensure social, economic and environmental well-being for present and future generations; however, it was found that Raimi (2024) limited the Deontological Theory as complementary framework that enrich the understanding and application of Islamic ethical principles within the context of sustainable development. This is consistent with the view from M Rahman et al. (2024), mentioning that Deontological Theory may not adequately address complex ethical dilemmas posed by artificial intelligence within the halal industry. Thus, this study proposed bridging Deontological Theory with Islamic theories to enhance ethical decision-making in Muslim contexts.

Table 3. Western theories underpinning Halal information systems

Western theories	Halal Information Systems
Deontological Theory	• Raimi (2024) limits the Deontological Theory as a complementary framework that enriches the understanding and application of Islamic ethical principles within the context of sustainable development. • Deontological Theory may not adequately address complex ethical dilemmas posed by artificial intelligence within the halal industry (M. Rahman et al., 2024).
Stakeholder Theory	• Companies should communicate with the stakeholders on the individuals who sit on the halal committee or halal advisory board (N. M. Ramli et al., 2020). • Each stakeholder should be ethical (Haleem et al., 2021). • Stakeholders are the key to realising halal tourism (Zarkasyi et al., 2022; Haleem et al., 2021).
Institutional Theory	• Participation intent in blockchain-empowered halal fashion traceability systems was mainly motivated by institutional pressures (Sumarliah et al., 2022) • There was a link between the theoretical isomorphic pressures of the institutional environment that shape the firm's decisions regarding halal certification (Gunsun & Chirapanda, 2024). • The Institutional Theory provides pressure to industry players on halal certification with a harmonious institutionalisation process (Susanty et al., 2024).
Diffusion of Innovation Theory	• Sumarliah et al. (2022) found that the participation intent in blockchain-empowered halal fashion traceability systems was mainly motivated by perceived desirability. • Qader et al. (2023) found that perceived compatibility, perceived relative advantage, perceived complexity, awareness and religious beliefs were the driving factors for halal supply chain adoption. • Sohail et al. (2024) found that there were significant correlations between knowledge, social influence, trust and acceptance of halal cosmetics.
Task-Technology Fit Theory	• Kumaladewi et al. (2020) used the revised Task-Technology Fit Theory, specifically the Human Organisation-Technology Fit model, in e-Halal certification system acceptance.

Stakeholder Theory

The Stakeholder Theory was founded by Freeman, R Edward. According to Freeman (1984), Stakeholder Theory proposes that a company should create value not only for its shareholders but for all stakeholders, groups or individuals who can affect or are affected by the company's actions. Ramli et al. (2020) stated that halal reporting to stakeholders through disclosures correctly stated in the annual reports and on the companies' websites is a basic rule to meet the demands of shariah. Companies should communicate with the stakeholders on the individuals who sit on the halal committee or halal advisory board (N. M. Ramli et al., 2020). Each stakeholder should be ethical, and their aim should not be to earn profit but to come forward voluntarily to create a global quality framework for halal logistics (Haleem et al., 2021). Therefore, consumers expect an ethical and transparent process, such as halal certification by Western companies, not just for profit but to respect religious values and expand halal market reach. Zarkasyi et al. (2022) mentioned that stakeholders are the main key to realising halal tourism, which includes the government (also mentioned by Haleem et al. (2021)), academia, media, business actors (also mentioned by Haleem et al. (2021)) and societies (also mentioned by Haleem et al. (2021)). The way forward in halal tourism development includes the needs of the local government to create clear guidelines, business actors to be clear with halal tourism, academicians to conduct halal tourism research, communities to be educated and empowered to develop halal tourism, and media to actively promote and share about halal tourism (Zarkasyi et al., 2022). Stakeholder Theory suggests that the business actors should consider the involved stakeholders' interests.

Institutional Theory

There were three elements or isomorphisms or external pressures to the institutions in Institutional Theory, which were referring to coercive, normative and mimetic (DiMaggio & Powell, 1983). However, Scott (1987) expanded Institutional Theory with institutional logic, such as religion, family and economics, among others. As relevant to this study, religious institutional logic was focused on. Abu Talib et al. (2020) and Mohaiyadin et al. (2022) used Institutional Theory with religious institutional logic in waqf studies, such as shariah compliance, *fatwa* and *ihsan*. Sumarliah et al. (2022) found that the participation intent in blockchain-empowered halal fashion traceability systems was mainly motivated by institutional pressures such as industry bodies (normative), competitors (mimetic) and regulators (coercive). In another study, Gunsun and Chirapanda (2024) utilised Institutional Theory in halal certification by The Central Islamic Council of Thailand and found a link between the theoretical isomorphic pressures of the institutional environment and the observable strategic forces shaping the firm's decisions of halal certification as a response to the competitive environment by highlighting the differences between industries and similarities between firms of different sizes. The Institutional Theory provides pressure (desire of halal institutions) that influences market formation, market transformation and the behaviour of companies within social networks; governments, policymakers and certifiers should engage industry players in halal certification through a harmonious institutionalisation process (Susanty et al., 2024).

Therefore, Institutional Theory highlights how organisations respond to regulatory pressures and evolving consumer expectations. For halal businesses, the pursuit of halal certification demands alignment with local laws and Islamic principles, driving the need for innovative, hybrid market adaptation strategies and a halal integration system between countries.

Diffusion of Innovation Theory

The founder of the Diffusion of Innovation Theory was Everett M. Rogers. Diffusion of Innovation Theory explains how, why and at what rate new ideas, technologies or products spread through a population or social system over time (Rogers, 1983). The authors identified that the Diffusion Innovation Theory aligns closely with the technology perspective of systems. Here, technology encompasses cutting-edge innovations like blockchain, artificial intelligence and the Internet of Things, the key enablers in the advancement of halal information systems. Sumarliah et al. (2022) found that the participation intent in blockchain-empowered halal fashion traceability systems was mainly motivated by perceived desirability. Qader et al. (2023) revealed that perceived compatibility, perceived relative advantage, perceived complexity, awareness and religious beliefs were the driving factors for halal supply chain adoption among exporters of meat associations in Pakistan. All factors describe the attributes of the Diffusion of Innovation Theory. Sohail et al. (2024) found that there were significant correlations between knowledge, social influence, trust and acceptance of halal cosmetics. The results confirmed that social influence and awareness were important factors in Pakistan's acceptance of halal cosmetics (Sohail et al., 2024). The Diffusion of Innovation Theory helps halal stakeholders understand and accept new technological advancements, such as perceived benefits, ease of use and regulatory support.

Task-Technology Fit Theory

The Task-Technology Fit Theory was founded by D Goodhue and Ronald L Thompson. According to Goodhue and Ronald (1995), Task-Technology Fit Theory explains how the effectiveness of technology depends on how well it supports the specific tasks a user needs to perform. Originally, Martono et al. (2020) mentioned that Task-Technology Fit Theory elements include task, technology, fit (utilisation) and result (performance), but Kumaladewi et al. (2020) added human element to the existing theory. Kumaladewi et al. (2020) employed the revised Task-Technology Fit Theory, which refers to the Human Organisation-Technology Fit model in e-halal certification system acceptance. Human here refers to system use (who uses it), level of user, training, knowledge, expectations, attitudes (acceptance or rejection) and user satisfaction. This adaptation reflects an important evolution of the original Task-Technology Fit Theory framework, as it recognises that system effectiveness is not determined by technology and task alignment alone, but also human factors. This inclusion acknowledges that user engagement and perception directly influence technology adoption and success, particularly in halal certification, where trust, usability and understanding are critical. At its core, Task-Technology Fit Theory focuses on how well technology supports users' tasks or the better the fit between technology and task, the more likely it will be used and be effective.

BRIDGING ISLAMIC AND WESTERN THEORIES IN HALAL INFORMATION SYSTEMS

Table 4 presents the conceptual framework of this study, aligning with its aim to develop a conceptual framework on the coalescence of Western and Islamic theories in halal information systems. The conceptual framework of this study was developed based on three key system perspectives: People, process and technology. The discussion of the people perspective includes suppliers, consumers and stakeholders. The discussion of the process perspective involves aspects such as compliance, fairness, transparency, accountability, ethics, policies, requirements, regulations and halal certification. Meanwhile, the technology perspective covers halal innovation and the application of technology within halal information systems. The discussion begins with the people perspective, described as follows.

People Perspective

The people perspective in halal information systems encompasses the human dimensions and ethical considerations that influence the system's design, governance and usage. This includes supplier integrity (ensures raw materials and processes follow halal standards), consumer trust (vital for system credibility and adoption), roles of governing bodies such as the board of directors and relevant stakeholders in halal information systems. This study discovered that shariah compliance aligns with Deontological Theory and Stakeholder Theory. By integrating these theories, this study emphasises that halal information systems should not merely function as technical platforms but also reflect ethical governance, religious accountability and inclusive stakeholder engagement. The discussion proceeds as follows.

Bridging Shariah Compliance with Deontological Theory

Based on Table 4, Abd Rashid et al. (2023) mentioned that personal factors are based on two moral philosophies: Deontological (rule-based views) and teleological evaluations (consequence-based views). According to Ab Rashid and N Bojei (2019), supplier ethics in pricing, efficiency and delivery time are also expected to impact their integrity in the halal industry. Ab Rashid and N Bojei (2019) also mentioned that suppliers in the halal industry must ensure that the livestock they provide meet shariah compliance, such as being fed with clean, lawful and nutritious food. Thus, supplier ethics are expected to impact the integrity to ensure their products meet shariah compliance. Both theories also emphasise the importance of justice and excellence in behaviour. Shariah compliance emphasises *adl* (justice) and *ihsan* (excellence in behaviour), whereas ethics concept emphasises justice ethics (fairness in treatment) and rights-based ethics (all individuals' rights are respected). For instance, the system platform should ensure all information is fair, equitable, clear and accurate to the users about halal products.

Table 4. Conceptual framework on coalescence of Islamic and Western theories in halal information systems

Perspective	Islamic theories	Bridging	Western theories
People	Shariah Compliance	1. Supplier integrity. 2. Consumer trust.	Deontological Theory.
		1. Clarification of stakeholders on shariah compliance solutions. 2. Shariah governance compliance ensures that the Board of Directors is responsible to the bank's stakeholders. 3. Greater significance in the sustainability score.	Stakeholder Theory.
Process	Shariah Compliance	1. Help stakeholders ensure shariah compliance transactions. 2. Shariah governance ensures fairness, transparency, and accountability to all stakeholders, aligning with stakeholder theory. 3. Encourage ethical and socially responsible practice in the multidimensional sustainability metrics. 4. Stakeholders' framework in Islam. 5. Helps companies comply with Islamic teachings for stakeholders	Stakeholder Theory.
		1. Designing the shariah governance framework. 2. Coercive pressure includes government policies, shariah requirements and regulations. 3. Describes how blockchain technology addresses challenges in halal certification.	Institutional Theory.

continued on following page

Table 4. Continued

Perspective	Islamic theories	Bridging	Western theories
Technology	*Maslahah*	*Maslahah* radical halal innovation.	Diffusion of Innovation Theory.
	Shariah Compliance	Islamic microfinance.	Task Technology Fit Theory.

According to Zulkifli and Yusuf (2023), incorporating the *maqasid* shariah principles enhances consumer trust in halal products and services to promote ethical and sustainable business practices within the halal industry. Najiha et al. (2024) used *maqasid* shariah and Deontology Theory on mandatory vaccination policy for children in Malaysia. At a high level, both theories can converge on the moral imperative to protect human life. Preservation of life is a primary objective of shariah, which gives strong normative weight to interventions that prevent death and serious illness. Deontology Theory recognises duties that protect persons and thus, when vaccination demonstrably prevents substantial harm, both theories can support a policy that seeks to secure broad protection for children and the community.

These highlight how shariah compliance aligns naturally with Deontological Theory in many contexts besides halal information systems and are maintained at every level of interaction. A halal information system guided by shariah is ethically grounded in obligatory compliance, like Deontological Theory that requires strict adherence to moral rules. Deontological Theory supports the ethical backbone of shariah compliance in halal information systems by reinforcing compliance, and both theories emphasise rule-following for the sake of moral, religious correctness, and obligatory adherence to the ethical principles; shariah compliance through divine command and Deontology Theory through rational duty. Consequently, Halal Information System can be governed by both theories, divine command and rational duty reinforce each other to uphold truth, trust, and accountability.

Bridging Shariah Compliance with Stakeholder Theory

Authors observed that while shariah compliance has limited connection to Stakeholder Theory in halal information systems, it has been widely explored in other Islamic contexts such as e-commerce, banking, Islamic accounting and Takaful operators. This issue also ties directly into halal matters, and this stands as a strong model for halal information systems to emulate. Ribadu et al. (2020) mentioned that stakeholders clarified shariah compliance for e-commerce by regularly proposing and evaluating alternative solutions. According to Alam et al. (2022), the shariah governance framework is a set of guidelines and practices prepared by regulators and the Board of Directors should consider the banking pressures, political situation and social limitations, as well as ensure responsibility, fairness and transparency with all stakeholders in the bank performance context. Puji Fajariani and Hermawan Adinugraha (2024) stated that shariah-related accounting helps companies comply with Islamic teachings in operations and finances, besides providing relevant and transparent information for stakeholders, including investors, customers and regulators.

Mohd Zain et al. (2025) mentioned that stakeholders' feedback highlighted that shariah compliance holds greater significance in the sustainability score for Takaful operators. These situations highlight how shariah compliance and Stakeholder Theory intersect across sectors like e-commerce, banking, Islamic accounting and Takaful, reinforcing the idea that shariah compliance is inherently stakeholder-oriented. These insights provide a conceptual foundation for developing halal information systems that are shariah-compliant with Stakeholder Theory in terms of stakeholder-responsive, regulator-aligned, as well as transparent and ethically grounded, as presented in Table 4.

Process Perspective

The process perspective in this study emphasises how operational workflows and procedures are designed and executed to ensure fair, transparent, accountable, ethical responsible transactions; strong governance aligned with shariah and government regulations; and supported by robust halal certification technology, as illustrated in Table 4. These processes include critical functions such as halal certification, supply chain traceability, audit and compliance monitoring, quality control and consumer assurance. This study observed that shariah compliance ensures that every step in the halal value chain maintains religious and legal integrity, seamlessly tied together with Stakeholder Theory and Institutional Theory, deeply embedded in a normative environment shaped by religious ethics. This theoretical integration ensures that halal information systems promote systematic trust, operational integrity and sustainable compliance, aligning with Islamic values and contemporary governance standards. The following section unpacks the key points of the discussion.

Bridging Shariah Compliance with Stakeholder Theory

Despite the limited direct links between both theories, they are still grounded in the Islamic perspective and may offer meaningful insights for the development of the conceptual framework in this study. Ribadu et al. (2020) stated that a shariah compliance e-commerce transaction algorithm was developed, proposing an intermediate shariah transaction party to act as a middle party of stakeholders to ensure shariah-compliant transactions. It emphasises a holistic approach that integrates shariah compliance throughout the development of lifecycle of the system. Shariah governance guides Stakeholder Theory by emphasising fairness, transparency and accountability to all stakeholders (Alam et al., 2022). Ullah et al. (2023) stated that Islamic jurisprudence or shariah law has received very special attention that can be linked with stakeholders' framework in Islamic labelling and corporate governance. Therefore, shariah compliance naturally aligns with Stakeholder Theory on transactional and organisational levels and blending these theories can build a strong conceptual framework for halal information systems. Besides, Mohd Zain et al. (2025) mentioned that to encourage ethical and socially responsible practice in the Takaful industry, *maqasid* shariah and stakeholder perspectives should be included for multidimensional sustainability metrics. Thus, the integration of both theories provides a solid foundation for the conceptual framework of this study, despite being applied in different contexts. This approach ensures that the systems do not just function efficiently but also align with Islamic principles.

Bridging Shariah Compliance with Institutional Theory

Bashir (2019) stated that coercive pressure, one of the Institutional Theory elements, includes government policies, regulations, shariah requirements and consumer expectations. At the individual level, halal consumers may experience coercive pressures from halal authorities, shariah requirements and food safety standards to consume halal food products. It shows that shariah compliance can be analysed not only as a personal or spiritual choice but also as an institutional force. The linkage between the two theories helps to contextualise religious adherence within broader institutional frameworks. Karbhari et al. (2020) stated that a well-designed shariah governance framework is driven by Institutional Theory, which could assist in providing guidelines, strategies and procedures for Islamic banks to better conduct, monitor and control their social, religious and accountability obligations. Karbhari et al. (2020) also mentioned that the Institutional Theory serves an important role in the enhancement of organisational structure and performance by balancing the stakeholders' roles, such as regulators, institutions, centralised shariah advisory board, the board of directors, shariah supervisory board, management and shariah officers in Islamic banks context through its capacity to deal with operational guidelines and procedures for organisations. By aligning shariah compliance with Institutional Theory, it becomes evident that compliance is not merely a spiritual obligation but also a strategic and structural necessity embedded within the organisational ecosystem.

Nasir et al. (2021) stated that key Islamic institutions should use existing shariah rules to create pressure through regulations and standards. Pressure on regulations and standards was an example of a coercive element in Institutional Theory. Mohaiyadin et al. (2024) used religious institutional logic, specifically shariah compliance, as an expansion from the institutional theory to describe how blockchain technology addresses challenges in halal certification. By linking these perspectives, it becomes clear that Institutional Theory provides regulatory (coercive) and value-driven (normative and religious logic) pathways for understanding shariah compliance. Therefore, shariah compliance ensures that all processes align with Islamic values and legal rulings. It covers coercive, normative, and mimetic isomorphisms of Institutional Theory for determining the permissibility and integrity of operations, guiding developers and users in ensuring the system functions within halal boundaries. It also implies that the system itself must support transparency, accountability and ethical conduct, in line with Islamic moral standards.

Technology Perspective

As shown in Table 4, the technology-driven halal innovation landscape is evolving through *maslahah*-inspired breakthroughs, such as blockchain-enabled traceability and artificial intelligence-based halal compliance monitoring. These innovations are not only improving the efficiency and transparency of Halal systems but are also being guided by Islamic ethical and economic principles, such as Islamic microfinance models. Islamic microfinance models promote financial inclusion, risk-sharing and ethical lending, which align with *maslahah* and shariah compliance. To meet the aims of this study from a technology perspective, the authors revealed a novel integration; *maslahah,* an Islamic theory, aligns with the Diffusion of Innovative Theory, while shariah compliance connects meaningfully with the Task Technology Fit Theory. This integrated theoretical approach enables a more holistic understanding of technology adoption and design within halal ecosystems. By combining *maslahah* with the Diffusion of Innovative Theory and shariah compliance with Task Technology Fit Theory, this study contributes a unique lens that respects religious foundations and technology relevance, paving the way for Islamic innovation frameworks that are principle-driven and practically viable. The following sub-section presents a discussion on this issue.

Bridging *Maslahah* with Diffusion of Innovative Theory

Haji Ahmad and Farid Shamsudin (2021) mentioned that man always revive and innovate through available resources to preserve the *maslahah* and ensure the sustainability of human lives. The precedence for innovation leads to *maslahah* as the most important principle that makes innovation as a necessity to be prioritised and implemented (Haji Ahmad & Farid Shamsudin, 2021). This shows that innovation is not merely an option but a moral imperative in Islam, driven by the pursuit of *maslahah* and the sustainability of human life. In the Diffusion of Innovative Theory, religious leaders and ethical institutions are the key players for public interest (*maslahah*). Additionally, Haji Ahmad & Farid Shamsudin (2021) also mentioned it is important for experts in fiqh (Islamic jurisprudence) to work together with professionals in fields related to *fardhu kifayah* (communal obligations). Sulistyawati et al. (2024) mentioned that *maslahah*-driven radical halal innovation in products represents a novelty, introducing various new tools and methods within small and medium industries in Indonesia. In the Diffusion of Innovative Theory, an innovation is anything perceived as new by a group, whereas *maslahah* radical halal innovation is the core innovation being diffused. *Maslahah* ensures that the innovation contributes to public interest, making it morally and socially advantageous while aligning with Islamic principles.

Bridging Shariah Compliance With Task Technology Fit Theory

While both theories have been explored within the wider Islamic framework, their intersection in the specific context of halal remains notably underexamined. Provita Wijayanti (2024) used both theories to examine the nature of the relationship between Task Technology Fit toward *maqasid* shariah implementation and sustainable performance in Islamic microfinance and found that *maqasid* shariah implementation mediated the relationship between Task Technology Fit and sustainable performance. Provita Wijayanti (2024) also mentioned that the prominent contribution of *maqasid* shariah implementation is a reference technology in Islamic microfinance. It revealed that *maqasid* shariah acts as a fundamental of Islamic theory for the Task Technology Fit of Western theory in Islamic microfinance and as a guiding framework for aligning technological solutions with shariah values, ensuring that the infrastructure does not host or promote haram content or unethical practices such as breaches and misuse. A significant gap was identified in existing research concerning the bridge between shariah compliance and Task Technology Fit Theory within the halal information system. Therefore, this limited coverage in the current literature signals the need for a more in-depth investigation moving forward.

CONCLUSION

This study explored how Islamic theories can be bridged with Western theories, particularly within the halal information systems context. Establishing this connection is crucial to address the shortcomings of Western theories when used as underpinning theories in research related to halal information systems. As such, this study aimed to develop a conceptual framework regarding the use of coalescence of Islamic and Western theories in halal information systems for halal industry players, academicians, researchers and students. This study identified and engaged the Western theories that can be aligned with Islamic perspectives without violating existing Islamic laws and principles. This offers a meaningful perspective for halal industry players, academicians, researchers and students to bridge both theories (Islamic and Western) in the halal information systems study. By employing a qualitative approach through journal articles and other publications, this study has successfully achieved its aims. Identified Islamic theories in this study included shariah compliance and *maslahah.* Meanwhile, the identified Western theories in this study included Deontological Theory, Stakeholder Theory, Institutional Theory, Diffusion of Innovation Theory and Task Technology Fit Theory.

The people perspective in this study reflects a dynamic interplay between Islamic theory, which refers to shariah compliance and Western theory, which refers to Deontological Theory. This integration jointly shapes ethical decision-making among individuals such as suppliers, developers, certifiers and consumers within the halal ecosystem. The emphasis on *adl* and *ihsan*, justice ethics and rights-based ethics underscores the expectation for ethical integrity in every interaction. On the other hand, the explicit intersection of shariah compliance and Stakeholder Theory in this study remains unexplored, demonstrating the strength of this integration. Shariah compliance functions through active stakeholder engagement, transparent communication and ethical governance frameworks. These findings affirmed that shariah compliance is not just a theological mandate but inherently stakeholder-oriented, requiring fairness, accountability and inclusivity in decision-making processes. Therefore, future studies on halal information systems should emulate these models by embedding shariah compliance within a stakeholder-responsive framework.

In the process perspective, the integration of shariah compliance with Stakeholder Theory and Institutional Theory provided a comprehensive and robust conceptual foundation for developing ethical and effective halal information systems. While Western theories originate from different domains, their convergence within the Islamic framework revealed shared values such as accountability, transparency, fairness and ethical governance. Bridging these theories affirmed that shariah compliance is not just a religious directive, but a comprehensive ethical framework embedded in organisational and societal structures. It shows that the halal information systems are not only operationally sound but also aligned with Islamic jurisprudence, delivering trust, integrity and accountability across all dimensions of system design and governance.

From a technology perspective, two pairs of Islamic theories were identified, which can be bridged with Western theories, referring to *Maslahah*-Diffusion of Innovative Theory and Shariah Compliance-Task Technology Fit Theory on halal information systems. Technologies like blockchain and artificial intelligence should be adapted to ensure that they are used in a manner that upholds Islamic values. Halal information systems should leverage technology to enhance the *maslahah* of people, while protecting people's rights and maintaining Islamic integrity. By applying Islamic theories, technology in halal information systems remains shariah-compliant. Both Western theories (Diffusion of Innovative Theory and Task Technology Fit Theory) align with Islamic theories (*maslahah* and shariah compliance), showing that halal is not just a religious concept but also a global framework. The integration of both theories, Western and Islamic, shows a cohesive information system that ensures halal compliance while respecting ethical and legal standards from both perspectives.

Practically, the contribution of this study is directed towards halal industry players, academicians, researchers and students researching the halal system. Three research areas have been suggested for emphasis, in-depth study, and exploration by bridging both theories. These include enhancing governance and accountability, navigating regulatory frameworks and technological compliance, and promoting ethical innovation and sustainability. In terms of enhancing governance and accountability, several stakeholders were identified as part of this study, which included suppliers, regulators, consumers, authority or certification bodies and system developers, by evaluating their impact on halal information systems using Shariah Compliance and Stakeholder Theory. For instance, in designing a new audit process, missing or inconsistent Halal certification data, managers uphold both stakeholder expectations for transparency and the Shariah mandate for ethical conduct. Thus, the Shariah Compliance-Stakeholder Theory bridge transforms Halal governance from a purely technical exercise into a value-based system that ensures integrity, trustworthiness, and continuous ethical assurance across the Halal supply chain.

In terms of navigating regulatory, through the alignment between shariah compliance and Institutional Theory, this study assists halal industry players and students to understand how these three isomorphisms force halal information systems to comply with shariah. For instance, coercive pressures from JAKIM, compelling firms to integrate traceability to ensure Halal data integrity, mimetic pressures encourage organisations to emulate the technological and ethical practices of successful Halal-certified entities, normative pressures emerge through professional education and Shariah governance training that embed ethical consciousness among system developers and auditors. Collectively, these institutional forces operationalise Shariah Compliance within the digital infrastructure of Halal Information Systems, that reinforcing both technical and spiritual legitimacy in Halal governance.

In terms of developing compliance with technologies, halal industry players, academicians, researchers and students are aware that each design and implementation of halal information systems should not only be efficient and technologically sound but also shariah-compliant by design. For example, system developers must provide a blueprint for integrating shariah governance at every stage of the system lifecycle, from design to monitoring. Theoretically, this study also contributes to the development of the theory integration between Islam and Western by compatibility of Islamic theories, such as shariah compliance and *maslahah,* with established Western theories such as Deontological Theory, Stakeholder Theory, Institutional Theory, Diffusion of Innovation Theory and Task Technology Fit Theory in each system's perspective.

Future research can be extended to empirical evidence and quantitative research to validate the conceptual findings. These would strengthen the reliability of the findings and offer more generalisable insights for academic and practical applications. By collecting and analysing data through surveys or case studies, researchers can assess the practical applicability and robustness of the conceptual framework of this study, as shown in Table 4. This would significantly strengthen the reliability and validity of the findings, providing more solid grounds for underpinning theories. Last but not least, it would offer more generalisable insights that are useful not only for theoretical development but also for participation, policymakers, and industry seeking to apply extended theoretical approaches.

ACKNOWLEDGEMENT

The authors gratefully acknowledge the financial support provided by the Research and Innovation Division, Universiti Pertahanan Nasional Malaysia.

REFERENCES

Abd Rashid, N. R., Ahmad, A. N., Md Dahlal, N., & Abdullah, M. A. (2023). Applying ethical climate theory in whistleblowing intentions study among employees in halal food companies: A protocol. *Halalsphere, 3*(1).

Abdul Jafar, W. (2022). Legality of Halal food certification on Maslahah Mursalah perspective. *Jurnal Ilmiah MIZANI, 9*(1), 85–108.

Abu Talib, N. Y., Abdul Latiff, R., & Aman, A. (2020). An institutional perspective for research in waqf accounting and reporting: A case study of Terengganu state Islamic Religious Council in Malaysia. *Journal of Islamic Accounting and Business Research, 11*(2), 400–427. DOI: 10.1108/JIABR-11-2016-0132

Ahmad, R. (2024). Integrating artificial intelligence and blockchain to improve the accuracy of Halal certification. *Jpurnal of Halal Review, 1*(1), 12–22.

Aizat Jamaludin, M., Kartika, B., & Anuar Ramli Senior Lecturer, M., & Hazrul Hamzah Postgraduate candidate, M. (2019). Muslim-friendly hospital services framework. *Halal Journal, 3*, 11–24.

Al Farisi, M. S., Anwar, S., Haryono, S., & Wahid, H. A. (2025). Sustainable Consumer Behavior of Halal Cosmetics in Indonesia E-Commerce: A Maslahah-Based Approach. *IQTISHODUNA: Jurnal Ekonomi Islam, 14*(1), 65–84. DOI: 10.54471/iqtishoduna.v14i1.2674

Alam, M. K., Rahman, M. M., Runy, M. K., Adedeji, B. S., & Hassan, M. F. (2022). The influences of Shariah governance mechanisms on Islamic banks performance and Shariah compliance quality. *Asian Journal of Accounting Research, 7*(1), 2–16. DOI: 10.1108/AJAR-11-2020-0112

Arifin, Z., & Hatoli, H. (2021). Application of Halal Certification by Indonesian Ulema Council on Electronic and Non-Consumption Products: Maslahah Perspective. *Justicia Islamica, 18*(1), 115–131. DOI: 10.21154/justicia.v18i1.2397

Awang, M. D., Yahaya, M. M., Sulaiman, M., Ismail, K., Baharum, N. B., & Abdullah, A. A. (2023). Perspectives on the role of National Fatwa Committee in handling food issues in Malaysia based on Maqasid Syariah. In *Food Research* (Vol. 6, pp. 60–66). Rynnye Lyan Resources., DOI: 10.26656/fr.2017.6(S3).5

Barney, S., Aurum, A., & Wohlin, C. (2008). A product management challenge: Creating software product value through requirements selection. *Journal of Systems Architecture*, *54*(6), 576–593. DOI: 10.1016/j.sysarc.2007.12.004

Bashir, A. M. (2019). Applying the Institutional Theory at the Level of Halal Consumers: The Case of Cape Town in South Africa. *Journal of Food Products Marketing*, *25*(5), 527–548. DOI: 10.1080/10454446.2019.1607645

Che Jamaludin, F. I., Abdullah, M. R. T. L., Endut, M. N. A. A., Saifuddeen, S. M., Hamimi, K. A., & Harun, S. (2025). Developing a Shariah-compliant medical services framework in Malaysia: An expert system approach using fuzzy Delphi method and interpretive structural modelling. *BMJ Open*, *15*(1), e082263. Advance online publication. DOI: 10.1136/bmjopen-2023-082263 PMID: 39762112

Creswell, J., & Poth, C. (2018). *Qualitative Inquiry and Research Design* (4th ed.). SAGE Publication.

Creswell, J. W., & Creswell, J. D. (2018). Research Designs Qualitative, Quantitative, and Mixed Methods Approaches. In *Fast Facts to Loving your Research Project* (Fifth Edit). SAGE Publications, Inc. DOI: 10.1891/9780826146373.0007

DiMaggio, P., & Powell, W. W. (1983). The Iron Cage Revisited: Institutional Isomorphism and Collective Rationality in Organizational Fields. *American Sociological Review*, *48*(2), 147–160. DOI: 10.2307/2095101

Freeman, R. E. (1984). A Stakeholder Approach to Strategic Management. In SSRN *Electronic Journal*. Pitman. DOI: 10.2139/ssrn.263511

Goodhue, D., & Ronald, L. (1995). Task-technology fit and individual performance. *Management Information Systems Quarterly*, *19*(2), 213–236. DOI: 10.2307/249689

Gunsun, A., & Chirapanda, S. (2024). Factors influencing the adoption of CICOT halal certification in Thai halal entrepreneurs: The institutional theory. *Journal of Family Business and Management Studies*, *16*(1), 169–192.

Haji Ahmad, A., & Farid Shamsudin, M. (2021). Innovation through delivery of tacit-explicit knowledge: A Maqasid approach. *Journal of Positive Psychology & Wellbeing*, *5*(3), 501–515. http://journalppw.com

Haleem, A., Khan, M. I., & Khan, S. (2021). *logistics Understanding the Adoption of Halal Logistics through Critical Success Factors and Stakeholder Objectives*. https://doi.org/DOI: 10.3390/logistics

Haron, A., Sahibuddin, S., Harun, M., Zakaria, N. H., & Mahrin, M. N. (2013). The important role of people, process and technology during software project requirement. *International Journal of Machine Learning and Computing*, *3*(1), 24–30. DOI: 10.7763/IJMLC.2013.V3.266

Hidayah, N. A., Amri, F. B., & Mutholib, A. (2024). Design and Integration of Information Systems for the Halal Inspection Institute (LPH) UIN Syarif Hidayatullah Jakarta with SiHalal Ministry of Religion of the Republic of Indonesia. [AISM]. *Applied Information System and Management*, *7*(2), 7–16. Advance online publication. DOI: 10.15408/aism.v7i2.36786

Ibrahim, I., Shuib, A., Yusoff, F. H., & Shariff, S. S. R. (2024). Planning of Halal Compliance Critical Control Points and IoT Integration in Halal Chicken Meat Supply Chain Traceability System. *Journal of Halal Industry & Services*, *7*(1). Advance online publication. DOI: 10.36877/jhis.a0000568

Kant, I. (1997). *Groundwork of the Metaphysics of Morals*. CAMBRIDGE University Press.

Karbhari, Y., Alam, M. K., & Rahman, M. M. (2020). Relevance of the application of institutional theory in Shariah governance of Islamic banks. *PSU Research Review*, *5*(1), 1–15. DOI: 10.1108/PRR-05-2020-0015

Kumaladewi, N., Ratnawati, S., Sugiarti, Y., & Umar Lubis, A. B. (2020, October). Evaluation of e-halal certification system acceptance to improve Halal certification services at LPPOM MUI. *The 8th International Conference on Cyber and IT Service Management*.

Mahmud Zuhudi, N. W., & Dolah, J. (2020). An experts' perspective based on consumers' perception of Halal-related issue. *Al-Risalah Journal*, *4*(3), 183–198.

Martono, S., Mukhibad, H., Anisykurlillah, I., & Nurkhin, A. (2020). Evaluation of acceptance of information systems in state university with theory of planned behavior and theory of acceptance model approaches. *Management Science Letters*, *10*(14), 3225–3234. DOI: 10.5267/j.msl.2020.6.016

Mas'ud, I., Fahmi, A. A., & Saputra, A. (2025). Dynamics of Islamic Legal Theory (Ushul al-Fiqh) toward Addressing Challenges of Halal Products in the 21st Century. *International Journal of Islamic Thought and Humanities*, *4*(1), 88–105. DOI: 10.54298/ijith.v4i1.403

Mohaiyadin, N. M. Hj., Aman, A., Palil, M. R., & Muhamad Said, S. (2022). Addressing Accountability and Transparency Challenges in Waqf Management using Blockchain Technology. *Journal of Islamic Monetary Economics and Finance, 8*(Special Issue: Islamic Finance). https://doi.org/https://doi.org/10.21098/jimf.v8i0.1413

Mohaiyadin, N. M. (2024). *Potensi Penggunaan Teknologi Blockchain Untuk Mengatasi Cabaran Akauntabiliti Dan Ketelusan Dalam Sistem Maklumat Pengurusan Wakaf Di Universiti Awam Malaysia*. Universiti Kebangsaan Malaysia.

Mohaiyadin, N. M. Hj., Mohd Zahari, H., & Mardzuki, K. (2024). Addressing Challenges in Halal Certification Using Blockchain Technology. In N. A. A. Rahman & M. H. Ali (Eds.), *Emerging Technology and Crisis Management in The Halal Industry: Issues and Recent Developments* (pp. 49–66). Springer Nature Singapore. DOI: 10.1007/978-981-97-1375-2_4

Mohd Zain, F. A., Wan Abdullah, W. A., Muhamad Nasir, M. N., & Hassan, M. F. (2025). Development of a comprehensive sustainability performance index for takaful operators: integrating Maqasid Al-Shariah and stakeholder perspectives. *International Journal of Islamic and Middle Eastern Finance and Management*. DOI: 10.1108/IMEFM-07-2024-0343

Moniruzzaan, & Hamid Aziz, A. (2022). Challenges in the development of Halal certification system in Bangladesh: A descriptive and analytical study based on Malaysian perspective. *Halalsphere, 2*(1).

Najiha, F., Abdullah, B., & Yusof, D. (2024). Islamic and western ethical perspective in mandatory vaccination policy for children in Malaysia. *Fikroh Jurnal Pemikiran Dan Pendidikan Islam, 17*(2), 135–150. DOI: 10.37812/fikroh.v17i2.1647

Nasir, N. M., Nair, M. S., & Ahmed, P. K. (2021). Institutional isomorphism and environmental sustainability: A new framework from the Shariah perspective. *Environment, Development and Sustainability, 23*(9), 13555–13568. DOI: 10.1007/s10668-021-01227-0

Naznii, H. (2023). Halal certification process by local governments and Muslim organizations in Australia. *Journal of International Islamic Business Studies, 1*(1), 46–53.

https://legacy.quran.com/2/185. (n.d.). *Surat Al-Baqarah (The Cow)*. Retrieved June 22, 2025, from https://legacy.quran.com/2/185

https://legacy.quran.com/45/18. (n.d.). *Surat Al-Jāthiyah (The Crouching)*.

Novianti, D., Haditjaroko, L., & Almunawar, M. N. (2022). Assurance information systems design for blockchain - Based micro, small and medium enterprises in Indonesia. *IOP Conference Series. Earth and Environmental Science*, *1063*(1), 012058. Advance online publication. DOI: 10.1088/1755-1315/1063/1/012058

Provita Wijayanti. (2024). *Computerized accounting information system, Maqashid Sharia and sustainable performance in Indonesia Islamic microfinance: An application of Task Technology of Fit*. Universiti Teknologi Mara.

Puji Fajariani, D., & Hermawan Adinugraha, H. (2024). Islamic accounting as an information system for Sharia-based companies. *Al-Muamalah: Jurnal Ekonomi Islam, Filatropi Dan Perbankan Syariah, 1*(1). https://journal.syamilahpublishing.com/index.php/muamalah/

Puspitasari, N., Luvian, V., & Mahardiyanto, A. (2023). *Phenomenological Study of the Application of Islamic Business Ethics in Fashion Sale and Purchase Transactions ARTICLE INFO*. https://jmrs.optima-science.com/index.php/jmrs

Qader, G., Shahid, Z. A., Junaid, M., Shaikh, I. M., & Qureshi, M. A. (2023). The role of diffusion of innovation theory towards the adoption of halal meat supply chain. *Journal of Islamic Marketing*, *14*(5), 1211–1228. DOI: 10.1108/JIMA-01-2021-0032

Raimi, L. (2024). Do Islamic epistemology and ethics advance the understanding and promotion of sustainable development? A systematic review using PRISMA. In *International Journal of Ethics and Systems*. Emerald Publishing., DOI: 10.1108/IJOES-04-2024-0115

Ramli, J. A., Hashim, H. A., & Salleh, Z. (2023). Governance of Malaysian Halal Food Industry: Conventional Governance vs Shariah Requirements. *Proceedings of the International Symposium & Exhibition on Business and Accounting 2022 (ISEBA 2022), 28 September 2022, Malaysia, 1*, 83–94. DOI: 10.15405/epfe.23081.8

Ramli, N. M., Abd Aziz, S., & Md Ali, N. S. A. (2020). Reporting on Halal Activities: What Companies Communicate to Stakeholders. *Journal of Fatwa Management and Research*, 42–58. DOI: 10.33102/jfatwa.vol19no1.4

Rashid, A., & Bojei, N. (2019). The relationship between halal traceability system adoption and environmental factors on halal food supply chain integrity in Malaysia. *Journal of Islamic Marketing*, *1*(11), 117–142. DOI: 10.1108/JIMA-01-2018-0016

Ribadu, M. B., Wan Wan Ab, W. N., Abd Ghani, A. A., Kamaruddin, A., & Othman, M. S. (2020). Sharia requirements framework for e-commerce systems: An exploratory study. *Journal of Theoretical and Applied Information Technology*, *98*(6), 994–1008. www.jatit.org

Ridwan, A. H., Hasanuddin, M., & Fatahillah, I. A. (2020). Authorization of Halal certification in Indonesia, Malaysia and Singapore. *International Journal of Psychosocial Rehabilitation*, *24*(08), 7992–8011.

Rogers, E. M. (1983). *Diffusion of innovations* (3rd ed.). The Free Press.

Schneier, B. (2015). *Secrets and Lies Digital Security in a Networked World*. Wiley. DOI: 10.1002/9781119183631

Scott, W. R. (1987). The Adolescence of Institutional Theory. *Administrative Science Quarterly*, *32*(4), 493. DOI: 10.2307/2392880

Sohail, N., Haque, A., & Aziz, S. (2024). Impact of diffusion of innovation among Pakistani consumers' adoption of Halal cosmetics. *Journal of Education and Social Sciences*, *26*(1), 11–21.

Suhartini, E., Hertiani, E., Djuniarsono, R., Rumatiga, H., & Nurfajrina, S. P. M. (2024). Analysis of Halal Certification for Micro and Small Business Actors from the Perspective of Maslahah Principles and Legal Certainty Theory. *Al-'Adalah*, *21*(2), 401–426. DOI: 10.24042/adalah.v21i2.23442

Sulistyawati, D. R., Mutamimah, M., & Hartono, S. (2024). Maslahah radical innovation: Breakthrough to achieve corporate sustainability in small and medium industries (SMI) batik in central Java province. *Edelweiss Applied Science and Technology*, *8*(6), 8740–8751. DOI: 10.55214/25768484.v8i6.3865

Sumarliah, E., Li, T., Wang, B., Fauziyah, F., & Indriya, I. (2022). Blockchain-empowered halal fashion traceability system in Indonesia. *International Journal of Information Systems and Supply Chain Management*, *15*(2), 1–24. Advance online publication. DOI: 10.4018/IJISSCM.287628

Susanty, A., Puspitasari, N. B., & Rosyada, Z. F. (2024). Prediction of the performance of halal food industry using a system dynamics simulation model. *Journal of Islamic Marketing*, *15*(11), 2785–2822. Advance online publication. DOI: 10.1108/JIMA-02-2023-0039

Ullah, S., Haroon, M., Hussain, S., & Rehman, A. U. (2023). Islamic labelling and corporate governance: A perspective of Shariah compliance firms. *Journal of Islamic Accounting and Business Research*, *14*(6), 849–867. DOI: 10.1108/JIABR-03-2021-0108

Vasudevan, H., & Aslan, I. (2021). Cosmetology advertising perspectives: Application of ethical theories during COVID-19 crisis. *Marketing and Management of Innovations*, *5*(4), 121–136. DOI: 10.21272/mmi.2021.4-10

Zarkasyi, M. R., Kurniawan, D. A., Surya, F., & Anggara, A. (2022). Stakeholders Approach in Halal Tourism Development Strategy: A Case Study in Ponorogo District. *Jurnal Ilmiah Bidang Ilmu Ekonomi, 17*(2), 171–181. http://journal.umpo.ac.id/index.php/ekuilibrium

Zhang, Y., Zhang, J., & Chen, J. (2013). Critical success factors in IT service management implementation: People, process, and technology perspectives. *Proceedings of International Conference on Service Science, ICSS, April 2013*, 64–68. DOI: 10.1109/ICSS.2013.38

Zulkifli, S. N., & Yusuf, S. N. S. (2023). Maqasid Syariah and Digital Transformation of Halal Supply Chain With Governance Elements. *Proceedings of the International Conference in Technology, Humanities and Management (ICTHM 2023),* 12-13 June, 2023, Istanbul, Turkey, *131*, 103–115. DOI: 10.15405/epsbs.2023.11.9

Chapter 3
Analysis of Halal Policy Based on Sustainability Principles to Realize Green Halal in Indonesia

Zulfia Hanum Alfi Syahr
http://orcid.org/0000-0003-0290-4559
National Research and Innovation Agency, Indonesia

Buyamin Buyamin
http://orcid.org/0000-0002-1435-6978
National Research and Innovation Agency, Indonesia

Dian Hafit Syaifullah
National Research and Innovation Agency, Indonesia

Zaenal Abidin
National Research and Innovation Agency, Indonesia

Nurhuda Firmansyah
National Research and Innovation Agency, Indonesia

ABSTRACT

As a country with a Muslim majority, the Indonesian government has regulations and policies to provide halal product guarantees to the public. However, regulations related to halal products are not only based on Islamic law but also need to follow the principles of the Sustainable Development Goals (SDGs) globally. Therefore, the problem that will be studied in this paper is how to structure halal regulations and policies based on the principles of a sustainable environment in Indonesia. To

DOI: 10.4018/979-8-3373-2792-1.ch003

achieve this, the study will develop a comprehensive policy framework grounded in sustainability principles and environmental stewardship. Based on an analysis of study documents, it was found that in halal regulations, both from the government and nongovernment agencies, no one explicitly explains the importance of implementing environmentally friendly, sustainable principles from manufacturing to production.

INTRODUCTION

As a country with a Muslim majority, the Indonesian government has the Halal Product Assurance law with the purpose of protecting Muslim consumers from non-halal goods. Implementing the provisions in the articles of the law is carried out by stipulating Government Regulation Number 31 of 2019. Then, it was continued with the stipulation of the Regulation of the Minister of Religion Number 26 of 2019, Government Regulation Number 39 of 2021, and Presidential Regulation Number 6 of 2023. These regulations aim to provide legal certainty and guarantee the halalness of public goods such as medicines, biological products, and medical devices that are traded in Indonesia.

Based on this, the development of the halal policy in Indonesia has been a significant and ongoing journey that reflects the country's commitment to ensuring that products align with Islamic principles. This journey began in earnest with a noteworthy fatwa issued by the Indonesian Ulema Council (Majelis Ulama Indonesia, or MUI) in 2003, formally recognizing the need for a halal certification process. The fatwa has an important role in this framework as a prominent non-governmental institution comprising esteemed Muslim scholars and religious authorities. These experts guide the community daily while adhering to Islamic values and principles.

Understanding the significant role of halal assurance, the government has embarked on a proactive journey to fortify the halal standard of products available to the public. This initiative spans extensive goods, including food, beverages, cosmetics, and pharmaceuticals, empowering consumers to make decisions that resonate with their beliefs and values. Throughout the years, a synergistic partnership between the Indonesian Ulema Council (MUI) and various government agencies has fostered a more robust regulatory framework, enhancing transparency and instilling confidence in the halal certification process. This collaborative effort has cultivated an environment of trustworthiness, ensuring consumers can confidently choose products that align with their commitment to halal principles. In 2014, the government finally introduced the Halal Product Assurance Law, a significant milestone that arrived a full eleven years after the initial halal fatwa was proclaimed. However, the subsequent response and development of derivative regulations proved sluggish. It wasn't until 2019 that the Minister of Religion published a regulation, followed by a Government Regulation in 2021, that aimed to explain how to implement the guarantee of halal products.

The pace at which halal regulations evolved has been frustratingly slow, particularly given the growing expectation that the halal concept should encompass sustainability principles, especially concerning environmental conservation. Unfortunately, the trio of these governmental regulations fails to address the numerous facets of ensuring adequate halal product guarantees. As a result, the public has turned to the Majelis Ulama Indonesia (MUI) for guidance, seeking clarity through fatwas to fill the apparent gaps left by government policies.

The environmentally friendly Green Halal concept has been known for applying the 3R principle: reduce-reuse-recycling in various halal products (Deuraseh et al., 2023). One of the things that has been done a lot is to use plastic materials as packaging no longer and replace them with materials easily decomposed by nature. In the study (Rahman et al., 2024), the principles of environmental sustainability have six dimensions, including: materials, energy, biodiversity, environmental compliance, water, and emissions, that important for the expansion of halal business. Then these six dimensions need to be implemented in the halal industry process by ensuring ingredients, preparation, processing, hygienic, and sanitation procedures are by halal principles and ensuring environmental sustainability (Hashim & Sulaiman, 2022). In addition, it is also necessary to improve infrastructure to ensure no physical contact with non-halal materials during the industrial process (Bux et al., 2022). The implementation of the sustainability concept in the industrial process will facilitate the halal product certification process and be able to meet global standards with the high value of halal products in the international market (W. S. T. Prince, 2024). The use of halal principles and environmental sustainability in every consumer product is expected to meet Islamic Sharia and provide guidelines and moral messages to maintain and protect nature (Deuraseh, 2022).

Therefore, the problems that will be discussed in this paper are: how has the current framework for halal policy been established and developed by the Indonesian government and the Indonesian Ulema Council (MUI)? This study aims to investigate the development of halal policy in Indonesia, mainly focusing on its adherence to sustainable practices emphasizing environmental preservation. Furthermore, to what extent does this framework embody sustainable principles that promote eco-friendly practices? The objective is to thoroughly analyze Indonesia's existing halal policies and evaluate their alignment with sustainability goals, ultimately contributing to the realization of green halal. This concept not only champions the principles of halal but also integrates crucial aspects of ecological responsibility.

METHOD

The method used in this study is qualitative, using the policy framework analysis based on the principle of environmental sustainability. The policy framework analysis focused on identifying stakeholders as policymakers, target policy users, and the objectives of policy-making based on the principles of environmental sustainability in halal policies. The policy documents analyzed are formal regulations related to halal in the form of laws, government regulations, regulations of ministries/institutions, namely the Ministry of Religion, and policies of non-governmental Islamic religious institutions from the Indonesian Ulema Council.

There are nine halal-related regulatory and policy documents to be analyzed, namely: 1) Law No. 33 of 2014; 2) Government Regulation No. 39 of 2021; 3) Regulation of the Minister of Religion No. 26 of 2019; 4) MUI Fatwa No. 4 of 2003 addresses the standardization of halal fatwas, laying a foundation for consistent and reliable halal certification; 5) MUI Fatwa No. 44 of 2020 clarifies the regulations surrounding the names, forms, and packaging of products that cannot be certified as halal, ensuring consumer transparency; 6) MUI Fatwa No. 11 of 2009 discusses the legalities surrounding alcohol, reinforcing the Islamic prohibition on its consumption and trade; 7) MUI Fatwa No. 12 of 2009 establishes the essential standards for halal slaughter, outlining humane practices that align with religious principles; 8) MUI Fatwa No. 26 of 2013 focuses on the halal standards for cosmetic products, ensuring that beauty and personal care goods comply with Islamic teachings; and 9) MUI Fatwa No. 56 of 2014 pertains to the tanning and utilization of animal skins in consumer goods, promoting ethical sourcing and processing methods.

DISCUSSION

Analysis of the Application of Sustainability Principles in the Environmental Sector in Law No. 33 of 2014

The establishment of Law Number 33 of 2014 is also an implementation of the mandate in the 1945 Constitution, which regulates the protection of consumer rights, especially those related to religious aspects (Rachmawati et al., 2023; Haryanti & Miru, 2024). The regulation states to guarantee every citizen to embrace their religion and beliefs when practising worship (Bagir et al., 2020). Therefore, products consumed by Muslims must be guaranteed halal. (Fawa'id & Mutafarida, 2024). The halal guarantee is shown by a halal certificate for the company's products, and halal label for the product packaging (Syahr et al., 2023). Halal certification is need to increase the competitiveness of Indonesian products in the international market, which increasingly prioritizes the halal aspect as one of the main criteria (Hartini & Malahayatie, 2024).

The enactment of Law Number 33 of 2014 is an initial regulation in the state's efforts to improve product quality and provide protection to consumers, especially Muslims. This law is expected to have an impact in terms of economic, social, and cultural (Abmi et al., 2024). Economically, this law encourages the halal industry sector to grow rapidly (Pratiwi & Vidiati, 2024). Business actors are required to guarantee that their products meet halal standards, which has the potential for global market opportunities (Rahmawati & Nugraha Triyan Putra , 2022). With the obligation of halal certification, business actors can gain consumer trust domestically and abroad. This will undoubtedly increase the quality of Indonesian halal products in the global market.

The social impact caused by Law Number 33 of 2014 is also significant (Putra & Ambariyanto, 2024). The public, especially Muslims, will feel more secure in consuming products that are meet the sharia principles (Al-Haq et al., 2024). This gives consumers a greater sense of trust, reduces doubt, and ensures that their basic needs can be met halal. In addition, implementing this law can also increase the competitiveness of manufactured goods by Islamic teachings (Hartini & Malahayatie, 2024). However, there are challenges in education and socialization, so many parties do not fully understand the importance of halal certification (Yuanitasari & Sardjono, 2023). Therefore, the government and relevant agencies must continue to conduct campaigns to increase public awareness of the benefits of this law.

The regulations in Law Number 33 of 2014 include the purpose and principles of regulation, product coverage, regulatory institutions, certification processes, obligations and sanctions, supervision and the evaluation of halal products development in Indonesia (Hosen et al., 2022). The ratification of Law Number 33 of 2014 aims to ensure the halal and safety of all products circulating in Indonesia for consumption by Muslims. Thus, this Law protects consumers from products that do not meet halal standards and simultaneously encourages the development of the halal industry in Indonesia.

The regulation in Law Number 33 of 2014 covers all products consumed by the public in the form of food, drinks, medicines, cosmetics, and other products used by Muslims. To ensure halal, the government assigns the task to the Halal Product Assurance Agency (BPJPH) to carry out halal product assurance providers, which previously had halal certification issued by the Indonesian Ulema Council (MUI) (Anjani et al., 2014). Meanwhile, the Halal Inspection Agency do the inspection of the halalness of a product and this institutions established by the community to obtain approval (Anjani et al., 2014).

In the halal certification process, producers or business actors must apply for halal certification to BPJPH (Chasanah & Muzammil, 2025). Certification includes inspecting raw materials, production processes, and final products (Hartini & Malahayatie, 2024). The MUI issues halal certificates after the product meets halal requirements. Furthermore, to improve the quality of the halal certification process, the government conducts periodic evaluations of the halal assurance system (Tsurayya Adilah & Dyah Kumalasari, 2023)(Zafitriani et al., 2024). The government also guarantees the development of the halal industry in Indonesia by strengthening infrastructure and standards in the certification process and expanding the domestic and international halal product market (Nurjannah et al., 2024).

Overall, the enactment of Law Number 33 of 2014 has excellent potential to bring positive changes in various aspects of the lives of the Indonesian people. Although there are challenges that must be faced, with the proper support and collaboration between the government, business actors, and the community. Implementing this law can be a strategic step in building a sustainable halal industry and improving the welfare of the people. The enactment of Law Number 33 of 2014 certainly did not run as expected and faced resistance from the public, which, among others, related to the cost of certification, procedures and length of the certification process, abuse of authority, product discrimination, business readiness of formal and non-formal sectors, and the possibility of violating World Trade Organization agreements (Nurul Fitri Amijaya et al., 2024).

One of the resistance to Law Number 33 of 2014 is the high cost incurred to obtain halal certification (Ningrum, 2022). Many business actors, from low and middle scale feel burdened by the considerable costs of meeting halal certification obligations. The halal certification process includes registration fees and periodic audit and checking fees that can burden entrepreneurs, especially those with limited resources. For some business actors, this can be an obstacle to continue operating or developing. The halal certification process, considered lengthy and complicated, also adds to the concerns of business actors (R. Putri, 2024). In some cases, they feel that the existing procedures are too bureaucratic and take a long time to get a decision. This can affect the smooth running of business operations, especially in highly dynamic sectors such as food and beverage, where new products are constantly being developed and introduced.

There is also resistance related to anxiety about irregularities in the declaration of halal certification. Less strict supervision by the government risks potential fraud by including halal certificates, by irresponsible parties (Masitah & Wiriani, 2024). Some parties who consistently follow the provisions of halal product assurance are worried about the inclusion of certificates or labels that do not by the provisions of Law Number 33 of 2014. On the other hand, some parties also feel that Law Number 33 of 2014 can give rise to discrimination against non-halal products, both from Indonesia and abroad. There are concerns that this law could create restrictions or stigma against products that do not get halal certification, even if they have good quality and nutritional value (Amantana et al., 2023). This can increase tensions between business actors who produce halal and non-halal products.

Resistance to Law Number 33 of 2014 can also be seen in the differences between business actors in the formal and informal sectors (Istianah & Dewi, 2022). The large informal sector has limited access to information and infrastructure to obtain halal certification. Beside that, the business actors in the formal sector, such as large companies, tend to adapt more easily to these regulations because they have adequate resources. Resistance also occurs because of the large number of business actors with diverse products in market demand. It can be the products of food, beverages, cosmetics, medicines, or other non-consumer products. The determination of the halal of each product becomes increasingly complex. New product innovations that continue to develop with the composition of each product are very diverse and present problems in keeping each product by the established halal standards (Nadila et al., 2024).

Analysis of the Concept of Green Halal in Government Regulation No. 39 of 2021

Government Regulation Number 39 of 2021 is a law and regulation in Indonesia that the President stipulates to enforce the law as it should. This regulation is implemented as a follow-up to Law No. 11 of 2020 (Sukri, 2021). The Halal Product Assurance Law emphasizes that all products traded in Indonesian territory must be halal certified. The halal certification in question is the recognition of the halalness of a product by the halal product assurance agency. The implementation of halal certification in Indonesia is a form of public awareness of the importance of halal certificates for a product. In this context, halal certification is an administrative tool and a moral and ecological instrument (Khairuddin & Zaki, 2021).

Halal products are an essential aspect of today's business world. This is because halal products are expected to have significant value and offer opportunities for the Muslim community and non-Muslims. As part of the government's duty to lawfully safeguard its citizens, halal products must be guaranteed. In addition to boosting the added value for business actors who create and sell halal products, the provision of a guarantee of the implementation of halal products seeks to give the public comfort, security, safety, and certainty of the availability of halal products when they consume and use them. This goal is essential, for advances in science and technology in food, medicine, and cosmetics, which are developing very rapidly. Food processing was still effortless in the past, and communication with producers could still be carried out directly, but nowadays, product processing has become very complex.

Indonesia already has a map of the national halal industry and the sharia economy, as an essential point for Indonesia as a reference or destination for halal tourism visits. The desire to make Indonesia as a halal destination in the world is indeed rational, considering that Indonesia has halal capital in the form of religious and demographic values. Generally, the need for products that are ensured to be halal be it processed food, medicine, cosmetics, agriculture, fisheries, pharmaceuticals, and fashion, continues to increase yearly (Al Mubarak et al., 2023). Halal trends and lifestyles are starting to emerge. This can be seen from consumers who are increasingly selective in paying attention to a product's halal label before deciding to buy. The shift in consumer behavior, especially Muslim consumers, who are increasingly selective, will encourage business actors to innovate and be more motivated to make halal-certified products. This is a positive signal for the future of Indonesia's halal industry because the synergy between consumer awareness and producer responsibility will open up space for strengthening the principle of sustainability in the halal production process.

Concept Green Halal is an approach that blends halal principles with environmental, social, and economic sustainability aspects. Halal products must be free of prohibited ingredients and produced through ethical, environmentally friendly, and socially responsible processes. This is to the principle *halalan tayyib*, which bold the importance of halal and good products (Mariatussifa, 2024). Green Halal also includes efforts to ensure that the entire supply chain, from raw materials to final distribution, is carried out responsibly, equitably, and efficiently. Although the term Green Halal is not explicitly mentioned in each government regulation, some of the provisions in this regulation reflect sustainability principles. Article 29 mandates that business actors maintain cleanliness, hygiene, and traceability of raw materials during production. In line with the concept of Green Halal, this study explains the need for environmentally friendly and sustainable production processes (Ratna, 2023). In addition, traceability is particularly relevant to transparency and accountability in the halal supply chain, as a key principle in sustainable food systems.

Application of the concept of Green Halal demands strong cross-institutional synergy. The synergy are needed between the government, industry players, and the community to encourage the principles of Green Halal in the Assurance System of Halal Products (Dewi, 2024). The supervision of halal product assurance implementation is also the focus of Government Regulation No. 39 of 2021. Thus, to reach the overall sustainability dimension, active cooperation with other ministries/institutions is needed, such as the Ministry of Environment and Forestry, the Ministry of Cooperatives and Small and Medium Enterprises, and the Ministry of Industry. This cooperation can be done by compiling environmental sustainability indicators for halal certification schemes, such as energy efficiency, waste management, and water conservation. It can also be done by providing technical assistance and financing support for small and medium business actors to apply the principles *of Green Halal*. In addition, as a halal fatwa issuer, the Indonesian Ulema Council

(MUI) can begin to include ethical and sustainability aspects in the substance of its fatwa (Ratna, 2023). The Halal Inspection Agency (LPH) must also develop an environmentally friendly halal audit system. Without this coordination between stakeholders, implementing *Green Halal* will be challenging to create and will only become normative jargon.

In its implementation, there are still several obstacles to applying the Green Halal product, among them public awareness. Awareness of halal products is increasing, but awareness of Green Halal products is still lacking. Product awareness of Green Halal is needed by suppliers, manufacturers, distributors, consumers, the government, and the private sector. Simultaneous awareness will make creating an ecosystem of Green Halal from upstream to downstream easier to realize economic, social, and environmental welfare simultaneously (Arifin et al., 2022). Meanwhile, the challenges faced in fostering public awareness can be addressed through various programs. First, collaboration between halal industry players, both from government agencies in collaboration with Non-Governmental Organizations (NGOs), and influencers who care about environmental issues. Cooperation can be achieved through content collaboration, practical activities, and socialization. Second, cooperation between the government as a regulator and researchers Green Halal together make practical regulations that concern all levels of society, from producers, packaging companies, and sellers to consumers. In practice, collaborate with NGOs and influencers to advance the halal industry while still protecting the environment and achieving the SDGs adopted by all United Nations (United Nations) members, including Indonesia. (Dewi, 2024).

Analysis of the Implementation of Green Halal in the Regulation of the Minister of Religion No. 26 of 2019

The word *thayyib* implies quality and does not harm health, whereas the Arabic word halal means allowed, justified, and welcome to be consumed by Islamic law. The items that have been deemed halal by Islamic law are known as halal items. To guarantee the halalness of products, several procedures must be followed, such as supplying materials, processing, storing, packaging, distributing, selling, and presenting the goods. Where products are items and/or services associated with consumables used, employed, or exploited by the community, as well as food, beverages, medications, cosmetics, chemicals, biological products, and genetic engineering products

Therefore, there is a need for Halal Product Assurance as legal certainty for the halalness of a product, as evidenced by a halal certificate from the state. So, the halal certification is mandatory, which was previously voluntary. Mandatory is something that must be done and must be followed, that all products are halal is compulsory.

Then, the Government establishes the Halal Product Assurance Agency, which has the authority to 1) establish norms, standards, procedures, and criteria for halal products; 2) issue and revoke halal certificates and labels; 3) conduct accreditation to the Halal Inspection Agency; 4) supervising halal products; and 5) conducting coaching for the human resources involved.

However, halal product assurance governance in Indonesia has not gone well. So, it needs good governance support or, more specifically, halal governance. Halal governance related to Sharia principles requires regulatory support, control management, supervision, and information disclosure. These problems can be categorized into four dimensions according to (Rusydiana et al., 2023), namely: 1) basic capital infrastructure/infrastructure/human resources for halal product guarantees; 2) technical elements outside the infrastructure; 3) regulations for halal products; and 4) inter-relations (relationships between institutions that take care of halal product assurance).

Next is the development of the concept of sustainability for the environment, which has not been mentioned in the regulation of the minister of religion. Muslim consumers' trust in quality goods and services with hygiene, hygienic standards, trust, and guaranteed nutrition are the primary needs for consumers. Moreover, the need for halal products continues to increase every year, especially in the halal food industry, which is the primary need of the Muslim community. Further, increasing the awareness of the Muslim community to make Islamic sharia a way of life and the basis for choosing a product is a consideration for manufacturers to use halal certification labels as a form of effort to distinguish their products from similar products that are not halal on the market. Therefore, the Halal Product Assurance Agency must work with different parties, ministries, and non-governmental organizations in other nations in the areas of industry, trade, health, agriculture, cooperatives, and small and medium businesses to fulfill its responsibilities and authorities. In the areas of food and drug monitoring, standardization and conformance, and the accreditation of conformity assessment organizations, collaboration is practiced.

Analysis of MUI Fatwa Related to Halal Based on Sustainability Aspects in Environmental Conservation

The Indonesian Ulema Council is a civil society forum for deliberations of Muslim scholars from a combination of Islamic community organizations throughout Indonesia. The role of the Indonesian Ulema Council in the halal certification process was strengthened by the issuance of Government Regulation Number 69 of 1999, which is a derivative of Law Number 7 of 1996. The Indonesian Ulema Council (MUI) has released a series of six pivotal fatwas to ensure the integrity and authenticity of halal products. These fatwas encompass a range of essential guidelines for halal standard certification.

a. MUI Fatwa No. 4 of 2003 addresses the standardization of halal fatwas, laying a foundation for consistent and reliable halal certification

Table 1. Analysis For MUI Fatwa No. 4 of 2003

No.	Fatwa	Main Theme	Subtheme	Explanation
1	As long as the animal is not harmed and remains alive after being stunned, the law allowing stunting of animals is acceptable (Hayat Mustaqirrah)	Animal Welfare	Ethics of Cutting	Stunning is allowed as long as it does not hurt, is related to ethical principles, and is sustainable in the treatment of animals.
2	The law is not allowed if you stun mechanically, electrically, chemically, or by other means that are considered to hurt animals.	Animal Welfare	Prohibition of Torture	Methods of stunting that hurt animals are prohibited, preserving the preservation of animals as part of the environment.
3	What is considered in the frog problem is environmental factors. The Prophet forbade the killing of frogs. So, it is haram to kill and eat frogs.	Environmental Conservation	Animal Conservation	Due to ecological considerations, the protection of toads shows concern for environmental sustainability.
4	Consumer products that use microbial products must be traced for halalness to the stage of the microbial refreshment process.	Product Safety and Hygiene	Sustainable Production	Keeping the microbial production process clean to ensure food safety and industrial sustainability aspects.

Source: Author's elaboration (2025)

Words such as “sustainability” or “environment” are not explicitly mentioned in this fatwa. However, sustainable values emerge through the etiquette of treating living things and hygiene standards. This is especially true for animal protection during slaughter and microbial production to maintain product cleanliness.

b. MUI Fatwa No. 11 of 2009 discusses the legalities surrounding alcohol, reinforcing the Islamic prohibition on its consumption and trade

Table 2. Analysis for MUI Fatwa No. 11 of 2009

No.	Fatwa	Main Theme	Subtheme	Explanation
1	Islam seeks to protect religion, the soul, the intellect, family, and property. This is the reason that beneficial things are commanded, and harmful things are forbidden.	Social Sustainability	Protection of the Soul and Mind	The purpose of sharia is to maintain the sustainability of human life, including health and social.
2	Alcohol is widely used in the manufacture of food, beverages, medicines, and cosmetics.	Products and Environmental Health	Chemicals in Products	Remind of the risks of alcohol to human health and the potential impact on the environmental quality of the product.
3	The harmful effects of alcoholic beverages are forgetting God, the source of evil, damage to organ health, decreased productivity, and undermining public safety.	Social Security and Environment	Health and Social Damage	Alcohol is seen as a threat to public health and social order, which can lead to socio-ecological damage.
4	Not to bring down to destruction.	Self-Preservation and the Environment	Prohibition of Self-Harm	Prevent self-destructive behaviors that also affect the community's and the environment's sustainability.
5	Not to do any damage to the earth.	Environmental Conservation	Anti-Destruction of Nature	The principle of preventing damage to the earth is part of Islamic environmental ethics.

Source: Author's elaboration (2025)

The MUI fatwa does not explicitly state the sustainability environment. Some of the things that are considered to refer to this statement are alcohol problems. Alcohol, when consumed by humans, will cause several environmental, social, and economic issues. Environmental impact: alcohol, with the disease burden, indirectly affects people's capacity to achieve the Sustainable Development Goals (SDGs), especially regarding health and well-being.

In the study (Cook et al., 2024) said that the production of alcohol (especially beer and wine) produces greenhouse gas emissions, especially during the fermentation and packaging process (CO_2 emissions). Then a study (Collin & Casswell, 2016) states that alcohol production requires a large amount of water and can contaminate the soil and water through organic waste from the production process. Furthermore, the study (Lourenco & Piotto, 2024) states that waste generated from the production process, such as glass bottles, cans, and plastics, contributes to CO_2 emissions. Packaging can increase the carbon footprint of alcohol products.

In addition, alcohol has a social impact if excessive consumption can cause health problems (cancer, liver disease), accidents, violence, and social inequality. This is conveyed by (Probst et al., 2020; Xu et al., 2023) that alcohol consumption exacerbates social disparities, especially in low-income countries, which are more vulnerable to its adverse impacts. Studies also say adolescents who are used to drinking a lot of alcohol will be more likely to consume illicit substances in adulthood. Economically, it will impact the emergence of health costs and decreased productivity due to alcohol, reducing sustainable economic growth (Silins et al., 2018).

c. MUI Fatwa No. 44 of 2020 clarifies the regulations surrounding the names, forms, and packaging of products that cannot be certified as halal, ensuring consumer transparency

Table 3. Analysis for MUI Fatwa No. 44 of 2020

No.	Fatwa	Main Theme	Subtheme	Explanation
1	Products are items and/ or services associated with consumables consumed, employed, or exploited by the community, as well as food, beverages, medications, cosmetics, chemicals, biological products, and genetic engineering products.	Sustainable Products	Product and Environmental Management	Show attention to the safety of consumption and the safe use of products, including biological and chemical products that have the potential to impact the environment.
2	The product is in the shape of a pig and a dog and has various designs.	Production Ethics	Prohibition of Negative Symbols	Avoid haram animal symbols to maintain the purity of the product and prevent negative perceptions in society about the value of ethical sustainability.
3	Products that use packaging with pigs and dogs as the primary focus.	Product Visual Ethics	Reputation of Environmentally Based Products	Focus on product visuals that are clean of symbols that contain negative social and cultural meanings.

continued on following page

Table 3. Continued

No.	Fatwa	Main Theme	Subtheme	Explanation
4	Products that use packaging that is in the form and/or of erotic and pornographic images.	Social Health	Protection of Community Morals	Protect consumers from potentially harmful social and environmental values.
5	The food and drinks consumed by humans must not only be halal but also must be tayyib (good and halal) not only in terms of content and health but also in the product's name, form, and packaging.	Consumer Environmental Health	Thayyiban Halalan Principles	Demonstrate the relationship between product feasibility, the sustainability of individual health, and the influence on the broader consumer environment.

Source: Author's elaboration (2025)

The fatwa above does not explicitly mention sustainability and the environment, but some keywords refer to it, namely halal and good (referring to the sustainability of consumer health). Previous studies have shown the relationship between these two things and sustainability. The study (Larranaga & Valor, 2022) mentions five indicators that show that consumer goods support sustainability, namely: 1) Labels and Certifications (Eco-labels), 2) Packaging Materials (Packaging Materials), 3) Color and Visual Design (Color and Visual Design), 4) Packaging Size and Structure (Packaging Size and Structure), 5) Additional Information (Additional Information).

Then, the concepts of halal and that in the Fatwa refer to the content of healthy products for consumption; the name, form, and packaging also follow the provisions of Islamic law. The provisions that are by Islamic law in this Fatwa are limited to symbols of disbelief, disobedience, and/or have negative connotations, prohibited objects/animals (pigs/dogs), erotic or pornographic. On the other hand, the concept of this in the discussion of Islamic academics is more developed than the fatwa in the scope of modern sustainability. Bringing the boundaries of Thayib closer to sustainability with goodness, cleanliness, health, economic sustainability, and social justice. Textually, this is attached to the concept of sustainability, which has become mainstream (Insani et al., 2019).

Research from (Jamaluddin & Ramli, 2022) interprets Thayyib as good, clean, safe, and healthy food, which includes innovative elements that are by environmental and social sustainability. They highlight that the concept of tayyib is not only related to religious aspects but also touches on food security, climate resilience, and economic justice by using more climate-resilient crops such as millet, sorghum, and beans. In this concept, the concept of this is connected to: Ecological sustainability (plants resistant to extreme climates), Economic sustainability (increasing smallholder income); and Social sustainability (food security and public health).

The same thing was conveyed by (Nafis, 2019) that the concept of thayib is more or less the same as in the fatwa, namely when the health aspect is interpreted as having healthy content; the product aspect is construed as having halal raw materials and processed with halal provisions, and the ethical element is interpreted with the ethics of the person in charge of the product to avoid mixing haram ingredients. In its thematic analysis of Qur'anic verses related to the concept of halal-tayyib, as well as its implications for the halal industry, especially in the context of food products (Arwani et al., 2022).

d. MUI Fatwa No. 12 of 2009 establishes the essential standards for halal slaughter, outlining humane practices that align with religious principles

Table 4. Analysis for MUI Fatwa No. 12 of 2009

No.	Fatwa	Main Theme	Sub Theme	Explanation
1	For the Muslim community to consume animal products, the slaughtering process must adhere to Islamic law.	Social Sustainability	Slaughter Ethics	Slaughter according to sharia rules to maintain the sustainability of halal and thayyib consumption.
2	Many slaughterhouses are utilizing modern equipment as technology evolves.	Innovation and Sustainability	Technology Adaptation	Showing the application of technology in slaughter while maintaining the principle of sharia sustainability.
3	Use all good way and avoid the bad way.	Preservation of Health and Morals	Good Consumption Standards	The principle is to maintain the sustainability of health and the moral environment with halal and good consumption.
4	Do the slaughter process in a good way.	Animal Welfare	Ethics of Animal Treatment	Ensure the slaughter process pays attention to animal welfare as part of environmental ethics and sustainability.
5	Use the sharp knife and hide it from the animals to be slaughtered.	Humane Slaughter	Minimize Animal Suffering	Technical aspects of slaughter that pay attention to the sustainability of animal welfare

Source: Author's elaboration (2025)

In the fatwa above, the practice of *humane slaughter* is not only related to animal welfare by minimizing stress and pain and reducing suffering but also has a significant impact on sustainability. In terms of the environment, it can reduce feed and water waste and greenhouse gas emissions (de Vries & de Boer, 2010). On the social aspect, it can reduce the risk of injury and psychological trauma in workers

(Slade & Alleyne, 2023). As well as producing better meat quality for consumers (Naldurtiker et al., 2022; William et al., 2023).

e. MUI Fatwa No. 26 of 2013 focuses on the halal standards for cosmetic products, ensuring that beauty and personal care goods comply with Islamic teachings

Table 5. Analysis for MUI Fatwa No. 26 of 2013

No.	Fatwa	Main Theme	Sub Theme	Explanation
1	Use natural resources for humans, which can be linked to the principle of sustainability.	Halal Consumption	Cosmetic & Environmental Ingredients	Utilization of Natural Resources in line with the concept of sustainability
2	Covers the environmental impact from the products.	Health and Hazards	Prohibition of Harming Yourself/Environment	The Prohibition of Harm covers environmental impacts.
3	The law prohibits cosmetics with unclean/haram ingredients (e.g., pigs or genetically modified microbes) that can damage the ecosystem or health.	Haram/impurities	Impact of illegal substances	Avoidance of Haram Materials (Pg. 7-8) that can impact the ecosystem.

Source: Author's elaboration (2025)

This fatwa encourages halal and holy ingredients, indirectly supporting sustainable practices by avoiding harmful or non-biodegradable ingredients. This fatwa does not directly use the terms "sustainability" or "environment" in Indonesian (such as "sustainability" or "environment"). However, there are relevant principles, such as the use of natural resources, the prohibition of harm, and the avoidance of haram materials. The concept of using natural resources broadly aligns with the idea of sustainability. In the fatwa, the redaction related to the utilization concept is left without restrictions and is freely associated with sustainable utilization. Meanwhile, the prohibition of harm in this Fatwa is aimed at humans who use the product and does not cover the environmental impact broadly. This fatwa encourages the use of halal and holy materials, the meaning of which must be read about the MUI Fatwa 44 of 2020, which indirectly supports sustainable practices at certain limits (religious subjective provisions).

f. MUI Fatwa No. 56 of 2014 pertains to the tanning and utilization of animal skins in consumer goods, promoting ethical sourcing and processing methods

Table 6. Analysis for MUI Fatwa No. 56 of 2014

No.	Fatwa	Main Theme	Sub Theme	Explanation
1	The skin of dogs, pigs, and their offspring remains unclean and haram to be used.	Illegal Materials & Environmental Impact	Avoidance of Hazardous Substances	The prohibition on using the skin of haram animals (such as pigs) can be associated with environmental and health contamination risks.
2	Recommendation: The government regulates the production of consumables according to the Fatwa	Regulation & Standardization	Eco-friendly product guarantee	Indirect implications: regulation can ensure the leather production process minimizes hazardous waste.

Source: Author's elaboration (2025)

The comparative narrative of the table above is made freely and limited to associate the MUI Fatwa with environmental and sustainability issues. In these freedoms and limitations, there are provisions in the fatwa that have the potential to be connected to sustainability and the environment. Although this fatwa does not directly use the term "sustainability" or "environment," there are several principles that can be freely associated with sustainability as other fatwas, namely: the use of natural resources, the prohibition of harm, the recycling of leather waste, and the avoidance of hazardous materials. On the other hand, this tanning narrative is closer to sustainability in terms of environmentally friendly tanning technology with organic materials than conventional chrome or other technologies that produce less waste than what currently exists. The recycled element of tanned leather products also has the potential to be included in the provisions to be closer to sustainability.

CONCLUSION

In general, various regulations and policies related to halal are issued by the government and non-government; in this case, the MUI has not explicitly stated the importance of ensuring the implementation of sustainable environmental principles. The regulation of providing a sustainable environment in every process and product that consumers will use can only be found in an implied meaning. In the Fatwa policy of the Indonesian Ulema Council, which is widely used as a guideline, more regulations can be interpreted about the principles of a sustainable environment.

The lack of clarity on the principle of a sustainable environment is explicitly stated in every regulation issued by the government due to the restrictions on conception. The restriction is presented only to solve the problem of Muslim consumption for its legal halal and has not led to religious ethics that are closer to environmental issues.

Thus, the regulations need to be revised to include sustainability indicators in the form of technical attachments or Operational Standards for halal certification procedures. Concrete recommendations include an environmental evaluation aspect in halal audits, where auditors are asked to assess waste management systems, energy and waste, and the sustainability of raw materials. This will expand the meaning of halal certification to a comprehensive evaluation of sharia compliance and compliance with sustainable industry principles. Furthermore, the supervision mechanism must be broadened to ensure compliance with *Green Halal* principles. This approach will provide enough moral and legal pressure to encourage industry players to be more responsible.

REFERENCES

Abmi, M., Fachrurrazy, M., & Hasan, H. (2024). The Implementation Of Halal Certification According To Law Number 33 Of 2014 Concerning Halal Product Assurance. *International Journal Mathla'ul Anwar Of Halal Issues, 4*(1), 76–86. Https://Doi.Org/10.30653/IJMA.202441.103

Al-Haq, F., Ismail, N., & Al-Ayubi, S. (2024). The Influence Of Student Knowledge, Attitudes And Beliefs On Halal Labeled Products (Food And Beverage Case Study). *I-ECONOMICS: A Research Journal On Islamic Economics, 10*(1), 68–78. Https://Doi.Org/10.19109/IECONOMICS.V10I1.22171

Al Mubarak, M. A. R., Malihah, L., Mu'minah, M., & Ma'mun, M. Y. (2023). Implementation Of Government Regulation Number 39 Of 2021 Concerning The Implementation Of The Halal Product Assurance Sector. *Al-Adl: Legal Journal, 15*(1), 214. Https://Doi.Org/10.31602/Al-Adl.V15i1.7072

Al Mustaqim, D. (2023). Halal Certification As A Form Of Muslim Consumer Protection: An Analysis Of Sharia Maqashid And Positive Law. *AB-JOIEC: Al-Bahjah Journal Of Islamic Economics, 1*(2), 54–67. Https://Doi.Org/10.61553/ABJOIEC.V1I2.26

Amantana, A. B., Zakiran, A. H., & Imaniyati, N. S. (2023). Inclusion Of Non-Halal Information On Pharmaceutical Products Of Medicinal Types Containing Pig DNA According To Law Number 33 Of 2014 Concerning Halal Product Assurance As An Effort To Protect Consumers. *Bandung Conference Series: Law Studies, 3*(1), 178–185. Https://Doi.Org/10.29313/BCSLS.V3I1.4936

Anjani, D., Hotimah, R. H., Sativa, S. O., Syifa, D. F., & Jaza, A. I. (2014). Analysis Of The Political Economy Of Halal Certification By The Indonesian Ulema Council. *JKAP (Journal Of Public Policy And Administration), 18*(1), 37–52. Https://Doi.Org/10.22146/JKAP.6870

Arifin, S., Ekonomi, F., Bisnis, D., Nahdlatul, I., & Jepara, U. (2022). The Effect Of Halal Green Packaging, Green Halal Product, Halal Green Perceived Value On Green Purchase Intention. *Scientific Journal Of Islamic Economics*, *8*(02), 1411–1424.

Arwani, W., Jaelani, A., Firdaus, S., & Hanim, T. F. (2022). Halal-Thayyib, Food Products, And The Halal Industry: A Thematic Analysis On The Verses Of The Qur'an. *Al-Amwal: Journal Of Sharia Economics And Banking, 14*(1). Https://Doi.Org/10.24235/Amwal.V14i1.10830

Bagir, Z. A. Asfinawati, Suhadi, & Arianingtyas, R. (2020). Limitations To Freedom Of Religion Or Belief In Indonesia: Norms And Practices. *Religion & Human Rights, 15*(1–2), 39–56. Https://Doi.Org/10.1163/18710328-BJA10003

Bux, C., Varese, E., Amicarelli, V., & Lombardi, M. (2022). Halal Food Sustainability Between Certification And Blockchain: A Review. *Sustainability (Switzerland), 14*(4), 1–18. Https://Doi.Org/10.3390/Su14042152

Chasanah, C. L., & Muzammil, S. (2025). Halal Certification Of The Halal Product Assurance Agency (BPJPH) In A Juridical Perspective. *Maslahah: Journal Of Sharia Management And Economics, 3*(1), 211–225. Https://Doi.Org/10.59059/MASLAHAH.V3I1.2022

Collin, J., & Casswell, S. (2016). Alcohol And The Sustainable Development Goals. In *The Lancet* (Vol. 387, Issue 10038). Https://Doi.Org/10.1016/S0140-6736(16)30827-3

Cook, M., Critchlow, N., O'Donnell, R., & Maclean, S. (2024). Alcohol's Contribution To Climate Change And Other Environmental Degradation: A Call For Research. In *Health Promotion International* (Vol. 39, Issue 1). Https://Doi.Org/10.1093/Heapro/Daae004

De Vries, M., & De Boer, I. J. M. (2010). Comparing Environmental Impacts For Livestock Products: A Review Of Life Cycle Assessments. *Livestock Science, 128*(1–3), 1–11. DOI: 10.1016/j.livsci.2009.11.007

Deuraseh, N. (2022). Reconstruction Of The Higher Objective Of Islamic Law (Maqasid Shariah) To Strengthen Halal Industry With Special Reference To Halal Envir. *Proceeding Of 2nd Malikussaleh Internasional Conference On Law, Legal Studies And Social Science (Micolls) 2022*, 1–9.

Deuraseh, N., Haji Matusin, S. N. I., Haji Abdul Aziz, A. A., Haji Sham, I. Z., Halid Khan, S. N. A., & Hashim, N. (2023). The Awareness Of Halal Green Among Postgraduate Students In UNISSA For Sustainable Campus. *Journal Of Halal Science And Technology*, 2(2), 76–91. Https://Doi.Org/10.59202/Jhst.V2i2.670. DOI: 10.59202/jhst.v2i2.670

Dewi, A. (2024). Green Halal: The Synergy Of The Halal Industry And Sustainable Development. *An-Natiq Journal Of Interdisciplinary Islamic Studies, 4*(2), 119–130.

Fawa'id, M. W., & Mutafarida, B. (2024). Indonesia And Malaysia Halal Certification Policy:Opportunities And Challenges. *Asean Journal Of Halal Industry, 1*(1), 28–38. Https://Doi.Org/Https://Journal.Unesa.Ac.Id/Index.Php/Ajhi/Article/View/35710

Hartini, H., & Malahayatie, M. (2024). Implications Of Halal Certificates In Food And Beverage Industry Business Management. *GREAT: Journal Of Islamic Management And Business, 1*(2), 3032–7253. Https://Doi.Org/10.62108/GREAT.V1I2.688

Haryanti, T., & Miru, A. (2024). The Consumer Protection Dynamics Of Halal Products In Indonesia. *Jambura Law Review, 6*(1), 102–123. Https://Doi.Org/10.33756/JLR.V6I1.19296

Hashim, N., & Sulaiman, N. S. (2022). A Case Study Of Halal Green Concept Integration In Halal Product Development. *Journal Of Halal Service Research, 3*(2), 55–67.

Hosen, M. N., Hutagalung, A. Z., & Suma, M. A. (2022). Analysis Of The Law On Halal Product Assurance And The Law On Job Creation (Between Reality And Sustainability). *JUDISIA: Journal Of Islamic Legal And Legal Thought, 13*(1), 103. Https://Doi.Org/10.21043/YUDISIA.V13I1.13721

Insani, T. D., Al-Faizin, A. W., & Ryandono, M. N. H. (2019). The Impact Of Halal At Thayyib And Consumption Ethics On Economic Growth: An Economic Tafsir Of Al-Baqarah 168. *Journal Of Islamic Monetary Economics And Finance*, *5*(2), 459–474. Https://Doi.Org/10.21098/Jimf.V5i2.1071. DOI: 10.21098/jimf.v5i2.1071

Istianah, I., & Dewi, G. (2022). Maslahah Analysis On The Concept Of Halal Self-Declare Before And After The Employment Law. *Al-Adl: Legal Journal, 14*(1), 85–109. Https://Doi.Org/10.31602/AL-ADL.V14I1.5870

Jamaluddin, M. A., & Ramli, S. N. H. (2022). Smart Food For Future Sustainability: Halal And Tayyib Perspectives. *Journal Of Halal Industry & Services*, *5*(1). Advance online publication. DOI: 10.36877/jhis.a0000309

Khairuddin & Zaki, M. (2021). PROGRESS OF HALAL CERTIFICATION IN INDONESIA Study On The Halal Product Assurance Agency (BPJPH) Of The Ministry Of Religion And The Institute For Assessment, Drugs And Cosmetics (LPPOM) Of The Central MUI. *Basics, 13*(1), 101–121.

Larranaga, A., & Valor, C. (2022). Consumers' Categorization Of Eco-Friendly Consumer Goods: An Integrative Review And Research Agenda. In *Sustainable Production And Consumption* (Vol. 34). Https://Doi.Org/10.1016/J.Spc.2022.10.005

Lourenco, C. E., & Piotto, V. (2024). Brewing Sustainability: Assessing Environmental Concerns And Consumers' Attitudes Towards Sustainable Craft Beer Purchase Intentions. *International Journal of Wine Business Research, 36*(2), 270–285. DOI: 10.1108/IJWBR-10-2023-0066

Mariatussifa, R. M. (2024). *Implementation Of Government Regulation No. 39 Of 2021 Concerning The Implementation Of Halal Product Assurance For Halal Product Process Assistance For Non-Muslim MSME Actors In Yogyakarta.*

Masitah, P. E. A., & Wiriani, E. (2024). Analysis Of Sharia Economic Law On Free Halal Certification Through The Self-Declare Mechanism. *Journal Of EMT KITA, 8*(4), 1665–1688. Https://Doi.Org/10.35870/EMT.V8I4.3389

Nadila, F., Ismail, M., & Mutia, A. (2024). Analysis Of Halal Product Assurance Using Halal Certification In Increasing Competitiveness: (Study On Banana Products For Sale In Purwo Bakti Village, Bathin III District). *Journal Of Nuansa: Publications Of Sharia Management And Economics*, *2*(3), 65–81. Https://Doi.Org/10.61132/NUANSA.V2I3.1090

Nafis, M. C. (2019). The Concept Of Halal And Thayyib And Its Implementation In Indonesia. *Journal Of Halal Product And Research*, *2*(1), 1. DOI: 10.20473/jhpr.vol.2-issue.1.1-5

Naldurtiker, A., Batchu, P., Kouakou, B., Terrill, T. H., Shaik, A., & Kannan, G. (2022). RNA-Seq Exploration Of The Influence Of Stress On Meat Quality In Spanish Goats. *Scientific Reports*, *12*(1), 20573. DOI: 10.1038/s41598-022-23269-8 PMID: 36446782

Ningrum, R. T. P. (2022). Problems Of Halal Certification Obligations For Micro And Small Enterprises (Mses) In Madiun Regency. *Istithmar, 6*(1), 43–58. Https://Doi.Org/10.30762/ISTITHMAR.V6I1.30

Nurjannah, N., Siradjuddin, S., Efendi, A., & Fadel, M. (2024). Pillar Of Indonesian Halal Industry Development. *Indonesia Journal Of Halal, 7*(2), 156–169. Https://Doi.Org/10.14710/HALAL.V7I2.21802

Nurul Fitri Amijaya, R., Prayarsni Korina, A., Alaika, R., Lutfiani, H., Jember, U., & Sharif Ali, S. (2024). Risk Assessment Of Trade Barriers: The Implications Of Indonesia's Halal Certification Law On International Commerce. *International Journal Of Islamic Economics, 6*(02), 132–145. Https://Doi.Org/10.32332/IJIE.V6I2.9028

Pratiwi, A. A., & Vidiati, C. (2024). The Development Of The Halal Industry In Indonesia Reviewed From The Strengthening Of The Sharia Economy. *De Banten-Bode: Journal Of Community Service (PKM) Setiabudhi, 5*(2), 61–71.

Probst, C., Kilian, C., Sanchez, S., Lange, S., & Rehm, J. (2020). The Role Of Alcohol Use And Drinking Patterns In Socioeconomic Inequalities In Mortality: A Systematic Review. *The Lancet. Public Health*, *5*(6), e324–e332. DOI: 10.1016/S2468-2667(20)30052-9 PMID: 32504585

Putra, I. A., & Ambariyanto, A. (2024). Analysis Of The Impact Of Halal Product Certification On Economic And Social Activities. *El-Mal: Journal Of Islamic Economic & Business Studies, 5*(7), 3408–3427. Https://Doi.Org/10.47467/ELMAL.V5I7.2649

Putri, R. (2024). Halal Certification Challenges For Micro, Small And Medium Enterprises (Msmes) Of Food Products In Pamekasan Regency. *Assyarikah: Journal Of Islamic Economic Business, 5*(2), 222–242. Https://Doi.Org/10.28944/ASSYARIKAH.V5I2.1911

Putri, W. S. T. (2024). The Impact Of Sustainable Sourcing On Halal Certification: A Literature Review On Ethical And Environmental Concerns. *Journal Of Halal Review, 1*(1), 51–64. DOI: 10.70764/gdpu-jhr.2025.1(1)-05

Rachmawati, R., Yaniza, T., Asikin, U., Ismawartati, I., & Rohani, S. (2023). The Role Of Halal Task Force Unit In Ensuring Halal Products In West Kalimantan Province. *Daengku: Journal Of Humanities And Social Sciences Innovation, 3*(5), 893–900. Https://Doi.Org/10.35877/454RI.DAENGKU2186

Rahman, M. M., Ahmad, Z., Mokal, M. N., Aziz, M. F., & Khotib, N. A. M. (2024). Green Sustainability And Financial Performance Of Halal Food Companies: Evidence Of Malaysia. *Journal Of Islamic Monetary Economics And Finance, 10*(4), 709–734. DOI: 10.21098/jimf.v10i4.2003

Rahmawati, T. H., & Nugraha Triyan Putra, Z. (2022). Overview Of The Halal Industry In Global Trade. *Company: Journal Of Sharia Economics, 5*(2), 72–81. Https://Doi.Org/10.25299/SYARIKAT.2022.VOL5(2).9657

Ratna, J. S. (2023). *Implementation Of Government Regulation No. 39 Of 2021 Concerning The Implementation Of The Halal Product Assurance Sector (Study At LPH LPPOM-MUI Lampung Province).* UIN Raden Intan Lampung.

Rusydiana, A. S., Ruhana, A. S., & As-Salafiyah, A. (2023, January-June). Problems In The Implementation Of Halal Product Assurance In Indonesia: An Analysis Of Halal Governance. *HARMONI Journal, 22*(1), 167–186. DOI: 10.32488/harmoni.v1i22.572

Silins, E., Horwood, L. J., Najman, J. M., Patton, G. C., Toumbourou, J. W., Olsson, C. A., Hutchinson, D. M., Degenhardt, L., Fergusson, D., Becker, D., Boden, J. M., Borschmann, R., Plotnikova, M., Youssef, G. J., Tait, R. J., Clare, P., Hall, W. D., & Mattick, R. P. (2018). Adverse Adult Consequences Of Different Alcohol Use Patterns In Adolescence: An Integrative Analysis Of Data To Age 30 Years From Four Australasian Cohorts. *Addiction (Abingdon, England), 113*(10), 1811–1825. DOI: 10.1111/add.14263 PMID: 29749666

Slade, J., & Alleyne, E. (2023). The Psychological Impact Of Slaughterhouse Employment: A Systematic Literature Review. In *Trauma, Violence, And Abuse* (Vol. 24, Issue 2). Https://Doi.Org/10.1177/15248380211030243

Sukri, I. F. (2021). Implementation Of The Job Creation Law On The Implementation Of Halal Certification And Halal Products In Indonesia. *National Law Magazine, 51*(1), 73–94. Https://Doi.Org/10.33331/Mhn.V51i1.139

Syahr, Z. H. A., Syaifullah, D. H., Buyamin, & Sally, N. U. (2023). Sustainable Development Goals Concept Overview In The Digital Service Halal Certification In Indonesia. *Springer Link*, 73–83. Https://Doi.Org/10.1007/978-981-99-5146-8_6

Tsurayya Adilah, A., & Dyah Kumalasari, I. (2023). Evaluation Of The Implementation Of The Halal Assurance System Based On The HAS 23000 Standard Criteria In Sakura Mochi Msmes. *Journal Of Halal Agroindustry*, *9*(1), 22–32. Https://Doi.Org/10.30997/JAH.V9I1.5528

William, M., Mokoboki, H. K., Manyeula, F., Mabelebele, M., & Sebola, N. A. (2023). Carcass Characteristics And Meat Quality Of Weaned New Zealand Rabbits Supplemented With Moringa Oleifera Leaves Meal. *Italian Journal of Animal Science*, *22*(1), 463–471. DOI: 10.1080/1828051X.2023.2206416

Xu, Y., Geldsetzer, P., Manne-Goehler, J., Theilmann, M., Marcus, M. E., Zhumadilov, Z., Quesnel-Crooks, S., Mwalim, O., Moghaddam, S. S., Koolaji, S., Karki, K. B., Farzadfar, F., Yuanitasari, D., & Sardjono, A. (2023). Halal Regulation Challenges For Micro And Small Business Actors: A Socio-Legal Study In Kupang East Nusa Tenggara. *DIURNAL ACTA Journal Of Notary Law, 6*(2), 254–267. Https://Doi.Org/10.23920/ACTA.V6I2.1474

Zafitriani, D. A., Khasanah, K., Abdurrahman, U. K., & Pekalongan, W. (2024). Legal Certainty In The Implementation Of Supervision Of Halal Certified Products In Indonesia. *El_Hisbah, 4*(1). Https://Doi.Org/10.28918/ELHISBAH.V4I1.7551

Chapter 4
Eco-Innovation by Islamic Boarding Schools (Pesantren) to Enhance the Sustainable Halal Industry Evidence From Indonesia

Ridan Muhtadi
http://orcid.org/0000-0003-3068-387X
IAI Miftahul Ulum Pamekasan, Indonesia & Kiai Haji Achmad Siddiq State Islamic University, Indonesia

Zaenol Hasan
http://orcid.org/0009-0008-7386-2660
Kiai Haji Achmad Siddiq State Islamic University, Indonesia & STIS Nurul Qarnain, Indonesia

Halili Halili
Kiai Haji Achmad Siddiq State Islamic University, Indonesia & STIS Nurul Qarnain, Indonesia

Khairunnisa Musari
http://orcid.org/0000-0003-0525-9903
Kiai Haji Achmad Siddiq State Islamic University, Indonesia

DOI: 10.4018/979-8-3373-2792-1.ch004

ABSTRACT

This chapter explores the strategic role of Islamic boarding schools (pesantren) in promoting eco-innovation within the halal industry. Focusing on the "One Pesantren One Product" (OPOP) initiative, the chapter highlights how pesantren-based business units integrate environmentally friendly practices to enhance the sustainability of halal production. Drawing on qualitative case studies from East Java Indonesia, the chapter presents a structured analysis across three dimensions: the implementation of eco-innovation by pesantren business units, their contribution to sustainable development, and the challenges and opportunities in embedding sustainability within pesantren-based enterprises. Findings show that pesantren possess inherent local wisdom and organizational capacity to act as agents of green transformation, supporting both the halal value chain and broader sustainable development goals. The chapter offers practical insights and policy recommendations to strengthen eco-friendly practices in Islamic educational institutions and align them with Indonesia's green economy agenda.

INTRODUCTION

The halal industry is growing swiftly. It includes a main sector like food and beverage, pharmaceuticals, cosmetics, as well as halal tourism (Hidayat & Musari, 2023; Musari et al., 2025). As the Muslim consumers globally are on the rise, the demand for halal products is stretching as we speak. Indonesia must be well-positioned to take the lead in this market due to being the country with the largest number of Muslims (Kismawadi, 2024; Muniarty et al., 2023).

Figure 1. Rank Indonesia in GIE most sector 2024

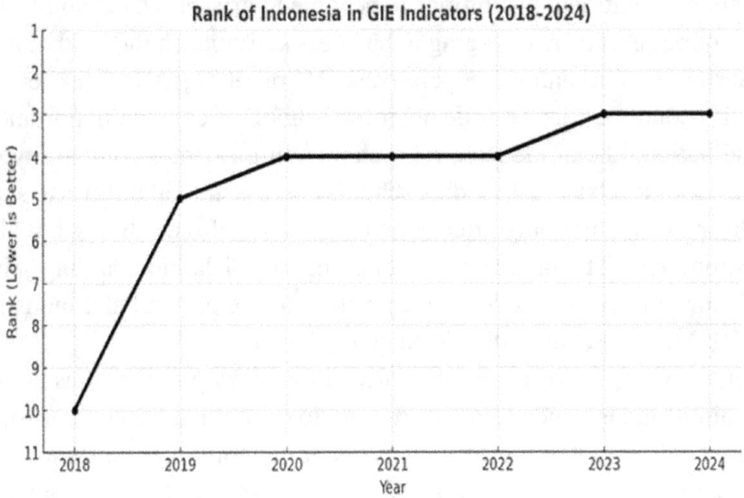

Table 1. Rank Indonesia in GIE most sector 2024

Sector	Rank
F&B Halal	2
Muslim Fashion	3
Pharmacy & Cosmetic Halal	5
Islamic Media & Recreation	6
Muslim Friendly Tourism	11
Islamic Finance	7

However, its contribution to the global halal value chain remains suboptimal. This gap indicates a substantial opportunity that has yet to be fully leveraged. To enhance national competitiveness in the halal sector, internal strengthening efforts are required—particularly in human resource development, local innovation, and the utilization of religious institutions with economic potential. In this regard, it is essential to examine the role of local actors such as *pesantren* as community-based drivers of a more inclusive and sustainable halal industry (Fadhilah & Syamsuri, 2022; Kholilah et al., 2022; Nurhayati & Dz, 2025; Qizam et al., 2024).

As the oldest Islamic educational institutions in Indonesia, *pesantren* have historically played a significant role in shaping the character, Islamic values, and socio-economic structures of Muslim communities (Isbah, 2020; Ningsih et al., 2023).

Islamic boarding schools (pesantren) have moved beyond their main function of being Islamic educational institutions to become Sharia-based economic activities. A number of pesantren are engaging in business activities in the field of halal food, organic farming, and Islamic cooperatives. (Mi'raj et al., 2023; Zaki et al., 2020) Within this economic role, Islamic boarding schools occupy an important position within the national halal industry ecosystem. With a strong community base and deep Islamic values, Islamic boarding schools possess the capabilities to support the halal industry which not only affects the accordance of the religion but also benefits the community. The involvement of pesantren or Islamic boarding schools is a crucial factor in fortifying Indonesia's position in the global halal industry (Ihsan et al., 2020; Muhtadi et al., 2022; Zaki et al., 2022).

The Indonesian government, especially in East Java province, has launched the One Pesantren One Product (OPOP) program to strengthen the economy of Islamic boarding schools. OPOP is a strategy to promote economic self-sufficiency through quality local products (Amalia et al., 2024; Muhtadi et al., 2022; Saputra et al., 2023). This program is not only expected to optimize the economy of the pesantren but also open up opportunities to insert eco-innovation values in the production process. Eco-innovation, which covers resource efficiency, eco-friendly materials, clean technology, and others, is closely related to the principles of Islam concerning environmental management. OPOP dijadwalkan untuk mempertemukan praktik industri halal dengan agenda pembangunan berkelanjutan di sektor green economy. OPOP (One Pesantren One Product) Garage thus plays a vital role in transforming Islamic boarding school institutions not only from a conventional educational institution but also into a vital organism for the halal food industry that is inclusive, innovative and environmentally friendly (Anshori & Pohl, 2022; Aulia et al., 2024).

Although they have a huge potential, the integration of green practices in halal businesses that located in Islamic boarding schools has a variety of structural constraints. Many *pesantren* still struggle with limited access to green technologies, funding, and managerial and technical skills (Bakri, 2021; Mandra & Ismail, 2022). Moreover, support from key stakeholders—such as the government, academics, and industry players—remains insufficient to drive the adoption of green innovation in these institutions. Without systemic support and adequate knowledge, the transformation toward eco-innovation in *pesantren* business units will be difficult to realize. Strategic approaches are therefore needed—ones that focus not only on economic outputs but also on ethical and sustainable production processes. In this framework, green innovation emerges as a central requirement for strengthening the halal value chain and ensuring that industry growth remains in harmony with environmental and Islamic values.

Although extensive literature has highlighted the contribution of *pesantren* to the socio-economic development of Muslim communities, studies explicitly linking *pesantren* to eco-innovation within the context of the halal industry remain limited. Previous research has tended to focus on the traditional educational role of *pesantren* or on the technical aspects of halal products, often neglecting environmental sustainability. The absence of an interdisciplinary approach that integrates Islamic, entrepreneurial, and sustainability perspectives has resulted in a lack of comprehensive understanding of the transformative potential of *pesantren*. Yet, the integration of sharia principles with green innovation through platforms such as OPOP offers significant opportunities to develop new business models that are ethical, sustainable, and globally relevant. Hence, there is an academic urgency to explore in greater depth how *pesantren* can serve as key agents in shaping a halal industry that is not only religiously compliant but also ecologically responsible (Hafidh et al., 2024; Huwaidi, 2023; S. Maulida & Ali, 2023; Thoha, 2024).

In 2019, the East Java provincial government initiated the program "One Pesantren One Product" (OPOP). The program is expected to achieve economic independence through the establishment of high-quality halal products in Islamic boarding schools. OPOP is expected to develop Islamic boarding schools from merely being educational institutions to productive economic entities (social enterprise) capable of producing halal goods and other added value services, which will be the first base of a broader community-based economic activation program. More than 1,200 Islamic boarding schools in fields such as food production, herbal medicine, textiles, and agroforestry have participated in OPOP by 2023 (Amalia et al., 2024).

OPOP was originally developed as a model for revitalizing local economies, but its importance has been greatly highlighted in the context of sustainable development. Integrating eco-friendly innovation into OPOP activities is becoming increasingly important in response to global demands related to climate change and the need to link Islamic economic activities with environmental values. Different OPOP pesantren (Islamic boarding schools) have been increasing eco-friendly practices such as composting, organic farming, eco-friendly printing with natural dyes, and energy-saving technologies.This is not merely a business strategy but also reflects Islamic ethics.

Observations in East Java show the businesses managed by Islamic boarding schools have varying levels of maturity for eco-innovation. There are already some Pesantren who have implemented a closed loop production system that recycles or utilizes resources locally. In contrast, there are also Pesantren which still does not utilize a closed loop production system caused by limited technical capacity and financial support (Aulia et al, 2024; Muhtadi et al, 2022). For instance, Pesantren A makes herbal drinks from local plants, processes organic waste into compost, and opens sustainability-based entrepreneurship classes for students. On the other hand, Pesantren B has produced environmentally friendly batik using natural dyes from plants. However, it does not have the infrastructure for the market.

OPOP has faced limitations despite raising expectations. In the face of low quality of green innovation in pesantren this study examines the pesantren program. Green education that works to support the access of green finance. Moreover, the marketing pattern of sustainable halal product is not integrated. Besides that, there is lack of policy coherence between OPOP implementation and broader halal industry development strategies, especially on the incorporation of sustainability indicators into the national halal certification system (Qizam et al., 2024).

This research is essential for fulfilling the demands of a more inclusive, sustainable and Islamic-based halal industry development model. The ongoing environmental crisis and economic disparity are prompting novel approaches for integrating entrepreneurship, sustainable development and spirituality. Through Pesantren, this study creates a significant gap and projection for the world of Islam in particular, as well as other communities in general through the environment-friendly economy to create the noble goods. The findings of this research are expected to be useful to policymakers, Islamic boarding schools, and halal industrial actors in creating a strategy oriented towards the development of the Islamic economy. The relevance of this research is the collaboration between the Islamic world and diverse modern innovations that will be able to create a sustainable and competitive halal industry ecosystem on a global scale. There has been an escalation of interest in integrating sustainable development into the Islamic economy and the halal industry in recent years. Nevertheless, studies showed that Islamic values, eco-innovation, and entrepreneurship at the local community level (especially from the Islamic boarding school context) is a scarce one. The aim of this study is to fill this critical gap.

Eco-innovation, originating from Western industrial concepts, refers to a new approach in business and production that not only reduces damage to the environment but also enhances economic and social value (Akhtar, 2025; Mady et al., 2024; Rafiki et al., 2023; Sikandar et al., 2024). In the Islamic framework, these principles are compatible with the key concepts of khilafah (stewardship), maslahah (public good), and izalat al-darar (removal of harm). Recent studies by Musari, (2024) indicate increased attention towards incorporating eco-friendly principles in a halal supply chain. The corporate level is the main focus of these studies; they haven't looked into grassroots institutions like Islam boarding schools for sustainable innovation.

While pesantren as religious educational institutions (Azra, 2006; Dhofier, 2011) are viewed within the context of classical literature, different studies take alternative perspectives. Research by Qizam et al., (2024) and Zaki et al., (2022) emphasizes *pesantren* as community-based economic actors operating cooperatives, halal food units, and Islamic micro-enterprises. Nevertheless, these studies often overlook environmental sustainability, focusing primarily on social and religious dimensions of *pesantren*-led entrepreneurship.

A growing body of research documents how several *pesantren* have begun implementing ecological values through education and practice. Studies by Anshori & Pohl, (2022), Fahrurrazi, (2019b), Hasan et al., (2022) highlight eco-*pesantren* initiatives such as composting, organic farming, waste recycling, and ecological literacy. However, these initiatives are largely educational or symbolic in nature, and rarely connected to *pesantren*'s economic ventures or integrated into scalable halal business models.

Existing literature lacks a comprehensive framework that synthesizes three key domains: (1) environmental sustainability, (2) Islamic ethics, and (3) *pesantren*-driven entrepreneurship. Very few empirical studies have systematically examined how eco-innovation principles are adopted in *pesantren*'s halal business units, or how theological values inform these practices.

In this context, the OPOP program occupies a critical position in bridging Islamic values, sustainability, and community-based entrepreneurship. However, to realize its transformative potential, there is a pressing need to institutionalize eco-innovation as a formal component of OPOP's operational framework, supported by government incentives, academic collaboration, and digital ecosystems. Thus, this chapter positions OPOP not merely as a halal business program, but as a platform for sustainable socio-religious transformation, with *pesantren* as its central actors.

Based on the previously outlined context and literature gap, this study aims to explore and analyze the role of the One *Pesantren* One Product (OPOP) program as an eco-innovation strategy to enhance the sustainability of the halal industry in Indonesia. The research focuses particularly on *pesantren* in East Java, a region actively implementing the OPOP initiative. This study also seeks to assess the extent to which environmentally friendly principles have been adopted in *pesantren* business activities and to evaluate their socio-economic impacts. Additionally, the research endeavors to identify both the challenges and opportunities in integrating sustainable practices into *pesantren*-based business units. Through this approach, the study aims to provide theoretical and practical contributions toward the development of ethical, innovative, and environmentally conscious community-based halal industry models.

SUSTAINABLE HALAL INDUSTRY IN INDONESIA

The halal industry in Indonesia encompasses all economic sectors producing goods and services compliant with Islamic sharia principles, including food and beverages, cosmetics, pharmaceuticals, Muslim fashion, Islamic finance, and halal tourism. This concept extends beyond mere product halal certification, ensuring safety, hygiene, and divine blessing (*barakah*) for Muslim consumers. Nationally, the government—through the Halal Product Assurance Agency (*Badan Penyelenggara Jaminan Produk Halal*, BPJPH) and the National Committee for Islamic Economics and Finance (*Komite Nasional Ekonomi dan Keuangan Syariah*, KNEKS)—emphasizes strengthening the halal industry as part of the national economic development strategy. Data from the *Global Islamic Economy Report* and KNEKS reveal Indonesia as one of the world's largest halal consumers, yet it remains a net importer rather than exporter. This disparity reflects untapped potential. Thus, understanding the definition and framework of Indonesia's halal industry is a critical first step in constructing narratives about its sustainability and assessing the integration of sustainability principles into national halal practices (Ali et al., 2024; Hidayat & Musari, 2022; Huwaidi, 2023; Kholilah et al., 2022).

The halal sector in Indonesia manifests in several key categories: halal food, halal cosmetics and pharmaceuticals, Islamic finance, Muslim fashion, and halal tourism. Each category exhibits distinct growth patterns and challenges. The halal food industry is a leader in domestic production and consumption, encompassing a wide range of players, from households to large industrial companies. Halal cosmetics and pharmaceuticals continue to grow, but face challenges in certification and production standardization. Islamic finance and halal tourism play a key role in supporting the broader halal ecosystem, as evidenced by the increasing number of Sharia-compliant financial institutions and certified halal tourism destinations. This reflects the growing awareness of Sharia compliance in daily life. Defining these categories not only highlights sectoral diversity but also provides a strategic framework for creating a comprehensive and integrated national halal system aimed at sustainable development (Chaniago et al., 2024; Hidayat & Musari, 2022; Iskandar et al., 2023; Musari, 2022).

Sustainable Halal refers to how to comply with Sharia principles in every halal production practice while considering environmental, social, and economic sustainability. These products are not only halal in terms of ingredients and processes, but also environmentally friendly, ethically sourced, and have a positive social impact. This trend responds to global demand for production models that combine profitability with global and social responsibility. Sustainable Halal embodies principles such as energy efficiency, carbon reduction, waste management, and worker rights protection, and aligns with Islamic values such as *Khalifah* (land stewardship) and *Maslahah* (public good). Thus, Sustainable Halal redefines the halal industry as a transformative force that values religious devotion and overall sustainability (Muniarty et al., 2023; Musari, 2024; Nurhayati & Dz, 2025).

The trend towards sustainable halal production is reflected in the approaches being pursued by various industries, from small and medium-sized enterprises to large corporations. In the food industry, organic farming, biodegradable packaging and low-carbon production methods are being integrated into the halal product system.

Halal cosmetics focus on natural ingredients and cruelty-free testing, reflecting environmental and ethical considerations. Islamic finance combines ethical investment with corporate social responsibility (CSR). Government measures such as the certification of 'green' halal products and cooperation with international organisations in the development of global halal product standards that take sustainability principles into account are increasingly supporting these initiatives. Halal industrial parks that have specifically adopted the principles of green industry illustrate this trend. These concrete examples show that sustainable halal products are not just a theoretical concept, but an innovative direction for responsible growth in the industry. Practical examples are important for understanding how the principles of sustainability are being implemented in the halal industry in a local context.

Case studies show how industry players are overcoming specific challenges, innovating and creating a halal ecosystem that is consistent with the values of Islam and sustainability. Previous studies have highlighted best practices from communities, multinational companies and educational institutions that have implemented a sustainable halal approach in the areas of production, distribution, waste management and consumer education. Successful implementation depends on leadership, regulation, community support and cross-sector collaboration. Analysing relevant case studies helps to identify patterns, barriers and key strategies for the transition to a sustainable halal industry and to link theory and practice. The case studies describe various sustainable halal approaches in regional and social contexts. Representative examples include pesantren, which develop sustainable halal activities such as organic farming and the production of healthy food at the community level. Large food and cosmetics companies focus on low-emission production, energy efficiency and transparent halal certification. Comparative examples from Malaysia and the United Arab Emirates provide insights into the strengthening of policy-based ecosystems. Another category is community-based economic empowerment programmes that combine Sharia principles with modern, environmentally friendly business practices. The sustainable halal products in this classifications are plural and contextual and shaped by the local socio-economic & cultural conditions.

THE ROLE OF *PESANTREN* IN INDONESIA

In Indonesia, pesantren (Islamic boarding schools) have a multifaceted role beyond the function of religion (Faruq et al., 2022; Putri et al., 2023; Susilo & Wulansari, 2020). In its conception, the pesantren is an essential unit in socio-economic development. The pesantren exists as a vital unit in society, which the community is developing. Pesantren not merely the place to transfer religious knowledge, but also the agent of social change. Through cooperatives, technical training and the promotion of micro-enterprises, they foster economic independence. Findings from Dhofier (2011) and Azra (2006) suggest that pesantren which have been considered as a good educational centre, is not foreign to the issues of sustainable development. This matter is of particular importance in indonesia, because the majority of farmers live in villages that are limited economic-resource and pesantren can play a role in regional growth.

The pesantren socio-economic role has an educational dimension, an economic dimension, and a social dimension. Pesantren widely offers education at an affordable rate, which includes skill-based curricula, e.g., agriculture, crafts or technology. In economic terms, a lot of pesantrens have organic farms, batik workshops, and coffee shops with students (santri) and the local community. In Pasuruan, the Pesantren Sidogiri is known for its productive waqf management supporting infrastructure development. Socially, pesantren aid in the resolution of disputes and the establishment of communal cooperation (gotong royong) through the networks formed by ulama (scholars) and community leaders (Van Bruinessen, 1995). Thus, pesantren not only acts as a spiritual centre but also acts as an economic and social centre (Ryandono, 2018; Wibowo et al., 2021).

The local wisdom of pesantren based sustainability is a local tradition that lives up to principles of environmental, green economics, and community resilience. Based on the philosophy of al-muhafazah ‘ala al-qadim al-shalih wa al-akhdzu bi al-jadid al-aslah (keeping the good old and grabbing the better new), pesantren can integrate values like islamic institution called khalifah (steward) in managing natural resources, e.g. through the implementan sustainable farming, water conservation, or renewable energy. This study shows that pesantren local wisdom has frugal consumption (zuhud), waste recycling, and respect for ecosystem balance. This method is believed to minimize environmental degradation while strengthening the self-sufficiency and sustainability of pesantren institutions (Fahrurrazi, 2019b; Hasan et al., 2022; Herdiansyah et al., 2019; Karman et al., 2023; Safei & Himayaturohmah, 2023).

Three forms of local wisdom are manifested, namely ecology, circular economy, and environmental education. The pesantren Daara Tauhid di Bandung also implements a biopore system and hydroponics. This is so that waste is reduced and food security is enhanced. In circular economies, they optimize resources by composting waste or crafting recycled products. Educationally, curricula incorporate Qur’anic environmental ethics, such as the prohibition of excess (QS. Al-A’raf: 31). Programs like *“Pesantren Hijau”* (Green *Pesantren*) in East Java engage *santri* in tree-planting and water conservation campaigns (Basri, 2022). Hence, *pesantren* local wisdom translates into tangible actions.

THEORETICAL REVIEW

The conceptual foundation of this study is built upon the intersection of eco-innovation theory, Islamic environmental ethics, and community-based enterprise models. Each of these frameworks contributes to understanding how pesantren—a unique Islamic institution—can act as a transformative agent in promoting sustainable halal industries.

1. Eco-Innovation Theory. Eco-innovation is broadly defined as the development and application of novel processes, products, or organizational models that reduce environmental risks, improve ecological efficiency, and create socio-economic value (Kant et al., 2025; Rafiki et al., 2023). It goes beyond conventional technological innovation by embedding ecological considerations into the entire innovation lifecycle. Eco-innovation involves both technical and non-technical elements, including behavioral shifts, regulatory changes, and institutional transformation. In the context of SMEs or grassroots enterprises, eco-innovation is not only about green technologies but also about adapting business models to local environmental realities, resource constraints, and cultural values (Al-Romeedy & Khairy, 2024; Mamta & Gupta, 2025; Wu et al., 2023).

The study interprets eco-innovation in the halal industry as the integration of eco-friendly processes within halal production. These processes can be the use of organic raw materials, waste reduction, renewable energy, and the use of recycled and eco-friendly packaging within pesantren's business process. Yet, micro-enterprise innovation capabilities are more likely to manifest due to access to technology and enabling institutional environments but also due to internal belief systems alignment.

2. Islamic Environmental Ethics. Islam has a rich ethical basis for the protection of the environment. The Qur'an views human beings as the khalifah (stewards) of the earth. Verses such as Surah Al-A'raf (7:31) instruct not to be excessive (israf). Surah Ar-Rum (30:41) has also indicated that corruption spreads, as a result of human hands which has spread. Thus, there is an inspirational theology which urges humankind to preserve the balance (mīzān). According to Anshori and Pohl (2022), through fiqh al-bi'ah (Islamic environmental jurisprudence), environmental actions are not seen as being social obligation but religious obligation.

The idea of maslahah (public goodness) also serve as a framework in Islamic economics to develop actions which will serve the interests of the community at large. In this case, eco-innovation in pesantren is not only a modern issue but also a case of Islamic tradition. Many pesantren have included values like the act of composting garbage as a form of zuhd (simplicity) or designing eco-products as one form of ibadah (worship).

3. Community-Based Enterprise and Embedded Economy. Theoretical lens three relies on the community-based development and embedded economy theory, particularly in application to faith-based institutions. The embedded economy, according to Polanyi (1944), is an economic concept which attributes social and cultural institutions with an economic action. Pesantren are not just moral and educational institutions, they are also economic players. These actors are not only driven by profit, but also by religious norms, community values, and historical traditions (Zaki et al., 2022).

The theory showcases the distinctiveness of pesantran entrepreneurship that is informal governance, value-based management, and community accountability. Innovation, within this framework, is not imposed from outside but rather grown from the inside, often inspired by the local wisdom, spirituality, and knowledge transfer across generations. Pesantren's role as producers of halal goods in the case of OPOP also offers a platform for da'wa, education, ecological awareness, and more; an integration of economic function with ethical mission.

4. Theoretical Integration and Research Relevance. This study proposes an interdisciplinary framework integrating eco-innovation theory, Islamic environmental ethics, and community-based enterprise for understanding pesantren's navigation of sustainable challenges and opportunities. The combination of these frameworks provides a perspective on eco-innovation that encapsulates more than a technological fix or a regulatory response; it is a social embedded and spiritual act. This framework is notably relevant in the context in Indonesia, where pesantren are centres of religious education, social welfare and microeconomic.

Consequently, the theoretical framework gives us the lens to examine the core research question: To what extent and in what ways do pesantren-based business units apply the principles of eco-innovation in their halal production systems and what factors enable or constrain this application.

RESEARCH METHODOLOGY

This study employs a qualitative research design using a case study approach to explore how pesantren-based halal enterprises adopt and implement eco-innovation principles within the framework of the One Pesantren One Product (OPOP) program. The qualitative paradigm was chosen due to the complex, context-bound nature of the research phenomenon—where religious values, institutional capacity, and environmental awareness intersect within localized economic systems. A case study method allows for an in-depth understanding of specific pesantren contexts, capturing both the practices and challenges surrounding the integration of eco-innovation.

1. Research Sites and Sampling Strategy. The research was conducted across three pesantren in East Java, a region considered the epicenter of the OPOP program implementation in Indonesia. The selection of pesantren was based on purposive sampling, with the following criteria: (1) active participation in the OPOP initiative, (2) operation of a functional business unit producing halal goods, and (3) documented or observable eco-friendly practices. These pesantren represent a variation in scale, product type, and organizational capacity, providing a diverse lens to examine eco-innovation dynamics.
2. Data Collection Techniques. To ensure rich and triangulated data, the study utilized three primary data collection methods, In-depth interviews were conducted with key stakeholders, including pesantren caretakers (kyai), business unit managers, students involved in production activities, and government facilitators of the OPOP program. The interviews explored their understanding of eco-innovation, operational challenges, and motivations for implementing sustainability values. Non-participant observations were conducted to examine daily production processes, environmental practices (e.g., composting, use of natural materials, waste management), and student involvement. Observations helped contextualize verbal accounts and identify practices not explicitly mentioned by informants. Document analysis was used to review brochures, product labels, internal business reports, training certificates, and OPOP-related materials to validate reported practices and assess the presence of sustainability narratives in pesantren branding. The triangulation of these data sources aimed to strengthen the validity of the findings and provide a multi-dimensional understanding of eco-innovation practices at the grassroots level.
3. Data Analysis Procedure. The data were analyzed using thematic analysis, guided by Sekaran & Bougie, (2016) framework. The process involved familiarization with transcripts and field notes, generating initial codes, searching for recurring themes, reviewing and refining themes, and synthesizing them into a coherent narrative. Key thematic categories that emerged included: (1) theological motivations for eco-innovation, (2) practical barriers in implementation, (3) community-based ecological entrepreneurship, and (4) institutional support structures.

4. Research Ethics. The study adhered to ethical research standards. Informed consent was obtained from all participants, and interviews were conducted with full confidentiality. The names of pesantren and participants are anonymized to protect their identities. Participation was voluntary, and the researcher clarified the academic purpose of the study prior to all engagements.
5. Limitations. As a qualitative case study focused on a specific geographical region, the findings are not statistically generalizable. However, they provide valuable analytical generalization and theoretical insights into the dynamics of eco-innovation in faith-based, community-driven halal enterprises. Future research could build upon these insights by employing longitudinal or comparative designs across provinces or involving quantitative assessments of economic or environmental outcomes.

PESANTREN AS CENTERS OF ENVIRONMENTAL MOVEMENTS: INTEGRATING RELIGIOUS VALUES AND NATURE CONSERVATION

Amid global environmental crises, Indonesian *pesantren* have emerged as unique actors harmonizing Islamic teachings with sustainability. Case studies reveal how these institutions produce not only devout generations but also resilient environmental advocates.

A prime example is *Eco-Pesantren* Ath-Thaariq in Garut, West Java, where environmental education adopts an inclusive, pluralist approach. *Kyai* (religious leaders) and *ustadz* (teachers) contextualize Qur'anic exegesis on ecology and interfaith dialogues. *Santri* regard nature as a "second sacred scripture" to be studied and protected, resulting in communities skilled in both religious rituals and grassroots reforestation/waste management.(Fahrurrazi, 2019a)

Other *pesantren* develop *"knowledge-based ecological pesantren"* models, transforming campuses into living labs with organic gardens, biogas systems, and solar panels. These technologies are studied through *fiqh al-bī'ah* (environmental jurisprudence), linking actions to Islamic principles. A *santri* at Daarut Tauhid noted: "Saving water isn't just cost-efficient—it's obedience to *hadith* prohibiting *israf* (waste)."(Muhardi et al., 2020)

Pesantren Selamat Kendal innovates with *"Qur'anic eco-theology,"* discussing verses like QS Ar-Rum:41 ("Corruption has appeared on land and sea due to human actions") while running a *"bank sampah pesantren"* (waste bank) that repurposes trash into lessons on *amanah* (trusteeship).(Karman et al., 2023)

Post-tsunami, *Dayah Terpadu* Inshafuddin in Banda Aceh built biopore systems for flood mitigation. "We learned that environmental destruction invites divine retribution," remarked an *ustadz.* Now, once-arid lands flourish with productive vegetation.(S. S. Maulida et al., 2024)

By farming maggots from organic waste, pesantren in Central Java supports the circular economy. At first, this project was met with disbelief, but it has now generated income and teaches entrepreneurs barokah. (Nurkhin et al., 2024)

The East Java Green Pesantren Movement is in line with Sustainable Development Goals (SDGs). A leader explained: "These bolsas de ocote yunqueros reduce single-use plastic thus fulfilling SDG 12; tree-planting helps fulfil SDG 13; and our collaboration with a government and NGO combine thus making pesantren a sustainability partner of choice.(Anabarja & Safril Mubah, 2021).

The environmental work happening is more than a project; it is a movement. Through climate prayers in mosques, pesantren institutions instill a deeper sensitivity to the environment. One anthropologist noticed – "Saving Earth is part of iman. Now that is more powerful than scientific talk." From Garut to Aceh, the pesantren exemplify a unique 'school of nature' that produces not only hafiz (Qur'an memorizers) but also guardians of creation. Islam rahmatan lil 'alamin (a mercy to all worlds) is an ideal religion that strikes a balance between devoting oneself to God and taking care of the planet. Eco-pesantren models are potentially replicable. Contextual dan non-didactic dapat menjadikan pesantren sebagai pelopor peradaban yang lebih hijau. As a pesantren saying goes, "Today makes a choice of investing in a better Earth, with a small environment."

IMPLEMENTATION OF ECO-INNOVATION IN *PESANTREN* BUSINESS UNITS

Eco-innovation practices began to be applied by several business units in the pesantren in East Java, the research results show. In interviews, pesantren administrators and caretakers convey that green behaviour is an Islamic value and has to be instilled in the students' character education. This strategy involves compost manure produced from kitchen waste, saving energy, and using organic raw materials. According to field observations, several pesantren have developed certain processed local food products and batik craft products using natural dyes. These claims are endorsed by visual evidence like green labels on products and brochures with sustainability messages. These initiatives, while still partial, indicate a collective awareness of the importance of the environment in halal production. The Application Of Eco-Innovation In Business Units Pesantren Is Something Different, But There Is An Intermediate An Effort Towards Green Industry.

A more in-depth investigation using interviews show that the pesantren adopts eco-innovation practices, not only for market purposes but rather for theological and cultural consciousness that is already firmly rooted in the principle of rahmatan lil 'alamin. Observations show that activities are not only done resourcewise but also in an environmental ethical manner. For example, not throwing away production waste into nature but recycling the by-products. Product labels bear sustainability symbols, but they're not standardized. This means that even though not all pesantren are capable of using eco-innovation in a systematic way due to technical and managerial limitations, but eco-innovation has now become an internal value among pesantren in managing business units. According to several sources, the process through which sustainability values are adopted is on a journey to a more extensive integration.

The findings from interviews, observations, and documentation indicate a correspondence between on-the-ground practices and the core issue explored in the research, namely the limited integration of sustainability values into the halal value chain based in *pesantren*. Although positive initiatives such as eco-innovation practices are evident, field realities show that their implementation still faces challenges such as limited technical training, financial constraints, and the absence of consistent documentation systems. These issues underscore the urgency of the research to identify the most effective strategies and models so that eco-innovation does not remain a partial initiative but becomes an integral part of *pesantren* business operations. Thus, these findings not only reflect the objective field conditions but also highlight the potential role of *pesantren* as transformative agents within a sustainable halal industry.

The *pesantren* business units observed demonstrated various forms of environmentally friendly practices. Through food production, handicrafts, and agriculture, *pesantren* utilize local resources and manage their waste in more eco-friendly ways. For instance, *Pesantren A* has developed organic farming and recycles kitchen waste into compost fertilizer, while *Pesantren B* produces eco-print batik using natural dyes derived from local leaves and roots. In addition, other *pesantren* use recycled materials for product packaging and reduce plastic usage in distribution. These activities were not only directly observed but were also supported by documentation such as brochures, halal certificates, and production reports that contain sustainability narratives. According to interviews, these practices are carried out with the awareness that environmental stewardship is part of a Muslim's moral responsibility. Although there is no standardized model yet, these initiatives reflect a spirit of commitment to building more environmentally responsible *pesantren* enterprises.

The elaboration of the data above indicates that eco-friendly practices within *pesantren* business units are carried out adaptively, in accordance with each institution's capacity and characteristics. Some *pesantren* have designated teams to manage environmental cleanliness, while others involve students directly in production and waste processing. Interviews also revealed that most *pesantren* business actors have not received formal training on eco-innovation, yet they strive to learn independently or through partnerships with government agencies and universities. Documentation shows that some *pesantren* have participated in training programs and obtained certifications that support sustainability practices. However, limitations in technology and management remain challenges in implementing these practices optimally. Therefore, while many initiatives are underway, these eco-friendly practices are still limited and require external support for further sustainable development.

The inconsistency in implementing eco-friendly practices, as previously described, reinforces the argument that there remains a gap between *pesantren* potential and the demands of a sustainable halal industry. One of the key issues identified in this research is the absence of a structured and sustainable eco-innovation implementation model within *pesantren* environments. Data from interviews and documentation clarify that many eco-friendly initiatives are undertaken spontaneously, lacking adequate technical guidelines or a clear evaluation framework. This poses a barrier to ensuring that such practices can meet the contemporary halal industry's expectations for efficiency, ethics, and sustainability simultaneously. Consequently, the realities presented by these findings are highly relevant to the urgency of the research, which seeks to build a deeper understanding of sustainability integration strategies that align with the socio-religious and operational contexts of *pesantren*.

Several concrete examples of halal products developed based efforts in various pesantren were identified in this study. The snacks or products consist of organic cassava chips, natural herbal drinks, eco-print batik, liquid soap made from herbs, and compost fertilizer made from fermented organic waste. The approach used is based on sustainable foresight for raw materials, low wastage production processes and eco-friendly packaging. The products do not just have economic implications but also ethical and spiritual meanings that reflect Islamic values, as explored through observance and documentation. Labelling halal and sustainability in the brochure strengthens the image of pesantren creations that are environmentally and socially responsible. Business managers in interviews said the products are appealing to consumers, especially young Muslims who are concerned about the environment and ethical consumption.

The findings reveal that halal products reliant on eco-innovation can serve not only as economic tools for pesantren, but also as medium for da'wa and character building. The whole production process of a product in a school like selection of material, packaging, marketing, etc can be done by students. Thus, production can become a space where the values of Islam along with care for the environment are integrated. Interviews with caretakers and business managers show that these products are considered not just for marketing purposes but also as an environment contribution. Nonetheless, quality standardization and market penetration continue to pose a challenge. Some products that appear promising do not have certification and their market access is rather limited, according to documentation. To make pesantren eco-innovation products more competitive, the efforts to improve quality and expand market access need to be enhanced.

The research findings on halal products based on eco-innovation reaffirm the core issue of the study, which is the need for developing pesantren halal business models that are shariah-compliant and environmentally friendly. Even though there are real product innovations that have environmental value, the implementation is still uneven and not yet a common practice in pesantren production systems. There is a disconnect between the potential and the limited resources available to pesantren to be a change agent. The findings of the study reveal that to overcome the challenges of the sustainable halal industry, an integrating approach that links Islamic values, environmental innovation and community-based economic empowerment strategies is needed.

This research shows that the application of environmentally friendly practices in pesantrean business units is not merely a reaction to market forces, but rather an expression of Islamic teachings in economic activities. The eco-innovation practices have not yet been structured or institutionalized on a wide scale, localized efforts are surfacing in the form of natural materials, organic waste recycling, and energy conservation. Environmental protection is consistent with the Islamic concepts of khalifah (stewardship) and maslahah (public good), and taking care of the environment is a religious obligation (Al-Jayyousi et al., 2022). The developed eco-innovation-based products show that pesantren have the potential to be shariah-compliant and sustainability-oriented producers in the halal industry. Challenges faced by this process include technical limitations, poor access to sustainable markets, and the absence of an adequate institutional ecosystem which hampers wide adoption (Harsanto et al., 2022).

The OPOP program initiated by pesantren has acted as a trigger for change at a grassroots level in the halal economy of Indonesia, although institutional reinforcement is still needed (Adawiyah et al., 2023; Oktafia et al., 2024). This research, in contrast to prior studies that largely picture pesantren as micro finance or religious education centres of the community, contributes to two aspects. First is the ecological dimension of pesantren entrepreneurship; the second is the case-based methodology that is grounded and triangulated through interview, observation, and document. Earlier studies seldom regard pesantren as potential eco-halalpreneurs. This study extends that discourse like through identifying pesantren as green innovators of halal ecosystem. which shifts their role from merely symbolic in religion to strategical in the economy as part of environmental sustainability (Musari, 2024; Nurhasanah et al., 2024).

In addition, this study proves that pesantren business which is included in a sustainability business is not only possible but also natural. Eco-innovation strengthens pesantren's values of tarbiyah (education), akhlaq (ethics), and da'wa (propagation of values) so that they can affect economic development or environmental awareness. This means that there is strong potential for pesantren to play the role of green institutional entrepreneurs that link Islamic values with SDGs.

The findings not only contribute to academic knowledge but also provide inputs for policy formulation. Regulatory agencies, such as the Regional Committee for Islamic Economics and Finance (KDEKS) of the East Java Province, need to expand halal certification criteria to include environmental and social indicators. Moreover, local government support is vital to create a training ecosystem and market platforms for pesantren eco-products. According to Mohamad et al., (2024), aligning the normative-Islamic pillars with the sustainability pillars will play a vital role in institutionalizing eco-innovation at the pesante. It is also expected that financial institutions and impact investors can formulate shariah-aligned and sustainability-linked financing that empower pesantren to scale their green halal innovations.

Figure 2. Implementation of eco-innovation in Pesantren bussiness unit

CONTRIBUTION TO SUSTAINABLE DEVELOPMENT

The result of the research conducted shows that the Pesantren business unit which participates in the OPOP program contributes directly to sustainable development at the local and national levels. Interviews with caretakers and business managers from pesantren (Islamic boarding schools) show that the implementation of organic agriculture, processing household waste and creating batik and food from natural ingredients as the real forms of pesantren's sustainability initiative. Observations show that it gives economic value and enhances students and surrounding society's engagement with the environment. The documentation of activities further proves the case (through training sessions and brochures communicating sustainability message) and certification obtained shows serious commitment to environment-friendly business practices. The pesantren activities also indirectly shape the awareness of the local community towards the environment while strengthening economic resilience based on Islamic values.

Interview data suggest that this contribution to sustainable development stems from a collective awareness that the continuity of *pesantren* enterprises depends heavily on maintaining a harmonious relationship with the surrounding environment. Caretakers associate the principle of environmental stewardship with the Islamic concepts of *amanah* (trust) and responsibility. From an observational standpoint, the existence of organic farming programs and recycling activities carried out by students strengthens character education rooted not only in religion but also in ecological awareness. Documentation reinforces this by showing halal product labeling that includes information on the use of natural, low-waste materials. Overall, these contributions reflect an integration of religious values, economic activity, and environmental practices within the operational framework of *pesantren* business units. Although these practices are not yet fully systematic, a gradual shift toward sustainable development is clearly underway.

These field-based contributions are directly linked to the research problem, which is the need for a *pesantren*-based halal industry model that upholds not only *shariah* compliance but also sustainability. The findings demonstrate that *pesantren* have significant potential as key actors in community-based green economic development. However, the fact that these contributions remain localized and have not been widely adopted indicates a persistent gap in policy formulation, technical support provision, and the development of standardized evaluation systems. Therefore, the data underscore the importance of systemic interventions to expand the sustainability impact already initiated by *pesantren* business units. .

The OPOP program has proven to have a positive impact on sustainable development, particularly in strengthening the local economy and fostering ecological awareness within *pesantren*. Interviews with program implementers and business managers reveal that *pesantren* revenues have increased, student participation in productive activities has grown, and awareness of environmental management has improved. Field observations show that business units engaged in the OPOP program not only prioritize economic profit but are also beginning to adopt more ethical and environmentally friendly production approaches. This is evident in their simple use of renewable energy, organic waste processing, and plastic reduction. Documentation from *pesantren* demonstrates progress in business reporting, the use of halal labels that highlight sustainability values, and participation in environmentally conscious halal product exhibitions. These activities reflect OPOP's positive influence in encouraging *pesantren* to become holistic development actors.

Further elaboration of these findings indicates that OPOP's positive impact extends beyond the economic domain to social and environmental aspects as well. The program provides *pesantren* with a platform to manage their own resources, empower students with entrepreneurial skills, and build networks with local communities and support institutions. Interviews reveal that caretakers believe OPOP-based production activities strengthen *pesantren* independence and broaden their role as community development centers. Observations show that *pesantren* active in the program also serve as models for others wishing to develop similar businesses. Documentation obtained highlights involvement in discussion forums, workshops, and technical mentoring aimed at enhancing business sustainability. All of this indicates that OPOP not only generates products but also builds a business ecosystem grounded in religious values and sustainable development principles.

The findings on OPOP's positive impact on sustainable development reinforce the program's relevance as a solution to the core issue of the study: the lack of an integrative model for managing *pesantren* halal industries. The continued limitations in implementation indicate that although OPOP has had a beneficial influence, its support system has not fully met the demands of scalability and long-term sustainability. This is directly related to the research question of how *pesantren*-based practices can be expanded systemically to support a sustainable national halal industry. The findings affirm that OPOP can be an effective model if supported by inclusive policies and institutional capacity building at the local level.

Pesantren actively embeds the halal value chain in their aspects through the development of products that are not only shariah-compliant but also sustainable. Based on interviews, business managers said that pesantren must ensure that the entire production process, from raw materials to products, is halal and environmentally friendly. Observations show that pesantren participate directly in the food and handicraft production process with low waste. Records of production activities, product labeling that mentions halal and green narratives, and training on the use of local raw materials support this. The involvement of pesantren along the whole value chain indicates that pesantren functions not only as an educational institution, halal product manufacturer, and distributor.

The data explained that the role of the pesantren in the halal value chain is quite strategic, in this case, maintaining the integrity of halal products and introducing sustainability values to consumers. Interviews indicate that the pesantren have an awareness of transparency in production practices and are beginning to set up simple documentation systems to show their ethical actions and quality in production. Our observations affirm that students are actively engaged in all production activities. This indicates that values that are halal and environmentally friendly have become a standard but also a learning process. Documentations such as product catalogs, promotional materials, and halal certificates from authorized bodies support this claim. This shows that pesantren have an important role as actors with integrity educators who internalize sustainability in everyday life.

The relationship between the descriptive data and previous explanations demonstrates that strengthening the pesantren-based halal value chain can effectively address long-standing challenges in Indonesia's halal industry, particularly the lack of business actors capable of bridging religious values with sustainability principles. Recent empirical findings confirm that pesantren-led enterprises, through internal religious motivation and educational orientation, can serve as environmental change agents (Harsanto et al., 2022; Syarifah et al., 2024). These initiatives are deeply embedded in Islamic epistemology, which aligns with the global shift toward value-based sustainable development (Al-Jayyousi et al., 2022). Findings suggest that *pesantren* can fill this gap through their involvement in both production processes and education. However, to scale this impact nationally, institutional structures must be strengthened, practices standardized, and cross-sectoral synergies established. Therefore, these findings not only clarify the strategic role of *pesantren* but also imply the need for a more comprehensive and collaborative policy framework to support their role in reinforcing the sustainable halal value chain.

This research indicates that *pesantren*'s contribution to sustainable development is no longer symbolic, but increasingly institutional in form. Business units developed under the OPOP program have internalized sustainability principles through practices such as waste management, use of natural materials, and engagement of local communities in productive activities. These practices are gradually shaping ecological awareness and economic independence grounded in Islamic values. Although implementation is still uneven, the *pesantren* ecosystem—combining education, production, and *da'wa*—positions these institutions as strategic actors in promoting a halal industry that is both *shariah*-compliant and consistent with sustainable development principles.

In contrast to most previous studies that frame *pesantren* in socio-religious or microeconomic empowerment contexts, this research offers a new perspective by positioning *pesantren* as central subjects in the transformation toward a sustainable halal industry. Compared to studies such as, which focus on the role of Islamic financial institutions in promoting a green economy, this research adds that religious educational institutions can also serve as environmental change agents. Its strength lies in an approach that integrates normative Islamic dimensions with environmentally conscious entrepreneurship practices, supported by triangulated field data. Thus, this study broadens the range of actors considered in the discourse on sustainable development in Muslim communities and enriches the literature on integrating spiritual values with environmental innovation in the economic sector.

The findings show that in order for pesantren to contribute to sustainable development they success not only through the technical capacity but also from the internal values that support their activities. The model of halal production that is produced by the integration of da'wa, character education, and economic activity is beyond law compliance. It has an ethical vision of the human-environment relationship. The aim of the research to identify the pesantren's contribution to the sustainable development by OPOP is highly relevant. This is because pesantren have already existed throughout Indonesia and their social outreach is socially significant. Not just economic value, but the values that students participating in the production and distribution gain through this achievement is also a positive result. The pesantren-based sustainable development can instill the character of the ecology from below, not from above.

These findings have both strategic implications but practical implications when developing Islamic-based sustainable development policies. Pesantren yang berhasil menerapkan prinsip eco-innovation menunjukkan bahwa lembaga pendidikan berbasis agama bukan hanya relevan untuk membentuk moral individu, tetapi juga untuk menghadapi persoalan ekologi dan ekonomi masa kini. This opens up the opportunities for pesantren to be positioned as development partners instead of just being the object of guidance within the halal industry context. In addition, these results could be used as a basis for the expansion of the OPOP programme to other regions in a more sustainability-based manner at the system level. The unique characteristics of the pesantren ecosystem can be used to develop incentive policies, enhancement of green technology-based training, and environmentally concerned halal certification systems. To reproduce the contribution to sustainable development identified in the research, it should be supported by suitable regulations and collaboration across sectors.

CHALLENGES AND OPPORTUNITIES

Based on the research findings, it was revealed that in the process of integrating sustainability principles into *pesantren*-based businesses, challenges and opportunities often coexist. Interviews with *pesantren* caretakers and business managers highlighted that one of the main challenges is the limited human resources who possess technical knowledge of environmentally friendly practices. In addition, infrastructure limitations—such as access to efficient production technology and policy support from the government—also hinder the comprehensive application of eco-innovation. Nevertheless, on the opportunity side, informants emphasized that *pesantren* inherently hold fundamental values aligned with sustainability, and many students show a strong interest in learning and engaging in green entrepreneurship activities. Observations revealed that while not all *pesantren* have been able to implement sustainability practices optimally, there are collective efforts underway to initiate change through waste management, energy-saving practices, and the use of natural materials. Documentation supports these findings by showcasing production and promotional activities with sustainability elements, along with training programs aimed at enhancing technical capacities.

An analysis of the collected data shows that the main challenge in implementing sustainability within *pesantren* lies not only in technical and facility limitations, but also in the absence of a structured sustainability-based business management system. Interviews revealed that many business managers still rely on traditional methods and have not integrated environmental indicators into production management. Observations support this with evidence of irregularities in record-keeping, distribution, and waste management systems across several *pesantren*. Documentation also shows that not all *pesantren* possess promotional materials or activity reports that explicitly present sustainability indicators. On the other hand, opportunities arise through the OPOP program, which offers training spaces, mentorship, and marketing networks for *pesantren* products. This serves as a foundation for capacity development that can enable *pesantren* businesses to transform toward more sustainability-oriented models in the future.

The findings on these challenges and opportunities are closely related to the main issue explored in this study—namely, the low level of sustainability integration within *pesantren*-based halal business systems. The data shows that while awareness of the importance of eco-innovation is already present, implementation is still hampered by structural factors and internal capacity limitations. This emphasizes the need for an approach that focuses not only on technical aspects but also on institutional strengthening and systemic support. The opportunities identified—such as students' innovative spirit and *pesantren*'s openness to training programs—indicate a strong social and cultural foundation to drive this transformation. Thus, the data descriptions and explanations reflect the actual field conditions and reinforce the urgency and relevance of this research.

The research also identifies various difficulties encountered in the application of sustainability in pesantren business activities. In this context, limited access to finance, low level managerial capacity, and weak strategic partnership network are among the obstacles. Business managers' interviews indicate that most business units operate on very limited internal capital and get no help from banks and other financial institutions. The observations confirmed these findings that basic production facilities were available. However, supporting infrastructure such as waste processing unit or storage space were not sufficient. In addition, documentation from internal reports also shows that many pesantren do not yet have standard operating procedures (SOPs) or quality assurance systems that consider sustainability. Due to technical and administrative barriers, the operational efficiency and sustainability of pesantren enterprise is hampered.

Based on interviews it could be explained that the lack of access to technical and managerial training has caused pesantren business managers to become more reliant on personal experience than data and strategic planning approach. An analysis of the written text shows that there are several pesantren who have a desire to apply environmentally friendly things. However, it is limited by the lack of information and skills to consistently implement it. The data we have gathered suggests that the handling of promotions, financial reporting and quality of products is not yet computerized and/or not compliant with the environment. The effective incorporation of sustainability, at these terms, becomes complicated to develop without either technical assistance or suitable support tools. The need for an all-out institution capacity development effort arises from the sporadic nature of sustainability efforts.

The conditions described in the previous two paragraphs are directly tied to the study's core issue—the absence of a systemic halal business model based on *pesantren* that is fully integrated with sustainability principles. Field data show that while there is intent and awareness, the lack of infrastructure, training, and internal regulation has made it difficult to address these challenges effectively. This reinforces the urgency of the research, which aims not only to depict the existing conditions but also to pave the way for system strengthening and more structured collaboration in integrating sustainability into the *pesantren*-based halal industry.

This study also uncovered several opportunities that can be leveraged to strengthen green innovation within the *pesantren* halal industry. Interviews indicated that student involvement in production processes creates a learning space open to sustainability values and innovation. *Pesantren* caretakers stated that a spirit of independence and empowerment is the main driving force behind exploring environmentally friendly production methods. Observations found that several *pesantren* have established partnerships with government agencies and universities to develop appropriate technologies and sustainability-based digital marketing. Documentation shows the success of some *pesantren* in producing products that blend halal values, local aesthetics, and environmental narratives, attracting urban consumers and young Muslim generations. All of this provides evidence that *pesantren* environments have the potential to continue evolving into incubators for sustainable halal innovation.

The opportunities found in this study can be further explained as the result of an acculturation process between religious values and entrepreneurial practices developed within a local context. In interviews, *pesantren* expressed that they do not view sustainability as a modern trend but rather as part of Islamic teachings that promote simplicity and responsibility toward nature. Observations showed that training programs and business incubations involving students not only develop products but also internalize ecological principles in the learning process. Documentation supports this with evidence of *pesantren* involvement in government programs and halal business events promoting environmentally friendly products. These opportunities open up the potential for scaling up green innovation-based businesses, provided they are supported with adequate mentoring systems and incentives.

The opportunities outlined in the previous two paragraphs illustrate an alignment between the internal potential of *pesantren* and the external need to build a more sustainable halal industry system. The main issue in this research—the weak integration of eco-innovation in *pesantren* halal businesses—can be addressed by optimizing these opportunities. However, in order for these opportunities to be fully realized, a cross-sectoral approach is required that brings together *pesantren*, government, academia, and industry players within a green innovation strengthening framework. Accordingly, the data confirms that beyond facing challenges, *pesantren* also possess strong social foundations and values to become centers of innovation in an environmentally conscious halal industry.

The research results provide evidence that pesantren business sustainability is structurally faced with technical limitations, minimal access to capital, and they do not have environmentally based managerial systems. On the other hand, pesantren are resilient and possess religious values supporting the environmental ethics of every human being. In addition, other benefits are the entrepreneurial spirit of students. This contradiction shows that the pesantren ecosystem is supportive of sustainable development in its value and social structure, but not in its institutional and technical capacity. Nonetheless, programs like OPOP provide spaces for potential development through training, partnerships, and access to market networks. In essence, the study illustrates the push and pull fundaments between opportunities and obstacles in the position of pesantren in the sustainable halal industry ecosystem.

This study fills a gap not widely addressed in previous research, which typically focuses on the economic success of *pesantren* without examining the extent to which sustainability dimensions have been integrated. Studies have highlighted the entrepreneurial potential of students in improving welfare, but without directly linking it to ecological issues. This study goes a step further by positioning *pesantren* not only as economic entities of the Muslim community but also as institutions capable of internalizing eco-innovation principles into their business models. The main strength of this research lies in its use of comprehensive field data and an integrative narrative approach that connects the social structure of *pesantren* with the sustainability challenges of the modern halal industry.

Reflections on these research findings reveal that sustainability cannot be imposed externally, but must grow from within the value structure and community system itself. In the *pesantren* context, sustainability values have great potential to be accepted because they align with Islamic teachings about *khalifah* (stewardship) and *maslahah* (public benefit). However, this reflection also emphasizes that values alone are not enough. A support system, technical capacity, and business models are needed to operationalize sustainability values within practical frameworks. Thus, the main contribution of this study is to demonstrate that integrating sustainability into *pesantren* environments requires a two-pronged strategy: internal strengthening (values and capacity) and external support (mentorship and incentives). Without the integration of these two components, sustainability will remain a moral discourse rather than a practical reality.

These findings have strategic implications for stakeholders—including government, academia, and halal industry players—that *pesantren* must be recognized as socio-ecological economic entities, not merely as religious educational institutions. The potential of *pesantren* to become drivers of an environmentally friendly halal industry lies in their moral and social strength. Therefore, national halal industry development policies must include special support schemes for *pesantren* business units, including incentives for green-labeled products, facilitation of sustainable halal certification, and the development of sustainability training modules based on *shariah*. This research also opens up opportunities for collaboration between *pesantren* and research institutions to develop business models oriented toward the *triple bottom line*: profit, people, and planet.

The primary reason why sustainability integration in *pesantren* businesses remains suboptimal lies in the disparity between values and capacity. Normatively, managers and students are very receptive to environmentally friendly practices because they align with Islamic values. But in practice, limitations in technology, managerial literacy, and support systems prevent these practices from developing systematically. In addition, government policies tend to be general and have yet to address the unique context of *pesantren*. Reliance on internal resources and lack of access to green technology and premium markets make it difficult for *pesantren* businesses to penetrate the global halal industry, where sustainability is increasingly a minimum standard. These findings underscore the importance of building a bridge between spiritual potential and an innovation-based economic system.

Table 2. Challenges and opportunities for integrating sustainability in Pesantren-based enterprises

Aspect	Challenges	Opportunities
Human Resources	- Limited technical knowledge on sustainability- Low managerial and strategic planning capacity	- High enthusiasm among students for green entrepreneurship- Pesantren readiness to engage in technical and managerial training
Infrastructure and Technology	- Limited access to environmentally friendly production technology- Lack of adequate waste processing facilities	- Emerging collaborations with universities and government institutions for sustainable technology development
Business Management Systems	- Absence of sustainability-oriented SOPs- Lack of quality control and digital-based financial reporting systems	- Willingness to adopt professional management systems through incubators and mentoring programs
Funding and Capital Access	- Dependence on limited internal capital- Minimal access to green or sharia-compliant financial institutions	- Potential support through OPOP programs, CSR schemes, and microfinance for green business initiatives
Institutional and Regulatory	- Lack of internal sustainability policies- Government policies not tailored to pesantren-specific contexts	- Policy opportunities to include pesantren in the national green halal industry development agenda
Pesantren Culture and Values	- Sustainability values not yet fully institutionalized	- Islamic teachings on *khalifah* (stewardship) and *maslahah* (public good) provide normative support for sustainability
Networking and Partnerships	- Weak strategic networks with government and industry	- Initiatives for partnerships with universities, ministries, and halal industry actors are emerging
Promotion and Marketing	- Lack of sustainability-oriented and digital-based promotion- Limited access to premium green markets	- Products appealing to younger urban Muslim consumers through narratives of halal, locality, and environmental responsibility
Business Orientation	- Traditional and short-term business focus	- Increasing awareness of the importance of sustainability and innovation among caretakers and students

Figure 3. Strategic action

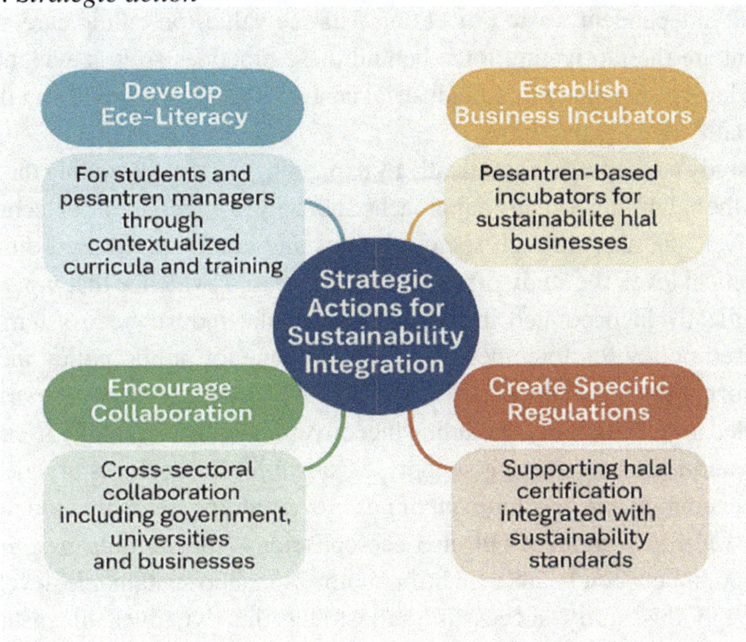

Based on the figure, immediate strategic actions are to be undertaken. In the initial stage, eco-literacy is developed for students and pesantren managers through contextualized curricula and training. The next step is to create pesantren sustainable Islamic business incubators in pesantren that link pesantren to green technology, Islamic financing, and digital markets. Third, it is necessary to foster cross-sectoral cooperation whereby the government, universities, and businesses can work together for the pesantren. In the fourth stage, build regulations to support halal certification that is integrated with sustainability standards. The In-Depth Study Steps That Become Development Programs By Pesantren Address Technical Problems And Realize The Value-Based Opportunities That Have Already Existed In The Pesantren Structure Thus, the integration of sustainability is not only possible but highly feasible by using a collaboration strategy that is context responsive..

CONCLUSION

One interesting finding is that pesantren (Islamic institutions) may have more potential to change the halal industry than previously thought. The study found that many pesantren in East Java area had performed eco-innovation, in relation to improper infrastructure and limited access to technology. They are creating halal products based on the values of sustainability, including organic agriculture, green batik, and independent waste processing. Islamic values on taking care of the environment are the motivating force behind these practices so it is evidence that it does not have to originate in an industrial centre. It can also come from the centre of spirituality and local culture.

This study contributes theoretically by expanding the understanding that sustainability in the halal industry can be approached not only from economic or technological perspectives, but also through socio-religious and community-based dimensions. On a practical level, the study offers strong field-based evidence that *pesantren* can be strategically incorporated into the national halal industry ecosystem through value-based policy reinforcement. The implications for public policy include the need to formulate regulations that support the development of *pesantren* business units rooted in sustainability, including incentives for environmentally friendly halal products and technical training support. Meanwhile, for business practices, these findings encourage the development of *pesantren* entrepreneurship models that are not only *shariah*-compliant but also eco-conscious—positioning *pesantren* as a meeting point between Islamic tradition, innovation, and sustainable development.

Although this study successfully illustrates the dynamics of sustainability integration in *pesantren* businesses, its geographical scope—limited to several *pesantren* in East Java—presents opportunities for broader exploration. This limitation should not be viewed as a weakness, but rather as a reflection of in-depth focus on a culturally and socially rich local context. Future studies may expand the scope to other provinces with *pesantren* of differing characteristics and explore in greater depth the influence of regional policies, *pesantren* leadership models, and the use of digital technologies in supporting eco-innovation. Additionally, applying quantitative methods or conducting longitudinal studies could enrich the findings by assessing the long-term impact of sustainability integration on the economic welfare of *pesantren* and their students. In this way, this research opens the door to the development of a broader and deeper research agenda in the future.

POLICY RECOMENDATION

1. Strengthening National Policies for *Pesantren*-Based Green Innovation

The government, through the Ministry of Religious Affairs and the National Committee for Islamic Economics and Finance (*Komite Nasional Ekonomi dan Keuangan Syariah*, KNEKS), should formulate specific policies that formally integrate *pesantren* into sustainable halal industry development strategies. This recommendation stems from evidence that *pesantren* have demonstrated internal capacity to manage eco-innovation business units despite technical and funding constraints. Therefore, regulations supporting technical training, environmentally conscious halal certification facilitation, and incentives for eco-friendly *pesantren* products must be prioritized. Empowering *pesantren* as community-based green entrepreneurship incubators will not only expand the halal industry's reach but also generate tangible socio-ecological impacts at the local level.

2. Integrating *Pesantren* into the Sustainable Halal Industry Ecosystem

Cross-sectoral policies are needed to connect *pesantren* with halal industry players, research institutions, and Islamic financing bodies. Central and regional governments should facilitate the establishment of *halal sustainability clusters*, positioning *pesantren* as both production hubs and training centers for environmentally responsible entrepreneurship. Such collaborative frameworks can promote technology transfer, digital market access, and the growth of locally rooted, innovative halal products. Additionally, digitizing *pesantren* business activity documentation must be prioritized to enhance accountability and transparency. Through this integration, *pesantren* enterprises will transition from informal entities into standardized, globally competitive components of the national halal value chain.

3. Mainstreaming Sustainability Values in *Pesantren* Education and Regulation

As educational institutions, *pesantren* hold a unique position to instill sustainability values in students (*santri*) from an early age. Thus, the Ministry of Religious Affairs should advocate for curricula integrating Islamic ecological literacy and environmentally based entrepreneurship. Long-term, this will produce a generation of young Muslims who are not only theologically devout but also ecologically conscious and economically productive. Such policies must be reinforced by regulatory frameworks that incentivize eco-friendly practices as operational standards for *pesantren* business units. Consequently, *pesantren* will serve dual roles as economic actors and agents of change in building an equitable and sustainable halal industry.

REFERENCES

Adawiyah, R., Ardiansyah, M., & Sholehah, N. A. (2023). A Islamic Boarding School Economic Empowerment Strategy Through an OPOP (One Persantren One Product) Model in The Digital (Case Study on Boarding School in Madura). *IQTISHADIA Jurnal Ekonomi & Perbankan Syariah*, *10*(1), 1. Advance online publication. DOI: 10.19105/iqtishadia.v10i1.8162

Akhtar, S. (2025). Introduction to Eco-Innovation, Green Marketing and Digital Transformation. In *Regulatory Frameworks and Digital Compliance in Green Marketing* (pp. 1–36). IGI Global Scientific Publishing., DOI: 10.4018/979-8-3693-9831-9.ch001

Al-Jayyousi, O., Tok, E., Saniff, S. M., Wan Hasan, W. N., Janahi, N. A., & Yesuf, A. J. (2022). Re-Thinking Sustainable Development within Islamic Worldviews: A Systematic Literature Review. *Sustainability (Basel)*, *14*(12), 12. Advance online publication. DOI: 10.3390/su14127300

Al-Romeedy, B. S., & Khairy, H. A. (2024). Eco-Innovation and Hospitality and Tourism Business Resilience: The Mediating Role of Green Dynamic Capabilities. In *Shifts in Knowledge Sharing and Creativity for Business Tourism* (pp. 17–36). IGI Global Scientific Publishing. DOI: 10.4018/979-8-3693-2619-0.ch002

Ali, J. A., Pambekti, G. T., Baroroh, H., Hassany, E. E. J. P., & Saibil, D. I. (2024). RESILIENSI EKONOMI PESANTREN MELALUI HOLDING BISNIS HEBITREN: APLIKASI ASSET BASED COMMUNITY DEVELOPMENT. *DEVOSI*, *5*(2), 2. Advance online publication. DOI: 10.33558/devosi.v5i2.9416

Amalia, D., Shofiyah, , Rif'ah, S., & Sa'idaturrohmah, N. (2024). Pemberdayaan Ekonomi Pesantren melalui One Pesantren One Product (OPOP) di Ponpes Kawasan Pantura Lamongan. *Amalee: Indonesian Journal of Community Research and Engagement*, *5*(2), 2. Advance online publication. DOI: 10.37680/amalee.v5i2.2426

Anabarja, S., & Safril Mubah, A. (2021). The Islamic Environmentalism in Eco-Pesantren Initiatives: Integrating the Sustainable Development Values in Islamic Boarding School. *Journal of International Studies on Energy Affairs*, *2*(1), 75–90. DOI: 10.51413/jisea.Vol2.Iss1.2021.75-90

Anshori, A. A., & Pohl, F. (2022). Environmental Education and Indonesia's Traditional Islamic Boarding Schools: Curricular and Pedagogical Innovation in the Green Pesantren Initiative. *Supporting Modern Teaching in Islamic Schools: Pedagogical Best Practice for Teachers*, 31–44. DOI: 10.4324/9781003193432-4

Aulia, R. N., Abbas, H., Nurhattati, N., Jasin, F. M., & Mushlihin, M. (2024). Eco-pesantren modeling for environmentally friendly behavior: New lessons from Indonesia. *International Journal of Evaluation and Research in Education*, *13*(1), 223–229. DOI: 10.11591/ijere.v13i1.25930

Azra, A. (2006). *Islam in the Indonesian world: An account of institutional formation*. Mizan Pustaka.

Bakri, M. (2021). ECO-Pesantren assessment study of Islamic Boarding School in Banda Aceh, Indonesia. *Journal of Islamic Architecture*, *6*(3), 143–150. DOI: 10.18860/jia.v6i3.7967

Basri, M. H. (2022). *Green Islam'and 'green Pesantren': An ethnographic study of Pesantren Annuqayah*. Western Sidney University.

Chaniago, S. A. C. S. A., Izza, M. I. M., Wijaya, B. S. W. B. S., & Rozi, F. F. P. R. F. F. P. (2024). Implementation of Halal Supply Chain in the Cooperative of Islamic Boarding School: Maqashid Syariah Perspective. *Jurnal Hukum Islam*, *22*(1), 1. Advance online publication. DOI: 10.28918/jhi_v22i1_3

Dhofier, Z. (2011). *Tradisi Pesantren: Studi Tentang Pandangan Hidup Kyai*. LP3ES.

Fadhilah, L. N., & Syamsuri, S. (2022). Depicthing Halal Value Chain At the Gontor Alumni Pesantren Forum (Fpag). *MIQOT: Jurnal Ilmu-Ilmu Keislaman, 46*(2), 162–185. DOI: 10.30821/miqot.v46i2.980

Fahrurrazi. (2019a). To be ecological is to become pluralist: Inclusive religious education at the eco-pesantren Ath-Thaariq, West Java. *Studies in Interreligious Dialogue, 9*(1), 23–42. DOI: 10.2143/SID.29.1.3286453

Fahrurrazi. (2019b). To be ecological is to become pluralist: Inclusive religious education at the eco-pesantren Ath-Thaariq, West Java. *Studies in Interreligious Dialogue, 9*(1), 23–42. DOI: 10.2143/SID.29.1.3286453

Faruq, A. K., Hepni, H., & Sujiwo, S. (2022). Technology and Noble Traditions in Pesantren. *Edukasi Islami: Jurnal Pendidikan Islam*, *11*(02). Advance online publication. DOI: 10.30868/ei.v11i02.2385

Hafidh, Z., Sururi, S., Nurdin, N., Adinata, A. R., & Ramadhan, R. A. (2024). Innovative Revenue Models for Islamic Boarding Schools: Achieving Economic Autonomy. *Indonesian Research Journal in Education |IRJE|*, *8*(2), Article 2. https://doi.org/DOI: 10.22437/irje.v8i2.36376

Harsanto, B., Mulyana, A., Faisal, Y. A., & Shandy, V. M. (2022). Open Innovation for Sustainability in the Social Enterprises: An Empirical Evidence. *Journal of Open Innovation*, *8*(3), 3. Advance online publication. DOI: 10.3390/joitmc8030160

Hasan, N., Mardhatillah, M., Abadi, M. M., & Hidayat, A. R. (2022). ENVIRONMENTAL ACTIVISM IN INDONESIAN PESANTREN: The Role of Lora in Mainstreaming Islamic Eco-theology in Tapal Kuda, East Java. *Teosofi: Jurnal Tasawuf Dan Pemikiran Islam*, *12*(2), 280–306. DOI: 10.15642/teosofi.2022.12.2.280-306

Herdiansyah, H., Sukmana, H., & Lestarini, R. (2019). Eco-Pesantren as A Basic Forming of Environmental Moral and Theology. *Kalam*, *12*(2), 303–326. DOI: 10.24042/klm.v12i2.2834

Hidayat, S. E., & Musari, K. (2022). ASEAN Towards a Global Halal Logistics Through the Digitally Enabled Community. [IJABIM]. *International Journal of Asian Business and Information Management*, *13*(2), 1–15. DOI: 10.4018/IJABIM.20220701.oa1

Hidayat, S. E., & Musari, K. (2023). Toward the Global Halal MSMEs Hub Through the Digitally Enabled Society: An Institutional Arrangement with Islamic N-Tuple Helix. In Rafiki, A. (Ed.), *Digitalization in Halal Management* (pp. 15–28). Springer Nature Singapore., DOI: 10.1007/978-981-99-5146-8_2

Huwaidi, M. H. (2023). MEMBIDIK POTENSI EKONOMI PESANTREN SEBAGAI PENUNJANG INDUSTRI HALAL INDONESIA. *Profit : Jurnal Kajian Ekonomi dan Perbankan Syariah, 7*(1), Article 1. DOI: 10.33650/profit.v7i1.5741

Ihsan, F. M., Permana, P. Y. E., Arifin, N. R., & Muhtadi, R. (2020). Islamic Boarding Schools Toward the Industrial Revolution 4.0; Opportunities and Challenges. *FIKROTUNA: Jurnal Pendidikan Dan Manajemen Islam*, *9*(01). Advance online publication. DOI: 10.32806/jf.v11i01.3940

Isbah, M. F. (2020). Pesantren in the Changing Indonesian Context: History and Current Developments. [Qudus International Journal of Islamic Studies]. *QIJIS*, *8*(1), 1. Advance online publication. DOI: 10.21043/qijis.v8i1.5629

Iskandar, W., Waridin, W., & Iskandar, D. D. (2023). The potential of Muslim Friendly Hospitality in the tourism industry in Central Java. *Indonesian Journal of Islam and Muslim Societies*, *13*(1), 169–197. DOI: 10.18326/ijims.v13i1.169-197

Kant, S., Adula, M., Kumari, M., & Nimbrain, N. (2025). Role of SMEs in Greening the Economy by Mediation of Eco-Innovation in the Horn of Africa. In *Examining Green Human Resources Management and Nascent Entrepreneurship* (pp. 173–200). IGI Global Scientific Publishing., DOI: 10.4018/979-8-3693-7046-9.ch007

Karman, A., Anwar, R., & Hakim, L. (2023). The Qur'anic Learning Based on Islamic Eco-Theology At Pesantren. *Jurnal Pendidikan Islam*, *9*(2), 169–186. DOI: 10.15575/jpi.v9i2.24933

Kholilah, K., Meylianingrum, K., Jaya, T. J., & Jouti, A. T. (2022). Halal Value Chain in the Holding Business: The Experience of Islamic-based School (Pesantren) in Indonesia. *Shirkah: Journal of Economics and Business*, *7*(3), 3. Advance online publication. DOI: 10.22515/shirkah.v7i3.522

Kismawadi, E. R. (2024). Halal food industry and sustainability. In *Economics and Environmental Responsibility in the Global Beverage Industry* (pp. 170–197). IGI Global Scientific Publishing., DOI: 10.4018/979-8-3693-2149-2.ch010

Mady, K., Abdelkareem, R. S., Halim, M. A. S. A., Omar, K., & Elsheikh, T. (2024). A systematic review and scientometric analysis of the driving factors of eco-innovation: Trends and future research. *International Journal of Procurement Management*, *19*(1), 74–105. DOI: 10.1504/IJPM.2024.135148

Mamta, M., & Gupta, S. (2025). Eco-Innovation and Sustainable Business Practices in the Textile Industry. In *Sustainable Business Ecosystems and Social Perspectives* (pp. 307–334). IGI Global Scientific Publishing., DOI: 10.4018/979-8-3693-8437-4.ch014

Mandra, M. A. S., & Ismail, R. (2022). Eco-pesantren Implementation Strategy Supports the Environmental Behavior of Islamic Boarding School Students in South Sulawesi. *Proceedings of the 1st World Conference on Social and Humanities Research (W-SHARE 2021), 654*, 28–33. DOI: 10.2991/assehr.k.220402.007

Maulida, S., & Ali, M. M. (2023). Pesantren in Indonesia and Sustainable Development Issues. *The Economic Review of Pesantren*, *2*(1). Advance online publication. DOI: 10.58968/erp.v2i1.267

Maulida, S. S., Nursaniah, C., & Sari, L. H. (2024). Study of implementation of the eco-pesantren concept at Dayah Terpadu Inshafuddin, Banda Aceh. In *IOP Conference Series: Earth and Environmental Science* (Vol. 1290, Issue 1). DOI: 10.1088/1755-1315/1290/1/012037

Mi'raj, D. A., Zaki, I., & Hasib, F. F. (2023). Economic Independence of Islamic Boarding Schools. *Amwaluna: Jurnal Ekonomi Dan Keuangan Syariah*, *7*(2), 2. Advance online publication. DOI: 10.29313/amwaluna.v7i2.7778

Mohamad, A., Yusoff, W. F. W., Rashid, U. K., & Adi, M. N. M. (2024). The Analysis of Sustainability Development Among MSMEs: Normative Pillar and Cultural-Cognitive Pillar. In Khamis, R., & Buallay, A. (Eds.), *Board Diversity and Corporate Governance* (pp. 673–691). Springer Nature Switzerland., DOI: 10.1007/978-3-031-53877-3_54

Muhardi, M., Nurdin, N., & Irfani, A. (2020). The role of knowledge-based ecological pesantren in environmental conservation. *Journal of Physics: Conference Series*, *1469*(1), 012126. DOI: 10.1088/1742-6596/1469/1/012126

Muhtadi, R., Ardiansyah, F., Sakinah, S., & Agustin, F. (2022). Waqf Forestry Integration Model with Islamic Boarding School in Optimizing the OPOP (One Pesantren One Product) Program. *Annual Conference on Islamic Economy and Law, 1*(2), Article 2. DOI: 10.21107/aciel.v1i2.88

Muniarty, P., Muhtadi, R., & Aziz, M. (2023). *Membangun Ekosistem Industri Halal Di Indonesia*. PT GLOBAL EKSEKUTIF TEKNOLOGI.

Musari, K. (2022). Circular Economy for Plastics and Digitally Enabled Community Towards ASEAN Halal Hub in Asia. In *Handbook of Research on Developing Circular, Digital, and Green Economies in Asia* (pp. 1–12). IGI Global Scientific Publishing. DOI: 10.4018/978-1-7998-8678-5.ch001

Musari, K. (2024). Driving Sustainable Supply Chain and Digitalization in the Halal Industry: Evidence in ASEAN-5. In *Strengthening Sustainable Digitalization of Asian Economy and Society* (pp. 87–100). IGI Global Scientific Publishing. DOI: 10.4018/979-8-3693-1942-0.ch005

Musari, K., Mahmudah, M., Hakim, Z., & Almunawar, M. N. (2025). Mapping the Implementation of Circular Economy and Reverse Logistics in the Sustainable Halal Supply Chain: Evidence in ASEAN-3. In Sakalayen, Q. M. H., Almunawar, M. N., & Yeakub Ali, M. (Eds.), *Sustainable Advanced Manufacturing and Logistics in ASEAN* (pp. 61–78). IGI Global., DOI: 10.4018/979-8-3693-5350-9.ch004

Ningsih, I. W., Basri, H., & Suhartini, A. (2023). HISTORY AND DEVELOPMENT OF PESANTREN IN INDONESIA. *JURNAL EDUSCIENCE*, *10*(1), 1. Advance online publication. DOI: 10.36987/jes.v10i1.3392

Nurhasanah, E., Mubarok, A. Z. S., Zahra, Q. S. A., & Rahmat, B. Z. (2024). DEVELOPING SUSTAINABLE ISLAMIC BOARDING SCHOOLS: ANALYSIS OF ONE PESANTREN ONE PRODUCT PROGRAM IN FOSTERING SELF-SUFFICIENCY. *Penamas*, *37*(2), 2. Advance online publication. DOI: 10.31330/penamas.v37i2.772

Nurhayati, E., & Dz, A. S. (2025). Developing Entrepreneurial Creativity through Creative Thinking Skills: Qualitative Study on Halal Industry SMEs in Pesantren. *Eduprof : Islamic Education Journal*, *6*(2), 1–14. DOI: 10.47453/eduprof.v6i2.302

Nurkhin, A., Martono, S., Fachrurrozie, F., Mukhibad, H., Rohman, A., Prabowo, W. T. J., & Rofiq, A. (2024). Promoting green-pesantren and circular economy; Improving santri's knowledge on food waste management and maggot cultivation. In *IOP Conference Series: Earth and Environmental Science* (Vol. 1414, Issue 1). DOI: 10.1088/1755-1315/1414/1/012026

Oktafia, R., Taufiq, M., & Utami, A. F. (2024). One Pesantren One Product: Can It Improve Economic Growth in East Java? *IQTISHODUNA: Jurnal Ekonomi Islam*, *13*(1), 131–152. DOI: 10.54471/iqtishoduna.v13i1.2519

Putri, A. Y., Mariza, E., & Alimni, A. (2023). Pesantren Sebagai Lembaga Pendidikan Islam (Sejarah Lahirnya Pesantren Sebagai Lembaga Pendidikan Islam Di Indonesia, Sejarah Perkembangan Pesantren/ Sistem Pendidikan, Dan Perkembangannya Masa Kini). *Innovative: Journal Of. Social Science Research*, *3*(2), 2.

Qizam, I., Berakon, I., & Ali, H. (2024). The role of halal value chain, Sharia financial inclusion, and digital economy in socio-economic transformation: A study of Islamic boarding schools in Indonesia. *Journal of Islamic Marketing*, *16*(3), 810–840. DOI: 10.1108/JIMA-03-2024-0108

Rafiki, A., Ramadhani, S. N., Ananda, R. F., & Harahap, I. (2023). Eco-Innovation Towards Increasing the Productivity of SMEs: A Case in Indonesia. In *Handbook of Research on Artificial Intelligence and Knowledge Management in Asia's Digital Economy* (pp. 223–232). IGI Global Scientific Publishing., DOI: 10.4018/978-1-6684-5849-5.ch013

Ryandono, M. N. H. (2018). Peran Pondok Pesantren dalam Pemberdayaan Sosial Ekonomi di Jawa Timur pada Abad ke-20. *MOZAIK HUMANIORA*, *18*(2), 2. Advance online publication. DOI: 10.20473/mozaik.v18i2.10934

Safei, A. A., & Himayaturohmah, E. (2023). Development of Environmentally Friendly Culture in the Islamic Boarding School through Social Intervention Strategy. *Al-Hayat: Journal of Islamic Education*, *7*(1), 1. Advance online publication. DOI: 10.35723/ajie.v7i1.323

Saputra, P. P., Setyawan, R. D., & Kurnia, M. (2023). Analysis of the Effectiveness of the One Pesantren One Product (OPOP) Program in Supporting the Economic Empowerment of Islamic Boarding Schools in Belitung Regency. *Society*, *11*(2), 2. Advance online publication. DOI: 10.33019/society.v11i2.660

Sekaran, U., & Bougie, R. (2016). *Research methods for business: A skill-building approach* (7th ed.). Wiley.

Sikandar, H., Kohar, U. H. A., Sanda, G., Salman, A., Cilan, T., Shabbir, M. S., & Ramos-Meza, C. S. (2024). Eco-innovation in Small and Medium Enterprises (SMEs): A Systematic Literature Review. *Journal of the Knowledge Economy*, *15*(2), 5841–5863. DOI: 10.1007/s13132-023-01367-w

Susilo, A. A., & Wulansari, R. (2020). Sejarah Pesantren Sebagai Lembaga Pendidikan Islam di Indonesia. *Tamaddun: Jurnal Kebudayaan dan Sastra Islam, 20*(2), Article 2. DOI: 10.19109/tamaddun.v20i2.6676

Syarifah, L., AJR, A. R., Solekah, N. A., & Wahyuni, S. S. (2024). Implementation of Eco-Innovation, Eco-Commitment, Eco-Opportunity in the Islamic Boarding School Environment: A Phenomenological Study on the Raudhatul Madinah Entrepreneur Islamic Boarding School. *ULIL ALBAB : Jurnal Ilmiah Multidisiplin, 4*(1), 149–161. DOI: 10.56799/jim.v4i1.6558

Thoha, A. F. K. (2024). Visionary Leadership and Dynamic Capabilities: Transforming Pesantren into a Social Enterprise. [International Journal of Islamic Business Ethics]. *IJIBE*, *9*(1), 1. Advance online publication. DOI: 10.30659/ijibe.9.1.46-62

Van Bruinessen, M. (1995). *Kitab Kuning Pesantren dan Tarekat: Tradisi-Tradisi Islam di Indonesia*. Mizan.

Wibowo, A., Muhammad, D. R. A., Lestari, E., & Karsidi, R. (2021). Community empowerment based on religious ecology leading to sustainable agricultural development (A case study of Isy Karima Islamic boarding school in Karanganyar, Central Java). *IOP Conference Series. Earth and Environmental Science*, *905*(1), 012035. DOI: 10.1088/1755-1315/905/1/012035

Wu, S., Zhou, X., & Zhu, Q. (2023). Green credit and enterprise environmental and economic performance: The mediating role of eco-innovation. *Journal of Cleaner Production*, *382*, 135248. DOI: 10.1016/j.jclepro.2022.135248

Zaki, I., Widiastuti, T., Yudha, A. T. R. C., Wijayanti, I., & Mi'raj, D. A. (2020). Implementation of Islamic entrepreneurial culture in Islamic boarding schools. *International Journal of Innovation. Creativity and Change*, *11*(11), 452–469.

Zaki, I., Zusak, M. B. F., Mi'raj, D. A., & Hasib, F. F. (2022). Islamic community-based business cooperation and sustainable development goals: A case of pesantren community in Indonesia. *International Journal of Ethics and Systems*, *38*(4), 621–632. DOI: 10.1108/IJOES-12-2021-0218

Chapter 5
Halal Business and Food Waste:
Examining Factors and Consumer Intentions in Brunei Darussalam

Zahidah Borhan
http://orcid.org/0009-0001-5029-9843
Universiti Brunei Darussalam, Brunei

Mohamed Syazwan Ab Talib
http://orcid.org/0000-0001-8190-9096
Universiti Brunei Darussalam, Brunei

ABSTRACT

Food waste is a growing environmental and economic concern, particularly within the halal food industry, where ethical consumption and sustainability are key principles. This study examines the factors influencing halal food waste prevention intentions in Brunei, applying the Theory of Planned Behaviour to assess the roles of subjective norms, perceived behavioural control, and attitudes. A survey of 105 respondents, analyzed using correlation and regression, found that attitudes and perceived behavioural control significantly influence food waste prevention, while subjective norms have minimal impact. These findings suggest that effective waste reduction strategies should focus on self-efficacy and positive attitudes. From a halal business perspective, this study highlights the role of Islamic values in promoting sustainability. Insights from this research can guide halal food producers, policymakers, and consumers in developing effective waste management strategies aligned with Brunei's Vision 2035 and the United Nations' Sustainable Development Goals.

DOI: 10.4018/979-8-3373-2792-1.ch005

INTRODUCTION

Global population growth, expected to reach 9.1 billion by 2050, has intensified the demand for food and, in turn, drawn attention to the growing issue of food waste. Although long overlooked, food waste has significant economic, political, and social consequences (Foti et al., 2018). According to the Food and Agriculture Organisation of the United Nations (FAO) Food and Agricultural Organization of the United Nations, 2017), approximately one-third of all food produced globally for human consumption is wasted.

Likewise, the global Muslim population is also expanding, with rising demand for halal-certified products across the supply chain. This surge in halal food consumption is evident in both Muslim-majority and minority countries. While increased availability and consumption of halal food signify improved access and market development, they also contribute to heightened levels of food surplus and eventual waste. Despite its relevance, the issue of halal food waste remains largely underexplored in current research. The existing literature tends to focus on halal certification, consumer trust, and supply chain integrity, with limited attention to the volume of halal food discarded at the consumer level. As such, the intersection between halal consumption practices and food waste merits closer examination, particularly in contexts where religious and cultural norms strongly influence food-related behaviours.

Brunei is no exception to this issue. Food waste constitutes 32% of the country's total municipal waste (Sulaiman, 2023). However, according to news from the Borneo Bulletin, only 11.3% of this food waste is recycled or otherwise utilised, and just 2% is compacted for disposal (Sulaiman, 2023). The problem worsens during festive seasons, such as Ramadhan and Eid, when food waste levels rise sharply (Mahmud, 2023). Globally, the average annual per capita household food waste is 74 kilograms, while in Brunei, the figure stands at 80 kilograms, six kilograms higher than the global average (UNEP, 2021). This disparity highlights the urgency of addressing food waste at the national level.

There are various ways to dispose of food waste, including composting, converting it to animal feed, or using garbage disposals. In Brunei, however, landfilling remains the most common method. Alwines (2020) notes that between 400 and 500 tonnes of waste are sent daily to the Sungai Paku landfill in Tutong. Without effective waste management, this landfill is projected to reach capacity by 2025 (Dariah et al., 2022). Although convenient, landfilling poses environmental risks, including the depletion of natural resources and the release of harmful gases. When food waste decomposes in landfills, it emits methane (CH_4), a major contributor to climate change. According to Shams et al. (2024), Brunei-Muara records the highest CH_4 emissions from landfills at 89,594 tonnes of CO_2e per year, followed by

Tutong at 21,423 tonnes, Kuala Belait at 15,132 tonnes, and Temburong, owing to its small population and dense forest cover, at 3,227 tonnes. Overall, landfill gases in Brunei could emit approximately 129,377 tonnes (0.13 million tonnes) of CO_2e annually. These figures stress the importance of reducing food waste to mitigate environmental impact and promote sustainability, while also improving food security, particularly in countries where food scarcity remains a challenge. Despite growing awareness of the need to reduce halal food waste, research and data on this issue remain limited in Brunei.

This study aims to explore the behavioural factors influencing halal food waste prevention in Brunei, specifically focusing on individuals' intentions and the determinants of their actions. Specifically, the study investigates three behavioural constructs, subjective norms, perceived behavioural control, and attitudes, to assess their relationship to reducing food waste. Accordingly, the research addresses three key questions: Is there a relationship between a) subjective norms, b) perceived behavioural control, and c) attitudes and the intention to prevent food waste?

This research offers practical relevance for policymakers, food retailers, producers, and consumers. Economically, reducing food waste can generate substantial savings across sectors, including households, where rising food prices continue to affect financial well-being (Philippidis et al., 2019). Retailers can also benefit from improved inventory and resource management. In Brunei, where the food retail and service sectors are expanding, addressing food waste may lead to greater efficiency and strengthen relationships with customers who increasingly value sustainability (Graham-Rowe et al., 2014). Policymakers, in turn, can develop targeted strategies, such as food waste reduction goals, while consumers can reflect on and improve their food management habits.

More broadly, this study supports Brunei's national development objectives. Its findings can inform policy initiatives aligned with Brunei Vision 2035, which prioritises resilience and sustainability. By understanding the behavioural drivers of food waste, authorities can implement awareness campaigns, community initiatives, and incentive-based programmes to reduce household waste. The study also contributes to global efforts under the United Nations (UN) Sustainable Development Goals (SDGs), particularly SDG 12 on Responsible Consumption and Production. Target 12.3 aims to halve global food waste per capita and reduce losses along production and supply chains by 2030. In this regard, the research provides valuable insights that can help align Brunei's domestic waste reduction efforts with international sustainability targets.

The scope of this study is limited to household food waste in Brunei, with a focus on subjective norms, perceived behavioural control, and attitudes. While the findings offer valuable insights, they are specific to Brunei's cultural, social, and economic context, which may limit their applicability elsewhere. Cultural factors such as the emphasis on generosity during festive occasions may not hold the same influence in other countries. Additionally, the study does not address food waste generated by schools, businesses, or the food service industry. It is confined solely to domestic food waste. The research employs a cross-sectional design, which captures a snapshot of food waste practices but does not account for how behaviours and attitudes may change over time, particularly in response to policy changes or shifts in public awareness.

The remainder of this paper is structured as follows. The next section presents a review of existing literature on food waste, with a focus on behavioural factors influencing consumer intentions. This is followed by the methodology section, which outlines the research design, data collection procedures, and analytical approach. The results and discussion section then presents the key findings and interprets them in relation to the study's objectives and existing literature. Finally, the conclusion summarises the main insights, discusses the implications for policy and practice, and suggests directions for future research.

1. LITERATURE REVIEW

Food waste remains a widespread challenge across both developed and developing nations. According to the Food and Agriculture Organization of the United Nations (Food and Agricultural Organization of the United Nations, 2017), an estimated 1.3 billion tonnes of food, approximately one-third of all food produced for human consumption, is wasted annually. Food is discarded at all stages of the supply chain, from agricultural production and post-harvest handling to retail and household consumption. However, growing evidence indicates that a significant proportion of food waste occurs at the consumer level in both industrialised and developing countries, largely due to over-purchasing, improper storage, and spoilage (UNEP, 2021).

The environmental consequences of food waste are considerable. Globally, food waste is responsible for approximately 8% of greenhouse gas (GHG) emissions, thereby exacerbating climate change and contributing to inefficient use of natural resources. For instance, the water used annually to grow food that ultimately goes to waste could meet the domestic water needs of nine billion people. Additionally, food discarded worldwide could feed up to two billion individuals, which would significantly alleviate hunger and malnutrition in food-insecure regions (Food and Agricultural Organization of the United Nations, 2011).

Alongside environmental concerns, food waste also results in substantial economic losses. The global economic cost of food loss and waste is estimated at USD 1 trillion annually (UN Climate Change, 2024). These losses affect multiple stakeholders, including governments, businesses, and consumers, highlighting the urgency of collective efforts to reduce food waste at every level of the supply chain.

1.1. Food Waste in Brunei

In Brunei, food waste has become increasingly problematic due to changing consumption patterns and rising affluence. Cultural values that encourage generosity, particularly during festive periods, often lead to the over-preparation of food. This behaviour is commonly observed during major celebrations such as Ramadhan and Hari Raya. Additionally, the popularity of buffet dining, large portion sizes, and limited public awareness of food waste mitigation practices contribute to rising waste levels in the food service industry, including hotels, restaurants, and catering businesses (De Moraes et al., 2020; Wu & Teng, 2022).

Although Brunei lacks detailed official statistics on food waste, existing estimates indicate that both households and commercial food establishments significantly contribute to the problem. In response, several awareness campaigns have emerged in recent years. Initiatives such as the Baja Buddies Project by Kumpulan Bumi, Zero Waste Brunei, and the Bank Islam Brunei Darussalam (BIBD) Eco-Alam Festival aim to promote sustainable consumption and food waste reduction (Borneo Bulletin, 2023; Bank Islam Brunei Darussalam, 2023; Kon, 2022). However, despite these efforts, food waste remains a persistent issue. This study seeks to examine the behavioural factors influencing household intentions to reduce food waste, contributing insights relevant to national strategies under Brunei Vision 2035 and the UN SDGs.

1.2. Theory of Planned Behaviour

The Theory of Planned Behaviour, introduced by Ajzen (1985), is one of the most widely adopted models for understanding and predicting human behaviour. It has frequently been used in research on consumer behaviour concerning environmental sustainability, including waste reduction and food-related practices (Tommasetti et al., 2018). According to Klöckner (2013), the Theory of Planned Behaviour was employed in approximately 40% of studies published in the field of environmental psychology.

The Theory of Planned Behaviour posits that individual behaviour is primarily influenced by three components: attitudes, subjective norms, and perceived behavioural control. These factors collectively shape a person's intention to perform a particular behaviour, which subsequently determines actual behavioural outcomes (Schrank et al., 2023). The model has proven effective in forecasting consumer decisions across a variety of sustainability-related contexts. For example, Qi and Ploeger (2019) found that the theory is useful in predicting consumers' willingness to purchase food. Its applicability in addressing complex behavioural issues, especially those relating to environmental responsibility, makes it an appropriate framework for this study (Wajon & Richter, 2019). Accordingly, this research adopts the Theory of Planned Behaviour to examine how subjective norms, perceived behavioural control, and attitudes influence Bruneian households' intentions to reduce food waste.

1.2.1. Subjective norms and food waste

Subjective norms refer to an individual's perception of social pressure to perform or refrain from a specific behaviour (La Barbera & Ajzen, 2020). Prior studies suggest that social influence, particularly from family and close social circles, can significantly shape food waste behaviours. For instance, Quested et al. (2013) found that people were more likely to reduce food waste when they believed their family members expected them to do so. Santos and Liguori (2020) further showed how subjective norms interact with other Theory of Planned Behaviour constructs, such as attitudes and perceived behavioural control, to influence intentions.

Nevertheless, the literature presents mixed findings. Schrank et al. (2023) reported that subjective norms were not significantly associated with intentions to reduce food waste. In some cases, cultural or social expectations may actually encourage over-preparation and excess, rather than moderation. Porpino et al. (2016) highlighted how the value placed on hospitality in certain cultures can lead individuals to serve large portions to guests, even if it results in food waste. This dynamic is particularly relevant in Brunei, where festive customs often emphasise abundance (Muhammad et al., 2013).

These inconsistencies underscore the need for more context-specific studies, especially in Southeast Asian societies. While the Theory of Planned Behaviour has been extensively applied in Western contexts, there is limited empirical work examining how subjective norms influence food waste intentions in Brunei. This study, therefore, proposes the following hypothesis:

H1: There is a positive relationship between subjective norms and intention to prevent halal food waste.

1.2.2. Perceived behavioural control and food waste

Perceived behavioural control refers to an individual's perception of their ability to perform a given behaviour, considering factors such as time, knowledge, and resources. Research consistently shows that when individuals feel confident in their food management skills, such as planning meals, storing leftovers, or freezing surplus, they are more likely to reduce food waste. Graham-Rowe et al. (2014) observed that participants with higher perceived control were more likely to adopt proactive food-saving behaviours. Similarly, Nair (2021) found that perceived behavioural control, along with attitude, significantly influenced the intention to prevent food waste among consumers in Qatar.

However, barriers such as limited time for meal planning, lack of storage knowledge, or inadequate food preservation practices can reduce perceived control, deterring individuals from adopting waste-reduction behaviours. This suggests that increasing consumers' self-efficacy and access to information can help strengthen their sense of control and promote more sustainable food practices.

While several studies highlight the importance of perceived behavioural control, few have examined this construct in the context of Bruneian households. Cultural and infrastructural factors unique to Brunei, such as reliance on domestic help, food availability, or shopping frequency, may influence how people perceive their control over food waste. Therefore, exploring this relationship can offer valuable insight into locally tailored interventions.

H2: There is a positive relationship between an individual's perceived behavioural control and intention to prevent halal food waste.

1.2.3. Attitudes and food waste

Attitudes represent an individual's overall evaluation of a behaviour and its outcomes. In the context of food waste, attitudes often reflect personal values related to environmental concern, resource conservation, and ethical consumption. Research shows that individuals who view food waste as environmentally harmful or morally unacceptable are more likely to engage in waste-reducing actions. Stancu et al. (2016) reported that pro-environmental attitudes correlated with lower levels of household food waste in Denmark, while Stefan et al. (2013) found that awareness of the environmental impacts of waste encouraged better food management.

Emotional responses also play a role in shaping attitudes. Ma et al. (2023) demonstrated that feelings of guilt associated with wasting food can motivate individuals to reduce their waste. However, Visschers et al. (2016) argued that while positive attitudes are necessary, they may not always lead to action, especially if individuals lack the time, knowledge, or resources to follow through.

Although attitudes toward food waste have been widely studied in general populations, there is a scarcity of research examining how these attitudes manifest in Brunei's cultural context. Local beliefs and traditions, particularly those tied to religion and hospitality, may shape people's evaluations of food waste differently than in Western countries. Thus, this study also investigates how attitudes influence the intention to prevent food waste in Bruneian households.

H3: There is a positive relationship between attitude and intention to prevent halal food waste.

The theoretical framework underpinning this study, along with the key constructs and hypotheses discussed, is illustrated in Figure 1 below. This framework applies the Theory of Planned Behaviour to the context of halal food waste prevention, focusing on how subjective norms, perceived behavioural control, and attitudes influence an individual's intention to reduce halal food waste. Each construct is hypothesised to have a positive relationship with intention, as shown by the directional arrows and hypothesis labels (H1, H2, and H3). This model guides the empirical investigation by offering a structured approach to examine behavioural determinants within the Bruneian context. The following section presents the research methodology, including details on data collection, sampling procedures, and analytical methods used to test the proposed framework.

Figure 1. Theoretical framework

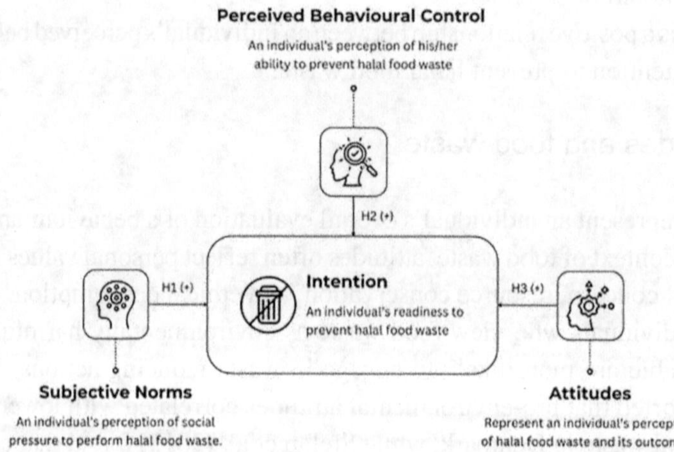

2. METHODOLOGY

2.1. Research Design

This study adopts a deductive, top-down research approach grounded in the Theory of Planned Behaviour to examine the behavioural factors influencing food waste in Brunei. A quantitative research strategy was employed, using primary data collected through an online survey. This method facilitated the measurement of respondents' subjective norms, perceived behavioural control, attitudes, and intentions to reduce food waste.

Surveys were chosen due to their efficiency in collecting data from a broad and diverse population within a limited timeframe. The use of quantitative analysis allowed for the systematic examination of relationships between the independent variables (subjective norms, perceived behavioural control, and attitudes) and the dependent variable, which is the intention to reduce food waste. Given the established relevance of the Theory of Planned Behaviour in studies on consumer behaviour and sustainability, this design was deemed suitable for the current research. A cross-sectional design was employed, with data gathered at a single point in time, offering a snapshot of current perceptions and practices related to food waste among Bruneian consumers.

2.2. Sampling Strategy

Given the limited duration of the study, a non-probability convenience sampling method was utilised. Participants were selected based on their availability and willingness to take part, with outreach conducted primarily through personal networks and digital platforms. Although this technique may affect the generalisability of findings, it was considered the most practical under the study's time and resource constraints.

The target population included Brunei residents aged 18 and above, encompassing both locals and non-locals. To enhance the diversity of the sample, efforts were made to include individuals from various demographic groups, including different age categories, genders, and socioeconomic backgrounds. Recruitment was carried out via social media platforms such as WhatsApp, Instagram, and Twitter, and further supported by word-of-mouth promotion and the distribution of printed participation cards. A small incentive was offered to participants who received the card to encourage engagement.

Initially, the study aimed to recruit at least 100 participants. According to Memon et al. (2020), a minimum of five observations per predictor variable is required for reliable regression analysis, while 15 to 20 observations per variable are preferred to detect smaller effect sizes. Ultimately, 105 respondents completed the survey, meeting the minimum requirement for statistical analysis. All participants were informed about the voluntary nature of the study and assured of anonymity and confidentiality. Maintaining participant anonymity also helped minimise social desirability bias, ensuring more honest and reliable responses.

2.3. Instrument and Data Collection

Primary data were collected using a structured Google Forms online survey, which was active from 25 July to 30 September 2024. The survey was developed using validated items adapted from previous theories of Planned Behaviour studies and was organised into five key sections: Subjective Norms, Perceived Behavioural Control, Attitudes, Intentions to Reduce Halal Food Waste, and Demographics.

The demographics section included questions related to gender, age, education level, occupation, residential district, income level, religion, ethnicity, and household size. All Theory of Planned Behaviour-related questions were close-ended and used a 5-point Likert scale (1 = Strongly Disagree to 5 = Strongly Agree) to capture the extent of agreement with each statement. This format allowed for ease of analysis while maintaining the reliability of responses. Table 1 presents the list of items used in each section of the Theory of Planned Behaviour constructs, including their descriptions and sources.

Table 1. Survey items

Variables	Code	Item Description	Source
Subjective Norm (SN)	SN1	Most people who are important to me believe that I should reduce food wastage.	Flowers et al., 2017
	SN2	People often ask me to reduce food wastage.	
	SN3	It is expected of me to reduce food wastage.	
	SN4	I feel under social pressure to reduce food wastage.	
	SN5	People who are similar to me reduce food wastage.	
Perceived Behavioural Control (PBC)	PBC1	I find it easy to prepare new meals from leftover foods.	Chun T'ing et al., 2021
	PBC2	I find it easy to ensure that only a small amount of food is discarded in my household.	
	PBC3	I find it easy to plan my food shopping so that all food is consumed.	
	PBC4	I feel that I can do something about the food I waste.	
	PBC5	People around me support my efforts to reduce food wastage.	

continued on following page

Table 1. Continued

Variables	Code	Item Description	Source
Attitudes (ATT)	ATT1	I prefer to waste less food at home.	Schrank et al., 2023
	ATT2	Food is valuable to me, so wasting it is undesirable.	
	ATT3	Reducing food waste at home benefits me personally.	
	ATT4	It is important to promote the reduction of food waste.	
Intention to Reduce Food Waste (INT)	INT1	I am willing to go out of my way to reduce food wastage.	Chun T'ing et al., 2021
	INT2	My personal goal is to minimise food wastage.	
	INT3	I will make every effort to generate as little food waste as possible.	
	INT4	I have seriously considered using all food leftovers.	
	INT5	I have a firm intention to reduce food wastage in the future.	

2.4. Data Analysis

The collected data were analysed using IBM SPSS Statistics 25. The analysis began with descriptive statistics to summarise demographic variables and provide an overview of the participant profile. Next, a reliability analysis using Cronbach's alpha was conducted to test the internal consistency of the survey scales.

Given the use of non-probability sampling and the results of the Shapiro-Wilk test (which indicated non-normality for several variables, with p-values < 0.05), non-parametric statistical tests were applied. Specifically, Spearman's rho correlation was used to explore associations between the Theory of Planned Behaviour constructs.

Additionally, multiple regression analysis was conducted to determine the extent to which the independent variables (subjective norms, perceived behavioural control, and attitudes) predicted the dependent variable (intention). Control variables were also included to test for potential relationships with intention, providing a more comprehensive understanding of the behavioural influences examined in the study.

3. RESULTS AND DISCUSSION

3.1. Respondent Profiles

A total of 105 participants completed the survey. Table 2 summarises the demographic characteristics of the respondents. Among them, 38.9% identified as male, while 58.3% were female. The majority of respondents (63.9%) were aged between 18 and 24, followed by 28.7% between the ages of 25 and 34. In terms of educational attainment, nearly half of the respondents held a Bachelor's degree (49.1%), with 22.2% having completed A-Level qualifications and 18.5% holding Diplomas. The professional profile revealed that a significant proportion of respondents were students (61.0%), followed by 21.0% who were employed.

Table 2. Respondent demographics

Category	Item	Responses (N=150)	Percentage (%)
Gender	Male	42	38.9
	Female	63	58.3
Age	18-24	69	63.9
	25-34	31	28.7
	35-44	1	0.9
	45-54	1	0.9
	55-64	3	2.8
	65 and above	0	0
Highest Education Level	A-Level	24	22.2
	Diploma	20	18.5
	Bachelor's Degree	53	49.1
	Master's Degree	6	5.7
	Doctoral Degree	2	1.9
Profession	Unemployed/Homemaker/Retired	18	17.1
	Employed	22	21.0
	Self-employed	1	1.0
	Student	64	61.0

continued on following page

Table 2. Continued

Category	Item	Responses (N=150)	Percentage (%)
Residing District	Brunei Muara	74	70.5
	Tutong	21	20
	Temburong	1	1
	Belait	9	8.6
Monthly Income (in BND)	< 1,000	93	88.6
	1,001 – 2,000	4	3.8
	2,001 – 3,000	3	2.9
	3,001 – 4,000	3	2.9
	> 4,001	2	1.9
Religion	Islam	92	87.6
	Christianity	6	5.7
	Buddhism	3	2.9
	Other	4	3.8
Race	Malay	88	83.8
	Chinese	8	7.6
	Filipino	3	2.9
	Other	6	5.7
Number of household members	1 – 4	17	16.2
	5 – 8	69	65.7
	9 or more	19	18.1

Geographically, most participants resided in Brunei-Muara (70.5%) and Tutong (20.0%), while smaller proportions were from Belait (8.6%) and Temburong (1.0%). Income distribution showed that 88.6% of participants earned less than BND1,000 per month. Household size varied, with 65.7% living in households of 5 to 8 members, 18.1% in households with 9 or more, and 16.2% in smaller households of 1 to 4 people.

These demographic patterns are significant in understanding food waste behaviours, particularly in contexts where cultural, social, and economic conditions influence consumption habits. For instance, the large representation of students and young adults may indicate higher awareness of environmental issues, while also reflecting potential constraints in food planning or preparation that influence waste generation.

3.2. Reliability Test

Cronbach's alpha was calculated to evaluate the internal consistency of the four main subscales: subjective norms (SN), perceived behavioural control (PBC), attitudes (ATT), and intentions to reduce food waste (INT). Table 3 presents the reliability values.

Table 3. Reliability test results

Variable	Cronbach's Alpha	No. of Items
SN	0.669	5
PBC	0.511	5
ATT	0.772	4
INT	0.883	5

The analysis showed that ATT ($\alpha = 0.772$) and INT ($\alpha = 0.883$) had acceptable to good reliability, while SN ($\alpha = 0.669$) was marginally acceptable. However, PBC ($\alpha = 0.511$) demonstrated poor internal consistency, falling below the threshold suggested by Nunnally (1978), who considers $\alpha \geq 0.70$ acceptable. While three of the four constructs were considered reliable, the PBC results suggest that some items within this subscale may not have been interpreted consistently by respondents.

Despite the weaker internal consistency for PBC, the construct still showed strong predictive power in later analyses. This indicates that while the measurement scale could be refined in future studies, the construct itself remains theoretically and empirically relevant.

3.3. Correlation Analysis

Spearman's rho was used to assess correlations between SN, PBC, ATT, and INT. Table 4 presents the correlation coefficients and significance levels.

Table 4. Spearman's Rho correlation results

Variable	Correlation with INT	Sig. (2-tailed)
SN	.048	.630
PBC	.451**	.000
ATT	.534**	.000

Note: Correlation is significant at the 0.01 level (2-tailed)

The analysis revealed that SN was not significantly correlated with INT ($r = 0.048$, $p = .630$), indicating that perceived social pressure did not play a substantial role in shaping food waste intentions among the participants. This result aligns with Schrank et al. (2023), who also found no significant relationship between subjective norms and food waste intention. Cultural factors may explain this. In Brunei, particularly during religious and festive occasions, generosity through food abundance is a norm. Social expectations may thus lean more toward hosting practices than waste reduction, weakening the influence of subjective norms on individual intentions (Hassan & Low, 2024; Porpino et al., 2016).

On the other hand, PBC showed a statistically significant moderate positive correlation with INT ($r = 0.451$, $p < .001$), supporting the notion that when individuals feel more in control of managing food through planning or resourcefulness, they are more likely to engage in waste-reducing behaviour. This finding echoes Graham-Rowe et al. (2014), who highlighted the role of self-efficacy in sustainable food practices.

The strongest correlation observed was between ATT and INT ($r = 0.534$, $p < .001$), indicating a strong link between positive attitudes toward food waste reduction and the intention to engage in such behaviour. This finding supports previous research by Stefan et al. (2013) and Stancu et al. (2016), suggesting that attitudes rooted in environmental concern and personal responsibility are key predictors of food waste-related actions.

3.4. Multiple Regression Analysis

A multiple regression analysis was conducted to evaluate the combined and individual influence of SN, PBC, and ATT on INT. As shown in Table 5, the model was statistically significant, $F(3, 101) = 20.641$, $p < .001$, with an R^2 of .380. This means that approximately 38% of the variance in INT could be explained by the three predictors. The adjusted R^2 value of .362 indicates that the model retains good explanatory power even after adjusting for the number of predictors.

Table 5. Model summary

R	R^2	Adjusted R^2	Std. Error
.617	.380	.362	3.07549

These findings are consistent with prior studies using the Theory of Planned Behaviour, suggesting that while these variables explain a substantial portion of the variance in intention, other unmeasured factors may also play a role. The strength of the model further supports the relevance of using the Theory of Planned Behaviour in the context of food waste prevention, especially in a culturally specific setting like Brunei.

Additionally, the ANOVA results in Table 6 confirm the model's significance ($F = 20.641$, $p < .001$), showing that the combination of SN, PBC, and ATT significantly predicts INT.

Table 6. ANOVA summary

Source	SS	df	MS	F	Sig.
Regression	585.553	3	195.184	20.641	.000
Residual	955.076	101	9.456		
Total	1540.639	104			

The coefficients in Table 7 provide insight into the strength of each predictor. SN ($B = .110$, $p = .190$) was not a statistically significant predictor, confirming the earlier correlation result. In contrast, PBC ($B = .384$, $p < .001$) and ATT ($B = .636$, $p < .001$) were both significant predictors of INT.

Table 7. Coefficients summary

Predictor	B	Std. Error	β	t	Sig.
Constant	-.242	2.726	-.089	.930	
SN	.110	.084	.105	1.321	.190
PBC	.384	.102	.317	3.779	.000
ATT	.636	.120	.437	5.282	.000

These results reinforce the earlier discussion: while subjective norms had limited influence, perceived control and attitudes played crucial roles. This again points to the importance of individual agency and internal motivation in food waste prevention.

Efforts to promote behavioural change should, therefore, focus on strengthening self-efficacy and shaping positive attitudes rather than relying solely on social pressure.

Overall, as shown in Table 8, These findings affirm that while attitudes and perceived behavioural control significantly shape intentions to reduce food waste, subjective norms appear to have little influence in this context. This aligns with other studies emphasising the value of personal conviction and confidence in influencing pro-environmental behaviours (Visschers et al., 2016; Qi & Roe, 2016).

Table 8. Hypotheses testing summary

Hypothesis	Relationship	Finding
H1	SN → INT	Not supported
H2	PBC → INT	Supported
H3	ATT → INT	Supported

4. CONCLUSION

This study aimed to explore the socio-behavioural factors influencing household intentions to reduce food waste in Brunei, using the Theory of Planned Behaviour as a guiding framework. The findings revealed that attitudes and perceived behavioural control significantly influenced intentions to minimise food waste, whereas subjective norms did not have a meaningful impact. The weak influence of subjective norms may be explained by deeply rooted cultural expectations around food abundance and hospitality, particularly during festive periods, which could override social pressure to reduce waste.

Perceived behavioural control emerged as a critical factor, highlighting the importance of individuals' confidence in their ability to manage food effectively. This suggests that enhancing food-management skills, such as meal planning, understanding food storage, and repurposing leftovers, could significantly reduce waste. Accordingly, community-based programmes that provide educational resources and practical tools could empower individuals to take proactive steps toward waste reduction. Furthermore, promoting positive attitudes through targeted campaigns could reshape public perceptions, encouraging environmentally responsible and ethically driven food practices. Reframing food waste as both an environmental and moral issue may also strengthen individuals' motivation to act.

Overall, the study provides actionable insights for reducing household food waste in Brunei. These include the importance of focusing on personal efficacy and environmental awareness over social influence. The findings also highlight the potential of integrating culturally specific approaches that align with national aspirations such as Brunei Vision 2035 and global objectives like the UN SDGs. Additionally, the exploration of digital and behavioural interventions could serve as a foundation for future programmes aimed at improving food sustainability practices at the household level.

4.1. Research Implications

The outcomes of this study have significant implications for consumers, policymakers, businesses, including those in the halal industry, and researchers. For consumers, the findings highlight the importance of individual responsibility and knowledge in managing food sustainably. By recognising how personal attitudes and a sense of control influence waste-related behaviour, consumers can make more conscious choices about portion sizes, food storage, and meal planning. Public education campaigns and household-level interventions could focus on building these capabilities, ultimately encouraging more thoughtful and waste-conscious food consumption practices.

For policymakers, the results call for greater investment in targeted programmes that address food waste at the individual and household levels. These could include educational outreach, incentive-based schemes, and the provision of tools and resources that enhance perceived behavioural control, such as training workshops on meal planning or subsidies for food storage technologies. Furthermore, culturally contextualised messaging, particularly during religious or festive periods, can play a role in shifting social norms related to food generosity and waste. By integrating food waste reduction into broader national sustainability agendas, such as Brunei Vision 2035 and the UN SDGs, policies can be made both impactful and inclusive.

For businesses, particularly those operating within the halal industry, the findings present an opportunity to take a more active role in waste reduction efforts. The halal sector, which emphasises cleanliness, ethical sourcing, and responsible consumption, is well positioned to lead in promoting food sustainability practices. Food retailers, producers, and service providers can implement inventory control systems, food redistribution programmes, or "halal-safe" surplus donation channels to manage excess food more effectively. Incorporating waste reduction strategies into halal certification frameworks or supply chain audits may also enhance consumer trust and brand reputation, aligning with the increasing demand for ethically and environmentally responsible halal products.

Additionally, halal-certified businesses, particularly in the food service and hospitality industries—can support consumer awareness by highlighting sustainable options, offering smaller portion sizes, or using digital platforms to inform customers about responsible consumption. By integrating food waste education into their customer engagement strategies, halal businesses can contribute to shaping positive attitudes and behaviours that extend beyond the point of sale.

For researchers, this study opens several pathways for further investigation. Future research could examine how behavioural drivers of food waste vary across demographic groups or cultural settings or explore how religious and ethical values embedded within halal principles influence consumer decision-making related to waste. Longitudinal studies could also provide insights into how attitudes and behaviours evolve, especially in response to national campaigns or shifts in policy.

4.2. Research Limitations

Despite the valuable insights provided, the study is subject to several limitations. Firstly, the use of non-probability convenience sampling and a relatively small sample size limits the generalisability of the findings. While this approach is acceptable for exploratory research, future studies would benefit from employing probability-based sampling methods and a larger, more representative sample to ensure broader applicability of the results across Brunei's diverse population.

Secondly, the reliability of the perceived behavioural control construct was lower than desirable, with a Cronbach's alpha of 0.511, falling short of the accepted threshold of 0.70 (Nunnally, 1978). This suggests inconsistencies in how respondents interpreted the items, which may affect the strength and clarity of the construct's impact on food waste intention. Future research should consider refining the PBC items to improve internal consistency and construct validity.

4.3. Future Research and Recommendations

Building on the current study, future research could explore other types of food waste (e.g., in restaurants, schools, or businesses) or examine behaviours across different market segments in Brunei. Additionally, investigating cultural and environmental influences, such as the impact of festivals, religious practices, or social gatherings, could offer richer insights into the context-specific drivers of food waste.

Additionally, future research could also further explore the role of subjective norms, especially in households where social influence may vary depending on age, gender, or cultural beliefs. Understanding when and how social pressure affects food waste behaviour could inform more targeted interventions, such as peer-driven campaigns or community-based initiatives. Moreover, studies could assess the effectiveness of educational programmes designed to improve perceived behavioural control. These programmes could incorporate traditional food management practices, local wisdom, and community values to enhance their relevance and impact. Evaluating such interventions would help determine whether improvements in food literacy translate into lasting behavioural change.

Finally, future work may investigate the adoption of technological solutions, such as smart kitchen tools, mobile applications for food tracking, or AI-based meal planners. Analysing the extent to which these innovations influence food waste behaviour would provide practical guidance for designing digital tools tailored to the Bruneian context. Such studies could also support national strategies aimed at modernising food systems and promoting sustainable consumption. Taken together, these directions offer a promising pathway to deepen understanding of food waste behaviours and develop culturally relevant, evidence-based solutions that support both environmental sustainability and social responsibility in Brunei and across Southeast Asia.

REFERENCES

Ajzen, I. (1985). From intentions to actions: A theory of planned behavior. In *Action Control: From Cognitive to Behaviour*. Springer. DOI: 10.1007/978-3-642-69746-3_2

Alwines, A. (2020, August 19). Brunei's first mass produced toilet tissue, made 100% from recycled paper. Biz Brunei. https://www.bizbrunei.com/2020/08/bruneis-first-mass-produced-toilet-tissue-made-100-from-recycled-paper-enevo/

Bank Islam Brunei Darussalam. (2023, January 24). BIBD eco-alam festival: Tackling food waste by going zero-waste, plastic-free and cashless. BIBD. https://bibd.com.bn/articles/news/bibd-eco-alam-festival-tackling-food-waste-by-going-zero-waste-plastic-free-and-cashless/

Borneo Bulletin. (2023, July 27). For a greener future. Borneo Bulletin. https://borneobulletin.com.bn/for-a-greener-future/

Chun T'ing, L., Moorthy, K., Gunasaygaran, N., Sek Li, C., Omapathi, D., Jia Yi, H., Anandan, K., & Sivakumar, K. (2021). Intention to reduce food waste: A study among Malaysians. *Journal of the Air & Waste Management Association*, *71*(7), 890–905. DOI: 10.1080/10962247.2021.1900001 PMID: 33689567

Dariah, A. R., Abdullah, R., Hidayat, A. R., & Matahir, F. (2022). Sustainable economic sectors in Indonesia and Brunei Darussalam. *Sustainability (Basel)*, *14*(5), 3044. DOI: 10.3390/su14053044

De Moraes, C. C., de Oliveira Costa, F. H., Pereira, C. R., Da Silva, A. L., & Delai, I. (2020). Retail food waste: Mapping causes and reduction practices. *Journal of Cleaner Production*, *256*, 120124. DOI: 10.1016/j.jclepro.2020.120124

Flowers, E. P., Freeman, P., & Gladwell, V. F. (2017). The development of three questionnaires to assess beliefs about green exercise. *International Journal of Environmental Research and Public Health*, *14*(10), 1172. DOI: 10.3390/ijerph14101172 PMID: 28976924

Food and Agricultural Organization of the United Nations. (2017). *The future of food and agriculture – Trends and challenges. Rome.*

Foti, V. T., Sturiale, L., & Timpanaro, G. (2018). An overview of food waste phenomenon: By problem to resource. *Calitatea*, *19*(S1), 232–240.

Graham-Rowe, E., Jessop, D. C., & Sparks, P. (2014). Identifying motivations and barriers to minimising household food waste. *Resources, Conservation and Recycling*, *84*, 15–23. DOI: 10.1016/j.resconrec.2013.12.005

Hassan, S. H., & Low, E. C. (2024). Spur of the moment: The unintended consequences of excessive food purchases and food waste during Ramadan. *British Food Journal*, *126*(7), 2732–2745. Advance online publication. DOI: 10.1108/BFJ-10-2023-0917

Klöckner, C. A. (2013). A comprehensive model of the psychology of environmental behaviour—A meta-analysis. *Global Environmental Change*, *23*(5), 1028–1038. DOI: 10.1016/j.gloenvcha.2013.05.014

Kon, J. (2022, February 25). Making use of food waste. Borneo Bulletin. https://borneobulletin.com.bn/making-use-of-food-waste/

La Barbera, F., & Ajzen, I. (2020). Control interactions in the theory of planned behavior: Rethinking the role of subjective norm. *Europe's Journal of Psychology*, *16*(3), 401–417. DOI: 10.5964/ejop.v16i3.2056 PMID: 33680190

Ma, Y., Al Mamun, A., Ali, M. H., Hoque, M. E., & Lili, Z. (2023). Modeling the intention and adoption of food waste prevention practices among Chinese households. *Humanities & Social Sciences Communications*, *10*(1), 1–12. DOI: 10.1057/s41599-023-02348-9

Mahmud, R. (2023). Fighting food waste during Ramadhan. Fighting Food Waste during Ramadhan. Borneo Bulletin. https://borneobulletin.com.bn/fighting-food-waste-during-ramadhan/

Memon, M. A., Ting, H., Cheah, J. H., Thurasamy, R., Chuah, F., & Cham, T. H. (2020). Sample size for survey research: Review and recommendations. *Journal of Applied Structural Equation Modeling*, *4*(2), i–xx. DOI: 10.47263/JASEM.4(2)01

Muhammad, R., Zahari, M. S. M., Ramly, A. S. M., & Ahmad, R. (2013). The roles and symbolism of foods in Malay wedding ceremony. *Procedia: Social and Behavioral Sciences*, *101*, 268–276. DOI: 10.1016/j.sbspro.2013.07.200

Nair, G. (2021). The food we waste: Antecedents of food wastage management behaviour. *International Journal of Social Economics*, *48*(6), 826–842. DOI: 10.1108/IJSE-01-2020-0029

Nunnally, J. C. (1978). An overview of psychological measurement. *Clinical diagnosis of mental disorders: A handbook*, 97-146.

Philippidis, G., Sartori, M., Ferrari, E., & M'Barek, R. (2019). Waste not, want not: A bio-economic impact assessment of household food waste reductions in the EU. *Resources, Conservation and Recycling*, *146*, 514–522. DOI: 10.1016/j.resconrec.2019.04.016 PMID: 31274960

Porpino, G., Wansink, B., & Parente, J. (2016). Wasted positive intentions: The role of affection and abundance on household food waste. *Journal of Food Products Marketing*, *22*(7), 733–751. DOI: 10.1080/10454446.2015.1121433

Qi, D., & Roe, B. E. (2016). Household food waste: Multivariate regression and principal components analyses of awareness and attitudes among US consumers. *PLoS One*, *11*(7), e0159250. DOI: 10.1371/journal.pone.0159250 PMID: 27441687

Qi, X., & Ploeger, A. (2019). Explaining consumers' intentions towards purchasing green food in Qingdao, China: The amendment and extension of the theory of planned behavior. *Appetite*, *133*, 414–422. DOI: 10.1016/j.appet.2018.12.004 PMID: 30537527

Quested, T. E., Marsh, E., Stunell, D., & Parry, A. D. (2013). Spaghetti soup: The complex world of food waste behaviours. *Resources, Conservation and Recycling*, *79*, 43–51. DOI: 10.1016/j.resconrec.2013.04.011

Santos, S. C., & Liguori, E. W. (2020). Entrepreneurial self-efficacy and intentions: Outcome expectations as mediator and subjective norms as moderator. *International Journal of Entrepreneurial Behaviour & Research*, *26*(3), 400–415. DOI: 10.1108/IJEBR-07-2019-0436

Schrank, J., Hanchai, A., Thongsalab, S., Sawaddee, N., Chanrattanagorn, K., & Ketkaew, C. (2023). Factors of food waste reduction underlying the extended theory of planned behavior: A study of consumer behavior towards the intention to reduce food waste. *Resources*, *12*(8), 93. DOI: 10.3390/resources12080093

Shams, S., Sahu, J. N., & Mubarak, N. M. (2024). A route for energy recovery from municipal solid waste and developing a framework for waste management in Brunei Darussalam. *Scientific Reports*, *14*(1), 19767. DOI: 10.1038/s41598-024-70845-1 PMID: 39187687

Stancu, V., Haugaard, P., & Lähteenmäki, L. (2016). Determinants of consumer food waste behaviour: Two routes to food waste. *Appetite*, *96*, 7–17. DOI: 10.1016/j.appet.2015.08.025 PMID: 26299713

Stefan, V., Van Herpen, E., Tudoran, A. A., & Lähteenmäki, L. (2013). Avoiding food waste by Romanian consumers: The importance of planning and shopping routines. *Food Quality and Preference*, *28*(1), 375–381. DOI: 10.1016/j.foodqual.2012.11.001

Sulaiman, N. S. (2023). Halal Industrial Food Waste Management: Lesson Learnt From Japan. *Dinar: Jurnal Ekonomi dan Keuangan Islam, 10*(1), 17-33.

Tommasetti, A., Singer, P., Troisi, O., & Maione, G. (2018). Extended theory of planned behavior (ETPB): Investigating customers' perception of restaurants' sustainability by testing a structural equation model. *Sustainability (Basel)*, *10*(7), 2580. DOI: 10.3390/su10072580

UN Climate Change. (2024). Food loss and waste account for 8-10% of annual global greenhouse gas emissions; cost USD 1 trillion annually. Unfccc.int. https://unfccc.int/news/food-loss-and-waste-account-for-8-10-of-annual-global-greenhouse-gas-emissions-cost-usd-1-trillion

UNEP. (2021, March 4). UNEP Food Waste Index Report 2021. UNEP – UN Environment Programme. https://www.unep.org/resources/report/unep-food-waste-index-report-2021

Visschers, V. H., Wickli, N., & Siegrist, M. (2016). Sorting out food waste behaviour: A survey on the motivators and barriers of self-reported amounts of food waste in households. *Journal of Environmental Psychology*, *45*, 66–78. DOI: 10.1016/j.jenvp.2015.11.007

Wajon, E., & Richter, J. (2019). *Students' Intention to Reduce Food Waste: An approach with an extended version of the Theory of Planned Behavior*. Uppsala University.

Wu, C. M. E., & Teng, C. C. (2022). Reducing food waste in buffet restaurants: A corporate management approach. *Foods*, *12*(1), 162. DOI: 10.3390/foods12010162 PMID: 36613378

Chapter 6

Halal Entrepreneurship a Catalyst for Sustainable and Ethical Global Business Ecosystem

Sevdie Alshiqi
http://orcid.org/0000-0002-1110-3078
University of Prishtina, Kosovo

Shujahat Ali
http://orcid.org/0000-0002-3760-9042
University of Kotli AJK, Pakistan

Wajahat Ali Ghulam
http://orcid.org/0000-0003-2835-580X
University of Science and Technology of China, China

ABSTRACT

Halal entrepreneurship is a business model rooted in Islamic principles, emphasizing ethical, socially responsible, and halal economic practices. Originating from the time of Prophet Muhammad (SAW), it is viewed as an honorable livelihood. The term "Halalpreneur" distinguishes entrepreneurs who offer shariah-compliant products and services from conventional counterparts. Despite its growth, the halal entrepreneurship ecosystem remains underexplored. This chapter conceptualizes halal entrepreneurship and investigates its key ecosystem components. Using a qualitative approach, it combines a structured literature review and global case studies to examine theoretical foundations, ecosystem actors, enabling factors, and sectoral implementation. The findings reveal challenges, research gaps, and offer

DOI: 10.4018/979-8-3373-2792-1.ch006

policy suggestions to foster halal entrepreneurship. This study contributes by integrating theory and practice, offering a framework to guide scholars, practitioners, and policymakers in developing global halal entrepreneurial ecosystems.

INTRODUCTION

Ethical entrepreneurial models have not been well researched or discussed over the years, particularly in the context of Islam (L. Raimi, Abdur-Rauf, & Raimi, 2023). However, with the passage of time and the operational, cultural, and religious nexus, researchers have attempted to develop improved methods. The Islamic economic system provides a better solution to these challenges. This approach is distinguished from traditional entrepreneurship by its integration with the Shariah Value system (M. Abdullah & M. Azam, 2020). The culture of conducting value-based ethical business activities is rooted in the teachings of Prophet Hazrat Muhammad (Yusmazida, Omar, Yusliza, Samad, & Abdul Mokmin, 2025). The Azhar (2025) business life of Prophet Hazrat Muhammad and his companions provide us a guidance and practical implementation of a value-based way to creating ventures. It formulates a pathway for upcoming entrepreneurs to conduct business in a halal manner. It brings into practice transparency, fairness, and societal welfare, while eliminating all odds from the traditional approach. This chapter aims to illustrate the relationship between the key variables of Halal Entrepreneurs and building ethical and sustainable businesses in alignment with the global Halal Market. The focus is to keep it more theoretical for ease of understanding the subject matter. This study examines how halal entrepreneurship contributes to ethical business practices. Any Muslim who produces and innovates halal products and services in Shari'ah compliance is called a "HALALPRENEUR' (M. A. Abdullah & M. Azam, 2020). Economic activity is vital to human growth and productivity. Every economic activity requires vital support from production factors. Businesses require a good ecosystem for their growth. Similarly, halal businesses require a supportive ecosystem. People intend to have an Islamic financial system, whether working with an online or physical business (Hermawati, Ali, Fettry, Hendarto, & Husin, 2021). The Islamic financial system is the main requirement for transactions and activities to create a Halal Entrepreneurial (HE) environment. The success of halal entrepreneurship is closely tied to the availability of a robust Islamic financial infrastructure and supportive entrepreneurial activities. The development of HE depends not only on individual initiatives but also on the creation of an ecosystem, including Islamic finance, regulatory compliance, and institutional facilitation, which collectively enable a Shari'ah Compliant growth system.

LITERATURE REVIEW

In recent era there has been increasing focus on the theory and practice of entrepreneurship. Similarly, the synthesis of Gümüsay (2015) and L. Raimi, Abdur-Rauf, and Olaide Raimi (2024) the concept of Halal Entrepreneurship has gained growing scholarly attention as an ethical faith-oriented approach to business and venture creation with deep roots of Islam and its principles as "Tawheed, Falah, Taqwas and it promotes not only profit but includes the spiritual accountability and justice. These sections examine and analyze the existing bodies of literature to find the theoretical underpinnings and themes with limitations and gaps in halal entrepreneurship.

Contrasting Paradigms Halal and Conventional Entrepreneurship

Entrepreneurial activities are known to be the finest practices for revitalizing economies and industries. The subject matter has superseded the traditional economic thought of will and power, as it has proven that will and suppress and overcome traditional economics thoughts and production factors (Shujat Ali, Lu, & Wang, 2013). The studies Shujahat Ali, Lu, Cheng, and Chaoge (2012) and Shujahat Ali, Ghulam, and Naseer (2025) have been synthesized and revealed it require more support from the ecosystem like academia, media, public policy and startup funding instead cannibalizing the one's own potential and resources with limited expansion chances. Historically, concepts and practices have been recorded to respond and react with respect to culture and religious value systems. Similarly, entrepreneurial thought and practice have been segmented into many thoughts and practices. As in this chapter we are contrasting the Halal entrepreneurship that is based on Sharia and Conventional that is based on traditional capitalistic mode. We focused more on HE in the beginning of this chapter but later also provided a contrasting viewpoint with conventional entrepreneurship.

Most studies have demonstrated that halal entrepreneurship (HE) is gaining scholarly and industry importance. Hereby the Changalima (2025) study resembled that there is exponential growth in the literature focusing on HE. The study of Kurniawati and Cakravastia (2023) also revealed the gaps and limited adoption and development of models and frameworks. The scholarly investigations have concentrated on the ongoing growth and acceptance of the global halal trade among both Muslim and other populations, thereby creating opportunities for enhanced buyer–seller relationships. Nevertheless, this growth also heightens the potential for conflict, which might stem from displeasure related to the non-observance of customer rights (Babatunde Bello, 2023). This study examines the factors driving the success of Malay halal food manufacturers in Northern Malaysia, focusing on religiosity, entrepreneurial mindset, halal supply chain, and structural challenges (I. J. Ismail, Marua, & Changalima, 2025). Numerous theories have been suggested to account for the rise of agro-entrepreneurship within the framework of Malaysian regulatory impact analysis. Consequently, this research offers an empirical evaluation of regulatory shape assessment grounded in consumer perceptions (Abdullah, Yusoff, Anumudu, & Zainol, 2020).

Brazil is among the leading exporters of halal poultry to Islamic markets. This includes the journey of an Islamic certifier from early initiatives to his present role in Brazil's halal poultry exports (Carneiro-Da-Cunha, Dos Santos, De Souza, Alssabak, & Macau, 2015). Emphasizing the mediating role of techno-entrepreneurship in halal supply chains. This study explores the role of innovation in fostering a sustainable halal environment in Ethiopia (Kant & Adula, 2025).

Several studies have documented the impact of digital transformation on global business operations. The Islamic digital economy is in its early stages, and the issues it encounters have yet to be resolved. However, there are considerable opportunities for Halal entrepreneurs to innovate within the digital economy (Salaheldeen, 2022). In recent times, there has been a surge in interest in this field, with Islamic Entrepreneurship (IE) research expanding, albeit with challenges. Upon examining the six IE models, several problematic inconsistencies emerged, which could be classified as sporadic IE objectives: differing core elements and varying levels of analysis (Tarip, 2024).

Numerous studies have examined the recent development of small-scale Muslim economies at the street level in Java, Indonesia, highlighting their significance as both cultural and material foundations for discussions on Islamic morality (Defend Islam Action 212). These small-scale economies illustrate the decentralization of halal consumerism in Indonesia, which emerged due to shifts in the political and Islamic spheres. These street-level economies provide political Islam with the unity of a Muslim cooperative framework, turning symbols linked to rallies into commodities (Savirani, Rafiq, & Baulch, 2024).

In recent decades, the harmful impact of human activities on the environment has become a major concern. Consequently, governments worldwide are working to minimize the ecological impact of human actions. To tackle these growing societal issues, companies are modifying their operations by integrating environmental considerations into their business practices (Salisu, Showole, & Moyosore, 2023).

Policymakers and Islamic financial institutions focus on sustainable development, examining sustainable finance practices. The Islamic sustainable finance (ISF) promotes sustainable development goals to manage risk in Islamic financial products (ISFP) (L. Raimi, Abdur-Rauf, & Ashafa, 2024). Numerous research groups have shown significant interest in this subject. The rise in Muslim tourism to countries where Islam is not the predominant religion underscores the importance of examining how well these destinations can accommodate the needs and lifestyles of Muslim visitors. This research focuses on Italy, where efforts have been made to gradually introduce halal products and provide accommodations and facilities that adhere to the fundamental principles of the Muslim faith (Halkias et al., 2014). To assess variables influencing halal entrepreneurial behavior among Thai entrepreneurs in Phuket, promoting the region as a halal destination (Soonsan, Jumani, Prasankarn, Thoomthong, & Tantha, 2025).

A framework connects the success of halal entrepreneurship with the ability to innovate and maintain sustainable innovation within the halal sector. By integrating and generating new approaches, the model transitions from existing literature to offer a theoretical contribution, linking halal entrepreneurial success with innovation capability and sustainability (Salaheldeen & Battour, 2024). The ongoing scholarly interest focuses on identifying the factors influencing global consumers in Malaysia to buy halal food products, with the acculturation effect playing a moderating role (Y. H. Lim, S. Lada, R. Ullah, & A. A. Abdul Adis, 2022). This research examines how Islamic entrepreneurship influences SME performance and proposes a framework to investigate Islamic entrepreneurship for competitive advantage. The study assesses Islamic entrepreneurship through a model incorporating two constructs: business and spirituality. These constructs serve as indicators of business performance (Raza et al., 2025).

Several theories have been proposed to explain this phenomenon. As the interest in incorporating Islamic principles into business practices grows, alongside a trend towards more ethical business behavior, the insufficient preparation of halal entrepreneurs has become a critical issue. The connections, both direct and indirect, between education in halal entrepreneurship and the intention to pursue halal entrepreneurship are viewed through the perspective of awareness (I. J. Ismail et al., 2025). In summary, halal entrepreneurship represents a dynamic intersection of religious values, ethical living, and consumption of day-to-day required products and services. It is critical for practitioners and researchers to understand and present better Halal Entrepreneurship practices, making it more valid to study its ecosystem.

Table 1.

Halal Entrepreneurship	Conventional Entrepreneurship
Rooted in Islamic worldview (Tawheed, Falah, Taqwa)	Rooted in capitalism, individualism, profit maximization
Business as Ibadah (act of worship)	Neutral toward religious/ethical values
Focus on social justice, fairness, ethical wealth creation	Driven by market opportunity, competition

Table 1 is based the synthesis of Halal and conventional entrepreneurship, and notable differences are mentioned The Halal entrepreneurship is deeply rooted in in the Islamic values systems based the foundation of Tawheed (Oneness of Allah), Falah (Success in life and the hereafter), and Taqwa (God-consciousness). As per Islamic values the Halal Entrepreneurship is not only generating profit but an act of worship, where the behavior of entrepreneurs aligns with religious and moral values. In comparison Dana (2010) conventional entrepreneurship is about making profit with a individualism emphasize grounding on capitalist ideology, by using market logics and gaining maximum profit. It is a value neutral and not aligned with religious dots the success is measured by competitive advantage and market share (Acs, Audretsch, Braunerhjelm, & Carlsson, 2012). The finding of Both paradigms pursues innovation and enterprise development, HE adds transformative dimension by embedding spiritual accountability, common good in the pursuit of entrepreneurial ventures. It's also affirmed by the view point of (Kuratko, 2005) and (Fauzi, Muhamad Tamyez, & Kumar, 2025).

COMPONENTS OF HALAL ENTREPRENEURIAL ECOSYSTEM

There is a notably high potential for positioning and marketing halal products and services (Syahril & Nugroho, 2024). The growth rate of Halal Entrepreneurship (HE) seeks attention from researchers is predicted to reach 7.4 trillion by 2032 (Zeybekci, 2025). The HE network includes entrepreneurs, Islamic Sharia-compliant financial institutions, regulatory bodies, certifications, and consumers, all of whom join hands to ensure that practices and products remain in accordance with Sharia guidelines (L. Raimi, Abdur-Rauf, & Raimi, 2024). As Muazu and Sjahrir (2023) suggest, socially responsible entrepreneurs with religious and value-based business practices are more productive and supportive of sustainability.

Education and Training

Education and training play pivotal roles in nurturing halal entrepreneurs. Without knowledge of the basis of Islamic Sharia law, the practice will not be up to mark, and it will be difficult to contrast traditional business practices with the HE. According to Zahro (2024), Sharia-compliant businesses are both a big challenge and an opportunity at the same time. Education and training can help overcome these challenges and facilitate their conversion into opportunities for women. Hence, "Halalpreneurs" need to link their lives with the belief and value system of Islam and provide products and services as per Islamic laws (Bella-Salsa, Kartika,

Jaiyeoba, and Jamaludin (2023) to achieve this effectively and efficiently, which is only possible through education and training.

Extensive studies have been carried out on the emergence of Muslim women as mompreneurs, particularly examining the views of younger Muslim women in Indonesia to understand what drives or deters them from pursuing this path. Emulating the example of Hazrat Khadijah (R.A) as a model for becoming successful Muslim mompreneurs was seen to harmonize professional and familial responsibilities while contributing socially among middle-class women. The growing focus on entrepreneurship education in universities and the swift expansion of digital marketplaces have further supported this movement (Minako Sakai, 2022). Recent studies have concentrated on determining the intention of consumers in Malaysia to buy halal food products, with the influence of acculturation acting as a moderating factor (Y. H. Lim, S. Lada, R. Ullah, & A.-A. Abdul Adis, 2022).

The creation of value through halal logistics (HLVC) is crucial for women-owned micro, small, and medium enterprises (MSMEs) in aviation. It explores how HLVC empowers female entrepreneurs and addresses halal-certified product demand in aviation through literature review and research methodology recommendations (Sabar, Anuar, & Hashom, 2025).

Studies show demand for integrating Islamic values into business and preparing halal entrepreneurs. This research examines links between halal entrepreneurship education and intention for halal entrepreneurial activities, focusing on entrepreneurial awareness (I. J. Ismail et al., 2025). Halal entrepreneurship is gaining importance globally due to rising Muslim consumer demand for halal products. Understanding this field's potential and challenges helps define its role in sustainable economy (Muazu & Sjahrir, 2023).

Research has identified resources for Islamic entrepreneurship stakeholders, including halal scholars, finance experts, and consultants specializing in halal business models. The exploration covered halal production ethics, Islamic entrepreneurship investment impact, Shariah principles for business innovation, and disruptive technologies like crowdfunding, Bitcoin, and blockchain. The study examined Islamic entrepreneurship's links to Sustainable Development Goals and Islamic-Fintech growth in Muslim-majority countries. Understanding of Islamic entrepreneurship remains limited among finance professionals and researchers (L. Raimi, Adekunle, & Shabbir, 2023). Education and training empower “Halalpreneurs” to acquire new skills and tools essential for mastering entrepreneurship. Both academia and industry recognize the pivotal role of education. This strategic investment in human capital not only ensures adherence to value-based practices but also facilitates compliance with Sharia Law.

ACCESS TO HALAL FUNDING

Research on sustainable development has intensified among policymakers and Islamic financial institutions. This study explores Islamic sustainable finance's role in achieving sustainable development goals and managing Islamic financial products' risks through qualitative analysis of literature (L. Raimi, I. A. Abdur-Rauf, et al., 2024). Interest in this subject has surged because Malaysia stands as a prominent leader in the global halal economy. At present, there is a noticeable increase in the involvement of young entrepreneurs in the halal food industry, spurred by Malaysian government initiatives that provide incentives, support, and a range of strategies or programs to foster the development of this sector. For young individuals, entrepreneurship offers a promising avenue to enhance their income, and the youth are a vital component of the country's economic progress (Nursalwani, Yumiemarnie, Sannasi, Amizi, & Ariff, 2021).

Islamic finance and halal entrepreneurship follow Shariah principles, with their integration boosting industry growth (Nurein, 2023). Islamic business practices can complement the Belt and Road Initiative (BRI), creating new halal markets as BRI expands into Muslim-populated nations (Zreik, 2023). Islamic entrepreneurship and business are studied in management due to the global business landscape, where culture and religion influence business relationships (Ramadani, Dana, Ratten, & Tahiri, 2015). While scholarly interest in ethical entrepreneurship remains strong, research gaps exist regarding Islamic financing models in the GCC's economic framework. This study examines the relationship between halal entrepreneurship and Islamic finance in developing a halal ecosystem (L. Raimi, Abdur-Rauf, & Olaide Raimi, 2025). Scholars are increasingly focusing on this subject. This research examines the inherent factors influencing entrepreneurs in Kelantan to embrace Al-Rahn. Al-rahn has evolved into a significant Islamic financial tool, offering swift and straightforward short-term funding, particularly amid the current economic uncertainties. Nevertheless, the acceptance of al-rahn among small entrepreneurs remains limited, as it is perceived to be utilized primarily in urgent situations for business needs (Yahaya & Mohamad, 2019).

This topic continues to receive increasing attention from scholars. Small entrepreneurs often face difficulties in obtaining capital due to a lack of trust in financial institutions, as they do not provide loan repayment guarantees. Therefore, Ar-Rahnu is an alternative for small entrepreneurs to obtain financing easily and quickly (Yahaya, 2020).

Research has shown that Malaysia is recognized as a global leader in the Halal economy. Currently, young entrepreneurs are becoming more involved in the halal food industry due to Malaysia's incentive programs, ongoing support, and various strategies. For young adults, entrepreneurship is a wise option to enhance their wealth compared to the current younger generation (Nursalwani & Ariff, 2023). Several This phenomenon has been reported in previous studies. Ensuring halal standards throughout the supply chain is vital for Indonesia given its Muslim population and growing global halal demand. Indonesia can become a Sharia economy hub by developing halal food and Islamic finance sectors, while strengthening the halal value chain ecosystem (Hasibuan & Lubis, 2024). Unlocking doors for halal funding is not only about capital. It is about having a value-driven ecosystem in which faith, finance, and innovation converge to empower a new era of ethical halal entrepreneurship.

CERTIFICATION

The Halal certification aids as a cornerstone to safeguard that entrepreneurial activities align with Islamic principles, offering credibility and market access to halal-compliance-based companies. Obtaining Hala certification involves the rigorous evaluation of products and services to guarantee compliance with Islamic dietary and ethical guidelines. The process typically includes documentation, on-site inspections, ingredient traceability checks, and approval by a recognized halal certification authority. The certification landscape varies from Muslim-majority to Muslim-minority and vice versa.

Ma'arif et al. (2024) explored the roles and obstacles faced by higher education in the halal certification value chain, the use of salt particles derived from seaweed processing by-products for creating low-sodium salt, and the factors influencing entrepreneurship in traditional culinary businesses. Earlier research has shown that halal certification serves as a marker of adherence to Islamic guidelines and should be implemented across various sectors, including the food industry. The Halal food market is experiencing rapid expansion and growth in numerous countries (Rafiki, 2019).

Halal has evolved from a religious concept into a global branding strategy for entrepreneurs seeking product expansion. This chapter delves into how halal contributes to the growth of entrepreneurship in response to the needs of Malaysian Muslim consumers. This chapter examines the Malaysian government's role in halal institutionalization, certification, and entrepreneurship development (Khalek, 2017). Research has shown that Halal certification is mainly associated with the product and its manufacturing process, yet the certification of price, place, and promotion—referred to as the 3Ps—has not been sufficiently addressed (Islam, Ab Talib, & Muhamad, 2025).

The topic continues to attract scholarly attention, as Muslim-owned restaurants in Malaysia face various obstacles in acquiring halal certification (Md Rodzi et al., 2023). The Indonesian Ulema Council's MUI fatwa on COVID-19 vaccination booster combines religious narratives and laboratory results, as religious texts provide effective ideological frameworks for influencing perception (Atabik & Muqtada, 2024). Achieving certification is vital for businesses to enhance consumer trust. Studies show MSMEs are communities' economic foundation, with their sustainability dependent on business legality compliance, particularly halal certification (Rahayu, Niravita, Anitasari, & Kamal, 2023).

Studies have explored the significance and necessity of effective halal certification through evaluation and accreditation. HCAA are crucial for enhancing customer satisfaction. To accomplish this, it is essential for all stakeholders to participate in policy development; therefore, this research aimed to uncover obstacles to the implementation of HCAA (Haleem, Khan, & Khan, 2020).

To address this issue, numerous researchers have suggested that halal certification for food products is crucial for safeguarding consumers and should be aligned with the practices of small-scale micro producers to ensure safety and shared advantages, in line with Islamic principles. Nevertheless, microbusinesses have diverse views on certification programs. With this in mind, the current study sought to classify the awareness of the benefits and legal aspects of digitalizing the certification process using a theoretical legal system approach (Sunardi, Bhari, & Abd Wakil, 2024).

In examining the link between halal certification and the performance of SMEs in a challenging setting like Palestine, it was found that certification positively influences the financial and operational outcomes of these businesses. Additionally, operational performance can serve as a mediator between certification and financial success (Amer, 2024).

They all need the availability of food and beverages that meet the provisions of Sharia, namely "halâlan thayyibâ" food and beverages. For this reason, the Government, concerning Halal Product Guarantee, requires every producer to produce food and beverages that are proven to have halal certificates (Suhartini et al., 2024).

Improvements are needed in halal certification recording applications due to missing data on micro and small enterprises' geographic references. Geographic Information System (GIS) technology could enhance halal industry data management by facilitating spatiotemporal and real-time data monitoring and analysis (Syaiful Huda et al., 2024). The global halal cosmetics market, valued at US$ 27.31 billion in 2021, was projected to reach US$ 54 billion by 2027. The industry lacked halal certification systems despite being dominated by multinational corporations (Adham, Muhamad, Masood, & Rahim, 2024).

The Malaysian Halal Certification by JAKIM verifies halal status for food enterprises. The non-conformance reports (NCR) among certified halal food SMEs in Malaysia and factors influencing NCR occurrence (Abdul Halim, Mutalib, Abd Ghani, & Hashim, 2024). Scholarly interest in this subject remains strong, and consumer demand for halal products is on the rise, accompanied by growing public alertness of the halal aspects of food consumption. The impact of halal credence, awareness, certification, and health consciousness on satisfaction with halal food is noteworthy (Fernando & Dewi, 2025).

The self-declaration process for small micro enterprises (MSEs) to obtain a halal logo presents both benefits and drawbacks. Advocates suggest that self-declaration simplifies the acquisition of a halal certificate for MSEs, shortens the submission timeline, and streamlines the certification process (Khalimy, Yusriyadi, Setyowati, Syahruddin, & Wadud, 2023). An examination of the Maldives' halal certification system addresses barriers to halal industry growth, particularly for fishery products. The certification process analyzed Maldivian laws and regulations to identify relevant issues (Muneeza & Mustapha, 2020). The literature explores how halal certification affects financial performance and supply chain resilience of micro, small, and medium enterprises in Indonesia's frozen food sector (Kristanto & Kurniawati, 2025).

Research focuses on product 'halalness' recognition by halal regulators based on Islamic law. Consumer and regulator intentions toward blockchain-based certification are valuable for storing halal certificates, enhancing trust since data remains unalterable (Karyani, Geraldina, Haque, & Zahir, 2024). Ultimately, halal certification merges religious principles with modern business practices, allowing halal entrepreneurs to maintain integrity, transparency, and competitiveness in both Muslim-majority and global markets. These certifications and standardizations meet the United Nations Sustainable Development Goals (SDGs) requirements for sustainable development and human progress.

DIGITAL PLATFORMS AND INNOVATIVE SOLUTIONS

In the era of AI and automation, “Halalpreneurs” also require stable and market-compatible work areas, either for physical presence or digital ones. These platforms are more than just tools; they function as catalysts for entrepreneurs with ethical considerations. To eliminate the barriers of time, space, and language, they offer more options and links.

Previous studies have indicated that rapid urbanization causes resource scarcity, infrastructure issues and social segregation. Nations are working to provide efficient solutions for deprived individuals and people living in deprivation (Kencono, Pradipta, & Agustiyara, 2024). This topic continues to receive increasing attention from scholars. Muslim women entrepreneurs, inspired by their role model Khadijah, have successfully managed both work and family responsibilities while making social contributions among middle-class women. The growing focus on entrepreneurship education in universities and the swift expansion of digital marketplaces have further supported this social movement (M. Sakai, 2022). Numerous studies have explored this trend, examining the connection between Halal Entrepreneurship (HE) and the Islamic Digital Economy (IDE) from a cultural standpoint (B. O. Raimi, 2023).

Several researchers have proposed methods to address this problem. Adapting the modern world to Sharia norms is one of the problems faced by Muslims today. Both Ulama and ordinary Muslims grasped part of the process of establishing the boundaries of what was permitted and forbidden. This study explores halal female Internet marketing using Instagram profiles as an example (Krapivin, 2021).

In addressing this issue, numerous scholars have suggested approaches that explore the potential for Islamic business practices to align with the Belt and Road Initiative (BRI). They assess how Islamic business principles might enhance the sustainability goals of the BRI, particularly as it extends into countries with predominantly Muslim populations. This expansion could lead to the development of new markets, halal industries, and Islamic Internet platforms (Zreik, 2023).

Strategies for digital entrepreneurship have been discussed extensively, gaining prominence with disruptive technologies that create startup opportunities. However, the process of achieving disruptive innovation in the digital economy remains unclear. Digital entrepreneurship is understudied, especially regarding halal entrepreneurs using disruptive technologies (Kartika, 2023).

In Pakistan, female entrepreneurs face significant barriers in male-dominated job markets, with women-only social media groups discussing obstacles and solutions. Unlike traditional networking channels, online platforms offer flexibility and constant connectivity (Din, 2023). In recent years, numerous theories have emerged in the literature about how business incubators (BIs) can foster entrepreneurship and innovation globally. Despite this, only a limited number of these incubators are dedicated to nurturing Sharia-compliant enterprises and halal products. The goal is to create a platform that supports Sharia business incubators in enhancing the competitiveness of halal products (Rozana, 2022).

While digital transformation impacts global business significantly, the Islamic digital economy remains nascent. The digital economy offers opportunities to halal entrepreneurs, yet challenges persist (Salaheldeen, 2022). In recent years, research in this area has become increasingly popular. Recently, faith-based entrepreneurship has emerged as a highly religious alternative to traditional approaches. This concept combines the influential elements of faith and entrepreneurship to create value, change lives, provide goods and services, and generate employment, thereby fostering prosperity for communities and nations. This section examines entrepreneurship rooted in Islamic faith, which is both well-developed and frequently misunderstood (B. O. Raimi, 2024).

Numerous studies have highlighted this as an essential asset for researchers in Islamic entrepreneurship: halal scholars, advocates of Islamic finance, and consultants specializing in halal business models in the rapidly evolving global economy. Their focus extends beyond Islamic and halal entrepreneurship to ethics of halal production and consumption, influencing Islamic investment. Shariah principles guide business model innovation and adoption of disruptive technologies like crowdfunding, bitcoin, cryptocurrency, and blockchain. The halalization of Sustainable Development Goals and Islamic Fintech in Muslim-majority countries is explored, including intersections with STEM. The understanding of Islamic and halal entrepreneurship continues to develop among finance professionals, consultants, researchers, and students (Shabbir, 2023). The fusion of Islamic values with digital innovation redefines entrepreneurship and creates a halal ecosystem. Ethical transactions, inclusive finance, and sustainable growth are the new standards. The embeddedness of Islamic principles in digital innovation and halal platforms ignites an entrepreneurial renaissance in the Muslim world. This will empower resilient and ethical ecosystems for future generations.

METHODOLOGY

This chapter adopts this approach to explore the paradigms, enablers, and impact of Halal Entrepreneurship as a catalyst for a sustainable and ethical global business ecosystem. To achieve these objectives, this chapter integrates two complementary methodological strategies: systematic literature access and illustrative global case studies. These case studies serve to contextualise and validate the conceptual insights derived from the literature and highlight cross-cultural practices within the HE ecosystem. The dual method approach enhances analytical rigor with practical links and increases relevance.

Global Case Studies of HE

Various approaches to entrepreneurship and public relations have been discussed in the literature. This case study is suitable for management, business, entrepreneurship, and communication courses. The case examines three issues in the Sarawak layered cake halal controversy: maintaining business resilience, fostering creativity, and implementing innovative strategies for growth (Latip, Md Yusoff, & Hanapi, 2015). Methods discussed in services marketing literature target postgraduate management students, helping them understand McKinsey's 7S framework and service sector's seven Ps through case studies (Nasreen, Siraj, & Beg, 2012)

Extensive research has been conducted on this topic. The rise in Muslim tourism to other countries underscores the insufficient examination of these destinations' ability and readiness to adequately meet the needs and lifestyles of Muslims. This study focuses on Italy, where there has been a gradual transition towards offering halal products and accommodations, as well as facilities that adhere to the fundamental principles of the Muslim faith (Halkias, Pizzurno, De Massis, & Fragoudakis, 2014).

This phenomenon has been reported in previous studies. This study examined the factors driving the success of Malay halal food manufacturers in Northern Malaysia, focusing on religiosity, entrepreneurial mindset, halal supply chain, and structural challenges. Despite validation and infrastructure development, participation in the halal sector remains low. This study used a qualitative case study to explore two halal-certified food manufacturers from Kedah and Perlis (R. M. Ismail, Hami, Jusop, & Muhardi, 2025).

Considerable research has been conducted on this subject. Investigating internal capabilities and geographical scope's moderating effect on the international presence of Malaysian halal food SMEs. While internationalization research has focused on developed nations, this study examines an emerging sector from the perspective of a developing nation. Studies overlook the geographical scope as a moderator, with inconclusive findings on elements impacting performance across foreign markets (N. A. Ismail & Kuivalainen, 2015).

Considerable research has been conducted on this subject to explore how geographical scope acts as a moderating factor in the connection concerning entrepreneurial orientation and the success of small and medium enterprises (SMEs) internationally. While most prior studies have identified a positive link between international entrepreneurial orientation and international performance, many have concentrated on developed nations and high-tech industries (N. A. Ismail, 2016)

This phenomenon has been observed in several studies. The connection between Islamic values and entrepreneurial endeavors aims to determine whether these values can enhance the visibility of Islamic entrepreneurship. A self-administered questionnaire was distributed to Saudi entrepreneurs in Riyadh to collect data and assess their perspectives on conventional and Islamic entrepreneurship. Results showed Saudi entrepreneurs view themselves as devout Muslims who consider entrepreneurship a religious and economic obligation, meant to generate halal income for financial responsibilities and contribute to the well-being (falah) of the Muslim community (ummah) in this life and hereafter (Kayed & Hassan, 2010)

This study extends prior research on illegal rural enterprises (IRE) by analyzing the concept from a macro-case perspective rather than a single-case approach within the farming industry. Understanding that IRE crimes require insider knowledge is crucial for studying these offences (Savirani et al., 2024). Numerous research teams have shown significant interest in this topic. To investigate how the level of geographical scope acts as a moderator in the connection between international entrepreneurial orientation and the international performance of SMEs within Malaysia's halal food sector, where a positive link between international entrepreneurial orientation and international performance has often been identified, many studies have concentrated on developed nations and the high-tech industry (N. A. Ismail, 2017).

The body of work on rural entrepreneurship is gradually growing, with numerous methods discussed. A recurring topic in this research is the generation of value and its extraction from the surroundings, which encompasses a broad spectrum of activities, including illegal activities (Smith, 2004).

Table 2.

Entity	Reference	Notes
Zaytuna College	Omar, I. A. (2012). *Zaytuna College and the American Muslim experience.* The Muslim World, 102(2), 347–356.	Islamic Education Entrepreneurship
Wardah Cosmetics	Suci, D. R., & Arifin, A. Z. (2019). *Halal cosmetic branding: The case of Wardah.* Journal of Islamic Marketing, 10(4), 1040–1056. https://doi.org/10.1108/JIMA-09-2018-0169	Branding Halal Cosmetics Successfully
Saffron Road	Durrani, A. (2015). *Bringing halal to Whole Foods.* Forbes. https://www.forbes.com/sites/abdullahidurrani/2015/03/20/saffron-road/	Entrepreneur Profile and Market Positioning
HalalBooking	Salaam Gateway. (2020). *Faith-based tourism rebounds post-COVID: HalalBooking insights.* https://salaamgateway.com	Digital Halal Tourism Case
Tanamera	Halal Development Corporation. (2019). *Malaysia Halal Industry Masterplan Case Studies.* https://www.hdcglobal.com	National Halal Reports
NoorVitamins	Islamic Services of America (ISA). (2021). *Case profile: NoorVitamins.* https://www.isahalal.com	Halal Supplements in U.S. Retail

From basic innovators to halal giants, the case studies affirm that when Islamic values are harmonized with entrepreneurial energy, the ecosystem not only flourishes but also inspires a movement rooted in purpose and prosperity (Table 2). The case studies echo that Halal Entrepreneurship is thriving, and more focus on its ecosystem proposes that market opportunities will grow for moral, clear, trustworthy, and in-depth sense of responsibility towards humanity.

DISCUSSION ON FINDINGS

Figure 1. The catalyst of success model for Halal entrepreneurship

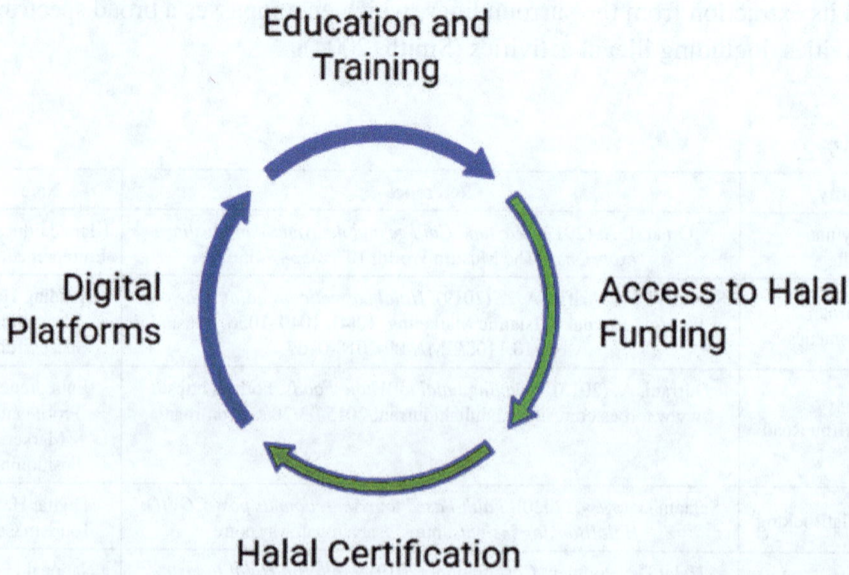

Based on our in-depth study of the literature and practices on Halal Entrepreneurship, Changalima (2025) proposed a model (Figure 01) that is not limited to the base of education and training, digital platforms, and halal access to funding. Based on the coupled and network analysis of Changalima (2025), it revealed from the key knowledge aspects and building nodes with existing knowledge and practice proposed this catalyst success model for halal entrepreneurship. However, entrepreneurial activities require incremental ecosystem support with variations in geopolitical and cultural boudoirs. It embodies a value-driven, holistic approach to business, grounded in the Islamic value system. Entrepreneurs must understand the market and respond to its products and services to ensure their survival.

CONCLUSION

Halal entrepreneurship is a compelling ethical alternative in the global entrepreneurial landscape, offering a robust integration of Islamic principles, social responsibility, and market relevance. Rooted in the traditions of Prophet Muhammad (SAW) and his companions, the concept extends beyond mere economic activity to encompass a comprehensive lifestyle of ethical production, consumption, and trade. The term "Halalpreneur" captures this evolving identity, which distinguishes itself from conventional entrepreneurship by embedding Shariah-compliant practices into every facet of business operations.

This chapter contributes to a more structured and theoretical understanding of Halal Entrepreneurship by examining its foundational principles, ecosystem requirements, and socioeconomic relevance. The Halal market, with an estimated value of USD 2.3 trillion and a steady growth rate, indicates not only the scale of opportunity but also the need for a more coherent and supportive ecosystem. A functioning Islamic financial system, ethical production chains, and awareness among consumers and producers are essential for fostering halal entrepreneurship.

However, despite the exponential growth of the market, academic- and policy-oriented attention to halal entrepreneurship ecosystems remains limited. This gap presents a vital area for further exploration, particularly in mapping best practices, evaluating institutional support, and integrating global case studies to guide practitioners and policymakers. Halal entrepreneurship addresses global concerns related to transparency, equity, and sustainability by drawing on Islamic ethical frameworks and advancing inclusive economic models. As this field continues to evolve, a multidisciplinary approach—blending religious insights, business innovation, and socioeconomic development— is essential for translating the promise of halal entrepreneurship into impactful global practice. The chapter covers the majority of HE and illustrates the proper use of digital technologies, education, and training, highlighting the need to incorporate it into national policy documents. However, it has limitations because it uses case study data and secondary sources. Future research is needed to identify the mode of training and education, whether formal or informal, vocational, in-person, or online. Future research must use primary data sources.

REFERENCES

Abdul Halim, N. R., Mutalib, S. A., Abd Ghani, M., & Hashim, H. (2024). Non-conformance report (NCR) on Malaysia halal certification: A case study among small-medium scale food enterprises (SMEs) in Malaysia. *Food Control, 160*(110298), 110298. DOI: 10.1016/j.foodcont.2024.110298

Abdullah, M., & Azam, M. (2020). Halal entrepreneurship from Maqasid-al-Sharia'h perspective: Inseparable concept for Halalpreneurs. *Journal of Food Science, 4*(S1), 34–42. DOI: 10.26656/fr.2017.4(S1).S07

Abdullah, M. A., & Azam, M. (2020). Halal entrepreneurship from Maqasid-al-Sharia'h perspective: Inseparable concept for Halalpreneurs. *Food Research, 4*(1), 34–42. DOI: 10.26656/fr.2017.4(S1).S07

Abdullah, Z., Yusoff, W. F. W., Anumudu, C. E., & Zainol, F. A. (2020). Regulatory impact analysis roles for agricultural products' qualities: Customers' perspectives for sustainability entrepreneurship. *Asian Journal of Agriculture and Rural Development, 10*(2), 563–577. DOI: 10.18488/journal.ajard.2020.102.563.577

Acs, Z. J., Audretsch, D. B., Braunerhjelm, P., & Carlsson, B. (2012). Growth and entrepreneurship. *Small Business Economics, 39*(2), 289–300. DOI: 10.1007/s11187-010-9307-2

Adham, K. A., Muhamad, N. S., Masood, A., & Rahim, A. A. (2024). Diagnosing a halal certification system for cosmetics: The viable system model approach. *Systemic Practice and Action Research, 37*(2), 139–159. DOI: 10.1007/s11213-023-09647-x

Ali, S., Ghulam, W. A., & Naseer, M. (2025). Public Policy and Startup Financing as Triggers of Entrepreneurial Intentions. *Annals of Human and Social Sciences, 6*(3), 719–727.

Ali, S., Lu, W., Cheng, C., & Chaoge, L. (2012). Media inattention for entrepreneurship in Pakistan. *European Journal of Business and Management, 4*(18), 96–100.

Ali, S., Lu, W., & Wang, W. (2013). Comparison of entrepreneurial intentions among college students in China and Pakistan. *International Journal of Pluralism and Economics Education, 4*(1), 51–60. DOI: 10.1504/IJPEE.2013.053588

Amer, M. (2024). Linkage among halal quality standard certification and SME's performance: Palestinian food halal certified SME's context. *Arab Gulf Journal of Scientific Research, 42*(4), 1414–1425. DOI: 10.1108/AGJSR-03-2023-0109

Atabik, A., & Muqtada, M. R. (2024). Maqashid Quran's critical view on Indonesian Ulema Council's fatwa on Halal certification of COVID-19 vaccine. *Hervormde Teologiese Studies*, *80*(1), a9050. Advance online publication. DOI: 10.4102/HTS.v80i1.9050

Azhar, M. M. T. (2025). PROPHET (SAW) AND SAHABA'S BUSINESS LIFE. *CONTEMPORARY JOURNAL OF SOCIAL SCIENCE REVIEW*, *03*(02), 89–105. DOI: 10.63878/cjssr.v3i2.753

Babatunde Bello, K. (2023). *Strengthen the Sustainability of Halal Entrepreneurs Through International Consumer Rights Laws*.

Bella-Salsa, A., Kartika, B., Jaiyeoba, H., & Jamaludin, M. (2023). Halal Lifestyle Entrepreneurship: Concept, Practice, Prospects and Challenges. *Journal of Halal Science and Technology*. DOI: 10.59202/jhst.v2i2.725

Carneiro-Da-Cunha, J. A., Dos Santos, M. G., De Souza, L. J., Alssabak, N. A. M., & Macau, F. R. (2015). The history of an Islamic entrepreneurship: Achieving exporting-network leadership through religious legitimacy. *International Journal of Business and Globalisation*, *15*(3), 272–293. DOI: 10.1504/IJBG.2015.071921

Changalima, I. A. (2025). Halal supply chain management: A bibliometric analysis of the 100 most-cited publications from Scopus-indexed journals. *Social Sciences & Humanities Open*, *11*, 101248. DOI: 10.1016/j.ssaho.2024.101248

Dana, L.-P. (2010). *Entrepreneurship and religion*. Edward Elgar Publishing. DOI: 10.4337/9781849806329

Din, F. M. (2023). Digital Connectivity as a Springboard to Professionalisation: Social Media Groups of Pakistani Women. *International Quarterly for Asian Studies*, *54*, 389-408. Retrieved from https://doi.org/DOI: 10.11588/iqas.2023.4.21080

Fauzi, M. A., Muhamad Tamyez, P. F., & Kumar, S. (2025). Social Entrepreneurship and Social Innovation in ASEAN: Past, Present, and Future Trends. *Journal of Social Entrepreneurship*, *16*(1), 146–168. DOI: 10.1080/19420676.2022.2143870

Fernando, F., & Dewi, C. K. (2025). Influence of halal credence, halal awareness, halal certification, and health consciousness to halal purchase intention through STHF (Satisfaction towards halal food) and religiosity as a moderation variable. *Edelweiss Applied Science and Technology*, *9*(4), 312–324. DOI: 10.55214/25768484.v9i4.5974

Gümüsay, A. A. (2015). Entrepreneurship from an Islamic perspective. *Journal of Business Ethics*, *130*(1), 199–208. DOI: 10.1007/s10551-014-2223-7

Haleem, A., Khan, M. I., & Khan, S. (2020). Halal certification, the inadequacy of its adoption, modelling and strategising the efforts. *Journal of Islamic Marketing*, *11*(2), 384–404. DOI: 10.1108/JIMA-05-2017-0062

Halkias, D., Pizzurno, E., De Massis, A., & Fragoudakis, M. (2014). Halal products and services in the italian tourism and hospitality industry: Brief case studies of entrepreneurship and innovation). *Journal of Developmental Entrepreneurship*, *19*(2), 1450012. DOI: 10.1142/S1084946714500125

Hasibuan, W. S., & Lubis, I. (2024). Halal value chain integration in food court establishment through Cash Waqf Linked Sukuk: Evidence from Indonesia. *Cogent Business & Management*, *11*(1), 2385075. DOI: 10.1080/23311975.2024.2385075

Hermawati, A., Ali, S., Fettry, S., Hendarto, T., & Husin, H. (2021). Freelancers Intentions Towards Adoption Of Islamic Banking. *Academy of Strategic Management Journal*, *20*(2), 1–16.

Islam, M. M., Ab Talib, M. S., & Muhamad, N. (2025). Halal certification of marketing mix focusing on cosmetics. *Journal of Islamic Marketing*, *16*(5), 1371–1409. DOI: 10.1108/JIMA-02-2024-0094

Ismail, I. J., Marua, N. M., & Changalima, I. A. (2025). Enhancing halal entrepreneurial intention: The impact of halal entrepreneurship education and halal entrepreneurial awareness. *Social Sciences & Humanities Open*, *11*, 101548. Advance online publication. DOI: 10.1016/j.ssaho.2025.101548

Ismail, N. A. (2016). The roles of international entrepreneur orientation and geographical scope level to determine international performance: A case in the malaysian halal food industry). *International Journal of Entrepreneurship*, *20*(1), 142–155.

Ismail, N. A. (2017). The roles of international entrepreneur orientation and geographical scope level to determine international performance: A case in the Malaysian Halal food industry). *International Journal of Entrepreneurship*, *21*(1), 46–59.

Ismail, N. A., & Kuivalainen, O. (2015). The effect of internal capabilities and external environment on small- and medium-sized enterprises' international performance and the role of the foreign market scope: The case of the Malaysian halal food industry; [Der Effekt von internen Kompetenzen und dem externen Umfeld auf den internationalen Unternehmenserfolg von KMU und die Moderator-Beziehung der geografische Reichweite: der Fall der Malaysischen Halal-Lebensmittelindustrie. *Journal of International Entrepreneurship*, *13*(4), 451–484. DOI: 10.1007/s10843-015-0160-x

Ismail, R. M., Hami, N., Jusop, M., & Muhardi, M. (2025). Halal food manufacturing: A case study on successful Bumiputera entrepreneurs in Malaysia). 2025. *International Journal of Innovative Research and Scientific Studies*, *8*(4), 1455–1456. DOI: 10.53894/ijirss.v8i4.8097

Kant, S., & Adula, M. (2025). *Innovation's effect on fostering a sustainable halal ecosystem by mediation of techno-preneurship in Ethiopia halal supply chain.*

Kartika, B. (2023). Halal Digital Entrepreneurship and Disruptive Technologies from the Lenses of Maqasid al-Shari'ah. In (pp. 179-197).

Karyani, E., Geraldina, I., Haque, M. G., & Zahir, A. (2024). Intention to adopt a blockchain-based halal certification: Indonesia consumers and regulatory perspective. *Journal of Islamic Marketing*, *15*(7), 1766–1782. DOI: 10.1108/JIMA-03-2023-0069

Kayed, R. N., & Hassan, M. K. (2010). Islamic entrepreneurship: A case study of Saudi Arabia). *Journal of Developmental Entrepreneurship*, *15*(4), 413–434. DOI: 10.1142/S1084946710001634

Kencono, D. S., Pradipta, R. N., & Agustiyara, A. (2024). *Managing Bandung City for a Smart Economy in Society: The Role of the Bandung City Government.* Paper presented at the E3S Web of Conferences. DOI: 10.1051/e3sconf/202459407002

Khalek, A. A. (2017). Entrepreneurship and the halal wave in Malaysia. In *Global Entrepreneurship and New Venture Creation in the Sharing Economy* (pp. 205-214).

Khalimy, A., Yusriyadi, Y., Setyowati, R., Syahruddin, S., & Wadud, A. M. A. (2023). The intersection of the progressive law theory and the self-declaration concept of MSEs halal certification. *J. Indonesian Leg. Stud.*, *8*(1), 159–198. DOI: 10.15294/jils.v8i1.66087

Krapivin, I. (2021). The "Faceless Brand": Muslim Women and Halal Internet Marketing. *Kunstkamera*, *2021*(4), 106–121. DOI: 10.31250/2618-8619-2021-4(14)-106-121

Kristanto, D., & Kurniawati, D. A. (2025). Financial performance of Indonesian frozen food MSMEs: halal supply chain resilience, certification and competitive advantage. *J. Islam. Mark.* DOI: 10.1108/JIMA-07-2024-0278

Kuratko, D. F. (2005). The emergence of entrepreneurship education: Development, trends, and challenges. *Entrepreneurship Theory and Practice*, *29*(5), 577–597. DOI: 10.1111/j.1540-6520.2005.00099.x

Kurniawati, D. A., & Cakravastia, A. (2023). A review of halal supply chain research: Sustainability and operations research perspective. *Cleaner Logistics and Supply Chain*, *6*, 100096. DOI: 10.1016/j.clscn.2023.100096

Latip, H. A., Md Yusoff, I. Y., & Hanapi, S. (2015). Strategizing business in times of crisis: The story of Sarawak layered cake). 2015. *Emerald Emerging Markets Case Studies.*, *5*(7), 7–13. DOI: 10.1108/EEMCS-09-2014-0233

Lim, Y. H., Lada, S., Ullah, R., & Abdul Adis, A.-A. (2022). Non-Muslim consumers' intention to purchase halal food products in Malaysia. *Journal of Islamic Marketing*, *13*(3), 586–607. Advance online publication. DOI: 10.1108/JIMA-06-2020-0172

Lim, Y. H., Lada, S., Ullah, R., & Abdul Adis, A. A. (2022). Non-Muslim consumers' intention to purchase halal food products in Malaysia. *Journal of Islamic Marketing*, *13*(3), 586–607. DOI: 10.1108/JIMA-06-2020-0172

Ma'arif, A., Amzeri, A., Caesarendra, W., Suwarno, I., Iqbal, J., Sharkawy, A.-N., . . . Herlambang, T. (2024). *2nd Biology Trunojoyo Madura International Conference, BTMIC 2024*. Paper presented at the BIO Web of Conferences.

Md Rodzi, Z. B., Mohd Amın, F. A., Jamiatun, N., Qaiyyum, A., Al-Sharqi, F., Zaharudin, Z. A., & Khair, M. H. M. (2023). Integrated Single-Valued Neutrosophic Normalized Weighted Bonferroni Mean (SVNNWBM)-DEMATEL for Analyzing the Key Barriers to Halal Certification Adoption in Malaysia. *International Journal of Neutrosophic Science*, *21*(3), 106–114. DOI: 10.54216/IJNS.210310

Muazu, M. H., & Sjahrir, E. R. (2023). Halal Entrepreneurship and Its Impact on Sustainable Economy: Opportunities and Challenges. In.

Muneeza, A., & Mustapha, Z. (2020). Halal certification process for fisheries products in Maldives. *Journal of Islamic Marketing*, *12*(2), 451–466. DOI: 10.1108/JIMA-02-2019-0035

Nasreen, R., Siraj, S., & Beg, S. (2012). Fast Trax - the Indian QSR chain). 2012. *Emerald Emerging Markets Case Studies.*, *2*(8), 14–27. DOI: 10.1108/20450621211289403

Nurein, S. A. (2023). Nexus of Halal Entrepreneurship and Islamic Finance for the Creation of a Strong Halal Ecosystem. In *Contemporary discourse of halal and Islamic entrepreneurship: Trends and future opportunities* (pp. 133-144). DOI: 10.1007/978-981-99-6427-7_9

Nursalwani, M., & Ariff, A. L. Z. (2023). *Influencing factors of young entrepreneur's participation in halal food products in Sarawak.* Paper presented at the AIP Conference Proceedings. DOI: 10.1063/5.0118113

Nursalwani, M., Yumiemarnie, J., Sannasi, A. P., Amizi, A. M., & Ariff, A. L. Z. (2021). *Factors influencing participation of youth entrepreneurs in halal food product labelling in Sabah.* Paper presented at the AIP Conference Proceedings. DOI: 10.1063/5.0053102

Rafiki, A. (2019). Perception and Challenges Due to Halal Certification: The Case of Zulaikha Shop). In *Management for Professionals, Part F561* (pp. 153-167).

Rahayu, S. A. P., Niravita, A., Anitasari, R. F., & Kamal, U. (2023). Halal Certification Imperatives for MSMEs: Navigating Sustainability, Consumer Confidence, and Policy Compliance (Case of Kenteng, Bandungan, Indonesia). *Indonesian Journal of Advocacy and Legal Services*, *5*(2), 143–160. DOI: 10.15294/ijals.v5i2.29861

Raimi, B. O. (2023). Halal Entrepreneurship in Islamic Digital Economy from a Cultural Perspective. In (pp. 115-132). DOI: 10.1007/978-981-99-6427-7_8

Raimi, B. O. (2024). Faith-Based Entrepreneurship as Ultra-Religious Entrepreneurship in Africa: Definition, Essence, Strands, Theoretical Underpinning, and Theological Foundation. In (pp. 251-279).

Raimi, L., Abdur-Rauf, I. A., & Ashafa, S. A. (2024). Does Islamic Sustainable Finance Support Sustainable Development Goals to Avert Financial Risk in the Management of Islamic Finance Products? A Critical Literature Review. *Journal of Risk and Financial Management, 17*(6), 236. Advance online publication. DOI: 10.3390/jrfm17060236

Raimi, L., Abdur-Rauf, I. A., & Olaide Raimi, B. (2024). Interdependence of halal entrepreneurship and Islamic finance for creating a strong halal ecosystem. *Journal of Islamic Marketing*.

Raimi, L., Abdur-Rauf, I. A., & Olaide Raimi, B. (2025). Interdependence of halal entrepreneurship and Islamic finance for creating a strong halal ecosystem. *Journal of Islamic Marketing*, *16*(3), 929–954. DOI: 10.1108/JIMA-05-2023-0162

Raimi, L., Abdur-Rauf, I. A., & Raimi, B. O. (2023). Halal Entrepreneurship in Islamic Digital Economy from a Cultural Perspective. In Raimi, L., Adekunle, S. M., & Shabbir, M. S. (Eds.), *Contemporary discourse of halal and Islamic entrepreneurship: Trends and future opportunities* (pp. 115–132). Springer Nature Singapore. DOI: 10.1007/978-981-99-6427-7_8

Raimi, L., Abdur-Rauf, I. A., & Raimi, B. O. (2024). Interdependence of halal entrepreneurship and Islamic finance for creating a strong halal ecosystem. *Journal of Islamic Marketing*. Advance online publication. DOI: 10.1108/JIMA-05-2023-0162

Raimi, L., Adekunle, S. M., & Shabbir, M. S. (2023). Contemporary Discourse of Halal and Islamic Entrepreneurship: Trends and Future Opportunities. In.

Ramadani, V., Dana, L. P., Ratten, V., & Tahiri, S. (2015). The context of Islamic entrepreneurship and business: Concept, principles and perspectives. *International Journal of Business and Globalisation*, *15*(3), 244–261. DOI: 10.1504/IJBG.2015.071906

Raza, M., Khalique, M., Khalid, R., Kasuma, J., Ali, W., & Selem, K. M. (2025). Achieving SMEs' excellence: Scale development of Islamic entrepreneurship from business and spiritual perspectives. *Journal of Islamic Accounting and Business Research*, *16*(1), 86–106. DOI: 10.1108/JIABR-02-2023-0060

Rozana, K. (2022). *SBI-Lab: Designing Sharia Business Incubator on Virtual Version for Developing Halal Product Competitiveness in Indonesia*. https://doi.org/ DOI: 10.1109/IBDAP55587.2022.9907598

Sabar, R., Anuar, N. K., & Hashom, H. (2025). *The Development of the Halal-Logistics Value Creation (HLVC)*. Concept for Women's Social-Entrepreneurship in the Aviation Business.

Sakai, M. (2022). To Be or Not to Be a Muslim Mompreneur in Indonesia. In (pp. 207-243). DOI: 10.1007/978-3-031-05954-4_6

Sakai, M. (2022). To Be or Not to Be a Muslim Mompreneur in Indonesia. In.

Salaheldeen, M. (2022). Opportunities for Halal Entrepreneurs in the Islamic Digital Economy: Future and Trends from a Cultural Entrepreneurship Perspective. In (pp. 95-107).

Salaheldeen, M., & Battour, M. (2024). Fostering innovation capability and sustainable innovation in halal industry: The role of halal entrepreneurs' success. *Journal of Islamic Marketing*, *15*(3), 777–799. DOI: 10.1108/JIMA-12-2022-0323

Salisu, M. A., Showole, R. K., & Moyosore, T. U. (2023). *Green Marketing as an Ethical Practice for Halal Entrepreneurs for a Sustainable Ecosystem.*

Savirani, A., Rafiq, D., & Baulch, E. (2024). Sharia Cooperatives and Mosque Ecosystems: The Devolution of Halal Entrepreneurship in Indonesia. *Asian Studies Review*, *48*(1), 86–101. DOI: 10.1080/10357823.2022.2134296

Shabbir, M. S. (2023). Contemporary Discourse of Halal and Islamic Entrepreneurship: Trends and Future Opportunities. In (pp. 1-263).

Smith, R. (2004). Rural rogues: A case story on the "smokies" trade). *International Journal of Entrepreneurial Behaviour & Research, 10*(4), 294–311. DOI: 10.1108/13552550410544231

Soonsan, N., Jumani, Z. A., Prasankarn, H., Thoomthong, T., & Tantha, B. (2025). Promoting Phuket as a halal destination: A perspective of SME's entrepreneur. *Journal of Islamic Marketing*, *16*(10), 2837–2857. Advance online publication. DOI: 10.1108/JIMA-06-2024-0239

Suhartini, E., Hertiani, E., Djuniarsono, R., Rumatiga, H., & PM, N. S. (2024). Analysis of Halal Certification for Micro and Small Business Actors from the Perspective of Maslahah Principles and Legal Certainty. *Al-'Adalah, 21*(2), 401-426.

Sunardi, D., Bhari, A., & Abd Wakil, M. N. B. (2024). Legal Awareness of Micro and Small Enterprise Operators Regarding Halal Certification: A Maslaha Perspective. *Ijtihad: Jurnal Wacana Hukum Islam dan Kemanusiaan, 24*(1), 23-45.

Syahril, S., & Nugroho, M. (2024). *Analysis of Halal Marketing Strategy for Food Products in Sharia-Based MSMEs*. Seriat Ekonomisi. DOI: 10.35335/qaz5a542

Syaiful Huda, I. A. i., Saadah, M., Sugiarto, A., Bin Ibrahim, M. H., Prasad, R. R., Putra, A. K., & Budianto, A. (2024). Revealing halal certification oversight gaps for MSEs through ArcGIS dashboard integration. *Indonesian Journal of Halal Research*, *6*(2), 58–69. DOI: 10.15575/ijhar.v6i2.33308

Tarip, I. (2024). Theorizing Islamic entrepreneurship from an Islamic governance perspective. *International Journal of Islamic and Middle Eastern Finance and Management*, *17*(2), 274–291. DOI: 10.1108/IMEFM-05-2023-0172

Yahaya, S. (2020). Intrinsic factors affecting the acceptance of muslim small entrepreneurs in kelantan towards ar-rahnu. *International Journal of Business and Society*, *21*(2), 507–520. DOI: 10.33736/ijbs.3268.2020

Yahaya, S., & Mohamad, S. S. (2019). Factors influence the acceptance of al-rahn among entrepreneurs. *Academy of Entrepreneurship Journal*, *25*(2), 1–6. DOI: 10.1080/85072152424

Yusmazida, M. Y., Omar, M. K., Yusliza, M. Y., Samad, S., & Abdul Mokmin, K. (2025). Developing an Islamic structural capital model: Perspectives from SMEs. *Journal of Islamic Marketing*, *16*(11), 3413–3455. Advance online publication. DOI: 10.1108/JIMA-06-2024-0238

Zahro, U. C. (2024). *Building A Sharia Entrepreneurial Ecosystem Through Halal Value Chain for MSMEs*. JURNAL PENGABDIAN TEKNOLOGI TEPAT GUNA., DOI: 10.47942/jpttg.v5i3.1793

Zeybekci, N. (2025, 2025, May 16). Halal is also a tool for protecting economic interests. Retrieved from https://russia-islworld.ru/en/novosti/nihat-zeybekci-halal-is-also-a-tool-for-protecting-economic-interests-2025-05-16-49192/

Zreik, M. (2023). Harnessing Islamic entrepreneurship for the belt and road initiative: Opportunities, challenges, and future directions. In (pp. 119-135).

Chapter 7
Halal Entrepreneurship Beyond Compliance

Jisu Kim
http://orcid.org/0009-0006-5528-4401
Institute for Mediterranean Studies, Busan University of Foreign Studies, South Korea

ABSTRACT

The paper utilizes qualitative research and relies much on previous literatures supported by examples of local cases. The research introduces 'theory and case' as a unit and drives conclusion from two cases and conclusively expects to foster subsequent research be expanded in sociological field. Ultimate goal of this research is to introduce conceptualized Halal entrepreneurship within non-Islamic context and examine the substance of Halal entrepreneurship in contemporary perspective. This chapter first provides concise overview of academic history regarding to entrepreneurship and elaborate the concept on Halal industry, discussing Halal entrepreneurship by re-evaluating the concept. Then, it introduces studies of locality which the author intends to integrate Halal studies with. The author claims that research of locality takes significant position in entrepreneurship, distinguishing the concept from entrepreneurial skills. Following part of the paper seeks cases that Halal entrepreneurship contributes in locality context especially in non-Islamic circumstances.

I. INTRODUCTION

Religion has served society in various way. From the concept of creator to shared social norm, religion has deeply involved to human life providing social regulation in multiple perspective. Amongst, Halal has guided Muslim community since early

DOI: 10.4018/979-8-3373-2792-1.ch007

Islamic period by suggesting boundary of allowance and therefore, distinguishing era of Islam from Jahiliyyah (جاهلية: age of ignorance). At the same time, however, Halal standard is observed to remain initial perspective of Islam, raising concern of discordancy in contemporary circumstances where complex standards coexist in multi-layered society. This paper considers entrepreneurship as contemporary elements that needs to be redefined according to social context and examine its reflection in Halal.

Halal entrepreneurship has been considered as business operation methodology based on Islamic ethics. It is compound of 'Halal' and 'Entrepreneurship', which forms discrete scholarly domain. Origin of entrepreneurship discourse still has much room for controversy, but it is widely known that it traces back to 18-19th century led by prominent scholars such as Richard Cantillon and Adam Smith. Consequence of the concept received limited attention from scholarly field until late 1980s when research with empirical experience became prevalent in academia, where role of SME (Small and Medium Enterprise) considered crucial to development of business and further, industry (Braunerhjelm, P., Andersson, M., & Eklund, J, 2022). On the other hand, however, perspective insisting collective approach to the topic has been suggested. Lindgren and Packendorff (2009) highlighted that current viewpoint toward entrepreneurship research is rooted on microeconomics with theoretical foundation and approach in individual disciplinary level, including microeconomics or psychology, which sometimes leave structural influence unnoticed. The authors proposed to discuss the entrepreneurship as outcome of interaction between individuals under the diverse social norms. For instance, H.E. Aldrich (2012) expands the standpoint to the entrepreneurship research after the 2000s by describing one of the characteristics of the topic as 'fragmentation', which indicates specialization of intellectual bases and formation of subfield. He suggests that contemporary status of entrepreneurship research concentrate on balancing between "specialization (as a result of fragmentation) and coherence" while pioneering its peculiar field in international academic community.

Meanwhile, research of Halal has yielded as rich amount of academic work as that of entrepreneurship. Halal entrepreneurship established its own definition that 'managing business with compliance of Shariah', which has positioned itself in dominance of the field. Despite that the subject has been accompanied the academic journey since the initiation of investigation of Islamic law, interpretation among the scholars regarding to the definition of term still show marginal disagreement. However, this chapter would like to employ the definition of Lukman Raimi (2024) that "Halal entrepreneurship indicates methods of business management according to the thought of Shari'ah in order to provide Halal products and services". While the author preserves conception that Halal entrepreneurship shows difference to general domain of entrepreneurship in terms of adherence to Islamic ethical rules, which leads to complementary consequences including economic growth or sustainable development of the business. Further, the author emphasized that combination of business practice in prevailing business under Islamic ethics based on Maqasid-ul-Shariah will strengthen customer loyalty.

Based on previous literatures of scholars from diverse disciplines, this chapter would like to introduce perspective toward Halal entrepreneurship through discovery of locality. The paper utilizes qualitative research and relies much on previous literatures supported by examples of local cases. The research considers combination of 'hypothesis & case' as a unit and drives conclusion from two cases and conclusively expects to foster subsequent research be expanded in sociological field.

Ultimate goal of this research is to introduce conceptualized Halal entrepreneurship within non-Islamic context and examine the substance of Halal entrepreneurship in 2025. In order for so, this chapter first provides concise overview of academic history regarding to entrepreneurship and elaborate the concept on Halal industry, discussing Halal entrepreneurship by re-evaluating the concept. Then, it introduces studies of locality which the author intends to integrate Halal studies with. The paper claims that research of locality takes significant position in entrepreneurship, distinguishing the concept from entrepreneurial skills. Following part of the paper seeks cases that Halal entrepreneurship contributes in locality context especially in non-Islamic circumstances. The paper introduces two cases of Halal entrepreneurship in non-Muslim majority countries; 1) Case of South Korea, and 2) Case of China. Each case is selected in accordance with two theoretical contexts within the process of integrating locality research to Halal entrepreneurship.

The paper endeavors to encourage readers not only to reconsider the existing framework to view the current definition of Halal entrepreneurship but to expand the concept and re-evaluate its functional significances.

II. ENTREPRENEURSHIP AND HALAL ENTREPRENEURSHIP

Cambridge dictionary defines word 'Entrepreneurship' as "Skills in starting new businesses, especially when this involves seeing new opportunities"[1]. The term 'Entrepreneurship' came from old French word 'entreprise', meaning "an undertaking", be known to mean "Adventrous disposition, readiness to undertake challenges, spirit of daring" since late 15th century CE[2]. That is, term 'Entrepreneurship' encompasses disposition to challenge and initiate innovation in business. Approach to entrepreneurship research has been practiced from diverse stance from individual cognition to social constructionism. Contemporary description of entrepreneurship is articulated in multiple publications including that of OECD's. The organization depicted entrepreneurship as strategic movement for resolution of high unemployment situation and aimed to build numerous job position through research conduct (OECD 1998). Lindgren and Packendorff (2009) analyzed entrepreneurship in societal level, suggesting that research about entrepreneurship should be examined within comprehensive framework of social constructionism. The authors denoted social phenomena that entrepreneurship today is being "less entrepreneurial" from confined analytical scope and proposed interdisciplinary approach as the subject should be regarded as compound of social interaction from various fields such as studies of gender, cultural, social movement, data analysis, etc.

Entrepreneurship research has been cultivated through several stages. Expansive scope that entrepreneurship contains culminated diverse approach and discourse to the topic. Empirical examination of the subject has undergone historical development, consequently facilitating cluster of leading intellectuals. Several taxonomies were utilized when discussing history of entrepreneurship research. For instance, Aldrich (2012) states entrepreneurship research has been conducted by individual scholars until the 1980s after which the field grew and expanded to be institutionalized. Regarding to the fact that contemporary studies of entrepreneurship launched with institutionalization, Aldrich analyzed six influencing factors, which are; 1) Social networking mechanism that leads to interconnection among scholars and their intellectual properties, 2) Increase of academic journal in the field, followed by formation of academic network, 3) Events that provide training and mentoring opportunities such as academic conference, 4) Standardized and expanded scale of funding source given to individual or group of researchers, 5) Amplification of scholarship to individual, and 6) Globalization as the field extends its transnational reach resulting increased opportunities of events in international scale. This paper would like to identify that the factors above culminate to singular conclusion, which is 'strengthening interconnection and encouraging collaboration of scholars in diverse discipline'. Entrepreneurship has indeed been recognized as an integrated field in an academic perspective, as publications from 2005 to 2010 indicate (Teixeria, 2011), but at the same time, "fragmented" (Aldrich, 2012) and formed individual subfield of several disciplines including economics, sociology, psychology, etc. Plurality in scholarly domain did pave the way for generating research cluster in multidiscipline circumstances. However, the characteristic is also identified as an obstacle lacking common theoretical paradigm or research framework (Carlsson et al., 2013).

In Arabic lexicon, Halal(حلال) is defined as 'permissible'. Being rooted on Islamic ethics, the concept has served Muslim society and believers not only as religious doctrine but also as social regulation, providing framework for moral conduct per diem. Halal industry today has been widened to be involved into general practice of Muslim consumption from food to pharmaceutical products, cosmetics, and even intangible services such as finance. Global Halal food market marked 2.71 trillion USD in 2024[3], and size of overall market is expected to increase considering the wide range that industry engage. Given its significant market size and extensive growth potential, the industry has emerged as compelling domain for entrepreneurial studies. Emergence of Halal Entrepreneurship is considered recent enough that consensus of definition has yet to be established. Abdullah M.A & Azam M.S.E (2020) describe Halal Entrepreneurship as "entrepreneurship in Halal industry that is conducted with compliance with Shariah". Authors highlighted that pivotal perspective in Halal Entrepreneurship is Shariah compliant business-running method over commercial activity. L.Raimi (2024) perceived Halal Entrepreneurship as "directing a firm based on Islamic finance aiming for complementing both dimensions". The author specifically discussed relation between Halal Entrepreneurship and Islamic finance, underscoring the role of Islamic finance in operating business and thus, strengthening Halal Entrepreneurship and further, Halal ecosystem. Similar discourse has been explored by name of 'Islamic Entrepreneurship', which prioritizes value of Shariah during practice of economic activity such as considering welfare of community or prohibition of Haram products (or services). To conclude, Halal Entrepreneurship (or Islamic Entrepreneurship) that has been widely discussed can be defined as 'Economic activities in every Halal area that are abiding Islamic law (Shariah), thus making entire process religiously wholesome (Tayyib)'.

However, despite the literal definition, current understanding of entrepreneurship would rather be closer to entrepreneurial awareness, thereby omitting essential element of recognition and embracement of 'pioneering' (Pittaway, 2005: Lindgreen & Packendorff, 2009). Equating notion of entrepreneurship to business opportunity has been frequently observed during the research from multiple scholarly works. For example, Venkataraman (2019) defined entrepreneurship as

> *"a scholarly field seeks to understand how opportunities to bring into existence 'future' goods and services are discovered, created, and exploited, by whom, and with what consequences..."*

which implies that the interpretation of entrepreneurship is connected to economic consequence rather than eliciting prospect. Although scholars including the author from previous quote do recognize the fact that entrepreneurship cannot be exclusively delineated by solitary viewpoint from specific discipline, conceptualization of entrepreneurship remain prejudiced to detecting venture potential. Primary field of interest to entrepreneurship researchers would be 'operation establishment', which raises question of "Where do opportunities come from" (Alvarez et al. 2010). That is, while shared discourse of entrepreneurship urges to examine the domain in multidisciplinary scale, it is still prejudiced that much of current research employs standpoint pondering the topic as extension of business (opportunity) strategy studies.

Furthermore, entrepreneurship research has struggled for continuous investigation due to the absence of unilateral theoretical structure. Entrepreneurship is cohesive scholarly domain spreading over wide range of influencing variables. On one hand,

Stevenson (2004) suggested six components of entrepreneurship as; 1) strategic orientation, 2) commitment to opportunity, 3) commitment process, 4) control of resources, 5) management structure, and 6) compensation and reward system while on the other hand, OECD report analyzed key factors of entrepreneurship are; 1) Framework conditions, 2) Government program, and 3) Supportive cultural attitudes.

Effort to approach to the inquiry from various perspective has been reflected to prevalent research and expanded to research of Halal entrepreneurship, which focuses on generating business conjunction by pursuing firm operation along with Islamic law while the derivation of the entrepreneurship underscores significance of recognition and incorporation of difference, to which one firm may determine their direction notwithstanding adversity. Thus, this paper would like to remind readers that it is time for us to remind the pristine essence of entrepreneurship and encourage them to take next step by raising a question: What makes Halal entrepreneurship HALAL?

III. LOCALITY

Locality, typically perceived as an inherent nature of particular geographic site, is a ramification of evolving conceptualization throughout academic interpretation. Theoretical re-evaluation and interpretation of the concept initiated from 'place', processing development to 'space', culminated in constitution of academic domain of 'local(ity)'. Oxford English Dictionary defines 'place' as "a particular position, point, or area in space", 'space' as "a continuous area or expanse which is free, available, or unoccupied", and 'local' as "a relating to or occurring in a particular area, city, or town". From the leading definitions of the terms, this paper would like to present extract lexical difference that 'place' indicates geographical and physical point, 'space' broadens the term by expanding dimension from scientific perspective where several notions and experiences may coexist and interact, therefore arrives at status of relativization, being 'local'. Origin of the logical discussion regarding to place and space traces back to ancient Greece, from discussion of Aristole about concept of the place. His interest to place stemmed from intellectual desire that wants to discover structure of the world by investigating capacity of human being for preserving ego in physical body. Aristole, according to his book, *Physics IV*, viewed space as an "interval and coextensive" element that is endowed with heterogeneous property to others. Ancient discourse about space is in closer proximity to ontological field where they considered space where human, embedded with achievement, exists in the universe (Korkmaz 2015: Ağarı M. 2024). However, it is widely acknowledged that while place entails irreplaceable feature of geographical site, space, as larger scale, has dimensional characteristic that accommodates matters (Agnew, 2011), taking more cohesive attitude.

Understanding locality invites wide range of disciplinaries to join. Although Oxford English dictionary defines locality as 'the position or site of something' and 'an area or neighborhood', "placing" the concept on cognitive extension of space, this paper would like to argue that locality lies within sociological discourse as relative concept that is highly influenced by context surround it. Locality is differentiated by several factors from regionality in terms of its postcolonial disposition. Semantic difference between the terms lies in analytic lens of dichotomy between 'center' and 'the other'. Region, as explained in the dictionary, depicts "an area, especially part of a country or the world having definable characteristics but not always fixed boundaries" while local refers to "relating or restricted to a particular area or one's neighborhood". That is, it would be able to conclude that region exists as independent variable while local modifies its status (of being local) depending on center at the moment, highlighting international dynamic attribute of the discourse, deconstructing conceptual boundary of immovable and absolute center.

Locality and local features are two constructs that are misused recurrently. Since locality implies inherent context, usage of the term is often considered not only as one of the methods of self-expression of users, but also as asserting voice for cultivating an atmosphere where one can find and develop their self-identity within the context (Kim, 2010). Elaborating such viewpoint, this paper would like to coincide scholarly opinions that have emphasized importance of non-parochial approach in locality research, proposing the conceptualization of locality as cohesive feature of the local, being understood within relational nexus. The nexus, namely 'Context' in locality research, serves as external agents that involves in establishment of identity of the environment (including local people). Context emerged in form of ethnographical discovery recognized as local feature, which limiting their sight rather than expanding the discovery in dimension of interaction (Appadurai, 2003). Interdepending relation between locality and entrepreneurship have been validated through academic output. For instance, Schutjens and Völker (2020) stated that social capital and local social capital (which function as context) served as influencing factors to define features of individual or firm[4]. In conclusion, locality research requires deliberation of context in addition to observation of phenomenon for profound and comprehensive result.

IV. INTRODUCING CASES

Connotating certain phenomenon is indeed interesting but adventurous work particularly in locality research since it requires extensive consideration in various span. This paper would like to employ articulation from Appadurai (2003) 's theory about relation between context and neighborhood in order to describe following cases. According to the author, neighborhood operates as space where locality is contained and concurrently, elicit context from interaction of localities it embraces. The premise is followed by two relation theories; 1) Neighborhood as context, and 2) Context of neighborhood, which this paper would like to present with corresponding case.

1. Neighborhood as Context: Case of South Korea (Halal Restaurant 'Asalam', Jeju Island)

When neighborhood is considered equivalent to context, it provides an environment to actors in which their practices are influenced, taking inductive approach. Jeju Island in South Korea faced influx of Yemenese nationals in 2018 who fled from civil war of their country. It is known that the asylum seekers first flew to Malaysia where they could enter the country without visa and stay for 90days, being told to leave the country, and found the Jeju Island offers visa-free entrance for foreign tourists from certain countries as strategy to foster the tourism of the Island. Around 500 people who had entered the Island soon applied for refugee status and lacking education of central and local government of Korea arouse social anxiety and hostility of residents toward the asylum seekers, calling them "fake refugees"[5]. Aggressive response from residents were intensified when Korean government made exceptional allowance of economic activities for Yemenese asylum seekers prior to the six-month-mark after application of refugee status, which Korean law regulates. As South Korea has been considered tacit exception of refugee acceptance for their consistent acceptance of every North Korean defector, the situation came up more foreign and sudden. Yemenese asylum seekers have faced legal restriction including range of appliable jobs or movement to mainland Korea while applying refugee in Jeju Island. Misunderstanding toward Muslim, derived from ignorance, provoked ambivalence emotions which are fierce enmity of residents with Islamophobic opinions and 'foreign but trying to understand'[6] at the same time. That is, hostile atmosphere and unstable social status correspond to context in this case, establishing circumstances of neighborhood (Jeju Island).

Within the situation, Halal restaurant 'Asalam' has served the neighborhood not only as the first authentic Yemenese restaurant but also as center of minority communities where they welcome all types of 'the local'. (Picture 1)

The restaurant, being operated by Yemenese husband(chef) and Korean wife, provides Yemenese cuisine used Halal meat, prohibits usage and consumption of alcohol and pork, and is Halal certified by Korean private certification body. They have supported local foreigners through hiring at the restaurant, or promoting awareness and fostering participation through various media including interviews, tv broadcasts, and literature publication. Halal restaurant 'Asalam' determines to state its identity not only as religious but as social minorities in non-Islamic nor Muslim majority country, expanding their scope of solidarity beyond religious boundary. (Picture 2&3)

2. Context of Neighborhood: Case of China (Conceptualization of 'Qingzhen')

Chinese vast territory has witnessed rise and fall of diverse cultures in the country. History of Muslim community in Chinese history traces back to 7th~10th century CE along to the Southeast coast of China estimated from excavated artefacts. China later encountered another large influx of Muslim immigrants from Arab, Persia, and Central Asia, who were mainly merchants crossing the land (Gladney, 2003). Consisting half of today's Chinese Muslim population, Hui tribe shows various discussion regarding to their emergence in Islamic history in China. One of the materials in early 18th century CE says

> *"... an emperor from Tang dynasty saw men in Turban (which was unfamiliar garment at the time) chasing evil ghost in his dream. An oneirocritic was called in, and said that the men are 'Huihui' and the dream indicates birth of sage in the west. With suggestion of a general, the emperor sent ambassador to the west and required Muslim king to dispatch a sage to exorcise the evil spirit in the palace ... "(Leslie, 1986; Lipman 1997)*

Although academic discussions over whether usage of the word 'Hui' meaning for Muslim should be accepted as common nouns or as signification of the source are still in progress, mentioning the term 'Hui' presents that identity of Hui people as Muslim has been historically acknowledged.

Literal definition of Qingzhen(淸眞) is '(spiritual) purity/cleanness', consisted of two components; 1) Qing(淸) refers 'clean, pure', and 2) Zhen(眞) indicates 'trueness, authenticity'. The concept is known to be rooted on Taoistic philosophy, guiding one to live within the value. Qingzhen can be found in multiple literatures from ancient era as commendation of life filled with genuine purity. Since its long history, assemblage of Qingzhen and Islam has been slow process as Taoism already had been served the country as one of the central philosophies when Islam began to be distributed in the country. Supported by scholarly work of Muslim intellectuals such as 'Ma Zhu' using the term in order to describe noble taught of Islam, concept of Qingzhen first considered equivalent to Islamic concept of 'Tayyib', meaning purity as well (Wang 2024). The prevalent phenomenon of paraphrasing Islamic concept to Chinese language is reflected in case such as the fact that masjid was called 'Qingzhensi(淸眞社: Temple of purity and genuine)' under the allowance of emperor during the Yuan dynasty (Ma, 2018), which has been regarded as localization of Islam (Ding, 2017: Ma, 2018). Majority of Chinese Muslim including Hui Muslims did not allow access of strangers and foreign culture to their community until 17th century CE maintaining their community-based lifestyle including not dining with non-Muslims or forbidding marriage to outsider of the community (Mai, 2024). Hui Muslims began to migrate to cities as they realized their isolation may starve their people, but majority of them ended up opening Qingzhen restaurant due to the low level of education they had received[7]. Increase of Qingzhen restaurant engaged another influx of Hui Muslims, planting Hui culture in territory of Han's (Ding,2017: Ma,2018). Qingzhen still remained on level of ideal lifestyle of Muslims until the establishment of People's Republic of China in 1950s when the government recognized and labeled Qingzhen as 'custom of minorities (Hui people)' and "food of Hui and Uygles people" (Sai, 2014). The definition is valid until today as one can observe from the fact that as BRI (Belt and Road Initiative) project amplified trade with Islamic countries since their inauguration, Qingzhen products were often labeled randomly as 'Halal' from prejudice of identifying Qingzhen as Halal.

Struggle of Hui Muslims persisted during the time of Cultural Revolution (1966-1971) when the national government adopted communism as national ideology and oppressed any belief that may stand against communist theory. Persecution included destroying religious buildings or forcing Hui Muslims to raise pig. However, the aged generation took the time to ruminate foundational signification of Qingzhen, concluding that it is spiritual cleanness that one should live for, liberating their guilty conscience by raising pig despite the critique that they are "secularized" (Ma, 2018). And conversely, revival movement of Hui Muslims were active after 1978 with support of liberating religious practice, from the reform movement of Deong Xiaoping (Gladney, 2003).

In conclusion, Qingzhen, originated from Taoistic ideology, was accepted to Muslims (usually Hui people) and was interpreted within Islamic context. Despite its initial interpretation as 'Unadulterated', practice of Hui Muslims confronted dynamic transition of Chinese society and was labeled as Islamic dietary regulation, neglecting its philosophical origin and process of interpretation through individual and communal practice. Thus, this paper would like to underscore that current scenery of Qingzhen in China was founded upon aggregation of discrete implement, thereby facilitating societal atmosphere, which builds deductive viewpoint toward the relation between neighborhood(human action) and context. (Picture 4&5)

IV. CONCLUSION

In 1998, OECD announced three key factors in fostering entrepreneurship; 1) Framework condition, 2) Government program, and 3) Supportive cultural attitudes.

The publication acknowledges difficulties to evaluate success of entrpereneurship for lacking universal indicator, but cleared that no indicator (or field) would be able to encompass entire status of entrepreneurship that collaborative approach among areas are essential in order to complete the blueprint of the concept. The statement linked corresponding factors to possibility of cooperation and further, valued 'others' as complimenting partners for concluding the work, which implies the significance of comprehensive understanding when discussing entrepreneurship. Entrepreneurship, from diverse perception, stands for pioneering disposition in discovering new business opportunities. While discussion from varied perspective in order to establish agreed definition of entrepreneurship is still persistent, consideration of the notion within multidisciplinary framework has been widely accepted approach. Being elaborated from the traditional idea of entrepreneurship, Halal Entrepreneurship (as a compound word) has focused on creating economic potential. Description of Halal Entrepreneurship is subject by researchers, but shows common interpretation that; 1) it should serve Halal products and 2) the whole process should be pursued within Islamic value. However, the exclusive prioritization of religious doctrine has overlooked foundational inherit essence of entrepreneurship; pioneering. Thus, this chapter sought to observe variation of Halal Entrepreneurship by contextual factors, ultimately highlighting need of locality studies in order to fertilize innovative approach in Halal Entrepreneurship study.

The paper introduced two cases based on foundational theoretical premises that regulates relation between context and neighborhood. The first theory 'Neighborhood as Context' was able to be perceived in case of South Korea (Halal Restaurant 'Asalam' in Jeju). The theory regulates that specific environmental condition are determinants of human action, which is illustrated in case of Halal restaurant operated by Yemenese asylum seeker in Jeju, South Korea, where they broadened scope their support to social minorities ('locals'[8]) in the hostile neighborhood and thereby serving as space of solidarity. The place maintained their religious identity as 'Halal restaurant' by prohibiting usage and consumption of pork and alcohol in the restaurant or providing prayer room to every Muslims (non customers also) but at the same time, expressed their communal support toward locals by promotings anti discrimination campaign or refugee issues abroad.

The second theory 'Context of Neighborhood' hypothesizes that the collective actions of individuals contribute to the constitution of the context, as case of Qingzhen in China demonstrates. Concept of Qingzhen is known to be derived from Taoistic philosophy, being employed by Hui Muslims as ideal lifestyle preserving purity in life. However, following foundation of PRC, Qingzhen was defined as 'custom of minorities' or 'food of Hui and Uygles people' as strategic neglect for reinforcement of Chinese citizenship over religious or tribal identity. Equation of Qingzhen with Halal was officialized since the launch of BRI project, driven by the clear purpose to foster commercial exchange between China and Islamic(or Muslim majority) countries. In summary, Qingzhen was introduced to Chinese Muslim community (Hui tribe) as Taoistic philosophy. The concept was adopted and utilized as expression of ultimate pursue by Hui Muslims, but persisted at the level of ideal way of life untill the establishment of PRC when the concept has been introduced as Islamic practice without its historical context. Therefore, the finding suggests that current landscape of Qingzhen in China is production of interpretation (by Hui Muslims) and reproduction (by Chinese government).

Halal Entrepreneurship has been recognized through the viewpoint closer to Halal entrepreneurial strategies, where one finds niche in marketing Halal products, often through wholesome process. This paper expects subsequent research initiatives as well as academic discussion should prioritize entrepreneurship rather than exclusive concentration on Halalness. Contemporary understanding of Halal encompasses broad spectrum of multiplicity and diversity of circumstances including non-Islamic environments, which application of locality research can suggest invaluable insights for developing entrepreneurship based on specificity. Accordingly, this paper asserts the significance of sociological approach to Halal entrepreneurship through profound understanding of locality, which, consequently, will widen our sights beyond the religious compliance.

REFERENCES

Abdullah, M. A., & Azam, M. S. E. (2020). In Abdullah, M. A., & Azam, M. S. E. (Eds.), *Halal entrepreneurship: Concept and business opportunities* (pp. 1–18). Entrepreneurship.

Ağarı, M. (2024). Concept of space: What is it – How is it perceived? *Karabük Türkoloji Dergisi*, *5*(9), 1–30.

Agnew, J. (2011). Space and place. In Agnew, J., & Livingstone, D. (Eds.), *Handbook of Geographical Knowledge* (pp. 1–34). Sage.

Aldrich, H. E. (2012). The emergence of entrepreneurship as an academic field: A personal essay on institutional entrepreneurship. *Research Policy*, *41*(7), 1240–1248. DOI: 10.1016/j.respol.2012.03.013

Alvarez, S. A., Barney, J. B., & Young, S. L. (2010). Debates in Entrepreneurship: Opportunity Formation and Implications for the Field of Entrepreneurship. In Z. J. Acs & D. B. Audretsch (Eds.), Handbook of Entrepreneurship Research (pp. 23–45). Springer Science+Business Media, LLC.

Appadurai, A. (2003). The production of locality. In *Counterworks* (pp. 208–229). Routledge. DOI: 10.4324/9780203450994-10

Braunerhjelm, P., Andersson, M., & Eklund, J. (2022). Pioneering entrepreneurship research: How, by whom, and when. *Foundations and Trends® in Entrepreneurship, 18*(2), 75–158.

Carlsson, B., Braunerhjelm, P., McKelvey, M., Olofsson, C., Persson, L., & Ylinenpää, H. (2013). The evolving domain of entrepreneurship research. *Small Business Economics*, *41*(4), 913–930. DOI: 10.1007/s11187-013-9503-y

Ding, M. (2017). The origin and the change of Qingzhen culture. *Journal of North Ethnic Studies*, (1)

Gladney, D. C. (2003). Islam in China: Accommodation or separatism? *The China Quarterly*, *174*, 451–467. DOI: 10.1017/S0009443903000275

Kim. (2010). Duality in the Discourse of Multiculture and Locality. *Locality Humanities*, (3), 75-105.

Leslie, D. D. (1986). *Islam in traditional China: A short history*. Canberra College of Advanced Education Lindgren, M., & Packendorff, J. (2009). Social constructionism and entrepreneurship: Basic assumptions and consequences for theory and research. *International Journal of Entrepreneurial Behaviour & Research*, *15*(1), 25–47.

Lipman, J. N. (1997). *Familiar strangers: A history of Muslims in Northwest China*. University of Washington Press.

Ma, M. (2018). Localization and sinicization: Understanding Qingzhen and halal in China. In *Proceedings of the International Workshop on Halal Food Consumption in East and West (with Appendix of Survey Report)* (pp. 77–104). Institute for Asian Muslim Studies, Waseda University.

Mai, J. (2024). The Hui Muslims in China: Muslim Hui di China. *Indonesian Journal of Islamic History and Culture*, *5*(1), 1–11.

Organisation for Economic Co-operation and Development(OECD). (1998). *Fostering Entrepreneurship*. OECD Publishing.

Pittaway, L. (2005). Philosophies in entrepreneurship: A focus on economic theories. *International Journal of Entrepreneurial Behaviour & Research, 11*(3), 201–221. DOI: 10.1108/13552550510598790

Raimi, L. 2024. "Interdependence of Halal Entrepreneurship and Islamic Finance for Creating a Strong Halal Ecosystem" *Journal of Islamic Marketing* pp.1-33.

Sai, Y. (2014). Policy, practice and perceptions of qingzhen (halal) in China. *Online Journal of Research in Islamic Studies*, *1*(2), 1–12.

Schutjens, V. A. J. M., & Völker, B. G. M. (2010). Space and social capital: The degree of locality in entrepreneurs' contacts and its consequences for firm success. *European Planning Studies*, *18*(6), 941–963. DOI: 10.1080/09654311003701480

Stevenson, D. (2004). "Civic gold" rush: Cultural planning and the politics of the third way. *International Journal of Cultural Policy*, *10*(1), 119–131. DOI: 10.1080/1028663042000212364

Teixeira, A. A. (2011). Mapping the (in) visible college (s) in the field of entrepreneurship. *Scientometrics*, *89*(1), 1–36. DOI: 10.1007/s11192-011-0445-3

Venkataraman, S. (2019). The distinctive domain of entrepreneurship research. In *Seminal ideas for the next twenty-five years of advances* (pp. 5–20). Emerald Publishing Limited. DOI: 10.1108/S1074-754020190000021009

Wang, Y. (2024). Islamization of the Term " "(Qing Zhen): Its Analysis for Purity and Authenticity for Muslim in China. *Journal of Al-Tamaddun*, *19*(1), 273–295. DOI: 10.22452/JAT.vol19no1.20

ENDNOTES

1 https://dictionary.cambridge.org/dictionary/english/entrepreneurship. Access Date: July 13th, 2025.

2 https://www.etymonline.com/word/enterprise. Access Date: July 13th.2025.

3 https://www.researchandmarkets.com/report/halal-food. Access Date: July 13th, 2025.

4 However, the research shows vulnerability in terms that they present case of Netherland, non-Islamic circumstances, under irrelevant topic to Islam nor Halal.

5 https://www.koreaherald.com/article/1919676 . Access Date: July 18th, 2025.

6 https://www.aljazeera.com/news/2018/8/23/residents-of-koreas-jeju-island-talk-about-yemeni-refugees. Access Date: July 18th, 2025.

7 Not only due to the restricted access to public education, Hui people are known to take education in communal Masjid, which functioned as religious as well as general school. However, since quality of education Masjid can provide was limited, educational tier was estimated low(Ma,2018). It was after 1986 when the Hui Muslims were able to access public education following the enactment of compulsory education law in the year (Shimbo,2018).

8 'Locals', as people who could not belong to dominant group.

Chapter 8
Halal Innovation in Sustainable Nutrition: Shariah-Compliant Insect Protein as a Future Food Source

Nazariyah Yahaya
http://orcid.org/0000-0001-9779-4967
Universiti Sains Islam Malaysia, Malaysia

Mohd Mahyeddin Mohd Salleh
http://orcid.org/0000-0001-5254-282X
Institute of Fatwa and Halal (IFFAH), Malaysia

Syamila Mansor
http://orcid.org/0000-0002-7133-4177
Independent Researcher, Malaysia

Syaza Azhari
http://orcid.org/0000-0002-5032-4949
Independent Researcher, Malaysia

A'wani Aziz Nurdalila
http://orcid.org/0000-0003-2752-8369
Institut Fatwa dan Halal (IFFAH), Malaysia

Hussein 'Azeemi Abdullah Thaidi
http://orcid.org/0000-0001-9512-2542
Independent Researcher, Malaysia

ABSTRACT

The chapter explores the potential of insect protein as a sustainable and halal-compliant food source. The aim of this study is to examine Shariah rulings (hukm) and address insect protein processing techniques to ensure food safety and enhance their nutritional value, with the ultimate goal of formulating halal guidelines tailored to insect protein enterprises. This guideline offers significant opportunities for economic growth and food security. In this study, we employ documentation, data analysis, and literature search.

DOI: 10.4018/979-8-3373-2792-1.ch008

INTRODUCTION

Food security is a critical issue we face globally, exacerbated by rising populations, environmental challenges, and the increasing demand for a sustainable food supply. Animal protein from traditional livestock farming has high demand but limited resources, which causes a significant environmental impact. As an alternative, edible insects are gaining people's attention, which not only are rich in nutrients but also benefit the environment. A high population of edible insect species is known worldwide, which could be an alternative source of food for the future (Kafle et al., 2024). However, the safety and clear regulation must be validated before an insect-based product is commercially available. As a Muslim, insect-based food must comply with halal standard guidelines.

The innovation of halal insect-based food, utilising advanced food technology, could potentially meet market demand. Advanced food technology, such as 3D-printed foods and lab-grown meat, could help innovate edible insects into more presentable, insect-based products with high nutritional value. The religious frameworks need to be developed to address the issues related to insect-based products, including halal status, regulation, safety, and acceptability. The advancement of technology can be used to produce, track, and distribute food products, but it cannot alter the fundamental basis of halal, making non-halal sources halal. In countries with a Muslim population, halal food with a trusted halal certification body is important to be taken in their everyday diet.

With the advancement of food technology, edible insects can serve as a source of protein. Insect protein is recognized as a sustainable replacement for human daily dietary intake, replacing conventional sources of protein, such as beef or poultry. As a human consumption, insect protein is not widely acceptable, especially in countries where Muslim is the majority. Consumer acceptance and the clear regulatory concerns associated with insect protein for human dietary intake must be addressed (Mohamad et al., 2025). As an animal feed, insect protein is now becoming a replacement for soybeans. As a replacement source of protein, insect protein has more benefits compared to traditional farm animal practice in terms of carbon footprint and is more environmentally friendly.

Regarding insects as a future human consumption source, in 2024, most of the food agencies in various countries, including Singapore, the United States of America, and Korea, recognized 16 species of insects for consumption, including locusts, grasshoppers, crickets, silkworms, and mealworms. Previously, the United Nations Food and Agriculture Organisation promoted insects as a sustainable replacement for meat due to their high protein content and less greenhouse gas emissions. With the growing interest in alternative protein sources to address food security and environmental concerns, examining the halal status of insect protein represents a significant area of innovation within the halal industry. Ants are not included in the 16 insects approved by SFA. However, there is rapid research regarding the use of ants as a potential future human consumption source, particularly due to their high lipid content. It is known that ant lipids are rich in dietary nutrients and contain a balanced mixture of bioactive compounds, sterols, saturated, monounsaturated fatty acids (MUFA), and polyunsaturated fatty acids (PUFA), and phospholipids, which can provide health benefits (Chetia et al., 2025).

However, what happens if an ant is no longer recognisable as an ant? The advancement of technology, like food printing, can turn the original food source into something else or unrecognisable. Food printing technologies can potentially produce customised foods (Neamah & Tandio, 2024). It has been reported that humans have been consuming insects for a long time (Tang et al., 2019). In this modern world, however, most people perceive eating insects as "disgusting," but not in certain cultural areas. In the future, ant biological materials could be used as ink for food printing to turn into delicious food. Is it permissible under Shariah rulings?

In response to growing global concerns and rapid technological advancements, this chapter explores Shariah rulings (ukm) and emerging technologies related to insect-based proteins. It includes a review of consumer acceptance and proposes halal guidelines for insect protein enterprises, aiming to support food security and empower sustainable development.

RESEARCH METHODOLOGY

To achieve the objectives of this study, we employed a four-pronged methodological approach. First, we conducted relevant *Shariah* rulings and issues pertaining to the permissibility of insects within Islamic jurisprudence. Second, we performed scientific analysis of various insect species to assess their suitability for halal. Third, a comprehensive literature review was undertaken to contextualize existing research and identify knowledge gaps. Finally, we developed key conceptual frameworks to inform the formulation of halal guidelines specific to insect-based products.

Examination of Shariah Rullings

A detailed examination of Shariah rulings (hukm) related to insect was conducted. This involved with reviewing relevant Islamic texts, including the Quran and Hadith.

Scientific Data Analysis

The phylogenetic tree for the 16 insects was constructed using MEGA 12, based on the *cytochrome c oxidase subunit III* gene sequence from the complete mitochondrial genome, obtained from the National Center for Biotechnology Information (NCBI) (Singh et al., 2024).

Literature Review

A comprehensive review of existing literature on insect species, processing techniques of insect to develop food product, the application of insect protein and their nutritional content of insect protein in insect-based product, consumer acceptance to insect-based products and safety issues.

Development of Key Concept in Halal Guidelines for Halal Insect-Based Products

Based on the syariah analysis and literature review approaches, a key concept of halal guidelines was developed.

RESULTS AND DISCUSSION

The primary theoretical lens for this study is the integration of Islamic jurisprudence (Fatwa) with phylogenetic classification. This dual framework enables a faith-based yet scientifically rigorous approach to identifying and processing halal insects, bridging traditional religious rulings with modern biological tools. It ensures that the development of insect-based foods is both Shariah-compliant and scientifically validated.

Insects as Future Food in Syariah and Fatwa Perspectives

Islamic dietary laws, commonly referred to as "halal" (permissible) and "haram" (forbidden), are a set of rules governing Muslim consumption. Their rules are stated in the Qur'an and the Hadith (Al-Qaradhawi, 2014). In the Qur'an and the hadith, there is mention of halal food and drink for Muslims to consume, which includes vegetables, fruits, grains, specific types of meat, and seafood. All food is generally allowed unless there is a specific rule that forbids it (Majlis Ugama Islam Singapura, 2024). This principle is based on the verse 145 of Surah al-An 'am:

Which means: "Say, O Prophet, 'I do not find in what has been revealed to me anything forbidden to eat except carrion, running blood, swine—which is impure— or a sinful offering in the name of any other than Allah. But if someone is compelled by necessity—neither driven by desire nor exceeding immediate need —then surely your Lord is All-Forgiving, Most Merciful."

Based on this verse, scholars have formulated a legal principle that says: *"The default ruling for things that are beneficial is permissibility"* (Al-Isnawi, 1999).

It means that prohibited food and drinks are restricted to a specific description specifically mentioned in the Qur'an and the Hadith. Among them, alcohol, pork, and its derivatives, and any food that contains dangerous or impure substances, or any religiously permissible farm animals that are not slaughtered according to Syariah laws. While the term "halal" principally refers to the lawfulness of consuming certain ingredients in Islamic dietary regulations, it is also important for Muslims to examine whether ethical and humane practices have been applied by food producers when selecting their halal food (Majlis Ugama Islam Singapura, 2024). The Qur'an assists Muslims to incorporate the features of mercy and compassion (*ra mah*) into all aspects of their lives, including the treatment of animals. Muslims are responsible for providing appropriate support, including food, water, and shelter, to the animals under their custody. Neglecting or mistreating animals is deemed a sin (Al-Qaradhawi, 2014).

The Islamic status of novel food, such as insect protein, can be examined according to core principles of Islamic ethics and jurisprudence. While the Qur'an and the Hadith may not specifically mention the "novel food" in the text, the permissibility of consuming such food can be examined within the wider context of Islamic principles related to food consumption and the environmental direction.

The Status of Insect in Islam

Generally, there is a difference of opinion among Islamic scholars regarding the ruling on consuming insects. The Hanafi, Shafi'i, and Hanbali schools of thought ruled it is forbidden (haram), while the Maliki school permitted it (Al-Nawawi et al., n.d).

The Hanafi, Shafi'i, and Hanbali jurisprudential schools forbid eating insects because they are considered repulsive (khabā'ith), as Allah says: *"He forbids them the impure things"* [Al-A'raf: 157]. Additionally, most of the Muslim community find insects disgusting to eat (Mohd Salleh & Jaffar, 2019). However, they exclude locusts, which are unanimously considered permissible, based on the saying of the Prophet : *"Two types of dead animals and two types of blood have been made lawful for us: the two dead animals are fish and locusts, and the two types of blood are the liver and spleen.*"(Reported by Ahmad and al-Bayhaqi from the narration of Abdullah ibn Umar)

However, the Shafi'is and Hanbalis added the dabb (spiny-tailed lizard) to the list of insects permitted for consumption, citing the hadith of Ibn Abbas (may Allah be pleased with them both): "Khalid ibn al-Walid and I entered the house of Maymunah with the Messenger of Allah , and a roasted dabb was brought. The Messenger of Allah reached for it but withdrew his hand. I said: "O Messenger of Allah, is it forbidden?" He said, "No, but it is not found in the land of my people, so I feel aversion toward it." Khalid then cut a piece and ate it while the Messenger of Allah looked on.' (Narrated by al-Bukhari). The Hanafis, however, considered it impermissible. The Hanbalis also made an exception for the jerboa and the rock hyrax, permitting their consumption. The Shafi'is added the hedgehog and the weasel to the list of permissible animals."

Otherwise, the Malikis ruled that all types of insects are lawful to eat (Al-Zuhaili, 2007). They stated that all animals and insects — from elephants to ants and worms — are permissible to consume, with the sole exception of pigs, which are unanimously prohibited (Majlis Ugama Islam Singapura, 2024).

Fatwa on Alternative Protein Sources

A fatwa is a ruling on a specific aspect of Islamic regulations issued by an authorized body (Al-Qaradhawi, 2014). Regarding insects as a food source for human consumption, the fatwa may differ between countries, depending on the school of thought adhered to by the halal authorities' body in those countries. In addition, differences in fatwas also arise due to differing views on the status of the carcass of animals whose blood does not flow, such as insects, whether they are considered impure (najis) or not from the view of Islamic regulations. Generally, those *fatwa*s can be divided into two categories: i) *fatwa*s that permit, and ii) *fatwa*s that prohibit.

(i) Fatwas That Permit

Referring to a fatwa issued by the Fatwa Committee of Singapore on 19 January 2023, the production of replacement animal proteins is considered a necessity (al-ājah) in today's world. Although there is currently an abundance of food sources, investing in replacement animal protein options now can help society prepare for a more sustainable food future. Replacement animal proteins, such as plant-based proteins and lab-grown meat, typically involve fewer resources, including land, water, and energy, compared to traditional animal farming. This replacement can help reduce the environmental impact of conventional food production. Therefore, the Fatwa Committee believes that the production of replacement animal proteins can also contribute to human well-being, the saving of life, and environmental sustainability (Majlis Ugama Islam Singapura, 2024).

The Fatwa Committee of Singapore considered various scholarly opinions on the matter. For instance, Ibn Ashūr (1984) describes the word *"khabā'ith"* as anything that is widely recognized as harmful or universally deemed impure, such as dirt, or anything that has a negative impact. The Fatwa Committee reviewed Ibn Ashūr's opinion, which highlights Islam's ability to embrace various cultures worldwide. The study also cites a fatwa issued by MUIS in 2009, permitting the use of a color extract derived from the cochineal insect. Similarly, Dar Ifta' Misriyyah (2013), an Egyptian Islamic advisory institution, has published a comparable judgement. Additionally, the Fatwa Committee of Singapore has determined that protein derived from insects is halal (Majlis Ugama Islam Singapura, 2024). This ruling is based on the isti ālah method, which involves a chemical transformation that changes a substance's composition and properties. When a substance no longer retains its original characteristics due to this process, its use is deemed permissible, as long as the final product does not contain any harmful elements.

In addition, the fatwa in Malaysia also permits it, as decided by the Muzakarah (Conference) of the Fatwa Committee of the National Council for Islamic Religious Affairs Malaysia in year 2012, regarding the issue of cochineal coloring derived from a type of insect (female beetle) (Salleh, Ahmad & Fadzillah, 2020). Among the arguments put forth are that the insect is not harmful and that the pigment produced from cochineal is beneficial to humans. The Muzakarah also adheres to the opinion of the majority of jurists (jumhur fuqaha') who unanimously agreed that the carcass of insects whose blood does not flow is considered pure, and cochineal coloring is obtained from dead cochineal insects whose blood does not flow. However, the permitted usage level is subject to the regulations set by the Ministry of Health Malaysia, as long as it does not cause harm (JAKIM, 2012).

The Jordanian Ifta' Committee (2016) also issued a similar ruling, allowing the use of Carmine E120 coloring derived from insects. One of the arguments for its permissibility is that, although it originates from a *khabith* (impure) animal—in this case, insects—which is originally prohibited, once the product has undergone complete *istihalah* (chemical and physical transformation), its ruling changes to halal. However, the Jordanian fatwa imposes several conditions for its use, such as the presence of necessity, the absence of alternative sources, limited use in minimal quantities, and that it does not cause harm

(ii) Fatwas That Prohibit

A fatwa prohibiting the utilize of insects as a replacement animal protein source has been issued by the Office of the State Mufti of Brunei (2022). According to them, insects such as cockroaches, beetles, worms, ants, lizards, scorpions, spiders, mosquitoes, bees, and flies are prohibited to be eaten in Islam, except for locusts. Insects are considered repulsive *(khabith)*, and therefore not permissible for consumption. Likewise, the carcasses of insects other than locusts are deemed haram to be used as food ingredients, including any parts extracted from them, such as colouring agents derived from insects.

The basis for this prohibition is particularly evident in the case of cochineal colouring, which is derived from a type of insect commonly used as a food colorant. Although cochineal is an insect whose blood does not flow, its carcass is considered impure (najis) and not permissible to consume. Even though cochineal is only used in extract form as a coloring agent, it is still considered haram because the colouring is a part of the insect's carcass, and thus impure, even if used in small amounts in a product. Furthermore, the colouring extracted from cochineal is said to significantly alter the characteristics of liquids, causing them to become impure (*mutanajjis*) or mixed with impurity (*najis*). Additionally, the use of this colouring is not due to necessity or unavoidability; rather, it is deliberately added to food products (Office of the State Mufti of Brunei, 2022).

Hence, according to the Brunei fatwa, if the carcass of a creature whose blood does not flow alters the nature of a liquid, or is intentionally added to a pure liquid, it renders the liquid impure (Office of the State Mufti of Brunei, 2022).

Scientific Background and Behaviour of Safe Consumption of Insect Species

Phylogenetics is the study of evolutionary relationships among species using genetic, morphological, or molecular data. In this study, phylogenetic trees are used to distinguish between halal and haram insects by grouping species based on their genetic similarities and evolutionary lineage. This approach allows researchers to identify which insects fall within the permissible categories, referring to the Hanafi, Shafi'i, and Hanbali schools of thought. Integrating Islamic jurisprudence with modern biological classification, this theory supports a scientifically grounded method for halal certification of insect species. Understanding the genetics of these insects and their diet is crucial before determining their permissibility. Additionally, the aspect of *Toyyib,* or cleanliness, of their habitat and diet must be considered before reviewing the halal hukm. Here, we summarize various insect species and their dietary habits, which are presented in Table 1. Insect represents a four-stage lifecycle: egg, larva, pupa, and adult, as illustrated in Figure 1 (Kulinčević & Rothenbuhler, 1982).

Figure 1. Life cycle of Apis mellifera (Honey Bee)

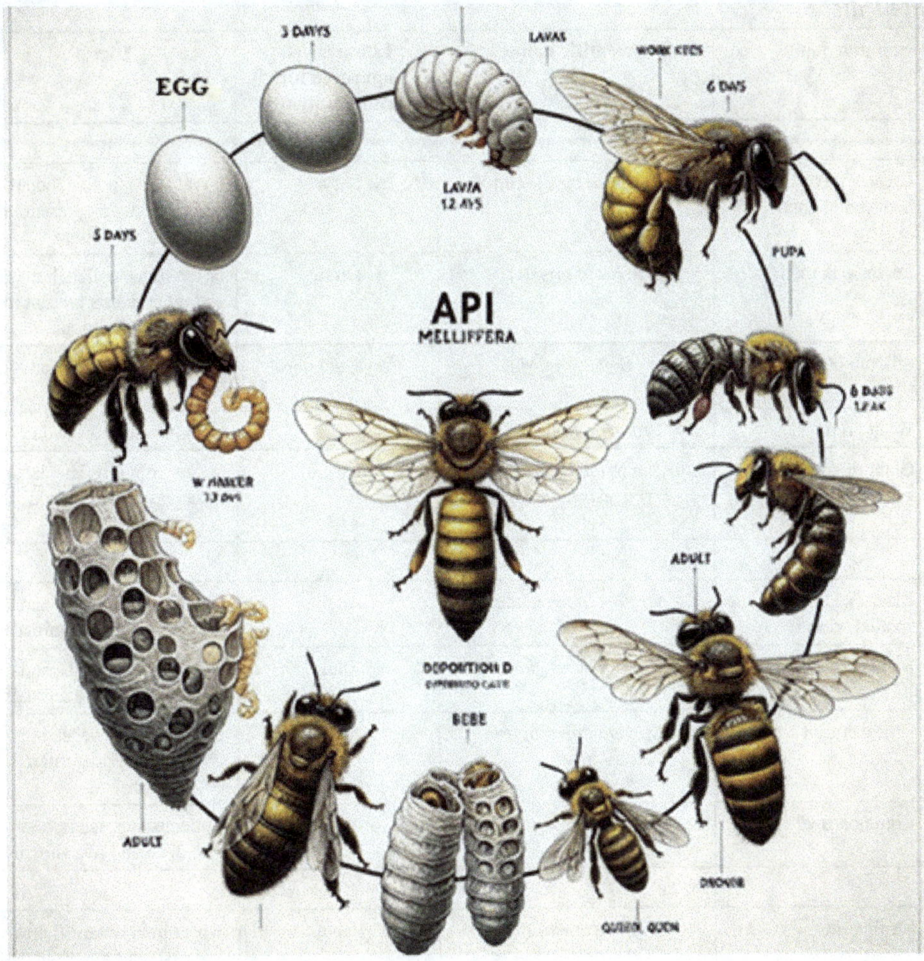

Table 1. Insect species approved by Singapore Food Agency (SFA) as food and their diet

Common name	Scientific name	Life stage (s) approved for consumption	Diet
Greater wax/ honeycomb moth	*Galleria mellonella*	Larva	larval skins, pollen, honey, and other debris present in the wax comb
Lesser wax moth	*Achroia grisella*	Larva	larval skins, pollen, honey, and other debris present in the wax comb
Silk moth/silkworm	*Bombyx mori*	Larva and pupa	mulberry leaves and lettuce
Whitegrub	*Protaetia brevitarsis*	Larva	oak-fermented sawdust
Giant rhino beetle grub	*Allomyrina dichotoma/ Trypoxylus dichotomus*	Larva	waste from Fagales plants such as chestnut, oaks, walnuts, pecans
Black field/two-spotted cricket	*Gryllus bimaculatus*	Adult	plant tissue, seeds, and both dead and live animals
Banded cricket	*Gryllodes sigillatus*	Adult	plant tissue, seeds, and both dead and live animals
House cricket	*Acheta domesticus*	Adult	cereals, fruits, vegetables, and small nocturnal insects
Common/field cricket	*Teleogryllus mitratus*	Adult	plant tissue, seeds, and both dead and live animals
Mealworm	*Tenebrio molitor*	Larva	wheat bran, wheat flakes, yeast, and rice flour
Superworm/giant mealworm beetle	*Zophobas atratus/Zophobas morio*	Larva	wheat bran and leaves of ivy gourd
Lesser mealworm	*Alphitobius diaperinus*	Larva	bird droppings, bat guano, waste, mold, eggs, feathers, and carrion
African migratory locust	*Locusta migratoria migratorioides*	Adult	stems and leaves
American desert/ desert locust	*Schistocerca americana/ Schistocerca gregaria*	Adult	stems and leaves
Grasshopper	*Oxya japonica*	Adult	stems and leaves
Western/European honey bee	*Apis mellifera*	Larva and adult	Pollen

Figure 2. Phylogenetic tree of insect genus approved by Singapore Food Agency (SFA) as food generated by using MEGA 12

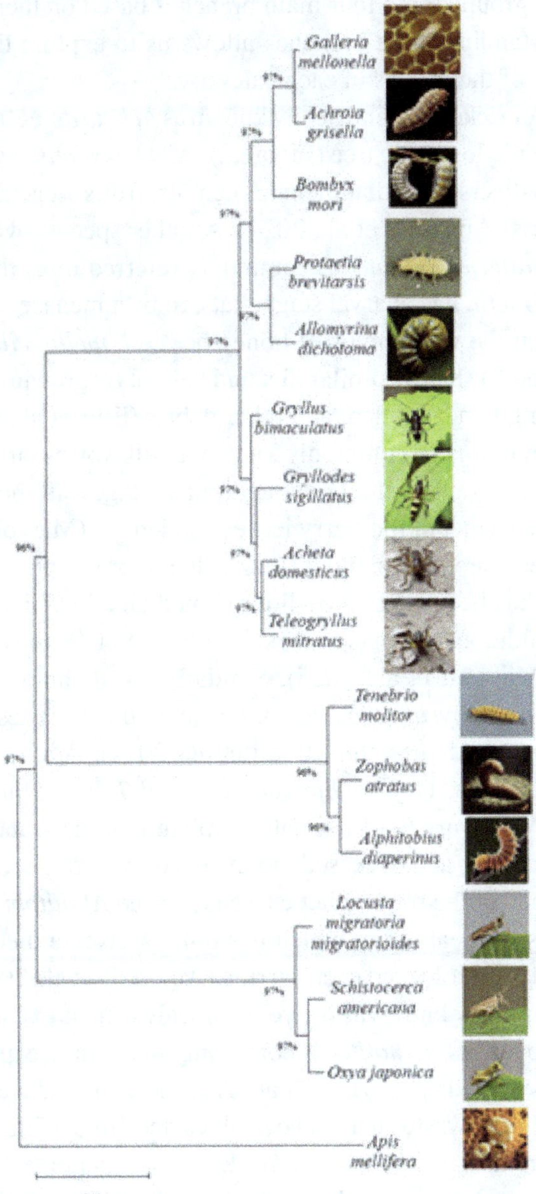

We take an in-depth look at the phylogenetic tree representing 16 insect species that have received approval from the Singapore Food Agency (SFA) (Figure 2). These species can be grouped into four main branches based on their evolutionary relationships. Understanding these branches allows us to explore the feeding behaviours and habitats of the insects in each category.

For instance, house crickets, scientifically known as *Acheta domesticus*, belong to the first branch of the phylogenetic tree (Figure 2). *A. domesticus* is an omnivorous insect and has quite a diverse diet that includes cereals, fruits, vegetables, and even small nocturnal insects (Amorello et al., 2024). Another species, which is located in the first branch, *Galleria mellonella*, commonly referred to as the greater wax worm or honeycomb moth, has a larval stage that can be a menace for beekeepers, as they like to feast on the wax combs of honey bees. *G. mellonella* and *Achroia grisella* (lesser wax moth) share a similar diet and habitat by growing vigorously in bee colonies and eating honey, pollen, and other debris (Ellis et al., 2013).

In addition, *Bombyx mori* or commonly known as silkworms, are harvested for their high-quality protein during the larval and pupal stages. In the silk industry, these silkworms are fed a diet of mulberry leaves and lettuce (Marzoli et al., 2022). In the group of beetles, the white-spotted flower chafer, or scientifically known as Protaetia brevitarsis, has been used in traditional medicine in China and Korea to treat minor health conditions for many years. The larvae of *P. brevitarsis* eat oak-fermented sawdust (Mansour et al., 2025). Similarly, giant rhino beetle grub, or scientically known as *Allomyrina dichotoma,* consume plant wastes from various trees, including walnuts and chestnuts (Uwai et al., 2014). Adult cricket species such as *Gryllodes sigillatus, Gryllus bimaculatus*, and *Teleogryllus mitratus* are omnivorous, feeding on a variety of animal and plant materials, including seeds, plant tissue, and both living and deceased organisms (Kwon & Lee, 2024).

In the second branch of the phylogenetic tree is located *Alphitobius diaperinus*, also known as the lesser mealworm, which has quite a diverse diet that includes bird droppings, bat guano, mold, and even carrion (Amorello et al., 2024). Whereas, *Tenebrio molitor*, commonly known as the yellow mealworm, is extensively used in fish meal to replace soybeans. *T. molitor* is commonly found in rice grains. In insect farming, *T. molitor* is feeded with wheat bran, flakes, yeast, and rice flour which is supplemented with food waste such as vegetables and fruits (Zunzunegui et al., 2024). In addition, larvae of *Zophobas atratus*, known as giant mealworm beetles, are fed leaves of ivy gourd and wheat bran (Zaelor & Kitthawee, 2018).

The third branch of the phylogenetic tree in Figure 2 consists of two species of locust, *Locusta migratoria migratorioides* and *Schistocerca americana,* and one species of grasshoppers (*Oxya japonica*). Locusts and grasshoppers are becoming known as novel protein sources due to their high muscle content, which is primarily composed of protein structures. They consume the stems and leaves of more than

300 plant species (Li et al., 2022). Meanwhile, *Apis mellifera* (honeybee), located in the fourth branch of the phylogenetic tree (Figure 2), consumes pollen as its food source (García-Vicente et al., 2024).

The phylogenetic tree constructed from insect species sequences identifies a group of halal insects located on branch three, distinct from other insect groups that are considered non-permissible (haram) for consumption according to the Hanafi, Shafi'i, and Hanbali schools of thought.

Processing Techniques to Formulate Insect-Based Product

Among the various edible insects, locust and grasshoppers are particularly significant in Islamic dietary law, as they are explicitly permitted (halal) by several major Islamic jurisprudential schools. By aligning modern food processing technologies with Islamic dietary laws, these insects can be transformed into acceptable, innovative food products that contribute to food security and economic empowerment in Muslim communities and beyond. Pre-processing, conventional, and commercial processing techniques to produce insect powder/insect flour, as well as oil extraction, can enhance the functional properties of insect proteins, such as solubility, gelling ability, and emulsifying capacity. These methods also alter physicochemical characteristics, such as protein structure and stability, improving their suitability for food applications (Yang et al., 2025). Table 2 summarizes the pre-processing and processing techniques applied to edible insects, along with their respective advantages and disadvantages, offering a consolidated reference for the development of safe and consumer-acceptable insect-based products.

Figure 3. Critical control point of halal insect product

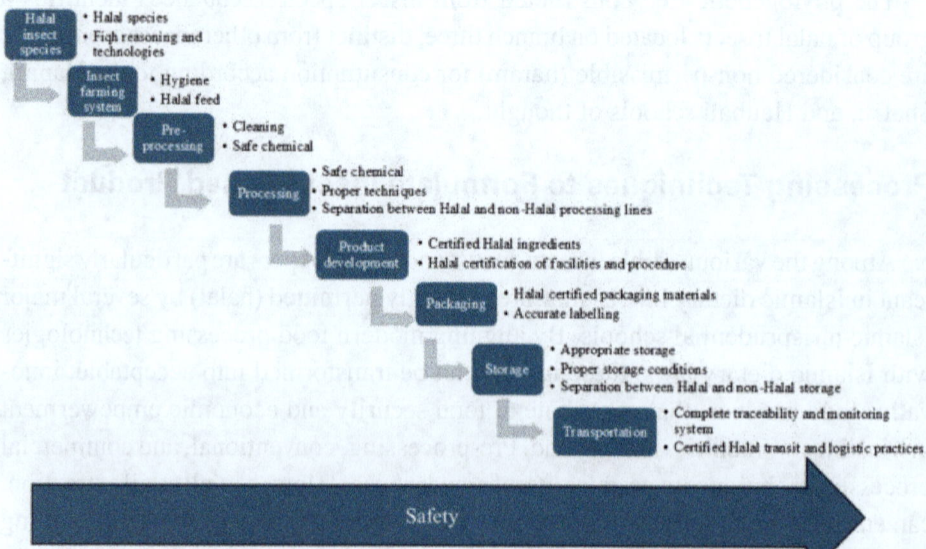

Table 2. Summary of pre-processing and processing techniques for edible insects with their advantages and disadvantages

Category	Processing Technique	Advantages	Disadvantages
Pre-processing	Starvation before harvesting	Reduces intestinal content, improves taste, lowers microbial load	May affect insect physiology and metabolism
	Washing with water	Removes debris and visible contaminants	Limited microbial reduction
	Washing with antimicrobials	Greater microbial reduction compared to water	Chemical residues, possible alteration of sensory quality
	Killing by blanching (boiling/steaming)	Effective microbial reduction, moisture retention, minimal oxidation	May affect color, induce non-enzymatic browning
	Killing by freezing	Convenient, preserves structure	Stress-induced glycolysis may alter pH and taste
	High-pressure or gas asphyxiation (CO_2/ N_2)	Non-thermal, minimal chemical changes	Requires specialized equipment, less accessible
Conventional Processing	Chilling (≤5°C)	Slows microbial growth, maintains freshness	Not a decontamination step, limited shelf life
	Freezing (≤-18°C)	Long shelf life, preserves sensory quality	Energy-intensive, may not inactivate all microbes
	Drying (sun/oven)	Reduces water activity, extends shelf life	Incomplete microbial inactivation without prior heat
	Boiling/steaming/ toasting	Significantly reduces microbial load	Alters texture, flavor, some nutrients
	Marination	Enhances flavor, inhibits microbial growth	May promote germination of bacterial spores
	Fermentation	Improves nutrition and shelf life, develops flavor	Requires controlled microbial cultures
Commercial Processing Technologies	Blanching and drying	High microbial reduction, enzyme inactivation	May impact color and texture
	Roasting (≈150°C, few minutes)	Enhances aroma, texture	Possible nutrient loss, over-browning
	Oven/air drying (60–80°C, 24–48h)	Scalable, reduces moisture	Changes sensory/ nutritional qualities
	Freeze-drying (lyophilization)	Retains shape, flavor, nutrients	Expensive, energy-intensive
	Refrigeration	Preserves freshness temporarily	Short shelf life, microbial growth resumes quickly
	Fermentation (commercial scale)	Produces novel products (e.g., insect sauce), enhances nutrition	Needs consistent fermentation control

Pre-Processing Techniques

The processing of edible insects involves several important steps to enhance nutritional value, improve sensory qualities, increase consumer acceptance, and safe to consume. The pre-processing stage involved the quality and microbial safety of insect-based food products (Akullo et al., 2025). It begins with harvesting, which can be performed manually or with automated systems, depending on the species of the insect and production scale. After the harvesting step, insects are placed in a starvation period or fasting to clear their guts, which could reduce microbial contamination and help to remove undesirable flavors. A crucial part of pre-processing is the humane killing of insects to conserve their nutritional content, at the same time to minimise the microbial contamination. Several methods are used for this purpose, including blanching, freezing, steaming, boiling, toasting, gas asphyxiation with carbon dioxide or nitrogen, and high-pressure processing (Hasnan et al., 2023).

Conventional Processing Techniques

Conventional processing techniques for edible insects are important steps to remove microbial contamination, to increase shelf-life, and to improve sensory qualities. Drying methods such as air drying, oven drying, or freeze drying are commonly used to reduce water activity, thus inhibiting microbial growth and enzymatic degradation (Akullo et al., 2025). However, drying alone may not ensure the microbiological contamination risk unless it is prolonged or combined with additional heat treatments. Heat-based methods, such as steaming, boiling, and toasting, are commonly combined with processing protocols, often in conjunction with blanching, which is known for its ability to quickly deactivate the asexual form of microbial cells (Ojha et al., 2021).

Additional conventional techniques, such as marination and fermentation, are commonly used in food processing. Marination, particularly using solutions like soy sauce, has demonstrated potential in reducing spoilage and modifying the sensory profile of insect products. Fermentation, on the other hand, offers multiple benefits, including enhancement of flavor, texture, and nutritional value. It can increase the bioavailability of certain nutrients, produce beneficial compounds such as vitamins and bioactive peptides, and extend shelf life (Hasnan et al., 2023).

Commercial Processing Technologies

At the commercial scale, the successful production of insect-based foods depends on the availability of standardized, scalable, and cost-effective processing technologies. Industrial practices commonly include blanching and pasteurization for microbial control, drying (via hot air, microwave, or freeze-drying) for shelf-life extension, and fermentation to improve nutritional and functional attributes (Akullo et al., 2025; Kozlu et al., 2024). Due to the diverse properties of insect species and their various product applications, processing conditions must be carefully optimized. Although interest and industrial advancements remain a major challenge for food safety assurance (Akullo et al., 2025; Ojha et al., 2021). Addressing this gap is crucial to ensure product quality and build consumer confidence consumer in the global insect-based food market.

Applications of Insect Protein in Food Products

The incorporation of insect protein into the global food chain is no longer a theoretical concept as it is becoming a reality. Insect-based ingredients are being used in a variety of culinary products, including protein-rich snacks, plant-based meat replacements, and functional health foods. Insects can now be transformed into various food components including powders, oils, and flours thanks to technological breakthroughs. These components improve not just the nutritional profile of foods, but also their sensory and functional features, such as moisture retention and stability (Cong et al., 2024). Table 3 outlines the use of insect protein in food items.

Table 3. Summary of food product from insect protein

Category	Benefits
Food Enrichment	1. Complete profile of essential amino acids and is rich in micronutrients such as iron, zinc, and vitamin B12. 2. Help address global challenges related to malnutrition and micronutrient deficiencies.
Protein-Enriched Snacks	1. Protein content ranging from 35% to 60%. 2. Rich source of iron, zinc, and vitamin B12 supports muscle growth and post-exercise recovery.
Baked Goods	1. Significantly enhance the protein content. 2. Improve moisture retention and crumb structure.
Meat Substitutes	1. Complete amino acid profile. 2. Bioavailable micronutrients and beneficial lipids. 3. Require approximately twelve times less feed than cattle to produce an equivalent amount of protein.
Dairy Alternatives	1. Sustainable and hypoallergenic for many consumers. 2. High levels of calcium, vitamin B12, and omega-3 fatty acids. 3. Essential for bone health and cognitive function.
Protein Supplements	1. High digestibility and protein content often exceeding 70% to 80% of dry weight. 2. Amino acid profile meets or exceeds the requirements for human nutrition. 3. Used in meal replacements, protein shakes, and nutrition bars.

continued on following page

Table 3. Continued

Category	Benefits
Functional Foods	1. Rich content of bioactive compounds. 2. Chitin improved gut health and reduced cholesterol levels. 3. Peptides and antioxidants contribute to anti-inflammatory, antimicrobial, and immunomodulatory effects.
Culinary Ingredients	1. Insect flours and pastes are being used to enrich sauces, spreads, and even desserts. 2. Incorporating crickets into pasta doughs, mealworm pastes into risottos, and black soldier fly larvae into exotic tasting menus.

(i) Food Enrichment

Food enrichment is a procedure that improves the nutritional value of food by introducing foods that have health-promoting properties. In this context, insect protein has proven to be an effective fortifier. It provides an extensive list of essential amino acids and is very rich in micronutrients including iron, zinc, and vitamin B12, which are all which are necessary for human health. Integrating insect protein into daily meals has the potential to aid in tackling global challenges such as nutritional deficiency and micronutrient deficiencies.

(ii) Protein-Enriched Snacks

The confectionery business was among the first to recognize insect protein in response to rising customer demand for environmentally conscious, high-protein food alternatives. Crickets, mealworms, and black army fly larvae contain protein levels ranging from 35% to 60%, depending on the species and processing techniques (Hasnan et al., 2023). They are also high in iron, zinc, and vitamin B12 (Lisboa et al., 2024), which makes them excellent for rich in nutrients snacks marketed to those who prioritize their health.

Crickets, for instance, deliver all the essential amino acids and may be easily ground into coarse flour for use in protein bars and energy treats. Cricket flour promotes muscular growth and after a workout recuperation, making it a tempting option for athletes and individuals who are active (Lampová et al., 2024). Furthermore, these insects provide dietary fiber via their content of chitin and possess beneficial lipids, such as omega-3 and omega-6 fatty acids. Their moderate flavor and versatility make them perfect for chips, crackers, and other popular snack formats, resulting in increased consumer acceptability.

(iii) Baked Goods

Baked foods are another intriguing application for insect protein incorporation. Insect flours are being utilized to reinforce common foods including bread, muffins, cookies, and cakes. Cricket flour made from the *Acheta domesticus* species is especially popular in the United States because of its delicate, nutty flavor and high level of protein (Gantner et al., 2024). Other species, such as mealworms (*Tenebrio molitor*) and black soldier fly larvae (H*ermetia illucens*), are gaining prominence due to their beneficial nutritional qualities (Macwan et al., 2023).

According to research studies, replacing insect flour for up to 15% of regular flour can dramatically increase the protein level in baked products while having no detrimental impact on taste or structure. In fact, insect flours have been shown to enhance retention of moisture and crumb structure, yielding smoother and more pleasant goods. This has resulted in the birth of a new type of baked food that provides both enjoyment and nutritional value, attracting to a growing audience of mindful of one's and environmentally sensitive consumers.

(iv) Meat Substitutes

Alongside increasing awareness of diets based on plants and worries about the environmental impact of traditional production of meat, meat replacements have emerged as a key focus of food inventiveness. In this field, insect proteins offer an exclusive solution. It provides a comprehensive amino acid profile and is nutritionally like animal proteins such as beef and poultry. Furthermore, insects provide bioavailable vitamins as well as beneficial fats, which increase the dietary content of meat substitutes (Orkusz, 2021).

Insect protein can be produced into flours, isolated compounds, and hydrolysates, which can then be used to make patty forms, sauerkraut, and meatballs. High-moisture extrusion technologies and enzymatic hydrolysis are employed to recreate meat's fibrous structure and taste. Fusion products containing insect and plant proteins have been shown to improve taste, texture, and acceptance among customers. The environmental benefits are enormous; for instance, crickets require nearly twelve times less feed than cattle to generate the same quantity of protein, making them a significantly more effective protein source.

(v) Dairy Alternatives

As the need for dairy-free options grows, insects are being considered as a new source of dairy replacement components. This development is being pushed by both sustainability concerns and the increasing prevalence of intolerance to lactose and dairy allergens. Insects provide a rich in nutrients, sustainable, and hypoallergenic choice for lots of consumers (Tello et al., 2021).

Protein isolates from crickets, mealworms, and black army fly larvae have been utilized to create milk alternatives, fermented goods such as yogurt, and ready-to-drink smoothies. These insects are rich in calcium, vitamin B12, and omega-3 fatty acids, all of those that are beneficial to bone health as well as cognitive performance. Enzymatic hydrolysis and enhanced homogenization are two manufacturing processes used to increase the solubility and flavour composition of insect-based alternatives to dairy, which makes them more pleasant and acceptable for everyday consumers.

(vi) Protein Supplements

Supplements made from proteins are a rapidly developing market, notably among athletes, elderly folks, and others with high protein requirements. Insects are ideal for this sector because of their high digestibility and levels of protein, which can surpass 70% to 80% of their dry mass. Their amino acid profile fulfills or surpasses the needs of humans' standards, making them among the best sources of dietary protein (Huis & Rumpold, 2023).

Insect proteins are commonly prepared into powders or concentrates for use in replacements for meals, protein shakes, and nutrition snacks. Their neutral taste, excellent emulsification characteristics, and capacity to generate durable gels provide them with extremely useful components (Queiroz et al., 2023). Enzymatic hydrolysis is one of the advanced manufacturing processes utilized to improve the absorption and bioavailability of insect protein. Integrating insect and plant proteins can also help balance amino acid compositions and boost popularity among consumers by tackling ethical and sensory challenges.

(vii) Functional Foods

Functional foods provide health advantages beyond simple nourishment. Because of their high concentration of bioactive chemicals, insect-derived substances are becoming more popular in this area. Chitin, a dietary fibre found in insect exoskeletons, has been linked to enhanced gut health and lower cholesterol levels. Furthermore, peptides and antioxidants found in insect protein may have anti-inflammatory, antibacterial, and immunomodulatory properties (Ferrazzano et al., 2023).

These functional qualities pave the way for insect-based diets to help avert illnesses and promote general health. Protein-enriched refreshments, functional snack bars, and nutritional supplements are being developed using insect protein in order to promote certain health outcomes (Placentino et al., 2021). Consumers looking for organic and successful solutions to improve their diets are increasingly embracing these technological advances, particularly when their advantages are clearly articulated and supported by evidence from scientific research.

(viii) Culinary Ingredients

Within food that is processed categories, insects are making their way into the world of cuisine. Their moderate flavor, adaptability, and distinct texture render them appropriate for a variety of meals. The whole insects can be baked or fried to serve as garnishes or components in savory dishes, while bug flours and pastes are employed to improve condiments, spreads, as well as desserts (Yazici & Ozer, 2021).

Insect-based culinary inventions are rising in popularity in premium restaurants and creative kitchens worldwide. Chefs are putting crickets in pasta batter, mealworm pastes in risottos, and black soldier fly larvae on unusual tasting platters. These kinds of uses not only highlight the taste versatility of edible insects but also serve to mainstream their use in regular cookery. The increasing demand of insect-based burgers and sausages indicates how culinary ingenuity can help mainstream insect protein (Krawczyk et al., 2024).

Consumer Acceptance

Despite the obvious dietary and environmental benefits of insect-based meals, broad consumer adoption remains a considerable challenge, especially in Western countries where entomophagy is not culturally embedded. Negative impressions about insects' look, taste, and generally perceived "ick factor" have hampered their uptake. However, studies show that these hurdles can be eliminated by clever marketing, education, and creative product development. One efficient technique is to employ insect protein in disguised forms, such as flours or isolates, so that consumers are able to utilize insect nutrition without having to deal with complete insects (Cong et al., 2024). Consumer tests show that products that highlight recognizable flavours, pleasant textures, and health or sustainability benefits outperform others.

Regulatory developments also play an important effect. The European Food Safety Authority (EFSA) has certified many insect species for consumption by humans, establishing legitimacy and paving the road toward business growth. Religious and ethical factors add to the complications. Some insects, such as locusts, are declared halal under Islamic dietary law, whilst others require expert interpretation. In contrast, kosher certification for insect-based foods remains limited, causing issues for Jewish customers (Precup et al., 2022). Finally, openness, consumer education, and culturally sensitive creation of goods are critical for increasing acceptability of insect-based meals. As consciousness of environmental and nutritional concerns rises and more customers seek alternate protein sources, insect protein is poised to become a growing vital component of the worldwide culinary scene (Ren et al., 2023).

Safety of Edible Insects as a Future Food Source for Human Consumption

As Islam emphasizes the safety of its followers and the *Halalan Toyyiban* aspect, it is important to ensure the sustainable dietary practices that are also safe for human consumption. The safety of edible insects as a prospective food source is crucial because the exposure and consumption of insects may pose health risks due to the presence of pathogens, toxins, and allergens. Previous research has identified numerous harmful bacteria colonizing insects throughout their lifecycle, which may cause significant health hazards when ingested by humans. For instance, the presence of *Bacillus cereus* in edible insects raises concerns for foodborne illness, as this bacterium is linked to gastrointestinal disorders (Vandeweyer et al., 2020). It has been reported that microbial cells are also present on insects' cuticles. The presence of microorganisms in insects, such as pathogenic bacteria, viruses, and fungi, is significantly influenced by insect farming conditions, which may be exposed to heavy metals, insecticides, mycotoxins, and other toxicants (Vandeweyer et al., 2021). Therefore, it is very relevant that the Food and Agriculture Organisation (FAO) establish insect farms guidelines which similar to food safety regulations and animal farms (FAO, 2013).

In addition to microbial issues in the safety of edible insects, insects were proven to cause allergic reactions, particularly for individuals with food allergies (Immunoglobulin E (IgE) mediated) related to exposure to crustacean (Broekman et al., 2017). In Western countries, low acceptance of insect consumption is due to food safety and allergic reactions (Huis, 2016). Scientifically, the presence of proteins that are analogous to tropomyosin and arginine kinase can induce insect allergies in individuals, specifically found in mealworms, crickets, and grasshoppers. Reactions may range from a minor skin rash, anaphylaxis and even death. Cases of anaphylaxis occurred in an individual with a crustacean allergy after consuming beverages containing cricket flour (Broekman et al., 2017). A subsequent investigation revealed that individuals allergic to mealworm protein may also exhibit allergies to other insect species, which complicates individual allergy management (Pali-Schöll et al., 2019; Truzzi et al., 2019). Due to these incidents, the FAO and other regulatory bodies have stressed the necessity of establishing explicit regulations for labelling insect-based products. It is important to use protein analysis and rapid methods to find specific allergens in different kinds of edible insects (Barre et al., 2021; Ruiz et al., 2025).

Hence, it is essential to address food safety issues through stringent hygiene standards, regulatory monitoring, allergen detection, and consumer education. The FAO has established standards and recommended methods for the production, processing, and storage of insects to mitigate the risks of allergies, infections, and other hazards associated with their consumption (FAO, 2013). Consistent chemical analysis of insect products and substrates is essential for safeguarding public safety (FAO, 2013). With the increasing global need for alternative protein sources, collaborative efforts among academics, legislators, and the food industry will be essential for the safe integration of edible insects into mainstream human diets.

Insects as a Future Food Source in the Halal Industry

Halal Control Points (HCPs) are crucial steps in the production process that protect the halal integrity of products. They come from the Hazard Analysis and Critical Control Points (HACCP) system. In insect husbandry and processing, HCPs can include factors such as the origin of the feed, the method of insect killing, the tool used for processing, and the materials used for packaging. National and international organisations, such as JAKIM, MUIS, and GAC, require that the entire supply chain, from procurement to distribution, adhere to halal standards. There must not be any ingredients from animals that are not allowed or that were not killed according to Shariah law, as well as any corrupt (*najis*) substances.

Following these rules exactly is crucial to maintain halal authenticity, as even small amounts of non-halal ingredients can render a product no longer halal. It is crucial to have a robust halal supply chain system, which begins with verifying the origin of raw materials (Figure 3). We need to examine and classify each type of insect individually to determine whether it is halal or haram. For example, Malaysia's Islamic dietary law states that grasshoppers and locusts are halal as long as they are not exposed to haram materials during farming, processing, or handling (Sabri et al., 2023).

To maintain halal integrity, all production activities must be conducted in facilities that are halal-certified. This makes sure that no haram materials are present in refining aids. All of the ingredients in the finished product must be halal-certified. Additionally, to prevent cross-contamination, halal production equipment and storage must be segregated or kept separate from non-halal products (Maqsood-ul-Haque & Veny, 2023). To ensure that halal products can be traced and that halal integrity is maintained at every stage, it is crucial to monitor their movement through the halal supply chain (Changalima, 2025).

CONCLUSION

Insect-based products that are certified halal must be available in the market. However, the innovation of the products must follow the key principles of Islamic ethics and rules. The diverse opinions of scholars regarding the permissibility of eating insects must be explored and acknowledged. The development of halal guidelines on insect-based products could increase confidence among the Muslim community to support the innovation of halal products and halal insect farming, which could benefit the economy and the environment. Market reception must be conducted from the consumer's perspective to assess the acceptability of insect-based products.

RECOMMENDATION

The framework and guidelines generated by this study are significant as references for the practices of halal industry players, halal agencies, and the Muslim community. The developed framework for halal insect-based products holds significance for the implementation and achievement of government policies and agendas, particularly in integrating them into the Food Security Policy.

FUTURE DIRECTION

The halal edible insect study has several limitations, stemming from the differing perspectives of Muslim scholars and the varying halal standards applied in different countries. Future research could explore a halal standard that integrates with good insect farming practices to make insect farming sustainable and economically viable. The Muslim perception of insect-based products must also be addressed for good reviews and a trustworthy halal standard. Halal innovation of insect-based products could open the opportunity for the advancement of food technology research. At the same time, the benefits of insect protein must be made known to consumers to encourage them to transition from conventional animal protein to insect protein.

CREDIT AUTHORSHIP CONTRIBUTION STATEMENT

Author contributions to this paper: Nazariyah Yahaya: Writing the original draft, and final approval; Mohd Mahyeddin Mohd Salleh, Syamila Mansor, Syaza

Azhari, A'wani Aziz Nurdalila: Writing the partial part of the original draft & Hussein 'Azeemi Abdullah Thaid: Concept and administration.

Grammarly contributed to this text by responding to these AI prompts: *Make it sound academic, improve it, simplify it.*

DECLARATION OF COMPETING INTEREST

The authors declare that they have no known competing financial interests or personal relationships that could have appeared to influence the work reported in this paper

ACKNOWLEDGEMENT

This research is funded by Universiti Sains Islam Malaysia under Projek Penyelidikan Transdisiplinari USIM 2023 (PPPI/TRANSDISIPLINARI/FST/USIM/18223) with the title "Halal Guidelines for Alternative Proteins Enterprises." We also thank the Institute Fatwa and Halal (IFFAH), Faculty of Science and Technology and Faculty of Syariah and Law, Universiti Sains Islam Malaysia (USIM) for the research facilities and support.

REFERENCES

Akullo, J. O., Egonyu, J. P., Ng'ang'a, J., Kiiru, S., Mmari, M., Ndiritu, A., Maimba, Z. W., Salano, F. M., & Kinyuru, J. (2025). Post-harvest handling, processing and value addition of edible insects as a sustainable food resource in Africa: A review. In *International Journal of Tropical Insect Science*. Springer Nature., DOI: 10.1007/s42690-024-01410-6

Al-Isnawi. (1999). *Nihāyat al-Sūl Shar Minhāj Al-Wu ūl*. Beirut: Dār al-Kutub al-'Ilmiyyah.

Al-Nawawi, Abu Zakariyya Muhyi al-Din Yahya bin Syaraf (n.d.). *al-Majmu' Syarh al-Muhazzab*. Beirut: Darul Fikr.

Al-Qaradhawi, Yusuf (2014). *Halal dan Haram Dalam Islam*. Nilai: Pustaka Cahaya Kasturi.

Al-Zuhaili, Wahbah bin Mustafa (2007). *Al-Fiqh al-Islami wa Adillatuhu*. Dimashq: Darul Fikr.

Amorello, D., Barreca, S., & Orecchio, S. (2024). Critical evaluation of hazardous pollutants in edible insects: A simple review. *Journal of Food Composition and Analysis*, *135*, 106675. DOI: 10.1016/j.jfca.2024.106675

Barre, A., Laisney, M., & De Oliveira, G. (2021). Microbiological safety of edible insects: A review. *Food Control*, *121*, 107658. DOI: 10.1016/j.foodcont.2020.107658

Broekman, H. C. H., Knulst, A. C., den Hartog Jager, C. F., van Bilsen, J., Raymakers, F. M., Kruizinga, A. G., & Houben, G. F. (2017). Anaphylaxis after eating insects in patients with known food allergy. *The Journal of Allergy and Clinical Immunology*, *139*(2), 883–885. DOI: 10.1016/j.jaci.2016.08.031

Chetia, J. R., S, S., Sahu, S., & Seth, D. (2025). Ant lipids: A comprehensive review of their major composition, health benefits, and potential as a future food. *Trends in Food Science & Technology*, *157*, 104895. DOI: 10.1016/j.tifs.2025.104895

Cong, L., Dean, D., Liu, C., Wang, K., & Hou, Y. (2024). The commercial application of insect protein in food products: A product audit based on online resources. *Foods*, *13*(21), 3509. DOI: 10.3390/foods13213509 PMID: 39517293

Dar Ifta' Misriyyah. (2013). Is it permissible to use carminic acid as a natural food colorant which is extracted from an insect? Retrieved from https://www.dar-alifta.org/en/fatwa/details/6888/is-it-permissible-to-use-carminic-acid-as-a-natural-food-colorant-which-is-extrac

Ellis, J. D., Graham, J. R., & Mortensen, A. (2013). Standard methods for wax moth research. *Journal of Apicultural Research*, *52*(1), 1–17. Advance online publication. DOI: 10.3896/IBRA.1.52.1.10

FAO. (2013). Edible insects: Future prospects for food and feed security. Rome: Food and Agriculture Organization of the United Nations. Retrieved on 16 July,2025 from https://www.fao.org/4/i3253e/i3253e.pdf

Ferrazzano, G. F., D'Ambrosio, F., Caruso, S., Gatto, R., & Caruso, S. (2023). Bioactive peptides derived from edible insects: Effects on human health and possible applications in dentistry. *Nutrients*, *15*(21), 4611. DOI: 10.3390/nu15214611 PMID: 37960264

Gantner, M., Sadowska, A., Piotrowska, A., Kulik, K., Sionek, B., & Kostyra, E. (2024). Wheat bread enriched with house cricket powder (*Acheta domesticus L.*) as an alternative protein source. *Molecules (Basel, Switzerland)*, *29*(3), 711. DOI: 10.3390/molecules29030711 PMID: 38338455

García-Vicente, E. J., Martín, M., Rey-Casero, I., Pérez, A., Martín, J., García, A., Alonso, J. M., & Risco, D. (2024). Effects of feeding with a protein liquid supplement on productivity, mortality and health of *Apis mellifera* hives in southwestern Spain. *Research in Veterinary Science*, *169*, 105173. https://doi.org/https://doi.org/10.1016/j.rvsc.2024.105173. DOI: 10.1016/j.rvsc.2024.105173 PMID: 38335895

Hasnan, F. F. B., Feng, Y., Sun, T., Parraga, K., Schwarz, M., & Zarei, M. (2023). Insects as valuable sources of protein and peptides: Production, functional properties, and challenges. *Foods*, *12*(23), 4243. DOI: 10.3390/foods12234243 PMID: 38231647

Huis, A. (2016). Edible insects are the future? *The Proceedings of the Nutrition Society*, *75*(3), 294–305. DOI: 10.1017/S0029665116000069 PMID: 26908196

Huis, A. V., & Rumpold, B. (2023). Strategies to convince consumers to eat insects: A review. *Food Quality and Preference*, *110*, 104927. DOI: 10.1016/j.foodqual.2023.104927

Ibn ʻĀshūr. (1984). *Al-Ta rīr wa al-Tanwīr*. Tunis: al-Dār al-Tūnisiyyah.

Jabatan Kemajuan Islam Malaysia [JAKIM]. (2012). Legal opinion of the MKI Muzakarah: Ruling on cochineal coloring substance: A review of the standard levels set by the Muzakarah of the Fatwa Committee of the National Council for Islamic Religious Affairs Malaysia. Retrieved from https://i-fiqh.islam.gov.my/portal/view.php?id=10301

Kafle, K., Subedi, S., & Poudel, A. (2024). A review on edible insects diversity, abundance, and conservation. *Journal of Entomology and Zoology Studies*, *12*(2), 137–142. DOI: 10.22271/j.ento.2024.v12.i2b.9306

Kozlu, A., Ngasakul, N., Klojdová, I., & Baigts-Allende, D. K. (2024). Edible insect-processing techniques: A strategy to develop nutritional food products and novelty food analogs. *European Food Research and Technology*, *250*(5), 1253–1267. DOI: 10.1007/s00217-024-04474-3

Krawczyk, A., Fernández-López, J., & Zimoch-Korzycka, A. (2024). Insect protein as a component of meat analogue burger. *Foods*, *13*(12), 1806. DOI: 10.3390/foods13121806 PMID: 38928748

Kulinčević, J. M., & Rothenbuhler, W. C. (1982). Selection for length of life in the honeybee (Apis mellifera). *Apidologie*, *13*(4), 347–352. DOI: 10.1051/apido:19820402

Kwon, W., & Lee, K. P. (2024). Macronutrient regulation in nymphs of the two-spotted cricket, *Gryllus bimaculatus* (Orthoptera: Gryllidae). *Journal of Insect Physiology*, *157*, 104684. DOI: 10.1016/j.jinsphys.2024.104684 PMID: 39074715

Lampová, B., Doskočil, I., Šmíd, P., & Kouřimská, L. (2024). Comparison of cricket protein powder and whey protein digestibility. *Molecules (Basel, Switzerland)*, *29*(15), 3598. DOI: 10.3390/molecules29153598 PMID: 39125003

Li, S., Feng, S., Ullah, H., Tu, X., & Zhang, Z. (2022). IPM - Biological and integrated management of desert locust. *Journal of Integrative Agriculture*, *21*(12), 3467–3487. DOI: 10.1016/j.jia.2022.09.017

Lisboa, H. M., Nascimento, A., Arruda, A., Sarinho, A., Lima, J., Batista, L., Dantas, M. F., & Andrade, R. (2024). Unlocking the potential of insect-based proteins: Sustainable solutions for global food security and nutrition. *Foods*, *13*(12), 1846. DOI: 10.3390/foods13121846 PMID: 38928788

Macwan, S. S. P., de Souza, T., Dunshea, F. R., DiGiacomo, K., & Suleria, H. A. (2023). Black soldier fly larvae (Hermetica illucens) as a sustainable source of nutritive and bioactive compounds, and their consumption challenges. *Animal Production Science, 64*(1), AN23192. DOI: 10.1071/AN23192

Majlis Ugama Islam Singapura. (2024). *From lab to table: Novel food for an Islamic perspective*. Office of the Mufti.

Mansour, A., Jeong, T., Lee, D., Song, J.-H., Kim, E., Lee, D.-W., Mannaa, M., & Seo, Y.-S. (2025). Fungal-bacterial interactions leading to increased insect mortality: *Trichoderma xixiacum* enhances the pathogenicity of *Serratia marcescens* in *Protaetia brevitarsis* larvae. *Journal of Invertebrate Pathology, 211*, 108327. DOI: 10.1016/j.jip.2025.108327 PMID: 40188938

Maqsood-ul-Haque, S., & Veny, H. (2023). Food processing aids: lubricants for halal manufacturing facilities. In *Innovation of Food Products in Halal Supply Chain Worldwide* (pp. 149–159). Academic Press. DOI: 10.1016/B978-0-323-91662-2.00019-3

Marzoli, F., Antonelli, P., Saviane, A., Tassoni, L., Cappellozza, S., & Belluco, S. (2022). *Bombyx mori* from a food safety perspective: A systematic review. *Food Research International, 160*, 111679. DOI: 10.1016/j.foodres.2022.111679 PMID: 36076388

Mohamad, A., Tan, C. K., Shah, N. N. A. K., Nayan, N., Ibrahim, A., Abdi, G., & Aadil, R. M. (2025). Insect protein: A pathway to sustainable protein supply chains, challenges, and prospects. *Journal of Agriculture and Food Research, 19*, 101678. DOI: 10.1016/j.jafr.2025.101678

Mohd Salleh, M. M., & Jaffar, M. N. (2019). *Halal Haram Haiwan Menurut Islam dan Fatwa di Malaysia*. Nilai: Penerbit USIM.

Neamah, H. A., & Tandio, J. (2024). Towards the development of foods 3D printer: Trends and technologies for foods printing. *Heliyon, 10*(13), e33882. DOI: 10.1016/j.heliyon.2024.e33882 PMID: 39050479

Office of the State Mufti of Brunei. (2022). Ramuan makanan sumber daripada serangga: adakah halal dimakan? *Media Permata*. Retrieved from https://mediapermata.com.bn/ramuan-makanan-sumber-daripada-serangga-adakah-halal-dimakan/

Ojha, S., Bußler, S., Psarianos, M., Rossi, G., & Schlüter, O. K. (2021). Edible insect processing pathways and implementation of emerging technologies. *Journal of Insects as Food and Feed, 7*(5), 877–900. DOI: 10.3920/JIFF2020.0121

Orkusz, A. (2021). Edible insects versus meat—Nutritional comparison: Knowledge of their composition is the key to good health. *Nutrients, 13*(4), 1207. DOI: 10.3390/nu13041207 PMID: 33917531

Pali-Schöll, I., Binder, R., Moens, Y., & Smulders, F. J. M. (2019). Edible insects—Defining a framework for risk assessment of novel foods. *Food and Chemical Toxicology, 126*, 108–118. DOI: 10.1016/j.fct.2019.02.018

Placentino, U., Sogari, G., Viscecchia, R., De Devitiis, B., & Monacis, L. (2021). The new challenge of sports nutrition: Accepting insect food as dietary supplements in professional athletes. *Foods, 10*(5), 1117. DOI: 10.3390/foods10051117 PMID: 34070020

Precup, G., Ververis, E., Azzollini, D., Rivero-Pino, F., Zakidou, P., & Germini, A. (2022). The safety assessment of insects and products thereof as novel foods in the European Union.

Queiroz, L. S., Nogueira Silva, N. F., Jessen, F., Mohammadifar, M. A., Stephani, R., Fernandes de Carvalho, A., Perrone, Í. T., & Casanova, F. (2023). Edible insect as an alternative protein source: A review on the chemistry and functionalities of proteins under different processing methods. *Heliyon, 9*(4), e14831. DOI: 10.1016/j.heliyon.2023.e14831 PMID: 37025786

Ren, L., Yang, F., & Gu, C. (2023). A study of the purchase intention of insect protein food as alternative foods for fitness proteins. *Heliyon, 9*(9), e20239. DOI: 10.1016/j.heliyon.2023.e20239 PMID: 37809624

Ruiz, F.E.A., Jácome, J.F.O., Tejera, E.. (2025). Edible insects as functional foods: bioactive compounds, health benefits, safety concerns, allergenicity, and regulatory considerations. frontiers in nutrition, 12. DOI: 10.3389/fnut.2025.1571084

Sabri, N. S. A., Kamardan, M. I. F., Wong, S. X., Azman, N. F., Akhir, F. N. M., Othman, N., Awang, N., Kuroki, Y., & Hara, H. (2023). Future aspects of insects' ingestion in Malaysia and Indonesia for human well-being and religion regulation. *Future Foods : a Dedicated Journal for Sustainability in Food Science, 8*, 100267. DOI: 10.1016/j.fufo.2023.100267

Salleh, M. M. M., Ahmad, N. M., & Fadzillah, N. A. (2020). Pewarna makanan dari serangga (cochineal) menurut perspektif halal: Analisis fatwa di beberapa negara ASEAN: Cochineal food coloring from halal perspective: A fatwa analysis in several ASEAN countries. *Journal of Fatwa Management and Research, 19*(1), 1–14. DOI: 10.33102/jfatwa.vol19no1.1

Singh, D., Mosahari, P. V., Sharma, P., Neog, K., & Bora, U. (2024). Comparative genomic and phylogenetic analysis of the complete mitochondrial genome of Cricula trifenestrata (Helfer) among lepidopteran insects. *Genome*, *67*(11), 424–439. Advance online publication. DOI: 10.1139/gen-2023-0037 PMID: 39047299

Tang, C., Yang, D., Liao, H., Sun, H., Liu, C., Wei, L., & Li, F. (2019). Edible insects as a food source: A review. *Food Production, Processing and Nutrition*, *1*(1), 8. DOI: 10.1186/s43014-019-0008-1

Tello, A., Aganovic, K., Parniakov, O., Carter, A., Heinz, V., & Smetana, S. (2021). Product development and environmental impact of an insect-based milk alternative. *Future Foods : a Dedicated Journal for Sustainability in Food Science*, *4*, 100080. DOI: 10.1016/j.fufo.2021.100080

The Jordanian Ifta' Committee. (2016). Hukm al-mawad al-mustakhrajah min al-a'yan al-najasah. Retrieved from https://www.aliftaa.jo/research-fatwas/3240/

Truzzi, C., Macedo, M. L. R., & De Oliveira, C. R. (2019). Nutritional composition of edible insects: A systematic review. *Critical Reviews in Food Science and Nutrition*, *59*(1), 1–17. DOI: 10.1080/10408398.2018.1437068 PMID: 28799777

Uwai, K., Okuyama, Y., Nakano, H., Furukawa, K., Hiroshima, E., Azuma, H., Watanabe, M., Matsumoto, T., Tokiwa, M., & Takeshita, M. (2014). Biotransformation of organic compounds in vivo using larvae of beetles (*Allomyrina dichotoma*) as biocatalysts. *Biocatalysis and Agricultural Biotechnology*, *3*(4), 129–133. DOI: 10.1016/j.bcab.2014.09.005

Vandeweyer, D., De Boeck, J., & Knapen, S. (2021). Food safety challenges in the use of edible insects for human consumption. *Journal of Food Safety*, *41*(3), e12854. DOI: 10.1111/jfs.12854

Vandeweyer, D., Lievens, B., & Campenhout, L. V. (2020). Microbiological safety of industrially reared insects for food: identification of bacterial endospores and targeted detection of foodborne viruses. https://doi.org/DOI: 10.1101/2020.04.22.055236

Yang, J., Chen, Y., Zhang, L., Zhou, S., You, L., & Song, J. (2025). Application of edible insects to food products: A review on the functionality, bioactivity and digestibility of insect proteins under high-pressure/ultrasound processing. *Food Chemistry*, *468*, 142469. DOI: 10.1016/j.foodchem.2024.142469 PMID: 39693885

Yazici, G. N., & Ozer, M. S. (2021). Using edible insects in the production of cookies, biscuits, and crackers: A review. *Biology and Life Sciences Forum, 6*(1), 80.

Zaelor, J., & Kitthawee, S. (2018). Growth response to population density in larval stage of darkling beetles (Coleoptera; Tenebrionidae) *Tenebrio molitor* and *Zophobas atratus*. *Agriculture and Natural Resources (Bangkok)*, *52*(6), 603–606. DOI: 10.1016/j.anres.2018.11.004

Zunzunegui, I., Martín-García, J., Santamaría, Ó., & Poveda, J. (2024). Analysis of yellow mealworm (*Tenebrio molitor*) frass as a resource for a sustainable agriculture in the current context of insect farming industry growth. *Journal of Cleaner Production*, *460*, 142608. DOI: 10.1016/j.jclepro.2024.142608

Chapter 9
A Shariah-Compliant Marketing Control Framework in Halal E-Commerce:
A Thematic Analysis of Prophetic Principles

Mohd Zohdi Mohd Amin
http://orcid.org/0000-0002-5143-3426
Universiti Sains Islam Malaysia, Malaysia

Mohd Sobri Ellias
http://orcid.org/0009-0007-0642-9966
Universiti Sains Islam Malaysia, Malaysia

Ahmad Obeid Jassim Hammadi
http://orcid.org/0000-0001-7751-1798
University of Anbar, Iraq

Abdulrahman Obeid Hussein
Universiti Sains Islam Malaysia, Malaysia

ABSTRACT

The halal online retail sector is growing rapidly, yet ethical challenges in digital marketing remain unresolved, including fake ads, misleading halal claims, and dishonest pricing that weaken consumer trust. This chapter proposes the Shariah-Compliant Online Marketing Control Framework (KKK-PEMASTI), developed

DOI: 10.4018/979-8-3373-2792-1.ch009

through thematic analysis of prophetic ḥadīths on trade and ethics. It highlights four principles—ṣidq (honesty), amānah (trustworthiness), the prohibition of tadlīs (fraud), and ʿadālah (justice)—to guide pricing, advertising, product information, and customer relations. Findings show that Sunnah-based ethics provide flexible yet prescriptive guidance aligned with maqāṣid al-sharīʿah, particularly in protecting wealth and life, thereby restoring trust and supporting sustainable growth in the halal ecosystem.

1. INTRODUCTION

The halal trade ecosystem is witnessing an increase in unethical business practices and fraud with its rapid expansion (Koswara & Herlina, 2025). According to recent reports, halal fraud has escalated, whereby careless individuals deceive consumers by fraudulently labelling products or making illegitimate claims of halal status (Voak, 2021). The credibility of the halal market has been undermined by incidents such as the use of counterfeit halal logos, fraudulent online sales, and scandals involving non-halal meat falsely labelled as halal (Daud et al., 2023; Rao et al., 2025). In recent years, Malaysian authorities have noted a significant increase in online fraud cases, primarily related to e-commerce fraud (Mohamad et al., 2024). The trust that halal branding and certification have gradually built up is at risk of being decreased by such developments, which raise serious concerns in the online marketplace (Alourani & Khan, 2024).

This perspective reveals troubling ethical shortcomings in many modern digital marketing practices aimed at Muslim consumers (Koswara & Herlina, 2025). Strategies that rely on deception, manipulation, or the promotion of excessive consumerism stand in clear contrast to Islamic moral values (Koswara & Herlina, 2025). Common examples include sexualised imagery (Islam, 2018), fabricated testimonials (Shahzad et al., 2019), unverified scientific claims, exaggerated promises, and high-pressure sales techniques—all of which compromise ethical integrity in e-commerce marketing. Furthermore, lavish expenditure on opulent advertising campaigns runs counter to Islamic principles that promote restraint and responsibility (Kusmidi, 2023). In addition to transgressing religious principles, such actions erode consumer confidence and may eventually damage the halal industry's long-term standing.

There is still a big hole in the regulations governing advertising content and digital marketing ethics, even with the strict halal standards for finance and products in place (Hadi et al., 2021). No comprehensive halal advertising standard has been formally established, and halal advertising is virtually non-existent in national regulatory frameworks (Fadhillah, 2022). Researchers have also noted that the scholarly conversation about Shariah-compliant marketing is still in its infancy and needs a well-defined framework to direct industry participants in conducting moral halal marketing strategies (Hadi et al., 2021). As noted in the literature, practitioners still lack useful advice for accomplishing this, even though the halal industry is urged to adopt marketing strategies based on Islamic principles (Sohail, 2001).

This context offers a robust foundation for addressing current deficiencies by drawing inspiration from prophetic teachings, particularly the ethical guidance of Prophet Muhammad concerning commerce. (Zuraidah & Aisyah, 2022). The Prophet serves as an example of Islamic business ethics, which place a strong emphasis on truthfulness, openness, fairness, and fulfilling contractual duties in all dealings (Beekun, 1997, n.d.). Integrity is a fundamental principle of marketplace ethics because the Prophet categorically denounced dishonesty, declaring, '*Whoever deceives is not of my community*' (Miswanto, 2021). Improving ethical marketing tactics fits with the halal industry's overarching objective of ethics and sustainability. Ethical marketing encourages social responsibility and reduces unneeded buying (Hashom et al., 2020).

This chapter presents a framework for marketing control that complies with Shariah, specifically designed for the halal online shopping ecosystem, in accordance with the ethical principles of Prophet Muhammad. It is a response to the issues the industry is presently encountering (Khalid et al., 2020). The system's goal is to bring e-commerce practices back in line with Islamic moral standards (Koswara & Herlina, 2025; Susanto, 2024). It also wants to stop unethical digital marketing. The framework incorporates prophetic values such as justice, honesty, trustworthiness, and moderation into modern marketing strategies to foster ethical growth, enhance sustainability, and rebuild consumer confidence in the halal market (Zuraidah & Aisyah, 2022; Koswara & Herlina, 2025; Atieqoh et al., 2023).

This study employs a thematic analysis of select hadiths of Prophet Muhammad to investigate business ethics, ethical transactions, and the prohibition of fraud (Kubaisi, 2024). To underscore the importance of compliance with Shariah law in e-commerce, particularly in marketing communications, several hadiths were selected from this study. The source was primarily derived from reliable and credible hadith compilations, including Ṣaḥīḥ al-Bukhārī, Sunan al-Tirmidhī, Sunan Ibn Mājah, and Ṣaḥīḥ Muslim. Two classical scholars, Imām al-Nawawī and Ibn Ḥajar al-ʿAsqalānī, have backed these up. Furthermore, this study determines the main moral lessons contained in these hadiths and categorises them into key themes, such as the significance of honesty, the prohibition against lying (*tadlīs*), honesty (*ṣidq*), and trust (*amānah*). These broad conclusions can direct the creation of a marketing control framework to address the current requirements and challenges of the digital halal landscape.

2. THE DEVELOPMENT OF HALAL E-COMMERCE AND THE NEED FOR ETHICAL MARKETING CONTROLS

These days halal e-commerce plays a significant role in the global digital economy. It has transformed the way Muslim consumers purchase Shariah-compliant goods and services. People are becoming more aware of their religious identity, and the digital economy is expanding. As a result, there is now more demand for trustworthy halal platforms for distribution, certification, and advertising. Malaysia has been important in this transformation. Two examples of halal-focused platforms that have expanded are HalalStreet and Zilzar. Businesses in the region are now providing business-to-business (B2B) and business-to-customer (B2C) services using Shariah-compliant models.

However, this rapid expansion has also raised significant ethical concerns. Misleading advertising, false claims, and dishonest business practices are the primary factors harming the integrity of halal marketing communications and undermining consumer confidence (Zuraidah & Aisyah, 2022). To address these issues, we require explicit ethical guidelines and a legislative framework that considers the demands of contemporary digital commerce alongside traditional Islamic principles. The Malaysian Communications and Multimedia Commission (MCMC) and Cybersecurity Malaysia have recently released data that shows the number of online fraud cases is still going up. One of the most common types of cybercrime in the country is e-commerce fraud. There were more than 3,000 incidents reported between January and October of 2023 (Azmi et al., 2025).

The reported cases encompass a broad spectrum of fraudulent activities. The reported cases include misleading product descriptions (Jusop et al., 2020; Zuraidah & Aisyah, 2022), price manipulation (Halim & Salleh, 2020), impersonating reputable halal brands (Halim & Salleh, 2020), false advertising (Voak, 2021), and failure to deliver goods post-payment (Arumugam et al., 2021). This situation raises serious concerns about the level of Shariah compliance in product processes and ingredients, as well as in marketing and information dissemination. In this instance, marketing functions as a communication tool to increase Muslim consumers' trust in each brand or product rather than just a sales tool (Alourani & Khan, 2024; Atieqoh et al., 2023). The transparency of information, including ingredients and halal claims, also affects consumer trust in halal products (Mohamed et al., 2013). The dangers of inconsistent marketing include misleading consumers, losing money, damaging Islam's image, and reducing confidence in the nation's halal certification system (Fadhillah, 2022). This goal stands in stark contrast to the goals of *maqāṣid al-sharīʿah*, which emphasise *ḥifẓ al-māl* (protection of wealth) and *ḥifẓ al-nafs* (protection of life) as fundamental principles in business transactions (Arsad et al., 2022).

Furthermore, current regulations from organisations like JAKIM, MCMC, and the Ministry of Domestic Trade and Consumer Affairs (KPDN) are generic and have not been specifically created to address problems in halal e-commerce. Despite the existence of Islamic advertising guidelines and codes of ethics, their application to digital advertising is still limited, particularly in the rapidly changing social media landscape (Fadhillah, 2022; Jaradt, 2020). This difficulty is worsened by the lax enforcement of viral advertising, whether it takes the shape of testimonial displays, brief videos, or soft-selling tactics that frequently inflate and play on consumer emotions (Koswara & Herlina, 2025). Consequently, there is an increasing demand for an online marketing control approach grounded in Shariah principles (Hadi et al., 2021). Such a model would serve as a basis for more extensive public policy and halal certification governance, in addition to providing guidance to industry participants and Muslim digital marketers on how to fulfil their social responsibilities ethically (Islam, 2018). It contributes to the larger goal of developing a sustainable halal industry, which places equal emphasis on consumer welfare, social justice, and the maintenance of Islamic dignity in addition to financial gain (Fageh, 2022). To combat fraud and promote change in the way the halal industry interacts with Muslim customers in an honest, reliable, and professional manner, it is pertinent and important to build a marketing control system that complies with Shariah.

The concept of Islamic marketing is rooted in both classical jurisprudential thought and contemporary scholarly analysis. From the perspective of classical scholars, marketing activities fall under the domain of *fiqh al-muʿāmalāt* (jurisprudence of transactions), where the emphasis is placed on honesty (*ṣidq*), trustworthiness (*amānah*), fairness (*ʿadālah*), and the prohibition of fraudulent concealment (*tadlīs*). Imam al-Nawawi, in his Sharḥ Ṣaḥīḥ Muslim, highlighted the obligation of transparency and truthful disclosure in all business transactions, while Ibn Ḥajar al-ʿAsqalānī, in Fatḥ al-Bārī, elaborated that the Prophet's conduct in marketplaces—such as disclosing product defects and ensuring fair measurement—established binding ethical norms for commercial life.

Building on these principles, contemporary scholars have attempted to articulate Islamic marketing as a distinct discipline within modern business studies. Beekun (1997) framed Islamic business ethics within the higher objectives of Shariah (*maqāṣid al-sharīʿah*), ensuring that marketing contributes to the preservation of wealth (*ḥifẓ al-māl*), the protection of wellbeing (*ḥifẓ al-nafs*), and the promotion of justice (*ʿadālah*). Wilson and Liu (2011) explored the role of emotion and cultural identity in Islamic branding, illustrating how Muslim consumers' behaviour is deeply shaped by faith-based values. More recent studies, such as Ahmad et al. (2016) and Abdullah (2018), examined halal certification and the adoption of Islamic marketing strategies among SMEs, whereas Ali & Suleiman (2017) and Ali et al. (2021) stressed the importance of integrity and transparency across the halal supply chain.

Taken together, these insights define Islamic marketing not simply as a set of promotional techniques for Muslim consumers, but as a comprehensive, Shariah-compliant framework that integrates prophetic ethics, juristic thought, and contemporary business scholarship. This synthesis demonstrates that Islamic marketing is distinguished by its rejection of manipulation and deception and its prioritisation of truthfulness, fairness, and social responsibility in both the physical and digital marketplaces.

In addition to ethical marketing practices, Halal Supply Chain Management (HSCM) has emerged as an essential component in maintaining integrity across the halal industry. At every stage of the value chain, from sourcing and production to storage, logistics, and final marketing, HSCM safeguards halal principles. Ali and Suleiman (2017) conceptualised food integrity from a halal supply chain perspective, identifying transparency and trust as critical elements in preventing contamination, fraud, and unethical practices. More recently, Ali et al. (2021) demonstrated that effective supply chain integration improves halal food supply chain integrity and product quality performance. These findings reinforce that marketing ethics cannot be separated from supply chain integrity: both must operate in tandem to uphold consumer trust, protect wealth (*ḥifẓ al-māl*), and ensure justice (*ʿadālah*) in halal e-commerce.

We can see the relationship between classical and modern Islamic digital marketing theories in the context of timeless ethical principles for contemporary marketplaces. Classical jurists such as Imam al-Nawawi and Ibn Hajar al-ʿAsqalānī, in their commentaries on *ḥadīth*, stressed that *ṣidq* (honesty), *amānah* (trust), the prohibition of *tadlīs* (fraud), and *ʿadālah* (justice) are indispensable to business conduct. Contemporary scholars have built upon this normative foundation by translating these values into frameworks and strategies suited to the digital era. Beekun (1997) conceptualised Islamic business ethics within the *maqāṣid al-sharīʿah*, Wilson and Liu (2011) examined Islamic branding and consumer emotions, while Ali & Suleiman (2017) and Ali et al. (2021) focused on halal supply chain integrity and transparency. Taken together, these works demonstrate that modern Islamic marketing theories are not separate from classical thought but rather extensions and contextual applications of prophetic ethics to the realities of e-commerce, social media, and digital advertising.

In light of this, there is a growing need for an online marketing control model based on Shariah principles (Hadi et al., 2021). Such a model would serve as a basis for more extensive public policy and halal certification governance, in addition to providing guidance to industry participants and Muslim digital marketers on how to fulfil their social responsibilities ethically (Islam, 2018). It contributes to the larger goal of developing a sustainable halal industry, which places equal emphasis on consumer welfare, social justice, and the maintenance of Islamic dignity in addition to financial gain (Fageh, 2022). To combat fraud and promote change in the way the halal industry interacts with Muslim customers in an honest, reliable, and professional manner, it is pertinent and important to build a marketing control system that complies with Shariah (Khalid et al., 2020).

In addition to global perspectives, several regional studies on Halal entrepreneurship further demonstrate the challenges and opportunities faced by Muslim entrepreneurs in Southeast Asia. For instance, research in Malaysia highlights both the motivations and limitations that firms encounter in implementing halal certification, especially among SMEs (Talib et al., 2016). Similarly, studies in Indonesia show that certification agencies have a major influence on halal product development and market acceptance (Hidayat & Siradj, 2015). Consumer religiosity has also been identified as a strong determinant in the intention to choose halal products, influencing entrepreneurial strategies in product positioning (Mukhtar & Butt, 2012). From a brand perspective, Wilson and Liu (2011) emphasise the emotional and cultural complexity of Islamic branding, which directly affects halal entrepreneurs seeking to build consumer trust. Beyond certification and branding, Ali, Tan, and Ismail (2017) propose a supply chain integrity framework that is critical for halal entrepreneurs to maintain transparency across production and distribution networks. Complementing this, Tieman and Ghazali (2014) discuss the importance of halal control activities and assurance mechanisms in logistics operations, which remain essential for ensuring the credibility of halal businesses. Collectively, these regional insights reinforce the urgent need for a Shariah-compliant framework for marketing control that supports ethical entrepreneurship and strengthens consumer trust in the halal e-commerce ecosystem.

3. METHODOLOGY

This study employs a qualitative approach using thematic analysis of selected prophetic traditions (*ḥadīth*) to investigate business ethics, ethical transactions, and the prohibition of fraud (Kubaisi, 2024). The sources were primarily drawn from canonical compilations that enjoy widespread scholarly consensus—Ṣaḥīḥ al-Bukhārī, Ṣaḥīḥ Muslim, Sunan al-Tirmidhī, and Sunan Ibn Mājah.

The analysis followed three systematic steps: (i) identification of *ḥadīths* related to ethical conduct in trade and marketing, (ii) coding of recurring ethical principles such as *ṣidq* (honesty), *amānah* (trust), *tadlīs* (fraudulent concealment), and *ʿadālah* (justice), and (iii) categorisation of these principles into broader thematic clusters.

To ensure scholarly rigour, the interpretations of the classical commentators Imām al-Nawawī in Sharḥ Ṣaḥīḥ Muslim and Ibn Ḥajar al-ʿAsqalānī in Fatḥ al-Bārī were consulted to contextualise the moral lessons derived from the selected traditions. This foundational understanding was subsequently linked to modern issues in digital marketing.

The chapter is theoretically anchored in *Maqāṣid al-sharīʿah* as its grand theory, particularly the objectives of protecting wealth (*ḥifẓ al-māl*) and wellbeing (*ḥifẓ al-nafs*). These objectives provide the normative framework, while the thematic analysis of the *ḥadīths* serves as the middle-range theory that operationalises prophetic ethics in the practical dimensions of Islamic digital marketing. Together, this methodological approach ensures both classical authenticity and contemporary relevance in developing the proposed Shariah-Compliant Online Marketing Control Framework (PEMASTI).

4. FOUNDATIONAL ETHICAL PRINCIPLES OF MARKETING IN ISLAM

In Islam, marketing activities are a type of social interaction that carries ethical, legal, and spiritual responsibility towards Allah and fellow humans, rather than just being commercial endeavours with the goal of boosting profit (Haryono, 2022). Justice, honesty, reliability, openness of information, and the prohibition of any kind of deception, coercion, or manipulation are the cornerstones of Islamic marketing ethics (Sulaiman et al., 2020). The guiding principles of Islamic marketing ethics are rooted in the Qur'an and the Sunnah, the two primary sources of Shariah, and later expanded through the traditional and contemporary scholarship of *fiqh al-muʿāmalāt*.

Sūrat al-Baqarah (2:188) says that Allah SWT does not allow people to take someone else's money without permission, especially if they do it in a dishonest or unfair way (Sahabi & Baide, 2021). This ban is a beneficial start for fighting against misleading ads or marketing that use information manipulation or take advantage of people's weaknesses (Li et al., 2022). In Sūrat al-Isrā' verse 35, Allah also wants fairness in weighing and measuring. This approach reflects the necessity for transparency and integrity in all business transactions and product communications (Sawandi et al., 2018).

Islamic marketing ethics also forbid *ikhtilāṭ al-ḥaqq bi al-bāṭil* (mixing truth with falsehood), *tadlīs* (hiding flaws), and *gharar* (too much uncertainty), according to Al-Suwailem (2000). In simple terms, this means that marketers or sellers can't hide flaws in their products, use deceiving visuals to change how people perceive them, or use psychological tricks like false scarcity or fear-based marketing (Wu et al., 2021). The Prophet Muhammad told people not to cheat in business many times. The Prophet said in a The Prophet said in an authentic *ḥadīth*, '*Whoever cheats is not of us*' (Miswanto, 2021). In a different story, the Prophet chastised a vendor for hiding moisture at the base of a grain pile, asking, '*Why didn't you put the wet portion on top so people could see it?*' He went on to stress that such dishonesty is incompatible with the integrity expected of a genuine Muslim businessperson (Humaidi & Muchtar, 2020). These *ḥadīths* are legal principles that directly affect whether or not commercial transactions are permitted, in addition to being moral precepts.

Islamic marketing ethics emphasises *amānah* (trustworthiness), in addition to honesty and transparency (Beekun, 1997). *Amānah* suggests that in the context of marketing, marketers should safeguard customers' interests just as they would their own. In Iḥyā᾽ ʿUlūm al-Dīn, Imām al-Ghazālī clarified that the prophets, the truthful, and the martyrs would be joined by genuinely honest and reliable traders in the Hereafter (Shuaib & Badmus, 2022). '*The honest and trustworthy merchant will be with the prophets, the truthful, and the martyrs,*' according to a *ḥadīth* recounted by al-Tirmidhī (Maishanu & Dutsin-ma, 2012). This demonstrates that in the Islamic perspective, the role of a marketer is far from insignificant and is respected when performed in line with prophetic ethics.

Furthermore, Islam forbids the use of sexual content, slander, or unfulfilled promises in marketing, as well as any other kind of coercion or extreme influence (Fadhillah, 2022). This includes strategies like clickbait, phoney ratings, phoney testimonials, and algorithms that are intended to deceive customers into making illogical decisions in the modern world (Koswara & Herlina, 2025). Under Islamic law, such acts are defined as *ghabn fāḥish*, or serious fraud of price or information, which may cancel a deal and make the attacker a sinner.

Maqāṣid al-sharīʿah's goals are to protect the five core values of religion, life, intellect, lineage, and wealth. These goals are closely related to marketing in Islam (Swadjaja et al., 2019). Marketing experts care about *hifẓ al-māl* (protecting wealth) and *ḥifẓ al-nafs* (protecting consumers from harm) (Arsad et al., 2022). Therefore, an Islamic marketing strategy based on *maqāṣid* wants to keep social trust, make online shopping fairer, and help customers as well as stop fraud. Recent studies indicate that Islamic marketing strategies can cultivate lasting, self-reinforcing producer-consumer relationships (Wilson & Grant, 2013).

5. THEMATIC ANALYSIS OF PROPHETIC PRINCIPLES IN MARKETING AND FRAUD PREVENTION

The second principle asserts that visual manipulation, misleading wording, or deceptive displays of information must not be employed to obscure flaws or mislead users. Furthermore, acts of fraud, distortion, or *tadlīs* are strictly prohibited (Kamilulloh & Ambardi, 2022; Lubis & Ismaulina, 2020). A *ḥadīth* narrated by Imām Muslim recounts an incident where the Prophet admonished a vendor who concealed moisture at the bottom of a grain pile, questioning, '*Why didn't you place the wet part on top so that the people could see it?*' He subsequently declared, '*Whoever cheats is not one of us.*' Classical commentators have offered profound explanations for these prophetic principles. Imam al-Nawawi, in his Sharḥ Ṣaḥīḥ Muslim, emphasised that honesty (*ṣidq*) and trustworthiness (*amānah*) are fundamental to all commercial transactions, asserting that any form of *tadlīs* (fraudulent concealment) is categorically forbidden. He articulated that the Prophet's declaration, "Whoever deceives is not of us," serves as definitive proof that ethical transparency is a religious obligation rather than merely a moral suggestion. Similarly, Ibn Ḥajar al-ʿAsqalānī, in Fatḥ al-Bārī, elaborated that the hadiths prohibiting deceit in trade encompass all forms of manipulation, including false advertising, misrepresentation of quality, and the concealment of product defects. He posited that the Prophet's practice of openly displaying goods and disclosing their condition established a binding precedent for Muslim entrepreneurs, rendering integrity and justice (*ʿadālah*) inseparable from Islamic business ethics.

These classical insights are relevant in today's digital marketplace, where manipulative techniques often mirror the very forms of *tadlīs* condemned in prophetic traditions. This *ḥadīth* serves as a stern reminder that any kind of dishonesty, even in trivial or obscure matters, is enough to disqualify someone from prophetic ethics. This ban is particularly related to digital marketing strategies like image manipulation, phoney testimonials, using 'halal' labels that are not verified, and fabricating reviews on e-commerce sites (Voak, 2021). All of these are classified as contemporary *tadlīs*, which are expressly prohibited by Shariah.

In Islam, marketing activities are a type of social interaction that carries ethical, legal, and spiritual responsibility towards Allah and fellow humans, rather than just being commercial endeavours with the goal of boosting profit (Haryono, 2022). Justice, honesty, reliability, openness of information, and the prohibition of any kind of deception, coercion, or manipulation are the cornerstones of Islamic marketing ethics (Sulaiman et al., 2020). The guiding principles of Islamic marketing ethics are rooted in the Qur'an and the Sunnah, the two primary sources of Shariah, and later expanded through the traditional and contemporary scholarship of fiqh al-muʿāmalāt.

Sūrat al-Baqarah (2:188) says that Allah SWT does not allow people to take someone else's money without permission, especially if they do it in a dishonest or unfair way (Sahabi & Baide, 2021). This ban is a beneficial start for fighting against misleading ads or marketing that use information manipulation or take advantage of people's weaknesses (Li et al., 2022). In Sūrat al-Isrāʾ verse 35, Allah also wants fairness in weighing and measuring. This is similar to how all business dealings and product communications should be open and honest (Sawandi et al., 2018).

Islamic marketing ethics also forbid *ikhtilāṭ al-ḥaqq bi al-bāṭil* (mixing truth with falsehood), *tadlīs* (hiding flaws), and *gharar* (too much uncertainty), according to Al-Suwailem (2000). In simple terms, this means that marketers or sellers can't hide flaws in their products, use deceiving visuals to change how people perceive them, or use psychological tricks like false scarcity or fear-based marketing (Wu et al., 2021). The Prophet Muhammad told people not to cheat in business many times. The Prophet stated in an authentic *ḥadīth*, "Whoever cheats is not of us" (Miswanto, 2021). In a different story, the Prophet chastised a vendor for hiding moisture at the base of a grain pile, asking, "Why didn't you put the wet portion on top so people could see it? He went on to stress that such dishonesty is incompatible with the integrity expected of a genuine Muslim businessperson (Humaidi & Muchtar, 2020). These *ḥadīths* are legal principles that directly affect whether or not commercial transactions are permitted, in addition to being moral precepts.

Islamic marketing ethics emphasises *amānah (trustworthiness),* in addition to honesty and transparency (Beekun, 1997). *Amānah* suggests that in the context of marketing, marketers should safeguard customers' interests just as they would their own. In Iḥyā᾽ 'Ulūm al-Dīn, Imām al-Ghazālī clarified that the prophets, the truthful, and the martyrs would be joined by genuinely honest and reliable traders in the Hereafter (Shuaib & Badmus, 2022). '*The honest and trustworthy merchant will be with the prophets, the truthful, and the martyrs*,' according to a *ḥadīth* recounted by al-Tirmidhī (Maishanu & Dutsin-ma, 2012). This demonstrates that in the Islamic perspective, the role of a marketer is far from insignificant and is respected when performed in line with prophetic ethics.

Furthermore, Islam forbids the use of sexual content, slander, or unfulfilled promises in marketing, as well as any other kind of coercion or extreme influence (Fadhillah, 2022). This includes strategies like clickbait, phoney ratings, phoney testimonials, and algorithms that are intended to deceive customers into making illogical decisions in the modern world (Koswara & Herlina, 2025). Under Islamic law, such acts are defined as *ghabn fāḥish*, or serious fraud of price or information, which may cancel a deal and make the attacker a sinner.

Maqāṣid al-sharī'ah's goals are to protect the five core values of religion, life, intellect, lineage, and wealth. These goals are closely related to marketing in Islam (Swadjaja et al., 2019). Marketing experts care about *hifẓ al-māl* (protecting wealth) and *ḥifẓ al-nafs* (protecting consumers from harm) (Arsad et al., 2022). Therefore, an Islamic marketing strategy based on *maqāṣid* wants to keep social trust, make online shopping fairer, and help customers as well as stop fraud. Recent studies indicate that Islamic marketing strategies can cultivate lasting, self-reinforcing producer-consumer relationships (Wilson & Grant, 2013).

6. DEVELOPING A SHARIAH-COMPLIANT ONLINE MARKETING CONTROL FRAMEWORK

The development of the Shariah-Compliant Online Marketing Control Framework (KKK-PEMASTI) is anchored in *Maqāṣid al-sharī'ah* as its grand theory. Within this paradigm, the thematic analysis of prophetic *ḥadīths* serves as a middle-range theory that operationalises the objectives of Shariah into practical marketing controls.

An approach that is grounded in revelatory sources, methodically organised, and practically in line with the current digital ecosystem is necessary for the creation of a truly Shariah-compliant online marketing control framework (Utami & Basrowi, 2021). A synthesis effort is required to convert those values into a set of control guidelines relevant to halal e-commerce platforms, based on the thematic analysis of prophetic marketing principles previously discussed (Hamdan et al., 2022). This framework acts as a moral compass and safeguard against deception and improper use in marketing communications (Koswara & Herlina, 2025). It must fulfil two principal functions: the normative function, based on *maqāṣid* and Shariah principles, and the operational function, significant to legislators, business proprietors, and marketers (Hadi et al., 2021).

The initial phase in the development process involves the examination of the Shariah foundations, which are sourced from the Qur'an, Sunnah, and *fiqh al-mu'āmalāt* discourse. These talks provide guidance on honesty, openness, not lying, and fairness in business deals (Shafin & Kasim, 2018). These principles are subsequently implemented in four primary domains of control: management of product information, oversight of pricing and promotional strategies, governance of social responsibility and consumer relations, and regulation of visual and narrative presentation (Nasir et al., 2020; Wulandari & Hasriadi, 2022). The framework mandates the provision of clear, accurate, and truthful information for all products advertised online (Jusop et al., 2020; Zuraidah & Aisyah, 2022). The data includes details about the product's halal certification status, ingredients, manufacturer and distributor, how to use it, and any side effects that might happen. To avoid confusion, this kind of information should be given in plain language instead of technical terms. This section is crucial because many fraud cases in halal e-commerce involve people lying about a product or leaving out important information (Shahzad et al., 2019).

The framework proposes guidelines for visual presentation in the available domain that involve voiceovers, images, videos, and marketing-related graphics. These presentations must not be misleading or manipulative, nor can they include false information about a product's actual functionality, recommendations, or images (Koswara and Herlina, 2021). They also need to follow Islamic moral rules about how to dress, act, and value moderation (Fadhillah, 2022). Marketing strategies that encourage extravagant lifestyles, objectify women, or exploit religious symbols for profit frequently result in unethical conduct on social media (Arbak et al., 2019; Harun et al., 2021).

The third area is controlling prices and marketing strategies. The framework states that all forms of price reduction, discounts, time-limited offers, or exclusive pricing must be based on authentic, original prices rather than artificially inflated ones (Mudrikah & Ayuningtyas, 2021). It is necessary to stop practices like raising the "original price" in advance to provide the appearance of a discount (Islam, 2018). The principles of *gharar* and *tadlīs*, which are forbidden in Shariah, are also incompatible with strategies like phoney urgency and fictitious limited quantities (Arianti & Yunarti, 2022; Febriandika et al., 2022; Handoko et al., 2022; Nasir et al., 2020). The framework also recommends the clear and upfront disclosure of hidden costs, including processing, delivery, and post-order fees (Zuraidah & Aisyah, 2022).

Consumer relations and marketers' social responsibility are the main topics of the fourth domain. Islam views the relationship between buyers and sellers as a social interaction founded on the concepts of maṣlaḥah and iḥsān, rather than just a transaction (Sodikin, 2020; Suhanda & Fahrullah, 2020). Because of this, digital marketers need to ensure that their guarantees, return policies, and customer service systems are all clear and easy to understand (Rahman & Ahamat, 2020; Sholikhin & Amijaya, 2019). They should also avoid using emotional tactics to change people's minds, like guilt-based messages or FOMO (Islam, 2018; Shahzad et al., 2019).

The Shariah-Compliant Online Marketing Control Framework (KKK-PEMASTI) will be the framework that connects all of these parts. This model could become the standard for halal e-commerce sites around the world as well as in the USA (Muslimin et al., 2022; Utami & Basrowi, 2021). As a result, people could obtain more certifications, like a Ministry of Trade Halal Digital Marketing Certificate or a JAKIM (Latif, 2020). Consumers, platform operators, regulators, and logistics providers all use this method to assess and balance online marketing content (Kamilulloh & Ambardi, 2022; Muhammad et al., 2019).

KKK-PEMASTI was developed with input from industry professionals, scholars of *fiqh al-muʿāmalāt*, and consumer law experts through sessions, interviews, and cross-validation. Thus, the framework is both practical and theoretical. Its main goals are to minimise fraud, boost Muslim consumers' trust in halal e-commerce, and support an ethical and responsible industry that corresponds with Malaysia Madani's vision and the principles of maqāṣid *al-sharīʿah* (Mohamad & Kashi, 2017)..

7. POLICY RECOMMENDATIONS AND PRACTICAL APPLICATIONS

The Shariah-Compliant Online Marketing Control Framework (KKK-PEMASTI) developed in this study is relevant to industry practices and policy implementation, in addition to being normative and conceptual. As the halal digital ecosystem becomes more competitive and complicated, the need for ethical and Shariah-based guidance is growing. As a result, this framework needs a lot of policy support and careful actions by the right authorities, not just individual efforts or corporate awareness.

Creating a specific halal digital marketing standard to supplement the current halal certification systems is one of the main policy suggestions. In Malaysia and many other Muslim-majority nations, halal certification has up until now mostly concentrated on ingredients, procedures, and logistics; marketing communication has not been vetted or closely watched. The creation of an extra certification module under JAKIM or other halal organisations, like the Shariah-Compliant Advertisement Compliance Certificate (SPIPS), would provide Islamically based promotional content legitimacy and stop the dissemination of deceptive advertising. This action is also in line with JAKIM's Pelan Transformasi *al-Falah* goals, which include ensuring human well-being via an integrated Islamic economic and social approach.

Policy-making organisations like the Malaysian Communications and Multimedia Commission (MCMC) and the Ministry of Domestic Trade and Cost of Living (KPDN) must also work together to develop a Shariah-based code of ethics for digital advertising that applies to all operators of e-commerce platforms, including foreign businesses doing business in Muslim countries. This code might be made mandatory for business licences or provided as a reward for industry participants who choose to abide by it. Since online marketing concerns touch on consumer protection, data governance, cyber law, social media supervision, and halal standards, such cross-agency collaboration is essential.

Education, training, and industry empowerment must be the main focuses of practical application initiatives in addition to policy formulation. Technology firms, halal industry training facilities, and higher education institutions should take the initiative to provide Shariah-compliant digital marketing training modules to Muslim business owners, especially those in small and medium-sized enterprises (SMEs). Some of these training modules are basic *fiqh al-muʿāmalāt*, media literacy, promotional ethics, understanding *maqāṣid al-sharīʿah*, and how to design ethical content. These kinds of programmes can help create a new generation of skilled and responsible Muslim marketers, which will help the industry grow in a way that values both honesty and making money.

Useful apps can also start at the platform level. Online stores like Shopee, Lazada, TikTok Shop, and HalalStreet could use tagging systems or special badges for ads that have been checked to ensure they follow Shariah law. For instance, they could implement "Shariah-Verified Promotion" or "Ethical Halal Ad". Not only does this system make customers feel surer about their choices, but it also pushes other advertisers to obey the rules so they can stay competitive. Additionally, platforms can collaborate with Islamic institutions and consumer NGOs to monitor the situation and provide users with specific methods to report ads that are misleading or do not adhere to the rules.

Subtle *da'wah* efforts can also be advantageous in helping Muslim communities create a marketing culture that follows Shariah. Mosques, independent preachers, and religious leaders can use social media to remind people how important it is to keep consumer information private, do business ethically, and promote themselves in the right way. If these values are taught from the ground up, it will be possible to create a more moral Muslim business culture that is based on understanding and following the teachings of Prophet Muhammad rather than just enforcing them.

All proposed initiatives for the expansion of the halal industry should align with the overarching framework of the Sustainable Development Goals (SDGs) and the Malaysia Madani agenda, which prioritise social sustainability, economic equity, and human welfare. Incorporating KKK-PEMASTI into the regulations for halal digital markets will enhance the Muslim e-commerce ecosystem and position the country as a global leader in establishing significant and trustworthy Islamic digital marketing standards.

8. CONCLUSION

Based on a thematic analysis of prophetic ethical principles, this chapter presents a scholarly and practical endeavour to develop a Shariah-compliant online marketing control framework in the context of halal e-commerce. The conversation began with the backdrop of the halal digital industry's explosive growth before outlining several new issues brought on by the absence of regulations in marketing communication, such as the increase in fraudulent activity, the improper use of halal symbols, and the transgression of Islamic ethical standards in advertising tactics. The industry's reputation as a whole could be harmed, and Muslim consumers' faith in the halal market could be undermined if these problems are not methodically resolved.

The study identified four fundamental principles that underpin Islamic marketing ethics by consulting primary Shariah sources and collections of authentic *ḥadīths*. These principles include honesty and trustworthiness, the prohibition of *tadlīs* and fraud, transparency in the presentation of product information, and fairness in pricing and promotional strategies. These principles not only direct Muslim marketers in making ethical decisions but also provide the framework for shaping a marketplace that is just, accountable, and sustainable.

These demands led to the proposal of a control framework known as KKK-PEMASTI, which includes four primary areas: social responsibility towards customers, visual and narrative presentation, pricing and promotional strategy, and product information control. The operational and normative framework is subject to change by a wide range of stakeholders, including lawmakers, platform operators, marketing firms, and halal certification organisations. It also allows for new rules, industry training, and special certifications to make Muslim digital marketers who are honest and deserving.

More importantly, the way this chapter demonstrates that prophetic ideas remain relevant despite changes in the digital economy. If the Sunnah of Prophet Muhammad is meticulously analysed and transformed into practical frameworks, it can serve as a reference for industrial and public policy strategies, as well as personal ethics. One of the goals of *Maqāṣid Al-sharīʿah* is to protect the Muslim community's wealth, honour, and trust, even in the increasingly complicated virtual economy. By aligning it with prophetic ethics, Muslims can elevate halal digital marketing beyond mere transactions. It becomes a way to build trust, protect consumers, and show how Islamic principles can help make modern economic systems more accountable and fairer. This programme helps rebuild public trust in the halal sector and supports an open, sustainable, and well-focused business ecosystem..

ACKNOWLEDGEMENT

The Ministry of Higher Education (MoHE) paid for this work through the Fundamental Research Grant Scheme (FRGS) programme, with project code USIM/FRGS/FPQS/KPT/52224. I am deeply grateful to the Ministry for providing the funding that enabled this study.

REFERENCES

Abdullah, J. B. (2018). Islamic marketing mix: Is there a role for Islamic-based strategies? *International Journal of Islamic Marketing and Branding*, *3*(1), 15. DOI: 10.1504/IJIMB.2018.091650

Ahmad, A. N., Rahman, R. A., Othman, M., & Abidin, U. F. U. Z. (2016). Critical success factors affecting the implementation of halal food management: Perspectives of halal executives, consultants, and auditors. *Food Control*, *74*, 70–78. DOI: 10.1016/j.foodcont.2016.11.031

Al-Suwailem, S. (2000). Towards An Objective Measure of *Gharar* in Exchange. *Islamic Economic Studies*, *61*. https://www.irti.org/English/Research/Documents/IES/119.pdf

Ali, M. H., Iranmanesh, M., Tan, K. H., Zailani, S., & Omar, N. A. (2021). Impact of supply chain integration on halal food supply chain integrity and food quality performance. *Journal of Islamic Marketing*, *13*(7), 1515–1534. DOI: 10.1108/JIMA-08-2020-0250

Ali, M. H., & Suleiman, N. (2017). Eleven shades of food integrity: A halal supply chain perspective. *Trends in Food Science & Technology*, *71*, 216–224. DOI: 10.1016/j.tifs.2017.11.016

Alourani, A., & Khan, S. (2024). A Blockchain and Artificial Intelligence-Based System for Halal Food Traceability. arXiv (Cornell University). https://doi.org//arxiv.2410.07305DOI: 10.48550

Arbak, S., Islam, R., & Rasyid, H. A. (2019). Influence of Islamic Advertising: Ethical Violation of Customer Purchase Intention of Halal Cosmetic Products in Malaysia. *Humanities & Social Sciences Reviews*, *7*(3), 671–682. DOI: 10.18510/hssr.2019.7398

Arianti, F., & Yunarti, S. (2022). Price Changes in A Limited Time in Home Shopping Program on RTV Television Media From the Perspective of Islamic Law. AL- ADALAH, 19(2), 357. DOI: 10.24042/adalah.v19i2.10316

Arsad, S., Said, R., Yusoff, H., & Ahmad, R. (2022). Islamic Corporate Social Responsibility Disclosure Index: The Application of Maqasid Shari'ah and Maslahah. *International Journal of Academic Research in Business & Social Sciences, 12*(7). Advance online publication. DOI: 10.6007/IJARBSS/v12-i7/14331

Arumugam, N., Mohamad, F., Shanthi, A., & Dharinee, S. (2021). A Study on Online Shopping Scams. *International Journal of Social Science Research, 10*(1), 22. DOI: 10.5296/ijssr.v10i1.19290

Atieqoh, S., Waseso, H. P., & Hamidi, A. (2023). *Halal Certificate and Public Trust Local Food and Beverage Business Development. In economics, business and management research/Advances in Economics, Business and Management Research.* Atlantis Press., DOI: 10.2991/978-94-6463-188-3_9

Azmi, S. N. S., Jais, Z., Samsudin, S. N., Hasini, N. F. M., Izhar, N. I., Idris, N. A., & Hashim, A. H. A. (2025). A Qualitative Approach of KAP Model Against Online Scams in Malaysia. *International Journal of Academic Research in Business & Social Sciences, 15*(2). Advance online publication. DOI: 10.6007/IJARBSS/v15-i2/24701

Beekun, R. I. (1997). *Islamic Business Ethics.* International Institute of Islamic Thought., DOI: 10.2307/j.ctvk8w1zv

Daud, A. H. M., Lee, U. H. M. S., & Ismail, A. (2023). The Practice of Halal Certification: A Case of Malaysia's Halal Meat-Based Industry. *International Journal of Academic Research in Business & Social Sciences, 13*(8). Advance online publication. DOI: 10.6007/IJARBSS/v13-i8/17666

Fadhillah, A. R. (2022). Contemporary Advertising in Islamic Perspective. *Jurnal Peurawi Media Kajian Komunikasi Islam, 5*(1), 1. DOI: 10.22373/jp.v5i1.12011

Fageh, A. (2022). Building a Synergy Between the Halal Industry and the Green Industry in the Maqasid Syari'ah Review as the Basis of Islamic Economics. *Journal of Islamic Economic Laws, 5*(1), 139–158. DOI: 10.23917/jisel.v5i1.17034

Febriandika, N. R., Tsany, N. P., & Sriplod, T. (2022). Marketing Strategy of *Gharar* Business Schemes: Mystery Box on the e-Commerce Shopee Platform. *ISLAMUNA Jurnal Studi Islam, 9*(1), 26–40. DOI: 10.19105/islamuna.v9i1.6028

Hadi, M. Q. A., Cahyo, E. N., & Budi, I. S. (2021). Marketing Ethics at Islamic Banks: Principles and Practices. *Journal of Islamic Economic Laws, 4*(2), 17–41. DOI: 10.23917/jisel.v4i2.14716

Halim, M. A. A., & Salleh, M. M. (2020). Consumer rights in halal products: A study based on legal and Syariah perspectives. *Food Research, 4*(S1), 281–290. DOI: 10.26656/fr.2017.4(S1).S31

Hamdan, U., Azzulala, B. N., & Nasifah. (2022). Urgensi Spiritual Marketing dan Marketing Syariah dalam Dunia Bisnis. IQTISHADIA Jurnal Ekonomi & Perbankan Syariah, 9(1), 27. DOI: 10.19105/iqtishadia.v9i1.5483

Handoko, P., Ibrahim, D., & Bukhari, K. (2022). the Law of Dropshipping Buying According to Madzhab Malikiyah and Syafi'iyah. *Nurani Jurnal Kajian Syari Ah Dan Masyarakat, 22*(1), 31–50. DOI: 10.19109/nurani.v22i1.11236

Harun, M. F. M., Albakry, N. S., Husain, A. H., & Arif, H. (2021). The Commodification of Religion as Symbolic Interactionism in Advertising. *International Journal of Academic Research in Business & Social Sciences, 11*(18). Advance online publication. DOI: 10.6007/IJARBSS/v11-i18/11426

Haryono, H. (2022). Awareness of the Islamic social reporting (ISR) disclosure: A case study of companies listed in the Jakarta Islamic Index (JII). [Jurnal Penelitian Pendidikan Indonesia]. *JPPI, 8*(2), 348. DOI: 10.29210/020221547

Hashom, H., Ariffin, A. S., Sabar, R., & Ahmad, H. (2020). Halal-Logistics Value Chain on Firm Performances: A Conceptual Framework. *International Journal on Food Agriculture and Natural Resources, 1*(2), 8–14. DOI: 10.46676/ij-fanres.v1i2.10

Humaidi, M. N., & Muchtar, A. M. (2020). the Salient Features of Medina Market in Early Islam and its Relevance Today. *El-Barka Journal of Islamic Economics and Business, 3*(2), 162–188. DOI: 10.21154/elbarka.v3i2.2434

Islam, M. M. (2018). Islamic marketing practice as a panacea to social marketing criticism. *International Journal of Islamic Marketing and Branding, 3*(2), 104. DOI: 10.1504/IJIMB.2018.094080

Jaradt, N. (2020). *Legitimacy Controls of Commercial Advertisements: A Comparative Study*. International Affairs and Global Strategy., DOI: 10.7176/IAGS/87-03

Jusop, M., Ismail, R. M., & Ismail, N. A. (2020). Managing Information Quality in B2C Companies: An Empirical Investigation on Halal e-Commerce Websites. [iJIM]. *International Journal of Interactive Mobile Technologies, 14*(17), 97. DOI: 10.3991/ijim.v14i17.16651

Kamilulloh, F., & Ambardi, P. (2022). Multi-Level Marketing Paradigm in Islam. *I-Best Islamic Banking & Economic Law Studies, 1*(2), 103–115. DOI: 10.36769/ibest.v1i2.252

Khalid, K., Aya, A., Ali, , Khaled, , & Ahmad, . (2020). Impact of Halal Digital Marketing on Consumer Behaviour: Jordan's Perspective. *International Journal of Economics and Business Administration, 202*(Special Issue 1), 202–215. Advance online publication. DOI: 10.35808/ijeba/537

Koswara, A., & Herlina, L. (2025). The Ethical Deviations of AI in Marketing Practices: A Critical Review from Halal Perspectives [Review of the Ethical Deviations of AI in Marketing Practices: A Critical Review from Halal Perspectives]. *Review of Islamic Economics, 2*(2), 105–116. DOI: 10.58777/rie.v2i2.393

Kubaisi, A. A. S. H. A. (2024). Ethics of Artificial Intelligence: A Purposeful and Foundational Study in Light of the Sunnah of Prophet Muhammad. *Religions, 15*(11), 1300. DOI: 10.3390/rel15111300

Kusmidi, H. (2023). An Overview of Islam and Religious Moderation: Concept, Principles, and Indicators. *Jurnal Ilmiah Syi Ar, 22*(2), 168. DOI: 10.29300/syr.v22i2.8752

Latif, M. A. (2020). *Halal International Standards and Certification.*, DOI: 10.1002/9781118823026.ch14

Li, C. H., Chan, O. L. K., Chow, Y. T., Zhang, X., Tong, P., Li, S. P., Ng, H. Y., & Keung, K. L. (2022). Evaluating the Effectiveness of Digital Content Marketing Under a Mixed Reality Training Platform on the Online Purchase Intention. *Frontiers in Psychology, 13*, 881019. Advance online publication. DOI: 10.3389/fpsyg.2022.881019 PMID: 35846680

Lubis, U. R., & Ismaulina, I. (2020). Tadlis Dalam Bisnis Jual Beli Online Perspektif Ekonomi Syariah (Studi Mahasiswa Ekonomi Syariah Febi Iain Lhokseumawe). [JESKaPe]. *Jurnal Ekonomi Syariah Akuntansi Dan Perbankan, 4*(2), 247–256. DOI: 10.52490/jeskape.v4i2.799

Maishanu, M. M., & Dutsin-ma, A. M. (2012). Business management and ethics: An Islamic approach. *Business Review (Federal Reserve Bank of Philadelphia)*, 7(2), 113–118. DOI: 10.54784/1990-6587.1208

Miswanto, A. (2021). Moral Hazard in Market Activities: A Textual and Contextual Perspective Review of Hadith. *Cakrawala Jurnal Studi Islam, 16*(1), 13–28. DOI: 10.31603/cakrawala.4222

Mohamad, A., & Kashi, A. (2017). Does an Islamic Finance Industry Need a Unification of Standards? A Qualitative Discussion. *Arab Law Quarterly, 31*(4), 336–362. DOI: 10.1163/15730255-12313031

Mohamad, A. R., Yaakop, M. R., & Razif, M. A. B. M. (2024). the Efficacy of the Malaysian Government's Response towards Cybercrime. *Open Journal of Political Science, 14*(1), 166–176. DOI: 10.4236/ojps.2024.141010

Mohamed, Z., Shamsudin, M. N., & Rezai, G. (2013). The Effect of Possessing Information About the Halal Logo on Consumer Confidence in Malaysia. *Journal of International Food & Agribusiness Marketing, 25*(sup1), 73–86. DOI: 10.1080/08974438.2013.800008

Mudrikah, S., & Ayuningtyas, R. D. (2021). Ethics of Islamic Consumption Behaviour on Discount Promotion and Flash Sale (Overview of Theoretical Economics of Umar bin Al-Khattab). *AKSES Jurnal Ekonomi Dan Bisnis, 16*(2). Advance online publication. DOI: 10.31942/akses.v16i2.5553

Muhammad, M. Z., Amboala, T., Salleh, M. Z. M., Abdullah, A., Tahrim, S. N. C., & Nawi, N. C. (2019). The Application of Shariah Principle in E-commerce Transaction: A Model Development. *Review of World Economics, 10*(2), 84. DOI: 10.5430/rwe.v10n2p84

Muslimin, J., Lubis, S., Putra, R., Nahartini, D., & Wafa, A. (2022). Islamic Branding and Digital Marketing: A Strategy to Attract Muslim Consumers' Buying Interest. DOI: 10.4108/eai.20-10-2021.2316313

Nasir, N. F., Roslin, R. M., Nasir, M., & Nasir, M. N. F. (2020). Marketing strategies from the Islamic perspective: Reviewing the relevance of elements of the marketing mix. *Journal of Emerging Economies and Islamic Research, 8*(3), 84. DOI: 10.24191/jeeir.v8i3.9952

Rahman, W. F. I. W. A., & Ahamat, H. (2020). Consumer Protection under Shariah Law in Islamic Religious Tourism. *International Journal of Asian Social Science, 10*(5), 262–272. DOI: 10.18488/journal.1.2020.105.262.272

Rao, S. X., Han, Z., Yin, H., Jiang, J., Zhang, Z., Zhao, Y., & Shan, Y. (2025). Fraud detection at eBay. *Emerging Markets Review, 101277*, 101277. Advance online publication. DOI: 10.1016/j.ememar.2025.101277

Sahabi, A., & Baide, K. (2021). Al-Amwal According to the Qur'an: Using the Maudhu'i Method. *Talaa Journal of Islamic Finance, 1*(1), 1–16. DOI: 10.54045/talaa.v1i1.253

Sawandi, N., Intan, T. P., Bakar, A. A., Shaari, H., Puteri, T., Saad, R. A. J., & Amran, N. A. (2018). The Delineation of the Islamic Accounting Concepts through the Narrative Reviews Interpretation. *The Journal of Social Sciences Research, 348*(SPI6), 348–352. Advance online publication. DOI: 10.32861/jssr.spi6.348.352

Shafin, N., & Kasim, R. (2018). Incorporating Islamic Ethical Elements into the Marketing Mix Paradigm. *Financial Risk and Management Reviews*, *4*(1), 24–33. DOI: 10.18488/journal.89.2018.41.24.33

Shahzad, A., Naseer, S., & Khurshid, A. (2019). Friend or Foe: An Islamic Ethical Perspective on the Online Consumers' Reviews. *Journal of Islamic Business and Management*, *9*(1). Advance online publication. DOI: 10.26501/jibm/2019.0901-013

Sholikhin, M., & Amijaya, R. N. F. (2019). E-Commerce Based on the Law of Buying and Selling in Islam. *KnE Social Sciences*, *3*(13), 1360. DOI: 10.18502/kss.v3i13.4290

Shuaib, A. J., & Badmus, S. S. (2022). Al-Ghazālī's Perspective of Salam and Its Relevance to E-Commerce in Nigeria. *Journal of Islamic Economic and Business Research*, *2*(2), 156–171. DOI: 10.18196/jiebr.v2i2.62

Sodikin, M. (2020). Competitive Advantages of Sharia Banks: Role of Ihsan Behaviour and Digital Marketing in the New Normal. *Journal of Digital Marketing and Halal Industry*, *2*(1), 1–14. DOI: 10.21580/jdmhi.2020.2.1.5769

Sohail, M. S. (2001). Strategies for Expanding and Promoting Business to and Beyond Muslim Markets. SSRN Electronic Journal. https://papers.ssrn.com/sol3/Delivery.cfm/SSRN_ID2649547_code811236.pdf?abstractid=2649547&mirid=1&type=2

Suhanda, R., & Fahrullah, A. (2020). Islamic Business Ethics on Customer Retention. DOI: 10.2991/icracos-19.2020.12

Sulaiman, S. M., Muhammad, A. D., & Sabiu, T. T. (2020). Islamic Business Ethics Practice among Muslim Entrepreneurs in Kano Metropolis, Nigeria. [IJIEF]. *International Journal of Islamic Economics and Finance*, *3*(3). Advance online publication. DOI: 10.18196/ijief.3233

Susanto, M. A.M. Arif Susanto. (2024). Islam dan Teknologi: Tantangan Etika dan Adaptasi dalam Era Digital. *Al-Muharrik*, *1*(2), 95–102. DOI: 10.59829/dq88ve47

Swadjaja, I., Sawarjuwono, T., & Ludigdo, U. (2019). Model of Islamic Wealth Management Based on Maqasid al-Shariah. *Journal of Innovation in Business and Economics*, *3*(2). Advance online publication. DOI: 10.22219/jibe.v3i02.7465

Utami, P., & Basrowi, B. (2021). Sharia Marketing Mix: A Model of the Digital Marketing Management Strategy of Zakat. *Mabsya Jurnal Manajemen Bisnis Syariah*, *3*(1), 44–59. DOI: 10.24090/mabsya.v3i1.4688

Voak, A. (2021). Fake: The Rise of Food Fraud in the Halal Supply Chain. [Halal Awareness Opinion Research and Initiative]. *Nusantara Halal Journal*, *2*(2), 82–88. DOI: 10.17977/um060.2021v2p082-088

Wilson, J. A. J., & Grant, D. (2013). Islamic marketing – a challenger to the classical marketing canon? *Journal of Islamic Marketing*, *4*(1), 7–21. DOI: 10.1108/17590831311306327

Wu, Q., Sang, Y., Wang, D., & Lu, Z. (2021). Malicious Selling Strategies in E-Commerce Livestream: A Case Study of Alibaba's Taobao and ByteDance's TikTok. arXiv (Cornell University). https://doi.org//arxiv.2111.10491DOI: 10.48550

Wulandari, S. R., & Hasriadi, . (2022). Online Marketing Strategy in a Sharia Economic Perspective. ETDC. *Indonesian Journal of Research and Educational Review*, *2*(1), 28–41. DOI: 10.51574/ijrer.v2i1.1166

Zakaria, Z., Majid, M. D. A., Ahmad, Z. A., Jusoh, Z., & Zakaria, N. (2018). Influence of Halal certification on customers' purchase intention. *Revue des Sciences Fondamentales et Appliquées*, *9*(5S), 772. DOI: 10.4314/jfas.v9i5s.55

Zuraidah, Z., & Aisyah, E. N. (2022). the Implementation of Islamic Business Ethical Theory in E-Commerce. Advances in Social Science, Education and Humanities Research. *Advances in Social Science, Education and Humanities Research*. Advance online publication. DOI: 10.2991/assehr.k.220206.021

Chapter 10

How Brand Experience and Emotional Attachment Build Trust, Satisfaction, and Loyalty to Drive Behavioural Intentions in the Halal Fast Food Sector

Syed Ahamed Suban
http://orcid.org/0000-0002-3543-6483
Alliance School of Business, Alliance University, Bangalore, India

ABSTRACT

The study intends to analyse the impact of brand experience on the dimensions of brand love and its subsequent effect on satisfaction, trust, and loyalty through a conceptual model. Moreover, it even investigates the impact of behavioural intention towards halal fast food.The study was conducted among Indian Muslim consumers of halal-certified fast-food chains via online surveys, employing a snowball sampling technique. .The study demonstrates that brand experience fosters significant brand affection by influencing intimacy and passion, highlighting how multisensory and emotionally engaging interactions cultivate profound consumer-brand connections. The two dimensions of brand love serve as crucial links between brand experience and crucial consumer outcomes. The correlation between intimacy and passion enhances customer trust and satisfaction, thereby fostering greater brand loyalty.

DOI: 10.4018/979-8-3373-2792-1.ch010

The model results imply that brand experience influences purchase intention through a sequential relationship involving brand love, trust, satisfaction, and ultimately, loyalty.

INTRODUCTION

The Arabic word "halal" describes something permissible as per Muslim law (Dashti et al., 2024). The principles of halal sustenance is the fundamental aspects of the Islamic faith (Bhutto, 2024). The expanding dominance of Islamic consumers in the global marketplace has prompted the hotel industry to adopt 'halal' branding as a strategy to differentiate its offerings (Zafar, 2025) Islam has established stringent standards for food to be deemed "halal." It must be confirmed as halal before any other purchasing factors ((Ahmed, 2008). The production process must exclude any of those animals banned as per Islamic law (Abd Rahim et al., 2018), and food must be produced using only clean equipment and utensils. Thus, the process of certifying food as halal is rigorous and multifaceted, necessitating the involvement of specialists from diverse organisations (Halimi et al., 2022). In today's technological landscape, consumers possess a heightened awareness of halal-certified foods that pursue products that adhere to Shariah law standards (Adekunle & Filson, 2020). These brands utilise trademarks or symbols to reassure consumers, especially Muslims, that ingredients and production procedures follow Islamic Shariah (Mayasari & Haryanto, 2025).

Consumers purchase halal products not solely for religious reasons; but because of certification, and purity (De Boni & Forleo, 2019). Fauzi (2024) asserts that, from a business standpoint, a rise in the number of individuals accepting Islam broadens the market for halal-certified food. Due to high predicted Islamic population, the halal industry has grown globally to suit Muslims' halal product demands (Fauzi, 2023). Hassan (2022) indicates that around US$2.2 trillion is expended by a Muslim population of 1.8 billion, indicating 5.2% yearly growth. It is projected that by 2025, the Muslim market will constitute approximately 3.2 trillion within the global economy (Mayasari & Haryanto, 2025). This provides a sizable opportunity for halal-based businesses to enter the market and leverage this highly profitable segment (Zafar et al., 2024). According to Azam and ABDULLAH (2020), millennials are more interested in halal cuisine and health-related items. Halal food requests in menus encompass major global fast food chains, including KFC and McDonald's. Similarly, Carrefour, Albert Heijn, and other prominent retailers incorporate halal meat into their product offerings(Sarstedt et al., 2024).

Brand experience was discussed in relation to different aspects in previous research, including love (Khabib and Anggara, 2022), trust (Huang, 2017; Wijayanti et al., 2023), satisfaction (Rohimah, 2024), brand loyalty (Huang and Chen, 2022), and behavioural intention (Pradana et al., 2024). Many studies suggest that emotion influences loyalty, such as (Drennan et al., 2015; Niyomart & Khanmwon, 2012), satisfaction (Rahman et al., 2021), and purchase intention (Huang & Chen, 2022; Muhammad, 2020). Research that emphasises brand affection and brand experience is mediated by emotion (Huang, 2017; Sarkar *et al.*, 2013). Muhammad (2020), and Joshi (2022) investigated the significance of affection towards brand in the halal skincare industries, highlighting that it emerges from brand experience and subsequently fosters trust, satisfaction, and loyalty. Ashraf (2019) finds that trustworthiness, religiosity, and emotional connectedness are crucial to halal buying behaviour in Bangladesh, China, Indonesia, and Malaysia. Also, the credibility of halal certification significantly enhances trust and intention to purchase (Bonne, Vermeir, Bergeaud-Blackler, et al., 2007; Harrison-walker & Harrison-walker, 2001; Pappu & Quester, 2006).

Notwithstanding the importance of vitality, most research is predominantly limited to the geographical confines of Malaysia(Muhammad, 2020), and China (Ali, Xiaoling, et al., 2017; Hong, 2019). Empirical evidence from India is limited, and a comprehensive empirical model has yet to be tested. Prior research, notably by Khan and Rahman (2015), has largely been qualitative, while studies like those by de Oliveira Santini et al. (2018)have relied on secondary data, leading to a significant gap in empirical, data-driven validation. Even though academics are increasingly focussing on the emotional experience of brand as distinct constructs, there exists a lack of research discovering the various dimensions of brand love, specifically passion and intimacy, within comprehensive frameworks that consider cognitive elements. The absence of research in this domain signifies a notable gap, especially considering that India is home to over 205 million Muslims (Bhutto, 2024; Supriani, 2024), emphasising the strategic value of its under-tapped halal consumer market. Hence, the authors have proposed the following research questions: How does brand experience influence the emotional aspects? What is the impact of brand love on loyalty, trust and satisfaction? How do these structures affect halal food restaurant customers' buying intentions? Given this research gap, this study empirically validates a complete framework that investigates brand experience's direct linkages with brand love (passion and intimacy). Second, we analyse how trust, satisfaction, and brand loyalty mediate purchase intention. This chapter is organised into a conceptual framework, hypothesis formation, research methods, results, discussion about the findings, implications and future scope.

BACKGROUND OF THE STUDY

The interest in halal food products has intensified, highlighting the cultural significance and growing economy (N. Ahmad et al., 2023). A complete review indicates that numerous studies on halal brands (M. F. Ahmad, 2015; Noor, 2025), halal industry (Hudaefi & Jaswir, 2019; Zafar et al., 2024), halal food (Ashraf, 2019; De Boni & Forleo, 2019), halal meat (Hanifasari, 2024) focus on the factors influencing consumer awareness (Yasin & Abdelkhair, 2024), attitude (Garg & Joshi, 2018; Hussain & Fayyaz, 2024), religiosity, (Ahmadova, 2019; Supriani, 2024), purchase intentions (Hanifasari, 2024), halal certification (Suhendri and Indra, 2024), towards Halal-branded products globally.

The global interest in halal products has grown through research conducted by scholars from Malaysia (Halimi et al., 2022; Muhammad, 2020), Indonesia (Febriandika et al., 2023; Suhendri & Indra, 2024), South Africa (Bashir et al., 2018), France (Bonne et al. 2007; Bonne, Vermeir, Bergeaud-Blackler, et al., 2007), Jordan (Otoum & Nimri, 2015), China (Ali, Xiaoling, et al., 2017; Hong, 2019), Japan (N. Ahmad et al., 2023) who studied consumer behavior and certification standards and market growth from different regional perspectives. Muhammad (2020) observed that there is a significant influence of experience of brnads on brands. Brand love also affects halal food trust, satisfaction, and loyalty. Hassan and Pandey (2020) showed that religious identification and emotional connection boost halal consumption among Indian young and how halal brandings emotionally connect with customers. Fauzi (2024) emphasises the importance of halal certification and its credibility, noting that it substantially increases customer trust and fosters favourable purchasing behaviour.

Brand love is a deep emotional relation to a brand that influences loyalty (Ali, Xiaoling, et al., 2017). Yasin and Abdelkhair (2024) concluded that brand recognition and trust are significantly influenced by brand experience. In contrast, Kennedy et al. (2024) found that brand affection and trust in Pekanbaru City have an impact on consumer satisfaction and repurchase intention. This research demonstrates how emotions and cognition affect customer decision-making in the halal market. Similar studies by Ashraf (2019) and Hong (2019) showed that trustworthiness strongly influences halal food purchases in China and Bangladesh. Keyword analysis showed that trust, satisfaction, and loyalty are major halal brand image study themes (Noor, 2025). J. Jo ˇsko Brakus et al. (2009) proved that customer satisfaction positively affects brand loyalty, and this is further backed up in hospitality research by (Assaker & Hallak, 2013; Huang & Chen, 2022; Liu et al., 2021). Most current research focuses on halal meat, indicating a deficiency in studies concerning halal branding as a whole. Halal branding, which encompasses food, travel, and apparel, must be studied. Branding's influence on halal food purchases has not been extensively studied despite continuous studies on consumer behaviour. This study identifies essential branding elements for marketers of halal products, which will guide the hypotheses formulations in the following sections.

CONCEPTUAL FRAMEWORK AND HYPOTHESIS FORMULATION

Brand Experience and Brand Love

J. Jo ˇsko Brakus et al. (2009) The term Brand involvement or experience refers to the internal response of customers towards product attributes. According to Padgett and Allen (1997). It is crucial to comprehend the brand image of companies in the service sector. Passion, defined as "the intense feeling of love or enthusiasm for a particular brand" (Maulani, 2023), is also intrinsic to the experience of relationships. Similarly, (Febriandika et al., 2023) brand love creates consumer experiences because customers and brands interact through consumer experiences. Furthermore, Roy et al. (2012) has placed significant emphasis on the notion that brand experience. The recent findings of Rodrigues and Brandão (2021) support the notion that engaging brand experiences foster intimacy and love, which in turn mediate the behavioural outcomes of advocacy and loyalty. So, it's reasonable to assume that customers will build a profound emotional bond with brands after having a positive brand experience.

H1: Brand experience has a positive impact on the intimacy dimension of brand love

H2: Brand experience significantly influences the passion element of brand love

The Impact of Brand Love and Brand Loyalty

The concept of "brand love" signifies the extent of passionate connection that customers possess towards halal products (Khabib & Anggara, 2022). Consumers and brands have a lasting bond known as "brand love" (Joshi & Garg, 2021). Customers with a preference for halal brands are likely to view these rands as irreplaceable, leading them to take measures to maintain their loyalty (Toshmirzaev et al., 2022). Numerous studies have specified this relationship among customers correlates with an increased likelihood of recommendations and loyalty (Bagozzi et al., 2017; Zhang et al., 2020). Niyomart and Khanmwon (2012) also demonstrates that it positively influences brand loyalty. Recent studies indicate that love and loyalty is interrelated (Huang & Chen, 2022; Mayasari & Haryanto, 2025; Niyomart & Khanmwon, 2012; Rahman et al., 2021).

H3: The intimacy aspect of brand love positively impacts loyalty in halal food consumption.

H4: The passion dimension significantly influences loyalty towards halal food.

The Effect of Brand Love and Satisfaction

The word "Brand love" is a significant concept to examine about brand attitude or satisfaction, as research indicates a stronger connection between brands and consumers (Karjaluoto et al., 2016). Consumers exhibit loyalty that extends to emotional and psychological involvement (Khabib & Anggara, 2022). Brand love's intimacy and passion affect customers' brand satisfaction. Huber et al. (2015) demonstrated that consumers who establish emotional connections with brands generally exhibit heightened satisfaction and loyalty. As per Batra et al (2012), the emotional intensity of passion enhances affective evaluations, thereby increasing satisfaction with brand interactions. Loureiro et al. (2012) provides evidence that passionate brand engagement enhances post-purchase satisfaction and strengthens consumer commitment. Research shows that emotional connectedness with brands drives customer satisfaction (Batra et al., 2012; Lada et al., 2009; Suki, 2014; Zehir et al., 2011).

H5: Brand love (intimacy) significantly impacts Customer satisfaction

H6: Brand love (passion) significantly affects Customer satisfaction

Effect of Brand Love and Trust

Brand trust is a long-lasting brand and consumer relationship, as evidenced by studies by Morgan and Hunt (1994). Brand trust is a cognitive construct that captures customer views about integrity and dependability, whereas brand love is a touching and affective construct (Odin et al., 2001; Padgett & Allen, 1997; Yoo & Donthu, 2001). Studies indicate a bidirectional influence between these constructs, with some studies suggesting that trust fosters brand love, while others propose it enhances brand trust (Assaker & Hallak, 2013; Loureiro et al., 2012; Niyomart & Khanmwon, 2012; Roy et al., 2012). Brand passion, which comprises emotional arousal and excitement, increases consumer involvement and brand sincerity perception, which builds trust (Anderson et al., 1994; Anwar, 2025; Aziz & Chok, n.d.; Elalfy et al., 2024). The emotional commitment in halal lifestyle branding enhances brand honesty and consistency, which are critical dimensions of trust as noted by Mayasari and Haryanto (2025). Through this evidence, we propose these hypotheses;

H7: The intimacy part of love positively affects trust.

H8: The passion element of brand love significantly impacts trust.

Impact of Brand Trust and Behavioural Outcome

Carroll and Ahuvia (2006) defines trust as the degree to which a consumer is convinced that a particular brand fulfils their needs. The concept of brand trust concerning halal branding pertains to the consumers' readiness to fulfil their halal commitments and declared assurances (Ali, Ali, et al., 2017). (Fauzi, 2024; Khabib & Anggara, 2022; Maulani, 2023) indicates that consumers experience increased satisfaction and a higher likelihood of repeat purchases due to trust derived from reliable halal certification. Brand trust arises from favourable brand experiences, resulting in heightened brand love and enhanced customer purchase intentions (Joshi, 2022). Trust serves as a crucial element in Indian halal food consumer decision-making, as customers prioritise religious compliance and brand integrity (Adekunle & Filson, 2020; Azam & ABDULLAH, 2020; Hassan & Pandey, 2020; Sosianika & Amalia, 2020; Zhang et al., 2020) thereby highlighting its significant role in fostering lasting brand-consumer relationships. Consequently, the following hypothesis context is implied by this study:

H9: Brand trust significantly impacts purchase intention.

Influence of Satisfaction and Purchase Intention

Richard (1999)characterised satisfaction as a post-purchase assessment that leads to favourable behavioural outcomes, including repeat purchases and recommendations to others regarding the product. Consumer satisfaction is a prominent subject in marketing literature, as it is essential for sustained business success (Pappu & Quester, 2006). The study conducted by Anderson et al. (1994) within retail contexts revealed that satisfaction significantly influences subsequent purchasing behaviours and the degree of customer loyalty. Suki (2014) established that satisfaction with halal personal care products influences purchase intention due to emotional and religious alignment. This argument posits that heightened satisfaction is anticipated to enhance purchasing intentions.

H10: Satisfaction has a positive impact on behavioural intention

Impact of Brand Loyalty and Behavioural Intentions

The term "brand loyalty", as defined by Dick (1978), encompasses the integration of attitudinal commitment and consistent repurchase behaviour, serving as a critical indicator for future purchasing decisions. The study by Chaudhuri and Holbrook (2001) shows that loyal consumers exhibit intent to repurchase and are less likely to move against competing brands. (Ismail, 2017)illustrated that loyalty in halal tourism arises from customer satisfaction and emotional connection, which in turn enhances behavioural intentions Zehir et al. (2011) and Alhaddad and Alhaddad (2015) demonstrated in their studies that loyalty serves as a mediating factor that converts trust and satisfaction into actual purchasing behaviours. Bianchi et al. (2014) illustrated that consumers who develop emotive connections associated with a brand are inclined to translate their preferences into consistent purchasing habits. Consequently, the following hypothesis context is implied by this study:

H11: Loyalty significantly impacts purchase intention.

As publicised in Figure 1, Proposed Conceptual framework and hypothesis formulation

METHODOLOGY

Sampling and Data Collection

The present research employed non-probabilistic sampling owing to the lack of a publicly accessible sampling frame that outlines Indian Muslim consumers who frequently visit halal fast-food establishments. The researchers have used the Snowball sampling technique because it worked well for reaching consumer groups with culturally unique needs but no established sample directory. The author residing in Bangalore during data collection disseminated the survey link via email and messaging applications, such as WhatsApp, to an extensive list of contacts, including students, colleagues, and professional associates.

In the email and message invites, the research purpose, survey completion instructions, and a secure link to Google Forms were provided. The questionnaire commenced with a compulsory consent form detailing data confidentiality protocols, voluntary participation criteria, and the academic research objectives to adhere to ethical research standards. The researcher chose online data collection due to its efficiency and scalability in accessing a diverse participant pool. Online surveys offer several benefits compared to traditional paper-based methods, including cost reduction, increased geographic reach, minimised human errors, and automated data processing.

The data were gathered during March in the year 2025. Certain responses were removed due to a low standard deviation, indicating a lack of engagement, while others were discarded because they did not meet the established criteria. Within the parameters of the sampling unit's definition. Consequently, the study exclusively encompassed Indian Muslim respondents aged 18 and above (n = 372), while others were excluded from consideration.

Questionnaire and Measurement

The study utilised multi-item scales that have been extensively validated in prior branding studies. J. Jo ˇsko Brakus et al. (2009) Brand Experience measuring tool assesses consumer-brand interactions through sensory, emotive, intellectual, and behavioural factors. Brand Love was assessed using (Sarkar et al., 2013) emotional intimacy and passionate attachment framework. Napoli et al. (2013) assessed brand trust using reliability, credibility, and honesty. Customer satisfaction is measured using (Şahin et al., 2011)'s post-consumption cognitive and emotional scale. The brand loyalty scale has been taken by Odin et al. (2001) identified attitudinal and behavioural components for brand loyalty. Purchase Intention was measured using Yoo and Donthu (2001) and Carroll and Ahuvia (2006) assessments assessing future behavioural intentions. The instruments were qualitatively pre-tested with 10 demographically compatible people. The group's suggestions led to minor semantic changes that improved clarity. A pilot study involving 60 participants assessed internal consistency and preliminary construct validity. The pilot study employed the measurement model with 0.70 Cronbach`s alpha values, where all constructs demonstrated satisfactory reliability.

Data Analysis

The PLS-SEM -SmartPLS 4.0 was used to validate the conceptual framework (Sarstedt et al., 2024). The initial analysis started with the outer model assessment, adhering to the methodology specified by Hair et al. (2017). This evaluation was conducted to ensure the indicator`s reliability and internal consistency using composite reliability as a measurement tool, along with this study analysed convergent and discriminant validity through "Fornell-Larcker criterion and HTMT ratios". The research team evaluated items with loadings below 0.70 for potential exclusion, guided by theoretical considerations.

RESULTS

Respondents Profile

The demographic profile of the respondents is depicted in table 1. It is revealed from the analysis that the gender has been distributed in a balanced manner, with

52.95% identified as male and 47.04% as female. A significant portion falls within the income brackets of 50,000 to 100,000 (21.8%) and 200,000 (28%), indicating a diverse representation across various economic strata. 49.2% of individuals are categorised as students, 42.2% as employed, and 8.6% as 'other' concerning employment status. Based on educational qualifications, 59.9 per cent hold postgraduate degrees, while 33.6 per cent possess undergraduate degrees. Married respondents constitute 57.8% of the sample, while unmarried respondents account for 42.2%. The predominant age demographic is 25–34 years, accounting for 43% of the total population. This is followed by individuals under 24 years at 27.4%, those aged 35–44 years at 24.5%, and finally, the group aged 45–55 years at 5.1%.

Table 1. Respondent`s profile

Category	Subcategory	Frequency	Percentage (%)
Gender	Male	197	52.95
	Female	175	47.04
Family Income (Indian rupees)	Below 50,000	90	24.2
	50001-100000	81	21.8
	100001-150001	49	13.2
	150001-200000	48	12.9
	Above 200000	104	28
Employment	Student	183	49.2
	Employed	157	42.2
	Other	32	8.6
Education	High school	10	2.7
	Undergraduate	125	33.6
	Postgraduate	223	59.9
	Other	14	3.76
Marital Status	Married	215	57.8
	Unmarried	157	42.2
Age	>24	102	27.4
	25–34	160	43
	35–44	91	24.5
	45–55	19	5.1

Source: by author

Measurement Model (Outer Model)

To ascertain the measurement quality, the initial stage entails the assessment of the outer model (Hofstede, 1980). Table 2 provides the details about "construct reliability, validity, and composite reliability as an outcome of the measurement model" by (Hair et al., 2017), results show that the factor loading of all items exceeded the threshold of 0.70, and the constructs have demonstrated AVE values that surpass, with a range from 0.741 to 0.920 as suggested by Bagozzi et al. (1981). Brand love intimacy (AVE = 0.898), brand love passion (AVE = 0.856), and trust (AVE = 0.920) exhibit robust psychometric properties. The results confirm that the "construct validity" and "reliability of the measurement model" have been established, demonstrating adherence to the ideal criteria of PLS-SEM. The assessment of discriminant validity for constructs is conducted using the "Fornell–Larcker Criterion", as illustrated in Table 3. Results show that diagonal values for each component are considerably bigger than off-diagonal values, proving discriminant validity for "Brand experience" (0.846), "brand love (Intimacy)" (0.951), "brand love (passion)" (0.927), "loyalty" (0.852), "purchase intention" (0.941), "satisfaction" (0.923), and "trust" (0.957). According to Henseler et al. (2015), this proves that every concept is different from the others in terms of empirical evidence.

Table 2. Measurement model assessment

Construct	Items	FL-Factor Loading	Cronbach's Alpha	CR	AVE
Brand Love Intimacy	BLI1	0.921	0.947	0.968	0.898
	BLI2	0.96			
	BLI3	0.971			
	BLI4	0.944			
	BLI5	0.943			
Brand Love Passion	BLP1	0.861	0.933	0.97	0.856
	BLP2	0.945			
	BLP3	0.99			
	BLP4	0.941			
	BLP5	0.928			

continued on following page

Table 2. Continued

Construct	Items	FL-Factor Loading	Cronbach's Alpha	CR	AVE
Brand Experience	BE1	0.855	0.914	0.991	0.742
	BE2	0.853			
	BE3	0.884			
	BE4	0.866			
	BE5	0.867			
	BE6	0.856			
	BE7	0.857			
	BE8	0.879			
	BE9	0.848			
	BE10	0.813			
	BE11	0.896			
	BE12	0.848			
Brand Loyalty	BL1	0.813	0.902	0.93	0.741
	BL2	0.898			
	BL3	0.835			
	BL4	0.794			
	BL5	0.852			
Purchase Intention	PI1	0.937	0.928	0.959	0.885
	PI2	0.953			
	PI3	0.927			
Satisfaction	S1	0.915	0.939	0.961	0.853
	S2	0.945			
	S3	0.933			
	S4	0.898			
Trust	T1	0.944	0.97	0.988	0.92
	T2	0.966			
	T3	0.976			
	T4	0.969			

Sources: by author

Table 3. Discriminant validity based Fornell–Larcker criterion

Constructs	Brand Experience (BI)	Brand Love Intimacy(BLI)	Brand Love Passion(BLP)	Loyalty(L)	Trust(T)	Satisfaction(S)	Purchase intention
Brand Experience	0.866						
Brand Love Intimacy	0.815	0.951					
Brand Love Passion	0.826	0.901	0.925				
Loyalty	0.483	0.474	0.562	0.852			
Trust	0.462	0.511	0.572	0.429	0.941		
Satisfaction	0.651	0.716	0.706	0.4	0.518	0.923	
Purchase Intention	0.715	0.726	0.711	0.388	0.486	0.85	0.957

Sources: by author

Inner model- Structural model

The inner model (structural model) was evaluated by examining 11 hypotheses based on the conceptual framework (Vinzi, 2013). The outcomes of the model are presented in Table 4. Of the 11 hypotheses evaluated, 9 were fully supported, 1 received partial support, and 1 was not supported. The results have demonstrated, that hypotheses (H1) and (H2) got support as brand experience has a direct influence on brand love intimacy "$\beta = 0.819$, $t = 25.342$, $p = 0.000$ and passion $\beta = 0.826$, $t = 28.915$, $p = 0.000$". The association between intimacy and loyalty is not significant (H3: 5= 1.123) as "$\beta = -0.009$, $t = 0.096$, $p = 0.924$". In contrast, brand loyalty has significantly affected passion (H4), it shows passion is essential for promoting loyalty in halal food ($\beta = 0.541$, $t = 7.593$, $p = 0.000$). Additionally, the Satisfaction was significantly improved by brand love intimacy (H5) and passion (H6) with coefficients of "$\beta = 0.37$ ($t = 6.72$, $p = 0.000$) and $\beta = 0.373$ ($t = 7.436$, $p = 0.000$)". Furthermore, the brand trust was statistically significant with coefficients of intimacy(H7) "$\beta = 0.486$, $t = 7.944$, $P = 0.000$, and (H8) passion $\beta = 0.263$, $t = 2.617$, $P = 0.009$", respectively. There exists a strong and significant relationship between brand trust and intention to purchase (H9) by a coefficient of "$\beta = 0.148$, a t-value of 1.9, and a p-value of 0.059." It suggests that trust may not be the most critical predictor of purchase behaviour. H10 suggests that satisfaction exerts a significant influence on purchase behaviour "($\beta = 0.298$, $t = 4.727$, $p = 0.000$)". The purchase intention has been significantly affected by loyalty (H11) as shown by "($\beta = 0.253$, $t = 4.046$, $p = 0.000$)". Further validation of the relationships of the effects was established, as all were found to be significant at the 1% level. The model demonstrates high reliability and validity, consistent with the optimal PLS-SEM indices. The findings provide strong support for the theoretical framework.

Table 4. Results

Construct Relationship	(β)	t-value	p-value	Decision
H1: BE → BLI	0.819*	25.342	0.000	Supported
H2: (BE) → BLP	0.826*	28.915	0	Supported
H3: BLI → BL	-0.009	0.096	0.924	Not Supported
H4: BLP → Brand Loyalty	0.541*	7.593	0	Supported
H5: Brand Love Intimacy → Satisfaction	0.37*	6.72	0	Supported
H6: Brand Love Passion → S-Satisfaction	0.373*	7.436	0	Supported
H7: Brand Love Intimacy → Trust	0.486*	7.944	0	Supported
H8: Brand Love Passion → T-Trust	0.263*	2.617	0.009	Supported
H9: Trust → PI-Purchase Intention	0.148**	1.9	0.059	Partially Supported
H10: Satisfaction → PI	0.298*	4.727	0	Supported
H11: Loyalty → Purchase Intention	0.253*	4.046	0	Supported
Note: *p < 0.01; **p < 0.05				

Sources: by author

DISCUSSION

The brand experience greatly affects brand love, fostering intimacy (H1) and passion (H2) in halal brands. It is a multi-faceted construct that includes sensory, emotional, cognitive, and behavioural components. These elements play an important role in fostering emotional attachment within halal consumption contexts, as noted by J. Jo ˇsko Brakus et al. (2009) and Muhammad (2020). The statistical analysis revealed no significant correlation between brand love (intimacy) and brand loyalty (H3). This suggests that emotional closeness alone does not result in behavioural commitment unless it is accompanied by passionate and energetic bonding. The research establishes that brand love passion has a direct effect on brand loyalty (H4), supporting (Drennan et al., 2015; Hussain & Fayyaz, 2024; Toshmirzaev et al., 2022; Yousef, 2018) findings that passionate engagement fosters enhanced loyalty within Islamic markets. Intimacy (H5) and passion (H6) exhibited statistical significance in influencing consumer satisfaction. Anwar (2025) confirms this finding by indicating that halal fashion consumers derive satisfaction from both self-expression and their affinity for brands that adhere to religious compliance. The emotional connection with a brand serves as a crucial mechanism for attaining satisfaction in consumption experiences. The analysis indicates that brand love, in both its forms, has a substantial effect on trust. Specifically, intimacy (H7) and passion (H8) were identified as significant factors. The research findings presented by (Bergkvist & Bech-larsen, 2010; Roy et al., 2012; Toshmirzaev et al., 2022; Zhang et al., 2020) indicate that emotional connections established between consumers and brands, facilitated by value-based and CSR-driven initiatives, result in increased trust and prolonged commitment among customers of halal restaurants.

The correlation between brand trust and behavioural intention (H9) received partial support, indicating that trust serves as a necessary condition but does not independently influence buying decisions. The study findings associated with the work of (Prasasti et al., 2024)(Garbarino & Johnson, 1999; Kennedy et al., 2024; Toshmirzaev et al., 2022), indicate that trust requires value congruence, brand communication, and religious alignment produce significant behavioural effects. The correlation between satisfaction and intention to purchase was significantly supported (H10), steady with outcomes from Quoquab et al. (2020), which indicated that satisfaction in halal-certified service encounters serves as a mediator between trust and loyalty. Consumers typically sustain their relationships with brands that meet their functional requirements as well as their emotional and ethical needs. The findings exhibit that brand loyalty significantly affects intention (H11), aligning with the results of Ali et al. (2017). Brand loyalty is established through a series of positive, repeated interactions, fostering both affection and trust in the brand. This results in both habitual and intentional purchasing behaviours. The model indicates that loyalty serves as a crucial intermediary between consumer advocacy and repeat behaviour. The analyses of indirect effects illustrate the progression from brand experience to brand love, which subsequently fosters trust and satisfaction, ultimately culminating in purchase intention via a sequential mediation pathway corroborated by various sources. The study validates the relational model proposed by Elalfy et al. (2024), indicating that emotional engagement and experiential branding significantly influence consumer happiness, brand affection, and purchasing decisions within service-oriented halal frameworks.

Managerial Implications

Brand managers should create multi-sensory experiences that integrate atmosphere, narrative, and visual branding to build emotional relationships with customers. Because religious compliance meets modern eating tastes, the Indian halal fast food business needs specific attention. Brand love serves as a significant predictor of brand loyalty and customer satisfaction, particularly through its passionate dimension. Brands should transition from an exclusive emphasis on product quality and certifications to fostering passionate customer engagement. This can be achieved through ongoing brand communication, alignment of values, and the implementation of cause-related marketing initiatives. The incorporation of shared religious, ethical, or cultural values in marketing campaigns enhances affective attachment, thereby fostering long-term customer loyalty. The research indicates that trust is an essential factor in shaping perceptions of halal brands; however, it requires satisfaction and loyalty to have a direct impact on purchase intentions. Research demonstrates that trust is insufficient to determine purchase intention without the backing of satisfaction and loyalty. A trusted strategy requires an integrated approach that combines transparent halal certification practices with regular updates on halal compliance, mechanisms for addressing customer concerns, and satisfaction programs that incorporate loyalty rewards and personalised service. Brands must monitor emotional engagement metrics alongside transactional satisfaction to establish lasting customer relationships. Indian halal consumers are categorised into distinct segments, with younger individuals seeking brands that maintain religious standards while also being contemporary. Digital platforms facilitate the establishment of trust and advocacy for brands by fostering the development of participatory brand communities. Managers ought to implement influencer marketing, halal ambassador campaigns, and customer co-creation initiatives to cultivate trusted relationships with their consumer base.

Theoretical Implications

The research enhances existing emotional branding theories (Carroll & Ahuvia, 2006) by demonstrating that intimacy, and passion function through distinct psychological processes that yield varying behavioural outcomes. The results demonstrate that brand love intimacy does not produce loyalty effects, while passion does. This challenges existing theories on emotional-brand relationships by suggesting that emotional closeness does not ensure behavioural commitment in halal food. The observed findings provide practical evidence for enhancing brand love models by demonstrating various emotional pathways, while also highlighting the necessity for further research into affective intensity within Islamic branding. The study shows love mediates trust and satisfaction, demonstrating a sequential connection with brands. The study endorses relational theories and PLS-SEM modelling techniques for examining complex emotional constructs in cross-cultural consumer contexts, particularly those related to religious and ethical dimensions. This study enhances the Theory of planned behaviour by incorporating affective elements (brand love) alongside cognitive factors (trust, satisfaction) and conative aspects (loyalty, purchase intention) within the framework of halal consumption. The study advocates for an enhanced Theory of Planned Behaviour model that aligns with Islamic consumer behaviour, emphasising emotional and experiential factors. Future research should examine the temporal changes of these constructs, their cultural variations, and the role of identity salience as a mediating factor.

CONCLUSION

According to the findings, brand love, intimacy, and passion are greatly influenced by the brand experience. Strong brand experience impacts love intimacy ($\beta = 0.819$) and passion ($\beta = 0.826$), highlighting the importance of multisensory and affect-rich interactions for emotionally engaged customers. The study demonstrates various impacts of two aspects on consumer loyalty. The research indicates that passion impacts loyalty ($\beta = 0.541$), whereas intimacy does not have a notable effect ($\beta = -0.009$). The research provides significant insights into consumer-brand relationship theory, indicating that emotional closeness alone does not foster loyalty in the absence of passionate engagement. Traditional models of brand love that merge intimacy and passion into a single construct require reevaluation, as they may not apply to culturally specific contexts, such as halal consumption.

The dimensions of love serve as connecting points between the brand experience and consumer results because of the favourable influence they have on customer happiness and trust. The results are in line with what is already known about consumer psychology and emotional marketing, especially as it pertains to Islamic marketing, where trust and happiness are strongly tied to conformity with ethics and shared values. Trust predicts purchase intention just partially, according to studies ($\beta = 0.148$), necessitating contextual assessment. The trust serves as a fundamental requirement in markets that operate under halal branding, as it establishes a standard rather than differentiating products. The research identified significant predictors of purchase intention, with satisfaction ($\beta = 0.298$) and loyalty ($\beta = 0.253$) emerging as key factors. This indicates that favourable brand assessments, coupled with attitudinal commitment, enhance the sustainability of consumer engagement. The analysis of indirect effects indicates that brand experience influences purchase intention via a sequential process involving brand love, trust, satisfaction, and loyalty.

The study substantiates the theoretical significance of integrating relational constructs (brand love, trust, satisfaction) with experiential variables to elucidate behavioural intentions in religious consumption contexts. This study confirms the appropriateness of PLS-SEM for modelling complex reflective latent variables and provides empirical evidence from previously under-researched geography, thereby enhancing the cross-cultural validity of Islamic marketing theory. Research suggests that marketers prioritise establishing emotional connections, particularly passionate attachments when developing brand narratives, designing products, and creating marketing messages. The research indicates that trust must be underpinned by emotional engagement and reliable service quality to influence actual purchasing decisions. The strategy for fostering customer loyalty must integrate innovative methods with community engagement and a strong commitment to halal principles.

Limitation and Future Scope

The study utilises self-reported survey data, which may lead to bias, particularly given the religious and ethical aspects of halal consumption. The mono-method design of this study may yield inflated correlations, notwithstanding the screening protocols and validity checks that were applied. Future research should employ mixed-methods approaches or behavioural tracking techniques to mitigate these biases. The study's cross-sectional approach prohibits cause-effect correlations and longitudinal consumer attitude studies. Research needs longitudinal research to examine the brand experience and love growth via repeated exposure and how life-stage, religion, and market dynamics affect these interactions. The analysed constructs exhibit temporal variations due to marketing campaigns, brand crises, and broader socio-political changes that this snapshot study did not capture. The study's emphasis on the Indian halal fast food market offers specific cultural insights; however, it restricts generalisability to other sectors such as halal cosmetics, finance, and tourism. The proposed model requires further validation through replication across product categories, as various sectors may employ different cognitive and emotional processes. The study identifies several promising avenues for future research.

The investigation identifies several potential research avenues for future studies. The model's descriptive power would improve with the enclosure of religiosity, generational differences, income level, and global halal trend exposure as moderating variables. Subsequent studies should examine the influence of religiosity on the passion-intimacy duality within brand love frameworks. Comparative studies between Muslim-majority and minority contexts could enhance the research by elucidating the impact of socio-cultural embeddedness on the development of trust and love. Investigating India, Singapore, Japan, China and the UAE, along with various cities exhibiting diverse levels of halal infrastructure, would yield significant cultural insights. The increasing digital dimension of brand interactions necessitates a comprehensive comprehension of how online contact points influence consumer emotional and perceptual responses. This study presents robust theoretical and empirical grounds for identifying the consumption behaviour of Indian halal fast food. However, further research addressing these limitations and exploring future directions will contribute to academic knowledge and practical applications in Islamic marketing and consumer behaviour.

REFERENCES

Abd Rahim, S. I., Mansor, S. K. M., Yakob, M. A., & Ismail, N. (2018). Food safety, sanitation and personal hygiene in food handling: An overview from islamic perspective. *International Journal of Civil Engineering and Technology*, *9*(9), 1524–1530.

Adekunle, B., & Filson, G. (2020). Understanding halal food market: Resolving asymmetric information. *Food Ethics*, *5*(1–2), 1–22. DOI: 10.1007/s41055-020-00072-7

Ahmad, M. F. (2015). *Antecedents of halal brand personality*. *6*(2), 209–223. DOI: 10.1108/JIMA-03-2014-0023

Ahmad, N., Halid Khan, A., Aziz, A., Mohd Raffi, R., Hasan, Q., Sumimura, Y., & Shimazono, Y. (2023). Determining Halal Food Preferences among Muslims Living in Osaka, Japan. *Journal of Halal Science and Technology*, *2*(2), 26–40. DOI: 10.59202/jhst.v2i2.696

Ahmadova, E. (2019). *Determinants of attitudes towards Halal products Empirical evidence from Azerbaijan*. *12*(1), 55–69. DOI: 10.1108/JIMA-04-2019-0068

Ahmed, A. (2008). Marketing of halal meat in the United Kingdom: Supermarkets versus local shops. *British Food Journal*, *110*(7), 655–670. DOI: 10.1108/00070700810887149

Alhaddad, A. A., & Alhaddad, A. (2015). Perceived Quality, Brand Image and Brand Trust as Determinants of Brand Loyalty. *Quest Journals Journal of Research in Business and Management*, *3*(4), 1–08. www.questjournals.org

Ali, A., Ali, A., Sherwani, M., Brand, H., & Intention, P. (2017). Shaping Halal Into a Brand? Factors Affecting Consumers ' Halal Brand Purchase Intention Shaping Halal Into a Brand? *Journal of International Food & Agribusiness Marketing*, *4438*(May), 234–259. Advance online publication. DOI: 10.1080/08974438.2017.1312657

Ali, A., Xiaoling, G., Sherwani, M., & Ali, A. (2017). *Factors affecting Halal meat purchase intention Evidence from international Muslim students in China*. *119*(3), 527–541. DOI: 10.1108/BFJ-10-2016-0455

Anderson, E. W., Fornell, C., & Lehmann, D. R. (1994). Customer Satisfaction, Market Share, and Profitability: Findings from Sweden. *Journal of Marketing*, *58*(3), 53–66. DOI: 10.1177/002224299405800304

Anwar, M. M. (2025). Halal fashion insights: Understanding brand dynamics in consumer perception. *Journal of Islamic Marketing*, *16*(8), 2294–2320. Advance online publication. DOI: 10.1108/JIMA-04-2024-0149

Ashraf, M. A. (2019). *Islamic marketing and consumer behavior toward halal food purchase in Bangladesh An analysis using SEM. 10*(3), 893–910. DOI: 10.1108/JIMA-03-2018-0051

Assaker, G., & Hallak, R. (2013). Moderating Effects of Tourists' Novelty-Seeking Tendencies on Destination Image, Visitor Satisfaction, and Short- and Long-Term Revisit Intentions. *Journal of Travel Research, 52*(5), 600–613. DOI: 10.1177/0047287513478497

Azam, M. S. E., & Abdullah, M. A. (2020). Global Halal Industry: Realities and Opportunities. *International Journal of Islamic Business Ethics, 5*(1), 47. DOI: 10.30659/ijibe.5.1.47-59

Aziz, Y. A., & Chok, N. V. (n.d.). *Journal of International Food & The Role of Halal Awareness, Halal Certification, and Marketing Components in Determining Halal Purchase Intention Among Non-Muslims in Malaysia : A Structural Equation Modeling Approach. December 2013*, 37–41. DOI: 10.1080/08974438.2013.723997

Bagozzi, R. P., Batra, R., & Ahuvia, A. (2017). Brand love: Development and validation of a practical scale. *Marketing Letters, 28*(1), 1–14. DOI: 10.1007/s11002-016-9406-1

Bagozzi, R. P., Fornell, C., & Larceer, D. P. (1981). Canonical correlation analysis as a special case of a structural relations model. *Multivariate Behavioral Research, 16*(4), 437–454. DOI: 10.1207/s15327906mbr1604_2 PMID: 26812673

Bashir, A. M., Bayat, A., Olutuase, S. O., & Ariff, Z. (2018). Factors affecting consumers ' intention towards purchasing halal food in South Africa : A structural equation modelling. *Journal of Food Products Marketing, 00*(00), 1–23. DOI: 10.1080/10454446.2018.1452813

Batra, R., Ahuvia, A., Bagozzi, R. P., & Love, B. (2012).. . *Brand Love., 76*(March), 1–16.

Bergkvist, L., & Bech-larsen, T. (2010). Two studies of consequences and actionable antecedents of brand love. *Journal of Brand Management, 17*(7), 504–518. DOI: 10.1057/bm.2010.6

Bhutto, M. Y. (2024). *Investigating EWOM and halal product knowledge on gen Z ' s halal cosmetics purchase intentions in Pakistan. 15*(11), 3266–3281. DOI: 10.1108/JIMA-09-2023-0292

Bianchi, C., Drennan, J., & Proud, B. (2014). Antecedents of consumer brand loyalty in the Australian wine industry. *Journal of Wine Research, 25*(2), 91–104. DOI: 10.1080/09571264.2014.888650

Bonne, K., Vermeir, I., & Bergeaud-blackler, F. (2007). *Determinants of halal meat consumption in France. 109*(5), 367–386. DOI: 10.1108/00070700710746786

Bonne, K., Vermeir, I., Bergeaud-Blackler, F., & Verbeke, W. (2007). Determinants of halal meat consumption in France. *British Food Journal, 109*(5), 367–386. DOI: 10.1108/00070700710746786

Carroll, B. A., & Ahuvia, A. C. (2006). *Some antecedents and outcomes of brand love*. 79–89. DOI: 10.1007/s11002-006-4219-2

Chaudhuri, A., & Holbrook, M. B. (2001). The chain of effects from brand trust and brand affect to brand performance: The role of brand loyalty. *Journal of Marketing, 65*(2), 81–93. DOI: 10.1509/jmkg.65.2.81.18255

Dashti, L. A. H. F., Jackson, T., West, A., & Jackson, L. (2024). Enhancing halal food traceability: A model for rebuilding trust and integrity in Muslim countries. *Journal of Islamic Marketing, 2018*(12), 3382–3408. Advance online publication. DOI: 10.1108/JIMA-06-2023-0167

De Boni, A., & Forleo, M. B. (2019). Italian halal food market development: Drivers and obstacles from experts' opinions. *Journal of Islamic Marketing, 10*(4), 1245–1271. DOI: 10.1108/JIMA-05-2018-0087

de Oliveira Santini, F., Ladeira, W. J., Sampaio, C. H., & Pinto, D. C. (2018). The brand experience extended model: A meta-analysis. *Journal of Brand Management, 25*(6), 519–535. DOI: 10.1057/s41262-018-0104-6

Dick, A. S. (1978). *Customer Loyalty : Toward an Integrated Conceptual Framework.*

Drennan, J., Bianchi, C., Cacho-Elizondo, S., Louriero, S., Guibert, N., & Proud, W. (2015). Examining the role of wine brand love on brand loyalty: A multi-country comparison. *International Journal of Hospitality Management, 49*, 47–55. DOI: 10.1016/j.ijhm.2015.04.012

Elalfy, R. M., Elayat, A. M. A., & Elsharnouby, M. H. (2024). Building good brand experience to sustain positive electronic word of mouth: The mediating effect of brand love. *Management and Sustainability, 4*(2), 217–236. DOI: 10.1108/MSAR-01-2024-0001

Fauzi, M. A. (2023). *Consumer purchase of halal certi fi ed product : a quantitative systematic literature review. 14*(6), 1397–1416. DOI: 10.1108/JIMA-09-2021-0299

Fauzi, M. A. (2024). *Halal certi fi cation in food products : science mapping of present and future trends. 2*, 3564–3580. DOI: 10.1108/JIMA-12-2023-0407

Febriandika, N. R., Wijaya, V., & Hakim, L. (2023). Gen-Z Muslims' purchase intention of halal food: Evidence from Indonesia. *Innovative Marketing*, *19*(1), 13–25. DOI: 10.21511/im.19(1).2023.02

Garbarino, E., & Johnson, M. S. (1999). The Different Roles of Satisfaction, Trust, and Commitment in Customer Relationships. *Journal of Marketing*, *63*(2), 70–87. DOI: 10.1177/002224299906300205

Garg, P., & Joshi, R. (2018). Purchase intention of "Halal" brands in India: The mediating effect of attitude. *Journal of Islamic Marketing*, *9*(3), 683–694. DOI: 10.1108/JIMA-11-2017-0125

Hair, J., Hollingsworth, C. L., Randolph, A. B., & Chong, A. Y. L. (2017). An updated and expanded assessment of PLS-SEM in information systems research. *Industrial Management & Data Systems*, *117*(3), 442–458. DOI: 10.1108/IMDS-04-2016-0130

Halimi, F. F., Gabarre, S., Rahi, S., Al-Gasawneh, J. A., & Ngah, A. H. (2022). Modelling Muslims' revisit intention of non-halal certified restaurants in Malaysia. *Journal of Islamic Marketing*, *13*(11), 2437–2461. DOI: 10.1108/JIMA-01-2021-0014

Hanifasari, D. (2024). *Millennial generation awareness of halal supply chain knowledge toward purchase intention for halal meat products : empirical evidence in Indonesia. 15*(7), 1847–1885. DOI: 10.1108/JIMA-01-2023-0012

Harrison-walker, L. J., & Harrison-walker, L. J. (2001). *The Measurement of Word-of-Mouth Communication and an Investigation of Service Quality and Customer*. DOI: 10.1177/109467050141006

Hassan, Y. (2022). A decade of research on Muslim entrepreneurship. *Journal of Islamic Marketing*, *13*(6), 1288–1311. DOI: 10.1108/JIMA-12-2019-0269

Hassan, Y., & Pandey, J. (2020). *Examining the engagement of young consumers for religiously sanctioned food : the case of halal food in India. 21*(2), 211–232. DOI: 10.1108/YC-01-2019-0940

Henseler, J., Ringle, C. M., & Sarstedt, M. (2015). A new criterion for assessing discriminant validity in variance-based structural equation modeling. *Journal of the Academy of Marketing Science*, *43*(1), 115–135. DOI: 10.1007/s11747-014-0403-8

Hofstede, G. (1980). Review Article : Geert Hofstede: Culture's Consequences: International Differences in Work Related Values. *Beverly Hills/London*, 390–391.

Hong, M. (2019). *Determinants of halal purchasing behaviour : evidences from China*. 410–425. DOI: 10.1108/JIMA-03-2018-0053

Huang, C. C. (2017). The impacts of brand experiences on brand loyalty: Mediators of brand love and trust. *Management Decision*, *55*(5), 915–934. DOI: 10.1108/MD-10-2015-0465

Huang, C. C., & Chen, S. E. (2022). Establishing and Deepening Brand Loyalty through Brand Experience and Customer Engagement: Evidence from Taiwan's Chain Restaurants. *Journal of Quality Assurance in Hospitality & Tourism*, *23*(1), 217–239. DOI: 10.1080/1528008X.2020.1864565

Huber, F., Meyer, F., & Schmid, D. A. (2015). Brand love in progress – the interdependence of brand love antecedents in consideration of relationship duration. *Journal of Product and Brand Management*, *24*(6), 567–579. DOI: 10.1108/JPBM-08-2014-0682

Hudaefi, F. A., & Jaswir, I. (2019). Halal Governance in Indonesia: Theory, Current Practices, and Related Issues. *Journal of Islamic Monetary Economics and Finance*, *5*(1), 89–116. DOI: 10.21098/jimf.v5i1.1049

Hussain, K., & Fayyaz, M. S. (2024). *Attitude, repurchase intention and brand loyalty toward halal cosmetics. 15*(2), 293–313. DOI: 10.1108/JIMA-08-2022-0210

Ismail, A. R. (2017). The influence of perceived social media marketing activities on brand loyalty: The mediation effect of brand and value consciousness. *Asia Pacific Journal of Marketing and Logistics*, *29*(1), 129–144. DOI: 10.1108/APJML-10-2015-0154

Jo ˇsko Brakus, , & Bernd, H. Schmitt, L. Z., & Brand. (2009). Brand Experience : What Is It? How Is It Measured? *Does It Affect Loyalty*, *73*(May), 52–68.

Joshi, R. (2022). *Assessing brand love, brand sacredness and brand fi delity towards halal brands. 13*(4), 807–823. DOI: 10.1108/JIMA-04-2020-0104

Joshi, R., & Garg, P. (2021). Role of brand experience in shaping brand love. In *International Journal of Consumer Studies* (Vol. 45, Issue 2). DOI: 10.1111/ijcs.12618

Karjaluoto, H., Munnukka, J., & Kiuru, K. (2016). Brand love and positive word of mouth: The moderating effects of experience and price. *Journal of Product and Brand Management*, *25*(6), 527–537. DOI: 10.1108/JPBM-03-2015-0834

Kennedy, N. F., Wijayanto, G., & Nursanti, A. (2024). The Influence Of Brand Love And Brand Trust On Repurchase Intention Through Consumer Satisfaction Of Indomie Products In Pekanbaru City. *InJEBA: International Journal of Economics. Business and Accounting*, *2*(2), 156–170.

Khabib, A., & Anggara, D. (2022). *How store attribute a ff ects customer experience, brand love and brand loyalty*. 2980–3006. DOI: 10.1108/JIMA-01-2022-0002

Lada, S., Tanakinjal, G. H., Amin, H., Lada, S., Tanakinjal, G. H., & Amin, H. (2009). *theory of reasoned action Predicting intention to choose halal products using theory of reasoned action*. DOI: 10.1108/17538390910946276

Liu, K. N., Tsai, T. I., Xiao, Q., & Hu, C. (2021). The impact of experience on brand loyalty: Mediating effect of images of Taiwan hotels. *Journal of China Tourism Research, 17*(3), 395–414. DOI: 10.1080/19388160.2020.1777238

Loureiro, S. M. C., Ruediger, K. H., & Demetris, V. (2012). Brand emotional connection and loyalty. *Journal of Brand Management, 20*(1), 13–27. DOI: 10.1057/bm.2012.3

Maulani, M. R. (2023). *Purchase intention behavior of halal cosmetics . Comparing study between Indonesia and Malaysia millennial generation. 547*, 1266–1292. DOI: 10.1108/JIABR-06-2021-0177

Mayasari, I., & Haryanto, H. C. (2025). *Investigating the role of brand love on brand advocacy in the local eco hijab fashion industry. 16*(3), 713–735. DOI: 10.1108/JIMA-04-2023-0117

Morgan, R. M., & Hunt, S. D. (1994). . . *The Commitment-Trust Theory of., 58*(July), 20–38.

Muhammad, S. (2020). *An integrated model of brand experience and brand love for halal brands : survey of halal fast food consumers in Malaysia*. DOI: 10.1108/JIMA-11-2019-0236

Napoli, J., Dickinson, S. J., Beverland, M. B., & Farrelly, F. (2013). Measuring consumer-based brand authenticity. *Journal of Business Research*. Advance online publication. DOI: 10.1016/j.jbusres.2013.06.001

Niyomart, S., & Khanmwon, A. (2012). Brand Love, Brand Loyalty, and Word of Mouth: A Case of AirAsia. *Conference of the International Journal of Arts & Sciences, 76*(2), 263–267.

Noor, N. (2025). *A closer look at halal brand image : systematic review and future directions*. DOI: 10.1108/JIMA-06-2024-0259

Odin, Y., Odin, N., & Valette-florence, P. (2001). *Conceptual and operational aspects of brand loyalty An empirical investigation. 53*.

Otoum, F. J. A.-, & Nimri, R. S. (2015). *Antecedents of Consumers ' Behavior towards Halal Food among Jordanian Customers : A Structural Equation Modeling (SEM) Approach*. 19–26.

Padgett, D., & Allen, D. (1997). Communicating experiences: A narrative approach to creating service brand image. *Journal of Advertising*, *26*(4), 49–62. DOI: 10.1080/00913367.1997.10673535

Pappu, R., & Quester, P. (2006). Does customer satisfaction lead to improved brand equity An empirical examination of two categories of retail brands. *Journal of Product and Brand Management*, *15*(1), 4–14. DOI: 10.1108/10610420610650837

Pradana, M., Rubiyanti, N., & Marimon, F. (2024). Measuring Indonesian young consumers' halal purchase intention of foreign-branded food products. *Humanities & Social Sciences Communications*, *11*(1), 150. Advance online publication. DOI: 10.1057/s41599-023-02559-0

Prasasti, R., Ashwat, N. U., Gunawan, S., & Azhar, J. A. (2024). Examining The Determinants of Halal Food Preferences in Gen Z: The Moderating Role of Motivation on Lifestyles and Purchasing Decisions. *Likuid Jurnal Ekonomi Industri Halal*, *4*(2), 49–76. DOI: 10.15575/likuid.v4i2.36853

Quoquab, F., Mohamed Sadom, N. Z., & Mohammad, J. (2020). Driving customer loyalty in the Malaysian fast food industry: The role of halal logo, trust and perceived reputation. *Journal of Islamic Marketing*, *11*(6), 1367–1387. DOI: 10.1108/JIMA-01-2019-0010

Rahman, R., Langner, T., & Temme, D. (2021). Brand love: conceptual and empirical investigation of a holistic causal model. In *Journal of Brand Management* (Vol. 28, Issue 6). Palgrave Macmillan UK. DOI: 10.1057/s41262-021-00237-7

Richard, L. (1999). Whence consumer loyalty ? *Journal of Marketing, 63*(Special Issue 1999), 33–44.

Rodrigues, C., & Brandão, A. (2021). Measuring the effects of retail brand experiences and brand love on word of mouth: A cross-country study of IKEA brand. *International Review of Retail, Distribution and Consumer Research*, *31*(1), 78–105. DOI: 10.1080/09593969.2020.1768577

Rohimah, R. (2024). The Influence of Price, Halal Brands, and Marketing Management Strategies on Consumer Satisfaction. *Journal of Halal Science, Industry, and Business*, *2*(1), 90–103. DOI: 10.31098/jhasib.v2i1.1991

Roy, S. K., Eshghi, A., & Sarkar, A. (2012). *Antecedents and consequences of brand love. March*, 1–8. DOI: 10.1057/bm.2012.24

Şahin, A., Zehir, C., & Kitapçi, H. (2011). The effects of brand experiences, trust and satisfaction on building brand loyalty; an empirical research on global brands. *Procedia: Social and Behavioral Sciences*, *24*, 1288–1301. DOI: 10.1016/j.sbspro.2011.09.143

Sarkar, A., Ponnam, A., & Murthy, B. K. (2013). Understanding and measuring romantic brand love. *Journal of Customer Behaviour*, *11*(4), 324–347. DOI: 10.1362/147539212X13546197909985

Sarstedt, M., Richter, N. F., Hauff, S., & Ringle, C. M. (2024). Combined importance–performance map analysis (cIPMA) in partial least squares structural equation modeling (PLS–SEM): a SmartPLS 4 tutorial. *Journal of Marketing Analytics*, 746–760. DOI: 10.1057/s41270-024-00325-y

Sosianika, A., & Amalia, F. A. (2020). Uncovering Indonesian Millennial's Halal Food Purchase Intention: Halal Value and Halal Logo as the Antecedents. *International Journal of Applied Business Research*, *2*(01), 31–45. DOI: 10.35313/ijabr.v2i01.91

Suhendri, & Indra. (2024). Halal Certification, Halal Understanding, and the Preference in Buying Halal Food Products: A Case in Indonesia. *Halal and Sustainability, 1*(1). DOI: 10.58968/hs.v1i1.424

Suki, N. M. (2014). Does celebrity credibility influence Muslim and non-Muslim consumers' attitudes toward brands and purchase intention? *Journal of Islamic Marketing*, *5*(2), 227–240. DOI: 10.1108/JIMA-04-2013-0024

Supriani, I. (2024). *How social media in fl uencers form Muslim consumers ' halal cosmetics purchase intention : religiosity concern*. DOI: 10.1108/JIMA-02-2024-0085

Toshmirzaev, D., Ahn, Y. J., Kiatkawsin, K., Sutherland, I., & Zielinski, S. (2022). The effect of corporate social responsibility on trustful relationship, supportive communication intention, and brand loyalty of ethnic halal restaurants. *Frontiers in Psychology*, *13*(October), 1–12. DOI: 10.3389/fpsyg.2022.1022835 PMID: 36312062

Vinzi, E. (2013). Editorial Partial Least Squares Structural Equation Modeling : Rigorous Applications. *Better Results and Higher Acceptance.*, *46*, 1–12. DOI: 10.1016/j.lrp.2013.01.001

Wijayanti, M., Giningroem, D. S. W. P., & Setyawati, N. W. (2023). Brand Fidelity Millennial Generation on Halal Cosmetic Brand Through Brand Experience and Brand Trust: The Role of Brand Love as Mediation. *Majalah Ilmiah Bijak*, *20*(1), 88–96. DOI: 10.31334/bijak.v20i1.3110

Yasin, F., & Abdelkhair, F. (2024). *Celebrate Branding: Brand Experience and Brand Trust Mediated by Brand Awareness Farah Yasin Farah Abdelkhair.*

Yoo, B., & Donthu, N. (2001). Developing and validating a multidimensional consumer-based brand equity scale. *Journal of Business Research*, *52*(1), 1–14. DOI: 10.1016/S0148-2963(99)00098-3

Yousef, W. (2018). A thesis submitted in partial fulfilment of the requirements for the degree of Doctor of Philosophy. *English, February.*

Zafar, M. B. (2025). *Halal purchasing decisions and consumer behavior : a multi method review*. DOI: 10.1108/JIMA-08-2024-0365

Zafar, M. B., Abu-Hussin, M. F., & Ali, H. (2024). Mapping the research on halal industry: A retrospective analysis. *Journal of Islamic Marketing*. Advance online publication. DOI: 10.1108/JIMA-08-2024-0348

Zehir, C., Şahin, A., Kitapçi, H., & Özçahin, M. (2011). The effects of brand communication and service quality in building brand loyalty through brand trust; the empirical research on global brands. *Procedia: Social and Behavioral Sciences*, *24*, 1218–1231. DOI: 10.1016/j.sbspro.2011.09.142

Zhang, S., Peng, M. Y. P., Peng, Y., Zhang, Y., Ren, G., & Chen, C. C. (2020). Expressive Brand Relationship, Brand Love, and Brand Loyalty for Tablet PCs: Building a Sustainable Brand. *Frontiers in Psychology*, *11*(March), 1–10. DOI: 10.3389/fpsyg.2020.00231 PMID: 32210865

Chapter 11
Leveraging AI in Halal Business Customer Relationship Management to Enhance Consumer Loyalty

Riza Fanny Meutia
Universitas Medan Area, Indonesia

Andre Hasudungan Lubis
http://orcid.org/0000-0002-4672-1060
Universitas Medan Area, Indonesia

ABSTRACT

This chapter investigates the impact of AI-based personalization in Customer Relationship Management (CRM) on consumer loyalty within the halal business sector, addressing the growing reliance on AI-driven marketing while balancing ethical, religious, and trust-related concerns. Despite the increasing adoption of AI in business, limited research has explored its effects in faith-driven markets. Through the Stimulus-Organism-Response framework, integrated with Expectation-Confirmation Theory and the Technology Acceptance Model, we conduct a quantitative approach with 700 respondents to examine how trust, satisfaction, and perceived value mediate AI-driven CRM effects, while religiosity and digital literacy moderate consumer responses. This study aims to provide fresh insights into how businesses can integrate AI-driven CRM strategies while maintaining consumer trust and ethi-

DOI: 10.4018/979-8-3373-2792-1.ch011

cal compliance. The findings are expected to contribute to both academic literature and industry practices, particularly in understanding how AI can enhance customer engagement in value-driven consumer segments.

1. INTRODUCTION

In recent times, the field of artificial intelligence (AI) has advanced at an extraordinary pace, leaving a noticeable impact on both society and industry (Mijwil & Abttan, 2021). Its growing capabilities have led to practical implementations across a wide array of sectors. For instance, AI is now frequently used to refine marketing strategies, improve the efficiency of supply chain management, enhance the quality of customer interactions, aid in financial analysis, and generally raise productivity across organizational operations (Bharadiya et al., 2023). AI can be defined as the process of using machines (mostly computer systems) to emulate human intelligence processes, the set of abilities regarded as human intelligence include learning, reasoning, problem solving, and for the purposes of this article, making decisions through algorithms and data-driven models. These systems are often capable of operating independently and adapting to new inputs (Sheikh et al., 2023). As such, AI presents substantial opportunities across a variety of sectors, including healthcare, finance, education, and other essential fields (Al-Ansi & Al-Ansi, 2023).

Furthermore, this technology also has become the key driver of sustainable innovation. It helps organizations use resources more efficiently, monitor emissions in real time, and operate smart systems that respond to environmental changes. In areas like energy grids, agriculture, and waste management, AI tools are being applied to support greener practices and cut down on environmental impact (Bolón-Canedo et al., 2024). For businesses, AI-driven sustainability initiatives improve operational efficiency, align corporate strategies with global environmental standards, and foster ethical stewardship—ultimately delivering both competitive advantages and meaningful societal contributions (Attaluri & Kotte, 2025).

In contemporary business practices, AI and AI-based tools are adopted to improve Customer Relationship Management (CRM), to automate supply chains, and use data to optimize decision-making, AI plays a vital role in developing business innovation and competitive advantage in uncertain and fluctuating markets. These capabilities not only foster business innovation but also create competitive advantages in volatile markets. Within the halal industry, AI offers transformative potential by improving product safety and quality, optimizing supply chain transparency, and ensuring strict compliance with halal standards—thereby strengthening consumer trust (Tobing et al., 2024). Furthermore, AI revolutionizes halal customer service through personalized experiences, deeper consumer engagement, and improved loyalty, all of which are central to modern CRM strategies (Patil, 2024). CRM, defined as a technology- and data-driven approach to managing customer interactions, prioritizes process efficiency, service quality, and long-term satisfaction (Ngelyaratan & Soediantono, 2022). CRM plays a pivotal role in the halal industry by addressing the unique needs of Muslim consumers, who prioritize halal compliance in their purchasing decisions. Effective CRM strategies enable businesses to cultivate stronger customer loyalty and trust, particularly in markets with significant Muslim populations (Rafiki, 2019).

Platform such as HalalBooking, AladdinStreet, and SalamWeb were used AI-related CRM tools to improve customer engagement and verification of their ethical standards in Shariah. For example, HalalBooking is a halal travel platform, and utilizes AI in the form of chatbots and recommendation engines to customize hotel and flight recommendations for Muslim travellers, ridding recommendations of non-Halal choices (including halal amenities such as prayer facilities and alcohol-free resorts). The consideration of *Amanah* in their CRM is noted, especially as they do not use misleading pricing algorithms. AladdinStreet is a halal e-commerce marketplace that employs AI to learn user patterns of behaviour, ensuring that suggestions for products are in line with Islamic values and automatically exclude haram options as well as only suggesting ethically sourced items. They have also added the use of blockchain in their CRM system for supply chain verification so have added an element of trust to their ethical compliance. SalamWeb is a Muslim-friendly browser and digital service provider that uses AI-powered sentiment analysis in their CRM to capture user feedback and improve the filtering of halal-related content. Their example captures also the principles around Islamic data privacy (*Hifz al-Khuluq*) and ensures that the data of its users is treated ethically and not subjected to profiling. Collectively, the examples serve to illustrate how additional value can be added through AI-enhanced CRM systems, which can support the Islamic marketing ethics discussed in this article to provide trust for consumers and ultimately the halal digital economy.

While the benefits of AI are significant in the role of CRM in this area, including creating personalization and increased efficiencies, there are also challenges. A major challenge, for example, is that AI-led personalization is aligned with halal and still trusted by consumers (Nasution et al., 2023). Despite its potential, several obstacles impede the seamless integration of AI into halal industry CRM strategies. One key issue is the lack of transparency in AI algorithms (often referred to as the "black box" problem), which raises concerns about biased recommendations and data privacy, ultimately increasing consumer scepticism (Ismail et al., 2024). This is compounded when looking at the many halal businesses which also experience infrastructure and financial challenges, extending the time it takes to incorporate AI-based technologies. Continued demand for qualified professionals who can deploy AI, rather than reverting to more basic systems creates further demands (Nurhayati, 2023). To address these challenges, halal businesses must carefully balance technological innovation with adherence to ethical and Sharia principles, ensuring that AI not only enhances efficiency but also fosters consumer trust and long-term loyalty.

Even as the role of AI in CRM becomes more entwined, empirical studies examining its contribution to the halal industry are limited. To date, while there has been academic attention to AI adoption in business more generally, no research has examined AI-based personalization in CRM or its subsequent impact on consumer loyalty in the halal industry. If halal enterprises (as part of a larger entity) had ideal CRM systems then many would adopt AI technologies that would lead to very personalized, ethical and Shariah compliant consumer experiences through decision legacy and limiting the impact of human biases and limitations, and maximize customer connection, while improving operational efficiencies and aligning systems to respect Islamic imperatives and halal compliance. What we find is that the halal industry has advanced toward the adoption of A.I. but the imperative to leverage the technology ethically with a focus on halal principles is lagging. While AI-enabled customer relationship management is widely implemented in mainstream markets, an ethical, religious, and contextual adaptation to halal business contexts remain unexplored and under-researched. Research has explored the application of artificial intelligence in generic business contexts, with attention to the efficiencies and customer satisfaction achieved through such applications, but empirical findings are typically inconsistent or inconclusive when translated to the halal context where the foundation of consumer loyalty comprises trust, religiosity, and ethical compliance rather than preferences. Furthermore, the role of affecting variables such as religiosity and digital literacy moderating the functions of AI-based CRM have not been researched extensively. Collectively, the research noted defines previous knowledge and gaps in contextual and theoretical knowledge; specifically, in understanding how AI-based personalization impacts consumers' loyalty within an ethically governed marketplace.

This study aims to address these gaps by integrating established technology adoption and consumer behaviour theories—namely S-O-R, TAM, and ECT—within the context of halal businesses. It offers a multi-dimensional framework that includes key mediators (perceived value, satisfaction) and moderators (digital literacy, religiosity) to better understand how AI-based personalization in CRM influences consumer loyalty. In doing so, the chapter provides both theoretical enrichment and practical guidance for halal industry stakeholders, researchers, and policymakers seeking to ethically leverage AI while preserving Islamic marketing ethics. Given that AI-driven CRM is reshaping consumer interactions, understanding these factors is crucial to ensure that AI applications align with halal consumer expectations.

Hence, in this chapter we address these gaps by examining the influence of AI-based personalization in CRM on consumer loyalty, while integrating several variables to provide a more comprehensive analysis of consumer behavior in halal businesses.

2. LITERATURE REVIEW

2.1. Islamic Marketing Ethics and Consumer Trust in Digital Tools.

Islamic marketing ethics consist of principles derived from the Sharia law, which detail requirements for honesty, fairness, transparency and social responsibility throughout the transaction process (Shah et al., 2022). This reflects the methods of marketing which can exhibit Islamic values and practices. The main purpose of Islamic marketing ethics is to create trusting and integrity bound relationship between consumers and buyers, where both parties abide by the Islamic principles derived from their transaction (Zeeshan, 2021). Recently, there has been a focus on multi-channel digital marketing tools in Muslim markets, which include; social media, e-commerce, AI and financial technology, as well as a wider adoption of internet use in these societies. The channel and methods to use in reaching out to and finding innovative ways to connect with these consumers provide many opportunities by shortening the process (Mohd Thas Thaker et al., 2021). Ethical marketing practices are critical to create trust and loyalty from consumers with brands in an ever digitally-focused digital marketing environment, where integrity - and connectedly the need for developing transparency and authenticity - should be underscored in a manner that had previously not provided the opportunity for consumers to capture Muslims interest in brands. When using digital marketing practices to connect with Muslim consumers, ethical marketing practices are important as consumers are more likely to engage with and share brands that exhibit honesty, fairness and social responsibility through online platforms rather than those don't demonstrate any ethical marketing practices (Suandi et al., 2023).

The primary Islamic business ethics that impact marketing practices consist of some core principles that are derived from the religion's teachings. Honesty (*Sidq*) prohibits deception (*Gharar*) and false advertising by making sure businesses provide truthful facts and avoid misleading consumers (Yasin et al., 2025). Fairness (*Adl*) addresses just pricing, and avoiding exploiting consumers; therefore, companies must treat all stakeholders equally (Jumaizi et al., 2022). Transparency (*Amanah*) includes open and clear communication in digital advertising, disclosing all product information, ensuring data privacy, and demonstrating trust and accountability (Fernando et al., 2025). Social Responsibility (*Maslahah*) encourages the marketing of halal products, and prohibits marketing harmful (*Haram*) or unethical goods, which might cause danger to a person, society, or group (Sholikah et al., 2021). Accountability (*Hisbah*) indicates the obligation of providing ethical oversight in all digital transactions; thus; businesses are accountable for their conduct, and must ensure they uphold Islamic ethical principles in their marketing engagements (Attahiru, 2021).

Those ethical principles permit marketers across the globe to operate ethically while being in line with an Islamic approach. Furthermore, trust is a foundational principle deeply rooted in the values of honesty (*Sidq*), transparency, and accountability (*Amanah*) in Islamic business ethics. More importantly, Trust is a spiritual and moral task that leads Muslims to evaluate their interactions with digital platforms (Qizwini & Perkasa, 2024). In an era of AI marketing, the use of AI chatbots, influencer marketing, and the rise of Islamic fintech can either empower or undermine trust. For example, AI chatbots that possess the capability of providing halal-compliant and transparent information can build trust by providing consistent and tailored guidance aligned to Islamic values. In contrast, other digital tools such as misleading advertisements, lack of transparency from brands, data privatisation, and algorithm use, can make it difficult for consumers to trust how a business is responding to their needs, all of which are barriers to making ethical decisions in the marketplace that are based on religious principles (Nasution et al., 2023). Even the physics of algorithmic bias can undermine consumer confidence when CCOs or CMOs decide to disregard a consumer group based on their characteristics (Hazarika & Dhaliwal, 2025). Nevertheless, emerging technologies also afford unique opportunities and/or offerings. Blockchain verification can help to increase consumer-trust levels through better transparency in halal supply chains, halal certification apps enable consumers to verify halal compliance independently (Chong, 2021), and Sharia-compliant digital payment systems reinforce and promote ethical financial practices (Latief et al., 2024). Thus, the ability to leverage trust-optimising technologies is a critical necessity, especially for businesses that must maintain trust within the digital marketplace.

2.2. Regulatory and Shariah Frameworks in Halal AI Systems

As the halal industry usage of AI grows, the establishment of a regulatory framework and the integration of principles within Islamic Shariah compliance will become ever more critical. Regulatory frameworks would ensure that AI-enabled tools not only provide technical efficiencies but are also Islamic-ethically compliant, which is an important component for halal commerce. Unlike conventional systems, halal ecosystems must adhere to both legal regulation and religious obligation, making the incorporation of AI technologies even more complicated (M. M. Rahman et al., 2024).

There are several institutions that play vital roles in this concern, including JAKIM (*Jabatan Kemajuan Islam Malaysia*) from Malaysia, BPJPH (*Badan Penyelenggara Jaminan Produk Halal*) from Indonesia, and MUIS (*Majlis Ugama Islam Singapura*) from Singapore. These institutions act to certifying products, auditing supply chains, and advising on Shariah governance in the halal ecosystem (Nuraini & Sucipto, 2021). As AI uses expand in established functions like CRM, e-commerce, and marketing automation, these authorities will need to add to their obligations to incorporate algorithmic transparency, ethics of data, and customized digital experiences. AI systems that make recommendations for halal items or create automated processes for religious content will need to be evaluated for Shariah compliance, which would incorporate improper targeting, avoiding misleading information, and consumer protection in terms of privacy. However it is more appropriate to have more general oversight of such AI functions, as they will have implications for the probity of the halal faith and the independent wholesomeness of the consumer experience in a digital halal ecosystem.

These regulatory bodies could also serve as advisors or auditors for AI system developers, ensuring that machine learning models used in halal contexts align with religious principles such as fairness (*Adl*), protection from harm (*Darar*), and public benefit (*Maslahah*). Furthermore, incorporating these standards into system design enhances consumer trust, especially among highly religious consumers, for whom Shariah compliance is not only a preference but a moral obligation. This is consistent with the model of this study, wherein religiosity moderates the relationship between trust and loyalty possibly demonstrating that well-regulated, faith-consistent digital resources can moderate and strengthen brand loyalty in halal markets. To fully realize the advantages of AI in halal ecosystems, it is important for there to be collaboration between technologists, Islamic Scholars and governance authorities to demonstrate how halal is safeguarded and promoted or enhanced, so Islamic values will not be compromised, but rather supported, in a system where consumers are progressively encroaching on digital territory.

2.3. AI-Based Personalization in CRM

AI-driven personalization in CRM represents a transformative shift in how organizations interact with customers. By leveraging advanced technologies like machine learning, natural language processing, and predictive analytics, businesses can analyse vast datasets to uncover deep insights into customer preferences, behaviours, and purchase histories (Venkateswaran, 2023). This capability enables hyper-personalized interactions, which enhance customer satisfaction and loyalty by tailoring services, recommendations, and communications to individual needs (Teepapal, 2025). Theoretical frameworks emphasize that AI's integration into CRM aligns with resource-based views of competitive advantage, where data-driven strategies create unique value propositions (Prasanthi et al., 2024). However, ethical challenges remain critical. The dependence on AI drives the need for rigorous data governance to respond to privacy concerns and to reduce algorithmic biases that could result in discriminatory outcomes (Sharma & Sharma, 2023). For example, if customers do not understand how their data is being processed and decisions made, their trust will dissipate irrespective of personalization because opaque systems create distrust. It has been shown that when trust erodes, satisfied customers can move disengage as quickly as they moved to engage. Researchers suggest that it is essential that a collaborative approach be taken to ensure equitable models for AI-CRM, which includes interdisciplinary components; technical, managerial, and ethical partnerships are vital (Oprea & Bâra, 2025). AI-driven customer service is transforming service environments, making them more customer-centric, responsive, and adaptable, which fosters long-term customer loyalty and satisfaction (Patil, 2024).

The integration of AI in customer relationship management systems presents a transformative opportunity for Halal businesses to enhance consumer loyalty through personalized experiences, efficient service delivery, and ethical operations (Wilson et al., 2024). By automating routine tasks, AI can free up human agents to handle complex customer issues, resulting in higher customer satisfaction and stronger relationships.

2.4. Consumer Loyalty in Halal Business

As Muslim consumers become more knowledgeable and develop a preference for Sharia-compliant products and services, consumer loyalty in halal businesses is proving to be relevant phenomenon. This shift in preference is driven not only by religious obligation, but also by trust in halal products and services being produced in a safer, cleaner and more ethical manner. As discussed by Tabelessy (2023), food quality and halal certification increase consumer satisfaction which ultimately contributes to their loyalty. It appears that halal attributes are not merely symbolic, but real markers of product integrity and value. In this regard, it makes theoretical sense since an overall product quality including halal features meet consumer expectations (Memon et al., 2020). Halal certification, as regulated by Indonesian government regulations (PP No. 33 of 2014), provides assurance to Muslim consumers that the products they consume have met strict halal standards (Darmalaksana, 2023). In a market where trust and transparency are increasingly valued, halal certification serves as a critical signal of both religious compliance and product credibility. This assurance not only increases consumer trust but also strengthens their Islamic identity and lifestyle (Dashti et al., 2024). It reinforces a sense of alignment between consumers' values and the brands they support, leading to a deeper emotional connection. Tabelessy's (2023) findings support the view that halal certification has a positive influence on consumer satisfaction and loyalty, consistent with previous research showing that restaurants with a halal identity increase customer satisfaction (Mursid & Wu, 2021; Sobari et al., 2022).

However, it is also worth noting that consumer satisfaction is an important mediating variable of the construct's food quality, halal certification, and customer loyalty. Tabelessy (2023) found consumer satisfaction as a positively significant variable to improve consumer loyalty, corroborated by studies across various industries (Gopi & Samat, 2020; Souki et al., 2020; Uddin, 2019). Satisfaction provides a psychological bridge that connects what consumers think about product quality and certification to the behavioural intention to remain loyal. When consumers believe their expectations have been fulfilled or exceeded, whether taste, cleanliness, or religious compliance, they become attached to the brand. Thus, satisfaction does not happen with separate transaction, but happened over time. Bandura expressed when we satisfy the consumer this increase consumer trust factors with brand and emotional commitment. This implies halal businesses need to focus on food quality, halal certification, and on delivering experiences that continuously fulfil customers' expectations in positive ways.

2.5. Theoretical Framework

This research adopts a theoretical model: Stimulus-Organism-Response (S-O-R) Model, Expectation-Confirmation Theory (ECT), and Technology Acceptance Model (TAM) to explore how AI-driven personalization in CRM influences customer loyalty in the halal industry. The main purpose to employs the S-O-R model is to capture the psychological mechanisms through which AI-driven personalization influences consumer emotions, cognition, and loyalty behaviours. The TAM is used to explain how users perceive and adopt AI-enabled CRM systems based on their usefulness and ease of use. Meanwhile, the reason behind the usage of ECT is to helps assess how consumers' prior expectations and actual experiences with AI personalization shape satisfaction and future loyalty within the halal business context.

These three frameworks have been widely used in marketing and business researches by previous studies, especially for the technology usage context. Elayat and Elalfy (2025) used S-O-R framework to explore the factors that determine the quality of AI chatbots from the perspective of young Egyptian fast food consumers, and to examine how these factors influence their satisfaction with the service and their propensity to recommend the brand. Vafaei-Zadeh et al. (2024) employed S-O-R and Task Technology Fit (TTF) framework to identify the key factors—such as technological features, user perceptions, and task alignment—that drive individuals' intentions to adopt AI customer service in Malaysia. Then, Ligaraba et al. (2023) also utilized the S-O-R framework to demonstrate how opt-in email marketing serves as an effective external stimulus that positively influences consumers' internal psychological states and subsequent purchasing behaviours. The S-O-R framework also used in halal domain research. For example, Ling et. Al. (2025) explore the key factors that influence consumers' intention to use mobile Halal verification applications, addressing the gap caused by limited existing evidence on their adoption, and to examine how religiosity moderates the relationships between these factors and users' use intention.

For the TAM usage, Nyagango et al. (2023) used this model to investigates the factors that influence the use of mobile phone technologies for accessing agricultural marketing information, which aims to identify the key drivers and barriers that affect farmers' adoption of mobile-based solutions, with the goal of enhancing the dissemination of valuable market information. Moreover, Na et al. (2022) conducted a research that explore the factors influencing end-users' intentions and acceptance of AI-based technology within construction companies, utilizing the Technology Acceptance Model (TAM). Meanwhile, Chatterjee et al. (2021) employed TAM to examine how environmental, technological, and social factors impact the adoption of Industry 4.0 within the realm of digital manufacturing. Similar to S-O-R framework, TAM also has been used in research that related to halal marketing. Anwar (2024) served TAM as a tool to examines how perceived usefulness and ease of use of shopping mobile apps influence consumers' flow experience, attitude, impulsive buying and the urge to engage in impulsive purchasing of halal fashion products.

ECT also has been used in may studies. Dhiman and Jimwal (2023) used this framework to resolve this debate by examining the factors that influence customers to persist in using AI chatbots for travel planning purposes. On the other hand, Rahi et al. (2021) employed ECT to examine the factors influencing users' continued intention to use Internet banking services. Bhatnagr and Rajesh (2024) reported a study to explore how AI features and ECT influence the usage and satisfaction of digital banking applications, specifically from the perspectives of Generation Y and Generation Z users. Besides conventional marketing, ECT also has been used in halal industry research. Taujiharrahman et al. (2022) used ECT to investigate how the the continuance intention of users in adopting M-Banking and Internet Banking services provided by Islamic banks.

This study can take advantage of applying S-O-R, TAM, and ECT together since they collectively add complementary breadth in examining the research objectives. While S-O-R describes the psychological mechanism of consumer decision-making, TAM accounts for perceived usefulness and use of technology and ECT represents the post-exposure satisfaction, there is a sound theoretical and conceptual basis for evaluating both the initial adoption and ongoing effectiveness of permission-based marketing techniques. The application of these three theories together can detail how AI operates as a stimulus thus modifying or influencing consumer perceptions and reactions that, in the end, determine loyalty to halal firms.

2.5.1. S-O-R Model

Beyond the popular models in psychology and marketing research, the S-O-R Model was proposed by Mehrabian and Russell in 1974, which is a theory foundation for comprehending how an individual is influenced by physical or digital environments according to the stimulus of his internal states drove responses (stimulus-organism-response). Over the years, the S-O-R Model has been extensively applied to study consumer behaviour, particularly in examining how environmental factors shape decision-making and emotional reactions. Its versatility makes it a valuable tool for analysing interactions in both traditional and digital settings (Sumardi et al., 2025).

The core of S-O-R Model deals with the stimulus, organism, and response (Z. Rahman et al., 2024). Stimulus refers to any outside or inside factor which affects an individual, including environmental stimuli or sensory inputs. The organism symbolizes the internal condition of the individual that processes the stimulus undertone between emotional or cognitive response. This mediation process is very important, for it establishes how the stimulus is experienced and felt. Response indicates the resultant behaviour of acceptance or rejection of the stimulus message. Each component contributes to the understanding of how individuals respond to perception, thus making the S-O-R Model suitable for describing behaviour in different contexts.

In this study, we proposed the AI-based personalization in CRM functions as the stimulus (S) that initiates a series of consumer psychological reactions (O), including trust, perceived value, engagement, and satisfaction. These cognitive and affective responses ultimately translate into a behavioural response (R) in the form of consumer loyalty toward halal businesses. AI personalization is doing this through deliveries of customized recommendations and predictive analytics and automated interactions. Positive perceptions of this help to build trust in the brand. In addition, engagement, satisfaction and the perceived value function as mediators that enhance this trust and empower long-term loyalty. Through the utilization of the S-O-R, this work captures the nuanced workings of AI-driven CRM in the halal industries influencing decision-making, organized along technological and psychological dimensions of customer engagement.

2.5.2. Expectation-Confirmation Theory (ECT)

In addition to S-O-R we propose Expectation-Confirmation Theory (ECT) as an approach to understanding how the AI-based personalized CRM experience has an impact on consumer satisfaction and loyalty in the halal industry. ECT is one of the most common theories used in consumer behaviour research and customer satisfaction and repurchase decisions fall under its application. The theory suggests that general satisfaction or dissatisfaction exists to the degree that expectations pre-consumption are disconfirmed at or post-consumption (Mamun et al., 2020). The ECT recognized that consumers typically form some first expectations about a product or service pre-use, and subsequently undertake an evaluation of whether the expectations were met or not based on the experience with the product or service. When the experience meets or exceeds expectations, perceived utility and satisfaction increases; when that is not met, utility and satisfaction decreases – this was an example of how expectation confirmation directly relates to overall satisfaction (Mbangata & Abayomi, 2022).

Figure 1. The original of ECT model (Majeed et al., 2018)

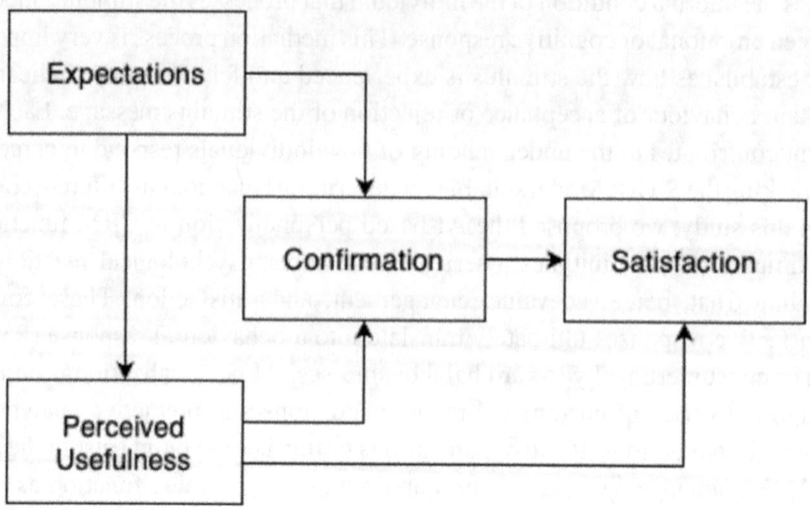

Based on Figure 1, ECT explains consumer behaviour through the interplay of expectation, confirmation, perceived usefulness, and satisfaction (D. M. Nguyen et al., 2021). Expectation is that which consumers want or wish to get out of a product or service before using it, based on marketing, reviews, or past experiences. Confirmation takes place when consumers compare their actual experience with these expectations-it may be positive if it is met, but negative otherwise. Based on this experience, perceived usefulness reflects how beneficial the product or service is perceived to be, significantly influencing its overall value to the consumer. Finally, satisfaction is the emotional conclusion as to whether the consumer is happy or not, as well as in determining whether he or she will be loyal to the brand or will make the repeat purchase (Rahi et al., 2021). All these factors reduplicate converging cycles of consumer decisions and loyalty.

As related to our work, these components play a crucial role in understanding how AI-based personalization in CRM influences consumer loyalty in the halal industry. Consumers develop expectations regarding AI-driven personalization based on prior experiences, brand reputation, and perceived alignment with halal values. When they interact with AI-powered CRM features, their actual experiences lead to confirmation—either reinforcing or challenging their initial expectations. This process shapes their perceived usefulness, determining whether AI-driven personalization enhances their engagement with the brand. Ultimately, satisfaction emerges as a key mediator, influencing trust and the consumer loyalty. By applying ECT, this study highlights the cognitive and emotional mechanisms that influence consumer responses to AI-driven CRM in halal businesses.

2.5.3. Technology Acceptance Model (TAM)

In this chapter, we also adopt the Technology Acceptance Model (TAM) to explain how AI-based personalization in CRM influences consumer behaviour and loyalty in the halal industry. TAM has become one of the most common models in information systems research in understanding how users accept and adopt new technologies (Al-Qaysi et al., 2020). According to Figure 2, the decision of a person to accept and use a new technology continuously is largely dependent on two constructs, namely Perceived Usefulness (PU) and Perceived Ease of Use (PEOU) (Davis et al., 2023). PU represents the degree to which a consumer believes that applying some sort of technology is useful in his or her occupational performance or will provide some significant advantage. Meanwhile, the PEOU means something in relation to how easy and simple the technology is to use (Alshammari & Rosli, 2020). In the case of AI-based CRM, the PU is whether consumers found value in AI-driven personalization in enhancing the shopping experience, in improving the convenience factor, or in providing relevant Halal product recommendations. On the other hand, PEOU describes the consumer would be more inclined to adopt AI-driven CRM tools should they be intuitive so that they could be easy to traverse and didn't press too much on the effort in interacting with.

Figure 2. The original of TAM model (Tella & Olasina, 2014)

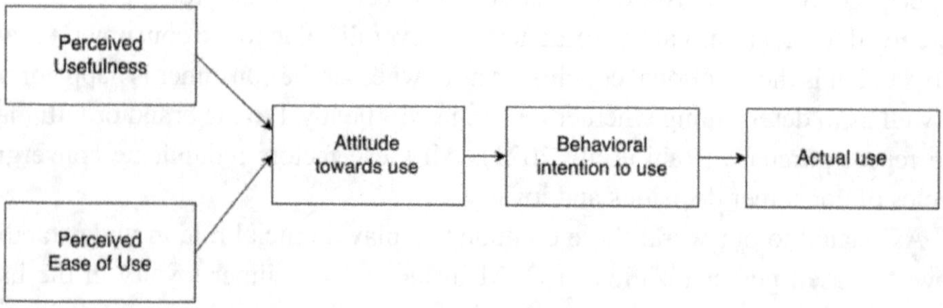

TAM is particularly relevant to this study because AI-driven personalization in CRM relies on consumers' willingness to interact with technology-based recommendations. Since PU and PEOU are influenced by digital literacy (Börekci & Çelik, 2024), meaning consumers with higher technological proficiency may perceive AI-based CRM as more useful and easier to use. Furthermore, PU directly influences perceived value, shaping whether consumers find AI-generated recommendations relevant and beneficial (Yin & Qiu, 2021). Then, the confirmation process from ECT also plays a role in strengthening consumers' trust in AI-based personalization (Bhatnagr et al., 2024), thereby impacting satisfaction and loyalty (Rane, 2023).

Integrating TAM in our work is an opportunity to provide a more holistic understanding of how the acceptance of AI-based personalization engenders customer engagement, satisfaction, and ultimately loyalty in the halal sector. This is based on the premise that the importance of trust and religious considerations for Muslim consumers means AI-led CRM needs to adhere to these value standards before positive consumer perceptions and adoption of the service can occur. The contribution of this study to the TAM model is the inclusion of consumer trust, engagement, and religiosity as moderating and mediating factors in the relationship between AI personalization and consumer loyalty. Technology Acceptance Model (TAM) stands out as the most resilient and significant in determining a user's inclination towards adopting technology. The TAM framework delves deep into the intricate dynamics that shape user behaviour when it comes to adopting new technologies, making it a cornerstone in understanding the decision-making processes involved in technology acceptance (Malatji et al., 2020).

2.6. Research Model

We develop a research model that integrates the S-O-R, ECT, and TAM frameworks to examine how AI-based personalization in CRM influences consumer loyalty in the halal industry. The model is designed to explain the mechanisms through which AI-driven personalization affects consumer behaviour by incorporating key mediating and moderating factors that shape consumer including four mediators (M1, M2, M3, M4) and two moderators (Z1, Z2) to provide a comprehensive explanation of consumer behavioural responses. S-O-R framework serves as the foundational structure for understanding consumer behavioural responses to AI-driven CRM.

In this model, AI-based personalization (X) acts as the stimulus (S), triggering various psychological and emotional reactions within the consumer. These internal reactions, or organisms (O), include customer engagement (M1), trust (M2), perceived value (M3), and satisfaction (M4)—all of which mediate the relationship between AI personalization and consumer loyalty. Finally, these organismic responses lead to consumer loyalty (Y) as the response (R), determining whether customers remain engaged with the brand in the long term.

Trust (M2) is essential to how consumers interpret AI-generated personalization, including whether the AI is viewed positively regarding ethics, reliability, and congruence with consumer values. In the Halal industry, religiosity (Z1) acts as a moderator, influencing this trust-building process—highly religious consumers assess AI personalization through the lens of Halal principles and Sharia compliance. When AI aligns with these values, it strengthens trust and paves the way for greater consumer loyalty. In accordance with the ECT framework, variable of expectation (ECT1) is established when consumers anticipate how AI-driven personalization in CRM will benefit them, based on prior experiences, brand reputation, or marketing efforts. Once they engage with the AI-enabled system, they compare their real experience with their expected one, a process called confirmation (ECT2). If the customization of the AI meets the expectations or exceeds those expectations, the consumer finds it useful, beneficial, and more trustworthy, satisfying, and loyal. On the other hand, if the personalization of AI does not meet the expectations, the consumers become dissatisfied and maybe disengaged with the brand.

Furthermore, TAM explains that there are two factors influence technology adoption, namely perceived ease of use (PEOU) and perceived usefulness (PU). In the current model, digital literacy (Z2) has an impact on both PEOU and PU, which will affect the consumer's perception and interaction with AI-based personalization. If consumers find the AI-based CRM easy to use and feel that it helps them make better purchase decisions, then their perception of usefulness (PU) will increase. This increases satisfaction and trust, and it allows for more consumer loyalty. It is important that Consumers accept and use features of an AI-driven CRM system. The effectiveness of the AI-based implementation in the long run usually depends on the acceptance of the consumer.

Our model integrates these three frameworks to explore how AI-driven personalization influences consumer behaviour in the Halal industry. The S-O-R model helps elucidate how AI acts as stimulus that leads to consumer engagement, trust, and satisfaction; ECT analyses the importance of expectations and confirmation in influencing a consumer's perceptions of AI; and TAM introduces the dimension of digital literacy, as it relates to consumer perception of ease of use and perceived usefulness. The outcome of the model is consumer loyalty (Y) shaped by the stimulus from AI-driven personalization, which is mediated by engagement, trust, value, and satisfaction, all while considering ethical and religious elements.

Figure 3. Proposed framework

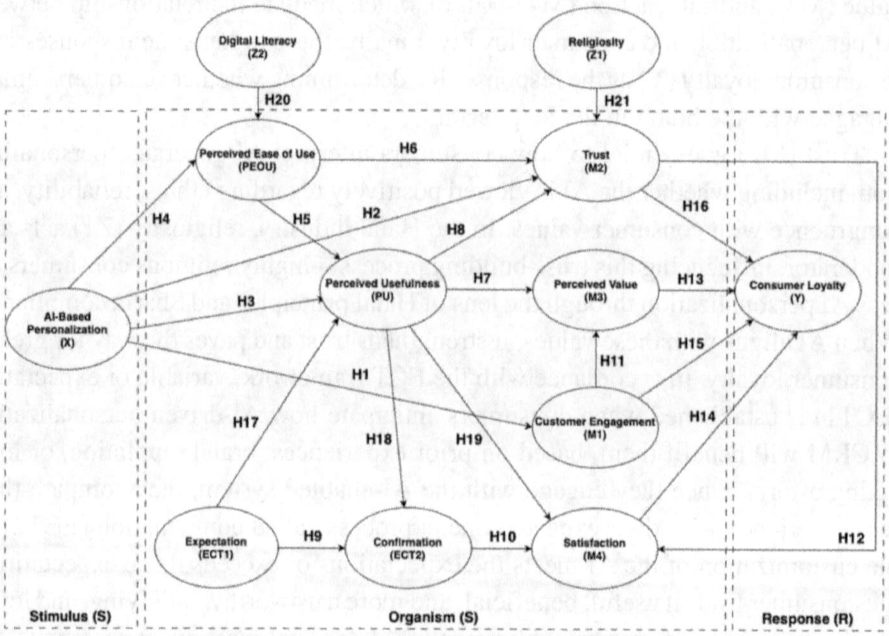

According to Figure 3, the framework consists of three main elements. The stimulus (S) is represented by AI-enabled personalization (X), which serves as the initiating variable that crystallizes consumer perception and experience. The organism (O) comprises the cognitive and emotional processes, such as trust, perceived usefulness, perceived ease of use, perceived value, customer engagement, and satisfaction, that mediate AI-enabled personalization impacts. Finally, the response (R) is consumer loyalty (Y), the resultant behavioural outcome of the interplay of the mediating variables in O.

Overall, this configuration presents a clear sequence explaining how AI-based personalization leads to consumer behaviour in the Halal industry context. The hypotheses in this study explore key psychological and behavioural mechanisms that influence consumer decision-making. AI-based personalization serves as the stimulus (S), shaping various consumer perceptions such as perceived ease of use, perceived usefulness, trust, and satisfaction (O), which ultimately impact consumer loyalty (R). Additionally, religiosity and digital literacy act as moderating variables that influence the strength of these relationships. The Table 1 below presents the hypotheses formulated based on this conceptual framework, outlining the expected relationships between the key constructs.

Table 1. List of hypotheses

Hypothesis	Statement
H1	AI-based personalization (X) positively influences customer engagement (M1).
H2	AI-based personalization (X) positively influences trust (M2).
H3	AI-based personalization (X) positively influences perceived usefulness (PU).
H4	AI-based personalization (X) positively influences perceived ease of use (PEOU).
H5	Perceived ease of use (PEOU) positively influences perceived usefulness (PU).
H6	Perceived ease of use (PEOU) positively influences trust (M2).
H7	Perceived usefulness (PU) positively influences perceived value (M3).
H8	Perceived usefulness (PU) positively influences trust (M2).
H9	Expectation (ECT1) positively influences confirmation (ECT2).
H10	Confirmation (ECT2) positively influences satisfaction (M4).
H11	Customer engagement (M1) positively influences perceived value (M3).
H12	Trust (M2) positively influences satisfaction (M4)
H13	Perceived value (M3) positively influences consumer loyalty (Y).
H14	Satisfaction (M4) positively influences consumer loyalty (Y).
H15	Customer engagement (M1) positively influences consumer loyalty (Y).
H16	Trust (M2) positively influences consumer loyalty (Y).
H17	Expectation (ECT1) positively influences perceived usefulness (PU).
H18	Perceived usefulness (PU) positively influences confirmation (ECT2).
H19	Perceived usefulness (PU) positively influences satisfaction (M4).
H20	Digital literacy (Z2) moderates the relationship between perceived ease of use (PEOU) and perceived usefulness (PU).
H21	Religiosity (Z1) moderates the relationship between trust (M2) and consumer loyalty (Y).

3. METHODOLOGY

3.1. Population and Sample

In this study, the population is made up of consumers familiar with AI-enabled personalization within CRM systems in the halal context. The population includes consumers with experience in AI-enabled features like personalized recommendations, chatbots, and personalized marketing across halal food, Islamic banking, modest fashion, and halal tourism activities. To enhance the representativeness of our sample, we apply a purposive sampling method, or non-probability sampling, to focus on respondents who meet certain criteria for our research objectives, including: (1) Experience with AI-based Personalization: Respondents must have interacted with AI-driven CRM features in a halal industry business; (2) Active Consumers: Participants should have engaged with AI-driven personalization within the past six months (e.g., received recommendations or used automated services), and (3) Awareness of Halal Values: Since religiosity is a moderating variable in this study, respondents should have a basic understanding of halal principles and how they influence their purchasing decisions.

To achieve robust analytical results, we collected responses from 700 participants, significantly exceeding the minimum sample size recommendation of 5-10 respondents per observed variable in structural equation modelling (SEM) proposed by Hair et al. (2010). The data collection employed two approaches. As the first one, the questionnaires were distributed through social media platforms, e-commerce applications, and halal business networks, specifically targeting consumers with prior experience using AI-powered CRM systems. Then, the complementary data was gathered through in-person surveys conducted at halal industry conferences, Islamic financial institutions, and specialty grocery stores as the second approach.

3.2. Research Instrument

To ensure a comprehensive measurement of the variables in this research, we propose the following questionnaire items. The instrument consists of multiple sections, ensuring a systematic approach to data collection while minimizing respondent fatigue. The first section gathers demographic information, including gender, age, education level, occupation, monthly income, and the frequency of interaction with AI-based features in halal business platforms. This foundational data allows for a deeper segmentation and analysis of how different user groups perceive and engage with AI-driven personalization in halal e-commerce. The subsequent sections contain items adapted from several previous studies, each aligned with the variables under investigation. Each item is designed to capture key constructs related to AI-based personalization, consumer perceptions, trust, engagement, religiosity, and consumer loyalty in the halal industry. Participants are asked to respond to these items using a five-point Likert scale, ranging from 1 (strongly disagree) to 5 (strongly agree). All questionnaire items and their respective indicators including the sources are listed in Table 2.

Table 2. Items in questionnaire

Construct	Item	Indicators	Sources
X	X1	The AI-based personalization in this CRM system provides recommendations that match my preferences.	(Hassan et al., 2025)
	X2	The personalized content offered by this AI system is relevant to my needs.	
	X3	I find that the AI-based personalization in this CRM system is helpful.	
	X4	I feel that the AI-based personalization enhances my experience with the brand.	
PEOU	PEOU1	The AI-driven CRM system is easy to navigate	(Lopes et al., 2024)
	PEOU2	I find it effortless to interact with AI-based personalization features	
	PEOU3	The AI system requires minimal effort to operate.	
	PEOU4	Learning how to use the AI-based personalization was simple for me	
PU	PU1	AI-based personalization improves my overall experience with the brand	(Wang et al., 2023)
	PU2	The AI-driven recommendations help me make better purchase decisions.	
	PU3	The system enhances my engagement with the brand.	
	PU4	I experience reduced time spent on tasks or activities.	
ECT1	ECT1.1	My shopping experience with AI system is better than my expectation.	(Alnaser et al., 2023)
	ECT1.2	The benefits of AI system are better than my expectation.	
	ECT1.3	The AI-based personalization had better service level than my expectation.	
ECT2	ECT2.1	Confirmation to the AI system in terms of ease of use and convenience.	(G.-D. Nguyen & Ha, 2021)
	ECT2.2	Confirmation to the service provided by the AI system	
	ECT2.3	Overall, the majority of my expectations regarding the use of AI system were met.	

continued on following page

Table 2. Continued

Construct	Item	Indicators	Sources
M1	M1.1	I am more likely to explore products/services because of AI recommendations.	(Asante et al., 2023; Elmashhara et al., 2024)
	M1.2	I spent a lot of time seeking ideas and information which provided by the AI system.	
	M1.3	I frequently interact with AI-based personalization features.	
	M1.4	The AI system makes me feel more engaged with the brand.	
M2	M2.1	I feel confident in relying on the AI-driven CRM system.	(Amil, 2024; Hassan et al., 2025; Sehgal et al., 2019; Wang et al., 2023)
	M2.2	I believe the AI system protects my personal data and privacy.	
	M2.3	The AI system provides transparency regarding the use of my personal information.	
	M2.4	The information provided by the AI system is reliable.	
M3	M3.1	AI-based personalization adds value to my shopping experience.	(Ram et al., 2024)
	M3.2	I perceive the AI-driven recommendations as beneficial.	
	M3.3	The AI system enhances my overall perception of the brand's worth.	
M4	M4.1	Customer contentment with prior shopping experiences.	(Hassan et al., 2025; G.-D. Nguyen & Ha, 2021)
	M4.2	Service quality in prior shopping experiences.	
	M4.3	Fulfilment of expectations in prior shopping experiences.	
	M4.4	Overall, I am satisfied when using AI-based personalization system.	
Z1	Z1.1	My purchasing decisions are influenced by my religious beliefs.	(Abdou et al., 2024)
	Z1.2	I prefer brands that align with my religious values.	
	Z1.3	My trust in AI-based personalization depends on whether it follows halal principles.	
	Z1.4	I follow strict Islamic rules to consume Halal products	
Z2	Z2.1	I can operate the AI-based personalization features.	(H. S. Hwang et al., 2023)
	Z2.2	I understand how AI-based personalization works.	
	Z2.3	I frequently use digital tools and AI-powered systems.	

continued on following page

Table 2. Continued

Construct	Item	Indicators	Sources
Y	Y1	I am more likely to stay loyal to halal businesses that personalize their services using AI technology	(Singh & Singh, 2024)
	Y2	AI-based personalization significantly influences my decision to continue using a halal brand's products or services	
	Y3	AI-driven personalization positively affects my long-term commitment to halal businesses	
	Y4	Positive experiences with AI-driven personalization features increase my loyalty to halal businesses.	

4. RESULT

The result of this study split in to two parts. The first part, we explain about the demographic profiles of the respondents, as these attributes provide context for interpreting the behavioural patterns reflected in the data. In the second part, we elaborate the analysis using Generalized Structured Component Analysis – Structural Equation Modelling (GSCA-SEM). GSCA-SEM is a component-based estimation technique that enables the simultaneous evaluation of both measurement and structural models in a single analytical step (H. Hwang et al., 2023). The GSCA-SEM procedure in this research was achieved using a two-step analytical approach: (1) Measurement Model Evaluation: This step asked for the evaluation of the reliability and validity of the latent constructs based on component-based estimation. To ensure the set of observed variables were measuring the corresponding construct properly, item loadings were analyzed and supported with model fit and internal consistency; and (2) Structural Model Evaluation: After the measurement model was validated, the process evaluated the structural model to see whether the hypothesized relationships among variables were supported. It evaluated both direct, indirect, and moderating effects hypothesized in the theoretical framework using path coefficients, and model fits.

4.1. Data Gathered

This study collected data from a total of 700 respondents who met the predetermined criteria for participation, ensuring a representative sample of the target population. The respondents were carefully screened based due to maintain relevance to the research objectives. The data collection process adhered to ethical guidelines, ensuring respondent anonymity and voluntary participation, which further strengthens the integrity of the study's outcomes. The demographic profile of respondents revealed meaningful diversity. As noted in Figure 4, the majority of participants were female (n = 384, 54.86%), while male respondents comprised 316 individuals (45.14%). In regard to respondents' age, the largest single group was Generation Z (ages 18-27) who made up 263 respondents (37.57%). This was followed by Millennials (ages 28-37) with 192 respondents (27.43%), and then Generation X (ages 38-47) with 145 respondents (20.71%). In contrast, there were only 78 respondents (11.14%) in the 48-57 age category and only a few 22 participants (3.14%) older than 57 years of age. Moreover, most respondents are high school students of educational level (n=296, 42.3%) indicating a relatively large share of adolescents among halal e-commerce users. The next largest group was bachelor's degree holders (n=236, 33.7%) which indicates approximately one-third of participants had some undergraduate training. Advanced degree holders included Masters graduates (n=118, 16.9%) and PhD graduates (n=50, 7.1%) which would indicate that 24% of the sample has have postgraduate training.

In term of respondents' occupation, the largest demographic segment comprised students (32.3%, n=226), indicating strong platform adoption among academic populations, likely due to greater technological familiarity and need for convenient shopping solutions. Traditional workforce participants collectively accounted for 36.3% of respondents, including office workers (19.3%, n=135) and healthcare professionals (17.0%, n=119). Meanwhile, entrepreneurs represented a substantial proportion (20.3%, n=142), reflecting the platform's relevance for business owners and self-employed individuals in the halal commerce ecosystem. However, non-active populations formed a smaller but notable segment (11.2% combined), consisting of unemployed individuals (8.6%, n=60) and retirees (2.6%, n=18). Furthermore, Figure 4 also shows the important socioeconomic differences in terms of income that stratified the sample. Most of the participants were below the low-income threshold of less than IDR 2 million (n=412, 58.9%). There are two groups that would be categorized as the middle-income range, as they are earning in the range of IDR 2 - 5 million (n=159, 22.7%) and IDR 5 - 10 million (n=89, 12.7%). Then, there are fewer participants like these high-income earners (n=40, 5.7%) earning more than IDR 10 million.

Ultimately, the study revealed significant variation in users' engagement with AI features on halal e-commerce platforms. The interaction frequencies followed a bimodal distribution: (1) Moderate Users (n=205, 29.3% "Sometimes") formed the largest group, suggesting cautious adoption; (2) Frequent Users (n=183, 26.1% "Often" + n=133, 19.0% "Always") represented substantial AI engagement (45.1% combined); (3) Limited Users (n=102, 14.6% "Rarely" + n=77, 11.0% "Almost Never") showed minimal interaction (25.6% combined). This distribution suggests that while nearly half of consumers (45.1%) use the AI features of the products they use routinely (occasionally) in relationship to the frequency of use, about one-quarter of consumers remain wary or hesitant adopters. The 29.3% of consumers that fall into the occasional use group are the critical target for improvement in usability and perceived value propositions of products or services incorporating AI or AI-like entities.

Figure 4. The distribution of respondents' demographic respectively: (a) Gender; (b) Age; (c) Education level; (d) Occupation; (e) Monthly income; (f) Frequency of AI interaction

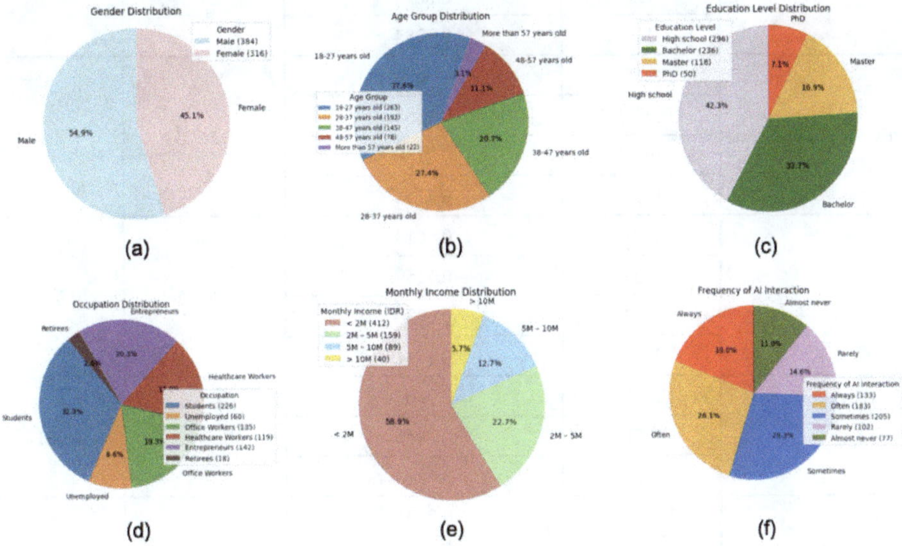

4.2. Measurement Model

GSCA adopts a component-based approach, where latent variables are estimated as weighted composites of their indicators. The analysis begins by assessing item loadings, which represent the strength of association between each observed variable and its construct. High item loadings (preferably above 0.70) indicate that the indicators adequately capture the intended latent construct. In addition, the constructs were assessed in terms of reliability and validity by assessing Construct Reliability (CR) and Average Variance Extracted (AVE). CR was then calculated to determine the internal consistency, with 0.70 (or greater) representing acceptable reliability, of each of the constructs. AVE was computed to assess convergent validity, which is the extent to which the indicators of a construct are related to one another and share the common variance in it. An AVE value of 0.50, or greater, means the construct explains more than 50% of the variance, of its observed variables (Mohd Dzin & Lay, 2021). The item loadings and the results of the validity and reliability is shown in Table 3.

Table 3. Measurement model evaluation

Construct	Item	Outer Loading	AVE	CR
X	X1	0.8625	0,5712	0,8417
	X2	0.8284		
	X3	0.8013		
	X4	0.7284		
PEOU	PEOU1	0,7036	0.5620	0.8364
	PEOU2	0,7562		
	PEOU3	0,8180		
	PEOU4	0,7154		
PU	PU1	0,6613	0.5015	0.8005
	PU2	0,7159		
	PU3	0,6936		
	PU4	0,7581		
ECT1	ECT1.1	0,7507	0.5463	0.7813
	ECT1.2	0,7415		
	ECT1.3	0,7248		
ECT2	ECT2.1	0,7201	0.5437	0.7807
	ECT2.2	0,7973		
	ECT2.3	0,6905		
M1	M1.1	0,8118	0.5561	0.8331
	M1.2	0,6805		
	M1.3	0,7319		
	M1.4	0,7528		
M2	M2.1	0,7819	0.5309	0.8184
	M2.2	0,7557		
	M2.3	0,7088		
	M2.4	0,6622		
M3	M3.1	0,7433	0.5766	0.8031
	M3.2	0,8002		
	M3.3	0,7328		

continued on following page

Table 3. Continued

Construct	Item	Outer Loading	AVE	CR
M4	M4.1	0,7965	0.6504	0.8802
	M4.2	0,6555		
	M4.3	0,8827		
	M4.4	0,8708		
Z1	Z1.1	0,5963	0.6057	0.8567
	Z1.2	0,6947		
	Z1.3	0,8930		
	Z1.4	0,8873		
Z2	Z2.1	0,6659	0.5133	0.7587
	Z2.2	0,7909		
	Z2.3	0,6861		
Y	Y1	0,7118	0.50174	0.8004
	Y2	0,7805		
	Y3	0,6819		
	Y4	0,6528		

According to Table 3, all constructs indicated acceptable levels of convergent validity and construct reliability according to the measurement model outputs. The outer loadings of the observed items ranged from 0.5963 (Z1.1) to 0.8930 (Z1.3), with the majority exceeding the recommended threshold of 0.70, indicating that the items were sufficiently correlated with their respective latent constructs. The AVE scores of constructs included were from 0.5015 (PU) to 0.6504 (M4), well over the minimum acceptable threshold of 0.50 for convergent validity.

In CR value, all constructs were above the 0.70, all surpassing the acceptable benchmark of 0.70, which suggests strong internal consistency across constructs. These results affirm that the measurement model in this study is both reliable and valid, providing a solid foundation for subsequent structural model analysis within the GSCA framework. Furthermore, the quality of the measurement model is further examined using overall model fit measures, which assess how well the specified model aligns with the empirical data. These including FIT (overall model fit), AFIT (adjusted FIT), FITs (FIT for the structural model), FITm (FIT for the measurement model), GFI (Goodness of Fit Index), SRMR (Standardized Root Mean Square Residual), OPE (overall predictive error), OPEs (predictive error for the structural model), and OPEm (predictive error for the measurement model). The result of those measures are shown in Table 4.

Table 4. Model fit measures

FIT	AFIT	FITs	FITm	GFI	SRMR	OPE	OPEs	OPEm
0.726	0.712	0.731	0.718	0.925	0.062	0.285	0.697	0.238

4.3. Structural Model Evaluation

After the measurement model was validated, the structural model was assessed to evaluate both the direction and strength of the hypothesized relationships between the latent constructs. In GSCA-SEM, structural models evaluate the estimated path coefficients and corresponding standard errors (SE) and 95% confidence intervals (CI) to examine how credibly they support the relationships posed in the hypothesis. Internationally recognized, path coefficients indicate the direction (positive or negative) and size (i.e., change) of the influence between constructs, and SE and confidence intervals provide perspective on the reliability and robustness of the estimates for a more nuanced interpretation of significance (H. Hwang et al., 2024). A causal relationship is considered statistically insignificant when the critical ratio (CR) falls within the range of -1.96 to +1.96, corresponding to a significance level of 0.05. The estimation results for the structural model, including the computed critical ratios, are presented in Table 5.

Table 5. Path coefficient

Path	Estimate	SE	95% CI Lower	95% CI Upper	Decision
X → M1	0.089	0.048	0.015	0,113	Accepted
X → M2	0.064	0.043	-0.012	0,092	Rejected
X → PU	0.077	0.036	0.009	0,100	Accepted
X → PEOU	0,072	0.045	0.018	0,114	Accepted
PEOU → PU	0.091	0.044	0.015	0,114	Accepted
PEOU → M2	0.071	0.042	-0.008	0,098	Rejected
PU → M3	0.058	0.033	0.003	0,077	Accepted
PU → M2	0.066	0.034	0.002	0,086	Accepted
ECT1 → ECT2	0.079	0.039	0.005	0,092	Accepted
ECT2 → M4	0.061	0.032	0.006	0,075	Accepted
M1 → M3	0.069	0.041	-0.007	0,086	Rejected
M2 → M4	0.061	0.043	-0.014	0,089	Rejected
M3 → Y	0.067	0.037	0.005	0,084	Accepted

continued on following page

Table 5. Continued

Path	Estimate	SE	95% CI Lower	95% CI Upper	Decision
M4 → Y	0.077	0.039	0.004	0,086	Accepted
M1 → Y	0.056	0.038	-0.012	0,081	Rejected
M2 → Y	0.088	0.036	0.014	0,093	Accepted
ECT1 → PU	0.091	0.041	0.011	0,103	Accepted
PU → ECT2	0.085	0.039	0.005	0,091	Accepted
PU → M4	0.061	0.033	0.002	0,081	Accepted
PEOU $\overrightarrow{Z2}$ PU	0.082	0.035	0.013	0,095	Accepted
M2 $\overrightarrow{Z1}$ Y	0.074	0.035	0.010	0,088	Accepted

Based on the structural model evaluation, 16 out of 21 hypotheses were statistically supported, as indicated by their 95% confidence intervals excluding zero. Firstly, the result shows that X has the significant and positive relationships on M1, PU, and PEOU. Then, it also present PEOU significantly influenced PU, while PU had significant effects on M3, M2 M4 and ECT2. Moreover, ECT1 positively influenced ECT2, while ECT2 in turn significantly predicted M4, supporting the sequential logic of expectation-confirmation affecting satisfaction. Moreover, M3 and M4 were found to significantly influence Y, confirming the importance of perceived value and satisfaction in fostering loyalty within the halal business ecosystem. Notably, M2 also demonstrated a direct and significant impact on Y, indicating the relevance of trust in mediating loyalty intentions. Furthermore, the analysis confirmed the presence of significant moderating effects, where Z2 (positively moderated the relationship between PEOU and PU, and Z1 moderated the relationship between M2 and Y, emphasizing the role of individual differences in shaping technology adoption and loyalty in faith-based consumer segments. Despite the majority of hypotheses being supported, five out of the 21 proposed paths were found to be statistically insignificant, as indicated by their 95% confidence intervals encompassing zero. These include the relationships between X and M2, PEOU and M2, M1 and M3, M2 → M4 and M1 and Y. The comprehensive of the result will be discuss in the next section.

5. DISCUSSION

The findings of the study provide a comprehensive perspective on how AI-driven technological, especially personalization in CRM dynamically engage with consumers' cognitive processes, emotional reactions, and behavioural outcomes.

In this study, we analysed how AI-based personalization in CRM shapes several consumers' attitude at the first stage. According to the statistical analysis, AI-based personalization positively influences both consumers' PU and PEOU. This in line with the empirical works by Lopes et al. (2024) and Yin et al. (2025) research on personalization in digital platforms. However, the relationship between AI-based personalization and trust was not statistically significant, suggesting that personalization alone is insufficient to build consumer trust in halal businesses. This finding contrasts with Sipos (2025), which argued that AI personalized has a positive impact on trust. Trust is more than the personalization of services; it is about transparency, ethical practices, and religious compliance especially when operating in a faith-driven market.

In the second stage, we examine the integration of the TAM in our analytical framework. The analysis remarks that consumers' perceived ease of use of AI technology only has an impact on significantly influences its perceived usefulness, but exhibits no statistically significant effect on trust. This finding contradicts established theoretical perspectives and empirical evidences which posit that perceived ease of use can enhance user trust formation in technological contexts. The divergence suggests that trust in AI-driven e-commerce systems may be governed more prominently by alternative factors, such as transparency (Abinesh & Dulloo, 2024), capability (Teodorescu et al., 2023), ethical design, or contextual cultural norms (Zimu, 2023). Conversely, we identify a divergent relationship between perceived usefulness and perceived ease of use in shaping consumer trust. While perceived ease of use demonstrates no statistically significant effect on trust, the perceived usefulness emerges as a robust predictor. This finding aligns with competence-based trust theory, where system utility - rather than usability - serves as the primary determinant of confidence in technological reliability (Schreibelmayr et al., 2023). Hence, it suggests that users prioritize functional benefits over interface simplicity when evaluating AI system trustworthiness in CRM contexts.

The user's perceived usefulness on AI in CRM also found significantly influences several factors. it is found that has an impact on consumers' perceived value, as it shapes their assessment of utilitarian benefits in relation to associated costs which is in line with Kanchanatanee (2024). When consumers recognize that AI provides practical advantages—such as improved efficiency, enhanced personalization, and superior decision-making—they are more likely to perceive greater value in its use. Moreover, it also influences the consumers' satisfaction, which is similar to the empirical study by Tan and Lim (2023). This suggestion is aligned with disconfirmation paradigm, where the fulfilment of task-oriented benefits creates positive expectancy-performance gaps that directly enhance user satisfaction (Chung, 2023). Then, perceived usefulness also has a positive impact on the technology confirmation operationalized through the expectation-confirmation paradigm. This relationship emerges as users' experiential assessments of functional performance converge with their a priori utility expectations. Such congruence between anticipated and realized technological benefits enhances users' post-adoption validation of the system's efficacy (Sundjaja et al., 2025). These findings collectively underscore that technology usefulness plays pivotal role as a central driver in the AI-CRM adoption cascade, operating through both cognitive (value, confirmation) and affective (trust, satisfaction) pathways.

Within the ECT framework, our analysis yields two key insights. Consumers' initial expectations demonstrate dual positive effects, simultaneously enhancing both subsequent technology confirmation and perceived usefulness. Consumers with the initial positive expectations about a technology may increase the likelihood that users will confirm or validate their experience with the technology. Additionally, they also contribute to the perception that the technology is useful. In other words, if consumers start with a favourable outlook, it reinforces their satisfaction and belief in the technology's value, creating a positive feedback loop that enhances their overall experience. Second, the confirmation process itself serves as a critical mediator, directly contributing to elevated satisfaction levels. The findings are in line with Jia et al. (2025). These relationships collectively illustrate a cascading cognitive-affective evaluation process, where pre-adoption expectations shape post-use assessments, which in turn drive emotional responses toward the AI-CRM system.

The next phase also reveals uncovers a nuanced landscape of mixed mediation effects for the proposed relationships, emphasizing the multilayered nature of consumer loyalty in relation to AI- enabled CRM systems. In our study, we first evaluated surveys and found customer engagement does not positively influence perceived value. The insignificant effect of customer engagement on perceived value may stem from multiple sources. First, perceived value is usually based on tangible characteristics including quality, price, and key features rather than the degree of engagement imparted by brand. A customer could be engaged in a brand, but they may be basing their assessment of the brand's value primarily on their own experience or the performance of other comparable products in the same category (Ko, 2024). Secondly, customer engagement could be unsuccessful because the engagement activity did not specifically recognize customer needs or preferences and consequently would not enhance their expected perceived value. Likewise, customer engagement could range from inconsistent to out of sync with customer expectations and rather lead to disengagement and lower perceived value (Chatzoglou et al., 2022). Lastly, the complexity of customer perceptions means that they can be affected by a myriad of factors outside of engagement (Parray et al., 2024), including brand reputation, trends in the market, and better competitors' offerings, diminishing the effect of engagement on perceived value (Mabkhot & Piaralal, 2023). Still, it is essential to build consumer loyalty through direct improvement. The analysis output indicated that customer engagement has a positive relationship to consumer loyalty as in Chen et al. (2022). Engaged customers also tend to contribute to the feedback errors, creating continuous improvement in products and services, thus reinforcing their loyalty (Somani et al., 2025).

Furthermore, trust is found that has contrast impact on consumer satisfaction and loyalty. Although it fails to mediate satisfaction meaning that higher levels of trust do not necessarily lead to increased customer satisfaction, it has a positive influence on loyalty outcomes. Trust creates feelings of security and confidence in the brand, causing customers to almost ignore minor failures in their experience overall, and trust leads customers to continue patronizing a brand they trust, to repeat purchase, refer others, etc., which illustrates the need to build trust and encourage customers to stick with the brand as a key strategy for improving loyalty outcomes (Alam et al., 2021). More intriguingly, both perceived value and satisfaction emerge as significant mediators, thereby demonstrating their essential roles in shaping consumer loyalty in this context. These findings suggest that the pathways to loyalty formation are not uniformly affected by all variables; rather, they underscore the importance of value perceptions and satisfaction as more reliable mediators than engagement or trust. This insight emphasizes the need for businesses to focus on cultivating these specific mediators to enhance loyalty in AI-driven environments, thus refining their strategies for customer relationship management.

At the final analysis stage, we present substantial moderation effects that challenge our fundamental understanding of the adoption process for AI-CRM features. The analysis identifies digital literacy as a key moderator that transparently mediates the relationship between perceived ease of use and perceived usefulness. This observation suggests that when developing marketing programs that promote AI-based personalization in CRM system, marketers interested in engaging customers should prioritize digital literacy education programs, as users with technological competence derive wider ranging benefit from the system's usability. Interestingly, Wideriyanti et al. (2024) indicates that digital literacy allows consumers to better utilize ecommerce by allowing consumers to engage and analyze product information more effectively to evaluate necessary information, associated with individual variables of digital literacy, it may also lead them to leverage enhanced features available as AI-generated recommendations allowing them to fully engage with the opportunities and increase their purchase frequency (Miraz et al., 2025). The moderation provided also expands the TAM in that it identifies that individual capability variables (e.g. talent level of digital literacy) can alter the fundamental perceptual relationships in technology adoption a systematic manner. For marketers, this suggests the necessity of developing segmented user experiences to account for the varying levels of users technological skills and abilities, even though we expect universal usability.

The current study contributes to an understanding of consumer loyalty in AI-enabled halal CRM through a complete model incorporating S-O-R, TAM, and ECT, however, we need to understand that with any technological adoption, practical implementation will always present challenges. In other words, beyond the theoretical frameworks, halal businesses exist in an environment where there are ethical boundaries with technology, beyond, AI transparency, consumer data privacy, and Shariah compliance. These concerns are especially sensitive in Muslim-majority markets where religious values deeply influence consumer trust. For instance, algorithmic opacity in AI-driven personalization can conflict with the Islamic principle of fairness (*adl*), while insufficient data governance may violate the trust expected in digital interactions. The ambiguity continues in regard to halal certification for digital tools because of unclear regulations. The current study's development of a conceptual model, and the applied challenges surrounding halal business in an AI-enabled CRM context, provides an inquiry into the complex ecosystem facing halal businesses when adopting AI in their CRM strategy.

6. RESEARCH IMPLICATIONS

The study has several important implications for academic research in the fields of marketing, practical, theoretical, and environmental. By examining the intersection of AI-based personalization, customer relationship management, and halal consumer behaviour, this research contributes to a deeper understanding of how emerging technologies interact with culturally and religiously sensitive markets. Firstly, the findings of this study provide critical insights for managers operating in halal industries who are seeking to adopt AI-based CRM systems. First, AI personalization must be implemented with sensitivity to Islamic values such as transparency, data ethics, and religious compliance to foster consumer trust and loyalty. Managers should prioritize the development of AI tools that exclude non-halal options, respect user privacy, and provide clear communication about how data is used. Additionally, since religiosity and digital literacy significantly influence consumer responses, businesses should segment their markets accordingly and design CRM strategies that reflect both behavioural and spiritual dimensions of their target audience. Training staff and aligning CRM systems with Shariah principles will not only boost loyalty but also strengthen brand credibility in Muslim-majority markets.

At the policy level, the study suggests a need for more formalized Shariah governance and regulatory guidelines for AI use in consumer-facing technologies. Policymakers and halal authorities (e.g., JAKIM, BPJPH, MUIS) should collaborate with tech developers to establish ethical standards for AI-driven personalization that align with halal certification. From a technology development perspective, AI systems should integrate faith-sensitive algorithms, especially in content curation, product recommendation, and customer interaction. Moreover, digital literacy programs should be promoted to empower Muslim consumers to make informed decisions in AI-mediated environments. Finally, the results can inform market design by encouraging the development of AI platforms that respect both religious values and consumer rights, creating a more inclusive digital economy

Furthermore, this study contributes to the theoretical literature by extending the S-O-R framework through the integration of technology adoption (TAM) and post-adoption (ECT) perspectives within a halal context. It introduces religiosity and digital literacy as key moderating variables—dimensions often overlooked in conventional models of AI adoption and CRM. By situating the analysis within the halal industry, the study offers a faith-driven theoretical lens that bridges behavioural science with religious consumerism. This approach not only enhances the explanatory power of existing models but also demonstrates how cultural and spiritual factors can shape the impact of AI technologies in niche markets.

The results of the research provide meaningful opportunities for increasing green, sustainable, and eco-friendly practices as part of the halal business ecosystem. As more corporations turn to AI-based personalization in CRM systems, this remodels the opportunity for not only increasing customer engagement but encouraging eco-friendly behaviour. As halal businesses use AI to streamline their operations and reduce waste and improve both digital and traditional communications, potentially aligning their marketing force and customer relationship strategy with sustainability goals. In addition, trust, satisfaction, and ethical alignment - key results from this research - suggest Muslim consumers want to do business with organizations that are environmentally responsible, aligning their consumption decisions with Islamic principles.To those end, the association of Shariah compliant AI tools coupled with environmental responsibility may create brand loyalty and assist with broader sustainability goals in faith based markets.

Future research could address longitudinal effects of AI-based personalization in halal CRM, especially how consumer loyalty develops over time as loyalty constructs evolve with consumers' interaction with faith-synchronised AI tools. Furthermore, it could also involve comparative studies of regional development (e.g. Europe versus Southeast Asia, or MENA) and across industry sectors (e.g. halal tourism, fintech, food) because regional, and situational contexts will influence how AI strategies are developed and executed and consumer's practice at some level. It would also be important to consider qualitative studies on consumer perceptions of AI ethics and religious compliance, given the inevitable collision of digital marketing with faith. Lastly expanding the model we have developed with perceived risk, Islamic consumer activism, or blockchain related to halal supply chains may help future researchers better understand the fluidity of AI and Islamic consumerism over time and space.

7. CONCLUSION

This study set out to examine the influence of AI-based personalization in CRM on consumer loyalty within the halal business sector, guided by an integrative framework combining the SOR Model, ECT, and TAM. The findings confirm that AI personalization plays a significant role in shaping consumer perceptions of usefulness and ease of use, which in turn impact their overall satisfaction and behavioural loyalty. While PU was consistently shown to be a pivotal predictor of positive outcomes across several constructs, trust was found to be moderated by religiosity—emphasizing the cultural and spiritual sensitivities in the halal market. Digital literacy was also confirmed as a moderating factor, especially in enhancing the usability and perceived value of AI-powered CRM tools. Then, religiosity emerges as a key moderator, amplifying the trust-loyalty relationship, suggesting that successful AI-CRM implementation requires culturally nuanced strategies that address both technological adoption barriers and religious values. These insights advance theoretical frameworks by extending TAM-ECT integration within cultural contexts and offer practical guidance for developing AI solutions that reconcile technological efficiency with Islamic ethical principles in halal commerce.

REFERENCES

Abdou, A. H., Chan, M. P., Rehman, S. U., Albakhit, A. I. A., & Almakhayitah, M. Y. (2024). Islamic food laws: Customer satisfaction effect halal purchase intention in China. Moderating role of religiosity. *British Food Journal*, *126*(8), 3088–3112. DOI: 10.1108/BFJ-10-2023-0875

Abinesh, R. C., & Dulloo, R. (2024). The Impact of AI-Driven Personalization on Customer Satisfaction in E-Commerce: Balancing Technology, Transparency, and Control. *Journal of Computational Analysis and Applications*, *33*(2).

Al-Ansi, A. M., & Al-Ansi, A. (2023). An overview of artificial intelligence (AI) in 6G: Types, advantages, challenges and recent applications. *Buletin Ilmiah Sarjana Teknik Elektro*, *5*(1), 67–75. DOI: 10.12928/biste.v5i1.7603

Al Mamun, M. R., Senn, W. D., Peak, D. A., Prybutok, V. R., & Torres, R. A. (2020). Emotional satisfaction and IS continuance behavior: Reshaping the expectation-confirmation model. *International Journal of Human-Computer Interaction*, *36*(15), 1437–1446. DOI: 10.1080/10447318.2020.1752478

Al-Qaysi, N., Mohamad-Nordin, N., & Al-Emran, M. (2020). A systematic review of social media acceptance from the perspective of educational and information systems theories and models. *Journal of Educational Computing Research*, *57*(8), 2085–2109. DOI: 10.1177/0735633118817879

Alam, M. M. D., Al Karim, R., & Habiba, W. (2021). The relationship between CRM and customer loyalty: The moderating role of customer trust. *International Journal of Bank Marketing*, *39*(7), 1248–1272. DOI: 10.1108/IJBM-12-2020-0607

Alnaser, F. M., Rahi, S., Alghizzawi, M., & Ngah, A. H. (2023). Does artificial intelligence (AI) boost digital banking user satisfaction? Integration of expectation confirmation model and antecedents of artificial intelligence enabled digital banking. *Heliyon*, *9*(8), e18930. DOI: 10.1016/j.heliyon.2023.e18930 PMID: 37600389

Alshammari, S. H., & Rosli, M. S. (2020). A review of technology acceptance models and theories. [ITLJ]. *Innovative Teaching and Learning Journal*, *4*(2), 12–22.

Amil, Y. (2024). *The Impact of AI-Driven Personalization Tools on Privacy Concerns and Consumer Trust in E-commerce*. Université de Liège.

Anwar, M. M. (2024). How does TAM affect impulsive buying on halal fashion products via shopping mobile apps? *Journal of Islamic Marketing*, *15*(10), 2481–2507. DOI: 10.1108/JIMA-03-2023-0096

Asante, I. O., Jiang, Y., Hossin, A. M., & Luo, X. (2023). Optimization of consumer engagement with artificial intelligence elements on electronic commerce platforms. *Journal of Electronic Commerce Research*, *24*(1), 7–28.

Attahiru, M. S. (2021). The Measurement of Hisbah Principles in the Islamic Marketing Context. *International Journal of Business and Management*, *9*(11).

Attaluri, V., & Kotte, K. R. (2025). Sustainable Business Strategies: A Data-Driven Approach to Eco-Friendly Practices. In *Driving Business Success Through Eco-Friendly Strategies* (pp. 357–374). IGI Global Scientific Publishing. DOI: 10.4018/979-8-3693-9750-3.ch019

Bharadiya, J. P., Thomas, R. K., & Ahmed, F. (2023). Rise of Artificial Intelligence in Business and Industry. *Journal of Engineering Research and Reports*, *25*(3), 85–103. DOI: 10.9734/jerr/2023/v25i3893

Bhatnagr, P., & Rajesh, A. (2024). Artificial intelligence features and expectation confirmation theory in digital banking apps: Gen Y and Z perspective. *Management Decision*.

Bhatnagr, P., Rajesh, A., & Misra, R. (2024). Continuous intention usage of artificial intelligence enabled digital banks: A review of expectation confirmation model. *Journal of Enterprise Information Management*, *37*(6), 1763–1787. DOI: 10.1108/JEIM-11-2023-0617

Bolón-Canedo, V., Morán-Fernández, L., Cancela, B., & Alonso-Betanzos, A. (2024). A review of green artificial intelligence: Towards a more sustainable future. *Neurocomputing*, *599*, 128096. DOI: 10.1016/j.neucom.2024.128096

Börekci, C., & Çelik, Ö. (2024). Exploring The Role of Digital Literacy in University Students' Engagement with AI through the Technology Acceptance Model. *Sakarya University Journal of Education*, *14*(2 (Special Issue-Artificial Intelligence Tools and Education)), 228–249. DOI: 10.19126/suje.1468866

Chatterjee, S., Rana, N. P., Dwivedi, Y. K., & Baabdullah, A. M. (2021). Understanding AI adoption in manufacturing and production firms using an integrated TAM-TOE model. *Technological Forecasting and Social Change*, *170*, 120880. DOI: 10.1016/j.techfore.2021.120880

Chatzoglou, P., Chatzoudes, D., Savvidou, A., Fotiadis, T., & Delias, P. (2022). Factors affecting repurchase intentions in retail shopping: An empirical study. *Heliyon*, *8*(9), e10619. DOI: 10.1016/j.heliyon.2022.e10619 PMID: 36158093

Chen, Y., Prentice, C., Weaven, S., & Hisao, A. (2022). The influence of customer trust and artificial intelligence on customer engagement and loyalty—The case of the home-sharing industry. *Frontiers in Psychology*, *13*, 912339. DOI: 10.3389/fpsyg.2022.912339 PMID: 35992434

Chong, F. H. L. (2021). Enhancing trust through digital Islamic finance and blockchain technology. *Qualitative Research in Financial Markets*, *13*(3), 328–341. DOI: 10.1108/QRFM-05-2020-0076

Chung, K. C. (2023). Customer satisfaction towards m-shopping and the significance of relational values and co-presence. *International Journal of Electronic Commerce Studies*, *14*(3), 21–48. DOI: 10.7903/ijecs.2242

Darmalaksana, W. (2023). How is the halal certification policy implemented? Perspective analysis of small and medium enterprises (SMEs) in Indonesia. *Journal of Islamic Accounting and Business Research*.

Dashti, L. A. H. F., Jackson, T., West, A., & Jackson, L. (2024). Enhancing halal food traceability: A model for rebuilding trust and integrity in Muslim countries. *Journal of Islamic Marketing*, *15*(12), 3382–3408. DOI: 10.1108/JIMA-06-2023-0167

Davis, F. D., Granić, A., & Marangunić, N. (2023). The technology acceptance model 30 years of TAM. *Technology*.

Dhiman, N., & Jamwal, M. (2023). Tourists' post-adoption continuance intentions of chatbots: Integrating task—technology fit model and expectation—confirmation theory. *Foresight*, *25*(2), 209–224. DOI: 10.1108/FS-10-2021-0207

Elayat, A. M. A., & Elalfy, R. M. (2025). Using SOR theory to examine the impact of AI Chatbot quality on Gen Z's satisfaction and advocacy within the fast-food sector. *Young Consumers*, *26*(2), 352–383. DOI: 10.1108/YC-08-2024-2199

Elmashhara, M. G., De Cicco, R., Silva, S. C., Hammerschmidt, M., & Silva, M. L. (2024). How gamifying AI shapes customer motivation, engagement, and purchase behavior. *Psychology and Marketing*, *41*(1), 134–150. DOI: 10.1002/mar.21912

Fernando, Y., Hendayani, R., Jawo, M., Rahamaddulla, S. R., Abdul Aziz, K., & Maimunah, N. (2025). Discovering Islamic marketing potential in shaping blockchain-based halal logistic services: A bibliometric analysis. *Journal of Islamic Marketing*, *16*(3), 870–905. DOI: 10.1108/JIMA-06-2024-0258

Gopi, B., & Samat, N. (2020). The influence of food trucks' service quality on customer satisfaction and its impact toward customer loyalty. *British Food Journal*, *122*(10), 3213–3226. DOI: 10.1108/BFJ-02-2020-0110

Hair, J. F., Black, W. C., Babin, B. J., & Anderson, R. E. (2010). *Multivariate data analysis* (Global edition). Pearson Higher Education Upper Saddle River.

Hassan, N., Abdelraouf, M., & El-Shihy, D. (2025). The moderating role of personalized recommendations in the trust—satisfaction—loyalty relationship: An empirical study of AI-driven e-commerce. *Future Business Journal*, *11*(1), 66. DOI: 10.1186/s43093-025-00476-z

Hazarika, D. D., & Dhaliwal, A. (2025). Harnessing Data for Enhanced Consumer Insights and Experiences: The Imperative for CMOs. In *Leadership Paradigms and the Impact of Technology* (pp. 157–172). IGI Global Scientific Publishing.

Hwang, H., Cho, G., & Choo, H. (2024). GSCA pro—Free stand-alone software for structural equation modeling. *Structural Equation Modeling*, *31*(4), 696–711. DOI: 10.1080/10705511.2023.2272294

Hwang, H., Sarstedt, M., Cho, G., Choo, H., & Ringle, C. M. (2023). A primer on integrated generalized structured component analysis. *European Business Review*, *35*(3), 261–284. DOI: 10.1108/EBR-11-2022-0224

Hwang, H. S., Zhu, L. C., & Cui, Q. (2023). Development and validation of a digital literacy scale in the artificial intelligence era for college students. [TIIS]. *KSII Transactions on Internet and Information Systems*, *17*(8), 2241–2258.

Ismail, J., Muchtar, A. H., Hanafi, M. I., Affandi, A. I., & Shofy, M. U. A. A. (2024). Integrating AI and Communication: A Study on Ethical Practices in Halal Supply Chain Management. *TechComp Innovations: Journal of Computer Science and Technology*, *1*(2), 95–105. DOI: 10.70063/techcompinnovations.v1i2.54

Jia, J., Chen, L., Zhang, L., Xiao, M., & Wu, C. (2025). A study on the factors that influence consumers' continuance intention to use artificial intelligence chatbots in a pharmaceutical e-commerce context. *The Electronic Library*, *43*(3), 303–321. DOI: 10.1108/EL-09-2024-0275

Jumaizi, C. W., bin M., & Tuzaka, E. (2022). Risk Management and Islamic Value: A Conceptual Development of Al-Adl Financing Risk Management. *Computational Intelligence in Security for Information Systems Conference*, 364–372.

Kanchanatanee, K. (2024). Factors Affecting The Acceptance of Artificial Intelligence in Electronic Commerce. *Asian Administration and Management Review*, *7*(2), 101–108.

Ko, H.-C. (2024). Exploring the Value of Live-Streaming Shopping and Its Impact on Customer Engagement from the Perspective of the Price-Quality-Value Model. *Proceedings of the 2024 7th International Conference on Computers in Management and Business*, 94–100. DOI: 10.1145/3647782.3647797

Latief, F., Suriyanti, S., Amin, A., Mahmud, A., Firman, A., & Dirwan, D. (2024). Ease and Risk Perception: Interest in Using Sharia Digital Payments, and the Users' Attitude Consequences. *Jurnal Minds: Manajemen Ide Dan Inspirasi*, *11*(2), 341–356.

Ligaraba, N., Chuchu, T., & Nyagadza, B. (2023). Opt-in e-mail marketing influence on consumer behaviour: A Stimuli—Organism—Response (S—O—R) theory perspective. *Cogent Business & Management*, *10*(1), 2184244. DOI: 10.1080/23311975.2023.2184244

Ling, P.-S., Yusof, F. I., & Wahab, A., A., & Bohari, S. A. (. (2025). Use intention on the Halal verification applications: The moderating role of religiosity in an SOR framework. *Journal of Islamic Marketing*. Advance online publication. DOI: 10.1108/JIMA-10-2024-0483

Lopes, J. M., Silva, L. F., & Massano-Cardoso, I. (2024). AI meets the shopper: Psychosocial factors in ease of use and their effect on E-Commerce purchase intention. *Behavioral Sciences (Basel, Switzerland)*, *14*(7), 616. DOI: 10.3390/bs14070616 PMID: 39062439

Mabkhot, H., & Piaralal, S. K. (2023). Enhancing Brand Reputation and Customer Citizenship Behaviour through Perceived Values in Hotel Industry: Role of CSR and Brand Credibility. *Transnational Marketing Journal*, *11*(2), 81–99.

Majeed, S., Lu, C., Majeed, M., & Shahid, M. N. (2018). Health resorts and multi-textured perceptions of international health tourists. *Sustainability (Basel)*, *10*(4), 1063. DOI: 10.3390/su10041063

Malatji, W. R., Van Eck, R., & Zuva, T. (2020). Understanding the usage, modifications, limitations and criticisms of technology acceptance model (TAM). *Advances in Science, Technology and Engineering Systems Journal*, *5*(6), 113–117. DOI: 10.25046/aj050612

Mbangata, L., & Abayomi, A. (2022). Learning Theories and Technology Adoption Models: A Review. *The Proceedings of the International Conference on Smart City Applications*, 388–403.

Memon, Y. J., Azhar, S. M., Haque, R., & Bhutto, N. A. (2020). Religiosity as a moderator between theory of planned behavior and halal purchase intention. *Journal of Islamic Marketing*, *11*(6), 1821–1836. DOI: 10.1108/JIMA-01-2019-0006

Mijwil, M. M., & Abttan, R. A. (2021). Artificial intelligence: A survey on evolution and future trends. *Asian Journal of Applied Sciences*, *9*(2). Advance online publication. DOI: 10.24203/ajas.v9i2.6589

Miraz, M. H., Rabiul, M. K., Adeyinka-Ojo, S., Nair, V., Tariq Hasan, M., Hossain, M. A., & Ha Jin, H. (2025). Digital literacy, marketing ability and tourist healthcare facilities influence tourists' intention to visit Asian countries through the moderation of AI. *Worldwide Hospitality and Tourism Themes*, *17*(3), 343–353. DOI: 10.1108/WHATT-02-2025-0055

Mohd Dzin, N. H., & Lay, Y. F. (2021). Validity and reliability of adapted self-efficacy scales in Malaysian context using PLS-SEM approach. *Education Sciences*, *11*(11), 676. DOI: 10.3390/educsci11110676

Mohd Thas Thaker, H., Khaliq, A., Ah Mand, A., Iqbal Hussain, H., Mohd Thas Thaker, M. A., & Allah Pitchay, A. B. (2021). Exploring the drivers of social media marketing in Malaysian Islamic banks: An analysis via smart PLS approach. *Journal of Islamic Marketing*, *12*(1), 145–165. DOI: 10.1108/JIMA-05-2019-0095

Mursid, A., & Wu, C. H.-J. (2021). The Antecedents of Customer Satisfaction and Customer-Company Identification in Enhancing Halal Restaurant Loyalty: Halal Company Identity Perspective. *International Journal of Religious Tourism and Pilgrimage*, *9*(1), 8.

Na, S., Heo, S., Han, S., Shin, Y., & Roh, Y. (2022). Acceptance model of artificial intelligence (AI)-based technologies in construction firms: Applying the Technology Acceptance Model (TAM) in combination with the Technology—Organisation—Environment (TOE) framework. *Buildings (Basel, Switzerland)*, *12*(2), 90. DOI: 10.3390/buildings12020090

Nasution, M. D. T. P., Astuti, D., Rahayu, S., Rossanty, Y., Harahap, R., & Rafiki, A. (2023). AI-Driven Chatbots in Halal Marketing Communication—Challenges and Opportunities. *Global Islamic Marketing Conference*, 403–421.

Ngelyaratan, D., & Soediantono, D. (2022). Customer relationship management (CRM) and recommendation for implementation in the defense industry: A literature review. *Journal of Industrial Engineering & Management Research*, *3*(3), 17–34.

Nguyen, D. M., Chiu, Y.-T. H., & Le, H. D. (2021). Determinants of continuance intention towards banks' chatbot services in Vietnam: A necessity for sustainable development. *Sustainability (Basel)*, *13*(14), 7625. DOI: 10.3390/su13147625

Nguyen, G.-D., & Ha, M.-T. (2021). The role of user adaptation and trust in understanding continuance intention towards mobile shopping: An extended expectation-confirmation model. *Cogent Business & Management*, *8*(1), 1980248. DOI: 10.1080/23311975.2021.1980248

Nuraini, S., & Sucipto, S. (2021). Comparison halal food regulation and practices to support halal tourism in Asia: A review. *IOP Conference Series. Earth and Environmental Science*, *733*(1), 12044. DOI: 10.1088/1755-1315/733/1/012044

Nurhayati, N. (2023). DIGITAL INNOVATION IN HALAL LOGISTICS: AN INDONESIAN CASE STUDY. *Agripreneur : Jurnal Pertanian Agribisnis*, *12*(2), 23–37. DOI: 10.35335/agripreneur.v12i2.4672

Nyagango, A. I., Sife, A. S., & Kazungu, I. (2023). Use of mobile phone technologies for accessing agricultural marketing information by grape smallholder farmers: A technological acceptance model (TAM) perspective. *Technological Sustainability*, *2*(3), 320–336. DOI: 10.1108/TECHS-01-2023-0002

Oprea, S.-V., & Bâra, A. (2025). Is Artificial Intelligence a Game-Changer in Steering E-Business into the Future? Uncovering Latent Topics with Probabilistic Generative Models. *Journal of Theoretical and Applied Electronic Commerce Research*, *20*(1), 16. DOI: 10.3390/jtaer20010016

Parray, Z. A., Iqbal, J., & Mushtaq, R. (2024). Customer perception of corporate social responsibility and its impact on customer engagement: Critical significance of corporate reputation. *Corporate Communications*, *29*(4), 592–606. DOI: 10.1108/CCIJ-05-2023-0063

Patil, D. (2024). Artificial Intelligence-Driven Customer Service: Enhancing Personalization, Loyalty, And Customer Satisfaction. *SSRN*.

Prasanthi, M., Sahu, S. R., Bakshi, M., Shanmugam, R., & Wable, P. M. (2024). Personalized Marketing in the Digital Age: The Role of AI in Consumer Behavior Analytics. *Library of Progress-Library Science, Information Technology & Computer, 44*(3).

Qizwini, J., & Perkasa, D. H. (2024). Analysis of Marketing Ethics from an Islamic Perspective. *Proceeding International Conference on Islamic Economics and Business (ICIEB), 3*(1), 46–57.

Rafiki, A. (2019). Customer Relationship Management Practices in Islamic Banks. In *Customer Relationship Management and IT*. IntechOpen.

Rahi, S., Othman Mansour, M. M., Alharafsheh, M., & Alghizzawi, M. (2021). The post-adoption behavior of internet banking users through the eyes of self-determination theory and expectation confirmation model. *Journal of Enterprise Information Management, 34*(6), 1874–1892. DOI: 10.1108/JEIM-04-2020-0156

Rahman, M. M., Al Mahi, A., & Hossian, M. A. Z. (2024). Application of AI in Halal Marketing: Navigating the Ethical Crossroads. *West Science Interdisciplinary Studies, 2*(04), 920–926. DOI: 10.58812/wsis.v2i04.866

Rahman, Z., Asadullah, J., Dodul, D. H., Shahrukh, T., Mebin, M. R., Akthar, N., Sharmin, S., Raju, Z. H., & Sonia, S. (2024). Literature Review on SOR Model from the Perspective of Social Media. *Pakistan Journal of Life and Social Sciences, 22*(2), 16630–16643. DOI: 10.57239/PJLSS-2024-22.2.001208

Ram, M., Maryam, P., & Bernard, A. T. (2024). *Beyond the Click: Unveiling the Influence of AI Personalization on E-commerce Impulse Buys.*

Rane, N. (2023). Enhancing customer loyalty through Artificial Intelligence (AI), Internet of Things (IoT), and Big Data technologies: improving customer satisfaction, engagement, relationship, and experience. *Internet of Things (IoT), and Big Data Technologies: Improving Customer Satisfaction, Engagement, Relationship, and Experience (October 13, 2023).*

Schreibelmayr, S., Moradbakhti, L., & Mara, M. (2023). First impressions of a financial AI assistant: Differences between high trust and low trust users. *Frontiers in Artificial Intelligence, 6*, 1241290. DOI: 10.3389/frai.2023.1241290 PMID: 37854078

Sehgal, A., La, H., Louis, S., & Nguyen, H. (2019). Deep reinforcement learning using genetic algorithm for parameter optimization. *2019 Third IEEE International Conference on Robotic Computing (IRC)*, 596–601. DOI: 10.1109/IRC.2019.00121

Shah, S. A., Bhutto, M. H., & Azhar, S. M. (2022). Integrative review of Islamic marketing. *Journal of Islamic Marketing, 13*(6), 1264–1287. DOI: 10.1108/JIMA-07-2020-0216

Sharma, A. K., & Sharma, R. (2023). Considerations in artificial intelligence-based marketing: An ethical perspective. *Applied Marketing Analytics, 9*(2), 162–172. DOI: 10.69554/RAPQ3226

Sheikh, H., Prins, C., & Schrijvers, E. (2023). Artificial intelligence: definition and background. In Mission, A. I. (Ed.), *The new system technology* (pp. 15–41). Springer.

Sholikah, S., Syukur, F., & Junaedi, M. (2021). Islamic education marketing discourse from maslahah perspective. *Nadwa: Jurnal Pendidikan Islam, 14*(02).

Singh, P., & Singh, V. (2024). The power of AI: Enhancing customer loyalty through satisfaction and efficiency. *Cogent Business & Management*, *11*(1), 2326107. DOI: 10.1080/23311975.2024.2326107

Sipos, D. (2025). The Effects of AI-Powered Personalization on Consumer Trust, Satisfaction, and Purchase Intent. *European Journal of Applied Science. Engineering and Technology*, *3*(2), 14–24.

Sobari, N., Kurniati, A., & Usman, H. (2022). The influence of Islamic attributes and religious commitments toward halal wellness services customer satisfaction and loyalty. *Journal of Islamic Marketing*, *13*(1), 177–197. DOI: 10.1108/JIMA-11-2018-0221

Somani, P. P., Behare, N., & Iyer, V. H. (2025). From Purchase to Metamorphosis: Cultivating Loyalty via Consumer Engagement and Experience. In *Resiliency Strategies for Long-Term Business Success* (pp. 233–256). IGI Global.

Souki, G. Q., Antonialli, L. M., Barbosa, A. A. da S., & Oliveira, A. S. (2020). Impacts of the perceived quality by consumers' of à la carte restaurants on their attitudes and behavioural intentions. *Asia Pacific Journal of Marketing and Logistics*, *32*(2), 301–321. DOI: 10.1108/APJML-11-2018-0491

Suandi, E., Herri, H., Yulihasri, Y., & Syafrizal, S. (2023). An empirical investigation of Islamic marketing ethics and convergence marketing as key factors in the improvement of Islamic banks performance. *Journal of Islamic Marketing*, *14*(6), 1438–1462. DOI: 10.1108/JIMA-07-2021-0225

Sumardi, R. S., Mahomed, A. S. B., & Aziz, Y. A. (2025). Bibliometric Analysis of Stimulus-Organism-Response Theory: Past Developments, Current Applications, and Future Trends. *International Journal of Academic Research in Business & Social Sciences*, *15*(01), 555–569. DOI: 10.6007/IJARBSS/v15-i1/23784

Sundjaja, A. M., Utomo, P., & Colline, F. (2025). The determinant factors of continuance use of customer service chatbot in Indonesia e-commerce: Extended expectation confirmation theory. *Journal of Science and Technology Policy Management*, *16*(1), 182–203. DOI: 10.1108/JSTPM-04-2024-0137

Tabelessy, W. (2023). The role of food quality and halal certificates to improve consumer satisfaction and loyalty. *International Journal of Social Service and Research*, *3*(05), 1127–1136. DOI: 10.46799/ijssr.v3i5.371

Tan, P. K., & Lim, C. M. (2023). Factors that affect user satisfaction of using e-commerce chatbot: A study on generation Z. *International Journal of Business and Technology Management*, *5*(1), 292–303.

Taujiharrahman, D., Mujibatun, S., & Agriyanto, R. (2022). The Combined Effect of Expectation Confirmation Model and Islam{\i}c Theory of Consumer Behavior on Continuance Intent of M and Internet Banking Users of Islamic Banks. *Annual International Conference on Islamic Economics and Business (AICIEB), 2*(1), 276–287.

Teepapal, T. (2025). AI-driven personalization: Unraveling consumer perceptions in social media engagement. *Computers in Human Behavior*, *165*, 108549. DOI: 10.1016/j.chb.2024.108549

Tella, A., & Olasina, G. (2014). Predicting users' continuance intention toward e-payment system: An extension of the technology acceptance model. [IJISSC]. *International Journal of Information Systems and Social Change*, *5*(1), 47–67. DOI: 10.4018/ijissc.2014010104

Teodorescu, D., Aivaz, K.-A., Vancea, D. P. C., Condrea, E., Dragan, C., & Olteanu, A. C. (2023). Consumer trust in AI algorithms used in e-commerce: A case study of college students at a Romanian public university. *Sustainability (Basel)*, *15*(15), 11925. DOI: 10.3390/su151511925

Tobing, F., Fauzan, H., Simatupang, K., & Aulia, R. (2024). *The Role of Artificial Intelligence in the Halal Industry*. Information Management and Business Review., DOI: 10.22610/imbr.v16i3(I)S.4050

Uddin, M. B. (2019). Customer loyalty in the fast food restaurants of Bangladesh. *British Food Journal*, *121*(11), 2791–2808. DOI: 10.1108/BFJ-02-2019-0140

Vafaei-Zadeh, A., Nikbin, D., Wong, S. L., & Hanifah, H. (2024). Investigating factors influencing AI customer service adoption: An integrated model of stimulus—organism—response (SOR) and task-technology fit (TTF) theory. *Asia Pacific Journal of Marketing and Logistics*.

Venkateswaran, N. (2023). AI-driven personalization in customer relationship management: Challenges and opportunities. *Journal of Theoretical and Applied Information Technology*, *101*(18), 7392–7399.

Wang, C., Ahmad, S. F., Ayassrah, A. Y. A. B. A., Awwad, E. M., Irshad, M., Ali, Y. A., Al-Razgan, M., Khan, Y., & Han, H. (2023). An empirical evaluation of technology acceptance model for Artificial Intelligence in E-commerce. *Heliyon*, *9*(8), e18349. DOI: 10.1016/j.heliyon.2023.e18349 PMID: 37520947

Widiyanti, E., Cahyadin, M., Santoso, A. I., Santoso, R. E., Widyamurti, N., & Ertimi, B. (2024). Synergy of Digital Literacy and E-Commerce in Boosting SME Performance. *EcceS. Economics Social and Development Studies*, *11*(1), 49–72.

Wilson, G., Johnson, O., & Brown, W. (2024). The Impact of Artificial Intelligence on Digital Marketing Strategies. *Journal of Digital Marketing*, *15*(3), 112–128. DOI: 10.20944/preprints202408.0276.v1

Yasin, R., Ariffin, Z. Z., Mohamed, H. A.-B., Zawawi, Z., Ghani, S. A., & Liaw, J. O. H. (2025). Islamic Values in Entrepreneurial Marketing Strategy. In *Dynamic Strategies for Entrepreneurial Marketing* (pp. 311–330). IGI Global Scientific Publishing. DOI: 10.4018/979-8-3693-3936-7.ch015

Yin, J., & Qiu, X. (2021). AI technology and online purchase intention: Structural equation model based on perceived value. *Sustainability (Basel)*, *13*(10), 5671. DOI: 10.3390/su13105671

Yin, J., Qiu, X., & Wang, Y. (2025). The Impact of AI-Personalized Recommendations on Clicking Intentions: Evidence from Chinese E-Commerce. *Journal of Theoretical and Applied Electronic Commerce Research*, *20*(1), 21. DOI: 10.3390/jtaer20010021

Zeeshan, A. (2021). Is Islamic Banking Another Marketing Gimmick? *International Journal of Business and Administrative Studies*, *7*(3), 42. DOI: 10.20469/ijbas.7.10004-3

Zimu, F. (2023). Exploring the impact of cultural factors on consumer behavior in E-commerce: A cross-cultural analysis. *Journal of Digitainability* [DREAM]. *Realism & Mastery*, *2*(03), 31–36. DOI: 10.56982/dream.v2i03.90

Chapter 12

Operational Challenges in Maintaining Halal Integrity in Cold Chain Logistics: A Study Based on Practitioner Interviews

Mohd Asyran Safwan Kamaruzaman
http://orcid.org/0000-0002-1811-0940
Universiti Teknologi MARA, Malaysia

Adli Iskandar Md Fauzi
Universiti Teknologi MARA, Malaysia

Mohamad Hasif Jaafar
Universiti Teknologi MARA, Malaysia

Nasif Sidquee Pauzi
Universiti Teknologi MARA, Malaysia

ABSTRACT

Maintaining halal integrity is becoming more important in cold chain logistics due to increasing global demand for halal-certified products. However, this integrity can be compromised if key operational issues are not properly managed, particularly in handling, temperature control, and storage. This study looks at the challenges faced by Bismi Cergas Sdn Bhd, a logistics company, in keeping its operations halal-compliant. A qualitative method was used, involving semi-structured interviews

DOI: 10.4018/979-8-3373-2792-1.ch012

with four company staff members. The interview data were analyzed using thematic analysis. The results identified several major challenges: unclear halal guidelines, issues with product thawing and refreezing, limited halal awareness among non-Muslim employees, and problems with animals or pests entering the premises. The study highlights that maintaining halal integrity in cold chain logistics depends on having proper standard operating procedures (SOPs), staff awareness, good infrastructure, and clear guidance from halal authorities.

INTRODUCTION

The global halal market has transcended its traditional religious boundaries to emerge as a formidable economic force, captivating a consumer base that includes both Muslims and non-Muslims alike. This surge is propelled by a powerful perception of halal certification as a universal benchmark for quality, safety, ethical sourcing, and hygiene (Utomo et al., 2021). As this demand proliferates across international markets, the complexity of the halal supply chain increases exponentially. The integrity of a halal product is no longer solely determined at the point of manufacture; instead, it is a fragile quality that must be meticulously preserved through every subsequent link in the logistical chain. This reality brings the field of halal logistics, particularly the highly sensitive cold chain, into sharp focus as a critical determinant of consumer trust and market viability.

Within this context, maintaining halal integrity is a multifaceted challenge that extends far beyond the basic avoidance of direct physical contamination with non-halal items. It encompasses a holistic system of protocols requiring rigorous segregation, unwavering commitment to hygiene, unambiguous labelling, and scrupulous compliance with standard operating procedures (SOPs) deeply rooted in Islamic principles. The cold chain, a temperature-controlled supply network designed to preserve perishable goods from production through storage, transportation, distribution, and final retailing, introduces a layer of profound complexity. The time-sensitive, high-pressure environment inherent to cold chain operations—characterized by rapid loading, limited storage space, and stringent delivery windows—creates a fertile ground for inadvertent breaches in halal protocols.

Recognizing these vulnerabilities, authoritative bodies like Malaysia's Department of Islamic Development (JAKIM) have pioneered comprehensive regulatory frameworks, most notably the MS2400:2019 series standard for Halal Logistics. These guidelines provide a crucial foundation for operational compliance. Yet, a significant and persistent chasm exists between the theoretical standards and their practical, day-to-day implementation. Empirical evidence suggests that numerous companies struggle to adhere to these guidelines effectively. Scholarly research has consistently identified key impediments, including prohibitive financial investments required for dedicated infrastructure, organizational resistance to change, and a critical shortage of personnel equipped with specialized halal logistics training (Talib et al., 2015). Consequently, tangible operational issues—such as the ethically and legally problematic thawing-refreezing cycle, a startling lack of halal awareness even among Muslim employees, and biosecurity threats like animal incursions into storage premises—continue to plague the industry.

While the existing academic literature has been instrumental in cataloging what these challenges are, a critical limitation remains. The current body of knowledge is largely constructed from macro-level analyses, quantitative surveys targeting mid-to-senior management, and theoretical model-building (Zailani et al., 2017). As Zailani et al. (2017) themselves note, this has resulted in a field that is somewhat "immature and incomplete," struggling to generate generalizable models that reflect on-the-ground realities. The consequence is a pronounced scarcity of rich, qualitative insights that delve into the lived experiences of frontline practitioners. These are the warehouse operators, truck drivers, loaders, and floor supervisors who are the first and last line of defense for halal integrity. Their daily decisions, made under immense operational pressure, ultimately determine success or failure. The "how," "why," and "when" of these operational breakdowns are stories that remain largely untold and unanalyzed in academic discourse.

Therefore, the fundamental issue is not merely the existence of operational challenges but a profound understanding gap regarding their root causes and manifestations in the field. This gap hinders the development of pragmatic, effective, and sustainable solutions. This study is designed to directly address this void. By shifting the analytical lens to the ground level, this research aims to provide a detailed, empirically-grounded exploration of the operational challenges in maintaining halal cold chain integrity from the perspective of the practitioners themselves. It is by illuminating these nuanced, everyday struggles that this study seeks to generate the insights necessary to bridge the implementation gap, inform more robust policy, and ultimately contribute to the strengthening of global halal assurance systems.

RESEARCH METHODOLOGY

Research Philosophy and Theoretical Foundation

This study is grounded in the interpretivist research philosophy. Interpretivism posits that social reality is not objective and singular but is rather subjective and constructed through human experiences and social contexts (Saunders et al., 2019). The core aim of this research is to explore the complex and context-laden operational challenges faced by practitioners. These challenges are not independent facts to be measured but are shaped by individual perceptions, organizational cultures, and specific situational factors. An interpretivist stance is, therefore, appropriate as it seeks to understand and interpret the meanings participants assign to their daily experiences in maintaining halal integrity within the cold chain.

Guided by this philosophy, a qualitative research methodology was adopted. This methodology is chosen for its ability to provide rich, detailed insights into complex, poorly understood social phenomena (Creswell & Poth, 2018). It is particularly suited to answering "how" and "why" questions, allowing for an exploration of the depth and complexity of human behavior. Given that the nature of halal practices in logistics is intricate and highly context-specific, a qualitative approach is essential to capture the lived experiences, perspectives, and tacit insights from frontline operators.

Research Design and Data Collection

The specific research design employed is an exploratory case study focused on the Malaysian halal cold chain logistics sector. A case study design is ideal for investigating a contemporary phenomenon within its real-life context, especially when the boundaries between the phenomenon and context are not clearly evident (Yin, 2018). This design supports the aim of achieving a deep, contextual understanding of real-world issues.

Data were collected through semi-structured interviews with four logistics practitioners. This method was selected because it provides a balanced structure, ensuring coverage of key topics while granting flexibility to probe deeper into emerging themes (Kallio et al., 2016). This approach is crucial for discovering detailed information and nuanced understandings that structured surveys would be unable to capture.

Validation and Ethical Considerations

Prior to data collection, this study received full approval from the UiTM Research Ethics Committee. The study adhered to strict ethical principles, including informed consent, confidentiality, and the right to withdraw. To enhance the validity of the instrument, the semi-structured interview protocol was reviewed and validated by an expert in the field, Dr. Mohd Hasif Jaafar.

Table 1. Developed interview questions

No.	Interview questions
1	How long have you worked in this company/or this field?
2	Can you please explain your role in the company's logistics operations?
3	Have you attended training / courses on halal logistics certification (e.g. MS 2400:2019)?
4	What can you explain briefly from the course?
5	What does halal integrity mean in the context of logistics for your company?
6	What steps are companies taking to ensure halal integrity is maintained throughout the logistics cold chain?
7	What are the main challenges faced in ensuring the separation between halal and non-halal products (in warehouses, in transportation, etc.)?
8	How do you address the risk of cross-contamination during transportation (e.g. in terms of cleaning, container/goods management, temperature control)?
9	What is the level of awareness and compliance of employees towards halal logistics requirements?
10	What technical or infrastructural constraints (e.g. storage facilities, vehicles, SOPs) that can affect halal compliance?
11	What challenges are faced or expected in preparing to obtain halal logistics certification?
12	To what extent is management supportive in investing towards halal logistics certification (in terms of training, facilities, procedures)?
13	How does the company ensure that halal integrity is maintained during the transition process in the cold chain (during unloading, transfer, temperature monitoring)?
14	Have you ever faced issues related to thawing and refreezing that could affect halal status?
15	What are the best practices that you can share with other companies that want to obtain halal logistics certification?
16	In your opinion, what form of support or policies from the authorities can help the logistics industry more easily implement halal standards?
17	Is there any additional information or additional comments?

Data Analysis

The interview data were analyzed using thematic analysis following the six-phase framework outlined by Braun and Clarke (2006). This method involves a systematic process of identifying, analyzing, and reporting patterns (themes) within qualitative data. The process included (a) familiarizing oneself with the data, (b) generating initial codes, (c) searching for themes, (d) reviewing potential themes, (e) defining and naming themes, and (f) producing the report. This iterative process allows for a rich and detailed account of the data, which aligns directly with the study's interpretivist foundation.

Conclusion

The chosen research design, grounded in interpretivism and executed through a qualitative case study approach, is robust and appropriate. It effectively supports the primary aim of the study, which is to develop a deeper, contextually rich understanding of the under-researched operational challenges in maintaining halal integrity within Malaysia's cold chain logistics sector.

FINDINGS

Need for Clear and Comprehensive Halal Logistics Guidelines

One of the existing issues that was raised by multiple participants is the lack of detailed and practical guidelines provided by halal authorities for logistics practitioners. Even though the halal standard like MS 2400:2019 exists, some participants felt that the guideline in it was too general for the implementation. They suggested that more operational guidance or modules from JAKIM must be made so it will help companies in implementing the halal requirements more effectively. The quotes from practitioners about this issue can be seen in Table 2.

Table 2. Interview transcript on item question 16

Question	Participant	Answer
In your opinion, what form of support or policy from the authorities can help the logistics industry more easily implement halal standards?	Participant 1	The authorities need to provide complete guidance to the halal logistics certificate applicants about the methods to perfectly maintain halal integrity in cold chain logistics.
	Participant 3	The authorities need to provide a clear explanation of the requirements of halal logistics so that companies will not make any inaccurate interpretations of the requirements. For example, halal awareness training. The Malaysian Standard for halal logistics does not provide a specific description of what modules and topics are required in the halal training.
	Participant 4	The industry needs more in-depth disclosure from the authorities about the halal logistics certification process from obtaining to maintaining the halal certificate so that they do not hesitate about the steps and interpretations that they make.

If the halal requirements are too general, logistics personnel might interpret it differently and they will struggle to translate those general requirements into real day-to-day procedures. This ambiguity will not only delay the approval of halal logistics applications, it also can terminate existing halal certificates from logistics companies. As halal logistics is a relatively new field and still growing in Malaysia, many companies, especially those who are in the early stages, are still developing their systems to adapt with halal requirements. Clear and detailed guidance from halal authorities will ensure proper compliance. This issue was raised by three out of four participants, showing that there is a need for halal logistics guidelines that are clear and detailed to the logistics practitioner. Plus, participant 3 has clearly mentioned about the halal awareness training aspects in the requirements that doesn't specify on any topic or module that should be the guide for them. This may cause the content of the training to be insufficient that can lead to the workers not gaining enough information about halal awareness.

Thawing-Refreezing Issue

Another important challenge that was identified to maintain halal integrity in cold chain logistics is the issue of thawing-refreezing issues of the poultry products during the storage process. It is a situation where the product defrosts because of the rise of temperature and refreeze it again. The participants reported the situation where the issue occurred sometimes in the cold room. Below is Table 3 stating the quotes from participants regarding this issue.

Table 3. Interview transcript on question 14 & 10

Question	Participant	Answer
Have you ever faced issues related to thawing and refreezing that could affect halal status?	Participant 1	We have faced that issue. Products that have this issue cannot be delivered to the customers and must go through a rework or disposal process for the damaged product.
	Participant 2	Products that experience the issue will be categorized as returns (products that will be returned to the factory). Then, the Quality Control team will then check the quality and safety of the product before moving it on to the next step. Then, they will investigate the cause leading to this issue.
	Participant 4	Sometimes this issue occurs in a cold room that is being upgraded because the cold room is being entered with the products exceeding the capacity limit that has been set.
What technical or infrastructural constraints (for example, storage facilities, vehicles, SOPs) that will affect the halal compliance in the halal logistics supply chain?	Participant 4	The storage area is still in the process of being upgraded to accommodate the increasing product order capacity, especially in the cold room.

The thawing-refreezing is a very important issue as it can directly spoil both the quality and halal integrity of poultry products. Even if the product thaws partially, it invites microbial growth and moisture contamination (Díaz et al., 2023), which can lead to doubts about the halal status, especially when the products are in direct contact with unclean surfaces. As has been reported by participant 4, the thawing-refreezing issue sometimes happens because the cold room is still in the upgrading process and the products in the current cold room sometimes exceed the limited quantity to withstand orders that keep increasing. This issue has been reported by three out of four participants, showing that the issue of products thawing-refreezing is a problem that happens frequently in the cold chain logistics.

Lack of Halal Awareness among Non-Muslim Employers

Another notable issue from the semi-structured interview is the lack of halal awareness among non-Muslim employers who are managing and owning the cold chain logistics business. One of the participants has expressed concern about some non-Muslim business owners not fully understanding and not prioritizing halal in their halal cold chain logistics company. While another one of them suggested that all involved parties including non-Muslim logistics business owners must be aware about halal practice. The quotes from participants that came up with this issue can be seen in Table 4 below.

Table 4. Interview transcript on question 7 & 15

Question	Participant	Answer
What are the main challenges faced in ensuring the separation between halal and non-halal products (in the warehouses and transportation, etc.)?	Participant 1	Non-Muslim company owners usually do not understand or care about the importance of maintaining halal status for Muslims. There are also buildings involved in logistics processes that are not fenced and covered to prevent animals such as cats from entering the logistics area.
What are the best practices that you can share with the other companies that want to apply for the halal logistics certification?	Participant 3	Every party who wants to apply for halal logistics even if they are non-Muslim needs to have awareness about the concept of halal logistics..

This issue is very important because in any logistics operation, employers and management will make key decisions about all aspects in cold chain logistics. If there is a lack of halal awareness and understanding among non-Muslim employers, it may lead to improper implementation of halal procedures, weak internal halal policies and the avoidance to invest in halal-compliant systems. This issue was specifically reported by one participant while another participant supported the report indirectly by suggesting that non-Muslim employers also must have halal awareness. Although this issue was not mentioned by majority of the participants like two previous issues, it still shows a real concern from the interviews, especially in the company that have diverse logistics environments where top management and business owners are not familiar with halal principles.

Animals Entering the Premise

The last theme and issue that was raised in the interviews was animals entering the logistics premise. The common animals mentioned by one of the participants were cats, cockroaches, rats and termites. The participants share this concern as these animals could compromise both halal integrity and cleanliness if not controlled properly. Cleanliness is one of key requirements in halal aspects, and these animals and pests can affect the halal the halal status of the products and the environment of the premise. This theme highlights the problem of animals and pests entering the premise that arise in halal logistics discussion. The quotes from one participant can be seen in Table 5.

Table 5. Interview transcript on question 7, 8 & 11

Question	Participant	Answer
What are the main challenges faced in ensuring the separation between halal and non-halal products (in warehouses, in transportation, etc.)?	Participant 1	Non-Muslim company owners usually do not understand or care about the importance of maintaining halal status for Muslims. There are also buildings involved in logistics processes that are not fenced and covered to prevent animals such as cats from entering the logistics area.
How do you handle the risk of cross-contamination during transportation (e.g. in terms of cleaning, container/ goods management, temperature control)?	Participant 1	Dealing with the entry of pests such as rats, cockroaches and termites into the logistics area by hiring insect repellants.
What challenges are faced or expected in preparing to obtain halal logistics certification?	Participant 1	Companies must register with the veterinary department (VHM) and close and fence off logistics areas to prevent the entry of animals such as cats.

This issue is very important because the entry of animals and pests like cats, cockroaches, rats and termites can be serious threats for two core principals in halal logistics, cleanliness and halal integrity. Animals and pests like them can bring in *najs mutawassitah* and carry filth from themselves. Plus, unfenced premise may also invite dogs that carry *najs mughallazah* that must be purified with the *sertu* method.

From a practical discussion, this issue reflects the weakness in pest control measures and premise design. In cold chain logistics where the products are being stored, entire batches of products can be affected even if it is entered by a small amount of infestation. Besides of compromising halal issue, the animal and pest infestation also can violate food safety as it can invite bacteria, fungi and virus, which put the halal certification and consumers' health at risk.

Even though this issue was only reported by one participant only, it was mentioned three times in three different questions during the interview. The repeated mention suggests that one participant views this issue as a significant concern that happens in daily operations. Although it was not mentioned by other participants in these interviews, the fact that one participant consistently repeated it can be the indicator that this issue may be underreported or not commonly acknowledged even it can have a huge impact on halal integrity and product cleanliness.

DISCUSSION

This study set out to explore the ground-level operational challenges of maintaining halal integrity in Malaysia's cold chain logistics sector. The findings reveal a complex interplay of procedural, human, and infrastructural factors that collectively threaten the halal assurance system. While each identified challenge—unclear guidelines, the thawing-refreezing cycle, a lack of awareness among non-Muslim employers, and animal intrusion—is significant on its own, their true impact is multiplicative. This discussion moves beyond describing these issues to interpret their deeper implications, synthesise them into a coherent narrative of systemic risk, and propose a theoretical lens for understanding halal logistics compliance. It concludes by outlining the practical and theoretical contributions of this work and acknowledging its limitations.

Synthesis and Interpretation of Key Findings

The Procedural Void: When Guidelines Lack Granularity

The finding that practitioners struggle with a "need for clear and comprehensive halal logistics guidelines" (Muhammad et al., 2020) points to a critical gap between policy and practice. While standards like MS2400:2019 provide a essential philosophical framework, our data suggest they fall short as operational manuals. The ambiguity in cleaning different types of *najis* (ritual impurities) is a prime example. This is not merely a communication gap but a procedural void that forces companies to interpret religious principles without expert guidance, risking inconsistent and potentially non-compliant practices. This finding is crucial because it shifts the blame from individual negligence to a systemic shortcoming. The "fragile" halal assurance system you describe stems from this very void. Without prescribed, standardised training modules, each company creates its own interpretation of halal, leading to a landscape of uneven compliance where the halal status (*halalan tayyiban*) of a product becomes uncertain (*shubhah*), not through malice, but through a lack of definitive direction.

The Clash of Logics: Operational Efficiency vs. Ritual Purity

The thawing-refreezing issue powerfully illustrates a fundamental conflict at the heart of halal logistics: the clash between the logic of operational efficiency and the imperative of ritual purity and safety. Cold chain logistics is driven by the relentless pressures of time, cost, and capacity utilisation (as seen during upgrades or peak seasons like Eid al-Adha). The act of refreezing thawed meat is, from a purely operational and economic logic, a way to avoid loss. However, from the logics of halal and food science, it is unequivocally unacceptable (Turgut et al., 2025; Opoku-Nkoom, 2015), compromising both safety and integrity. Participants are caught in this clash. Their suggested solutions—stricter FIFO (Abd-El Aziz et al., 2012) and third-party logistics—are attempts to reconcile these logics by creating operational workarounds that protect halal integrity without crippling efficiency. This tension is a central, under-theorised challenge in the halal industry that requires management strategies that genuinely integrate these two competing imperatives.

The Critical Role of Leadership in Cultural Compliance

The finding regarding the lack of halal awareness among non-Muslim employers extends the work of Ernest and Lau (2012) and Prabowo et al. (2015) into a critical management insight. Halal compliance cannot be viewed solely as a procedural or floor-level worker issue; it is fundamentally a top-down organisational and cultural commitment. The decision-making power of managers and owners directly dictates resource allocation for training, infrastructure, and time-consuming procedures like *sertu* (ritual cleansing). If leadership perceives halal as merely a certificate for market access rather than a core value proposition, compliance becomes a check-box exercise, vulnerable to being overridden by efficiency pressures. Therefore, the "awareness" deficit is not just a knowledge gap but a strategic risk. Building a robust halal culture requires targeted engagement with leadership, convincing them of the brand equity, consumer trust, and market longevity that genuine halal commitment provides, transforming it from a religious obligation into a strategic business advantage.

Infrastructural Neglect as a Form of Contamination

The issue of animals entering the premise (Ismail et al., 2022, 2023) seems like a simple pest control problem but symbolises a deeper issue of infrastructural neglect. A facility with poor barriers, uncovered drains, and inadequate pest control is a facility that is inherently non-compliant. It represents a passive, constant threat of contamination that can invalidate halal status instantly, regardless of how careful workers are. This finding underscores that halal integrity is not just about active processes but also about passive, built-environment factors. Investing in physical infrastructure is as important as training staff. The participant's solution of hiring a licensed pest control company and the literature's suggestion of AI-powered monitoring (Olatunde et al., 2024) highlight a shift from reactive to proactive, technology-driven integrity management, representing the future of halal assurance.

Theoretical and Practical Implications

This study offers a key theoretical implication: effective halal logistics management requires a Integrated Compliance Framework that addresses three interconnected levels:

1. **The Systemic Level:**
   Regulatory bodies must close the procedural void with detailed, practical directives.
2. **The Organisational Level:**
   Companies must foster a halal culture from the top down, reconciling operational and ritual logics.
3. **The Infrastructural Level:**
   Physical facilities must be designed and maintained as the first line of defense against contamination.

This framework moves beyond checklists and argues that halal integrity is a dynamic outcome of interacting systems, culture, and infrastructure.

Practical Implications

1. **For Halal Authorities (JAKIM):**
   Develop mandatory, detailed annexes to MS2400 for cold chain operations, specifically outlining cleaning methods for different *najis* and standardised training modules.
2. **For Logistics Companies:**

Implement advanced facility management (e.g., AI monitoring) and advocate for clearer standards. Develop internal halal leadership training programs aimed at all levels of management.

3. **For Industry Associations:**
   Create platforms for knowledge-sharing on best practices for overcoming the efficiency-purity clash, such as models for collaborative cold storage during peak demand.

Limitations and Future Research

This study's findings, while insightful, are constrained by its focus on a single company, limiting generalisability. Future research should expand to a multi-case study design across various regions and company sizes in Malaysia. Furthermore, relying solely on interviews introduces the potential for social desirability bias; future studies should incorporate ethnographic methods and direct observation to capture the actual practices, not just the reported ones. Finally, a specific investigation into the decision-making processes of non-Muslim stakeholders in the halal industry would provide invaluable depth to the understanding of organisational commitment.

CONCLUSION

The journey through the operational realities of Malaysia's halal cold chain logistics reveals a landscape fraught with intricate challenges. This study has identified that the threats to halal integrity are not merely isolated operational hiccups but are symptomatic of deeper, systemic gaps within the national halal ecosystem. The ambiguity in guidelines creates a procedural void, leaving well-intentioned practitioners without a clear roadmap. The thawing-refreezing cycle exemplifies a fundamental conflict between the relentless pressures of logistical efficiency and the non-negotiable demands of ritual purity and food safety. Furthermore, a lack of halal-centric leadership, particularly among non-Muslim decision-makers, points to a critical cultural and strategic gap that can undermine even the most robust standard operating procedures. Finally, issues like animal intrusion underscore that halal is as much about physical infrastructure and proactive investment as it is about process and protocol.

Collectively, these challenges form a chain of vulnerability where a single weak link—be it an unclear rule, a compromised temperature, an uninformed decision, or an unsealed entry point—can irrevocably break the trust of consumers and nullify the hard-earned halal certification. This erodes Malaysia's brand equity as a global halal hub, transforming a powerful competitive advantage into a potential liability.

Addressing this multifaceted problem demands an equally sophisticated and collaborative multi-stakeholder strategy. The way forward is clear:

1. **For Regulatory Bodies (JAKIM, etc.):** The call to action is to evolve from setting principles to prescribing practices. This means developing detailed, actionable, and enforceable annexes to existing standards like MS2400:2019 that offer granular guidance on critical issues like *sertu* and *najs* cleaning methods, and mandating standardized training modules to ensure consistency across the industry.
2. **For Logistics Companies:** Compliance must be reframed from a cost center to a core value proposition. Investment in advanced operational technologies—such as AI-driven hygiene monitoring and real-time temperature tracking—is no longer optional but essential. Adopting best practices like strict FIFO systems and forming strategic partnerships with certified third-party logistics providers during peak periods are crucial steps to mitigate risk.
3. **For Industry Leadership:** Building a true "halal culture" requires moving beyond the warehouse floor to the boardroom. Targeted engagement and awareness programs for non-Muslim employers and managers are imperative to align strategic decision-making with halal requirements, ensuring that resource allocation and corporate priorities reflect a genuine commitment to integrity.

While this study offers a critical, ground-level perspective, it also acknowledges its limitations, primarily its focus on a single company. This very limitation, however, serves as a springboard for future research. It underscores the urgent need for large-scale, multi-company studies that can validate and generalize these findings. Furthermore, it highlights the potential for rich, ethnographic research involving on-site observation to move beyond what participants *say* they do to reveal what they *actually* do in practice.

In the final analysis, preserving halal integrity in the complex cold chain is a daunting but essential endeavor. It is a continuous process of improvement, vigilance, and adaptation. By closing the procedural voids, reconciling operational logics, fostering enlightened leadership, and embracing technological innovation, Malaysia can fortify its halal logistics framework. This will not only fulfill a religious obligation but will also solidify a formidable commercial advantage, ensuring that the promise of "halalan tayyiban" (permissible and wholesome) is a guarantee delivered from farm to fork, thereby securing consumer confidence and ensuring long-term market sustainability for the nation.

REFERENCES

Abd-El Aziz, N. A., Moharram, Y. G., Attia, R. S., & Kotit, S. M. (2012). Application of HACCP system during meat slices preparation. *GIDA-Journal of Food*, *2*, 59–66.

Braun, V., & Clarke, V. (2006). Using thematic analysis in psychology. *Qualitative Research in Psychology*, *3*(2), 77–101. DOI: 10.1191/1478088706qp063oa

Creswell, J. W., & Poth, C. N. (2018). *Qualitative inquiry and research design: Choosing among five approaches* (4th ed.). SAGE Publications.

Díaz, A. V., Calleja, C. A., Escámez, P. F., Abuín, C. M. F., Sillué, S. M., & Moragas, G. S. (2023). Report of the Scientific Committee of the Spanish Agency for Food Safety and Nutrition (AESAN) on the determination of the date of minimum durability for frozen meat in retail establishments (Vol. 1, No. 1, p. 0001E).

Ernest, C. D., & Lau, W. M. (2012). Will those targeted pay more? The Issue of Halal Logo. Osman MohdZain. Reading in Marketing: An Islamic Perspective.

Ismail, I. A., Rozar, N. M., Usman, I., Menhat, M., Kamaruddine, S. A., & Razik, M. A. (2023). Challenges faced by Halal Warehouse during the Implementation of Islamic Shariah Compliance: Malaysian Perspective. *Journal for Maritime Research*, *20*(2), 135–140.

Ismail, S., Nazarudin, N., & Muhamad, M. Z. (2022). Governance of halal logistics compliance. *Journal of Contemporary Islamic Studies*, *8*(3), 1–20. DOI: 10.24191/jcis.v8i3.6

Kallio, H., Pietilä, A.-M., Johnson, M., & Kangasniemi, M. (2016). Systematic methodological review: Developing a framework for a qualitative semi-structured interview guide. *Journal of Advanced Nursing*, *72*(12), 2954–2965. DOI: 10.1111/jan.13031 PMID: 27221824

Muhammad, M. A., Elistina, A. B., & Ahmad, S. (2020). The challenges faced by halal certification authorities in managing the halal certification process in Malaysia. *Food Research*, *4*(1), 170–178. DOI: 10.26656/fr.2017.4(S1).S17

Olatunde, T. M., Okwandu, A. C., Akande, D. O., & Sikhakhane, Z. Q.Tosin Michael OlatundeAzubuike Chukwudi OkwanduDorcas Oluwajuwonlo AkandeZamathula Queen Sikhakhane. (2024). Reviewing the role of artificial intelligence in energy efficiency optimization. *Engineering Science & Technology Journal*, *5*(4), 1243–1256. DOI: 10.51594/estj.v5i4.1015

Opoku-Nkoom, W. (2015). Safety and quality characteristics of freeze-defrost cycles in muscle foods. *EC Nutr, 1*, 140–144.

Prabowo, S., Abd Rahman, A., Ab Rahman, S., & Samah, A. A. (2015). Revealing factors hindering halal certification in East Kalimantan Indonesia. *Journal of Islamic Marketing, 6*(2), 268–291. DOI: 10.1108/JIMA-05-2014-0040

Saunders, M. N. K., Lewis, P., & Thornhill, A. (2019). *Research methods for business students* (8th ed.). Pearson.

Talib, M. S. A., Hamid, A. B. A., Zulfakar, M. H., & Chin, T. A. (2015). Barriers to Halal logistics operation: Views from Malaysian logistics experts. *International Journal of Logistics Systems and Management, 22*(2), 193–209. DOI: 10.1504/IJLSM.2015.071545

Turgut, S. S., Myustedzhebov, A., & Feyissa, A. H. (2025). Low-cost multispectral sensor reveals cold chain breaks, meat type, and storage time in chicken meat samples. *Food Control, 167*, 110816. DOI: 10.1016/j.foodcont.2024.110816

Utomo, S. B., Sekaryuni, R., Widarjono, A., Tohirin, A., & Sudarsono, H. (2021). Promoting Islamic financial ecosystem to improve halal industry performance in Indonesia: A demand and supply analysis. *Journal of Islamic Marketing, 12*(5), 992–1011. DOI: 10.1108/JIMA-12-2019-0259

Yin, R. K. (2018). *Case study research and applications: Design and methods* (6th ed.). SAGE Publications.

Zailani, S., Iranmanesh, M., Aziz, A. A., & Kanapathy, K. (2017). Halal logistics opportunities and challenges. *Journal of Islamic Marketing, 8*(1), 127–139. DOI: 10.1108/JIMA-04-2015-0028

Chapter 13
The Role of Maqasid al-Shari'ah in Influencing Halal Travel Intentions:
Evidence From Muslim-Friendly Tourism in Yogyakarta, Indonesia

Wahyu Wibowo
http://orcid.org/0009-0000-5176-7103
Sunan Kalijaga State Islamic University, Yogyakarta, Indonesia

Siti Nur Azizah
http://orcid.org/0000-0003-3554-9637
Sunan Kalijaga State Islamic University, Yogyakarta, Indonesia

ABSTRACT

This study examines the impact of religious experience, visitor satisfaction, service quality, destination image, and affordability on Muslim tourists' intentions to visit Muslim-friendly destinations in Yogyakarta, Indonesia. Using the Maqāṣid al-Sharīʿah framework, the research applies a Shariah-oriented lens to understand travel behavior. A structured survey was conducted with 300 Muslim tourists, and data were analyzed using SPSS version 30, including validity, reliability, and regression tests. Results indicate that religious experience, satisfaction, service quality, and destination image significantly influence travel intention, with religious experience being the strongest predictor. Affordability, however, showed no significant effect. The findings validate the relevance of Maqāṣid al-Sharīʿah in explaining Muslim travel behavior. The study is limited to one location and does not account for variables such as religiosity or cultural background. Future research is encouraged to use broader, comparative, or longitudinal designs.

DOI: 10.4018/979-8-3373-2792-1.ch013

1. INTRODUCTION

The Muslim-friendly tourism sector has continued to undergo transformation in recent years, which has become a new chapter for the global tourism industry (Moshin et al., 2020; Suban et al., 2023; Wibowo et al., 2025; Restuti et al., 2025). Hashim et al. (2025) argues that several structural and socio-cultural factors, such as rising incomes, the growth of the Muslim middle class, and the growing global awareness of halal values, have been the main drivers behind the increasing demand for Muslim-friendly tourism.According to the Global Muslim Travel Index (GMTI, 2024), in 2019 the number of Muslim tourists from all over the world reached 160 million, and is expected to increase to 230 million by 2028. These tourists will contribute more than USD 300 billion to the global economy. The main reasons for this growth are marked by increasing purchasing power, strengthening Islamic identity, and increasing number of services available (Battour & Ismail, 2016; Han et al., 2019).

In addition, millennials and Gen Z Muslims are emerging with ethical and sustainability awareness that adds a new dimension to consumer expectations (Amalia et al., 2024). As spiritual awareness grows, there is also a new tendency among Muslim travelers, especially millennials and Gen Z, to associate their travel choices with good and ecologically responsible consumption. These trends include a preference for destinations that not only offer halal services, but also seek to implement sustainable practices such as the use of renewable energy, good waste management, and the preservation of local culture. Studies by Amalia et al. (2024) and Maulida et al. (2024) show that young Muslim tourists are more likely to judge destinations based on the values of environmental sustainability and social justice, rather than just worship facilities or low prices. Therefore, the ethical and ecological dimensions are important in the behavior of modern tourism that is friendly to Muslims. (Saffinee et al., 2024), but also address complex environmental and social challenges.

Indonesia, as a country with the largest Muslim population in the world of around 246.63 million people (RISSC, 2024), has a strategic position in the development of Muslim-friendly tourism. Based on the Indonesian Muslim Travel Index (IMTI, 2023) report, Indonesia has always consistently been in the top five positions as a global destination for Muslim-friendly tourism. The evaluation conducted by IMTI is based on the availability of worship facilities, halal-certified food, and national policy support. This strategic position is even strengthened by the National Committee for Sharia Economics and Finance (KNEKS) which has designated Muslim-friendly tourism as a national priority in the Indonesian Halal Industry Master Plan 2023–2029 (KNEKS, 2023). However, these achievements need to be more aligned with the sustainable development agenda in order to not only meet the preferences of Muslim tourists (Saffinee et al., 2024), but also address complex environmental and social challenges.

Unfortunately, scientific studies still focus on the determinants of tourist behavior that are functional and psychological such as value perception, destination image, and service quality (Eid & El-Gohary, 2015; Battour et al., 2018; Hanafiah et al., 2020; Sodawan & Hsu, 2022; Joseph et al., 2022; Ratnasari et al., 2024). There is also a lot of literature that has examined the psychological constructs of the consumer level, including trust, religiosity, and brand loyalty (Mustikawati et al., 2022; Maulida et al., 2024; Zaki & Elseidi, 2024; Martaleni et al., 2025). In addition, many studies still use Western frameworks such as *the Theory of Planned Behavior* (TPB), which emphasizes more rationality and social norms, but has not been able to fully represent Islamic spiritual values and ethics (Ajzen, 1991; Junaidi, 2020).

Although research can be a source of knowledge and enrich humans about tourist behavior. This framework is indeed useful as a universal starting point, but in the context of Muslim tourists this kind of understanding often fails to grasp the transcendental, spiritual, and ethical dimensions that shape their decisions (Henderson, 2010; Zamani-Farahani & Eid, 2016; Suban et al., 2023). Therefore, a number of researchers call for the need for an alternative framework that is not only theoretically compatible, but also epistemologically aligned with Islamic values (Fauzi & Battour, 2024; Muradi, 2022). The framework is *Maqāṣid al-Sharīʿah* which emphasizes the protection of religion (*hifz ad-dīn*), soul (*hifz an-nafs*), intellect (*hifz al-'aql*), heredity (*hifz an-nasl*), and property (*hifz al-māl*). *Maqāṣid al-Sharīʿah* can be the basis for understanding and designing the behavior of Muslim tourists in more depth (Auda, 2008; Chapra, 2008).

Maqāṣid al-Sharīʿah as a normative framework that assesses tourism practices not only from the halal-formal aspect, but also from the ethical aspects, social justice, and ecological sustainability. For example, *hifz an-nafs* not only covers the physical protection of tourists, but also includes environmental health, air quality, and access to clean water. *Hifz al-māl* is not only talking about friendly prices, but also energy efficiency and resource conservation (Khuluq & Asmuni, 2024; Shompa et al., 2025; Klongrua et al., 2025; Tumiran et al, 2025). The interpretation of *Maqāṣid al-Sharīʿah* in the context of sustainability can bring Muslim-friendly tourism closer to environmental, *social, and governance* (ESG) principles which in turn become global standards for responsible industry practices (Mohd Zain et al., 2024).

Several studies have linked *Maqāṣid al-Sharīʿah* to ecotourism and green tourism activities. Nglanggeran and Pentingsari in Yogyakarta can be an example that can be learned from community-based tourism villages that prioritize cultural preservation, natural harmony, and community economic empowerment, even without the formal label of "halal" (Purbasari & Manaf, 2018; Azizah et al., 2023: Very, 2025). Such a model actually substantively embodies *Maqāṣid al-Sharīʿah* in the context of local and participatory development (Akmal et al., 2021; Nurjannah et al., 2023).

Environmental sustainability aspects can also be strengthened through the integration of policies such as green certification, halal ecotourism audits, and the preparation of environmentally friendly accommodation standards. Lodgings that use renewable energy, a good waste management system, and environmental education programs for tourists are real implementations of *the values of Maqāṣid al-Sharīʿah* (Dwicahyani et al., 2025). Some recent research even suggests the need for *an eco-fatwa* framework to be the basis for implementing tourism in accordance with sustainability-oriented sharia principles.

On a broader scale, there are a number of initiatives that encourage the success of halal tourism and ecotourism, such as Islamic Eco-Resorts in Turkey and Malaysia that combine sharia-standard comfort with environmentally friendly principles. Research by Kayal (2023), Afifi et al. (2021), and Fisol et al. (2019) reveals that Muslim tourists are now increasingly considering ecological impacts in destination selection. In addition to also thinking about the availability of worship facilities or halal food, as well as the consistency of Islamic values in services have a significant impact on the loyalty and satisfaction of visitors.

In this regard, the integration of *Maqāṣid al-Sharīʿah* in Muslim-friendly tourism is not only symbolic, but needs to be a philosophical, ethical, and operational foundation in designing policies, governance, and shaping consumer behavior (Ruhaeni et al., 2024). This study aims to develop a conceptual and normative framework for the development of sustainable Muslim tourism that combines Islamic spiritual values, social justice, and ecological preservation in an integrated manner. This paper is expected to be of great benefit to academics, policymakers, and tourism actors who want to explore how *Maqāṣid al-Sharīʿah* can be translated into environmental sustainability strategies in Muslim-friendly tourism practices, especially in Indonesia and the Muslim world at large.

2. CONCEPTUAL FRAMEWORK AND HYPOTHESIS DEVELOPMENT

This research is based on the premise that Muslim tourists' tourist intentions are shaped by factors that are in line with Islamic values, in particular as articulated within the framework of *Maqāṣid al-Sharīʿah*. This classical Islamic legal theory emphasizes the importance of safeguarding five important elements: safeguarding religion (*hifz al-dīn*), safeguarding the soul (*hifz an-nafs*), safeguarding the intellect (*hifz al-aql),* safeguarding one's offspring (*hifz an-nasl*), and safeguarding one's property (*hifz al-mal*). In the context of Muslim-friendly tourism, these dimensions provide a normative structure to evaluate how the tourism experience contributes not only to consumer satisfaction but also to the preservation of Islamic ethical values (Auda, 2008; Chapra, 2008).

Figure 1 illustrates the five proposed determinants of travel intentions in Muslim-friendly tourism to be identified in this study. Those variables are religious experience, quality of service, visitor satisfaction, destination image, and affordability, conceptually attributable to one of the five dimensions of *Maqā id al-Sharī ah.* This mapping forms a Shariah-compliant model of behavior that reflects individual motivations and communal Islamic principles.

Figure 1. Conceptual framework for Halal travel intentions

Religious Experience

The variables of religious experience reflect the spiritual engagement and fulfillment experienced by Muslim tourists, such as access to prayer facilities, halal food, and the religious atmosphere in the destination. This is directly related to *hifz ad-din* (safeguarding religion), as the availability and quality of religious services are very important for Muslim tourists (Battour & Ismail, 2016; Zakaria & Othman, 2023). These elements not only contribute to a higher spiritual fulfillment, but also reinforce the principle of *hifz ad-dīn (*safeguarding religion), which is at the core of Muslim identity. When tourists feel that their religious obligations can be fulfilled easily and with dignity, they tend to choose destinations that facilitate and respect these religion-based practices (Junaidi, 2020).

H1: Religious Experiences Have a Positive Influence on Halal Travel Intentions

Visitor Satisfaction

Visitor satisfaction reflects an overall evaluation of the traveler's experience. This is conceptually related to *hifz al-ʿaql* (keeping the mind), since satisfaction often arises from the process of learning, personal reflection, and emotional fulfillment (Han et al., 2019; Rahayu & Candera, 2023). Tourist satisfaction indicates the extent to which the overall tourist experience is in line with or exceeding tourist expectations (Haryanto et al., 2024). This satisfaction includes cognitive assessments such as perception of service quality and affective responses, including feelings of security, comfort, and emotional satisfaction (Syed & Kaliappen, 2024). Within the framework *of Maqāṣid al-Sharīʿah*, this construct corresponds to *hifz an-nafs* (safeguarding the soul), since a satisfying tourist experience contributes to emotional well-being, psychological security, and protection from mental stress. When Muslim tourists feel that their physical and emotional needs are well met, they are more likely to revisit or recommend Muslim-friendly destinations to others (Rahayu & Candera, 2023).

H2: Visitor Satisfaction has a Positive Effect on Halal Tourism Intentions

Quality of Service

Quality of service refers to the tourists' perception of the standards and reliability of the services provided during their trip, which includes the dimensions of safety, cleanliness, and hospitality. Within the framework *of Maqāṣid al-Sharīʿah*, it relates to *hifz an-nafs* (safeguarding the soul), which emphasizes the importance of ensuring overall physical well-being, safety, and comfort during the journey (Fauzi & Battour, 2024). The quality of service is characterized by professionalism, safety, cleanliness and responsiveness, not only fostering trust but also contributing to a rational and enriching tourist experience. This is in line with *Maqāṣid al-Sharīʿah's principle, hifz al-ʿaql* (keeping one's mind), as high-quality services empower travelers to make informed decisions, feel intellectually valued, and have a mentally and emotionally satisfying experience. In the context of Muslim-friendly tourism, ethically provided services reinforce positive perceptions and play an important role in shaping tourists' intentions to revisit or recommend the destination (Han et al., 2019; Rahayu & Candera, 2023).

H3: The Quality of Service has a Positive Effect on Halal Travel Intentions

Destination Image

Destination imagery can include tourists' perception of the destination's key attributes, including cultural suitability, family friendliness, and moral or ethical ambience. This dimension is closely related to *the principle of Maqāṣid al-Sharīʿah*, namely *hifz an-nasl* (safeguarding offspring), as it reflects the role of destinations in supporting family-friendly values, ethical behavior, and moral development of future generations (Junaidi, 2020; Fairuz, 2024). A positive and culturally aligned image of the destination will significantly shape the expectations and perceptions of tourists before traveling. For Muslim tourists, a destination that is considered morally supportive, family-oriented, and respects Islamic norms. Such destinations are seen as a safe and supportive environment to strengthen family ties, moral development, and strengthen Islamic identity (Zaki & Elseidi, 2024).

H4: The Image of the Destination has a Positive Effect on Halal Travel Intentions

Affordability

Affordability refers to tourists' perception of the economic feasibility of visiting a destination. This concept is in line with *Maqāṣid al-Sharīʿah's principle of hifz al-māl* (safeguarding wealth), which emphasizes financial responsibility and fair access. Muslim-friendly travel offerings at affordable prices that provide perceived value encourage sound financial decision-making and encourage inclusivity by making the experience accessible beyond the high-income segment. Thus, affordability not only facilitates a wider market reach but also reinforces the ethical imperative of economic justice in Islamic tourism (Junaidi, 2020; Zidni et al., 2022).

H5: Affordability has a Significant Positive Effect on Halal Travel Intentions

3. METHODOLOGY

This study uses a cross-sectional research design and quantitative approach to look at how religious experience, quality of service, visitor satisfaction, destination image, and affordability affect travel intentions in Muslim-friendly tourism (Sugiyono, 2021). Based on the *framework of Maqāṣid al-Sharīʿah*, this design facilitates the empirical validation of the conceptual relationship between Islamic ethical principles and the behavioral intentions of Muslim tourists. The structured nature of this research instrument allows statistical accuracy in assessing the strength and direction of the hypothetical relationship.

In this study, the population consisted of Muslim tourists who had previously visited Muslim-friendly tourist destinations in Yogyakarta, Indonesia. The selection of respondents was through *purposive sampling* based on three main criteria of other Muslims, having visited at least one Muslim-friendly location in Yogyakarta, and being 17 years old and above. As shown in Table 1, a total of 300 Muslim respondents from various regions throughout Indonesia participated in this study. The demographic characteristics of the respondents in this study included gender, age, educational background, and frequency of visits to Muslim-friendly tourist destinations. This data provides an important picture of the study population and can then help contextualize subsequent analysis by providing information about the profiles of Muslim tourists relevant to the study (Creswell, 2016; Bougie & Sekaran, 2020).

This research uses instruments consisting of a structured questionnaire and is divided into seven parts, including demographic information, tourist intentions, and five latent constructs. These constructs are religious experience, service quality, visitor satisfaction, destination image, affordability, and tourist intentions, which are operationalized using several items to be measured on a five-point Likert scale (1 = strongly disagree to 5 = strongly agree). The research measurement items were adapted and improved from validated instruments used in previous studies on Muslim-friendly tourism (Eid & El-Gohary, 2015; Junaidi, 2020). For example, the construct of religious experience includes indicators related to the spiritual atmosphere and availability of worship facilities, while service quality includes items that assess responsiveness, cleanliness, and friendliness of staff.

Data analysis was carried out using SPSS version 30. The analysis begins with descriptive statistics to profile the respondents and summarize the main variables. The validity of the construct was checked, and the internal consistency was verified via Cronbach alpha, with a threshold of ≥ 0.70 considered acceptable (Hair et al., 2019). Hypothesis testing was carried out using multiple linear regression to determine the influence of independent variables on halal travel intentions. To ensure the robustness of the regression model, classical assumption tests, including normality, multicollinearity, and heteroscedasticity tests were also performed.

Table 1. Demographic characteristics of Muslim tourists visiting Yogyakarta

Demographic characteristics	**Frequency**	**(%)**
Gender		
Male	103	34,33
Female	197	65,67
Age		
17-27	131	43,67
28-38	103	34,44
39-49	39	13
50-60	27	9
Pulau asal		
Sumatera	145	48,33
Jawa	99	33
Kalimantan	12	4
Sulawesi	16	5,33
Bali and Nusa Tenggara	19	6,33
Other	9	3
Education Level		
High school	26	8,67
Bachelor	166	55,33
Postgraduate	101	33,67
Other	7	2,33
Marital status		
Married	161	53,67
Single	139	46,33
Work		
Student	104	34,67
Civil Servant / Government Employee	80	26,67
Private Sector Employees	35	11,67
Businessman	18	6
Other	63	21

continued on following page

Table 1. Continued

Demographic characteristics	Frequency	(%)
Income Levels		
< Rp 1.000.000	101	33,67
Rp 1.000.000-2.499.900	58	19,33
Rp 2.500.000-5.000.000	87	29
> Rp 5.000.000	54	18
Destinations Visited		
Malioboro	258	86
pantai (Parangtritis, Depok, Cemara Sewu)	170	56,67
Alun-alun Kidul	169	56.33
Candi Prambanan	161	53.67
Masjid (Jogokariyan and Gedhe Kauman)	140	46.67
Keraton	137	45.67
Taman Pintar	126	42
Gunung Merapi	122	40.67
Taman Sari	102	34
Wisata Alam Mangunan	101	33.67

Source: Author's own work (research results)

As shown in Table 1, the majority of the 300 Muslim respondents were women (65.67%), while men accounted for 34.33%. Most participants were between the ages of 17 and 27 (43.67%), followed by those aged 28–38 (34.33%), which showed the dominance of young tourists in the sample.

In terms of education, respondents are highly educated: 55.33% have a bachelor's degree and 33.67% have a postgraduate degree. Geographically, almost half of the respondents came from Sumatra (48.33%), the rest from Java (33%), Bali and Nusa Tenggara (6.33%), Sulawesi (5.33%), and Kalimantan (4%), which reflects Yogyakarta's cross-regional appeal as a Muslim-friendly destination.

In terms of employment, students are the largest segment (34.67%), followed by civil servants (26.67%) and private employees (11.67%). Regarding monthly income, 33.67% earned less than IDR 1,000,000, and 29% earned between IDR 2,500,000 and IDR 5,000,000, indicating the dominance of middle-to-lower income tourists. This demographic profile reflects the diversity and inclusivity of the Muslim tourism market, which reinforces Yogyakarta's relevance in the broader halal tourism landscape.

4. RESULT

Reliability and Validity Test

The validity test is carried out to ensure that the questionnaire instrument is accurate and reliable in measuring the desired variable. All responses from 300 participants were analyzed, and all items in all six constructs measured showed a significance level (p-value) of less than 0.05, as shown in Table 2. This shows that each item in the questionnaire is statistically valid and effectively reflects the construct it wants to measure.

Table 2. Validity test results

Variabel	Thing	P value	Information
Intention	Int1	0,001	Valid
	Int2	0,001	Valid
	Int3	0,001	Valid
	Int4	0,001	Valid
	Int5	0,001	Valid
Religious Experience	REx1	0,001	Valid
	REx2	0,001	Valid
	REx3	0,001	Valid
	REx4	0,001	Valid
	REx5	0,001	Valid
Visitor Satisfaction	VSa1	0,001	Sah
	VSa2	0,001	Valid
	VSa3	0,001	Valid
	VSa4	0,001	Valid
	VSa5	0,001	Valid
Quality of Service	SQu1	0,001	Valid
	SQu2	0,001	Valid
	SQu3	0,001	Valid
	SQu4	0,001	Valid
	SQu5	0,001	Valid

continued on following page

Table 2. Continued

Variabel	Thing	P value	Information
Destination Image	DIm1	0,001	Valid
	DIm2	0,001	Valid
	DIm3	0,001	Valid
	DIm4	0,001	Valid
	DIm5	0,001	Valid
Affordability	Aff1	0,001	Valid
	Aff2	0,001	Valid
	Aff3	0,001	Valid
	Aff4	0,001	Valid
	Aff5	0,001	Valid

Source: SPSS, processed by the author (2025)

Reliability testing is performed using Cronbach's Alpha method to assess the internal consistency of each construct. All variables show a Cronbach's Alpha coefficient that exceeds the acceptable threshold, which is 0.70, which indicates high reliability: Intention (0.924), Religious Experience (0.905), Visitor Satisfaction (0.863), Quality of Service (0.926), Destination Image (0.873), and Price Affordability (0.900), as shown in Table 3. These results confirm that the measurement instruments used in this study show strong internal consistency and can be considered a reliable tool for obtaining accurate data from respondents.

Table 3. Reliability test results

Variabel	Number of Items	Cronbach's Alpha	Information
Intention	5	0,924	Reliable
Religious Experience	5	0,905	Reliable
Visitor Satisfaction	5	0,863	Reliable
Quality of Service	5	0,926	Reliable
Destination Image	5	0,873	Reliable
Price Affordability	5	0,900	Reliable

Source: SPSS, processed by the author (2025)

Uji Hypothesis

The results of the hypothesis test showed that four of the five variables had a statistically significant influence on Muslim tourism intentions, as detailed in Table 4. Religious experience ($t = 4.304$, $p < 0.001$), service quality ($t = 2.838$, $p = 0.005$), and destination image ($t = 3.725$, $p < 0.001$) showed a positive and significant relationship with tourism intentions. In contrast, visitor satisfaction ($t = -3.652$, $p < 0.001$) showed a significant but negative influence. Meanwhile, price affordability ($t = 0.537$, $p = 0.592$) did not have a statistically significant effect on tourist intentions.

Table 4. Summary of regression results for hypothesis testing

NO	Variabel	Regression Coefficient (B)	t-value	Sig. (p)	Conclusion
1	Religious Experience	0.103	4.304	0,001	Significant
2	Visitor Satisfaction	-0,194	-3.652	0,001	Significant*
3	Quality of Service	0,193	2.838	0,005	Significant
4	Destination Image	0.112	3.725	0,001	Significant
5	Price Affordability	0,003	0,537	0,592	Insignificant

Source: SPSS, processed by the author (2025)

As a continuation of the regression results presented in Table 4, the following Table 5 summarizes the hypotheses that have been tested, complete with supporting statistical values, the decision to accept or reject the hypothesis, and the underlying academic references. This information provides a more structured picture of the contribution of each variable to travel intentions in Muslim-friendly tourism.

Table 5. Hipotesis, Dukungan Statistik, dan Referensi Akademis

NO	Hypothesis	Independent Variable → Dependent Variable	t-value	Sig. (P)	Results	Academic References
H1	Religious experiences influence halal travel intentions	Religious Experiences → Halal Travel Intentions	4.304	0,001	Accepted	(Battour et al., 2011; Idul Fitri & El-Gohary, 2015)
H2	Visitor satisfaction affects halal tourism intentions	Visitor Satisfaction → Halal Tourism Intention	- 3.652	0,001	Accepted (negative)	(Yoon & Uysal, 2005)
H3	The quality of service affects the intention of halal travel	Service Quality → Halal Travel Intention	2.838	0,005	Accepted	(Idul Fitri & El-Gohary, 2015; Mohsin dkk., 2016)
H4	The image of the destination affects halal travel intentions	Halal Travel Destination Photos → Intentions	3.725	0,001	Accepted	(Zulaikhah dkk., 2023)
H5	Price affordability affects halal travel intentions	Affordable Prices → Halal Travel Intentions	0,537	0,592	Rejected	(Stephenson, 2014; Zailani et al., 2011)

Source: SPSS, processed by the author (2025)

The results of the hypothesis test showed that four of the five variables significantly influenced travel intentions in the context of Muslim-friendly tourism: religious experience, quality of service, image of the destination, and visitor satisfaction. Visitor satisfaction shows a significant but negative relationship, indicating a potential mismatch between travelers' expectations and their actual experience. In contrast, affordability was found to be statistically insignificant, implying that Muslim travelers may prioritize spiritual alignment, service excellence, and destination perception over financial considerations. These findings underscore the important role of Islamic values in shaping travel behavior that is in harmony with the goals *of Maqāṣid al-Sharīʿah.* In particular, religious experiences support *hifz ad-dīn* (safeguarding religion), visitor satisfaction is associated with *hifz an-nafs* (safeguarding the soul), the image of the destination is aligned with *hifz al-māl* (safeguarding of property), and the quality of service reflects *hifz al-ʿaql* (intellectual preservation) through services that foster ethical and cognitive well-being.

5. DISCUSSION

Although the findings of this study show that the dimensions of halal tourism intentions and religious perceptions are the main drivers in the behavior of Muslim tourists, there is still a gap between these intentions and the factual conditions of services on the ground. Many tourist destinations have accommodated aspects of worship and halal food, but have not been integrated with environmental sustainability principles such as energy efficiency, waste management, or the preservation of local culture. In contrast, some sustainable tourism initiatives do not fully understand the specific needs of Muslim travelers, including privacy, worship facilities, and halal products. This gap signals the need for a more comprehensive approach, which not only prioritizes satisfaction and loyalty, but also unifies *Maqā id al-Sharī ah* with global ethical values such as Environmental, Social, and Governance (ESG).

5.1. The Primacy of Religious Experience in Travel Intent

Religious experiences stand out as an important factor influencing Muslim travelers' travel decisions, beyond the motivation of entertainment or simply the search for something new. This is in line with *hifz ad-dīn* (religious preservation), one of the basic goals of *Maqāṣid al-Sharīʿah*, which demands that religious values be integrated into every aspect of life, including recreation and tourism (Auda, 2008). With the presence of representative worship facilities and the presentation of Islamic historical narratives, the destination is able to offer a spiritual depth that distinguishes this experience from conventional tourism.

The availability of prayer rooms, halal-certified menus, gender-based facilities, and an atmosphere that supports moral and spiritual reflection strengthens an authentic impression for visitors (Stephenson, 2014; Mohsin et al., 2016). Battour and Ismail (2016) emphasized that the success of halal tourism is measured by the extent to which tourists feel spiritually respected, not just the fulfillment of logistical requirements. Meanwhile, Eid and El-Gohary (2015) show that the harmony between services and religious beliefs increases the credibility of the destination and the confidence of tourists in its commitment.

For the younger generation, travel is an important means to strengthen religious identity that may be reduced in the midst of daily life (Jafari & Scott, 2014). Destinations that provide spiritual context such as *Maqāṣid al-Sharīʿah* introductory sessions or community religious activities to help tourists build long-term emotional bonds. This approach not only meets the needs of worship, but also affirms the role of tourism as a vehicle for strengthening values and identity.

5.2. Quality of Service and Ethical-Cognitive Experience

High-quality services characterized by Islamic norms, cleanliness, hospitality, and safety have been shown to have a significant impact in influencing travel intentions on Muslim-friendly tourism. These attributes reflect *hifz al-ʿaql* (keeping reason), which suggests that service is more than just functionality, but also supports the intellectual and emotional comfort of travelers. As emphasized by Han et al. (2019), service quality that is aligned with spiritual values increases trust, builds a perception of professionalism, and fosters loyalty through ethical interaction with increasingly vital components of the Muslim-friendly tourism industry.

5.3. Destination Image and Family-Oriented Ethos

The image of the destination also significantly affects tourism intentions, especially if the destination is considered Islamic, inclusive, and family-friendly (Adham et al., 2025). This supports the *principle of hifz an-nasl* (safeguarding one's offspring), which reflects Muslim tourists' preference for an environment that upholds moral values and encourages the inheritance of Islamic principles between generations. Muslim-friendly tourism destinations that are considered to be able to provide ethical harmony in fostering a sense of security for families who travel and play an important role in encouraging visits to occur again.

5.4. The Paradox of Visitor Satisfaction

In contrast to the general assumption, it turns out that for visitor satisfaction informs a negative relationship with travel intention in this study. Although satisfaction is generally thought to be a driver of loyalty and behavioral intent, these findings suggest that satisfaction that lacks spiritual substance can be perceived as unstable or temporary. This highlights the need to distinguish between surface satisfaction and spiritually meaningful engagement. In line with Auda's (2008) interpretation of *Maqāṣid al-Sharīʿah*, meaningful well-being encompasses both material and spiritual dimensions, the goal of which is not only temporary pleasure, but also long-term ethical fulfillment.

The results of the study found a negative relationship between visitor satisfaction and traveller intention which shows the complexity of perceptions in Muslim-friendly tourism experiences (Ekka & Bhardwaj, 2024). One possible interpretation is that the visitor satisfaction aspect that respondents reported is more likely to be pragmatic and short-term, without touching on the deeper dimensions of sustainability or spirituality values. In this context, it can be assumed that satisfaction with facilities, comforts, or services has not consistently reflected ecological awareness. In fact, within the framework of *Maqāṣid al-Sharīʿah*, environmental preservation is an inseparable part of *hifz an-nafs* and *hifz al-māl*. Thus, efforts are needed to expand the dimension of satisfaction that also includes aspects of environmental ethics, for example through green tourism education, participation in conservation programs, or transparency of sustainability practices from destination managers.

In this context, the dimension of environmental sustainability has not been fully reflected in the perception of tourist satisfaction, even though the practice of conservation and concern for nature can increase emotional and spiritual attachment. By including elements of environmental education or tourist participation in conservation, such as tree planting activities or recycling workshops at tourist sites, visitor satisfaction is not only pragmatic but also touches moral awareness. This can be a space to form a deep impression that travel is also a form of worship in caring for God's creation.

5.5. Rethinking Affordability in Muslim-Friendly Tourism

Interestingly, the affordability of the price was found to be not statistically significant. This is different from the conventional tourism behavior model, which places cost as a major factor. In the framework *of hifz al-māl* (wealth protection), these results show that Muslim tourists view spending from the perspective of ethical consumption by prioritizing spiritual values, adherence to sharia, and the pursuit *of blessings* (divine blessings) over financial efficiency. These insights reinforce the growing awareness of value-based spending in Muslim travel behavior.

The affordability of prices that are insignificant in their influence on travel intentions can be re-read through the lens of maqāṣid and sustainability. In the Islamic view, *hifz al-māl* not only means efficiency of spending, but also includes the principle of prudence in consumption and responsibility for long-term impacts. Tourism that is too cheap but ignores the preservation of nature, the well-being of local communities, or the exploitation of resources can be contrary to *Maqāṣid al-Sharīʿah*. Therefore, affordability in Muslim-friendly tourism must be reinterpreted: it is not just a matter of low prices, but how wise the price represents the social and ecological costs incurred. This is in line with the ESG (*Environmental, Social, Governance*) approach that is increasingly relevant in contemporary Islamic business practices.

5.6. Technology and Sustainability Dimension

According to the World Tourism Barometer, by 2024 the number of international tourist arrivals will reach 1.4 billion people, or 99% of pre-pandemic levels. (UNWTO, 2024). Meanwhile, the Religious Tourism Market Report 2024 estimates the global Hramah Muslim tourism market value at US$ 284.5 billion by 2024 with a projected compound annual growth (CAGR) of 14.2% until 2030 (Research and Markets, 2025).

Digital technology is now the backbone of the Muslim-friendly tourism experience. Booking sites with sharia filters allow Muslim tourists to find halal-certified accommodations, restaurants, and attractions while displaying sustainability indicators such as the use of renewable energy and waste management policies (Chantarungsri et al., 2024). Studies in Indonesia show that green service quality is integrated with halal attributes and is known as *greensmart service quality*, which significantly improves the image of the destination and the intention of Muslim tourists to revisit (Alfarizi et al., 2025). With an easy-to-use interface and transparent certifications, the platform enables travel planning without the hassle of research. The real-time information available makes Muslim-friendly destinations superior and attractive to the global market.

Certification practices and green policies are increasingly becoming a benchmark for the competitiveness of halal destinations at the global level. Eco-halal labels and sharia ecotourism certificates unite environmental, social, and economic criteria in a single standard, so that tourists not only get a guarantee of sharia compliance, but also certainty of environmental conservation commitments (Khan et al., 2025). Destinations that have these certifications often include indicators of waste management, water conservation, and local community empowerment support in their promotional materials. Collaboration between tourism operators, local governments, and certification bodies accelerates the adoption of green practices, establishing a reputation for destinations that are not only halal, but also sustainable and responsible.

5.7. Maqāṣid al-Sharīʿah as a Framework of Interpretation

The integration *of Maqāṣid al-Sharīʿah* into this study provides a deeper and more holistic understanding of Muslim tourist behavior. Far beyond its normative-theological function, *the Maqāṣid* serves as a dynamic analytical tool that bridges rational decision-making with spiritual and ethical commitment. In contrast to conventional models of consumer behavior such as Planned Behavior Theory (TPB), *the Maqāṣid al-Sharīʿah* framework allows for an integrated analysis of values, virtues, beliefs, and actions. As emphasized by Fauzi and Battour (2024), this approach not only enriches theoretical research but also informs practices in Islamic marketing and Muslim-friendly tourism development.

5.8. Spiritual Journey as a Purposeful Experience

Furthermore, the study also reflects the growing aspirations of Muslim tourists, especially among the spiritually conscious younger generation such as backpackers. Travel is no longer seen as just recreation, but as a form of *worship* and the search for meaning in life. For these tourists, travel is an opportunity to strengthen faith, affirm identity, and practice Islamic values. Therefore, tourist destinations should aspire to be spaces that combine spiritual reflection with a wealth of experience—aligning adventure with devotion, and recreation with purpose.

5.9. Environmental Dimension in Muslim Tourist Behavior

In the context of *Maqāṣid al-Sharīʿah*, environmental preservation is not just an additional element, but inherent in the purpose of safeguarding life (*hifz an-nafs*) and property (*hifz al-māl*). This becomes even more important when considering that tourism activities often involve consuming energy, water, and producing a lot of waste. Value-conscious Muslim tourists are now beginning to question the ecological footprint of each of their visits. Therefore, the existence of inns with green certification, mosques with clean water and waste management systems, and environmentally friendly halal restaurants are starting to become an added value in their chosen destinations.

Studies by Mohd Zain et al. (2024) and Shompa et al. (2025) underline that the integration of ESG principles in halal services can strengthen Muslim tourists' confidence. In this case, *green tourism* and *eco-fatwa* are important approaches in uniting Islamic values and environmental sustainability. Even in a local study in Yogyakarta, community-based ecotourism practices in the villages of Nglanggeran and Pentingsari are tangible evidence that sustainability can be integrated into a form of tourism that is substantively aligned with *Maqāṣid.*

Tourists who care about the environment will also respond positively to ecotourism education such as reducing single-use plastics, promoting environmentally friendly transportation, and *managing homestays* that support the local economy without exploiting natural resources. This kind of preference shows that halal tourism is not enough to meet the needs of worship, but also needs to answer the aspiration for a more sustainable world.

6. GENERAL MANAGER IMPLICATIONS, LIMITATIONS AND THE FUTURE OF RESEARCH

6.1. Practical and Theoretical Implications

This study underlines the important role of religious experience, visitor satisfaction, service quality, and destination image as the main predictors of travel intention in Muslim-friendly tourism, especially among Muslim tourists visiting Yogyakarta. For destination managers and tourism stakeholders, these findings emphasize the importance of designing experiences that go beyond recreational value and include spiritual meaning. This includes the provision of adequate prayer facilities, access to halal food (Alam et al., 2024), and the development of an Islamic spiritual atmosphere that is in harmony with the values and identity of Muslim tourists.

The quality of service, if it is in line with Sharia principles defined by hospitality, cleanliness, safety, and adherence to Islamic ethical norms, should be institutionalized as the minimum standard in Muslim-friendly tourism. In addition, local governments and tourism business actors are encouraged to integrate *Maqāṣid al-Syarīʿah* into strategic tourism planning and policymaking. Such integration is important to deliver a travel experience that is not only enjoyable but also spiritually enriching. These recommendations are consistent with the emerging global trend in Islamic tourism that advocates sustainability, authenticity, and deep Sharia compliance (Battour et al., 2018; Fauzi & Battour, 2024).

In addition to affirming the role of religious experience and destination imagery, this study also opens up opportunities to reformulate a value-based approach to tourism intentions, taking into account ecological sustainability as an inherent dimension of maqāṣid. In practice, destination managers can start compiling sustainability indicators that are relevant to the Islamic context, such as water use efficiency, plastic waste reduction, or contribution to local conservation. These elements not only serve as a social responsibility, but also part of worship in safeguarding Allah's creation (*hifz al-ʿālam*). Thus, the intention of travel in a Muslim context can be enriched by deep ecological values, making travel part of social and spiritual piety.

In the context of Muslim-friendly tourism, *Maqāṣid al-Syarīʿah* can serve as a normative bridge linking Islamic environmental ethical principles with the global sustainability agenda. The dimensions of *hifz an-nafs* and *hifz al-māl*, for example, not only emphasize the protection of life and property, but also contain ecological implications in the form of responsibility for nature conservation, ecosystem balance, and equitable distribution of benefits. These values demonstrate substantial conformity with the ESG (Environmental, Social, and Governance) framework and the Sustainable Development Goals (SDGs). Therefore, the sharia framework is not just a tool of ritual ethics, but can be positioned as a foundation of values that can give direction to tourism policies and practices that are ecologically just, long-term-oriented, and transformative.

As an illustration, the practice of sharia-based waste management at the Jogokariyan Mosque, Yogyakarta, shows how ecological awareness can be practiced within the framework *of Maqāṣid al-Syarī'ah*, especially *hifz al- 'ālam*. Through activities to reduce the use of plastic waste, waste sorting systems, and education of worshippers about cleanliness as part of worship, this mosque is a concrete example of how spiritual values can be directly linked to environmental ethics. A study by Wibowo et al. (2025) highlights that an ecological approach based on Islamic values not only strengthens individual piety, but also forms an environmentally conscious society that is integrated with religious practices. Thus, the integration of narratives or case studies such as this can enrich quantitative approaches and strengthen the ecological relevance in *Maqāṣid al-Sharī'ah-based Muslim tourism behavior models.*

6.2. Limitations

Despite its contributions, the study has some methodological limitations. First, the geographic focus is limited to Yogyakarta, thus limiting the generalization of the findings to other Muslim-friendly destinations. Implementation in the broader field requires careful interpretation and contextual adaptation. Second, the proposed model does not take into account potential moderator variables such as social norms, cultural interpretations, or the level of religious commitment that may influence travel behavior.

Third, reliance on self-report data collected through online surveys poses a risk of social desire bias and may not fully capture the spiritual depth of respondents' travel motivations. Fourth, the quantitative approach used in this study may ignore the emotional and subjective dimensions of travel that are particularly prominent in the context of sharia-compliant tourism.

6.3. Future Research Directions

To overcome these limitations and advance this field, several promising research paths are proposed in the future. First, a cross-cultural comparative study in different regions or contexts of Muslim majorities and minorities will broaden generalizations and deepen the contextual understanding of *the Maqāṣid al-Sharī'ah-based* framework. This research can reveal how the principles of maqāṣid are interpreted and embodied differently according to cultural norms will result in richer theoretical insights.

Second, future research on the expansion of existing behavioral models can be conducted by integrating distinctive spiritual constructs such as destination loyalty sustained by religious values, the search for *blessings* (divine blessings), and the recognition of travel as worship (*ʿibādah*). This addition will offer a more nuanced understanding of the motivations and behavioural commitments of Muslim tourists.

Third, the application of a mixed-methods approach will allow for a more in-depth exploration of spiritual experiences, emotional responses, and psychological meanings that may be underrepresented in quantitative models. Qualitative insights, including narrative investigations or in-depth interviews, can offer a more in-depth perspective on the life experiences of Muslim travelers.

Fourth, longitudinal research is encouraged to explore the dynamics of changing Muslim tourist intentions and preferences over a longer period of time, especially in response to global disruptions such as pandemics, economic instability, or geopolitical crises. Such studies can uncover how values, motivations, and behavior patterns evolve over time.

Fifth, future studies should start integrating sustainability indicators that are in line with sharia principles into the construction of tourism behavior. Perceptions of ecotourism practices, natural resource conservation, and support for local economies and communities can be operationalized as variables in the intention model. This integration will expand the scope of maqāṣid from the moral and ritual dimensions to ecological justice and social sustainability. With this approach, the study of travel intentions not only avoids hedonistic and secular biases, but also voices a more transformative perspective of Islamic ethics in tourism governance.

Finally, interdisciplinary collaborations between the fields of Islamic economics, tourism studies, environmental sociology, and religious psychology can result in a more comprehensive and integrative framework for understanding Muslim travel behavior. This approach allows for the development of holistic knowledge that brings together ethical, spiritual, economic, and experiential dimensions in the study of Muslim-friendly tourism.

At the global level, the integration of halal tourism services and environmental sustainability principles has been implemented in a number of countries. Japan, for example, has developed *eco-halal tourism* practices that combine environmental education with halal services in rural tourism packages and cultural conservation (Pratama, 2022). Turkey introduced a *green-halal hotels* certification program, which combines halal standards with efficient energy, water, and waste management (Zulvianti et al., 2022). Meanwhile, the United Arab Emirates encourages the concept *of smart halal tourism* based on advanced technology to improve personalization services while monitoring the environmental impact of destinations (Echchabi et al., 2022). This comparison shows that the integration between *Maqāṣid al-Sharīʿah* and the principles of Environmental, Social, and Governance (ESG) is not just a normative ideal, but has been adopted as a competitive advantage in the global tourism industry. Indonesia, especially destinations such as Yogyakarta, can learn from these models to strengthen the framework for sustainable Muslim-friendly tourism development.

In Indonesia, several tourist villages such as Nglanggeran and Pentingsari in Yogyakarta have implemented the principles of community-based ecotourism that are in line with Islamic values (Manaf et al., 2018). Practices such as Muslim-friendly homestay management, environmentally conscious training, and preservation of local culture show that the integration between *Maqāṣid al-Sharīʿah* and sustainability is not utopian. Such a model can be replicated and expanded with policy support and certification frameworks that combine halal and green aspects.

7. CONCLUSION

This research confirms the conceptual and practical relevance *of Maqāṣid al-Sharīʿah* as a comprehensive framework for understanding halal tourism intentions among Muslim tourists. By aligning five key determinants: religious experience, visitor satisfaction, service quality, destination image, and affordability, with the five higher goals of Islamic law (*hifz ad-dīn, hifz an-nafs*, *hifz al-ʿaql*, *hifz an-nasl*, and *hifz al-māl*), the study contributes to the development of a spiritually grounded behavioral model in the study of Islamic tourism.

The results of the study empirically show that religious experience, visitor satisfaction, service quality, and destination image significantly influence Muslim tourists' intention to travel, while affordability does not show a statistically significant influence. This shows that Muslim tourists generally prioritize spiritual harmony, ethical integrity, and religious conformity over financial considerations in making travel decisions. This insight underscores the growing importance of spiritual and moral values in shaping tourism behavior in a Muslim-friendly context.

Furthermore, the results of this study emphasize the importance of implementing a value-based approach in the development of Muslim-friendly tourism, especially in Indonesia. Muslim tourists are increasingly looking for destinations that offer not only tourism, but also spiritual enrichment, moral resonance, and affirmation of their religious identity. Destinations that successfully integrate *the principles of Maqāṣid al-Sharīʿah* into their offerings both through services and branding are more likely to attract and retain loyal Muslim tourists.

The study also provides a foundation for tourism policy innovation, encouraging stakeholders to design strategies that go beyond conventional market logic by instilling Islamic ethical values in a sustainable and contextually meaningful manner. Thus, Muslim-friendly tourism can evolve into a transformative platform that balances commercial success with spiritual goals and cultural authenticity.

Although the quantitative approach in this study managed to systematically map the determinants of halal tourism intentions, it is important to balance it with a qualitative approach that captures the ecological dimension, local spirituality, and contextual sustainability practices. An in-depth study of destinations such as Nglanggeran in Yogyakarta, which combines community participation, halal services, and environmental conservation, can complement the empirical understanding that has been built. Interdisciplinary collaboration between Islamic economics, religious psychology, and environmental studies will enrich the discourse of Muslim-friendly tourism in the future. Thus, the integration between *Maqāṣid al-Sharīʿah* and ESG principles will not only have an impact on individual intentions, but also on more ethical and sustainable destination practices.

REFERENCES

Adham, K. A., Nasir, N. M., Muhamad, N. S., Sarkam, S. F., & Ramli, R. M. (2025). Halal Tourism with the Family: Destination – Local Islands of the Maldives. *Journal of Islamic Marketing*, *16*(8), 2321–2346. Advance online publication. DOI: 10.1108/ JIMA-03-2024-0117

Afifi, MF, Mohsin, A., & Farouk, M. (2021). Perhotelan Halal Mendunia: Tantangan (Tidak) Menyajikan Alkohol di Destinasi Wisata Islam: Studi Kasus Mesir. *Kritik Pariwisata: Praktik dan Teori, 2* (2), 134–152. DOI: 10.1108/TRC-12-2020-0022

Ajzen, I. (1991). The Theory of Planned Behavior. *Organizational Behavior and Human Decision Processes*, *50*(2), 179–211. Advance online publication. DOI: 10.1016/0749-5978(91)90020-T

Akmal, H., & Lahuri, S.bin, Ghozali, M., & Nurizal, N. (. (2021). Mengembangkan Panduan Pariwisata Halal di Indonesia Berbasis Pendekatan Maqashid al-Shari'a. *Justicia Islamica*, *18*(2), 243–259. DOI: 10.21154/justicia.v18i2.2650

Alam, A., Ratnasari, R. T., Prasetyo, A., Hapnitasari, I., & Rahmawati, E. (2024). Tinjauan Pustaka Sistematis tentang Studi Label Halal dalam Pariwisata Halal. TEM Journal, 13(1), 635–645. https://doi.org/DOI: 10.18421/TEM131-66

Alfarizi, M., Ngatindriatun, N., Arifian, R., & Widiharjanti, I. (2025). Green-Smart Service Quality and Halal Tourism Attributes on Revisit Intention and Quality of Life: A Case Study From Indonesia. *International Journal of Halal Industry*, *1*(1), 1–20. Advance online publication. DOI: 10.20885/IJHI.vol1.iss1.art1

Amalia F A, Nova M, Koh C dan Suhartanto D. (2024). Sustainable Development in Halal Tourism Industry: The Role of Innovation and Environmental Concern. *E3S Web of Conferences*, 479: 07038. DOI: 10.1051/e3sconf/202447907038

Auda, J. (2008). *Maqasid al-Syariah sebagai Filsafat Hukum Islam: Pendekatan Sistem. Dalam*. Institut Pemikiran Islam Internasional.

Azizah, N., Salam, A. N., & Arifin, A. Z. (2023). Model design of sociopreneurship: Halal based-development of micro, small and medium enterprises through zakat institutions. *ISRA International Journal of Islamic Finance*, *15*(3), 46–63. DOI: 10.55188/ijif.v15i3.610

Battour, M., Hakimian, F., Ismail, M., & Boğan, E. (2018). Persepsi Wisatawan Non-Muslim terhadap Pariwisata Halal: Bukti dari Turki dan Malaysia. *Jurnal Pemasaran Islam*, *9*(4). Advance online publication. DOI: 10.1108/JIMA-07-2017-0072

Battour, M., & Ismail, M. N. (2016). *Pariwisata halal: Konsep, Praktik, Tantangan, dan Masa Depan. Dalam* (Vol. 19). Perspektif Manajemen Pariwisata., DOI: 10.1016/j.tmp.2015.12.008

Battour, M., Ismail, M. N., & Battor, M. (2011). Dampak Atribut Destinasi terhadap Pilihan Wisatawan Muslim. *Jurnal Riset Pariwisata Internasional, 13*(6). Advance online publication. DOI: 10.1002/jtr.824

Bougie, R., & Sekaran, U. (2020). *Metode Penelitian untuk Bisnis: Pendekatan Pengembangan Keterampilan Edisi ke-8, Asia*. Wiley.

Chantarungsri, C., Popichit, N., Rugthangam, S., Wattana, N., Chuanchom, J., & Sukmak, M. (2024). Mapping the landscape of halal tourism: A bibliometric analysis. *Cogent Social Sciences, 10*(1), 2365507. DOI: 10.1080/23311886.2024.2365507

Chapra, MU. (2008). Visi Pembangunan Islam dalam Cahaya Maqasid al-Syariah. Dalam *makalah sesekali seri 15* .

Creswell, W. J. (2016). *Penelitian Kualitatif dan Desain Riset*. Penelitian Kualitatif.

Dwicahyani R R, Shafira A H, Maulana N dan Mandalia S. (2025). Halal tourism among Gen Z: Analyzing the effect of halal awareness and destination trust on visit intention with religiosity as a mediator. *Jurnal Ekonomi dan Bisnis Islam*, 11(1): 1–21. DOI: 10.20473/jebis.v11i1.59898

Echchabi, A., Bocanet, A., & Grassa, R. (2022). Determinants of Selection of Halal Tourism Destination: A Case Study of the UAE. *Global Journal Al-Thaqafah, 12*(1), 186–203. DOI: 10.7187/GJAT072022-12

Eid, R., & El-Gohary, H. (2015). Nilai yang Dirasakan Wisatawan Muslim dalam Industri Perhotelan dan Pariwisata. *Jurnal Riset Perjalanan, 54*(6). Advance online publication. DOI: 10.1177/0047287514532367

Ekka, P. M., & Bhardwaj, S. (2024). Customers' Satisfaction as a Critical Success Factor in Halal Tourism: Literature Review and Research Agenda. *Journal of Islamic Marketing, 15*(8), 2069–2085. DOI: 10.1108/JIMA-02-2023-0059

Fairuz, A. (2024). Environmental sustainability in the Hajj pilgrimage. *International Journal of Academic Research in Business & Social Sciences, 14*(12), 222–6990. DOI: 10.6007/IJARBSS/v14-i12/23913

Fauzi, M. A., & Battour, M. (2024). Pariwisata Halal dan Islam: Pemetaan Ilmiah Tren Saat Ini dan Masa Depan. Dalam. *Tourism Review*. Advance online publication. DOI: 10.1108/TR-08-2023-0533

Fisol, WNM, Suid, IS, Mohd Saufi, MSA, & Bahari, A. (2019). Pengembangan Pariwisata Islam Berbasis Keilmuan Kerangka Maqasid Syariah. *Jurnal Internasional Riset Akademik Bisnis dan Ilmu Sosial, 9* (5).

GMTI. (2024). *Edisi ke-9 Mastercard-Crescentrating Global Muslim Travel Index (GMTI).* Global Muslim Travel Index (GMTI). https://www.crescentrating.com/reports/global-muslim-travel-index-2024.html

Hair, JF, Risher, JJ, Sarstedt, M., & Ringle, CM (2019). Kapan Menggunakan dan Bagaimana Melaporkan Hasil PLS-SEM. Dalam *European Business Review* (Vol. 31, Edisi 1). DOI: 10.1108/EBR-11-2018-0203

Han, H., Al-Ansi, A., Olya, H. G. T., & Kim, W. (2019). Menjelajahi Atribut Destinasi Ramah Halal di Korea Selatan: Persepsi dan Perilaku Wisatawan Muslim terhadap Destinasi Non-Muslim. *Manajemen Pariwisata, 71.* Advance online publication. DOI: 10.1016/j.tourman.2018.10.010

Hanafiah, A., Wibowo, M. W., & Damayanti, F. (2020). Pengaruh Electronic Word of Mouth, Promosi dan Kualitas Pelayanan terhadap Minat Berkunjung Generasi Z pada Destinasi Wisata Halal Provinsi Jawa Barat. *Jurnal Ilmiah Manajemen Dan Bisnis*, *6*(3), 347–364. DOI: 10.22441/JIMB.V6I3.10095

Haryanto, R., Anwar, M. M., Harisah, H., & Fadllan, F. (2024). Tourist satisfaction toward halal tourism: The role of tourism governance and branding. *Journal of Islamic Marketing*, *15*(9), 2229–2244. DOI: 10.1108/JIMA-09-2023-0282

Hashim, N., Sulaiman, N. S., & Muslim, H. (2025). *Maqasid Syariah as a framework for halal tourism in Brunei Darussalam.* In: *The Halal Industry in Asia.* pp.179–201 https://link.springer.com/chapter/10.1007/978-981-99-7681-9_11

Henderson, J. C. (2010). Islam and Tourism. In Scott, N., & Jafari, J. (Eds.), *Tourism in the Muslim world: Bridging tourism theory and practice* (Vol. 2, pp. 75–89). Emerald Group Publishing Limited., DOI: 10.1108/S2042-1443(2010)0000002009

IMTI. (2023). *Indeks Perjalanan Muslim Indonesia 2023.* Crescent Rating. https://www.crescentrating.com/reports/indonesia-muslim-travel-index-2023.html

Jafari, J., & Scott, N. (2014). Dunia Muslim dan pariwisatanya. *Annals of Tourism Research*, *44*, 1–19. DOI: 10.1016/j.annals.2013.08.011

Junaidi, J. (2020). Halal-Friendly Tourism and Factors Influencing Halal Tourism. *Management Science Letters*, *10*(8), 1755–1762. DOI: 10.5267/j.msl.2020.1.004

Kayal, G. (2023). Persona dan Motivasi Wisatawan Religi dan Dampaknya terhadap Niat Mengunjungi Tempat-Tempat Religi di Arab Saudi. *Jurnal Internasional Kota Wisata*, *9*(1). Advance online publication. DOI: 10.1108/IJTC-04-2022-0092

Khan, N., Falahat, M., Ullah, I., Sikandar, H., & Van, N. T. (2025). Integrating Halal Tourism with Sustainable Development Goals Through Islamic Values Environmental Responsibility and Technological Innovation. *Discover Sustainability*, *6*(1), 648. Advance online publication. DOI: 10.1007/s43621-025-01503-3

Khuluq, M. K., & Asmuni, A. (2024). Hifz al-Bi'ah as part of Maqashid al-Shari'ah and its Relevance in the Context of Global Climate Change. *Indonesian Journal of Interdisciplinary Islamic Studies*, *7*(2), 3. Advance online publication. DOI: 10.20885/ijiis.vol7.iss2.art3

Klongrua, S., Umuri, K., & Muftahuddin, M. (2025). Maqasid Al-Shariah and Environmental Sustainability: An Islamic Economic Perspective. *International Journal of Kita Kreatif*, *2*(1). Advance online publication. DOI: 10.24815/ijkk.v2i1.44790

KNEKS. (2023). *Komite Nasional Ekonomi dan Keuangan Syariah*. https://kneks.go.id/berita/644/katalog-buku-master-plan-industri-halal-indonesia-2023-2029?category=1

Manaf, A., Purbasari, N., Damayanti, M., Aprilia, N., & Astuti, W. (2018). Pariwisata pedesaan berbasis komunitas dalam kolaborasi antar-organisasi: Bagaimana cara kerjanya yang berkelanjutan? pelajaran dari Desa Wisata Nglanggeran, Kabupaten Gunungkidul, Yogyakarta, Indonesia. *Sustainability*, *10*(7), 2142. DOI: 10.3390/su10072142

Martaleni, M., Mulyono, S., & Utami, E. S. (2025). Peran Religiusitas dalam Meningkatkan Loyalitas Wisatawan Melalui Pariwisata Halal dan Layanan Berkualitas. *Pemasaran Inovatif*, *21*(1), 50–64. DOI: 10.21511/im.21(1).2025.05

Maulida, A., Dwi, R., & Hapsari, V. (2024). Memahami pengaruh religiusitas, label halal, label ramah lingkungan, dan persepsi halal hijau terhadap loyalitas pelanggan: studi pada perempuan Muslim Generasi Z di Kota Malang. *Jurnal Internasional Riset Bisnis dan Ilmu Sosial (2147-4478), 13* (4), 64–75. DOI: 10.20525/ijrbs.v13i4.3303

Mohd Zain, F. A., Muhamad, S. F., Abdullah, H., Sheikh Ahmad Tajuddin, S. A. F., & Wan Abdullah, W. A. (2024). Integrating Environmental, Social and Governance (ESG) Principles With Maqasid al-Shariah: A Blueprint for Sustainable Takaful Operations. *International Journal of Islamic and Middle Eastern Finance and Management*, *17*(3), 461–484. DOI: 10.1108/IMEFM-11-2023-0422

Mohsin, A., Ramli, N., & Alkhulayfi, B. A. (2016). *Pariwisata Halal: Peluang yang Muncul. Dalam* (Vol. 19). Perspektif Manajemen Pariwisata., DOI: 10.1016/j.tmp.2015.12.010

Moshin, A., Brochado, A., & Rodrigues, H. (2020). Pariwisata Halal Berkembang Pesat: Persepsi dan Implikasi Komunitas. *Jurnal Pemasaran dan Manajemen Destinasi, 18.* DOI: 10.1016/j.jdmm.2020.100503

Mustikawati, R., Arafah, W., & Mariyanti, T. (2022). Pengaruh Religiusitas dan Nilai yang Dirasakan Pelanggan Muslim terhadap Loyalitas dan Kepuasan Pelanggan dalam Pariwisata Halal di Indonesia. *Jurnal Internasional Bisnis Islam*, *7*(2). Advance online publication. DOI: 10.32890/ijib2022.7.2.4

Nurjannah, Awalauddin, M., K, A., Fadel, M., & Asti, MJ (2023). Urgensi Maqāṣid Sharīa untuk Regulasi Pariwisata Halal di Indonesia. *Al-Risalah Jurnal Ilmu Syariah Dan Hukum*. DOI: 10.24252/al-risalah.vi.35026

Pratama, D. P. (2022). The future of the halal tourism market in Japan after COVID-19: an economic pragmatism perspective. In International Conference on Humanities and Social Sciences, KnE Social Sciences, pp. 21–43. DOI: 10.18502/kss.v7i4.10512

Purbasari, N. & Manaf, A. (2018). Comparative Study on the Characteristics of Community-Based Tourism between Pentingsari and Nglanggeran Tourism Village, Special Region Yogyakarta. E3S Web of Conferences, 31, 09007. DOI: 10.1051/e3sconf/20183109007

Rahayu, S., & Candera, M. (2023). Tourist loyalty to halal tourism in Indonesia: The role of services quality, satisfaction, and experience quality. *Jurnal Manajemen Bisnis*, *14*(1), 198–213. DOI: 10.18196/mb.v14i1.17790

Ratnasari, R. T., Sari, N. S., Ahmi, A., & Ismail, S. (2024). Research trends of halal tourism: A bibliometric analysis. *Journal of Islamic Accounting and Business Research.* Advance online publication. DOI: 10.1108/JIABR-08-2023-0246

Research and Markets. (2025). Religious Tourism Market Report 2024. Research and Markets. https://www.researchandmarkets.com/report/faith-based-tourism-market?srsltid=AfmBOorf3z9ILEW2xMC8oQ9wtPSLwk2ym2gQrakTMOIRGOJQEHsMQcG8

Restuti, D. P., Kasdi, A., & Cahya, B. T. (2025). Isu Ekonomi Industri Halal. In *Exploring the Halal Industry and Its Business Ecosystem Prospects* (pp. 1–22). IGI Global., DOI: 10.4018/979-8-3693-8618-7.ch001

RISSC. (2024). *The Muslim 500 | Muslim Paling Berpengaruh di Dunia.* https://themuslim500.com/books/TheMuslim500-2025-lowres.pdf

Ruhaeni, N., Yusdiansyah, E., & Aqimuddin, E. A. (2024). Revisiting Indonesia halal tourism policy in light of GATS. *Journal of International Trade Law & Policy, 23*(2–3), 154–167. DOI: 10.1108/JITLP-12-2023-0064

Saffinee, S. S., Jamaludin, M. A., Rosli, N. L. I., Amid, A., & Has-Yun Hashim, K. S. (2024). *Sustainable and ethical vicegerency in halal tourism practices*. Journal of Event. *Tourism and Hospitality Studies*, *4*, 111–126. DOI: 10.32890/jeth2024.4.8

Shompa, Z. A., Akbar, M. A., & Mohadis, H. M. (2025). Harmonizing Maqasid al-Shari'ah with Sustainable Waste Management Practices: A Conceptual Framework for Principles and Implementation. *International Journal of Islamic and Middle Eastern Finance and Management*, *18*(1), 142–165. DOI: 10.1108/IMEFM-02-2024-0061

Sodawan, A., & Hsu, R. L. W. (2022). Atribut Ramah Halal dan Niat Berkunjung Muslim: Menggali Peran Nilai yang Dirasakan dan Kepercayaan terhadap Destinasi. *Sustainability (Swiss)*, *14*(19). Advance online publication. DOI: 10.3390/su141912002

Stephenson, M. L. (2014). Menguraikan "Perhotelan Islami": Perkembangan, Tantangan, dan Peluang. *Manajemen Pariwisata*, *40*. Advance online publication. DOI: 10.1016/j.tourman.2013.05.002

Suban, S. A., Madhan, K., & Shagirbasha, S. (2023). Analisis Bibliometrik Pariwisata Halal dan Islam. *International Hospitality Review*, *37*(2). Advance online publication. DOI: 10.1108/IHR-05-2021-0038

Tumiran, M. A., Ponari, M. H. A., Mohamad, S. P., & Mohamed, Z. I. (2025). Integrating Sustainable Agriculture and Maqasid al-Shariah Principles for Ethical and Environmental Stewardship. *QJSSH*, *6*(3), 79–95. Advance online publication. DOI: 10.55197/qjssh.v6i3.654

United Nations World Tourism Organization (UNWTO). (2024). International Tourism to Reach Pre-Pandemic Levels in 2024. World Tourism Barometer. UNWTO. https://www.unwto.org/news/international-tourism-to-reach-pre-pandemic-levels-in-2024

Very. (2025). Menteri Pariwisata Kunjungi Desa Wisata Pentingsari, Peraih Community Best Tourism dari ASEAN Tourism Award 2025. indonews.id, 12 Mei 2025. https://indonews.id/artikel/344004/Menteri-Pariwisata-Kunjungi-Desa-Wisata-Pentingsari-Peraih-Community-Best-Tourism-dari-ASEAN-Tourism-Award-2025

Wibowo, W., Ariga, A., Azizah, S.N., Panggabean, N.A. and Irfaniah, N.R. (2025). Kampung Ramadhan Jogokariyan (KRJ): Peran Manajemen Masjid dalam Pariwisata Ramah Muslim dan Ekonomi Lokal. AKUA: Jurnal Akuntasi dan Keuangan, 4(2), pp.161–170. .DOI: 10.54259/akua.v4i2.4258

Wibowo, W., Choiri, A., Aminuddin, A., Emilda, P. and Salim, F. (2025). Sustainable Islamic tourism: Jogokariyan Ramadan Village as a sustainable religious and economic tourism destination (case study in Jogokariyan Ramadan Village). Ecopreneur: Jurnal Ekonomi dan Bisnis Islam, 6(1), pp.61–76. .DOI: 10.47453/ecopreneur.v6i1.3091

Yoon, Y., & Uysal, M. (2005). Kajian Pengaruh Motivasi dan Kepuasan terhadap Loyalitas Destinasi: Sebuah Model Struktural. *Manajemen Pariwisata*, *26*(1), 45–56. DOI: 10.1016/j.tourman.2003.08.016

Zailani, S., Omar, A., & Kopong, S. (2011). Studi Eksploratif tentang Faktor-Faktor yang Mempengaruhi Ketidakpatuhan terhadap Standar Halal di Kalangan Pengusaha Hotel di Malaysia. *Manajemen Bisnis Internasional*, *5*(1). Advance online publication. DOI: 10.3923/ibm.2011.1.12

Zakaria, N. S., & Othman, A. (2023). *Pelestarian Agama (Hifz Al-Din) dalam Paket Wisata Syariah.* Jurnal Studi Islam Internasional Al-Qanatir.

Zaki, R. M., & Elseidi, R. I. (2024). *Religiusitas dan niat beli: perspektif kepribadian merek pakaian Islami.* Jurnal Pemasaran Islam., DOI: 10.1108/JIMA-09-2022-0257

Zamani-Farahani, H. & Eid, R. (2016). Muslim World: A Study of Tourism & Pilgrimage Among OIC Member States. Tourism Management Perspectives, vol. 19, part B, pp. 144–149, .DOI: 10.1016/j.tmp.2015.12.009

Zidni, A. R., Sholihin, M., Hanafi, S. M., & Maulana, A. I. (2022). *Pariwisata Halal: Tinjauan Literatur yang Sistematis.* https://journal2.uad.ac.id/index.php/ijiefb/article/view/6490

Zulaikhah, S., Wusko, A. U., & Kusumawati, A. (2023). Pengaruh Citra Destinasi dan Nilai Islam terhadap Nilai Persepsi dan Kepuasan (Survei pada Wisatawan Muslim Wisata Halal di Banyuwangi). *Jurnal Studi Administrasi Publik*, *8*(1). Advance online publication. DOI: 10.21776/ub.jpas.2023.008.01.6

Zulvianti, N., Aimon, H., & Abror, A. (2022). The Influence of Environmental and Non-Environmental Factors on Tourist Satisfaction in Halal Tourism Destinations in West Sumatra, Indonesia. *Sustainability (Basel)*, *14*(15), 9185. DOI: 10.3390/su14159185

Chapter 14
Halal as a Means of Kalimatun Sawa': A Unifying Element among Religious Communities in Malaysia

Nur Farhana Abdul Rahman
http://orcid.org/0000-0001-7039-8411
National University of Malaysia, Malaysia

Jaffary Awang
National University of Malaysia, Malaysia

ABSTRACT

This chapter explores halal elements in Islam as a medium for Kalimatun Sawa, highlighting its role in fostering interfaith harmony in Malaysia. Within Malaysia's diverse society, certain non-Muslim groups perceive halal in a negative light, mainly associating it with religious sensitivity. However, various other religious traditions also highlight values that align with halal principles, such as cleanliness, safety, and the prevention of harm. Through qualitative analysis of Muslim and non-Muslim perspectives, it reveals shared values of cleanliness and safety, positioning halal as a unifying principle promoting tolerance and cooperative coexistence.The results indicate that while some non-Muslims regard halal solely as an Islamic requirement, most acknowledge cleanliness and safety as universal principles shared across all religions. These results illustrate that halal can become a point of strengthening harmonious coexistence (ta'ayush) and fostering positive interactions among the diverse religious communities in Malaysia.

DOI: 10.4018/979-8-3373-2792-1.ch014

1. INTRODUCTION

Malaysia is recognised as a uniquely multicultural, multi-religious, and multi-ethnic nation, where the majority Muslim population coexists alongside significant non-Muslim minorities including Buddhists, Christians, Hindus, and adherents of Chinese traditional religions. This plural reality necessitates more than passive tolerance, it demands an ethos of mutual respect and the cultivation of shared values. Within this framework, the Qur'anic concept of kalimatun sawa' (Āl 'Imrān 3:64) a "common word" where diverse groups converge on universal values provides a normative foundation for interfaith cooperation.

Today, halal has become a globally recognised system for quality assurance. It not only ensures compliance with Islamic legal rulings but also covers hygiene, food safety, supply chain transparency, animal welfare, and environmental sustainability. Malaysia's halal standards, such as MS1500:2019, have created a strict and thorough framework that is considered an international benchmark. In the context of Malaysia's plural society, however, halal should not be perceived as an exclusively Muslim concern. Rather, it represents a value system that can be appreciated across religious and cultural boundaries.

For Malaysia, implementing halal through the spirit of kalimatun sawa' means reframing it from being seen as a religious imposition to being recognised as a common standard that benefits all. This requires inclusive education campaigns, transparent certification processes, and interfaith dialogues that highlight halal's universal elements food safety, consumer protection, and corporate integrity. By doing so, Malaysia can reduce misperceptions among non-Muslims who may view halal certification merely as an extension of Islamic identity politics. Instead, halal can be promoted as a unifying platform for ethical governance and public trust, fostering stronger social cohesion in a multicultural nation.

At the policy level, Malaysia can leverage its role as a global halal hub to demonstrate how halal aligns with universal aspirations for sustainability, accountability, and justice. Initiatives such as the Global Halal Data Pool (HDC, 2022) and the adoption of blockchain technology in halal traceability can further strengthen this inclusive positioning. When halal is framed as a guarantee of transparency, safety, and integrity, it transcends religious boundaries and becomes an embodiment of shared human values. In doing so, Malaysia not only fulfils its responsibility to uphold Islamic principles but also advances the Qur'anic vision of kalimatun sawa' as a practical model for peaceful coexistence and collective progress in a plural society.

This chapter looks at the issue by focusing on three main aspects. First, it explores the idea of halal and its connection to kalimatun sawa'. Second, it examines halal governance in Malaysia, covering standards, enforcement, and challenges. Third, it investigates how halal can be a basis for social unity and a platform for interfaith dialogue.

2. HALAL IN THE MALAY WORLD: HISTORICAL TRAJECTORIES

In the Malay Archipelago, the spread of Islam between the 13th and 15th centuries integrated halal principles into social, economic, and political life.Historical records note that the Sultanate of Melaka (15th century) institutionalised Islamic dietary laws and legal principles (Shariah) in its courts and marketplaces, integrating halal as part of its governance framework (Azra, 2004). This institutionalisation elevated halal from a private religious observance to a public legal and political standard, thereby ensuring that Muslim and non-Muslim traders operating in Melaka adhered to a shared system of trust, transparency, and accountability(Azra, 2004).

The institutionalization of halal also had a diplomatic aspect. The Melaka Sultanate, as a maritime power, used halal-compliant trade policies to strengthen ties with other Muslim states like Aceh, Pasai, and Demak. At the same time, it built trust among Chinese, Indian, and European merchants. Halal served as both an identity marker for Islamic civilization and a cultural bridge that encouraged interreligious exchange. In this regard, halal was not exclusive; it was seen as a universal symbol of integrity, cleanliness, and fairness. This made it widely accepted in diverse port cities throughout the Archipelago.

Moreover, the incorporation of halal principles into political administration illustrates the early Islamisation of governance and law in Southeast Asia. Texts such as the Undang-Undang Melaka and Undang-Undang Laut Melaka embedded Islamic legal concepts, including rules on halal slaughter, trade honesty, and prohibition of fraudulent practices, as part of the judicial system. These codifications demonstrate that halal was not viewed as a peripheral issue but as an essential component of governance, reinforcing social cohesion and ensuring just trade practices.

The colonial period disrupted this natural growth. During British rule in Malaya, food imports, including meat and processed goods, created new challenges for halal compliance. Without a central authority, Muslim communities depended on religious scholars and local Majlis Agama Islam Negeri for guidance (Hooker, 1984). This fragmentation continued until the post-independence era, when Malaysia started to create national systems for halal certification.

In contemporary Malaysia, these historical precedents continue to resonate. The legacy of Melaka as a centre of halal governance underlines the enduring role of halal as both a religious duty and a public good. This dual character strengthens the argument that halal should be positioned not as a sectarian requirement but as a universal standard of quality assurance that transcends religious boundaries (Fischer, 2016). The formalisation of halal governance began in 1974 with the introduction of a national halal logo. This made Malaysia the first Muslim-majority country to centralise halal certification at the federal level (HDC, 2020). The establishment of the Department of Islamic Development Malaysia (JAKIM) in 1994 further consolidated authority and led to more systematic halal standardisation. Since the establishment of the Halal Hub Division within the Department of Islamic Development Malaysia (JAKIM) and the implementation of systematic halal certification, Malaysia has become as a global leader in the halal industry. According to the Thomson Reuters Report (2021), the global halal economy was valued at USD 2.09 trillion in 2021, with the halal food sector making the largest contribution. This phenomenon not only reflects the economic potential of halal but also demonstrates its universal appeal that transcends religious boundaries.

Nevertheless, a key challenge lies in public perception, particularly among non-Muslims. Several studies (Rezai et al., 2012; Haque et al., 2015) have shown that while many non-Muslims acknowledge halal as a marker of quality and safety, misconceptions persist in viewing halal as an exclusively Muslim concept. Therefore, communication methods that highlight shared values are important for presenting halal as a true kalimatun sawa' space for dialogue and agreement among people of different faiths.

3. ISSUES AND FACTOR OF MISCONCEPTIONS AMONG NON-MUSLIMS IN MALAYSIA REGARDING THE CONCEPT OF HALAL IN ISLAM

The concept of halal in Islam is most visibly manifested in Malaysia through the implementation of halal certification. This certification functions not only as a religious instrument but also as a quality and food safety standard recognised internationally. However, some non-Muslims still hold misconceptions about halal certification.

One common misconception is that halal only means "free from pork and alcohol." Golnaz et al. (2010) found in their study of non-Muslim consumers in Malaysia that many participants did not realize that halal includes a broader principle called halālan ṭayyiban. This principle involves cleanliness, safety, animal welfare, and business ethics. This limited view leads some to see halal certification as unimportant, focusing only on Islamic dietary rules.

In addition, halal certification is often seen as a sign of the Islamisation of public spaces. Some non-Muslims view the JAKIM halal logo as a sign of religious exclusivity rather than a universal quality standard. Haque et al. (2015) point out that this misunderstanding mainly comes from political discussions that portray halal as a majority agenda, not as an inclusive measure of food safety. These views create mistrust and make non-Muslims hesitant to appreciate the positive values associated with halal.

From an economic standpoint, non-Muslim business operators sometimes view halal certification as a financial burden. The stringent certification process, audit costs, and strict compliance requirements lead them to perceive halal as favouring large corporations (Zailani et al., 2010). This misconception emerges when halal certification is seen merely as a mechanism of religious control, rather than as an opportunity to access broader global markets.

Culturally, in a diverse society like Malaysia, food signifies identity. Some non-Muslims perceive halal as a threat to their culinary traditions, particularly among the Malaysian Chinese community, which is well known for its use of pork. According to Ng (2021), such misconceptions arise when halal is perceived as an attempt to "erase" traditional foods, whereas in reality halal certification is only mandated for products intended for Muslim consumers.

These misunderstandings come from limited knowledge, personal experiences, communication issues, and the effects of media and identity politics. These factors work together to challenge the idea of halal as a universal concept, instead of one limited to Islamic practice. A closer look at these aspects shows both the reasons for confusion and chances to create a more inclusive and positive view of halal in multi-religious societies like Malaysia.

Firstly, limited knowledge remains a central barrier. Many non-Muslims perceive halal only in its narrow sense as a religious dietary requirement, without appreciating its wider implications in hygiene, safety, ethics, and transparency. Golnaz et al. (2010) emphasise that a significant proportion of non-Muslim consumers in Malaysia misunderstand halal as a purely religious matter. However, the same study shows that perceptions improve considerably once halal is reframed in terms of universal human values such as food safety and consumer protection. Similarly, Haque et al. (2015) found that educational initiatives and awareness campaigns positively influence non-Muslim trust in halal-certified products by highlighting its alignment with global food safety standards.

Secondly, personal experiences strongly shape consumer perceptions. Positive experiences with halal-certified products, particularly in terms of quality and safety, reinforce non-Muslim confidence. Conversely, negative experiences, such as those associated with scandals, can lead to suspicion and distrust. For instance, the 2014 Malaysian meat cartel scandal, which involved allegations of fraudulent halal certification, significantly affected consumer trust, both Muslim and non-Muslim alike (Ali, Jie, & Karnik, 2017). Bonne and Verbeke (2008) argue that trust in halal certification is fragile, and even isolated incidents of malpractice can disproportionately damage perceptions, especially among consumers who are not deeply familiar with its religious foundations.

Thirdly, communication issues further complicate halal's acceptance. Certification bodies and policymakers frequently use religiously framed language, focusing on Islamic jurisprudence, which can alienate non-Muslim stakeholders.

Fourth, Media also plays a decisive role in shaping perceptions of halal, often in contradictory ways. On the one hand, the media highlights the economic value of the halal industry, portraying it as a driver of tourism, trade, and global competitiveness. On the other hand, sensationalist reporting especially in Western contexts tends to frame halal within discourses of religious exclusivity or political dominance. Bonne and Verbeke (2008) note that halal is often simplified in media narratives as a symbol of Islamic identity, thereby reducing its universal appeal. In the tourism sector, Battour and Ismail (2016) demonstrate that negative portrayals of halal in media coverage can discourage wider acceptance, particularly when linked to stereotypes of religious conservatism.

Finally, the role of identity politics cannot be ignored. Halal, while intended as an inclusive standard of safety and ethical production, is sometimes politicised and framed as a marker of religious or cultural dominance. Cornille (2013) observes that interreligious dialogue often falters when religious practices are co-opted into political narratives of identity and power. In Malaysia, although halal is promoted as part of the national economic and branding strategy, its association with Muslim identity has sometimes generated suspicion among non-Muslim communities, who perceive it as privileging one group over others (Othman, Hashim, & Musa, 2016).

Based on this analysis, in a plural society such as Malaysia, halal often becomes a point of contention when it is misunderstood as an exclusively Islamic religious demand. These misunderstandings manifest in various forms, such as assuming halal is only about prohibitions against pork and alcohol, linking it to Islamic political dominance, or perceiving certification as an economic burden. Consequently, halal is not viewed as a universal meeting point (kalimatun sawa'), but rather as an exclusive Muslim instrument. Yet, grounded in the theory of interfaith relations, halal can be reframed as a concept containing universal values that serve as a kalimatun sawa' a common ground that can be shared across all religious and cultural traditions. By highlighting shared ethical, moral, and humanitarian values, halal holds the potential to become a universal platform that supports social harmony in Malaysia. These misconceptions can be rectified through public education, interfaith awareness campaigns, and emphasising the universal dimensions of halal, namely halālan ṭayyiban.

4. THEORETICAL FRAMEWORK: THE CONCEPT OF KALIMATUN SAWA' IN ISLAM AND SHARE VALUES IN INTERFAITH RELATIONS THEORY

The discussion in this chapter is grounded in a dual theoretical framework: (i) the Qur'ānic imperative of seeking common ground (kalimatun sawa'), and (ii) the search for universal shared values within Interfaith Relations Theory.

4.1 The Concept of Kalimatun Sawa' (Common Ground) in Islam

In Islam, there exists a normative imperative to seek common ground (kalimatun sawa'), as articulated in Surah Āl 'Imrān (3:64), which provides a theological foundation in line with the principles of interfaith relations. The Qur'ān states:
كِرْشُنْ الَوَ هّٰللا الَّا دَبُعْنَ الَّا مْكُنَيْبَوَ انَنَيْبَ ءٍاوَسَ ةٍمَلِكَ ىلٰا اوْلَاعَتَ بِتٰكِلْا لَهْاَيٰ لْقُ
اوْدُهَشْا اوْلُوْقُفَ اوْلَّوَتَ نْاِفَ ۗ هّٰللا نِوْدُ نْمِّ ابًابَرْاَ اضًعْبَ انَضُعْبَ ذَخِتَّيَ الَوَّ اًـٔيْشَ هٖبِ
نَوْمُلِسْمُ انَّاَبِ. *(Al-Quran Ali Imran: 64)*

Translation

Say, "O People of the Book! Come to a word that is equitable between us and you—that we shall not worship except Allah, and that we shall not associate anything with Him, and that none of us shall take others as lords besides Allah." But if they turn away, then say, "Bear witness that we are Muslims who submit to Him" (Mukhtasar al-Bayān Translation).

Classical exegetes such as al-Ṭabarī (2001) and Ibn Kathīr (1999) interpreted kalimatun sawa' as a call to monotheism and the rejection of polytheism. However, contemporary scholars such as Alwi Shihab (2005) and Ardiansyah & Prihantoro (2023) have expanded its meaning to encompass universal ethical values, including honesty, cleanliness, justice, and safety. These values, being universal, are applicable in social life and create an ethical meeting point that transcends doctrinal differences. Thus, kalimatun sawa' can be understood not only as a theological call to faith but also as a foundation for harmonious social interaction.

Moreover, integrating kalimatun sawa' into halal governance makes Malaysia a unique model. Malaysia's diverse population needs policies that uphold Islamic law and build trust among different religious communities. By presenting halal certification through shared values like justice, honesty, safety, and welfare, the Malaysian model can put kalimatun sawa' into practical governance structures. This approach reduces views of religious exclusivity and positions halal as a public good available to all citizens, no matter their beliefs .

In summary, kalimatun sawa' goes beyond its traditional role as a marker of doctrinal boundaries. In today's interfaith situations, it acts as an ethical bridge. It offers theological support for cooperation, coexistence, and mutual growth. When included in the halal discussion, this Qur'ānic principle reshapes halal into a space of ethical agreement. Here, both Muslims and non-Muslims can engage in a system that promotes justice, safety, and integrity. In this way, kalimatun sawa' shows that Islam remains relevant in tackling the ethical challenges present in diverse modern societies.

4.2 Interfaith Relations Theory

Interfaith Relations Theory has evolved into a multidimensional framework that recognises the complexity of pluralistic societies. Beyond mere dialogue, the theory underscores the importance of cultivating structures of sustained engagement, where communities move from tolerance to genuine collaboration. Scholars such as Swidler (1983) established foundational guidelines, famously articulated in his Dialogue Decalogue, which stresses the necessity of honesty, empathy, and reciprocity in interfaith exchanges. Cornille (2013) expanded this further by addressing the inherent difficulties such as doctrinal differences, power imbalances, and historical wounds—that make dialogue both necessary and challenging. She argues that acknowledging these challenges openly is itself a precondition for authentic interreligious engagement.

Contemporary applications of Interfaith Relations Theory show that social harmony needs more than agreement on beliefs. It requires real cooperation in everyday life. Coward (2016) points out that interfaith ethics flourish when communities demonstrate genuine solidarity. When people cooperate in areas like education, health, and the economy, they put into practice values of compassion and justice that go beyond strict beliefs. Interfaith Relations Theory, as elaborated by Swidler (1983) and Cornille (2013), emphasises that social harmony in plural societies can only be achieved through sustained efforts to foster understanding among religious communities. This approach extends beyond theological dialogue to include social interaction, economic cooperation, and joint activities that allow different communities to recognise shared values and norms.

In the Malaysian context, this theory is highly significant, as the country is characterised by religious pluralism with Islam as the religion of the Federation (Article 3(1) of the Federal Constitution) and freedom of religion guaranteed under Article 11. This reality requires mechanisms that can manage theological differences while maximising common ethical ground. By viewing halal certification as both a religious necessity and a public benefit, Malaysia can turn halal into a means of interfaith cooperation. This illustrates how interfaith relations move from abstract dialogue to concrete collaboration in daily life. Furthermore, Interfaith Relations Theory stressed the necessity of dialogical inclusivity ensuring that diverse voices are represented in shaping social norms. Within Malaysia's halal industry, this could involve structured engagement between Muslim authorities, non-Muslim stakeholders, and global partners to reinforce transparency and trust.Ultimately, Interfaith Relations Theory helps reframe halal as not just an Islamic legal category. It presents halal as a shared ethical platform that connects with universal human values. In this way, Malaysia upholds its identity as a Muslim-majority nation. It also shows how religious principles can promote unity in diversity. This vision aligns with the Qur'ānic idea of kalimatun sawa'.

4.3 Halal as a Value of Common Ground (Kalimatun Sawa') and Universality

Drawing on both the Qur'ānic concept of kalimatun sawa' (Āl 'Imrān 3:64) and Interfaith Relations Theory (Swidler, Cornille), it can be argued that the main idea behind promoting interreligious harmony is to identify shared ethical values. This search for common ground does not require claiming that all religions are equally true. Instead, it emphasizes values that go beyond theological differences. In this context, halal acts as a practical means for expressing a shared ethical language. It enables followers of different faiths to converge around values such as food safety, cleanliness, and ethical production. For instance, Rezai, Mohamed, and Shamsudin (2012) found that non-Muslim consumers in Malaysia accept the concept of halal when it is framed in terms of quality and safety, rather than exclusively as a religious requirement. Similarly, Haque et al. (2015) demonstrated that trust in halal certification, transparency of information, and the effectiveness of audit systems significantly enhance interfaith acceptance. These findings affirm the potential of halal as a concrete kalimatun sawa' that unites a religiously diverse society.

From the perspective of interfaith relations, halal can be regarded as an "institutionalised kalimatun sawa'," that is, a shared value operationalised through national standards, legal enforcement, and international recognition. Through halal certification administered by JAKIM and guided by standards such as MS1500:2019 (Department of Standards Malaysia, 2019), the universal values inherent in halal are realised in systematic procedures recognised across communities and industries. This not only builds consumer trust but also establishes a framework for collaboration between industries and religiously diverse communities.

Accordingly, within the theoretical framework of this study, halal operates as a bridge between the normative principle of kalimatun sawa' and inclusive socio-economic practice. By emphasising shared ethical dimensionscleanliness, safety, justice, and trustworthiness halal fosters positive interaction across different communities. Ultimately, this analysis asserts that the inclusive implementation of halal has the capacity to enhance interreligious understanding, build social trust, and strengthen national harmony.

5. RESEARCH FINDINGS AND DISCUSSION

This chapter discusses three main discussion: (i) the concept of halal from the perspectives of history, maqāṣid al-sharīʿah, and modern standards; (ii) values constituting common ground (kalimatun sawa') in the context of halal; (iii) non-Muslim perceptions of halal based on values of cleanliness, safety, justice, and trustworthiness.

5.1 The Concept of Halal: History, Maqāṣid al-Sharīʿah, and Modern Standards

The concept of halal has existed since the early days of Islam, rooted in the Qur'ān and Sunnah, which distinguish between the permissible (ḥalāl) and the prohibited (ḥarām). Halal does not only concern food and beverages but also encompasses finance, tourism, pharmaceuticals, cosmetics, and the broader Muslim lifestyle (Shafie & Othman, 2006).During the classical Islamic civilisation, the institution of ḥisbah played a central role in enforcing halal principles in public markets. The muḥtasib (market inspector) was tasked with monitoring quality control, preventing fraud, and ensuring compliance with Islamic ethical standards in food and trade. In Baghdad, Cairo, and Cordoba, the ḥisbah functioned as a proto-regulatory mechanism that safeguarded consumers regardless of religious affiliation. Non-Muslim minorities (ahl al-dhimmah) who lived under Muslim rule were also subject to fair trade regulations, which ensured halal integrity in public markets. This demonstrates that halal, even in its early historical development, functioned as a universal principle of justice and accountability.

From the perspective of maqāṣid al-sharīʿah, halal is closely linked to the five higher objectives of Islamic law (al-ḍarūriyyāt al-khams): protection of religion (ḥifẓ al-dīn), life (ḥifẓ al-nafs), intellect (ḥifẓ al-ʿaql), lineage (ḥifẓ al-nasl), and wealth (ḥifẓ al-māl) (Dusuki & Abozaid, 2007). Compliance with halal in production and service delivery guarantees consumer safety, prevents harm, and preserves the integrity of the supply chain. The principle of ḥalālan ṭayyiban is also consistent with universal values recognised in other religions. In Hinduism and Buddhism, the principle of ahimsa emphasises the avoidance of harm to living beings, while in Christianity, the Book of Leviticus chapter 11 provides guidance on clean and unclean foods aimed at safeguarding health and preventing harm. Such convergence reinforces the argument that halal can function as kalimatun sawa', an ethical common ground shared across religions.

In Malaysia, the MS1500:2019 standard is the main reference for halal certification. It addresses raw materials, hygiene, handling, packaging, storage, transportation, and food preparation. This standard is widely recognized and has set a standard for other countries (Tieman, 2011). The principles are established through the national standard MS1500:2019 (Halal Food – General Requirements), which was developed by the Department of Standards Malaysia. Tieman (2011) claims that Malaysia's halal certification has become a global reference because it effectively combines sharīʿah principles with modern industry practices. This shows that halālan ayyiban has many practical uses in today's economy.

In Malaysia, halal is not just a religious norm, it has become an important tool of Islamic governance that includes legal, economic, and social aspects. Malaysia was one of the first countries to set up a centralized halal certification system through the Department of Islamic Development Malaysia (JAKIM) in 1974. This was later strengthened by the Trade Descriptions Act 2011 (Act 730), which controls the use of the halal logo. As a result, Malaysia has gained recognition as a global leader in halal systems, especially with the creation of the MS1500:2019 standard, which is now used by other countries (Talib et al., 2016; Aziz & Chok, 2013). In governance, JAKIM serves as the main authority that issues halal certification. It works together with the Ministry of Domestic Trade and Cost of Living (KPDN) and the Ministry of Health Malaysia (MOH) to enforce these standards. This approach helps people see halal not just as a religious practice but also as a measure of quality, cleanliness, food safety, and supply chain trust.

However, halal governance in Malaysia also faces structural challenges. Among the most debated issues are the 2020 meat cartel scandal, which undermined the integrity of the system, the problem of counterfeit halal products, and the perception and the view that small non-Muslim entrepreneurs face too much bureaucracy when trying to get certification (Zailani et al., 2010). Nevertheless, the government has introduced several reforms. These include the digitalization of halal certification through MYeHALAL and the creation of the Halal Development Corporation (HDC). These steps aim to improve the halal industry based on the Malaysia Halal Industry Master Plan 2030.

5.2 Shared and Universal Values in the Concept of Halal as a Point of Convergence of Kalimatun Sawa' Across Religions

International research shows that halal is increasingly seen as an ethical brand that includes safety, cleanliness, and social responsibility (Wilson & Liu, 2010). In non-Muslim majority countries like Thailand and Japan, halal certification is used not just to attract Muslim tourists but is also promoted as a quality guarantee for non-Muslim consumers (Bonne & Verbeke, 2008). In Malaysia, various studies point out the potential of halal to promote social unity. For example, Ahmad et al. (2015) found that non-Muslim consumers often view halal as a sign of quality, and their knowledge and familiarity with the halal industry affect this positive view.

The Qur'anic concept of kalimatun sawa' in Surah Āl 'Imrān (3:64) highlights the importance of finding common ground among religious groups based on shared values. In the case of halal, these shared values are clearly seen in the focus on cleanliness and safety and the value of Justice and Trustworthiness in Halal Concept.

a. The Values of Cleanliness and Safety

A major misconception is that halal is limited to ritualistic practices. However, looking at it through the lens of interfaith relations, cleanliness and food safety emerge as universal values shared among religions. Cleanliness (ṭahārah) is central to Islamic teaching, with the Prophet Muhammad ﷺ stating that "cleanliness is half of faith" (Ṣaḥīḥ Muslim, 223).

Cleanliness ia a main element in the term halālan ṭayyiban . This term refers to two complementary demands. First, halal signifies what is permissible under Shariah, free and clean from prohibited elements such as carrion, blood, pork, and animals slaughtered without invoking the name of Allah (see Qur'an, al-Baqarah 2:173; al-Mā'idah 5:3). It also includes the prohibition of illicit income sources such as fraud, usury, and corruption. Second, ṭayyib refers to what is wholesome, clean, safe, beneficial, and non-harmful to the body, intellect, or morals. It encompasses aspects of quality, food safety, hygiene, animal welfare, and environmental sustainability. The Qur'an affirms this principle:

"O mankind, eat from whatever is on earth [that is] lawful and good (ayyiban), and do not follow the footsteps of Satan. Indeed, he is to you a clear enemy" (al-Baqarah 2:168).

Similarly, in Surah al-Mā'idah (5:88), Allah reminds humanity to consume what is lawful and good while maintaining piety. This demonstrates that halālan ayyiban is not limited to the legal status of food but extends to ensuring that what is consumed brings benefit and avoids harm.

Within the halal framework, cleanliness is not limited to ritual purity but extends to hygiene in food preparation, storage, and consumption. The halal certification system requires strict compliance with hygiene protocols, ensuring that food is free from contamination, harmful substances, or unhygienic practices (MS 1500:2019; Department of Standards Malaysia, 2019). From a public health perspective, this intersects with global standards such as the Codex Alimentarius, demonstrating that halal principles align with universal norms of safety and consumer protection.

Non-Muslims also care about cleanliness and safety in food. Studies in Malaysia show that non-Muslim consumers often connect halal certification with better quality and stricter hygiene standards. This connection boosts their trust in halal products, even if they do not have a religious duty to eat them (Golnaz et al., 2010; Haque et al., 2015). This highlights how halal's focus on cleanliness and safety creates a common ground for discussion and collaboration, going beyond religious differences. These values can act as common ethical points that cross religious lines and align with the moral principles embedded in Malaysia's main religious traditions, including Hinduism, Buddhism, and Christianity.

In Hinduism, the principle of ahimsa represents the highest moral law. It demands avoiding any form of violence or harm towards all living beings. Harold Coward (2016)[1] explains that ahimsa is not just the absence of violence; it is an active commitment to preventing harm to humans, animals, and the environment. . In Hinduism, the principle of ahimsa represents the highest moral law. It demands avoiding any form of violence or harm towards all living beings. Harold Coward (2016) explains that ahimsa is not just the absence of violence; it is an active commitment to preventing harm to humans, animals, and the environment. The classical expression ahimsa paramo dharmah means "non-violence is the highest dharma (moral duty)." When it comes to diet, this principle encourages choosing food that prevents unnecessary animal suffering. This value aligns with the Islamic notion of ayyib, which calls for ethical slaughter practices, animal welfare, and maintaining cleanliness and food safety.

Buddhism equally emphasises ahimsa through its First Precept (Pancasila), stated in Pali as pānātipātā veramanī sikkhāpadam samādiyāmi "I undertake the precept to abstain from destroying living beings". Peter Harvey (2013)[2] explains that this precept is rooted in compassion (karuṇā) and the recognition that all beings fear death and suffering. Thus, Buddhists are encouraged to refrain from actions that cause suffering, whether directly or indirectly. As in Islam, this principle advocates the production and consumption of food that avoids harmful or destructive elements, aligning with the spirit of ṭayyib.

In Christianity, particularly in the Book of Leviticus, clear guidelines are provided regarding clean and unclean foods (Leviticus 11:1–47)[3]. These include prohibitions on animals that do not both chew cud and have split hooves, fish without fins and scales, and birds of prey or carrion eaters. While rooted in religious law, these dietary rules embody concerns for cleanliness, health, and disease prevention. In the modern context, such regulations bear strong similarities to halālan ṭayyiban, which prohibits the consumption of harmful, unclean, or unethically produced foods.

The convergence of these shared values demonstrates that halālan ṭayyiban, ahimsa in Hinduism and Buddhism, and the Christian principles of clean foods all rest on the same moral foundation, such as respect for life, the avoidance of harm, and the preservation of well-being. Empirical evidence reinforces backs this up. For example, Rezai, Mohamed, and Shamsudin (2012) found that non-Muslim consumers were more likely to accept the halal concept when it was associated with safety, cleanliness, and ethical production. Similarly, Haque et al. (2015) emphasised that trust in halal certification increased when supported by transparent audit systems and quality control mechanisms. Thus, by highlighting the shared values among ahimsa, Christian food purity laws, and ṭayyib in Islam, halal can serve as a positive foundation for more inclusive interfaith dialogue.

b. The Values of Justice and Trustworthiness in Economics

Justice ('adl) and trustworthiness (amānah) are equally central in the halal system. In Islam, justice is a divine command: "Indeed, Allah commands you to render trusts to whom they are due and when you judge between people to judge with justice" (Qur'ān, 4:58). Within halal governance, justice manifests in the fair treatment of producers, distributors, and consumers, ensuring that all stakeholders in the supply chain are protected from exploitation or fraud. Trustworthiness, meanwhile, is a moral requirement for those involved in halal certification, as any breach of integrity undermines consumer confidence and damages the credibility of the halal system.

One of the recurring issues in Malaysian society is the misuse of fake halal logos by some non-Muslim traders. For instance, in 2019, the Department of Islamic Development Malaysia (JAKIM) and the Ministry of Domestic Trade and Consumer Affairs (KPDNHEP) seized several products with unauthorized halal logos. This incident received significant media attention, raising concerns among both Muslims and non-Muslim consumers who felt misled about labeling and product quality (Berita Harian, 2019). Such actions clearly go against the ethical principles of business across various religious traditions. In the halal framework, fairness and trustworthiness are key aspects of certification. This aligns with ethical standards from different faiths, where fairness and honesty are seen as universal values.

In Islam, the prohibition of gharar, which means fraud or deception, is clearly emphasized. Gharar refers to uncertainty, deception, or unclear transactions that may violate the rights of one party. The Prophet Muhammad (peace be upon him) stated: "The Messenger of Allah forbade transactions involving gharar" (Sahih Muslim, no. 1513). Gharar is harmful in commerce because it allows for exploitation, fraud, and unfair loss. As a result, halal standards in the food industry focus not only on lawful ingredients and preparation but also on maintaining the integrity of the supply chain to ensure it is free from fraudulent practices.This principle reflects the maqāṣid al-sharī'ah (objectives of Islamic law) in protecting wealth (ḥifẓ al-māl) and ensuring consumer welfare.

In Christianity, honesty is strongly emphasized in both social and commercial relations. The Book of Ephesians 4:25 instructs: "Therefore each of you must put off falsehood and speak truthfully to your neighbor, for we are all members of one body." This verse highlights that deception is not only an economic violation but also a disruption of communal bonds. Therefore, truthfulness in trade is understood as a moral duty that sustains community trust. This principle aligns with halal, which rejects fraudulent practices in certification and labeling. It highlights the need for transparency as a basic moral requirement (Guthrie, 2014).

In Hinduism, the principle of satya (truth) is one of the yamas (moral codes) in Patanjali's Yoga Sutras. Satya entails steadfast commitment to truth in speech, conduct, and commerce (Vivekananda, 2012). A Hindu merchant who faithfully upholds satya would avoid all forms of forgery or deceit, asbecause these actions go against dharma, which is our cosmic and moral responsibility. Hence, When halal certification is seen as a promise of transparency, it aligns with the Hindu devotion to satya, which requires honesty and integrity in all economic dealings.

In Buddhism, Buddhist teachings likewise stress honesty in economic life. In the Anguttara Nikaya (AN 5.177), the Buddha enumerates five types of trade that should be avoided, including trade in weapons, humans, meat, intoxicants, and poisons since these cause harm and suffering. Furthermore, the Digha Nikaya emphasizes that a devout Buddhist should avoid musāvāda (false speech or deceit) in both words and business dealings. "Right Speech" (sammā-vācā), part of the Noble Eightfold Path, requires individuals to speak truthfully, avoid deception, refrain from slander, and abstain from harmful speech (Harvey, 2013). From this perspective, honesty in commerce is considered a way of reducing suffering for other beings. When halal is interpreted as a mechanism of integrity in food trade, it harmonizes with Buddhist teachings that reject deception and demand honesty in economic practices.

Therefore, halal standards protect the integrity of the supply chain while prohibiting fraud, aligning with the ethical business values rom various faith traditions. This demonstrates that the integrity embodied in halal is a shared value that protects all consumers, not just a requirement for Muslims.. When halal certification is understood as a system of economic integrity, it becomes part of a universal ethical framework for interfaith commerce. This affirms that halal should not be perceived as a burden but rather as a guarantee of quality and market justice.

When viewed as a whole, cleanliness and safety focus on the physical and material aspects of human well-being. Justice and trustworthiness support the ethical and relational parts of social life. Together, they elevate halal beyond a simple religious practice; they create a broad ethical system. This complexity positions halal as a reliable example of kalimatun sawa', connecting communities through shared values.

In practice, Malaysia's halal industry can see itself not just as serving Muslim consumers but as providing universal benefits like safe food, transparent governance, and ethical accountability. These benefits appeal to people beyond religious lines. This approach aligns with the ideas in Interfaith Relations Theory (Swidler, 1983; Cornille, 2013), which suggests that working together based on shared values is a better way to achieve harmony than discussing abstract doctrines.

5.3 The Impact of the Universal Values of Halal on Positive Non-Muslim Perceptions of Halal in Malaysia

The idea of halal is mainly linked to the religious duties of Muslims. However, the growth of the halal industry in Malaysia shows that its importance goes beyond just religion. Halal, especially within the idea of halālan ṭayyiban, is now viewed not only as a way to comply with religious rules, but also as a standard for quality, food safety, hygiene, and supply chain integrity. This acceptance reaches beyond Muslim communities and has received support from non-Muslim communities in Malaysia as well. In a multi-ethnic and multi-religious context such as Malaysia, the perception of non-Muslims towards halal carries strategic importance. First, they represent a significant proportion of consumers, producers, and contributors to the halal ecosystem. Second, their positive engagement positions halal as a point of convergence or kalimatun sawa', uniting diversity through shared values. Non-Muslim communities in Malaysia generally hold positive perceptions of halal, particularly in the following areas:

a. Trust in Halal Certification

One of the most notable dimensions of non-Muslim perceptions of halal is their trust in halal certification issued by authorized bodies, particularly the Department of Islamic Development Malaysia (JAKIM). Halal certification is not only seen as evidence of compliance with Islamic law but also as a guarantee of product quality, hygiene, and safety. According to Bonne and Verbeke (2008), although halal originates from an Islamic context, non-Muslim consumers frequently associate the halal logo with safer, cleaner, and healthier products.

In Malaysia, the study by Rezai, Mohamed, and Shamsudin (2012) found that many non-Muslim consumers view halal certification as a trust mark that aids them in product selection, especially in the food and beverage categories. This is consistent with Haque et al. (2015), who reported that non-Muslim consumers believe halal certification protects them from food contamination and harmful substances. In other words, halal is perceived as a credible quality control mechanism, comparable to international food safety standards.

Furthermore, the JAKIM halal logo carries high credibility at the global level, making it relevant not only to Muslims but also to non-Muslims who value quality assurance. This demonstrates that the concept of halal in Malaysia has successfully penetrated universal dimensions that are acceptable within a plural society.

b. Halal as an Ethical Brand

Beyond trust in certification, halal is increasingly recognized as an ethical brand that reflects social responsibility. The principles of halālan ayyiban focus on welfare, cleanliness, and safety. These principles align with universal values found in various religions and cultures. For example, non-Muslim consumers often link halal with practices that benefit consumers, promote environmental sustainability, and ensure transparent production. Wilson and Liu (2010) emphasize that halal is more than a religious label; it is a global ethical brand that represents universal values of justice, welfare, and social responsibility. In Malaysia, non-Muslims view halal as a sign that a product is suitable for Muslims and also offers high quality.

In the business world, non-Muslim companies that seek halal certification often see it as part of their social responsibility strategies. A study by Othman, Hashim, and Musa (2016) found that many non-Muslim companies in Malaysia incorporate halal into their ethical marketing plans to build consumer trust. This shows the positive response to halal as a shared business value. Awareness of the importance of halal certification is rising. Rezai, Mohamed, and Shamsudin (2012) conducted a pioneering study in the Klang Valley and found that while most non-Muslims had a moderate understanding of halal principles, their acceptance grew significantly when halal was connected with safety and hygiene.

c. Growing Public Awareness of Halal

Positive views of halal among non-Muslims are growing due to increased public awareness. Urbanization, education, and better access to information have improved non-Muslim understanding that halal is not just related to Islam but also to food safety and healthy living. Rezai et al. (2015) found that younger non-Muslims in Malaysia's big cities are more open to the idea of halal, seeing it mainly in terms of health rather than religion. Additionally, government efforts to promote the halal industry through projects like Halal Malaysia (MyHalal) and the Halal Development Corporation (HDC) have strengthened the idea that halal is a national resource that benefits everyone.

This awareness has also grown with the rise of halal tourism. Many non-Muslim operators in the tourism sector see that halal certification adds value. It attracts Muslim tourists and also improves how non-Muslim tourists view cleanliness and professionalism (Battour & Ismail, 2016).

d. Halal Certification as a Product Marketing Strategy

The acceptance of halal by non-Muslims is clear in market trends. Many non-Muslim entrepreneurs, especially in the food, beverage, logistics, pharmaceutical, and cosmetics sectors, pursue halal certification for their products. This choice is not only about meeting Muslim consumer demand; it also comes from the understanding that halal certification improves product competitiveness in both local and international markets. Furthermore, many non-Muslim consumers in Malaysia prefer international food and beverage brands that are halal certified. For example, global brands like Nestlé and KFC, owned by non-Muslim companies, have long received halal certification to cater to the Malaysian market.

In the tourism sector, non-Muslim operators who provide halal-friendly facilities such as food, prayer spaces, and Muslim-friendly amenities have found that these enhance the appeal of their businesses not only for Muslims but also for non-Muslim tourists, who interpret such provisions as indicators of professionalism and hygiene (Battour et al., 2010). Ali, Jie, and Karnik (2017) found that many non-Muslim entrepreneurs in Malaysia regard halal as a passport for exports to Muslim-majority countries, thereby expanding their business opportunities. This demonstrates that halal is accepted not merely as a religious requirement but as a significant source of economic value.

Based on the discussion above, the main factors affecting non-Muslim purchase intentions are trust in certification, attitudes, and awareness. These findings show how important it is to keep the certification system trustworthy and to communicate its universal values, rather than presenting halal only as a religious requirement.

6. CONCLUSION

The earlier discussion shows that the values in the Islamic idea of halal and the role of halal certification in Malaysia go beyond just religious issues. They also address universal questions like the need for honesty and transparency, which are important in Islam, Christianity, Hinduism, and Buddhism. Additionally, they highlight the significance of food safety and consumer rights, which are shared human values, and the need for integrity in governance, which builds social trust among different religions.

The detailed discussion of halal as a medium of kalimatun sawa' shows that the concept of halal in Islam goes beyond sharīʿah requirements related to food. It has a universal aspect that crosses religious, cultural, and ethnic lines. The principle of halālan ṭayyiban, which includes cleanliness, safety, and universal justice, connects with moral teachings in other religions. For example, it relates to ahimsa in Hinduism, the avoidance of dukkha in Buddhism, dietary purity in the Old Testament of Christianity, and the emphasis on integrity and honesty found in both Islam (gharar) and Hinduism (satya).

From the perspective of halal governance in Malaysia, the history of JAKIM's halal certification, the MS1500:2019 standard, and the role of government agencies have shaped an ecosystem that has positioned halal as a global brand. It is embraced by Muslims and respected by non-Muslim consumers for its role as a quality assurance marker. However, challenges such as counterfeit halal logos, the meat cartel scandal, and confusion over halal labels show that the system still faces mixed views. Some see halal as linked to quality and cleanliness, while others view it as a symbol of dominance or an economic burden. However, when viewed through the lens of kalimatun sawa' theory and the interfaith relations approach, halal can serve as a point of convergence for shared values. The values of honesty, integrity, and social responsibility found in halal are universal and align with the moral teachings of other religions. This, in turn, promotes mutual understanding and creates opportunities for cooperation in areas like trade, food security, and market integrity.

In conclusion, this article shows that halal can serve as a unifying element in Malaysia's plural society. This idea aligns with the concept of kalimatun sawa', which highlights common ground for everyone's well-being. The future potential of halal lies not only in strengthening social harmony but also in positioning Malaysia as a global reference center for halal governance grounded in universal values. Therefore, ongoing efforts in public education, inclusive policies, and interfaith dialogue are crucial. These efforts will help ensure that halal is seen not as an exclusive symbol, but as a promise of a good quality of life for all.

ACKNOWLEDGEMENT

Special thanks to the Ministry of Higher Education Malaysia for the Fundamental Research Grant Scheme (FRGS/1/2017/SS06/UKM/03/1). This grant is titled Guidelines for Religious Tolerance in Muslim and Non-Muslim Relations in Malaysia from the Perspective of Religious Leaders. They also appreciate Universiti Kebangsaan Malaysia for the University Research Grant (GGPM-2017-018), which is called Perceptions of Religious Adherents on Issues of Religious Sensitivities in Malaysia. Both grants were important for collecting data for this study.

REFERENCES

Alwi Shihab. (2005). *Nilai-nilai Pluralisme dalam Islam*. Mizan.

Ardiansyah, A., & Prihantoro, Y. (2023). Towards "Kalimatun Sawa": A Dialogue between Islam and Battour, M., & Ismail, M. N. (2016). Halal tourism: Concepts, practises, challenges and future. *Tourism Management Perspectives*, *19*(1), 150–154. DOI: 10.46362/jrsc.v4i1.96

Aziz, Y. A., & Chok, N. V. (2013). The role of halal awareness, halal certification, and marketing components in determining halal purchase intention among non-Muslims in Malaysia. *International Journal of Business and Social Science*, *4*(1), 1–7.

Azra, A. (2004). *The Origins of Islamic Reformism in Southeast Asia: Networks of Malay-Indonesian and Middle Eastern 'Ulama' in the Seventeenth and Eighteenth Centuries*. University of Hawai'i Press. DOI: 10.1163/9789004488199

Battour, M., & Ismail, M. N. (2016). Halal tourism: Concepts, practices, challenges and future. *Tourism Management Perspectives*, *19*, 150–154. DOI: 10.1016/j.tmp.2015.12.008

Battour, M., Ismail, M. N., & Battor, M. (2010). Toward a halal tourism market. *Tourism Analysis*, *15*(4), 461–470. DOI: 10.3727/108354210X12864727453304

Bonne, K., & Verbeke, W. (2008). Muslim consumer trust in halal meat status and control in Belgium. *Meat Science*, *79*(1), 113–123. DOI: 10.1016/j.meatsci.2007.08.007 PMID: 22062604

Cornille, C. (2013). *The Im-Possibility of Interreligious Dialogue*. Crossroad Publishing.

Department of Standards Malaysia. (2019). [*Halal Food – General Requirements*. Putrajaya: Standards Malaysia.]. *Ms*, *1500*, 2019.

Dusuki, A. W., & Abozaid, A. (2007). Maqasid al-Shariah, Maslahah, and corporate social responsibility. *The American Journal of Islamic Social Sciences*, *24*(1), 25–45. DOI: 10.35632/ajiss.v24i1.415

Fischer, J. (2016). I*slam, Standards, and Technoscience*. In *Global Halal Zones*. Routledge.

Golnaz, R., Zainalabidin, M., Shamsudin, M. N., & Chiew, F. C. E. (2010). Non-Muslim consumers' understanding of halal principles in Malaysia. *Journal of Islamic Marketing*, *1*(1), 62–74. DOI: 10.1108/17590831011026245

Guthrie, S. (2014). *Christian Ethics: A Historical Introduction*. Wiley-Blackwell.

Haque, A., Sarwar, A., Yasmin, F., Tarofder, A. K., & Hossain, M. A. (2015). Non-Muslim consumers' perception toward purchasing halal food products in Malaysia. *Journal of Islamic Marketing*, *6*(1), 133–147. DOI: 10.1108/JIMA-04-2014-0033

Harvey, P. (2013). *An Introduction to Buddhism: Teachings, History and Practices* (2nd ed.). Cambridge University Press.

Hooker, M. B. (1984). *Islamic Law in South-East Asia*. Oxford University Press.

Ibn Kathir, I. (1999). *Tafsir al-Qur'an al-'Azim*. Beirut: Dar al-Kutub al-'Ilmiyyah.

Othman, B., Hashim, N. H., & Musa, R. (2016). Conceptualizing the influences of knowledge and religiosity on halal certification trust: The perspectives of non-Muslim consumers. *Asian Academy of Management Journal*, *21*(1), 23–48.

Rezai, G., Mohamed, Z., & Shamsudin, M. N. (2012). Non-Muslim consumers' understanding of halal principles in Malaysia. *Journal of Islamic Marketing*, *3*(1), 35–46. DOI: 10.1108/17590831211206572

Swidler, L. (1983). The dialogue decalogue: Ground rules for interreligious dialogue. *Journal of Ecumenical Studies*, *20*(1), 1–4.

The Holy Bible. (2001). [Grand Rapids: Zondervan.]. *Leviticus*, *11*, 1–47.

Tieman, M. (2011). The application of halal in supply chain management: In-depth interviews. *Journal of Islamic Marketing*, 2(2), 186–195. DOI: 10.1108/17590831111139893

Vivekananda, S. (2012). *The Yoga Sutras of Patanjali*. CreateSpace Independent Publishing.

Wilson, J. A. J., & Liu, J. (2010). Shaping the halal into a brand? *Journal of Islamic Marketing*, *1*(2), 107–123. DOI: 10.1108/17590831011055851

Zailani, S., Arrifin, Z., Wahid, N. A., Othman, R., & Fernando, Y. (2010). Halal traceability and halal tracking systems in strengthening halal food supply chain for food industry in Malaysia (A review). *Journal of Food Technology*, *8*(3), 74–81. DOI: 10.3923/jftech.2010.74.81

ENDNOTES

1 Ahimsa, as articulated in Hindu traditions, is not merely the absence of violence but an active commitment to avoid causing harm to any living being. It embodies the highest dharma, guiding moral behaviour towards compassion, non-injury, and respect for life." (Coward, 2016, The Perfectibility of Human Nature in Eastern and Western Thought, Albany: SUNY Press.)

2 "The first precept requires abstaining from killing or causing harm to living beings. This is rooted in compassion (karu ā) and the understanding that all beings fear death and suffering. Thus, the practitioner refrains from acts that cause injury, directly or indirectly." — Harvey, 2013, An Introduction to Buddhism: Teachings, History and Practices, Cambridge: Cambridge University Press.

3 (Leviticus 11:1–47) Clean and Unclean Food: " 11 The Lord said to Moses and Aaron, 2 "Say to the Israelites: 'Of all the animals that live on land, these are the ones you may eat: 3 You may eat any animal that has a divided hoof and that chews the cud. 4 "'There are some that only chew the cud or only have a divided hoof, but you must not eat them. The camel, though it chews the cud, does not have a divided hoof; it is ceremonially unclean for you. 5 The hyrax, though it chews the cud, does not have a divided hoof; it is unclean for you. 6 The rabbit, though it chews the cud, does not have a divided hoof; it is unclean for you. 7 And the pig, though it has a divided hoof, does not chew the cud; it is unclean for you. 8 You must not eat their meat or touch their carcasses; they are unclean for you.9 "'Of all the creatures living in the water of the seas and the streams you may eat any that have fins and scales. 10 But all creatures in the seas or streams that do not have fins and scales—whether among all the swarming things or among all the other living creatures in the water—you are to regard as unclean. 11 And since you are to regard them as unclean, you must not eat their meat; you must regard their carcasses as unclean. 12 Anything living in the water that does not have fins and scales is to be regarded as unclean by you.13 "'These are the birds you are to regard as unclean and not eat because they are unclean: the eagle,[a] the vulture, the

black vulture, 14 the red kite, any kind of black kite, 15 any kind of raven, 16
the horned owl, the screech owl, the gull, any kind of hawk, 17 the little owl,
the cormorant, the great owl, 18 the white owl, the desert owl, the osprey, 19
the stork, any kind of heron, the hoopoe and the bat.20 "'All flying insects that
walk on all fours are to be regarded as unclean by you. 21 There are, however,
some flying insects that walk on all fours that you may eat: those that have
jointed legs for hopping on the ground. 22 Of these you may eat any kind of
locust, katydid, cricket or grasshopper. 23 But all other flying insects that
have four legs you are to regard as unclean.24 "'You will make yourselves
unclean by these; whoever touches their carcasses will be unclean till evening.
25 Whoever picks up one of their carcasses must wash their clothes, and they
will be unclean till evening. 26 "'Every animal that does not have a divided
hoof or that does not chew the cud is unclean for you; whoever touches the
carcass of any of them will be unclean. 27 Of all the animals that walk on all
fours, those that walk on their paws are unclean for you; whoever touches their
carcasses will be unclean till evening. 28 Anyone who picks up their carcasses
must wash their clothes, and they will be unclean till evening. These animals
are unclean for you. 29 "'Of the animals that move along the ground, these are
unclean for you: the weasel, the rat, any kind of great lizard, 30 the gecko, the
monitor lizard, the wall lizard, the skink and the chameleon. 31 Of all those
that move along the ground, these are unclean for you. Whoever touches them
when they are dead will be unclean till evening. 32 When one of them dies
and falls on something, that article, whatever its use, will be unclean, whether
it is made of wood, cloth, hide or sackcloth. Put it in water; it will be unclean
till evening, and then it will be clean. 33 If one of them falls into a clay pot,
everything in it will be unclean, and you must break the pot. 34 Any food you
are allowed to eat that has come into contact with water from any such pot is
unclean, and any liquid that is drunk from such a pot is unclean. 35 Anything
that one of their carcasses falls on becomes unclean; an oven or cooking pot
must be broken up. They are unclean, and you are to regard them as unclean.
36 A spring, however, or a cistern for collecting water remains clean, but
anyone who touches one of these carcasses is unclean. 37 If a carcass falls on
any seeds that are to be planted, they remain clean. 38 But if water has been
put on the seed and a carcass falls on it, it is unclean for you.39 "'If an animal
that you are allowed to eat dies, anyone who touches its carcass will be unclean
till evening. 40 Anyone who eats some of its carcass must wash their clothes,
and they will be unclean till evening. Anyone who picks up the carcass must
wash their clothes, and they will be unclean till evening.41 "'Every creature
that moves along the ground is to be regarded as unclean; it is not to be eaten.
42 You are not to eat any creature that moves along the ground, whether it

moves on its belly or walks on all fours or on many feet; it is unclean. 43 Do not defile yourselves by any of these creatures. Do not make yourselves unclean by means of them or be made unclean by them. 44 I am the Lord your God; consecrate yourselves and be holy, because I am holy. Do not make yourselves unclean by any creature that moves along the ground. 45 I am the Lord, who brought you up out of Egypt to be your God; therefore be holy, because I am holy. 46 "'These are the regulations concerning animals, birds, every living thing that moves about in the water and every creature that moves along the ground. 47 You must distinguish between the unclean and the clean, between living creatures that may be eaten and those that may not be eaten.'"

Compilation of References

Ab Rashid, N., & Bojei, J. (2020). The relationship between halal traceability system adoption and environmental factors on halal food supply chain integrity in Malaysia. *Journal of Islamic Marketing*, *11*(1), 117–142. Advance online publication. DOI: 10.1108/JIMA-01-2018-0016

Ab Talib, M. S., Mohd. Riaz, M., & Johan, M. R. M. (2022). Halal Supply Chain Digitalisation: Enhancing Traceability and Consumer Trust. *Journal of Islamic Marketing*, *13*(7), 1423–1440. DOI: 10.1108/JIMA-10-2020-0316

Abd Rahim, S. I., Mansor, S. K. M., Yakob, M. A., & Ismail, N. (2018). Food safety, sanitation and personal hygiene in food handling: An overview from islamic perspective. *International Journal of Civil Engineering and Technology*, *9*(9), 1524–1530.

Abd Rashid, N. R., Ahmad, A. N., Md Dahlal, N., & Abdullah, M. A. (2023). Applying ethical climate theory in whistleblowing intentions study among employees in halal food companies: A protocol. *Halalsphere, 3*(1).

Abd-El Aziz, N. A., Moharram, Y. G., Attia, R. S., & Kotit, S. M. (2012). Application of HACCP system during meat slices preparation. *GIDA-Journal of Food*, *2*, 59–66.

Abdou, A. H., Chan, M. P., Rehman, S. U., Albakhit, A. I. A., & Almakhayitah, M. Y. (2024). Islamic food laws: Customer satisfaction effect halal purchase intention in China. Moderating role of religiosity. *British Food Journal*, *126*(8), 3088–3112. DOI: 10.1108/BFJ-10-2023-0875

Abdul Halim, N. R., Mutalib, S. A., Abd Ghani, M., & Hashim, H. (2024). Non-conformance report (NCR) on Malaysia halal certification: A case study among small-medium scale food enterprises (SMEs) in Malaysia. *Food Control*, *160*(110298), 110298. DOI: 10.1016/j.foodcont.2024.110298

Abdul Jafar, W. (2022). Legality of Halal food certification on Maslahah Mursalah perspective. *Jurnal Ilmiah MIZANI*, *9*(1), 85–108.

Abdullah, J. B. (2018). Islamic marketing mix: Is there a role for Islamic-based strategies? *International Journal of Islamic Marketing and Branding*, *3*(1), 15. DOI: 10.1504/IJIMB.2018.091650

Abdullah, M. A., & Azam, M. S. E. (2020). In Abdullah, M. A., & Azam, M. S. E. (Eds.), *Halal entrepreneurship: Concept and business opportunities* (pp. 1–18). Entrepreneurship.

Abdullah, M., & Azam, M. (2020). Halal entrepreneurship from Maqasid-al-Sharia'h perspective: Inseparable concept for Halalpreneurs. *Journal of Food Science*, *4*(S1), 34–42. DOI: 10.26656/fr.2017.4(S1).S07

Abdullah, Z., Yusoff, W. F. W., Anumudu, C. E., & Zainol, F. A. (2020). Regulatory impact analysis roles for agricultural products' qualities: Customers' perspectives for sustainability entrepreneurship. *Asian Journal of Agriculture and Rural Development*, *10*(2), 563–577. DOI: 10.18488/journal.ajard.2020.102.563.577

Abinesh, R. C., & Dulloo, R. (2024). The Impact of AI-Driven Personalization on Customer Satisfaction in E-Commerce: Balancing Technology, Transparency, and Control. *Journal of Computational Analysis and Applications*, *33*(2).

Abmi, M., Fachrurrazy, M., & Hasan, H. (2024). The Implementation Of Halal Certification According To Law Number 33 Of 2014 Concerning Halal Product Assurance. *International Journal Mathla'ul Anwar Of Halal Issues*, *4*(1), 76–86. Https://Doi.Org/10.30653/IJMA.202441.103

Abu Talib, N. Y., Abdul Latiff, R., & Aman, A. (2020). An institutional perspective for research in waqf accounting and reporting: A case study of Terengganu state Islamic Religious Council in Malaysia. *Journal of Islamic Accounting and Business Research*, *11*(2), 400–427. DOI: 10.1108/JIABR-11-2016-0132

Acs, Z. J., Audretsch, D. B., Braunerhjelm, P., & Carlsson, B. (2012). Growth and entrepreneurship. *Small Business Economics*, *39*(2), 289–300. DOI: 10.1007/s11187-010-9307-2

Adawiyah, R., Ardiansyah, M., & Sholehah, N. A. (2023). A Islamic Boarding School Economic Empowerment Strategy Through an OPOP (One Persantren One Product) Model in The Digital (Case Study on Boarding School in Madura). *IQTISHADIA Jurnal Ekonomi & Perbankan Syariah*, *10*(1), 1. Advance online publication. DOI: 10.19105/iqtishadia.v10i1.8162

Adekunle, B., & Filson, G. (2020). Understanding halal food market: Resolving asymmetric information. *Food Ethics*, *5*(1–2), 1–22. DOI: 10.1007/s41055-020-00072-7

Adham, K. A., Muhamad, N. S., Masood, A., & Rahim, A. A. (2024). Diagnosing a halal certification system for cosmetics: The viable system model approach. *Systemic Practice and Action Research*, *37*(2), 139–159. DOI: 10.1007/s11213-023-09647-x

Adham, K. A., Nasir, N. M., Muhamad, N. S., Sarkam, S. F., & Ramli, R. M. (2025). Halal Tourism with the Family: Destination – Local Islands of the Maldives. *Journal of Islamic Marketing*, *16*(8), 2321–2346. Advance online publication. DOI: 10.1108/JIMA-03-2024-0117

Afifi, MF, Mohsin, A., & Farouk, M. (2021). Perhotelan Halal Mendunia: Tantangan (Tidak) Menyajikan Alkohol di Destinasi Wisata Islam: Studi Kasus Mesir. *Kritik Pariwisata: Praktik dan Teori, 2* (2), 134–152. DOI: 10.1108/TRC-12-2020-0022

Ağarı, M. (2024). Concept of space: What is it – How is it perceived? *Karabük Türkoloji Dergisi*, *5*(9), 1–30.

Agnew, J. (2011). Space and place. In Agnew, J., & Livingstone, D. (Eds.), *Handbook of Geographical Knowledge* (pp. 1–34). Sage.

Ahmad, H., Fazullah, A., Borham, A. J., & Hashim, H. (2011). Halal Studies In Universities : A Way Forward To Manage Halal Introduction to Fundamental Halal Halal Industry and Awareness. *International Jornal of Arts and Sciences Conference, 4*(09), 1–9.

Ahmad, M. F. (2015). *Antecedents of halal brand personality. 6*(2), 209–223. DOI: 10.1108/JIMA-03-2014-0023

Ahmad, A. N., Rahman, R. A., Othman, M., & Abidin, U. F. U. Z. (2016). Critical success factors affecting the implementation of halal food management: Perspectives of halal executives, consultants, and auditors. *Food Control*, *74*, 70–78. DOI: 10.1016/j.foodcont.2016.11.031

Ahmad, N., Halid Khan, A., Aziz, A., Mohd Raffi, R., Hasan, Q., Sumimura, Y., & Shimazono, Y. (2023). Determining Halal Food Preferences among Muslims Living in Osaka, Japan. *Journal of Halal Science and Technology*, *2*(2), 26–40. DOI: 10.59202/jhst.v2i2.696

Ahmadova, E. (2019). *Determinants of attitudes towards Halal products Empirical evidence from Azerbaijan. 12*(1), 55–69. DOI: 10.1108/JIMA-04-2019-0068

Ahmad, R. (2024). Integrating artificial intelligence and blockchain to improve the accuracy of Halal certification. *Jpurnal of Halal Review*, *1*(1), 12–22.

Ahmed, A. (2008). Marketing of halal meat in the United Kingdom: Supermarkets versus local shops. *British Food Journal, 110*(7), 655–670. DOI: 10.1108/00070700810887149

Aizat Jamaludin, M., Kartika, B., & Anuar Ramli Senior Lecturer, M., & Hazrul Hamzah Postgraduate candidate, M. (2019). Muslim-friendly hospital services framework. *Halal Journal, 3*, 11–24.

Ajzen, I. (1985). From intentions to actions: A theory of planned behavior. In *Action Control: From Cognitive to Behaviour*. Springer. DOI: 10.1007/978-3-642-69746-3_2

Ajzen, I. (1991). The Theory of Planned Behavior. *Organizational Behavior and Human Decision Processes, 50*(2), 179–211. Advance online publication. DOI: 10.1016/0749-5978(91)90020-T

Akhtar, S. (2025). Introduction to Eco-Innovation, Green Marketing and Digital Transformation. In *Regulatory Frameworks and Digital Compliance in Green Marketing* (pp. 1–36). IGI Global Scientific Publishing., DOI: 10.4018/979-8-3693-9831-9.ch001

Akmal, H., & Lahuri, S.bin, Ghozali, M., & Nurizal, N. (. (2021). Mengembangkan Panduan Pariwisata Halal di Indonesia Berbasis Pendekatan Maqashid al-Shari'a. *Justicia Islamica, 18*(2), 243–259. DOI: 10.21154/justicia.v18i2.2650

Akullo, J. O., Egonyu, J. P., Ng'ang'a, J., Kiiru, S., Mmari, M., Ndiritu, A., Maimba, Z. W., Salano, F. M., & Kinyuru, J. (2025). Post-harvest handling, processing and value addition of edible insects as a sustainable food resource in Africa: A review. In *International Journal of Tropical Insect Science*. Springer Nature., DOI: 10.1007/s42690-024-01410-6

Al Farisi, M. S., Anwar, S., Haryono, S., & Wahid, H. A. (2025). Sustainable Consumer Behavior of Halal Cosmetics in Indonesia E-Commerce: A Maslahah-Based Approach. *IQTISHODUNA: Jurnal Ekonomi Islam, 14*(1), 65–84. DOI: 10.54471/iqtishoduna.v14i1.2674

Al Mamun, M. R., Senn, W. D., Peak, D. A., Prybutok, V. R., & Torres, R. A. (2020). Emotional satisfaction and IS continuance behavior: Reshaping the expectation-confirmation model. *International Journal of Human-Computer Interaction, 36*(15), 1437–1446. DOI: 10.1080/10447318.2020.1752478

Al Mubarak, M. A. R., Malihah, L., Mu'minah, M., & Ma'mun, M. Y. (2023). Implementation Of Government Regulation Number 39 Of 2021 Concerning The Implementation Of The Halal Product Assurance Sector. *Al-Adl: Legal Journal, 15*(1), 214. Https://Doi.Org/10.31602/Al-Adl.V15i1.7072

Al Mustaqim, D. (2023). Halal Certification As A Form Of Muslim Consumer Protection: An Analysis Of Sharia Maqashid And Positive Law. *AB-JOIEC: Al-Bahjah Journal Of Islamic Economics, 1*(2), 54–67. Https://Doi.Org/10.61553/ABJOIEC.V1I2.26

Alam, A., Ratnasari, R. T., Prasetyo, A., Hapnitasari, I., & Rahmawati, E. (2024). Tinjauan Pustaka Sistematis tentang Studi Label Halal dalam Pariwisata Halal. TEM Journal, 13(1), 635–645. https://doi.org/DOI: 10.18421/TEM131-66

Alam, M. K., Rahman, M. M., Runy, M. K., Adedeji, B. S., & Hassan, M. F. (2022). The influences of Shariah governance mechanisms on Islamic banks performance and Shariah compliance quality. *Asian Journal of Accounting Research, 7*(1), 2–16. DOI: 10.1108/AJAR-11-2020-0112

Alam, M. M. D., Al Karim, R., & Habiba, W. (2021). The relationship between CRM and customer loyalty: The moderating role of customer trust. *International Journal of Bank Marketing, 39*(7), 1248–1272. DOI: 10.1108/IJBM-12-2020-0607

Al-Ansi, A. M., & Al-Ansi, A. (2023). An overview of artificial intelligence (AI) in 6G: Types, advantages, challenges and recent applications. *Buletin Ilmiah Sarjana Teknik Elektro, 5*(1), 67–75. DOI: 10.12928/biste.v5i1.7603

Aldrich, H. E. (2012). The emergence of entrepreneurship as an academic field: A personal essay on institutional entrepreneurship. *Research Policy, 41*(7), 1240–1248. DOI: 10.1016/j.respol.2012.03.013

Alfarizi, M., Ngatindriatun, N., Arifian, R., & Widiharjanti, I. (2025). Green-Smart Service Quality and Halal Tourism Attributes on Revisit Intention and Quality of Life: A Case Study From Indonesia. *International Journal of Halal Industry, 1*(1), 1–20. Advance online publication. DOI: 10.20885/IJHI.vol1.iss1.art1

Alhaddad, A. A., & Alhaddad, A. (2015). Perceived Quality, Brand Image and Brand Trust as Determinants of Brand Loyalty. *Quest Journals Journal of Research in Business and Management, 3*(4), 1–08. www.questjournals.org

Al-Haq, F., Ismail, N., & Al-Ayubi, S. (2024). The Influence Of Student Knowledge, Attitudes And Beliefs On Halal Labeled Products (Food And Beverage Case Study). *I-ECONOMICS: A Research Journal On Islamic Economics, 10*(1), 68–78. Https://Doi.Org/10.19109/IECONOMICS.V10I1.22171

Ali, A., Xiaoling, G., Sherwani, M., & Ali, A. (2017). *Factors affecting Halal meat purchase intention Evidence from international Muslim students in China. 119*(3), 527–541. DOI: 10.1108/BFJ-10-2016-0455

Ali, M. H., & Suleiman, N. (2018). Eleven shades of food integrity: A halal supply chain perspective. In *Trends in Food Science and Technology* (Vol. 71). DOI: 10.1016/j.tifs.2017.11.016

Ali, A., Ali, A., Sherwani, M., Brand, H., & Intention, P. (2017). Shaping Halal Into a Brand? Factors Affecting Consumers ' Halal Brand Purchase Intention Shaping Halal Into a Brand? *Journal of International Food & Agribusiness Marketing*, *4438*(May), 234–259. Advance online publication. DOI: 10.1080/08974438.2017.1312657

Ali, A., & Suleiman, N. (2023). Digital Transformation and Sustainability in the Halal Industry: A Maqasid al-Shariah Perspective. *International Journal of Islamic Business and Management*, *7*(1), 55–68. DOI: 10.46281/ijibm.v7i1.1909

Ali, J. A., Pambekti, G. T., Baroroh, H., Hassany, E. E. J. P., & Saibil, D. I. (2024). RESILIENSI EKONOMI PESANTREN MELALUI HOLDING BISNIS HEBITREN: APLIKASI ASSET BASED COMMUNITY DEVELOPMENT. *DEVOSI*, *5*(2), 2. Advance online publication. DOI: 10.33558/devosi.v5i2.9416

Ali, M. H., Iranmanesh, M., Tan, K. H., Zailani, S., & Omar, N. A. (2021). Impact of supply chain integration on halal food supply chain integrity and food quality performance. *Journal of Islamic Marketing*, *13*(7), 1515–1534. DOI: 10.1108/JIMA-08-2020-0250

Ali, S., Ghulam, W. A., & Naseer, M. (2025). Public Policy and Startup Financing as Triggers of Entrepreneurial Intentions. *Annals of Human and Social Sciences*, *6*(3), 719–727.

Ali, S., Lu, W., Cheng, C., & Chaoge, L. (2012). Media inattention for entrepreneurship in Pakistan. *European Journal of Business and Management*, *4*(18), 96–100.

Ali, S., Lu, W., & Wang, W. (2013). Comparison of entrepreneurial intentions among college students in China and Pakistan. *International Journal of Pluralism and Economics Education*, *4*(1), 51–60. DOI: 10.1504/IJPEE.2013.053588

Al-Isnawi. (1999). *Nihāyat al-Sūl Shar Minhāj Al-Wu ūl*. Beirut: Dār al-Kutub al-'Ilmiyyah.

Al-Jayyousi, O., Tok, E., Saniff, S. M., Wan Hasan, W. N., Janahi, N. A., & Yesuf, A. J. (2022). Re-Thinking Sustainable Development within Islamic Worldviews: A Systematic Literature Review. *Sustainability (Basel)*, *14*(12), 12. Advance online publication. DOI: 10.3390/su14127300

Alnaser, F. M., Rahi, S., Alghizzawi, M., & Ngah, A. H. (2023). Does artificial intelligence (AI) boost digital banking user satisfaction? Integration of expectation confirmation model and antecedents of artificial intelligence enabled digital banking. *Heliyon*, *9*(8), e18930. DOI: 10.1016/j.heliyon.2023.e18930 PMID: 37600389

Al-Nawawi, Abu Zakariyya Muhyi al-Din Yahya bin Syaraf (n.d.). *al-Majmu' Syarh al-Muhazzab*. Beirut: Darul Fikr.

Alourani, A., & Khan, S. (2024). A blockchain and artificial intelligence based system for halal food traceability [Preprint]. arXiv. https://doi.org//arXiv.2410.07305DOI: 10.48550

Al-Qaradhawi, Yusuf (2014). *Halal dan Haram Dalam Islam*. Nilai: Pustaka Cahaya Kasturi.

Al-Qaysi, N., Mohamad-Nordin, N., & Al-Emran, M. (2020). A systematic review of social media acceptance from the perspective of educational and information systems theories and models. *Journal of Educational Computing Research*, *57*(8), 2085–2109. DOI: 10.1177/0735633118817879

Al-Romeedy, B. S., & Khairy, H. A. (2024). Eco-Innovation and Hospitality and Tourism Business Resilience: The Mediating Role of Green Dynamic Capabilities. In *Shifts in Knowledge Sharing and Creativity for Business Tourism* (pp. 17–36). IGI Global Scientific Publishing. DOI: 10.4018/979-8-3693-2619-0.ch002

Alshammari, S. H., & Rosli, M. S. (2020). A review of technology acceptance models and theories. [ITLJ]. *Innovative Teaching and Learning Journal*, *4*(2), 12–22.

Al-Suwailem, S. (2000). Towards An Objective Measure of *Gharar* in Exchange. *Islamic Economic Studies*, *61*. https://www.irti.org/English/Research/Documents/IES/119.pdf

Alvarez, S. A., Barney, J. B., & Young, S. L. (2010). Debates in Entrepreneurship: Opportunity Formation and Implications for the Field of Entrepreneurship. In Z. J. Acs & D. B. Audretsch (Eds.), Handbook of Entrepreneurship Research (pp. 23–45). Springer Science+Business Media, LLC.

Alwi Shihab. (2005). *Nilai-nilai Pluralisme dalam Islam*. Mizan.

Alwines, A. (2020, August 19). Brunei's first mass produced toilet tissue, made 100% from recycled paper. Biz Brunei. https://www.bizbrunei.com/2020/08/bruneis-first-mass-produced-toilet-tissue-made-100-from-recycled-paper-enevo/

Al-Zuhaili, Wahbah bin Mustafa (2007). *Al-Fiqh al-Islami wa Adillatuhu*. Dimashq: Darul Fikr.

Amalia F A, Nova M, Koh C dan Suhartanto D. (2024). Sustainable Development in Halal Tourism Industry: The Role of Innovation and Environmental Concern. *E3S Web of Conferences*, 479: 07038. DOI: 10.1051/e3sconf/202447907038

Amalia, D., Shofiyah, , Rif'ah, S., & Sa'idaturrohmah, N. (2024). Pemberdayaan Ekonomi Pesantren melalui One Pesantren One Product (OPOP) di Ponpes Kawasan Pantura Lamongan. *Amalee: Indonesian Journal of Community Research and Engagement*, *5*(2), 2. Advance online publication. DOI: 10.37680/amalee.v5i2.2426

Amantana, A. B., Zakiran, A. H., & Imaniyati, N. S. (2023). Inclusion Of Non-Halal Information On Pharmaceutical Products Of Medicinal Types Containing Pig DNA According To Law Number 33 Of 2014 Concerning Halal Product Assurance As An Effort To Protect Consumers. *Bandung Conference Series: Law Studies, 3*(1), 178–185. Https://Doi.Org/10.29313/BCSLS.V3I1.4936

Amer, M. (2024). Linkage among halal quality standard certification and SME's performance: Palestinian food halal certified SME's context. *Arab Gulf Journal of Scientific Research*, *42*(4), 1414–1425. DOI: 10.1108/AGJSR-03-2023-0109

Amil, Y. (2024). *The Impact of AI-Driven Personalization Tools on Privacy Concerns and Consumer Trust in E-commerce*. Université de Liège.

Amin, H., & Isa, M. S. (2021). Transparency and Accountability in Halal Certification: The Role of Digital Technologies. *Journal of Halal Studies*, *3*(2), 45–59.

Amorello, D., Barreca, S., & Orecchio, S. (2024). Critical evaluation of hazardous pollutants in edible insects: A simple review. *Journal of Food Composition and Analysis*, *135*, 106675. DOI: 10.1016/j.jfca.2024.106675

Anabarja, S., & Safril Mubah, A. (2021). The Islamic Environmentalism in Eco-Pesantren Initiatives: Integrating the Sustainable Development Values in Islamic Boarding School. *Journal of International Studies on Energy Affairs*, *2*(1), 75–90. DOI: 10.51413/jisea.Vol2.Iss1.2021.75-90

Anderson, E. W., Fornell, C., & Lehmann, D. R. (1994). Customer Satisfaction, Market Share, and Profitability: Findings from Sweden. *Journal of Marketing*, *58*(3), 53–66. DOI: 10.1177/002224299405800304

Anjani, D., Hotimah, R. H., Sativa, S. O., Syifa, D. F., & Jaza, A. I. (2014). Analysis Of The Political Economy Of Halal Certification By The Indonesian Ulema Council. *JKAP (Journal Of Public Policy And Administration), 18*(1), 37–52. Https://Doi .Org/10.22146/JKAP.6870

Anshori, A. A., & Pohl, F. (2022). Environmental Education and Indonesia's Traditional Islamic Boarding Schools: Curricular and Pedagogical Innovation in the Green Pesantren Initiative. *Supporting Modern Teaching in Islamic Schools: Pedagogical Best Practice for Teachers*, 31–44. DOI: 10.4324/9781003193432-4

Anwar, M. M. (2024). How does TAM affect impulsive buying on halal fashion products via shopping mobile apps? *Journal of Islamic Marketing*, *15*(10), 2481–2507. DOI: 10.1108/JIMA-03-2023-0096

Anwar, M. M. (2025). Halal fashion insights: Understanding brand dynamics in consumer perception. *Journal of Islamic Marketing*, *16*(8), 2294–2320. Advance online publication. DOI: 10.1108/JIMA-04-2024-0149

Appadurai, A. (2003). The production of locality. In *Counterworks* (pp. 208–229). Routledge. DOI: 10.4324/9780203450994-10

Arbak, S., Islam, R., & Rasyid, H. A. (2019). Influence of Islamic Advertising: Ethical Violation of Customer Purchase Intention of Halal Cosmetic Products in Malaysia. *Humanities & Social Sciences Reviews*, *7*(3), 671–682. DOI: 10.18510/hssr.2019.7398

Ardiansyah, A., & Prihantoro, Y. (2023). Towards "Kalimatun Sawa": A Dialogue between Islam and Battour, M., & Ismail, M. N. (2016). Halal tourism: Concepts, practises, challenges and future. *Tourism Management Perspectives*, *19*(1), 150–154. DOI: 10.46362/jrsc.v4i1.96

Arianti, F., & Yunarti, S. (2022). Price Changes in A Limited Time in Home Shopping Program on RTV Television Media From the Perspective of Islamic Law. AL- ADALAH, 19(2), 357. DOI: 10.24042/adalah.v19i2.10316

Arifin, S., Ekonomi, F., Bisnis, D., Nahdlatul, I., & Jepara, U. (2022). The Effect Of Halal Green Packaging, Green Halal Product, Halal Green Perceived Value On Green Purchase Intention. *Scientific Journal Of Islamic Economics*, *8*(02), 1411–1424.

Arifin, Z., & Hatoli, H. (2021). Application of Halal Certification by Indonesian Ulema Council on Electronic and Non-Consumption Products: Maslahah Perspective. *Justicia Islamica*, *18*(1), 115–131. DOI: 10.21154/justicia.v18i1.2397

Arsad, S., Said, R., Yusoff, H., & Ahmad, R. (2022). Islamic Corporate Social Responsibility Disclosure Index: The Application of Maqasid Shari'ah and Maslahah. *International Journal of Academic Research in Business & Social Sciences*, *12*(7). Advance online publication. DOI: 10.6007/IJARBSS/v12-i7/14331

Arumugam, N., Mohamad, F., Shanthi, A., & Dharinee, S. (2021). A Study on Online Shopping Scams. *International Journal of Social Science Research, 10*(1), 22. DOI: 10.5296/ijssr.v10i1.19290

Arwani, W., Jaelani, A., Firdaus, S., & Hanim, T. F. (2022). Halal-Thayyib, Food Products, And The Halal Industry: A Thematic Analysis On The Verses Of The Qur'an. *Al-Amwal: Journal Of Sharia Economics And Banking, 14*(1). Https://Doi .Org/10.24235/Amwal.V14i1.10830

Asadullah, A., Faik, I., & Kankanhalli, A. (2018). Digital platforms: A review and future directions. *Proceedings of the 22nd Pacific Asia Conference on Information Systems - Opportunities and Challenges for the Digitized Society: Are We Ready? PACIS 2018.*

Asante, I. O., Jiang, Y., Hossin, A. M., & Luo, X. (2023). Optimization of consumer engagement with artificial intelligence elements on electronic commerce platforms. *Journal of Electronic Commerce Research*, *24*(1), 7–28.

Ashraf, M. A. (2019). *Islamic marketing and consumer behavior toward halal food purchase in Bangladesh An analysis using SEM. 10*(3), 893–910. DOI: 10.1108/ JIMA-03-2018-0051

Asif, M., & Akhlaq, M. (2024). Sharia Compliance in Modern Business Practices. *Tanazur, 5*(2), 285–301. https://tanazur.com.pk/index.php/tanazur/article/view/305

Assaker, G., & Hallak, R. (2013). Moderating Effects of Tourists' Novelty-Seeking Tendencies on Destination Image, Visitor Satisfaction, and Short- and Long-Term Revisit Intentions. *Journal of Travel Research*, *52*(5), 600–613. DOI: 10.1177/0047287513478497

Atabik, A., & Muqtada, M. R. (2024). Maqashid Quran's critical view on Indonesian Ulema Council's fatwa on Halal certification of COVID-19 vaccine. *Hervormde Teologiese Studies*, *80*(1), a9050. Advance online publication. DOI: 10.4102/HTS. v80i1.9050

Atieqoh, S., Waseso, H. P., & Hamidi, A. (2023). *Halal Certificate and Public Trust Local Food and Beverage Business Development. In economics, business and management research/Advances in Economics, Business and Management Research.* Atlantis Press., DOI: 10.2991/978-94-6463-188-3_9

Attahiru, M. S. (2021). The Measurement of Hisbah Principles in the Islamic Marketing Context. *International Journal of Business and Management*, *9*(11).

Attaluri, V., & Kotte, K. R. (2025). Sustainable Business Strategies: A Data-Driven Approach to Eco-Friendly Practices. In *Driving Business Success Through Eco-Friendly Strategies* (pp. 357–374). IGI Global Scientific Publishing. DOI: 10.4018/979-8-3693-9750-3.ch019

Atzori, L., Iera, A., & Morabito, G. (2010). The Internet of Things: A survey. *Computer Networks*, *54*(15), 2787–2805. Advance online publication. DOI: 10.1016/j.comnet.2010.05.010

Auda, J. (2008). *Maqasid al-Syariah sebagai Filsafat Hukum Islam: Pendekatan Sistem. Dalam.* Institut Pemikiran Islam Internasional.

Aulia, R. N., Abbas, H., Nurhattati, N., Jasin, F. M., & Mushlihin, M. (2024). Eco-pesantren modeling for environmentally friendly behavior: New lessons from Indonesia. *International Journal of Evaluation and Research in Education*, *13*(1), 223–229. DOI: 10.11591/ijere.v13i1.25930

Awang, M. D., Yahaya, M. M., Sulaiman, M., Ismail, K., Baharum, N. B., & Abdullah, A. A. (2023). Perspectives on the role of National Fatwa Committee in handling food issues in Malaysia based on Maqasid Syariah. In *Food Research* (Vol. 6, pp. 60–66). Rynnye Lyan Resources., DOI: 10.26656/fr.2017.6(S3).5

Azam, M. S. E., & Abdullah, M. A. (2020). Global Halal Industry: Realities and Opportunities. *International Journal of Islamic Business Ethics*, *5*(1), 47. DOI: 10.30659/ijibe.5.1.47-59

Azhar, M. M. T. (2025). PROPHET (SAW) AND SAHABA'S BUSINESS LIFE. *CONTEMPORARY JOURNAL OF SOCIAL SCIENCE REVIEW*, *03*(02), 89–105. DOI: 10.63878/cjssr.v3i2.753

Aziz, Y. A., & Chok, N. V. (n.d.). *Journal of International Food & The Role of Halal Awareness, Halal Certification, and Marketing Components in Determining Halal Purchase Intention Among Non-Muslims in Malaysia : A Structural Equation Modeling Approach. December 2013*, 37–41. DOI: 10.1080/08974438.2013.723997

Azizah, N., Salam, A. N., & Arifin, A. Z. (2023). Model design of sociopreneurship: Halal based-development of micro, small and medium enterprises through zakat institutions. *ISRA International Journal of Islamic Finance*, *15*(3), 46–63. DOI: 10.55188/ijif.v15i3.610

Aziz, Y. A., & Chok, N. V. (2013). The role of halal awareness, halal certification, and marketing components in determining halal purchase intention among non-Muslims in Malaysia. *International Journal of Business and Social Science*, *4*(1), 1–7.

Azmi, S. N. S., Jais, Z., Samsudin, S. N., Hasini, N. F. M., Izhar, N. I., Idris, N. A., & Hashim, A. H. A. (2025). A Qualitative Approach of KAP Model Against Online Scams in Malaysia. *International Journal of Academic Research in Business & Social Sciences, 15*(2). Advance online publication. DOI: 10.6007/IJARBSS/v15-i2/24701

Azra, A. (2004). *The Origins of Islamic Reformism in Southeast Asia: Networks of Malay-Indonesian and Middle Eastern 'Ulama' in the Seventeenth and Eighteenth Centuries*. University of Hawai'i Press. DOI: 10.1163/9789004488199

Azra, A. (2006). *Islam in the Indonesian world: An account of institutional formation*. Mizan Pustaka.

Babatunde Bello, K. (2023). *Strengthen the Sustainability of Halal Entrepreneurs Through International Consumer Rights Laws*.

Bagir, Z. A. Asfinawati, Suhadi, & Arianingtyas, R. (2020). Limitations To Freedom Of Religion Or Belief In Indonesia: Norms And Practices. *Religion & Human Rights, 15*(1–2), 39–56. Https://Doi.Org/10.1163/18710328-BJA10003

Bagozzi, R. P., Batra, R., & Ahuvia, A. (2017). Brand love: Development and validation of a practical scale. *Marketing Letters*, *28*(1), 1–14. DOI: 10.1007/s11002-016-9406-1

Bagozzi, R. P., Fornell, C., & Larceer, D. P. (1981). Canonical correlation analysis as a special case of a structural relations model. *Multivariate Behavioral Research*, *16*(4), 437–454. DOI: 10.1207/s15327906mbr1604_2 PMID: 26812673

Bakar, M. A., Noor, A. M., Ismail, S., & Yusoff, M.Marina Abu BakarAfiffudin Mohammed NoorSyaimak Ismail @ Mat Yusoff. (2025). Halal Meets Biotech: Exploring Integration Opportunities and Challenges in Malaysian Universities: Halal Bertemu Bioteknologi: Meneroka Peluang dan Cabaran Integrasi di Universiti-Universiti Malaysia. *Sains Insani*, *10*(1), 62–74. DOI: 10.33102/sainsinsani.vol10no1.721

Bakri, M. (2021). ECO-Pesantren assessment study of Islamic Boarding School in Banda Aceh, Indonesia. *Journal of Islamic Architecture*, *6*(3), 143–150. DOI: 10.18860/jia.v6i3.7967

Bank Islam Brunei Darussalam. (2023, January 24). BIBD eco-alam festival: Tackling food waste by going zero-waste, plastic-free and cashless. BIBD. https://bibd.com.bn/articles/news/bibd-eco-alam-festival-tackling-food-waste-by-going-zero-waste-plastic-free-and-cashless/

Barney, S., Aurum, A., & Wohlin, C. (2008). A product management challenge: Creating software product value through requirements selection. *Journal of Systems Architecture*, *54*(6), 576–593. DOI: 10.1016/j.sysarc.2007.12.004

Barre, A., Laisney, M., & De Oliveira, G. (2021). Microbiological safety of edible insects: A review. *Food Control, 121*, 107658. DOI: 10.1016/j.foodcont.2020.107658

Bashir, A. M. (2019). Applying the Institutional Theory at the Level of Halal Consumers: The Case of Cape Town in South Africa. *Journal of Food Products Marketing, 25*(5), 527–548. DOI: 10.1080/10454446.2019.1607645

Bashir, A. M., Bayat, A., Olutuase, S. O., & Ariff, Z. (2018). Factors affecting consumers ' intention towards purchasing halal food in South Africa : A structural equation modelling. *Journal of Food Products Marketing, 00*(00), 1–23. DOI: 10.1080/10454446.2018.1452813

Basri, M. H. (2022). *Green Islam'and 'green Pesantren': An ethnographic study of Pesantren Annuqayah.* Western Sidney University.

Batra, R., Ahuvia, A., Bagozzi, R. P., & Love, B. (2012).. . *Brand Love., 76*(March), 1–16.

Battour, M., Hakimian, F., Ismail, M., & Boğan, E. (2018). Persepsi Wisatawan Non-Muslim terhadap Pariwisata Halal: Bukti dari Turki dan Malaysia. *Jurnal Pemasaran Islam, 9*(4). Advance online publication. DOI: 10.1108/JIMA-07-2017-0072

Battour, M., & Ismail, M. N. (2016). *Pariwisata halal: Konsep, Praktik, Tantangan, dan Masa Depan. Dalam* (Vol. 19). Perspektif Manajemen Pariwisata., DOI: 10.1016/j.tmp.2015.12.008

Battour, M., Ismail, M. N., & Battor, M. (2010). Toward a halal tourism market. *Tourism Analysis, 15*(4), 461–470. DOI: 10.3727/108354210X12864727453304

Battour, M., Ismail, M. N., & Battor, M. (2011). Dampak Atribut Destinasi terhadap Pilihan Wisatawan Muslim. *Jurnal Riset Pariwisata Internasional, 13*(6). Advance online publication. DOI: 10.1002/jtr.824

Beekun, R. I. (1997). *Islamic Business Ethics*. International Institute of Islamic Thought., DOI: 10.2307/j.ctvk8w1zv

Bella-Salsa, A., Kartika, B., Jaiyeoba, H., & Jamaludin, M. (2023). Halal Lifestyle Entrepreneurship: Concept, Practice, Prospects and Challenges. *Journal of Halal Science and Technology*. DOI: 10.59202/jhst.v2i2.725

Bergkvist, L., & Bech-larsen, T. (2010). Two studies of consequences and actionable antecedents of brand love. *Journal of Brand Management, 17*(7), 504–518. DOI: 10.1057/bm.2010.6

BERNAMA. (2025). "Malaysia to Issue Halal Certificates Electronically from May 5." *BERNAMA News Agency*, January 15, 2025. https://www.bernama.com

Bharadiya, J. P., Thomas, R. K., & Ahmed, F. (2023). Rise of Artificial Intelligence in Business and Industry. *Journal of Engineering Research and Reports*, *25*(3), 85–103. DOI: 10.9734/jerr/2023/v25i3893

Bhatnagr, P., & Rajesh, A. (2024). Artificial intelligence features and expectation confirmation theory in digital banking apps: Gen Y and Z perspective. *Management Decision.*

Bhatnagr, P., Rajesh, A., & Misra, R. (2024). Continuous intention usage of artificial intelligence enabled digital banks: A review of expectation confirmation model. *Journal of Enterprise Information Management*, *37*(6), 1763–1787. DOI: 10.1108/JEIM-11-2023-0617

Bhatt, T., Hickey, C., & McEntire, J. C. (2013). Pilot projects for improving product tracing along the food supply system. *Journal of Food Science*, *78*(s2, Suppl 2.). Advance online publication. DOI: 10.1111/1750-3841.12298 PMID: 24171802

Bhutto, M. Y. (2024). *Investigating EWOM and halal product knowledge on gen Z ' s halal cosmetics purchase intentions in Pakistan. 15*(11), 3266–3281. DOI: 10.1108/JIMA-09-2023-0292

Bianchi, C., Drennan, J., & Proud, B. (2014). Antecedents of consumer brand loyalty in the Australian wine industry. *Journal of Wine Research*, *25*(2), 91–104. DOI: 10.1080/09571264.2014.888650

Bolón-Canedo, V., Morán-Fernández, L., Cancela, B., & Alonso-Betanzos, A. (2024). A review of green artificial intelligence: Towards a more sustainable future. *Neurocomputing*, *599*, 128096. DOI: 10.1016/j.neucom.2024.128096

Bonne, K., Vermeir, I., & Bergeaud-blackler, F. (2007). *Determinants of halal meat consumption in France. 109*(5), 367–386. DOI: 10.1108/00070700710746786

Bonne, K., & Verbeke, W. (2008). Muslim consumer trust in halal meat status and control in Belgium. *Meat Science*, *79*(1), 113–123. DOI: 10.1016/j.meatsci.2007.08.007 PMID: 22062604

Börekci, C., & Çelik, Ö. (2024). Exploring The Role of Digital Literacy in University Students' Engagement with AI through the Technology Acceptance Model. *Sakarya University Journal of Education*, *14*(2 (Special Issue-Artificial Intelligence Tools and Education)), 228–249. DOI: 10.19126/suje.1468866

Borneo Bulletin. (2023, July 27). For a greener future. Borneo Bulletin. https://borneobulletin.com.bn/for-a-greener-future/

Bougie, R., & Sekaran, U. (2020). *Metode Penelitian untuk Bisnis: Pendekatan Pengembangan Keterampilan Edisi ke-8, Asia*. Wiley.

Braunerhjelm, P., Andersson, M., & Eklund, J. (2022). Pioneering entrepreneurship research: How, by whom, and when. *Foundations and Trends® in Entrepreneurship, 18*(2), 75–158.

Braun, V., & Clarke, V. (2006). Using thematic analysis in psychology. *Qualitative Research in Psychology, 3*(2), 77–101. DOI: 10.1191/1478088706qp063oa

Broekman, H. C. H., Knulst, A. C., den Hartog Jager, C. F., van Bilsen, J., Raymakers, F. M., Kruizinga, A. G., & Houben, G. F. (2017). Anaphylaxis after eating insects in patients with known food allergy. *The Journal of Allergy and Clinical Immunology, 139*(2), 883–885. DOI: 10.1016/j.jaci.2016.08.031

Bux, C., Varese, E., Amicarelli, V., & Lombardi, M. (2022). Halal Food Sustainability Between Certification And Blockchain: A Review. *Sustainability (Switzerland), 14*(4), 1–18. Https://Doi.Org/10.3390/Su14042152

Carlsson, B., Braunerhjelm, P., McKelvey, M., Olofsson, C., Persson, L., & Ylinenpää, H. (2013). The evolving domain of entrepreneurship research. *Small Business Economics, 41*(4), 913–930. DOI: 10.1007/s11187-013-9503-y

Carneiro-Da-Cunha, J. A., Dos Santos, M. G., De Souza, L. J., Alssabak, N. A. M., & Macau, F. R. (2015). The history of an Islamic entrepreneurship: Achieving exporting-network leadership through religious legitimacy. *International Journal of Business and Globalisation, 15*(3), 272–293. DOI: 10.1504/IJBG.2015.071921

Carroll, B. A., & Ahuvia, A. C. (2006). *Some antecedents and outcomes of brand love*. 79–89. DOI: 10.1007/s11002-006-4219-2

Changalima, I. A. (2025). Halal supply chain management: A bibliometric analysis of the 100 most-cited publications from Scopus-indexed journals. *Social Sciences & Humanities Open, 11*, 101248. DOI: 10.1016/j.ssaho.2024.101248

Chaniago, S. A. C. S. A., Izza, M. I. M., Wijaya, B. S. W. B. S., & Rozi, F. F. P. R. F. F. P. (2024). Implementation of Halal Supply Chain in the Cooperative of Islamic Boarding School: Maqashid Syariah Perspective. *Jurnal Hukum Islam, 22*(1), 1. Advance online publication. DOI: 10.28918/jhi_v22i1_3

Chantarungsri, C., Popichit, N., Rugthangam, S., Wattana, N., Chuanchom, J., & Sukmak, M. (2024). Mapping the landscape of halal tourism: A bibliometric analysis. *Cogent Social Sciences, 10*(1), 2365507. DOI: 10.1080/23311886.2024.2365507

Chapra, MU. (2008). Visi Pembangunan Islam dalam Cahaya Maqasid al-Syariah. Dalam *makalah sesekali seri 15* .

Chasanah, C. L., & Muzammil, S. (2025). Halal Certification Of The Halal Product Assurance Agency (BPJPH) In A Juridical Perspective. *Maslahah: Journal Of Sharia Management And Economics, 3*(1), 211–225. Https://Doi.Org/10.59059/MASLAHAH.V3I1.2022

Chatterjee, S., Rana, N. P., Dwivedi, Y. K., & Baabdullah, A. M. (2021). Understanding AI adoption in manufacturing and production firms using an integrated TAM-TOE model. *Technological Forecasting and Social Change*, *170*, 120880. DOI: 10.1016/j.techfore.2021.120880

Chatzoglou, P., Chatzoudes, D., Savvidou, A., Fotiadis, T., & Delias, P. (2022). Factors affecting repurchase intentions in retail shopping: An empirical study. *Heliyon*, *8*(9), e10619. DOI: 10.1016/j.heliyon.2022.e10619 PMID: 36158093

Chaudhuri, A., & Holbrook, M. B. (2001). The chain of effects from brand trust and brand affect to brand performance: The role of brand loyalty. *Journal of Marketing*, *65*(2), 81–93. DOI: 10.1509/jmkg.65.2.81.18255

Che Jamaludin, F. I., Abdullah, M. R. T. L., Endut, M. N. A. A., Saifuddeen, S. M., Hamimi, K. A., & Harun, S. (2025). Developing a Shariah-compliant medical services framework in Malaysia: An expert system approach using fuzzy Delphi method and interpretive structural modelling. *BMJ Open*, *15*(1), e082263. Advance online publication. DOI: 10.1136/bmjopen-2023-082263 PMID: 39762112

Chen, Y., Prentice, C., Weaven, S., & Hisao, A. (2022). The influence of customer trust and artificial intelligence on customer engagement and loyalty—The case of the home-sharing industry. *Frontiers in Psychology*, *13*, 912339. DOI: 10.3389/fpsyg.2022.912339 PMID: 35992434

Chetia, J. R., S, S., Sahu, S., & Seth, D. (2025). Ant lipids: A comprehensive review of their major composition, health benefits, and potential as a future food. *Trends in Food Science & Technology*, *157*, 104895. DOI: 10.1016/j.tifs.2025.104895

Chong, F. H. L. (2021). Enhancing trust through digital Islamic finance and blockchain technology. *Qualitative Research in Financial Markets*, *13*(3), 328–341. DOI: 10.1108/QRFM-05-2020-0076

Chun T'ing, L., Moorthy, K., Gunasaygaran, N., Sek Li, C., Omapathi, D., Jia Yi, H., Anandan, K., & Sivakumar, K. (2021). Intention to reduce food waste: A study among Malaysians. *Journal of the Air & Waste Management Association*, *71*(7), 890–905. DOI: 10.1080/10962247.2021.1900001 PMID: 33689567

Chung, K. C. (2023). Customer satisfaction towards m-shopping and the significance of relational values and co-presence. *International Journal of Electronic Commerce Studies, 14*(3), 21–48. DOI: 10.7903/ijecs.2242

Collin, J., & Casswell, S. (2016). Alcohol And The Sustainable Development Goals. In *The Lancet* (Vol. 387, Issue 10038). Https://Doi.Org/10.1016/S0140-6736(16)30827-3

Cong, L., Dean, D., Liu, C., Wang, K., & Hou, Y. (2024). The commercial application of insect protein in food products: A product audit based on online resources. *Foods, 13*(21), 3509. DOI: 10.3390/foods13213509 PMID: 39517293

Cook, M., Critchlow, N., O'Donnell, R., & Maclean, S. (2024). Alcohol's Contribution To Climate Change And Other Environmental Degradation: A Call For Research. In *Health Promotion International* (Vol. 39, Issue 1). Https://Doi.Org/10.1093/Heapro/Daae004

Cornille, C. (2013). *The Im-Possibility of Interreligious Dialogue*. Crossroad Publishing.

Creswell, J. W., & Creswell, J. D. (2018). Research Designs Qualitative, Quantitative, and Mixed Methods Approaches. In *Fast Facts to Loving your Research Project* (Fifth Edit). SAGE Publications, Inc. DOI: 10.1891/9780826146373.0007

Creswell, J. W., & Poth, C. N. (2018). *Qualitative inquiry and research design: Choosing among five approaches* (4th ed.). SAGE Publications.

Creswell, J., & Poth, C. (2018). *Qualitative Inquiry and Research Design* (4th ed.). SAGE Publication.

Creswell, W. J. (2016). *Penelitian Kualitatif dan Desain Riset*. Penelitian Kualitatif.

Dana, L.-P. (2010). *Entrepreneurship and religion*. Edward Elgar Publishing. DOI: 10.4337/9781849806329

Dar Ifta' Misriyyah. (2013). Is it permissible to use carminic acid as a natural food colorant which is extracted from an insect? Retrieved from https://www.dar-alifta.org/en/fatwa/details/6888/is-it-permissible-to-use-carminic-acid-as-a-natural-food-colorant-which-is-extrac

Dariah, A. R., Abdullah, R., Hidayat, A. R., & Matahir, F. (2022). Sustainable economic sectors in Indonesia and Brunei Darussalam. *Sustainability (Basel), 14*(5), 3044. DOI: 10.3390/su14053044

Darmalaksana, W. (2023). How is the halal certification policy implemented? Perspective analysis of small and medium enterprises (SMEs) in Indonesia. *Journal of Islamic Accounting and Business Research.*

Dashti, L. A. H. F., Jackson, T., West, A., & Jackson, L. (2024). Enhancing halal food traceability: A model for rebuilding trust and integrity in Muslim countries. *Journal of Islamic Marketing*, *2018*(12), 3382–3408. Advance online publication. DOI: 10.1108/JIMA-06-2023-0167

Daud, A. H. M., Lee, U. H. M. S., & Ismail, A. (2023). The Practice of Halal Certification: A Case of Malaysia's Halal Meat-Based Industry. *International Journal of Academic Research in Business & Social Sciences, 13*(8). Advance online publication. DOI: 10.6007/IJARBSS/v13-i8/17666

Davis, F. D., Granić, A., & Marangunić, N. (2023). The technology acceptance model 30 years of TAM. *Technology.*

De Boni, A., & Forleo, M. B. (2019). Italian halal food market development: Drivers and obstacles from experts' opinions. *Journal of Islamic Marketing*, *10*(4), 1245–1271. DOI: 10.1108/JIMA-05-2018-0087

De Moraes, C. C., de Oliveira Costa, F. H., Pereira, C. R., Da Silva, A. L., & Delai, I. (2020). Retail food waste: Mapping causes and reduction practices. *Journal of Cleaner Production*, *256*, 120124. DOI: 10.1016/j.jclepro.2020.120124

de Oliveira Santini, F., Ladeira, W. J., Sampaio, C. H., & Pinto, D. C. (2018). The brand experience extended model: A meta-analysis. *Journal of Brand Management*, *25*(6), 519–535. DOI: 10.1057/s41262-018-0104-6

De Vries, M., & De Boer, I. J. M. (2010). Comparing Environmental Impacts For Livestock Products: A Review Of Life Cycle Assessments. *Livestock Science*, *128*(1–3), 1–11. DOI: 10.1016/j.livsci.2009.11.007

Department of Standards Malaysia. (2019). [– *Halal Food – General Requirements] [Third Revision] [*. Putrajaya: Standards Malaysia.]. *Ms*, *1500*, 2019.

Deuraseh, N. (2022). Reconstruction Of The Higher Objective Of Islamic Law (Maqasid Shariah) To Strengthen Halal Industry With Special Reference To Halal Envir. *Proceeding Of 2nd Malikussaleh Internasional Conference On Law, Legal Studies And Social Science (Micolls) 2022*, 1–9.

Deuraseh, N., Haji Matusin, S. N. I., Haji Abdul Aziz, A. A., Haji Sham, I. Z., Halid Khan, S. N. A., & Hashim, N. (2023). The Awareness Of Halal Green Among Postgraduate Students In UNISSA For Sustainable Campus. *Journal Of Halal Science And Technology*, *2*(2), 76–91. Https://Doi.Org/10.59202/Jhst.V2i2.670. DOI: 10.59202/jhst.v2i2.670

Dewi, A. (2024). Green Halal: The Synergy Of The Halal Industry And Sustainable Development. *An-Natiq Journal Of Interdisciplinary Islamic Studies*, *4*(2), 119–130.

Dhiman, N., & Jamwal, M. (2023). Tourists' post-adoption continuance intentions of chatbots: Integrating task—technology fit model and expectation—confirmation theory. *Foresight*, *25*(2), 209–224. DOI: 10.1108/FS-10-2021-0207

Dhofier, Z. (2011). *Tradisi Pesantren: Studi Tentang Pandangan Hidup Kyai*. LP3ES.

Díaz, A. V., Calleja, C. A., Escámez, P. F., Abuín, C. M. F., Sillué, S. M., & Moragas, G. S. (2023). Report of the Scientific Committee of the Spanish Agency for Food Safety and Nutrition (AESAN) on the determination of the date of minimum durability for frozen meat in retail establishments (Vol. 1, No. 1, p. 0001E).

Dick, A. S. (1978). *Customer Loyalty : Toward an Integrated Conceptual Framework.*

DiMaggio, P., & Powell, W. W. (1983). The Iron Cage Revisited: Institutional Isomorphism and Collective Rationality in Organizational Fields. *American Sociological Review*, *48*(2), 147–160. DOI: 10.2307/2095101

DinarStandard. (2023). *State of the Global Islamic Economy Report 2023*. Dubai: DinarStandard. Retrieved from: https://www.dinarstandard.com/post/state-of-the-global-islamic-economy-report-2023

Din, F. M. (2023). Digital Connectivity as a Springboard to Professionalisation: Social Media Groups of Pakistani Women. *International Quarterly for Asian Studies, 54*, 389-408. Retrieved from https://doi.org/DOI: 10.11588/iqas.2023.4.21080

Ding, M. (2017). The origin and the change of Qingzhen culture. *Journal of North Ethnic Studies*, (1)

Dorsemaine, B., Gaulier, J. P., Wary, J. P., Kheir, N., & Urien, P. (2016). Internet of Things: A Definition and Taxonomy. *Proceedings - NGMAST 2015: The 9th International Conference on Next Generation Mobile Applications, Services and Technologies*. DOI: 10.1109/NGMAST.2015.71

Drennan, J., Bianchi, C., Cacho-Elizondo, S., Louriero, S., Guibert, N., & Proud, W. (2015). Examining the role of wine brand love on brand loyalty: A multi-country comparison. *International Journal of Hospitality Management*, *49*, 47–55. DOI: 10.1016/j.ijhm.2015.04.012

Dusuki, A. W., & Abozaid, A. (2007). Maqasid al-Shariah, Maslahah, and corporate social responsibility. *The American Journal of Islamic Social Sciences*, *24*(1), 25–45. DOI: 10.35632/ajiss.v24i1.415

Dusuki, A. W., & Abozaid, A. (2021). Trust and Responsibility in Islamic Business Ethics. *International Journal of Islamic and Middle Eastern Finance and Management*, *14*(6), 1004–1020. DOI: 10.1108/IMEFM-05-2020-0223

Dwicahyani R R, Shafira A H, Maulana N dan Mandalia S. (2025). Halal tourism among Gen Z: Analyzing the effect of halal awareness and destination trust on visit intention with religiosity as a mediator. *Jurnal Ekonomi dan Bisnis Islam*, 11(1): 1–21. DOI: 10.20473/jebis.v11i1.59898

Dwivedi, Y. K., Hughes, L., Wang, Y., Alalwan, A. A., Ahn, S. J., Balakrishnan, J., Barta, S., Belk, R., Buhalis, D., Dutot, V., Felix, R., Filieri, R., Flavián, C., Gustafsson, A., Hinsch, C., Hollensen, S., Jain, V., Kim, J., Krishen, A. S., & Wirtz, J. (2023). Metaverse marketing: How the metaverse will shape the future of consumer research and practice. *Psychology and Marketing*, *40*(4), 750–776. DOI: 10.1002/mar.21767

Echchabi, A., Bocanet, A., & Grassa, R. (2022). Determinants of Selection of Halal Tourism Destination: A Case Study of the UAE. *Global Journal Al-Thaqafah*, *12*(1), 186–203. DOI: 10.7187/GJAT072022-12

Eid, R., & El-Gohary, H. (2015). Nilai yang Dirasakan Wisatawan Muslim dalam Industri Perhotelan dan Pariwisata. *Jurnal Riset Perjalanan*, *54*(6). Advance online publication. DOI: 10.1177/0047287514532367

Ekka, P. M., & Bhardwaj, S. (2024). Customers' Satisfaction as a Critical Success Factor in Halal Tourism: Literature Review and Research Agenda. *Journal of Islamic Marketing*, *15*(8), 2069–2085. DOI: 10.1108/JIMA-02-2023-0059

Elalfy, R. M., Elayat, A. M. A., & Elsharnouby, M. H. (2024). Building good brand experience to sustain positive electronic word of mouth: The mediating effect of brand love. *Management and Sustainability*, *4*(2), 217–236. DOI: 10.1108/MSAR-01-2024-0001

Elayat, A. M. A., & Elalfy, R. M. (2025). Using SOR theory to examine the impact of AI Chatbot quality on Gen Z's satisfaction and advocacy within the fast-food sector. *Young Consumers*, *26*(2), 352–383. DOI: 10.1108/YC-08-2024-2199

Ellahi, R. M., Wood, L. C., Khan, M., & Bekhit, A. E. D. A. (2025). Integrity challenges in halal meat supply chain: Potential industry 4.0 technologies as catalysts for resolution. *Foods*, *14*(7), 1135. DOI: 10.3390/foods14071135 PMID: 40238310

Ellis, J. D., Graham, J. R., & Mortensen, A. (2013). Standard methods for wax moth research. *Journal of Apicultural Research*, *52*(1), 1–17. Advance online publication. DOI: 10.3896/IBRA.1.52.1.10

Elmashhara, M. G., De Cicco, R., Silva, S. C., Hammerschmidt, M., & Silva, M. L. (2024). How gamifying AI shapes customer motivation, engagement, and purchase behavior. *Psychology and Marketing*, *41*(1), 134–150. DOI: 10.1002/mar.21912

Ernest, C. D., & Lau, W. M. (2012). Will those targeted pay more? The Issue of Halal Logo. Osman MohdZain. Reading in Marketing: An Islamic Perspective.

Fadhilah, L. N., & Syamsuri, S. (2022). Depicthing Halal Value Chain At the Gontor Alumni Pesantren Forum (Fpag). *MIQOT: Jurnal Ilmu-Ilmu Keislaman, 46*(2), 162–185. DOI: 10.30821/miqot.v46i2.980

Fadhillah, A. R. (2022). Contemporary Advertising in Islamic Perspective. *Jurnal Peurawi Media Kajian Komunikasi Islam*, *5*(1), 1. DOI: 10.22373/jp.v5i1.12011

Fageh, A. (2022). Building a Synergy Between the Halal Industry and the Green Industry in the Maqasid Syari'ah Review as the Basis of Islamic Economics. *Journal of Islamic Economic Laws*, *5*(1), 139–158. DOI: 10.23917/jisel.v5i1.17034

Fahrurrazi. (2019a). To be ecological is to become pluralist: Inclusive religious education at the eco-pesantren Ath-Thaariq, West Java. *Studies in Interreligious Dialogue, 9*(1), 23–42. DOI: 10.2143/SID.29.1.3286453

Fairuz, A. (2024). Environmental sustainability in the Hajj pilgrimage. *International Journal of Academic Research in Business & Social Sciences*, *14*(12), 222–6990. DOI: 10.6007/IJARBSS/v14-i12/23913

FAO. (2013). Edible insects: Future prospects for food and feed security. Rome: Food and Agriculture Organization of the United Nations. Retrieved on 16 July,2025 from https://www.fao.org/4/i3253e/i3253e.pdf

Faruq, A. K., Hepni, H., & Sujiwo, S. (2022). Technology and Noble Traditions in Pesantren. *Edukasi Islami: Jurnal Pendidikan Islam*, *11*(02). Advance online publication. DOI: 10.30868/ei.v11i02.2385

Fauzan, A.Rezki Akbar Norrahman. (2025). Smart Contracts in Increasing Sharia Compliance on Peer To Peer Lending Platforms in Sharia Fintech. *Journal of Society and Scientific Studies*, *1*(1), 45–55. DOI: 10.62504/scientival

Fauzi, M. A. (2023). *Consumer purchase of halal certi fi ed product : a quantitative systematic literature review. 14*(6), 1397–1416. DOI: 10.1108/JIMA-09-2021-0299

Fauzi, M. A., & Battour, M. (2024). Pariwisata Halal dan Islam: Pemetaan Ilmiah Tren Saat Ini dan Masa Depan. Dalam. *Tourism Review*. Advance online publication. DOI: 10.1108/TR-08-2023-0533

Fauzi, M. A., Mohd Ali, N. S., Mat Russ, N., Mohamad, F., Battour, M., & Mohd Zaki, N. N. (2024). Halal certification in food products: Science mapping of present and future trends. *Journal of Islamic Marketing*, *15*(12), 3564–3580. DOI: 10.1108/JIMA-12-2023-0407

Fauzi, M. A., Muhamad Tamyez, P. F., & Kumar, S. (2025). Social Entrepreneurship and Social Innovation in ASEAN: Past, Present, and Future Trends. *Journal of Social Entrepreneurship*, *16*(1), 146–168. DOI: 10.1080/19420676.2022.2143870

Fawa'id, M. W., & Mutafarida, B. (2024). Indonesia And Malaysia Halal Certification Policy:Opportunities And Challenges. *Asean Journal Of Halal Industry, 1*(1), 28–38. Https://Doi.Org/Https://Journal.Unesa.Ac.Id/Index.Php/Ajhi/Article/View/35710

Febriandika, N. R., Tsany, N. P., & Sriplod, T. (2022). Marketing Strategy of *Gharar* Business Schemes: Mystery Box on the e-Commerce Shopee Platform. *ISLAMUNA Jurnal Studi Islam*, *9*(1), 26–40. DOI: 10.19105/islamuna.v9i1.6028

Febriandika, N. R., Wijaya, V., & Hakim, L. (2023). Gen-Z Muslims' purchase intention of halal food: Evidence from Indonesia. *Innovative Marketing*, *19*(1), 13–25. DOI: 10.21511/im.19(1).2023.02

Fernando, F., & Dewi, C. K. (2025). Influence of halal credence, halal awareness, halal certification, and health consciousness to halal purchase intention through STHF (Satisfaction towards halal food) and religiosity as a moderation variable. *Edelweiss Applied Science and Technology*, *9*(4), 312–324. DOI: 10.55214/25768484.v9i4.5974

Fernando, Y., Hendayani, R., Jawo, M., Rahamaddulla, S. R., Abdul Aziz, K., & Maimunah, N. (2025). Discovering Islamic marketing potential in shaping blockchain-based halal logistic services: A bibliometric analysis. *Journal of Islamic Marketing*, *16*(3), 870–905. DOI: 10.1108/JIMA-06-2024-0258

Ferrazzano, G. F., D'Ambrosio, F., Caruso, S., Gatto, R., & Caruso, S. (2023). Bioactive peptides derived from edible insects: Effects on human health and possible applications in dentistry. *Nutrients*, *15*(21), 4611. DOI: 10.3390/nu15214611 PMID: 37960264

Fischer, J. (2016). I*slam, Standards, and Technoscience*. In *Global Halal Zones*. Routledge.

Fisol, WNM, Suid, IS, Mohd Saufi, MSA, & Bahari, A. (2019). Pengembangan Pariwisata Islam Berbasis Keilmuan Kerangka Maqasid Syariah. *Jurnal Internasional Riset Akademik Bisnis dan Ilmu Sosial, 9* (5).

Flowers, E. P., Freeman, P., & Gladwell, V. F. (2017). The development of three questionnaires to assess beliefs about green exercise. *International Journal of Environmental Research and Public Health, 14*(10), 1172. DOI: 10.3390/ijerph14101172 PMID: 28976924

Food and Agricultural Organization of the United Nations. (2017). *The future of food and agriculture – Trends and challenges. Rome.*

Foti, V. T., Sturiale, L., & Timpanaro, G. (2018). An overview of food waste phenomenon: By problem to resource. *Calitatea, 19*(S1), 232–240.

Freeman, R. E. (1984). A Stakeholder Approach to Strategic Management. In SSRN *Electronic Journal.* Pitman. DOI: 10.2139/ssrn.263511

Gantner, M., Sadowska, A., Piotrowska, A., Kulik, K., Sionek, B., & Kostyra, E. (2024). Wheat bread enriched with house cricket powder (*Acheta domesticus L.*) as an alternative protein source. *Molecules (Basel, Switzerland), 29*(3), 711. DOI: 10.3390/molecules29030711 PMID: 38338455

Garbarino, E., & Johnson, M. S. (1999). The Different Roles of Satisfaction, Trust, and Commitment in Customer Relationships. *Journal of Marketing, 63*(2), 70–87. DOI: 10.1177/002224299906300205

García-Vicente, E. J., Martín, M., Rey-Casero, I., Pérez, A., Martín, J., García, A., Alonso, J. M., & Risco, D. (2024). Effects of feeding with a protein liquid supplement on productivity, mortality and health of *Apis mellifera* hives in southwestern Spain. *Research in Veterinary Science, 169*, 105173. https://doi.org/https://doi.org/10.1016/j.rvsc.2024.105173. DOI: 10.1016/j.rvsc.2024.105173 PMID: 38335895

Garg, P., & Joshi, R. (2018). Purchase intention of "Halal" brands in India: The mediating effect of attitude. *Journal of Islamic Marketing, 9*(3), 683–694. DOI: 10.1108/JIMA-11-2017-0125

Ghalih, M., & Chang, C.-H. (n.d.). *Aligning Halal Supply Chain Management Improvements with Global Sustainability Standards: A DEMATEL-Based Analysis.* DOI: 10.2478/mdke-2025-0012

Gladney, D. C. (2003). Islam in China: Accommodation or separatism? *The China Quarterly, 174*, 451–467. DOI: 10.1017/S0009443903000275

GMTI. (2024). *Edisi ke-9 Mastercard-Crescentrating Global Muslim Travel Index (GMTI).* Global Muslim Travel Index (GMTI). https://www.crescentrating.com/reports/global-muslim-travel-index-2024.html

Golnaz, R., Zainalabidin, M., Shamsudin, M. N., & Chiew, F. C. E. (2010). Non-Muslim consumers' understanding of halal principles in Malaysia. *Journal of Islamic Marketing, 1*(1), 62–74. DOI: 10.1108/17590831011026245

Goodhue, D., & Ronald, L. (1995). Task-technology fit and individual performance. *Management Information Systems Quarterly, 19*(2), 213–236. DOI: 10.2307/249689

Gopi, B., & Samat, N. (2020). The influence of food trucks' service quality on customer satisfaction and its impact toward customer loyalty. *British Food Journal, 122*(10), 3213–3226. DOI: 10.1108/BFJ-02-2020-0110

Graham-Rowe, E., Jessop, D. C., & Sparks, P. (2014). Identifying motivations and barriers to minimising household food waste. *Resources, Conservation and Recycling, 84*, 15–23. DOI: 10.1016/j.resconrec.2013.12.005

GS1. 2022. *EPCIS and Core Business Vocabulary Standard, Version 2.0.* Brussels: GS1 AISBL. https://www.gs1.org/standards/epcis

Gümüsay, A. A. (2015). Entrepreneurship from an Islamic perspective. *Journal of Business Ethics, 130*(1), 199–208. DOI: 10.1007/s10551-014-2223-7

Gunsun, A., & Chirapanda, S. (2024). Factors influencing the adoption of CICOT halal certification in Thai halal entrepreneurs: The institutional theory. *Journal of Family Business and Management Studies, 16*(1), 169–192.

Guthrie, S. (2014). *Christian Ethics: A Historical Introduction*. Wiley-Blackwell.

Hadi, M. Q. A., Cahyo, E. N., & Budi, I. S. (2021). Marketing Ethics at Islamic Banks: Principles and Practices. *Journal of Islamic Economic Laws, 4*(2), 17–41. DOI: 10.23917/jisel.v4i2.14716

Hafidh, Z., Sururi, S., Nurdin, N., Adinata, A. R., & Ramadhan, R. A. (2024). Innovative Revenue Models for Islamic Boarding Schools: Achieving Economic Autonomy. *Indonesian Research Journal in Education |IRJE|, 8*(2), Article 2. https://doi.org/DOI: 10.22437/irje.v8i2.36376

Hair, JF, Risher, JJ, Sarstedt, M., & Ringle, CM (2019). Kapan Menggunakan dan Bagaimana Melaporkan Hasil PLS-SEM. Dalam *European Business Review* (Vol. 31, Edisi 1). DOI: 10.1108/EBR-11-2018-0203

Hair, J. F., Black, W. C., Babin, B. J., & Anderson, R. E. (2010). *Multivariate data analysis* (Global edition). Pearson Higher Education Upper Saddle River.

Hair, J., Hollingsworth, C. L., Randolph, A. B., & Chong, A. Y. L. (2017). An updated and expanded assessment of PLS-SEM in information systems research. *Industrial Management & Data Systems*, *117*(3), 442–458. DOI: 10.1108/IMDS-04-2016-0130

Haji Ahmad, A., & Farid Shamsudin, M. (2021). Innovation through delivery of tacit-explicit knowledge: A Maqasid approach. *Journal of Positive Psychology & Wellbeing*, *5*(3), 501–515. http://journalppw.com

Halal Times. (2025). Malaysia's halal certification goes fully digital via MYeHALAL platform.

Haleem, A., Khan, M. I., & Khan, S. (2021). *logistics Understanding the Adoption of Halal Logistics through Critical Success Factors and Stakeholder Objectives*. https://doi.org/DOI: 10.3390/logistics

Haleem, A., Khan, M. I., & Khan, S. (2020). Halal certification, the inadequacy of its adoption, modelling and strategising the efforts. *Journal of Islamic Marketing*, *11*(2), 384–404. DOI: 10.1108/JIMA-05-2017-0062

Halimi, F. F., Gabarre, S., Rahi, S., Al-Gasawneh, J. A., & Ngah, A. H. (2022). Modelling Muslims' revisit intention of non-halal certified restaurants in Malaysia. *Journal of Islamic Marketing*, *13*(11), 2437–2461. DOI: 10.1108/JIMA-01-2021-0014

Halim, M. A. A., & Salleh, M. M. (2020). Consumer rights in halal products: A study based on legal and Syariah perspectives. *Food Research*, *4*(S1), 281–290. DOI: 10.26656/fr.2017.4(S1).S31

Halkias, D., Pizzurno, E., De Massis, A., & Fragoudakis, M. (2014). Halal products and services in the italian tourism and hospitality industry: Brief case studies of entrepreneurship and innovation). *Journal of Developmental Entrepreneurship*, *19*(2), 1450012. DOI: 10.1142/S1084946714500125

Hamdan, U., Azzulala, B. N., & Nasifah. (2022). Urgensi Spiritual Marketing dan Marketing Syariah dalam Dunia Bisnis. IQTISHADIA Jurnal Ekonomi & Perbankan Syariah, 9(1), 27. DOI: 10.19105/iqtishadia.v9i1.5483

Hanafiah, A., Wibowo, M. W., & Damayanti, F. (2020). Pengaruh Electronic Word of Mouth, Promosi dan Kualitas Pelayanan terhadap Minat Berkunjung Generasi Z pada Destinasi Wisata Halal Provinsi Jawa Barat. *Jurnal Ilmiah Manajemen Dan Bisnis*, *6*(3), 347–364. DOI: 10.22441/JIMB.V6I3.10095

Handoko, P., Ibrahim, D., & Bukhari, K. (2022). the Law of Dropshipping Buying According to Madzhab Malikiyah and Syafi'iyah. *Nurani Jurnal Kajian Syari Ah Dan Masyarakat*, *22*(1), 31–50. DOI: 10.19109/nurani.v22i1.11236

Han, H., Al-Ansi, A., Olya, H. G. T., & Kim, W. (2019). Menjelajahi Atribut Destinasi Ramah Halal di Korea Selatan: Persepsi dan Perilaku Wisatawan Muslim terhadap Destinasi Non-Muslim. *Manajemen Pariwisata, 71*. Advance online publication. DOI: 10.1016/j.tourman.2018.10.010

Hanifasari, D. (2024). *Millennial generation awareness of halal supply chain knowledge toward purchase intention for halal meat products : empirical evidence in Indonesia. 15*(7), 1847–1885. DOI: 10.1108/JIMA-01-2023-0012

Haque, A., Sarwar, A., Yasmin, F., Tarofder, A. K., & Hossain, M. A. (2015). Non-Muslim consumers' perception toward purchasing halal food products in Malaysia. *Journal of Islamic Marketing, 6*(1), 133–147. DOI: 10.1108/JIMA-04-2014-0033

HARA AgriTech. (2019). *HARA and Sreeya collaborate to invent halal traceability with the first blockchain technology in Indonesia*. Medium.

Haron, A., Sahibuddin, S., Harun, M., Zakaria, N. H., & Mahrin, M. N. (2013). The important role of people, process and technology during software project requirement. *International Journal of Machine Learning and Computing, 3*(1), 24–30. DOI: 10.7763/IJMLC.2013.V3.266

Harrison-walker, L. J., & Harrison-walker, L. J. (2001). *The Measurement of Word-of-Mouth Communication and an Investigation of Service Quality and Customer*. DOI: 10.1177/109467050141006

Harsanto, B., Mulyana, A., Faisal, Y. A., & Shandy, V. M. (2022). Open Innovation for Sustainability in the Social Enterprises: An Empirical Evidence. *Journal of Open Innovation, 8*(3), 3. Advance online publication. DOI: 10.3390/joitmc8030160

Hartini, H., & Malahayatie, M. (2024). Implications Of Halal Certificates In Food And Beverage Industry Business Management. *GREAT: Journal Of Islamic Management And Business, 1*(2), 3032–7253. Https://Doi.Org/10.62108/GREAT.V1I2.688

Harun, M. F. M., Albakry, N. S., Husain, A. H., & Arif, H. (2021). The Commodification of Religion as Symbolic Interactionism in Advertising. *International Journal of Academic Research in Business & Social Sciences, 11*(18). Advance online publication. DOI: 10.6007/IJARBSS/v11-i18/11426

Harvey, P. (2013). *An Introduction to Buddhism: Teachings, History and Practices* (2nd ed.). Cambridge University Press.

Haryanti, T., & Miru, A. (2024). The Consumer Protection Dynamics Of Halal Products In Indonesia. *Jambura Law Review, 6*(1), 102–123. Https://Doi.Org/10.33756/JLR.V6I1.19296

Haryanto, R., Anwar, M. M., Harisah, H., & Fadllan, F. (2024). Tourist satisfaction toward halal tourism: The role of tourism governance and branding. *Journal of Islamic Marketing, 15*(9), 2229–2244. DOI: 10.1108/JIMA-09-2023-0282

Haryono, H. (2022). Awareness of the Islamic social reporting (ISR) disclosure: A case study of companies listed in the Jakarta Islamic Index (JII). [Jurnal Penelitian Pendidikan Indonesia]. *JPPI, 8*(2), 348. DOI: 10.29210/020221547

Hasan, N., Mardhatillah, M., Abadi, M. M., & Hidayat, A. R. (2022). ENVIRONMENTAL ACTIVISM IN INDONESIAN PESANTREN: The Role of Lora in Mainstreaming Islamic Eco-theology in Tapal Kuda, East Java. *Teosofi: Jurnal Tasawuf Dan Pemikiran Islam, 12*(2), 280–306. DOI: 10.15642/teosofi.2022.12.2.280-306

Hashim, N., Sulaiman, N. S., & Muslim, H. (2025). *Maqasid Syariah as a framework for halal tourism in Brunei Darussalam*. In: *The Halal Industry in Asia*. pp.179–201 https://link.springer.com/chapter/10.1007/978-981-99-7681-9_11

Hashim, N., & Sulaiman, N. S. (2022). A Case Study Of Halal Green Concept Integration In Halal Product Development. *Journal Of Halal Service Research, 3*(2), 55–67.

Hashom, H., Ariffin, A. S., Sabar, R., & Ahmad, H. (2020). Halal-Logistics Value Chain on Firm Performances: A Conceptual Framework. *International Journal on Food Agriculture and Natural Resources, 1*(2), 8–14. DOI: 10.46676/ij-fanres.v1i2.10

Hasibuan, W. S., & Lubis, I. (2024). Halal value chain integration in food court establishment through Cash Waqf Linked Sukuk: Evidence from Indonesia. *Cogent Business & Management, 11*(1), 2385075. DOI: 10.1080/23311975.2024.2385075

Hasnan, F. F. B., Feng, Y., Sun, T., Parraga, K., Schwarz, M., & Zarei, M. (2023). Insects as valuable sources of protein and peptides: Production, functional properties, and challenges. *Foods, 12*(23), 4243. DOI: 10.3390/foods12234243 PMID: 38231647

Hassan, Y., & Pandey, J. (2020). *Examining the engagement of young consumers for religiously sanctioned food : the case of halal food in India. 21*(2), 211–232. DOI: 10.1108/YC-01-2019-0940

Hassan, N., Abdelraouf, M., & El-Shihy, D. (2025). The moderating role of personalized recommendations in the trust—satisfaction—loyalty relationship: An empirical study of AI-driven e-commerce. *Future Business Journal, 11*(1), 66. DOI: 10.1186/s43093-025-00476-z

Hassan, S. H., & Low, E. C. (2024). Spur of the moment: The unintended consequences of excessive food purchases and food waste during Ramadan. *British Food Journal, 126*(7), 2732–2745. Advance online publication. DOI: 10.1108/BFJ-10-2023-0917

Hassan, Y. (2022). A decade of research on Muslim entrepreneurship. *Journal of Islamic Marketing*, *13*(6), 1288–1311. DOI: 10.1108/JIMA-12-2019-0269

Hazarika, D. D., & Dhaliwal, A. (2025). Harnessing Data for Enhanced Consumer Insights and Experiences: The Imperative for CMOs. In *Leadership Paradigms and the Impact of Technology* (pp. 157–172). IGI Global Scientific Publishing.

Henderson, J. C. (2010). Islam and Tourism. In Scott, N., & Jafari, J. (Eds.), *Tourism in the Muslim world: Bridging tourism theory and practice* (Vol. 2, pp. 75–89). Emerald Group Publishing Limited., DOI: 10.1108/S2042-1443(2010)0000002009

Henseler, J., Ringle, C. M., & Sarstedt, M. (2015). A new criterion for assessing discriminant validity in variance-based structural equation modeling. *Journal of the Academy of Marketing Science*, *43*(1), 115–135. DOI: 10.1007/s11747-014-0403-8

Herdiansyah, H., Sukmana, H., & Lestarini, R. (2019). Eco-Pesantren as A Basic Forming of Environmental Moral and Theology. *Kalam*, *12*(2), 303–326. DOI: 10.24042/klm.v12i2.2834

Hermawati, A., Ali, S., Fettry, S., Hendarto, T., & Husin, H. (2021). Freelancers Intentions Towards Adoption Of Islamic Banking. *Academy of Strategic Management Journal*, *20*(2), 1–16.

Hidayah, N. A., Amri, F. B., & Mutholib, A. (2024). Design and Integration of Information Systems for the Halal Inspection Institute (LPH) UIN Syarif Hidayatullah Jakarta with SiHalal Ministry of Religion of the Republic of Indonesia. [AISM]. *Applied Information System and Management*, *7*(2), 7–16. Advance online publication. DOI: 10.15408/aism.v7i2.36786

Hidayat, S. E., & Musari, K. (2022). ASEAN Towards a Global Halal Logistics Through the Digitally Enabled Community. [IJABIM]. *International Journal of Asian Business and Information Management*, *13*(2), 1–15. DOI: 10.4018/IJABIM.20220701.oa1

Hidayat, S. E., & Musari, K. (2023). Toward the Global Halal MSMEs Hub Through the Digitally Enabled Society: An Institutional Arrangement with Islamic N-Tuple Helix. In Rafiki, A. (Ed.), *Digitalization in Halal Management* (pp. 15–28). Springer Nature Singapore., DOI: 10.1007/978-981-99-5146-8_2

Hofstede, G. (1980). Review Article : Geert Hofstede: Culture's Consequences: International Differences in Work Related Values. *Beverly Hills/London*, 390–391.

Hong, M. (2019). *Determinants of halal purchasing behaviour : evidences from China*. 410–425. DOI: 10.1108/JIMA-03-2018-0053

Hooker, M. B. (1984). *Islamic Law in South-East Asia*. Oxford University Press.

Hosen, M. N., Hutagalung, A. Z., & Suma, M. A. (2022). Analysis Of The Law On Halal Product Assurance And The Law On Job Creation (Between Reality And Sustainability). *JUDISIA: Journal Of Islamic Legal And Legal Thought, 13*(1), 103. Https://Doi.Org/10.21043/YUDISIA.V13I1.13721

https://legacy.quran.com/2/185. (n.d.). *Surat Al-Baqarah (The Cow)*. Retrieved June 22, 2025, from https://legacy.quran.com/2/185

https://legacy.quran.com/45/18. (n.d.). *Surat Al-Jāthiyah (The Crouching)*.

Huang, C. C. (2017). The impacts of brand experiences on brand loyalty: Mediators of brand love and trust. *Management Decision*, *55*(5), 915–934. DOI: 10.1108/MD-10-2015-0465

Huang, C. C., & Chen, S. E. (2022). Establishing and Deepening Brand Loyalty through Brand Experience and Customer Engagement: Evidence from Taiwan's Chain Restaurants. *Journal of Quality Assurance in Hospitality & Tourism*, *23*(1), 217–239. DOI: 10.1080/1528008X.2020.1864565

Huber, F., Meyer, F., & Schmid, D. A. (2015). Brand love in progress – the interdependence of brand love antecedents in consideration of relationship duration. *Journal of Product and Brand Management*, *24*(6), 567–579. DOI: 10.1108/JPBM-08-2014-0682

Hudaefi, F. A., & Jaswir, I. (2019). Halal Governance in Indonesia: Theory, Current Practices, and Related Issues. *Journal of Islamic Monetary Economics and Finance*, *5*(1), 89–116. DOI: 10.21098/jimf.v5i1.1049

Huis, A. (2016). Edible insects are the future? *The Proceedings of the Nutrition Society*, *75*(3), 294–305. DOI: 10.1017/S0029665116000069 PMID: 26908196

Huis, A. V., & Rumpold, B. (2023). Strategies to convince consumers to eat insects: A review. *Food Quality and Preference*, *110*, 104927. DOI: 10.1016/j.foodqual.2023.104927

Humaidi, M. N., & Muchtar, A. M. (2020). the Salient Features of Medina Market in Early Islam and its Relevance Today. *El-Barka Journal of Islamic Economics and Business*, *3*(2), 162–188. DOI: 10.21154/elbarka.v3i2.2434

Hussain, K., & Fayyaz, M. S. (2024). *Attitude, repurchase intention and brand loyalty toward halal cosmetics. 15*(2), 293–313. DOI: 10.1108/JIMA-08-2022-0210

Huwaidi, M. H. (2023). MEMBIDIK POTENSI EKONOMI PESANTREN SEBAGAI PENUNJANG INDUSTRI HALAL INDONESIA. *Profit : Jurnal Kajian Ekonomi dan Perbankan Syariah, 7*(1), Article 1. DOI: 10.33650/profit.v7i1.5741

Hu, Y., & Ghadimi, P. (2022). A review of blockchain technology application on supply chain risk management. *IFAC-PapersOnLine*, *55*(10), 958–963. Advance online publication. DOI: 10.1016/j.ifacol.2022.09.472

Hwang, H. S., Zhu, L. C., & Cui, Q. (2023). Development and validation of a digital literacy scale in the artificial intelligence era for college students. [TIIS]. *KSII Transactions on Internet and Information Systems*, *17*(8), 2241–2258.

Hwang, H., Cho, G., & Choo, H. (2024). GSCA pro—Free stand-alone software for structural equation modeling. *Structural Equation Modeling*, *31*(4), 696–711. DOI: 10.1080/10705511.2023.2272294

Hwang, H., Sarstedt, M., Cho, G., Choo, H., & Ringle, C. M. (2023). A primer on integrated generalized structured component analysis. *European Business Review*, *35*(3), 261–284. DOI: 10.1108/EBR-11-2022-0224

Ibn ʻĀshūr. (1984). *Al-Ta rīr wa al-Tanwīr*. Tunis: al-Dār al-Tūnisiyyah.

Ibn Kathir, I. (1999). *Tafsir al-Qur'an al-'Azim*. Beirut: Dar al-Kutub al-'Ilmiyyah.

Ibrahim, I., Shuib, A., Yusoff, F. H., & Shariff, S. S. R. (2024). Planning of Halal Compliance Critical Control Points and IoT Integration in Halal Chicken Meat Supply Chain Traceability System. *Journal of Halal Industry & Services*, *7*(1). Advance online publication. DOI: 10.36877/jhis.a0000568

Ihsan, F. M., Permana, P. Y. E., Arifin, N. R., & Muhtadi, R. (2020). Islamic Boarding Schools Toward the Industrial Revolution 4.0; Opportunities and Challenges. *FIKROTUNA: Jurnal Pendidikan Dan Manajemen Islam*, *9*(01). Advance online publication. DOI: 10.32806/jf.v11i01.3940

Imani, S., Mi'raj, D. A., Bawana, T. A., & Malik, A. R. (2022). E-Commerce Platform As a Halal Life Style Ecosystem Innovation of The Maqashid Shariah Approach. *Journal of Digital Business and Innovation Management*, *1*(2), 101–118. DOI: 10.26740/jdbim.v1i2.50498

IMTI. (2023). *Indeks Perjalanan Muslim Indonesia 2023*. Crescent Rating. https://www.crescentrating.com/reports/indonesia-muslim-travel-index-2023.html

Insani, T. D., Al-Faizin, A. W., & Ryandono, M. N. H. (2019). The Impact Of Halal At Thayyib And Consumption Ethics On Economic Growth: An Economic Tafsir Of Al-Baqarah 168. *Journal Of Islamic Monetary Economics And Finance*, *5*(2), 459–474. Https://Doi.Org/10.21098/Jimf.V5i2.1071. DOI: 10.21098/jimf.v5i2.1071

Irfany, M. I., Nekha, A., Tieman, M., & Haq, D. A. (2025). Halal procurement strategy for the halal pharmaceutical industry in Indonesia. *Journal of Islamic Marketing*, *16*(4), 1073–1094. DOI: 10.1108/JIMA-09-2023-0274

Isbah, M. F. (2020). Pesantren in the Changing Indonesian Context: History and Current Developments. [Qudus International Journal of Islamic Studies]. *QIJIS*, *8*(1), 1. Advance online publication. DOI: 10.21043/qijis.v8i1.5629

Iskandar, W., Waridin, W., & Iskandar, D. D. (2023). The potential of Muslim Friendly Hospitality in the tourism industry in Central Java. *Indonesian Journal of Islam and Muslim Societies*, *13*(1), 169–197. DOI: 10.18326/ijims.v13i1.169-197

Islam, M. M. (2018). Islamic marketing practice as a panacea to social marketing criticism. *International Journal of Islamic Marketing and Branding*, *3*(2), 104. DOI: 10.1504/IJIMB.2018.094080

Islam, M. M., Ab Talib, M. S., & Muhamad, N. (2025). Halal certification of marketing mix focusing on cosmetics. *Journal of Islamic Marketing*, *16*(5), 1371–1409. DOI: 10.1108/JIMA-02-2024-0094

Ismail, A. R. (2017). The influence of perceived social media marketing activities on brand loyalty: The mediation effect of brand and value consciousness. *Asia Pacific Journal of Marketing and Logistics*, *29*(1), 129–144. DOI: 10.1108/APJML-10-2015-0154

Ismail, I. A., Rozar, N. M., Usman, I., Menhat, M., Kamaruddine, S. A., & Razik, M. A. (2023). Challenges faced by Halal Warehouse during the Implementation of Islamic Shariah Compliance: Malaysian Perspective. *Journal for Maritime Research*, *20*(2), 135–140.

Ismail, I. J., Marua, N. M., & Changalima, I. A. (2025). Enhancing halal entrepreneurial intention: The impact of halal entrepreneurship education and halal entrepreneurial awareness. *Social Sciences & Humanities Open*, *11*, 101548. Advance online publication. DOI: 10.1016/j.ssaho.2025.101548

Ismail, J., Muchtar, A. H., Hanafi, M. I., Affandi, A. I., & Shofy, M. U. A. A. (2024). Integrating AI and Communication: A Study on Ethical Practices in Halal Supply Chain Management. *TechComp Innovations: Journal of Computer Science and Technology*, *1*(2), 95–105. DOI: 10.70063/techcompinnovations.v1i2.54

Ismail, N. A. (2016). The roles of international entrepreneur orientation and geographical scope level to determine international performance: A case in the malaysian halal food industry). *International Journal of Entrepreneurship, 20*(1), 142–155.

Ismail, N. A. (2017). The roles of international entrepreneur orientation and geographical scope level to determine international performance: A case in the Malaysian Halal food industry). *International Journal of Entrepreneurship, 21*(1), 46–59.

Ismail, N. A., & Kuivalainen, O. (2015). The effect of internal capabilities and external environment on small- and medium-sized enterprises' international performance and the role of the foreign market scope: The case of the Malaysian halal food industry; [Der Effekt von internen Kompetenzen und dem externen Umfeld auf den internationalen Unternehmenserfolg von KMU und die Moderator-Beziehung der geografische Reichweite: der Fall der Malaysischen Halal-Lebensmittelindustrie. *Journal of International Entrepreneurship, 13*(4), 451–484. DOI: 10.1007/s10843-015-0160-x

Ismail, R. M., Hami, N., Jusop, M., & Muhardi, M. (2025). Halal food manufacturing: A case study on successful Bumiputera entrepreneurs in Malaysia). 2025. *International Journal of Innovative Research and Scientific Studies, 8*(4), 1455–1456. DOI: 10.53894/ijirss.v8i4.8097

Ismail, S., Nazarudin, N., & Muhamad, M. Z. (2022). Governance of halal logistics compliance. *Journal of Contemporary Islamic Studies, 8*(3), 1–20. DOI: 10.24191/jcis.v8i3.6

Istianah, I., & Dewi, G. (2022). Maslahah Analysis On The Concept Of Halal Self-Declare Before And After The Employment Law. *Al-Adl: Legal Journal, 14*(1), 85–109. Https://Doi.Org/10.31602/AL-ADL.V14I1.5870

Jabatan Kemajuan Islam Malaysia [JAKIM]. (2012). Legal opinion of the MKI Muzakarah: Ruling on cochineal coloring substance: A review of the standard levels set by the Muzakarah of the Fatwa Committee of the National Council for Islamic Religious Affairs Malaysia. Retrieved from https://i-fiqh.islam.gov.my/portal/view.php?id=10301

Jafari, J., & Scott, N. (2014). Dunia Muslim dan pariwisatanya. *Annals of Tourism Research, 44*, 1–19. DOI: 10.1016/j.annals.2013.08.011

Jamaluddin, M. A., & Ramli, S. N. H. (2022). Smart Food For Future Sustainability: Halal And Tayyib Perspectives. *Journal Of Halal Industry & Services, 5*(1). Advance online publication. DOI: 10.36877/jhis.a0000309

Jaradt, N. (2020). *Legitimacy Controls of Commercial Advertisements: A Comparative Study*. International Affairs and Global Strategy., DOI: 10.7176/IAGS/87-03

Jia, J., Chen, L., Zhang, L., Xiao, M., & Wu, C. (2025). A study on the factors that influence consumers' continuance intention to use artificial intelligence chatbots in a pharmaceutical e-commerce context. *The Electronic Library*, *43*(3), 303–321. DOI: 10.1108/EL-09-2024-0275

Jo ˇsko Brakus, , & Bernd, H. Schmitt, L. Z., & Brand. (2009). Brand Experience : What Is It? How Is It Measured? *Does It Affect Loyalty*, *73*(May), 52–68.

Joshi, R. (2022). *Assessing brand love, brand sacredness and brand fi delity towards halal brands. 13*(4), 807–823. DOI: 10.1108/JIMA-04-2020-0104

Joshi, R., & Garg, P. (2021). Role of brand experience in shaping brand love. In *International Journal of Consumer Studies* (Vol. 45, Issue 2). DOI: 10.1111/ijcs.12618

Jumaizi, C. W., bin M., & Tuzaka, E. (2022). Risk Management and Islamic Value: A Conceptual Development of Al-Adl Financing Risk Management. *Computational Intelligence in Security for Information Systems Conference*, 364–372.

Junaidi, J. (2020). Halal-Friendly Tourism and Factors Influencing Halal Tourism. *Management Science Letters*, *10*(8), 1755–1762. DOI: 10.5267/j.msl.2020.1.004

Jusop, M., Ismail, R. M., & Ismail, N. A. (2020). Managing Information Quality in B2C Companies: An Empirical Investigation on Halal e-Commerce Websites. [iJIM]. *International Journal of Interactive Mobile Technologies*, *14*(17), 97. DOI: 10.3991/ijim.v14i17.16651

Kafle, K., Subedi, S., & Poudel, A. (2024). A review on edible insects diversity, abundance, and conservation. *Journal of Entomology and Zoology Studies*, *12*(2), 137–142. DOI: 10.22271/j.ento.2024.v12.i2b.9306

Kallio, H., Pietilä, A.-M., Johnson, M., & Kangasniemi, M. (2016). Systematic methodological review: Developing a framework for a qualitative semi-structured interview guide. *Journal of Advanced Nursing*, *72*(12), 2954–2965. DOI: 10.1111/jan.13031 PMID: 27221824

Kamali, M. H. (2022). *Maqasid al-Shariah, Ijtihad and Civilisational Renewal: A Reformist Approach to Shariah Governance*. IAIS Malaysia.

Kamilulloh, F., & Ambardi, P. (2022). Multi-Level Marketing Paradigm in Islam. *I-Best Islamic Banking & Economic Law Studies*, *1*(2), 103–115. DOI: 10.36769/ibest.v1i2.252

Kanchanatanee, K. (2024). Factors Affecting The Acceptance of Artificial Intelligence in Electronic Commerce. *Asian Administration and Management Review*, *7*(2), 101–108.

Kant, S., & Adula, M. (2025). *Innovation's effect on fostering a sustainable halal ecosystem by mediation of techno-preneurship in Ethiopia halal supply chain.*

Kant, I. (1997). *Groundwork of the Metaphysics of Morals*. CAMBRIDGE University Press.

Kant, S., Adula, M., Kumari, M., & Nimbrain, N. (2025). Role of SMEs in Greening the Economy by Mediation of Eco-Innovation in the Horn of Africa. In *Examining Green Human Resources Management and Nascent Entrepreneurship* (pp. 173–200). IGI Global Scientific Publishing., DOI: 10.4018/979-8-3693-7046-9.ch007

Karbhari, Y., Alam, M. K., & Rahman, M. M. (2020). Relevance of the application of institutional theory in Shariah governance of Islamic banks. *PSU Research Review*, *5*(1), 1–15. DOI: 10.1108/PRR-05-2020-0015

Karjaluoto, H., Munnukka, J., & Kiuru, K. (2016). Brand love and positive word of mouth: The moderating effects of experience and price. *Journal of Product and Brand Management*, *25*(6), 527–537. DOI: 10.1108/JPBM-03-2015-0834

Karman, A., Anwar, R., & Hakim, L. (2023). The Qur'anic Learning Based on Islamic Eco-Theology At Pesantren. *Jurnal Pendidikan Islam*, *9*(2), 169–186. DOI: 10.15575/jpi.v9i2.24933

Kartika, B. (2023). Halal Digital Entrepreneurship and Disruptive Technologies from the Lenses of Maqasid al-Shari'ah. In (pp. 179-197).

Karyani, E., Geraldina, I., Haque, M. G., & Zahir, A. (2024). Intention to adopt a blockchain-based halal certification: Indonesia consumers and regulatory perspective. *Journal of Islamic Marketing*, *15*(7), 1766–1782. DOI: 10.1108/JIMA-03-2023-0069

Kayal, G. (2023). Persona dan Motivasi Wisatawan Religi dan Dampaknya terhadap Niat Mengunjungi Tempat-Tempat Religi di Arab Saudi. *Jurnal Internasional Kota Wisata*, *9*(1). Advance online publication. DOI: 10.1108/IJTC-04-2022-0092

Kayed, R. N., & Hassan, M. K. (2010). Islamic entrepreneurship: A case study of Saudi Arabia). *Journal of Developmental Entrepreneurship*, *15*(4), 413–434. DOI: 10.1142/S1084946710001634

Kencono, D. S., Pradipta, R. N., & Agustiyara, A. (2024). *Managing Bandung City for a Smart Economy in Society: The Role of the Bandung City Government.* Paper presented at the E3S Web of Conferences. DOI: 10.1051/e3sconf/202459407002

Kennedy, N. F., Wijayanto, G., & Nursanti, A. (2024). The Influence Of Brand Love And Brand Trust On Repurchase Intention Through Consumer Satisfaction Of Indomie Products In Pekanbaru City. *InJEBA: International Journal of Economics. Business and Accounting*, *2*(2), 156–170.

Khabib, A., & Anggara, D. (2022). *How store attribute a ff ects customer experience, brand love and brand loyalty*. 2980–3006. DOI: 10.1108/JIMA-01-2022-0002

Khairuddin & Zaki, M. (2021). PROGRESS OF HALAL CERTIFICATION IN INDONESIA Study On The Halal Product Assurance Agency (BPJPH) Of The Ministry Of Religion And The Institute For Assessment, Drugs And Cosmetics (LPPOM) Of The Central MUI. *Basics, 13*(1), 101–121.

Khalek, A. A. (2017). Entrepreneurship and the halal wave in Malaysia. In *Global Entrepreneurship and New Venture Creation in the Sharing Economy* (pp. 205-214).

Khalid, K., Aya, A., Ali, , Khaled, , & Ahmad, . (2020). Impact of Halal Digital Marketing on Consumer Behaviour: Jordan's Perspective. *International Journal of Economics and Business Administration*, *202*(Special Issue 1), 202–215. Advance online publication. DOI: 10.35808/ijeba/537

Khalimy, A., Yusriyadi, Y., Setyowati, R., Syahruddin, S., & Wadud, A. M. A. (2023). The intersection of the progressive law theory and the self-declaration concept of MSEs halal certification. *J. Indonesian Leg. Stud.*, *8*(1), 159–198. DOI: 10.15294/jils.v8i1.66087

Khan, N., Falahat, M., Ullah, I., Sikandar, H., & Van, N. T. (2025). Integrating Halal Tourism with Sustainable Development Goals Through Islamic Values Environmental Responsibility and Technological Innovation. *Discover Sustainability*, *6*(1), 648. Advance online publication. DOI: 10.1007/s43621-025-01503-3

Khan, S., Rahman, N. A., & Yusoff, R. (2024). Blockchain and AI Integration for Halal Traceability: A Systematic Review. *Food Control*, *156*, 110123. DOI: 10.1016/j.foodcont.2023.110123

Kholilah, K., Meylianingrum, K., Jaya, T. J., & Jouti, A. T. (2022). Halal Value Chain in the Holding Business: The Experience of Islamic-based School (Pesantren) in Indonesia. *Shirkah: Journal of Economics and Business*, *7*(3), 3. Advance online publication. DOI: 10.22515/shirkah.v7i3.522

Khuluq, M. K., & Asmuni, A. (2024). Hifz al-Bi'ah as part of Maqashid al-Shari'ah and its Relevance in the Context of Global Climate Change. *Indonesian Journal of Interdisciplinary Islamic Studies*, *7*(2), 3. Advance online publication. DOI: 10.20885/ijiis.vol7.iss2.art3

Kim. (2010). Duality in the Discourse of Multiculture and Locality. *Locality Humanities*, (3), 75-105.

Kismawadi, E. R. (2024). Halal food industry and sustainability. In *Economics and Environmental Responsibility in the Global Beverage Industry* (pp. 170–197). IGI Global Scientific Publishing., DOI: 10.4018/979-8-3693-2149-2.ch010

Klöckner, C. A. (2013). A comprehensive model of the psychology of environmental behaviour—A meta-analysis. *Global Environmental Change*, *23*(5), 1028–1038. DOI: 10.1016/j.gloenvcha.2013.05.014

Klongrua, S., Umuri, K., & Muftahuddin, M. (2025). Maqasid Al-Shariah and Environmental Sustainability: An Islamic Economic Perspective. *International Journal of Kita Kreatif*, *2*(1). Advance online publication. DOI: 10.24815/ijkk.v2i1.44790

KNEKS. (2023). *Komite Nasional Ekonomi dan Keuangan Syariah*. https://kneks.go.id/berita/644/katalog-buku-master-plan-industri-halal-indonesia-2023-2029?category=1

Ko, H.-C. (2024). Exploring the Value of Live-Streaming Shopping and Its Impact on Customer Engagement from the Perspective of the Price-Quality-Value Model. *Proceedings of the 2024 7th International Conference on Computers in Management and Business*, 94–100. DOI: 10.1145/3647782.3647797

Kon, J. (2022, February 25). Making use of food waste. Borneo Bulletin. https://borneobulletin.com.bn/making-use-of-food-waste/

Koswara, A., & Herlina, L. (2025). The Ethical Deviations of AI in Marketing Practices: A Critical Review from Halal Perspectives [Review of the Ethical Deviations of AI in Marketing Practices: A Critical Review from Halal Perspectives]. *Review of Islamic Economics*, *2*(2), 105–116. DOI: 10.58777/rie.v2i2.393

Kozlu, A., Ngasakul, N., Klojdová, I., & Baigts-Allende, D. K. (2024). Edible insect-processing techniques: A strategy to develop nutritional food products and novelty food analogs. *European Food Research and Technology*, *250*(5), 1253–1267. DOI: 10.1007/s00217-024-04474-3

Krapivin, I. (2021). The "Faceless Brand": Muslim Women and Halal Internet Marketing. *Kunstkamera*, *2021*(4), 106–121. DOI: 10.31250/2618-8619-2021-4(14)-106-121

Krawczyk, A., Fernández-López, J., & Zimoch-Korzycka, A. (2024). Insect protein as a component of meat analogue burger. *Foods*, *13*(12), 1806. DOI: 10.3390/foods13121806 PMID: 38928748

Kristanto, D., & Kurniawati, D. A. (2025). Financial performance of Indonesian frozen food MSMEs: halal supply chain resilience, certification and competitive advantage. *J. Islam. Mark.* DOI: 10.1108/JIMA-07-2024-0278

Kubaisi, A. A. S. H. A. (2024). Ethics of Artificial Intelligence: A Purposeful and Foundational Study in Light of the Sunnah of Prophet Muhammad. *Religions*, *15*(11), 1300. DOI: 10.3390/rel15111300

Kulinčević, J. M., & Rothenbuhler, W. C. (1982). Selection for length of life in the honeybee (Apis mellifera). *Apidologie*, *13*(4), 347–352. DOI: 10.1051/apido:19820402

Kumaladewi, N., Ratnawati, S., Sugiarti, Y., & Umar Lubis, A. B. (2020, October). Evaluation of e-halal certification system acceptance to improve Halal certification services at LPPOM MUI. *The 8th International Conference on Cyber and IT Service Management*.

Kuratko, D. F. (2005). The emergence of entrepreneurship education: Development, trends, and challenges. *Entrepreneurship Theory and Practice*, *29*(5), 577–597. DOI: 10.1111/j.1540-6520.2005.00099.x

Kurniawati, D. A., & Cakravastia, A. (2023). A review of halal supply chain research: Sustainability and operations research perspective. *Cleaner Logistics and Supply Chain*, *6*, 100096. Advance online publication. DOI: 10.1016/j.clscn.2023.100096

Kurniawati, D. A., & Rochman, M. A. (2023). Two stages of halal food distribution model for perishable food products. *International Journal of Production Management and Engineering*, *11*(2), 147–166. Advance online publication. DOI: 10.4995/ijpme.2023.18233

Kusmidi, H. (2023). An Overview of Islam and Religious Moderation: Concept, Principles, and Indicators. *Jurnal Ilmiah Syi Ar*, *22*(2), 168. DOI: 10.29300/syr.v22i2.8752

Kwon, W., & Lee, K. P. (2024). Macronutrient regulation in nymphs of the two-spotted cricket, *Gryllus bimaculatus* (Orthoptera: Gryllidae). *Journal of Insect Physiology*, *157*, 104684. DOI: 10.1016/j.jinsphys.2024.104684 PMID: 39074715

La Barbera, F., & Ajzen, I. (2020). Control interactions in the theory of planned behavior: Rethinking the role of subjective norm. *Europe's Journal of Psychology*, *16*(3), 401–417. DOI: 10.5964/ejop.v16i3.2056 PMID: 33680190

Lada, S., Tanakinjal, G. H., Amin, H., Lada, S., Tanakinjal, G. H., & Amin, H. (2009). *theory of reasoned action Predicting intention to choose halal products using theory of reasoned action*. DOI: 10.1108/17538390910946276

Lampová, B., Doskočil, I., Šmíd, P., & Kouřimská, L. (2024). Comparison of cricket protein powder and whey protein digestibility. *Molecules (Basel, Switzerland), 29*(15), 3598. DOI: 10.3390/molecules29153598 PMID: 39125003

Larranaga, A., & Valor, C. (2022). Consumers' Categorization Of Eco-Friendly Consumer Goods: An Integrative Review And Research Agenda. In *Sustainable Production And Consumption* (Vol. 34). Https://Doi.Org/10.1016/J.Spc.2022.10.005

Latief, F., Suriyanti, S., Amin, A., Mahmud, A., Firman, A., & Dirwan, D. (2024). Ease and Risk Perception: Interest in Using Sharia Digital Payments, and the Users' Attitude Consequences. *Jurnal Minds: Manajemen Ide Dan Inspirasi, 11*(2), 341–356.

Latif, M. A. (2020). *Halal International Standards and Certification.*, DOI: 10.1002/9781118823026.ch14

Latif, M. N. A., Aziz, N. A. A., Hussin, N. S. N., & Aziz, Z. A. (2021). Cyber security in supply chain management: A systematic review. *LogForum, 17*(1), 49–57. DOI: 10.17270/J.LOG.2021555

Latip, H. A., Md Yusoff, I. Y., & Hanapi, S. (2015). Strategizing business in times of crisis: The story of Sarawak layered cake). 2015. *Emerald Emerging Markets Case Studies., 5*(7), 7–13. DOI: 10.1108/EEMCS-09-2014-0233

León-Ecay, S., Insausti, K., López-Maestresalas, A., & Prieto, N. (2025). Non-destructive spectroscopy-based technologies for meat and meat product discrimination - A review. *Meat Science, 228*, 109893. https://doi.org/https://doi.org/10.1016/j.meatsci.2025.109893. DOI: 10.1016/j.meatsci.2025.109893 PMID: 40570613

Leslie, D. D. (1986). *Islam in traditional China: A short history.* Canberra College of Advanced Education Lindgren, M., & Packendorff, J. (2009). Social constructionism and entrepreneurship: Basic assumptions and consequences for theory and research. *International Journal of Entrepreneurial Behaviour & Research, 15*(1), 25–47.

Li, C. H., Chan, O. L. K., Chow, Y. T., Zhang, X., Tong, P., Li, S. P., Ng, H. Y., & Keung, K. L. (2022). Evaluating the Effectiveness of Digital Content Marketing Under a Mixed Reality Training Platform on the Online Purchase Intention. *Frontiers in Psychology, 13*, 881019. Advance online publication. DOI: 10.3389/fpsyg.2022.881019 PMID: 35846680

Ligaraba, N., Chuchu, T., & Nyagadza, B. (2023). Opt-in e-mail marketing influence on consumer behaviour: A Stimuli—Organism—Response (S—O—R) theory perspective. *Cogent Business & Management, 10*(1), 2184244. DOI: 10.1080/23311975.2023.2184244

Lim, Y. H., Lada, S., Ullah, R., & Abdul Adis, A.-A. (2022). Non-Muslim consumers' intention to purchase halal food products in Malaysia. *Journal of Islamic Marketing*, *13*(3), 586–607. Advance online publication. DOI: 10.1108/JIMA-06-2020-0172

Ling, P.-S., Yusof, F. I., & Wahab, A., A., & Bohari, S. A. (. (2025). Use intention on the Halal verification applications: The moderating role of religiosity in an SOR framework. *Journal of Islamic Marketing*. Advance online publication. DOI: 10.1108/JIMA-10-2024-0483

Lipman, J. N. (1997). *Familiar strangers: A history of Muslims in Northwest China*. University of Washington Press.

Li, S., Feng, S., Ullah, H., Tu, X., & Zhang, Z. (2022). IPM - Biological and integrated management of desert locust. *Journal of Integrative Agriculture*, *21*(12), 3467–3487. DOI: 10.1016/j.jia.2022.09.017

Lisboa, H. M., Nascimento, A., Arruda, A., Sarinho, A., Lima, J., Batista, L., Dantas, M. F., & Andrade, R. (2024). Unlocking the potential of insect-based proteins: Sustainable solutions for global food security and nutrition. *Foods*, *13*(12), 1846. DOI: 10.3390/foods13121846 PMID: 38928788

Liu, K. N., Tsai, T. I., Xiao, Q., & Hu, C. (2021). The impact of experience on brand loyalty: Mediating effect of images of Taiwan hotels. *Journal of China Tourism Research*, *17*(3), 395–414. DOI: 10.1080/19388160.2020.1777238

Lopes, J. M., Silva, L. F., & Massano-Cardoso, I. (2024). AI meets the shopper: Psychosocial factors in ease of use and their effect on E-Commerce purchase intention. *Behavioral Sciences (Basel, Switzerland)*, *14*(7), 616. DOI: 10.3390/bs14070616 PMID: 39062439

Loureiro, S. M. C., Ruediger, K. H., & Demetris, V. (2012). Brand emotional connection and loyalty. *Journal of Brand Management*, *20*(1), 13–27. DOI: 10.1057/bm.2012.3

Lourenco, C. E., & Piotto, V. (2024). Brewing Sustainability: Assessing Environmental Concerns And Consumers' Attitudes Towards Sustainable Craft Beer Purchase Intentions. *International Journal of Wine Business Research*, *36*(2), 270–285. DOI: 10.1108/IJWBR-10-2023-0066

Lubis, U. R., & Ismaulina, I. (2020). Tadlis Dalam Bisnis Jual Beli Online Perspektif Ekonomi Syariah (Studi Mahasiswa Ekonomi Syariah Febi Iain Lhokseumawe). [JESKaPe]. *Jurnal Ekonomi Syariah Akuntansi Dan Perbankan*, *4*(2), 247–256. DOI: 10.52490/jeskape.v4i2.799

Ma'arif, A., Amzeri, A., Caesarendra, W., Suwarno, I., Iqbal, J., Sharkawy, A.-N., . . . Herlambang, T. (2024). *2nd Biology Trunojoyo Madura International Conference, BTMIC 2024*. Paper presented at the BIO Web of Conferences.

Mabkhot, H., & Piaralal, S. K. (2023). Enhancing Brand Reputation and Customer Citizenship Behaviour through Perceived Values in Hotel Industry: Role of CSR and Brand Credibility. *Transnational Marketing Journal*, *11*(2), 81–99.

Macwan, S. S. P., de Souza, T., Dunshea, F. R., DiGiacomo, K., & Suleria, H. A. (2023). Black soldier fly larvae (Hermetica illucens) as a sustainable source of nutritive and bioactive compounds, and their consumption challenges. *Animal Production Science*, *64*(1), AN23192. DOI: 10.1071/AN23192

Mady, K., Abdelkareem, R. S., Halim, M. A. S. A., Omar, K., & Elsheikh, T. (2024). A systematic review and scientometric analysis of the driving factors of eco-innovation: Trends and future research. *International Journal of Procurement Management*, *19*(1), 74–105. DOI: 10.1504/IJPM.2024.135148

Mahmud Zuhudi, N. W., & Dolah, J. (2020). An experts' perspective based on consumers' perception of Halal-related issue. *Al-Risalah Journal*, *4*(3), 183–198.

Mahmud, R. (2023). Fighting food waste during Ramadhan. Fighting Food Waste during Ramadhan. Borneo Bulletin. https://borneobulletin.com.bn/fighting-food-waste-during-ramadhan/

Mai, J. (2024). The Hui Muslims in China: Muslim Hui di China. *Indonesian Journal of Islamic History and Culture*, *5*(1), 1–11.

Maishanu, M. M., & Dutsin-ma, A. M. (2012). Business management and ethics: An Islamic approach. *Business Review (Federal Reserve Bank of Philadelphia)*, *7*(2), 113–118. DOI: 10.54784/1990-6587.1208

Majeed, S., Lu, C., Majeed, M., & Shahid, M. N. (2018). Health resorts and multi-textured perceptions of international health tourists. *Sustainability (Basel)*, *10*(4), 1063. DOI: 10.3390/su10041063

Majlis Ugama Islam Singapura. (2024). *From lab to table: Novel food for an Islamic perspective*. Office of the Mufti.

Malatji, W. R., Van Eck, R., & Zuva, T. (2020). Understanding the usage, modifications, limitations and criticisms of technology acceptance model (TAM). *Advances in Science, Technology and Engineering Systems Journal*, *5*(6), 113–117. DOI: 10.25046/aj050612

Malay Mail. (2024). Jakim developing AI system to simplify halal certification approval.

Ma, M. (2018). Localization and sinicization: Understanding Qingzhen and halal in China. In *Proceedings of the International Workshop on Halal Food Consumption in East and West (with Appendix of Survey Report)* (pp. 77–104). Institute for Asian Muslim Studies, Waseda University.

Mamta, M., & Gupta, S. (2025). Eco-Innovation and Sustainable Business Practices in the Textile Industry. In *Sustainable Business Ecosystems and Social Perspectives* (pp. 307–334). IGI Global Scientific Publishing., DOI: 10.4018/979-8-3693-8437-4.ch014

Manaf, A., Purbasari, N., Damayanti, M., Aprilia, N., & Astuti, W. (2018). Pariwisata pedesaan berbasis komunitas dalam kolaborasi antar-organisasi: Bagaimana cara kerjanya yang berkelanjutan? pelajaran dari Desa Wisata Nglanggeran, Kabupaten Gunungkidul, Yogyakarta, Indonesia. *Sustainability*, *10*(7), 2142. DOI: 10.3390/su10072142

Mandra, M. A. S., & Ismail, R. (2022). Eco-pesantren Implementation Strategy Supports the Environmental Behavior of Islamic Boarding School Students in South Sulawesi. *Proceedings of the 1st World Conference on Social and Humanities Research (W-SHARE 2021), 654*, 28–33. DOI: 10.2991/assehr.k.220402.007

Mansour, A., Jeong, T., Lee, D., Song, J.-H., Kim, E., Lee, D.-W., Mannaa, M., & Seo, Y.-S. (2025). Fungal-bacterial interactions leading to increased insect mortality: *Trichoderma xixiacum* enhances the pathogenicity of *Serratia marcescens* in *Protaetia brevitarsis* larvae. *Journal of Invertebrate Pathology*, *211*, 108327. DOI: 10.1016/j.jip.2025.108327 PMID: 40188938

Maqsood-ul-Haque, S., & Veny, H. (2023). Food processing aids: lubricants for halal manufacturing facilities. In *Innovation of Food Products in Halal Supply Chain Worldwide* (pp. 149–159). Academic Press. DOI: 10.1016/B978-0-323-91662-2.00019-3

Mariatussifa, R. M. (2024). *Implementation Of Government Regulation No. 39 Of 2021 Concerning The Implementation Of Halal Product Assurance For Halal Product Process Assistance For Non-Muslim MSME Actors In Yogyakarta.*

Martaleni, M., Mulyono, S., & Utami, E. S. (2025). Peran Religiusitas dalam Meningkatkan Loyalitas Wisatawan Melalui Pariwisata Halal dan Layanan Berkualitas. *Pemasaran Inovatif*, *21*(1), 50–64. DOI: 10.21511/im.21(1).2025.05

Martono, S., Mukhibad, H., Anisykurlillah, I., & Nurkhin, A. (2020). Evaluation of acceptance of information systems in state university with theory of planned behavior and theory of acceptance model approaches. *Management Science Letters*, *10*(14), 3225–3234. DOI: 10.5267/j.msl.2020.6.016

Marzoli, F., Antonelli, P., Saviane, A., Tassoni, L., Cappellozza, S., & Belluco, S. (2022). *Bombyx mori* from a food safety perspective: A systematic review. *Food Research International*, *160*, 111679. DOI: 10.1016/j.foodres.2022.111679 PMID: 36076388

Mas'ud, I., Fahmi, A. A., & Saputra, A. (2025). Dynamics of Islamic Legal Theory (Ushul al-Fiqh) toward Addressing Challenges of Halal Products in the 21st Century. *International Journal of Islamic Thought and Humanities*, *4*(1), 88–105. DOI: 10.54298/ijith.v4i1.403

Masitah, P. E. A., & Wiriani, E. (2024). Analysis Of Sharia Economic Law On Free Halal Certification Through The Self-Declare Mechanism. *Journal Of EMT KITA*, *8*(4), 1665–1688. Https://Doi.Org/10.35870/EMT.V8I4.3389

Maulani, M. R. (2023). *Purchase intention behavior of halal cosmetics . Comparing study between Indonesia and Malaysia millennial generation. 547*, 1266–1292. DOI: 10.1108/JIABR-06-2021-0177

Maulida, A., Dwi, R., & Hapsari, V. (2024). Memahami pengaruh religiusitas, label halal, label ramah lingkungan, dan persepsi halal hijau terhadap loyalitas pelanggan: studi pada perempuan Muslim Generasi Z di Kota Malang. *Jurnal Internasional Riset Bisnis dan Ilmu Sosial (2147-4478), 13* (4), 64–75. DOI: 10.20525/ijrbs.v13i4.3303

Maulida, S. S., Nursaniah, C., & Sari, L. H. (2024). Study of implementation of the eco-pesantren concept at Dayah Terpadu Inshafuddin, Banda Aceh. In *IOP Conference Series: Earth and Environmental Science* (Vol. 1290, Issue 1). DOI: 10.1088/1755-1315/1290/1/012037

Maulida, S., & Ali, M. M. (2023). Pesantren in Indonesia and Sustainable Development Issues. *The Economic Review of Pesantren*, *2*(1). Advance online publication. DOI: 10.58968/erp.v2i1.267

Ma, Y., Al Mamun, A., Ali, M. H., Hoque, M. E., & Lili, Z. (2023). Modeling the intention and adoption of food waste prevention practices among Chinese households. *Humanities & Social Sciences Communications*, *10*(1), 1–12. DOI: 10.1057/s41599-023-02348-9

Mayasari, I., & Haryanto, H. C. (2025). *Investigating the role of brand love on brand advocacy in the local eco hijab fashion industry. 16*(3), 713–735. DOI: 10.1108/JIMA-04-2023-0117

Mbangata, L., & Abayomi, A. (2022). Learning Theories and Technology Adoption Models: A Review. *The Proceedings of the International Conference on Smart City Applications*, 388–403.

Md Rodzi, Z. B., Mohd Amın, F. A., Jamiatun, N., Qaiyyum, A., Al-Sharqi, F., Zaharudin, Z. A., & Khair, M. H. M. (2023). Integrated Single-Valued Neutrosophic Normalized Weighted Bonferroni Mean (SVNNWBM)-DEMATEL for Analyzing the Key Barriers to Halal Certification Adoption in Malaysia. *International Journal of Neutrosophic Science, 21*(3), 106–114. DOI: 10.54216/IJNS.210310

Memon, M. A., Ting, H., Cheah, J. H., Thurasamy, R., Chuah, F., & Cham, T. H. (2020). Sample size for survey research: Review and recommendations. *Journal of Applied Structural Equation Modeling, 4*(2), i–xx. DOI: 10.47263/JASEM.4(2)01

Memon, Y. J., Azhar, S. M., Haque, R., & Bhutto, N. A. (2020). Religiosity as a moderator between theory of planned behavior and halal purchase intention. *Journal of Islamic Marketing, 11*(6), 1821–1836. DOI: 10.1108/JIMA-01-2019-0006

Mi'raj, D. A., Zaki, I., & Hasib, F. F. (2023). Economic Independence of Islamic Boarding Schools. *Amwaluna: Jurnal Ekonomi Dan Keuangan Syariah, 7*(2), 2. Advance online publication. DOI: 10.29313/amwaluna.v7i2.7778

Mijwil, M. M., & Abttan, R. A. (2021). Artificial intelligence: A survey on evolution and future trends. *Asian Journal of Applied Sciences, 9*(2). Advance online publication. DOI: 10.24203/ajas.v9i2.6589

Miraz, M. H., Rabiul, M. K., Adeyinka-Ojo, S., Nair, V., Tariq Hasan, M., Hossain, M. A., & Ha Jin, H. (2025). Digital literacy, marketing ability and tourist healthcare facilities influence tourists' intention to visit Asian countries through the moderation of AI. *Worldwide Hospitality and Tourism Themes, 17*(3), 343–353. DOI: 10.1108/WHATT-02-2025-0055

Miswanto, A. (2021). Moral Hazard in Market Activities: A Textual and Contextual Perspective Review of Hadith. *Cakrawala Jurnal Studi Islam, 16*(1), 13–28. DOI: 10.31603/cakrawala.4222

Mohaiyadin, N. M. Hj., Aman, A., Palil, M. R., & Muhamad Said, S. (2022). Addressing Accountability and Transparency Challenges in Waqf Management using Blockchain Technology. *Journal of Islamic Monetary Economics and Finance, 8*(Special Issue: Islamic Finance). https://doi.org/https://doi.org/10.21098/jimf.v8i0.1413

Mohaiyadin, N. M. Hj., Mohd Zahari, H., & Mardzuki, K. (2024). Addressing Challenges in Halal Certification Using Blockchain Technology. In N. A. A. Rahman & M. H. Ali (Eds.), *Emerging Technology and Crisis Management in The Halal Industry: Issues and Recent Developments* (pp. 49–66). Springer Nature Singapore. DOI: 10.1007/978-981-97-1375-2_4

Mohaiyadin, N. M. (2024). *Potensi Penggunaan Teknologi Blockchain Untuk Mengatasi Cabaran Akauntabiliti Dan Ketelusan Dalam Sistem Maklumat Pengurusan Wakaf Di Universiti Awam Malaysia*. Universiti Kebangsaan Malaysia.

Mohamad, A. R., Yaakop, M. R., & Razif, M. A. B. M. (2024). the Efficacy of the Malaysian Government's Response towards Cybercrime. *Open Journal of Political Science*, *14*(1), 166–176. DOI: 10.4236/ojps.2024.141010

Mohamad, A., & Kashi, A. (2017). Does an Islamic Finance Industry Need a Unification of Standards? A Qualitative Discussion. *Arab Law Quarterly*, *31*(4), 336–362. DOI: 10.1163/15730255-12313031

Mohamad, A., Tan, C. K., Shah, N. N. A. K., Nayan, N., Ibrahim, A., Abdi, G., & Aadil, R. M. (2025). Insect protein: A pathway to sustainable protein supply chains, challenges, and prospects. *Journal of Agriculture and Food Research*, *19*, 101678. DOI: 10.1016/j.jafr.2025.101678

Mohamad, A., Yusoff, W. F. W., Rashid, U. K., & Adi, M. N. M. (2024). The Analysis of Sustainability Development Among MSMEs: Normative Pillar and Cultural-Cognitive Pillar. In Khamis, R., & Buallay, A. (Eds.), *Board Diversity and Corporate Governance* (pp. 673–691). Springer Nature Switzerland., DOI: 10.1007/978-3-031-53877-3_54

Mohamed, Z., Shamsudin, M. N., & Rezai, G. (2013). The Effect of Possessing Information About the Halal Logo on Consumer Confidence in Malaysia. *Journal of International Food & Agribusiness Marketing*, *25*(sup1), 73–86. DOI: 10.1080/08974438.2013.800008

Mohammed, A., Wang, Q., & Li, X. (2017). A cost-effective decision-making algorithm for an RFID-enabled HMSC network design A multi-objective approach. *Industrial Management & Data Systems*, *117*(9), 1782–1799. Advance online publication. DOI: 10.1108/IMDS-02-2016-0074

Mohd Dzin, N. H., & Lay, Y. F. (2021). Validity and reliability of adapted self-efficacy scales in Malaysian context using PLS-SEM approach. *Education Sciences*, *11*(11), 676. DOI: 10.3390/educsci11110676

Mohd Salleh, M. M., & Jaffar, M. N. (2019). *Halal Haram Haiwan Menurut Islam dan Fatwa di Malaysia*. Nilai: Penerbit USIM.

Mohd Thas Thaker, H., Khaliq, A., Ah Mand, A., Iqbal Hussain, H., Mohd Thas Thaker, M. A., & Allah Pitchay, A. B. (2021). Exploring the drivers of social media marketing in Malaysian Islamic banks: An analysis via smart PLS approach. *Journal of Islamic Marketing*, *12*(1), 145–165. DOI: 10.1108/JIMA-05-2019-0095

Mohd Zain, F. A., Wan Abdullah, W. A., Muhamad Nasir, M. N., & Hassan, M. F. (2025). Development of a comprehensive sustainability performance index for takaful operators: integrating Maqasid Al-Shariah and stakeholder perspectives. *International Journal of Islamic and Middle Eastern Finance and Management*. DOI: 10.1108/IMEFM-07-2024-0343

Mohd Zain, F. A., Muhamad, S. F., Abdullah, H., Sheikh Ahmad Tajuddin, S. A. F., & Wan Abdullah, W. A. (2024). Integrating Environmental, Social and Governance (ESG) Principles With Maqasid al-Shariah: A Blueprint for Sustainable Takaful Operations. *International Journal of Islamic and Middle Eastern Finance and Management*, *17*(3), 461–484. DOI: 10.1108/IMEFM-11-2023-0422

Mohsin, A., Ramli, N., & Alkhulayfi, B. A. (2016). *Pariwisata Halal: Peluang yang Muncul. Dalam* (Vol. 19). Perspektif Manajemen Pariwisata., DOI: 10.1016/j.tmp.2015.12.010

Moniruzzaan, & Hamid Aziz, A. (2022). Challenges in the development of Halal certification system in Bangladesh: A descriptive and analytical study based on Malaysian perspective. *Halalsphere, 2*(1).

Morgan, R. M., & Hunt, S. D. (1994)... *The Commitment-Trust Theory of.*, *58*(July), 20–38.

Moshin, A., Brochado, A., & Rodrigues, H. (2020). Pariwisata Halal Berkembang Pesat: Persepsi dan Implikasi Komunitas. *Jurnal Pemasaran dan Manajemen Destinasi, 18*. DOI: 10.1016/j.jdmm.2020.100503

Muazu, M. H., & Sjahrir, E. R. (2023). Halal Entrepreneurship and Its Impact on Sustainable Economy: Opportunities and Challenges. In.

Mudrikah, S., & Ayuningtyas, R. D. (2021). Ethics of Islamic Consumption Behaviour on Discount Promotion and Flash Sale (Overview of Theoretical Economics of Umar bin Al-Khattab). *AKSES Jurnal Ekonomi Dan Bisnis*, *16*(2). Advance online publication. DOI: 10.31942/akses.v16i2.5553

Muhammad, S. (2020). *An integrated model of brand experience and brand love for halal brands : survey of halal fast food consumers in Malaysia*. DOI: 10.1108/JIMA-11-2019-0236

Muhammad, M. A., Elistina, A. B., & Ahmad, S. (2020). The challenges faced by halal certification authorities in managing the halal certification process in Malaysia. *Food Research*, *4*(1), 170–178. DOI: 10.26656/fr.2017.4(S1).S17

Muhammad, M. Z., Amboala, T., Salleh, M. Z. M., Abdullah, A., Tahrim, S. N. C., & Nawi, N. C. (2019). The Application of Shariah Principle in E-commerce Transaction: A Model Development. *Review of World Economics*, *10*(2), 84. DOI: 10.5430/rwe.v10n2p84

Muhammad, R., Zahari, M. S. M., Ramly, A. S. M., & Ahmad, R. (2013). The roles and symbolism of foods in Malay wedding ceremony. *Procedia: Social and Behavioral Sciences*, *101*, 268–276. DOI: 10.1016/j.sbspro.2013.07.200

Muhardi, M., Nurdin, N., & Irfani, A. (2020). The role of knowledge-based ecological pesantren in environmental conservation. *Journal of Physics: Conference Series*, *1469*(1), 012126. DOI: 10.1088/1742-6596/1469/1/012126

Muhtadi, R., Ardiansyah, F., Sakinah, S., & Agustin, F. (2022). Waqf Forestry Integration Model with Islamic Boarding School in Optimizing the OPOP (One Pesantren One Product) Program. *Annual Conference on Islamic Economy and Law*, *1*(2), Article 2. DOI: 10.21107/aciel.v1i2.88

Muneeza, A., & Mustapha, Z. (2020). Halal certification process for fisheries products in Maldives. *Journal of Islamic Marketing*, *12*(2), 451–466. DOI: 10.1108/JIMA-02-2019-0035

Muniarty, P., Muhtadi, R., & Aziz, M. (2023). *Membangun Ekosistem Industri Halal Di Indonesia*. PT GLOBAL EKSEKUTIF TEKNOLOGI.

Mursid, A., & Wu, C. H.-J. (2021). The Antecedents of Customer Satisfaction and Customer-Company Identification in Enhancing Halal Restaurant Loyalty: Halal Company Identity Perspective. *International Journal of Religious Tourism and Pilgrimage*, *9*(1), 8.

Musari, K. (2022). Circular Economy for Plastics and Digitally Enabled Community Towards ASEAN Halal Hub in Asia. In *Handbook of Research on Developing Circular, Digital, and Green Economies in Asia* (pp. 1–12). IGI Global Scientific Publishing. DOI: 10.4018/978-1-7998-8678-5.ch001

Musari, K. (2024). Driving Sustainable Supply Chain and Digitalization in the Halal Industry: Evidence in ASEAN-5. In *Strengthening Sustainable Digitalization of Asian Economy and Society* (pp. 87–100). IGI Global Scientific Publishing. DOI: 10.4018/979-8-3693-1942-0.ch005

Musari, K., Mahmudah, M., Hakim, Z., & Almunawar, M. N. (2025). Mapping the Implementation of Circular Economy and Reverse Logistics in the Sustainable Halal Supply Chain: Evidence in ASEAN-3. In Sakalayen, Q. M. H., Almunawar, M. N., & Yeakub Ali, M. (Eds.), *Sustainable Advanced Manufacturing and Logistics in ASEAN* (pp. 61–78). IGI Global., DOI: 10.4018/979-8-3693-5350-9.ch004

Muslimin, J., Lubis, S., Putra, R., Nahartini, D., & Wafa, A. (2022). Islamic Branding and Digital Marketing: A Strategy to Attract Muslim Consumers' Buying Interest. DOI: 10.4108/eai.20-10-2021.2316313

Mustikawati, R., Arafah, W., & Mariyanti, T. (2022). Pengaruh Religiusitas dan Nilai yang Dirasakan Pelanggan Muslim terhadap Loyalitas dan Kepuasan Pelanggan dalam Pariwisata Halal di Indonesia. *Jurnal Internasional Bisnis Islam*, *7*(2). Advance online publication. DOI: 10.32890/ijib2022.7.2.4

Nadila, F., Ismail, M., & Mutia, A. (2024). Analysis Of Halal Product Assurance Using Halal Certification In Increasing Competitiveness: (Study On Banana Products For Sale In Purwo Bakti Village, Bathin III District). *Journal Of Nuansa: Publications Of Sharia Management And Economics*, *2*(3), 65–81. Https://Doi.Org/10.61132/NUANSA.V2I3.1090

Nafis, M. C. (2019). The Concept Of Halal And Thayyib And Its Implementation In Indonesia. *Journal Of Halal Product And Research*, *2*(1), 1. DOI: 10.20473/jhpr.vol.2-issue.1.1-5

Nair, G. (2021). The food we waste: Antecedents of food wastage management behaviour. *International Journal of Social Economics*, *48*(6), 826–842. DOI: 10.1108/IJSE-01-2020-0029

Najiha, F., Abdullah, B., & Yusof, D. (2024). Islamic and western ethical perspective in mandatory vaccination policy for children in Malaysia. *Fikroh Jurnal Pemikiran Dan Pendidikan Islam*, *17*(2), 135–150. DOI: 10.37812/fikroh.v17i2.1647

Naldurtiker, A., Batchu, P., Kouakou, B., Terrill, T. H., Shaik, A., & Kannan, G. (2022). RNA-Seq Exploration Of The Influence Of Stress On Meat Quality In Spanish Goats. *Scientific Reports*, *12*(1), 20573. DOI: 10.1038/s41598-022-23269-8 PMID: 36446782

Napoli, J., Dickinson, S. J., Beverland, M. B., & Farrelly, F. (2013). Measuring consumer-based brand authenticity. *Journal of Business Research*. Advance online publication. DOI: 10.1016/j.jbusres.2013.06.001

Na, S., Heo, S., Han, S., Shin, Y., & Roh, Y. (2022). Acceptance model of artificial intelligence (AI)-based technologies in construction firms: Applying the Technology Acceptance Model (TAM) in combination with the Technology—Organisation—Environment (TOE) framework. *Buildings (Basel, Switzerland)*, *12*(2), 90. DOI: 10.3390/buildings12020090

Nasir, N. F., Roslin, R. M., Nasir, M., & Nasir, M. N. F. (2020). Marketing strategies from the Islamic perspective: Reviewing the relevance of elements of the marketing mix. *Journal of Emerging Economies and Islamic Research*, *8*(3), 84. DOI: 10.24191/jeeir.v8i3.9952

Nasir, N. M., Nair, M. S., & Ahmed, P. K. (2021). Institutional isomorphism and environmental sustainability: A new framework from the Shariah perspective. *Environment, Development and Sustainability*, *23*(9), 13555–13568. DOI: 10.1007/s10668-021-01227-0

Nasreen, R., Siraj, S., & Beg, S. (2012). Fast Trax - the Indian QSR chain). 2012. *Emerald Emerging Markets Case Studies.*, *2*(8), 14–27. DOI: 10.1108/20450621211289403

Nasution, M. D. T. P., Astuti, D., Rahayu, S., Rossanty, Y., Harahap, R., & Rafiki, A. (2023). AI-Driven Chatbots in Halal Marketing Communication—Challenges and Opportunities. *Global Islamic Marketing Conference*, 403–421.

Naznii, H. (2023). Halal certification process by local governments and Muslim organizations in Australia. *Journal of International Islamic Business Studies*, *1*(1), 46–53.

Neamah, H. A., & Tandio, J. (2024). Towards the development of foods 3D printer: Trends and technologies for foods printing. *Heliyon*, *10*(13), e33882. DOI: 10.1016/j.heliyon.2024.e33882 PMID: 39050479

Ngelyaratan, D., & Soediantono, D. (2022). Customer relationship management (CRM) and recommendation for implementation in the defense industry: A literature review. *Journal of Industrial Engineering & Management Research*, *3*(3), 17–34.

Nguyen, D. M., Chiu, Y.-T. H., & Le, H. D. (2021). Determinants of continuance intention towards banks' chatbot services in Vietnam: A necessity for sustainable development. *Sustainability (Basel)*, *13*(14), 7625. DOI: 10.3390/su13147625

Nguyen, G.-D., & Ha, M.-T. (2021). The role of user adaptation and trust in understanding continuance intention towards mobile shopping: An extended expectation-confirmation model. *Cogent Business & Management*, *8*(1), 1980248. DOI: 10.1080/23311975.2021.1980248

Ningrum, R. T. P. (2022). Problems Of Halal Certification Obligations For Micro And Small Enterprises (Mses) In Madiun Regency. *Istithmar, 6*(1), 43–58. Https://Doi.Org/10.30762/ISTITHMAR.V6I1.30

Ningsih, I. W., Basri, H., & Suhartini, A. (2023). HISTORY AND DEVELOPMENT OF PESANTREN IN INDONESIA. *JURNAL EDUSCIENCE, 10*(1), 1. Advance online publication. DOI: 10.36987/jes.v10i1.3392

Niyomart, S., & Khanmwon, A. (2012). Brand Love, Brand Loyalty, and Word of Mouth: A Case of AirAsia. *Conference of the International Journal of Arts & Sciences*, *76*(2), 263–267.

Noman, A., Al, , Afif, M. M., Huq, A. M. R., Rahman, A. F. F., & Islam, M. (2025). Blockchain-Driven Halal Supply Chains: Enhancing Transparency and Efficiency While Ensuring Shariah Adherence. *International Journal of Innovative Science and Research Technology*, (April), 1992–1997. DOI: 10.38124/ijisrt/25apr1001

Noor, N. (2025). *A closer look at halal brand image : systematic review and future directions*. DOI: 10.1108/JIMA-06-2024-0259

Novianti, D., Haditjaroko, L., & Almunawar, M. N. (2022). Assurance information systems design for blockchain - Based micro, small and medium enterprises in Indonesia. *IOP Conference Series. Earth and Environmental Science*, *1063*(1), 012058. Advance online publication. DOI: 10.1088/1755-1315/1063/1/012058

Nunnally, J. C. (1978). An overview of psychological measurement. *Clinical diagnosis of mental disorders: A handbook*, 97-146.

Nuraini, S., & Sucipto, S. (2021). Comparison halal food regulation and practices to support halal tourism in Asia: A review. *IOP Conference Series. Earth and Environmental Science*, *733*(1), 12044. DOI: 10.1088/1755-1315/733/1/012044

Nurein, S. A. (2023). Nexus of Halal Entrepreneurship and Islamic Finance for the Creation of a Strong Halal Ecosystem. In *Contemporary discourse of halal and Islamic entrepreneurship: Trends and future opportunities* (pp. 133-144). DOI: 10.1007/978-981-99-6427-7_9

Nurhasanah, E., Mubarok, A. Z. S., Zahra, Q. S. A., & Rahmat, B. Z. (2024). DEVELOPING SUSTAINABLE ISLAMIC BOARDING SCHOOLS: ANALYSIS OF ONE PESANTREN ONE PRODUCT PROGRAM IN FOSTERING SELF-SUFFICIENCY. *Penamas, 37*(2), 2. Advance online publication. DOI: 10.31330/penamas.v37i2.772

Nurhayati, E., & Dz, A. S. (2025). Developing Entrepreneurial Creativity through Creative Thinking Skills: Qualitative Study on Halal Industry SMEs in Pesantren. *Eduprof : Islamic Education Journal, 6*(2), 1–14. DOI: 10.47453/eduprof.v6i2.302

Nurhayati, N. (2023). DIGITAL INNOVATION IN HALAL LOGISTICS: AN INDONESIAN CASE STUDY. *Agripreneur : Jurnal Pertanian Agribisnis, 12*(2), 23–37. DOI: 10.35335/agripreneur.v12i2.4672

Nurjannah, Awalauddin, M., K, A., Fadel, M., & Asti, MJ (2023). Urgensi Maqāṣid Sharīa untuk Regulasi Pariwisata Halal di Indonesia. *Al-Risalah Jurnal Ilmu Syariah Dan Hukum*. DOI: 10.24252/al-risalah.vi.35026

Nurjannah, N., Siradjuddin, S., Efendi, A., & Fadel, M. (2024). Pillar Of Indonesian Halal Industry Development. *Indonesia Journal Of Halal, 7*(2), 156–169. Https://Doi.Org/10.14710/HALAL.V7I2.21802

Nurkhin, A., Martono, S., Fachrurrozie, F., Mukhibad, H., Rohman, A., Prabowo, W. T. J., & Rofiq, A. (2024). Promoting green-pesantren and circular economy; Improving santri's knowledge on food waste management and maggot cultivation. In *IOP Conference Series: Earth and Environmental Science* (Vol. 1414, Issue 1). DOI: 10.1088/1755-1315/1414/1/012026

Nursalwani, M., & Ariff, A. L. Z. (2023). *Influencing factors of young entrepreneur's participation in halal food products in Sarawak.* Paper presented at the AIP Conference Proceedings. DOI: 10.1063/5.0118113

Nursalwani, M., Yumiemarnie, J., Sannasi, A. P., Amizi, A. M., & Ariff, A. L. Z. (2021). *Factors influencing participation of youth entrepreneurs in halal food product labelling in Sabah.* Paper presented at the AIP Conference Proceedings. DOI: 10.1063/5.0053102

Nurul Fitri Amijaya, R., Prayarsni Korina, A., Alaika, R., Lutfiani, H., Jember, U., & Sharif Ali, S. (2024). Risk Assessment Of Trade Barriers: The Implications Of Indonesia's Halal Certification Law On International Commerce. *International Journal Of Islamic Economics, 6*(02), 132–145. Https://Doi.Org/10.32332/IJIE.V6I2.9028

Nusran, M., Nasution, E. N., Prayitno, M. A., & Sudarmanto, E. (2023). Halal Certification in The Digital Age: Leveraging Online Platforms for Enhanced Transparency and Accessibility. *Jurnal Ekonomi. Akuntansi Dan Manajemen Indonesia*, *2*(01), 105–115. DOI: 10.58471/jeami.v2i01.379

Nyagango, A. I., Sife, A. S., & Kazungu, I. (2023). Use of mobile phone technologies for accessing agricultural marketing information by grape smallholder farmers: A technological acceptance model (TAM) perspective. *Technological Sustainability*, *2*(3), 320–336. DOI: 10.1108/TECHS-01-2023-0002

Odin, Y., Odin, N., & Valette-florence, P. (2001). *Conceptual and operational aspects of brand loyalty An empirical investigation. 53.*

Office of the State Mufti of Brunei. (2022). Ramuan makanan sumber daripada serangga: adakah halal dimakan? *Media Permata*. Retrieved from https://mediapermata.com.bn/ramuan-makanan-sumber-daripada-serangga-adakah-halal-dimakan/

Ogbuke, N. J., Yusuf, Y. Y., Dharma, K., & Mercangoz, B. A. (2022). Big data supply chain analytics: Ethical, privacy and security challenges posed to business, industries and society. *Production Planning and Control*, *33*(2-3), 123–137. DOI: 10.1080/09537287.2020.1810764

Ojha, S., Bußler, S., Psarianos, M., Rossi, G., & Schlüter, O. K. (2021). Edible insect processing pathways and implementation of emerging technologies. *Journal of Insects as Food and Feed*, *7*(5), 877–900. DOI: 10.3920/JIFF2020.0121

Oktafia, R., Taufiq, M., & Utami, A. F. (2024). One Pesantren One Product: Can It Improve Economic Growth in East Java? *IQTISHODUNA: Jurnal Ekonomi Islam*, *13*(1), 131–152. DOI: 10.54471/iqtishoduna.v13i1.2519

Olatunde, T. M., Okwandu, A. C., Akande, D. O., & Sikhakhane, Z. Q.Tosin Michael OlatundeAzubuike Chukwudi OkwanduDorcas Oluwajuwonlo AkandeZamathula Queen Sikhakhane. (2024). Reviewing the role of artificial intelligence in energy efficiency optimization. *Engineering Science & Technology Journal*, *5*(4), 1243–1256. DOI: 10.51594/estj.v5i4.1015

Ologeanu-Taddei, R., Hönigsberg, S., Weritz, P., Wache, H., Mittermeier, F., Tana, S., Dang, D., Hautala-Kankaanpää, T., & Pekkola, S. (2025). The relationship of digital transformation and corporate sustainability: Synergies and tensions. *Technological Forecasting and Social Change*, *210*, 123809. https://doi.org/https://doi.org/10.1016/j.techfore.2024.123809. DOI: 10.1016/j.techfore.2024.123809

Opoku-Nkoom, W. (2015). Safety and quality characteristics of freeze-defrost cycles in muscle foods. *EC Nutr*, *1*, 140–144.

Oprea, S.-V., & Bâra, A. (2025). Is Artificial Intelligence a Game-Changer in Steering E-Business into the Future? Uncovering Latent Topics with Probabilistic Generative Models. *Journal of Theoretical and Applied Electronic Commerce Research*, *20*(1), 16. DOI: 10.3390/jtaer20010016

Organisation for Economic Co-operation and Development(OECD). (1998). *Fostering Entrepreneurship*. OECD Publishing.

Orkusz, A. (2021). Edible insects versus meat—Nutritional comparison: Knowledge of their composition is the key to good health. *Nutrients*, *13*(4), 1207. DOI: 10.3390/nu13041207 PMID: 33917531

Othman, B., Hashim, N. H., & Musa, R. (2016). Conceptualizing the influences of knowledge and religiosity on halal certification trust: The perspectives of non-Muslim consumers. *Asian Academy of Management Journal*, *21*(1), 23–48.

Otoum, F. J. A.-, & Nimri, R. S. (2015). *Antecedents of Consumers ' Behavior towards Halal Food among Jordanian Customers : A Structural Equation Modeling (SEM) Approach*. 19–26.

Oye, E., & Emma, O. (2024). *The Role of Big Data Analytics in Enhancing Corporate Social Responsibility (CSR) Initiatives in American Firms*. https://www.researchgate.net/publication/388005010

Padgett, D., & Allen, D. (1997). Communicating experiences: A narrative approach to creating service brand image. *Journal of Advertising*, *26*(4), 49–62. DOI: 10.1080/00913367.1997.10673535

Pali-Schöll, I., Binder, R., Moens, Y., & Smulders, F. J. M. (2019). Edible insects—Defining a framework for risk assessment of novel foods. *Food and Chemical Toxicology*, *126*, 108–118. DOI: 10.1016/j.fct.2019.02.018

Pappu, R., & Quester, P. (2006). Does customer satisfaction lead to improved brand equity An empirical examination of two categories of retail brands. *Journal of Product and Brand Management*, *15*(1), 4–14. DOI: 10.1108/10610420610650837

Parray, Z. A., Iqbal, J., & Mushtaq, R. (2024). Customer perception of corporate social responsibility and its impact on customer engagement: Critical significance of corporate reputation. *Corporate Communications*, *29*(4), 592–606. DOI: 10.1108/CCIJ-05-2023-0063

Patil, D. (2024). Artificial Intelligence-Driven Customer Service: Enhancing Personalization, Loyalty, And Customer Satisfaction. *SSRN*.

Philippidis, G., Sartori, M., Ferrari, E., & M'Barek, R. (2019). Waste not, want not: A bio-economic impact assessment of household food waste reductions in the EU. *Resources, Conservation and Recycling, 146*, 514–522. DOI: 10.1016/j.resconrec.2019.04.016 PMID: 31274960

Pittaway, L. (2005). Philosophies in entrepreneurship: A focus on economic theories. *International Journal of Entrepreneurial Behaviour & Research, 11*(3), 201–221. DOI: 10.1108/13552550510598790

Placentino, U., Sogari, G., Viscecchia, R., De Devitiis, B., & Monacis, L. (2021). The new challenge of sports nutrition: Accepting insect food as dietary supplements in professional athletes. *Foods, 10*(5), 1117. DOI: 10.3390/foods10051117 PMID: 34070020

Porpino, G., Wansink, B., & Parente, J. (2016). Wasted positive intentions: The role of affection and abundance on household food waste. *Journal of Food Products Marketing, 22*(7), 733–751. DOI: 10.1080/10454446.2015.1121433

Prabowo, S., Abd Rahman, A., Ab Rahman, S., & Samah, A. A. (2015). Revealing factors hindering halal certification in East Kalimantan Indonesia. *Journal of Islamic Marketing, 6*(2), 268–291. DOI: 10.1108/JIMA-05-2014-0040

Pradana, M., Rubiyanti, N., & Marimon, F. (2024). Measuring Indonesian young consumers' halal purchase intention of foreign-branded food products. *Humanities & Social Sciences Communications, 11*(1), 150. Advance online publication. DOI: 10.1057/s41599-023-02559-0

Prasanthi, M., Sahu, S. R., Bakshi, M., Shanmugam, R., & Wable, P. M. (2024). Personalized Marketing in the Digital Age: The Role of AI in Consumer Behavior Analytics. *Library of Progress-Library Science, Information Technology & Computer, 44*(3).

Prasasti, R., Ashwat, N. U., Gunawan, S., & Azhar, J. A. (2024). Examining The Determinants of Halal Food Preferences in Gen Z: The Moderating Role of Motivation on Lifestyles and Purchasing Decisions. *Likuid Jurnal Ekonomi Industri Halal, 4*(2), 49–76. DOI: 10.15575/likuid.v4i2.36853

Pratama, D. P. (2022). The future of the halal tourism market in Japan after COVID-19: an economic pragmatism perspective. In International Conference on Humanities and Social Sciences, KnE Social Sciences, pp. 21–43. DOI: 10.18502/kss.v7i4.10512

Pratiwi, A. A., & Vidiati, C. (2024). The Development Of The Halal Industry In Indonesia Reviewed From The Strengthening Of The Sharia Economy. *De Banten-Bode: Journal Of Community Service (PKM) Setiabudhi, 5*(2), 61–71.

Precup, G., Ververis, E., Azzollini, D., Rivero-Pino, F., Zakidou, P., & Germini, A. (2022). The safety assessment of insects and products thereof as novel foods in the European Union.

Probst, C., Kilian, C., Sanchez, S., Lange, S., & Rehm, J. (2020). The Role Of Alcohol Use And Drinking Patterns In Socioeconomic Inequalities In Mortality: A Systematic Review. *The Lancet. Public Health*, *5*(6), e324–e332. DOI: 10.1016/S2468-2667(20)30052-9 PMID: 32504585

Provita Wijayanti. (2024). *Computerized accounting information system, Maqashid Sharia and sustainable performance in Indonesia Islamic microfinance: An application of Task Technology of Fit*. Universiti Teknologi Mara.

Puji Fajariani, D., & Hermawan Adinugraha, H. (2024). Islamic accounting as an information system for Sharia-based companies. *Al-Muamalah: Jurnal Ekonomi Islam, Filatropi Dan Perbankan Syariah, 1*(1). https://journal.syamilahpublishing.com/index.php/muamalah/

Purbasari, N. & Manaf, A. (2018). Comparative Study on the Characteristics of Community-Based Tourism between Pentingsari and Nglanggeran Tourism Village, Special Region Yogyakarta. E3S Web of Conferences, 31, 09007. DOI: 10.1051/e3sconf/20183109007

Puspitasari, N., Luvian, V., & Mahardiyanto, A. (2023). *Phenomenological Study of the Application of Islamic Business Ethics in Fashion Sale and Purchase Transactions ARTICLE INFO*. https://jmrs.optima-science.com/index.php/jmrs

Putra, I. A., & Ambariyanto, A. (2024). Analysis Of The Impact Of Halal Product Certification On Economic And Social Activities. *El-Mal: Journal Of Islamic Economic & Business Studies, 5*(7), 3408–3427. Https://Doi.Org/10.47467/ELMAL.V5I7.2649

Putri, R. (2024). Halal Certification Challenges For Micro, Small And Medium Enterprises (Msmes) Of Food Products In Pamekasan Regency. *Assyarikah: Journal Of Islamic Economic Business, 5*(2), 222–242. Https://Doi.Org/10.28944/ASSYARIKAH.V5I2.1911

Putri, A. Y., Mariza, E., & Alimni, A. (2023). Pesantren Sebagai Lembaga Pendidikan Islam (Sejarah Lahirnya Pesantren Sebagai Lembaga Pendidikan Islam Di Indonesia, Sejarah Perkembangan Pesantren/ Sistem Pendidikan, Dan Perkembangannya Masa Kini). *Innovative: Journal Of. Social Science Research*, *3*(2), 2.

Putri, W. S. T. (2024). The Impact Of Sustainable Sourcing On Halal Certification: A Literature Review On Ethical And Environmental Concerns. *Journal Of Halal Review*, *1*(1), 51–64. DOI: 10.70764/gdpu-jhr.2025.1(1)-05

Qader, G., Shahid, Z. A., Junaid, M., Shaikh, I. M., & Qureshi, M. A. (2023). The role of diffusion of innovation theory towards the adoption of halal meat supply chain. *Journal of Islamic Marketing*, *14*(5), 1211–1228. DOI: 10.1108/JIMA-01-2021-0032

Qi, D., & Roe, B. E. (2016). Household food waste: Multivariate regression and principal components analyses of awareness and attitudes among US consumers. *PLoS One*, *11*(7), e0159250. DOI: 10.1371/journal.pone.0159250 PMID: 27441687

Qi, X., & Ploeger, A. (2019). Explaining consumers' intentions towards purchasing green food in Qingdao, China: The amendment and extension of the theory of planned behavior. *Appetite*, *133*, 414–422. DOI: 10.1016/j.appet.2018.12.004 PMID: 30537527

Qizam, I., Berakon, I., & Ali, H. (2024). The role of halal value chain, Sharia financial inclusion, and digital economy in socio-economic transformation: A study of Islamic boarding schools in Indonesia. *Journal of Islamic Marketing*, *16*(3), 810–840. DOI: 10.1108/JIMA-03-2024-0108

Qizwini, J., & Perkasa, D. H. (2024). Analysis of Marketing Ethics from an Islamic Perspective. *Proceeding International Conference on Islamic Economics and Business (ICIEB)*, *3*(1), 46–57.

Queiroz, L. S., Nogueira Silva, N. F., Jessen, F., Mohammadifar, M. A., Stephani, R., Fernandes de Carvalho, A., Perrone, Í. T., & Casanova, F. (2023). Edible insect as an alternative protein source: A review on the chemistry and functionalities of proteins under different processing methods. *Heliyon*, *9*(4), e14831. DOI: 10.1016/j.heliyon.2023.e14831 PMID: 37025786

Quested, T. E., Marsh, E., Stunell, D., & Parry, A. D. (2013). Spaghetti soup: The complex world of food waste behaviours. *Resources, Conservation and Recycling*, *79*, 43–51. DOI: 10.1016/j.resconrec.2013.04.011

Quoquab, F., Mohamed Sadom, N. Z., & Mohammad, J. (2020). Driving customer loyalty in the Malaysian fast food industry: The role of halal logo, trust and perceived reputation. *Journal of Islamic Marketing*, *11*(6), 1367–1387. DOI: 10.1108/JIMA-01-2019-0010

Rachmawati, R., Yaniza, T., Asikin, U., Ismawartati, I., & Rohani, S. (2023). The Role Of Halal Task Force Unit In Ensuring Halal Products In West Kalimantan Province. *Daengku: Journal Of Humanities And Social Sciences Innovation, 3*(5), 893–900. Https://Doi.Org/10.35877/454RI.DAENGKU2186

Rafiki, A. (2019). Perception and Challenges Due to Halal Certification: The Case of Zulaikha Shop). In *Management for Professionals, Part F561* (pp. 153-167).

Rafiki, A. (2019). Customer Relationship Management Practices in Islamic Banks. In *Customer Relationship Management and IT*. IntechOpen.

Rafiki, A., Ramadhani, S. N., Ananda, R. F., & Harahap, I. (2023). Eco-Innovation Towards Increasing the Productivity of SMEs: A Case in Indonesia. In *Handbook of Research on Artificial Intelligence and Knowledge Management in Asia's Digital Economy* (pp. 223–232). IGI Global Scientific Publishing., DOI: 10.4018/978-1-6684-5849-5.ch013

Rahayu, S. A. P., Niravita, A., Anitasari, R. F., & Kamal, U. (2023). Halal Certification Imperatives for MSMEs: Navigating Sustainability, Consumer Confidence, and Policy Compliance (Case of Kenteng, Bandungan, Indonesia). *Indonesian Journal of Advocacy and Legal Services*, *5*(2), 143–160. DOI: 10.15294/ijals.v5i2.29861

Rahayu, S., & Candera, M. (2023). Tourist loyalty to halal tourism in Indonesia: The role of services quality, satisfaction, and experience quality. *Jurnal Manajemen Bisnis*, *14*(1), 198–213. DOI: 10.18196/mb.v14i1.17790

Rahi, S., Othman Mansour, M. M., Alharafsheh, M., & Alghizzawi, M. (2021). The post-adoption behavior of internet banking users through the eyes of self-determination theory and expectation confirmation model. *Journal of Enterprise Information Management*, *34*(6), 1874–1892. DOI: 10.1108/JEIM-04-2020-0156

Rahman, R., Langner, T., & Temme, D. (2021). Brand love: conceptual and empirical investigation of a holistic causal model. In *Journal of Brand Management* (Vol. 28, Issue 6). Palgrave Macmillan UK. DOI: 10.1057/s41262-021-00237-7

Rahman, M. M., Ahmad, Z., Mokal, M. N., Aziz, M. F., & Khotib, N. A. M. (2024). Green Sustainability And Financial Performance Of Halal Food Companies: Evidence Of Malaysia. *Journal Of Islamic Monetary Economics And Finance*, *10*(4), 709–734. DOI: 10.21098/jimf.v10i4.2003

Rahman, M. M., Al Mahi, A., & Hossian, M. A. Z. (2024). Application of AI in Halal Marketing: Navigating the Ethical Crossroads. *West Science Interdisciplinary Studies*, *2*(04), 920–926. DOI: 10.58812/wsis.v2i04.866

Rahman, M. M., & Razimi, M. S. A. (2023). Halal biotechnology product: halal supply chain compliance and integrity risk. In *Innovation of food products in Halal supply chain worldwide* (pp. 195–204). Academic Press. DOI: 10.1016/B978-0-323-91662-2.00016-8

Rahman, W. F. I. W. A., & Ahamat, H. (2020). Consumer Protection under Shariah Law in Islamic Religious Tourism. *International Journal of Asian Social Science, 10*(5), 262–272. DOI: 10.18488/journal.1.2020.105.262.272

Rahman, Z., Asadullah, J., Dodul, D. H., Shahrukh, T., Mebin, M. R., Akthar, N., Sharmin, S., Raju, Z. H., & Sonia, S. (2024). Literature Review on SOR Model from the Perspective of Social Media. *Pakistan Journal of Life and Social Sciences, 22*(2), 16630–16643. DOI: 10.57239/PJLSS-2024-22.2.001208

Rahmawati, T. H., & Nugraha Triyan Putra, Z. (2022). Overview Of The Halal Industry In Global Trade. *Company: Journal Of Sharia Economics, 5*(2), 72–81. Https://Doi.Org/10.25299/SYARIKAT.2022.VOL5(2).9657

Raimi, B. O. (2023). Halal Entrepreneurship in Islamic Digital Economy from a Cultural Perspective. In (pp. 115-132). DOI: 10.1007/978-981-99-6427-7_8

Raimi, B. O. (2024). Faith-Based Entrepreneurship as Ultra-Religious Entrepreneurship in Africa: Definition, Essence, Strands, Theoretical Underpinning, and Theological Foundation. In (pp. 251-279).

Raimi, L. 2024. "Interdependence of Halal Entrepreneurship and Islamic Finance for Creating a Strong Halal Ecosystem" *Journal of Islamic Marketing* pp.1-33.

Raimi, L., Adekunle, S. M., & Shabbir, M. S. (2023). Contemporary Discourse of Halal and Islamic Entrepreneurship: Trends and Future Opportunities. In.

Raimi, L. (2024). Do Islamic epistemology and ethics advance the understanding and promotion of sustainable development? A systematic review using PRISMA. In *International Journal of Ethics and Systems*. Emerald Publishing., DOI: 10.1108/IJOES-04-2024-0115

Raimi, L., Abdur-Rauf, I. A., & Ashafa, S. A. (2024). Does Islamic Sustainable Finance Support Sustainable Development Goals to Avert Financial Risk in the Management of Islamic Finance Products? A Critical Literature Review. *Journal of Risk and Financial Management, 17*(6), 236. Advance online publication. DOI: 10.3390/jrfm17060236

Raimi, L., Abdur-Rauf, I. A., & Olaide Raimi, B. (2024). Interdependence of halal entrepreneurship and Islamic finance for creating a strong halal ecosystem. *Journal of Islamic Marketing*.

Ram, M., Maryam, P., & Bernard, A. T. (2024). *Beyond the Click: Unveiling the Influence of AI Personalization on E-commerce Impulse Buys.*

Ramadani, V., Dana, L. P., Ratten, V., & Tahiri, S. (2015). The context of Islamic entrepreneurship and business: Concept, principles and perspectives. *International Journal of Business and Globalisation, 15*(3), 244–261. DOI: 10.1504/IJBG.2015.071906

Ramli, N. M., Abd Aziz, S., & Md Ali, N. S. A. (2020). Reporting on Halal Activities: What Companies Communicate to Stakeholders. *Journal of Fatwa Management and Research*, 42–58. DOI: 10.33102/jfatwa.vol19no1.4

Ramli, J. A., Hashim, H. A., & Salleh, Z. (2023). Governance of Malaysian Halal Food Industry: Conventional Governance vs Shariah Requirements. *Proceedings of the International Symposium & Exhibition on Business and Accounting 2022 (ISEBA 2022), 28 September 2022, Malaysia, 1*, 83–94. DOI: 10.15405/epfe.23081.8

Rane, N. (2023). Enhancing customer loyalty through Artificial Intelligence (AI), Internet of Things (IoT), and Big Data technologies: improving customer satisfaction, engagement, relationship, and experience. *Internet of Things (IoT), and Big Data Technologies: Improving Customer Satisfaction, Engagement, Relationship, and Experience (October 13, 2023).*

Rangkuti, M. Y. (2023). Toward a Holistic Framework of Islamic Business Ethics: Insights from Leadership, Halal Practices, and Finance in a Digital Age. *Sinergi International Journal of Islamic Studies, 1*(3), 114–127. DOI: 10.61194/ijis.v1i3.593

Rao, S. X., Han, Z., Yin, H., Jiang, J., Zhang, Z., Zhao, Y., & Shan, Y. (2025). Fraud detection at eBay. *Emerging Markets Review, 101277*, 101277. Advance online publication. DOI: 10.1016/j.ememar.2025.101277

Rasyidah, A. N., Azizi, A. Q., & Kholis, N. (2025). Digital Ecosystems in Supporting Global Trade of Halal Products: Innovation and Challenges. *ADPEBI International Journal of Business and Social Science, 5*(2), 1–11.

Ratna, J. S. (2023). *Implementation Of Government Regulation No. 39 Of 2021 Concerning The Implementation Of The Halal Product Assurance Sector (Study At LPH LPPOM-MUI Lampung Province).* UIN Raden Intan Lampung.

Ratnasari, R. T., Sari, N. S., Ahmi, A., & Ismail, S. (2024). Research trends of halal tourism: A bibliometric analysis. *Journal of Islamic Accounting and Business Research.* Advance online publication. DOI: 10.1108/JIABR-08-2023-0246

Raza, M., Khalique, M., Khalid, R., Kasuma, J., Ali, W., & Selem, K. M. (2025). Achieving SMEs' excellence: Scale development of Islamic entrepreneurship from business and spiritual perspectives. *Journal of Islamic Accounting and Business Research*, *16*(1), 86–106. DOI: 10.1108/JIABR-02-2023-0060

Rejeb, A., Rejeb, K., Zailani, S., Treiblmaier, H., & Hand, K. J. (2021). Integrating the Internet of Things in the halal food supply chain: A systematic literature review and research agenda. In *Internet of Things (Netherlands)* (Vol. 13). DOI: 10.1016/j.iot.2021.100361

Ren, L., Yang, F., & Gu, C. (2023). A study of the purchase intention of insect protein food as alternative foods for fitness proteins. *Heliyon*, *9*(9), e20239. DOI: 10.1016/j.heliyon.2023.e20239 PMID: 37809624

Research and Markets. (2025). Religious Tourism Market Report 2024. Research and Markets. https://www.researchandmarkets.com/report/faith-based-tourism-market?srsltid=AfmBOorf3z9ILEW2xMC8oQ9wtPSLwk2ym2gQrakTMOIRGOJQEHsMQcG8

Restuti, D. P., Kasdi, A., & Cahya, B. T. (2025). Isu Ekonomi Industri Halal. In *Exploring the Halal Industry and Its Business Ecosystem Prospects* (pp. 1–22). IGI Global., DOI: 10.4018/979-8-3693-8618-7.ch001

Ribadu, M. B., Wan Wan Ab, W. N., Abd Ghani, A. A., Kamaruddin, A., & Othman, M. S. (2020). Sharia requirements framework for e-commerce systems: An exploratory study. *Journal of Theoretical and Applied Information Technology*, *98*(6), 994–1008. www.jatit.org

Richard, L. (1999). Whence consumer loyalty ? *Journal of Marketing, 63*(Special Issue 1999), 33–44.

Ridho, A. (2025). Integrating artificial intelligence and blockchain to improve the accuracy of halal certification. *Journal of Halal Review*, *1*(1), 12–22. Advance online publication. DOI: 10.70764/gdpu-jhr.2025.1(1)-02

Ridwan, A. H., Hasanuddin, M., & Fatahillah, I. A. (2020). Authorization of Halal certification in Indonesia, Malaysia and Singapore. *International Journal of Psychosocial Rehabilitation*, *24*(08), 7992–8011.

RISSC. (2024). *The Muslim 500 | Muslim Paling Berpengaruh di Dunia*. https://themuslim500.com/books/TheMuslim500-2025-lowres.pdf

Rodrigues, C., & Brandão, A. (2021). Measuring the effects of retail brand experiences and brand love on word of mouth: A cross-country study of IKEA brand. *International Review of Retail, Distribution and Consumer Research, 31*(1), 78–105. DOI: 10.1080/09593969.2020.1768577

Rogers, E. M. (1983). *Diffusion of innovations* (3rd ed.). The Free Press.

Rohimah, R. (2024). The Influence of Price, Halal Brands, and Marketing Management Strategies on Consumer Satisfaction. *Journal of Halal Science, Industry, and Business*, *2*(1), 90–103. DOI: 10.31098/jhasib.v2i1.1991

Roy, S. K., Eshghi, A., & Sarkar, A. (2012). *Antecedents and consequences of brand love. March*, 1–8. DOI: 10.1057/bm.2012.24

Rozana, K. (2022). *SBI-Lab: Designing Sharia Business Incubator on Virtual Version for Developing Halal Product Competitiveness in Indonesia.* https://doi.org/ DOI: 10.1109/IBDAP55587.2022.9907598

Ruhaeni, N., Yusdiansyah, E., & Aqimuddin, E. A. (2024). Revisiting Indonesia halal tourism policy in light of GATS. *Journal of International Trade Law & Policy*, *23*(2–3), 154–167. DOI: 10.1108/JITLP-12-2023-0064

Ruiz, F.E.A., Jácome, J.F.O., Tejera, E.. (2025). Edible insects as functional foods: bioactive compounds, health benefits, safety concerns, allergenicity, and regulatory considerations. frontiers in nutrition, 12. DOI: 10.3389/fnut.2025.1571084

Russo, I., Patrucco, A. S., Klumpp, M., & Stanton, D. (2025). Leveraging social media to bridge academia and industry in supply chain management research: A framework for integrated strategies. *International Journal of Physical Distribution & Logistics Management*, *55*(11), 144–162. DOI: 10.1108/IJPDLM-10-2024-0387

Rusydiana, A. S., Ruhana, A. S., & As-Salafiyah, A. (2023, January-June). Problems In The Implementation Of Halal Product Assurance In Indonesia: An Analysis Of Halal Governance. *HARMONI Journal*, *22*(1), 167–186. DOI: 10.32488/harmoni.v1i22.572

Ryandono, M. N. H. (2018). Peran Pondok Pesantren dalam Pemberdayaan Sosial Ekonomi di Jawa Timur pada Abad ke-20. *MOZAIK HUMANIORA*, *18*(2), 2. Advance online publication. DOI: 10.20473/mozaik.v18i2.10934

Sabar, R., Anuar, N. K., & Hashom, H. (2025). *The Development of the Halal-Logistics Value Creation (HLVC).* Concept for Women's Social-Entrepreneurship in the Aviation Business.

Sabri, N. S. A., Kamardan, M. I. F., Wong, S. X., Azman, N. F., Akhir, F. N. M., Othman, N., Awang, N., Kuroki, Y., & Hara, H. (2023). Future aspects of insects' ingestion in Malaysia and Indonesia for human well-being and religion regulation. *Future Foods : a Dedicated Journal for Sustainability in Food Science*, *8*, 100267. DOI: 10.1016/j.fufo.2023.100267

Safei, A. A., & Himayaturohmah, E. (2023). Development of Environmentally Friendly Culture in the Islamic Boarding School through Social Intervention Strategy. *Al-Hayat: Journal of Islamic Education*, *7*(1), 1. Advance online publication. DOI: 10.35723/ajie.v7i1.323

Saffinee, S. S., Jamaludin, M. A., Rosli, N. L. I., Amid, A., & Has-Yun Hashim, K. S. (2024). *Sustainable and ethical vicegerency in halal tourism practices*. Journal of Event. *Tourism and Hospitality Studies*, *4*, 111–126. DOI: 10.32890/jeth2024.4.8

Sahabi, A., & Baide, K. (2021). Al-Amwal According to the Qur'an: Using the Maudhu'i Method. *Talaa Journal of Islamic Finance*, *1*(1), 1–16. DOI: 10.54045/talaa.v1i1.253

Şahin, A., Zehir, C., & Kitapçi, H. (2011). The effects of brand experiences, trust and satisfaction on building brand loyalty; an empirical research on global brands. *Procedia: Social and Behavioral Sciences*, *24*, 1288–1301. DOI: 10.1016/j.sbspro.2011.09.143

Sai, Y. (2014). Policy, practice and perceptions of qingzhen (halal) in China. *Online Journal of Research in Islamic Studies*, *1*(2), 1–12.

Sakai, M. (2022). To Be or Not to Be a Muslim Mompreneur in Indonesia. In (pp. 207-243). DOI: 10.1007/978-3-031-05954-4_6

Sakai, M. (2022). To Be or Not to Be a Muslim Mompreneur in Indonesia. In.

Salaam Gateway. (2019). *Malaysia's B2B halal e-commerce platforms DagangHalal, Zilzar, AladdinStreet: Where are they now? Standards and Metrology Institute for Islamic Countries. (2021). OIC/SMIIC Standards on Halal Food and Certification.* SMIIC.

Salaheldeen, M. (2022). Opportunities for Halal Entrepreneurs in the Islamic Digital Economy: Future and Trends from a Cultural Entrepreneurship Perspective. In (pp. 95-107).

Salaheldeen, M., & Battour, M. (2024). Fostering innovation capability and sustainable innovation in halal industry: The role of halal entrepreneurs' success. *Journal of Islamic Marketing*, *15*(3), 777–799. DOI: 10.1108/JIMA-12-2022-0323

Salisu, M. A., Showole, R. K., & Moyosore, T. U. (2023). *Green Marketing as an Ethical Practice for Halal Entrepreneurs for a Sustainable Ecosystem.*

Salleh, M. M. M., Ahmad, N. M., & Fadzillah, N. A. (2020). Pewarna makanan dari serangga (cochineal) menurut perspektif halal: Analisis fatwa di beberapa negara ASEAN: Cochineal food coloring from halal perspective: A fatwa analysis in several ASEAN countries. *Journal of Fatwa Management and Research, 19*(1), 1–14. DOI: 10.33102/jfatwa.vol19no1.1

Santos, S. C., & Liguori, E. W. (2020). Entrepreneurial self-efficacy and intentions: Outcome expectations as mediator and subjective norms as moderator. *International Journal of Entrepreneurial Behaviour & Research, 26*(3), 400–415. DOI: 10.1108/IJEBR-07-2019-0436

Saputra, P. P., Setyawan, R. D., & Kurnia, M. (2023). Analysis of the Effectiveness of the One Pesantren One Product (OPOP) Program in Supporting the Economic Empowerment of Islamic Boarding Schools in Belitung Regency. *Society, 11*(2), 2. Advance online publication. DOI: 10.33019/society.v11i2.660

Sarkar, A., Ponnam, A., & Murthy, B. K. (2013). Understanding and measuring romantic brand love. *Journal of Customer Behaviour, 11*(4), 324–347. DOI: 10.13 62/147539212X13546197909985

Sarstedt, M., Richter, N. F., Hauff, S., & Ringle, C. M. (2024). Combined importance–performance map analysis (cIPMA) in partial least squares structural equation modeling (PLS–SEM): a SmartPLS 4 tutorial. *Journal of Marketing Analytics*, 746–760. DOI: 10.1057/s41270-024-00325-y

Saunders, M. N. K., Lewis, P., & Thornhill, A. (2019). *Research methods for business students* (8th ed.). Pearson.

Savirani, A., Rafiq, D., & Baulch, E. (2024). Sharia Cooperatives and Mosque Ecosystems: The Devolution of Halal Entrepreneurship in Indonesia. *Asian Studies Review, 48*(1), 86–101. DOI: 10.1080/10357823.2022.2134296

Sawandi, N., Intan, T. P., Bakar, A. A., Shaari, H., Puteri, T., Saad, R. A. J., & Amran, N. A. (2018). The Delineation of the Islamic Accounting Concepts through the Narrative Reviews Interpretation. *The Journal of Social Sciences Research, 348*(SPI6), 348–352. Advance online publication. DOI: 10.32861/jssr.spi6.348.352

Schneier, B. (2015). *Secrets and Lies Digital Security in a Networked World.* Wiley. DOI: 10.1002/9781119183631

Schrank, J., Hanchai, A., Thongsalab, S., Sawaddee, N., Chanrattanagorn, K., & Ketkaew, C. (2023). Factors of food waste reduction underlying the extended theory of planned behavior: A study of consumer behavior towards the intention to reduce food waste. *Resources*, *12*(8), 93. DOI: 10.3390/resources12080093

Schreibelmayr, S., Moradbakhti, L., & Mara, M. (2023). First impressions of a financial AI assistant: Differences between high trust and low trust users. *Frontiers in Artificial Intelligence*, *6*, 1241290. DOI: 10.3389/frai.2023.1241290 PMID: 37854078

Schutjens, V. A. J. M., & Völker, B. G. M. (2010). Space and social capital: The degree of locality in entrepreneurs' contacts and its consequences for firm success. *European Planning Studies*, *18*(6), 941–963. DOI: 10.1080/09654311003701480

Scott, W. R. (1987). The Adolescence of Institutional Theory. *Administrative Science Quarterly*, *32*(4), 493. DOI: 10.2307/2392880

Sehgal, A., La, H., Louis, S., & Nguyen, H. (2019). Deep reinforcement learning using genetic algorithm for parameter optimization. *2019 Third IEEE International Conference on Robotic Computing (IRC)*, 596–601. DOI: 10.1109/IRC.2019.00121

Sekaran, U., & Bougie, R. (2016). *Research methods for business: A skill-building approach* (7th ed.). Wiley.

Shabbir, M. S. (2023). Contemporary Discourse of Halal and Islamic Entrepreneurship: Trends and Future Opportunities. In (pp. 1-263).

Shafin, N., & Kasim, R. (2018). Incorporating Islamic Ethical Elements into the Marketing Mix Paradigm. *Financial Risk and Management Reviews*, *4*(1), 24–33. DOI: 10.18488/journal.89.2018.41.24.33

Shah, S. A., Bhutto, M. H., & Azhar, S. M. (2022). Integrative review of Islamic marketing. *Journal of Islamic Marketing*, *13*(6), 1264–1287. DOI: 10.1108/JIMA-07-2020-0216

Shahzad, A., Naseer, S., & Khurshid, A. (2019). Friend or Foe: An Islamic Ethical Perspective on the Online Consumers' Reviews. *Journal of Islamic Business and Management*, *9*(1). Advance online publication. DOI: 10.26501/jibm/2019.0901-013

Shams, S., Sahu, J. N., & Mubarak, N. M. (2024). A route for energy recovery from municipal solid waste and developing a framework for waste management in Brunei Darussalam. *Scientific Reports*, *14*(1), 19767. DOI: 10.1038/s41598-024-70845-1 PMID: 39187687

Sharma, A. K., & Sharma, R. (2023). Considerations in artificial intelligence-based marketing: An ethical perspective. *Applied Marketing Analytics*, *9*(2), 162–172. DOI: 10.69554/RAPQ3226

Sheikh, H., Prins, C., & Schrijvers, E. (2023). Artificial intelligence: definition and background. In Mission, A. I. (Ed.), *The new system technology* (pp. 15–41). Springer.

Sholikah, S., Syukur, F., & Junaedi, M. (2021). Islamic education marketing discourse from maslahah perspective. *Nadwa: Jurnal Pendidikan Islam, 14*(02).

Sholikhin, M., & Amijaya, R. N. F. (2019). E-Commerce Based on the Law of Buying and Selling in Islam. *KnE Social Sciences*, *3*(13), 1360. DOI: 10.18502/kss.v3i13.4290

Shompa, Z. A., Akbar, M. A., & Mohadis, H. M. (2025). Harmonizing Maqasid al-Shari'ah with Sustainable Waste Management Practices: A Conceptual Framework for Principles and Implementation. *International Journal of Islamic and Middle Eastern Finance and Management*, *18*(1), 142–165. DOI: 10.1108/IMEFM-02-2024-0061

Shuaib, A. J., & Badmus, S. S. (2022). Al-Ghazālī's Perspective of Salam and Its Relevance to E-Commerce in Nigeria. *Journal of Islamic Economic and Business Research*, 2(2), 156–171. DOI: 10.18196/jiebr.v2i2.62

Sikandar, H., Kohar, U. H. A., Sanda, G., Salman, A., Cilan, T., Shabbir, M. S., & Ramos-Meza, C. S. (2024). Eco-innovation in Small and Medium Enterprises (SMEs): A Systematic Literature Review. *Journal of the Knowledge Economy*, *15*(2), 5841–5863. DOI: 10.1007/s13132-023-01367-w

Silins, E., Horwood, L. J., Najman, J. M., Patton, G. C., Toumbourou, J. W., Olsson, C. A., Hutchinson, D. M., Degenhardt, L., Fergusson, D., Becker, D., Boden, J. M., Borschmann, R., Plotnikova, M., Youssef, G. J., Tait, R. J., Clare, P., Hall, W. D., & Mattick, R. P. (2018). Adverse Adult Consequences Of Different Alcohol Use Patterns In Adolescence: An Integrative Analysis Of Data To Age 30 Years From Four Australasian Cohorts. *Addiction (Abingdon, England)*, *113*(10), 1811–1825. DOI: 10.1111/add.14263 PMID: 29749666

Singh, D., Mosahari, P. V., Sharma, P., Neog, K., & Bora, U. (2024). Comparative genomic and phylogenetic analysis of the complete mitochondrial genome of Cricula trifenestrata (Helfer) among lepidopteran insects. *Genome*, *67*(11), 424–439. Advance online publication. DOI: 10.1139/gen-2023-0037 PMID: 39047299

Singh, P., & Singh, V. (2024). The power of AI: Enhancing customer loyalty through satisfaction and efficiency. *Cogent Business & Management*, *11*(1), 2326107. DOI: 10.1080/23311975.2024.2326107

Sipos, D. (2025). The Effects of AI-Powered Personalization on Consumer Trust, Satisfaction, and Purchase Intent. *European Journal of Applied Science. Engineering and Technology*, *3*(2), 14–24.

Slade, J., & Alleyne, E. (2023). The Psychological Impact Of Slaughterhouse Employment: A Systematic Literature Review. In *Trauma, Violence, And Abuse* (Vol. 24, Issue 2). Https://Doi.Org/10.1177/15248380211030243

Smith, R. (2004). Rural rogues: A case story on the "smokies" trade). *International Journal of Entrepreneurial Behaviour & Research*, *10*(4), 294–311. DOI: 10.1108/13552550410544231

Sobari, N., Kurniati, A., & Usman, H. (2022). The influence of Islamic attributes and religious commitments toward halal wellness services customer satisfaction and loyalty. *Journal of Islamic Marketing*, *13*(1), 177–197. DOI: 10.1108/JIMA-11-2018-0221

Sodawan, A., & Hsu, R. L. W. (2022). Atribut Ramah Halal dan Niat Berkunjung Muslim: Menggali Peran Nilai yang Dirasakan dan Kepercayaan terhadap Destinasi. *Sustainability (Swiss)*, *14*(19). Advance online publication. DOI: 10.3390/su141912002

Sodikin, M. (2020). Competitive Advantages of Sharia Banks: Role of Ihsan Behaviour and Digital Marketing in the New Normal. *Journal of Digital Marketing and Halal Industry*, *2*(1), 1–14. DOI: 10.21580/jdmhi.2020.2.1.5769

Sohail, M. S. (2001). Strategies for Expanding and Promoting Business to and Beyond Muslim Markets. SSRN Electronic Journal. https://papers.ssrn.com/sol3/Delivery.cfm/SSRN_ID2649547_code811236.pdf?abstractid=2649547&mirid=1&type=2

Sohail, N., Haque, A., & Aziz, S. (2024). Impact of diffusion of innovation among Pakistani consumers' adoption of Halal cosmetics. *Journal of Education and Social Sciences*, *26*(1), 11–21.

Somani, P. P., Behare, N., & Iyer, V. H. (2025). From Purchase to Metamorphosis: Cultivating Loyalty via Consumer Engagement and Experience. In *Resiliency Strategies for Long-Term Business Success* (pp. 233–256). IGI Global.

Soonsan, N., Jumani, Z. A., Prasankarn, H., Thoomthong, T., & Tantha, B. (2025). Promoting Phuket as a halal destination: A perspective of SME's entrepreneur. *Journal of Islamic Marketing*, *16*(10), 2837–2857. Advance online publication. DOI: 10.1108/JIMA-06-2024-0239

Sosianika, A., & Amalia, F. A. (2020). Uncovering Indonesian Millennial's Halal Food Purchase Intention: Halal Value and Halal Logo as the Antecedents. *International Journal of Applied Business Research*, *2*(01), 31–45. DOI: 10.35313/ijabr.v2i01.91

Souki, G. Q., Antonialli, L. M., Barbosa, A. A. da S., & Oliveira, A. S. (2020). Impacts of the perceived quality by consumers' of à la carte restaurants on their attitudes and behavioural intentions. *Asia Pacific Journal of Marketing and Logistics*, *32*(2), 301–321. DOI: 10.1108/APJML-11-2018-0491

Stancu, V., Haugaard, P., & Lähteenmäki, L. (2016). Determinants of consumer food waste behaviour: Two routes to food waste. *Appetite*, *96*, 7–17. DOI: 10.1016/j.appet.2015.08.025 PMID: 26299713

Stefan, V., Van Herpen, E., Tudoran, A. A., & Lähteenmäki, L. (2013). Avoiding food waste by Romanian consumers: The importance of planning and shopping routines. *Food Quality and Preference*, *28*(1), 375–381. DOI: 10.1016/j.foodqual.2012.11.001

Stephenson, M. L. (2014). Menguraikan "Perhotelan Islami": Perkembangan, Tantangan, dan Peluang. *Manajemen Pariwisata*, *40*. Advance online publication. DOI: 10.1016/j.tourman.2013.05.002

Stevenson, D. (2004). "Civic gold" rush: Cultural planning and the politics of the third way. *International Journal of Cultural Policy*, *10*(1), 119–131. DOI: 10.1080/1028663042000212364

Suandi, E., Herri, H., Yulihasri, Y., & Syafrizal, S. (2023). An empirical investigation of Islamic marketing ethics and convergence marketing as key factors in the improvement of Islamic banks performance. *Journal of Islamic Marketing*, *14*(6), 1438–1462. DOI: 10.1108/JIMA-07-2021-0225

Suban, S. A., Madhan, K., & Shagirbasha, S. (2023). Analisis Bibliometrik Pariwisata Halal dan Islam. *International Hospitality Review*, *37*(2). Advance online publication. DOI: 10.1108/IHR-05-2021-0038

Suhanda, R., & Fahrullah, A. (2020). Islamic Business Ethics on Customer Retention. DOI: 10.2991/icracos-19.2020.12

Suhartini, E., Hertiani, E., Djuniarsono, R., Rumatiga, H., & Nurfajrina, S. P. M. (2024). Analysis of Halal Certification for Micro and Small Business Actors from the Perspective of Maslahah Principles and Legal Certainty Theory. *Al-'Adalah, 21*(2), 401–426. DOI: 10.24042/adalah.v21i2.23442

Suhartini, E., Hertiani, E., Djuniarsono, R., Rumatiga, H., & PM, N. S. (2024). Analysis of Halal Certification for Micro and Small Business Actors from the Perspective of Maslahah Principles and Legal Certainty. *Al-'Adalah, 21*(2), 401-426.

Suhendri, & Indra. (2024). Halal Certification, Halal Understanding, and the Preference in Buying Halal Food Products: A Case in Indonesia. *Halal and Sustainability, 1*(1). DOI: 10.58968/hs.v1i1.424

Suki, N. M. (2014). Does celebrity credibility influence Muslim and non-Muslim consumers' attitudes toward brands and purchase intention? *Journal of Islamic Marketing*, *5*(2), 227–240. DOI: 10.1108/JIMA-04-2013-0024

Sukri, I. F. (2021). Implementation Of The Job Creation Law On The Implementation Of Halal Certification And Halal Products In Indonesia. *National Law Magazine, 51*(1), 73–94. Https://Doi.Org/10.33331/Mhn.V51i1.139

Sulaiman, N. S. (2023). Halal Industrial Food Waste Management: Lesson Learnt From Japan. *Dinar: Jurnal Ekonomi dan Keuangan Islam, 10*(1), 17-33.

Sulaiman, S. M., Muhammad, A. D., & Sabiu, T. T. (2020). Islamic Business Ethics Practice among Muslim Entrepreneurs in Kano Metropolis, Nigeria. [IJIEF]. *International Journal of Islamic Economics and Finance*, *3*(3). Advance online publication. DOI: 10.18196/ijief.3233

Sulistyawati, D. R., Mutamimah, M., & Hartono, S. (2024). Maslahah radical innovation: Breakthrough to achieve corporate sustainability in small and medium industries (SMI) batik in central Java province. *Edelweiss Applied Science and Technology*, *8*(6), 8740–8751. DOI: 10.55214/25768484.v8i6.3865

Sumardi, R. S., Mahomed, A. S. B., & Aziz, Y. A. (2025). Bibliometric Analysis of Stimulus-Organism-Response Theory: Past Developments, Current Applications, and Future Trends. *International Journal of Academic Research in Business & Social Sciences*, *15*(01), 555–569. DOI: 10.6007/IJARBSS/v15-i1/23784

Sumarliah, E., Li, T., Wang, B., Fauziyah, F., & Indriya, I. (2022). Blockchain-empowered halal fashion traceability system in Indonesia. *International Journal of Information Systems and Supply Chain Management*, *15*(2), 1–24. Advance online publication. DOI: 10.4018/IJISSCM.287628

Sunardi, D., Bhari, A., & Abd Wakil, M. N. B. (2024). Legal Awareness of Micro and Small Enterprise Operators Regarding Halal Certification: A Maslaha Perspective. *Ijtihad: Jurnal Wacana Hukum Islam dan Kemanusiaan, 24*(1), 23-45.

Sundjaja, A. M., Utomo, P., & Colline, F. (2025). The determinant factors of continuance use of customer service chatbot in Indonesia e-commerce: Extended expectation confirmation theory. *Journal of Science and Technology Policy Management*, *16*(1), 182–203. DOI: 10.1108/JSTPM-04-2024-0137

Sunmola, F., Baryannis, G., Tan, A., Co, K., & Papadakis, E. (2025). Holistic framework for blockchain-based halal compliance in supply chains enabled by artificial intelligence. *Systems, 13*(1), 21. DOI: 10.3390/systems13010021

Supriani, I. (2024). *How social media in fl uencers form Muslim consumers ' halal cosmetics purchase intention : religiosity concern*. DOI: 10.1108/JIMA-02-2024-0085

Susanto, M. A.M. Arif Susanto. (2024). Islam dan Teknologi: Tantangan Etika dan Adaptasi dalam Era Digital. *Al-Muharrik, 1*(2), 95–102. DOI: 10.59829/dq88ve47

Susanty, A., et al. (2025). Consumer acceptance of halal food traceability systems. Cleaner Logistics and Supply Chain.

Susanty, A., Puspitasari, N. B., & Rosyada, Z. F. (2024). Prediction of the performance of halal food industry using a system dynamics simulation model. *Journal of Islamic Marketing, 15*(11), 2785–2822. Advance online publication. DOI: 10.1108/JIMA-02-2023-0039

Susilo, A. A., & Wulansari, R. (2020). Sejarah Pesantren Sebagai Lembaga Pendidikan Islam di Indonesia. *Tamaddun: Jurnal Kebudayaan dan Sastra Islam, 20*(2), Article 2. DOI: 10.19109/tamaddun.v20i2.6676

Swadjaja, I., Sawarjuwono, T., & Ludigdo, U. (2019). Model of Islamic Wealth Management Based on Maqasid al-Shariah. *Journal of Innovation in Business and Economics, 3*(2). Advance online publication. DOI: 10.22219/jibe.v3i02.7465

Swidler, L. (1983). The dialogue decalogue: Ground rules for interreligious dialogue. *Journal of Ecumenical Studies, 20*(1), 1–4.

Syahr, Z. H. A., Syaifullah, D. H., Buyamin, & Sally, N. U. (2023). Sustainable Development Goals Concept Overview In The Digital Service Halal Certification In Indonesia. *Springer Link*, 73–83. Https://Doi.Org/10.1007/978-981-99-5146-8_6

Syahril, S., & Nugroho, M. (2024). *Analysis of Halal Marketing Strategy for Food Products in Sharia-Based MSMEs*. Seriat Ekonomisi. DOI: 10.35335/qaz5a542

Syaiful Huda, I. A. i., Saadah, M., Sugiarto, A., Bin Ibrahim, M. H., Prasad, R. R., Putra, A. K., & Budianto, A. (2024). Revealing halal certification oversight gaps for MSEs through ArcGIS dashboard integration. *Indonesian Journal of Halal Research, 6*(2), 58–69. DOI: 10.15575/ijhar.v6i2.33308

Syarifah, L., AJR, A. R., Solekah, N. A., & Wahyuni, S. S. (2024). Implementation of Eco-Innovation, Eco-Commitment, Eco-Opportunity in the Islamic Boarding School Environment: A Phenomenological Study on the Raudhatul Madinah Entrepreneur Islamic Boarding School. *ULIL ALBAB : Jurnal Ilmiah Multidisiplin, 4*(1), 149–161. DOI: 10.56799/jim.v4i1.6558

Syed Hamzah, S. A., Johari, S., Yusof, Y. A., Ramlan, M. A., & Mohd Azmi, P. U. B. (2024). a Research Trend: Talent Management Practice in Halal Management. *International Journal of Entrepreneurship and Management Practices, 7*(28), 559–584. DOI: 10.35631/IJEMP.728040

Tabelessy, W. (2023). The role of food quality and halal certificates to improve consumer satisfaction and loyalty. *International Journal of Social Service and Research, 3*(05), 1127–1136. DOI: 10.46799/ijssr.v3i5.371

Talib, M. S. A., Hamid, A. B. A., Zulfakar, M. H., & Chin, T. A. (2015). Barriers to Halal logistics operation: Views from Malaysian logistics experts. *International Journal of Logistics Systems and Management, 22*(2), 193–209. DOI: 10.1504/IJLSM.2015.071545

Tang, C., Yang, D., Liao, H., Sun, H., Liu, C., Wei, L., & Li, F. (2019). Edible insects as a food source: A review. *Food Production, Processing and Nutrition, 1*(1), 8. DOI: 10.1186/s43014-019-0008-1

Tan, P. K., & Lim, C. M. (2023). Factors that affect user satisfaction of using e-commerce chatbot: A study on generation Z. *International Journal of Business and Technology Management, 5*(1), 292–303.

Tarip, I. (2024). Theorizing Islamic entrepreneurship from an Islamic governance perspective. *International Journal of Islamic and Middle Eastern Finance and Management, 17*(2), 274–291. DOI: 10.1108/IMEFM-05-2023-0172

Taujiharrahman, D., Mujibatun, S., & Agriyanto, R. (2022). The Combined Effect of Expectation Confirmation Model and Islam{\i}c Theory of Consumer Behavior on Continuance Intent of M and Internet Banking Users of Islamic Banks. *Annual International Conference on Islamic Economics and Business (AICIEB), 2*(1), 276–287.

Teepapal, T. (2025). AI-driven personalization: Unraveling consumer perceptions in social media engagement. *Computers in Human Behavior, 165*, 108549. DOI: 10.1016/j.chb.2024.108549

Teixeira, A. A. (2011). Mapping the (in) visible college (s) in the field of entrepreneurship. *Scientometrics, 89*(1), 1–36. DOI: 10.1007/s11192-011-0445-3

Tella, A., & Olasina, G. (2014). Predicting users' continuance intention toward e-payment system: An extension of the technology acceptance model. [IJISSC]. *International Journal of Information Systems and Social Change*, *5*(1), 47–67. DOI: 10.4018/ijissc.2014010104

Tello, A., Aganovic, K., Parniakov, O., Carter, A., Heinz, V., & Smetana, S. (2021). Product development and environmental impact of an insect-based milk alternative. *Future Foods : a Dedicated Journal for Sustainability in Food Science*, *4*, 100080. DOI: 10.1016/j.fufo.2021.100080

Teodorescu, D., Aivaz, K.-A., Vancea, D. P. C., Condrea, E., Dragan, C., & Olteanu, A. C. (2023). Consumer trust in AI algorithms used in e-commerce: A case study of college students at a Romanian public university. *Sustainability (Basel)*, *15*(15), 11925. DOI: 10.3390/su151511925

The Holy Bible. (2001). [Grand Rapids: Zondervan.]. *Leviticus*, *11*, 1–47.

The Jordanian Ifta' Committee. (2016). Hukm al-mawad al-mustakhrajah min al-a'yan al-najasah. Retrieved from https://www.aliftaa.jo/research-fatwas/3240/

Thoha, A. F. K. (2024). Visionary Leadership and Dynamic Capabilities: Transforming Pesantren into a Social Enterprise. [International Journal of Islamic Business Ethics]. *IJIBE*, *9*(1), 1. Advance online publication. DOI: 10.30659/ijibe.9.1.46-62

Tieman, M. (2011). The application of halal in supply chain management: In-depth interviews. *Journal of Islamic Marketing*, *2*(2), 186–195. DOI: 10.1108/17590831111139893

Tieman, M., & Van Nistelrooy, M. (2014). Perception of Malaysian food manufacturers toward halal logistics. *Journal of International Food & Agribusiness Marketing*, *26*(3), 218–233. DOI: 10.1080/08974438.2013.833572

Tobing, F., Fauzan, H., Simatupang, K., & Aulia, R. (2024). The Role of Artificial Intelligence in the Halal Industry. *Information Management and Business Review*, *16*(3), 159–166. DOI: 10.22610/imbr.v16i3(I)S.4050

Tommasetti, A., Singer, P., Troisi, O., & Maione, G. (2018). Extended theory of planned behavior (ETPB): Investigating customers' perception of restaurants' sustainability by testing a structural equation model. *Sustainability (Basel)*, *10*(7), 2580. DOI: 10.3390/su10072580

Toshmirzaev, D., Ahn, Y. J., Kiatkawsin, K., Sutherland, I., & Zielinski, S. (2022). The effect of corporate social responsibility on trustful relationship, supportive communication intention, and brand loyalty of ethnic halal restaurants. *Frontiers in Psychology*, *13*(October), 1–12. DOI: 10.3389/fpsyg.2022.1022835 PMID: 36312062

Truzzi, C., Macedo, M. L. R., & De Oliveira, C. R. (2019). Nutritional composition of edible insects: A systematic review. *Critical Reviews in Food Science and Nutrition*, *59*(1), 1–17. DOI: 10.1080/10408398.2018.1437068 PMID: 28799777

Tsurayya Adilah, A., & Dyah Kumalasari, I. (2023). Evaluation Of The Implementation Of The Halal Assurance System Based On The HAS 23000 Standard Criteria In Sakura Mochi Msmes. *Journal Of Halal Agroindustry*, *9*(1), 22–32. Https://Doi.Org/10.30997/JAH.V9I1.5528

Tumiran, M. A., Ponari, M. H. A., Mohamad, S. P., & Mohamed, Z. I. (2025). Integrating Sustainable Agriculture and Maqasid al-Shariah Principles for Ethical and Environmental Stewardship. *QJSSH*, *6*(3), 79–95. Advance online publication. DOI: 10.55197/qjssh.v6i3.654

Turgut, S. S., Myustedzhebov, A., & Feyissa, A. H. (2025). Low-cost multispectral sensor reveals cold chain breaks, meat type, and storage time in chicken meat samples. *Food Control*, *167*, 110816. DOI: 10.1016/j.foodcont.2024.110816

Uddin, M. B. (2019). Customer loyalty in the fast food restaurants of Bangladesh. *British Food Journal*, *121*(11), 2791–2808. DOI: 10.1108/BFJ-02-2019-0140

Ullah, S., Haroon, M., Hussain, S., & Rehman, A. U. (2023). Islamic labelling and corporate governance: A perspective of Shariah compliance firms. *Journal of Islamic Accounting and Business Research*, *14*(6), 849–867. DOI: 10.1108/JIABR-03-2021-0108

UN Climate Change. (2024). Food loss and waste account for 8-10% of annual global greenhouse gas emissions; cost USD 1 trillion annually. Unfccc.int. https://unfccc.int/news/food-loss-and-waste-account-for-8-10-of-annual-global-greenhouse-gas-emissions-cost-usd-1-trillion

UNEP. (2021, March 4). UNEP Food Waste Index Report 2021. UNEP – UN Environment Programme. https://www.unep.org/resources/report/unep-food-waste-index-report-2021

United Nations World Tourism Organization (UNWTO). (2024). International Tourism to Reach Pre-Pandemic Levels in 2024. World Tourism Barometer. UNWTO. https://www.unwto.org/news/international-tourism-to-reach-pre-pandemic-levels-in-2024

Utami, P., & Basrowi, B. (2021). Sharia Marketing Mix: A Model of the Digital Marketing Management Strategy of Zakat. *Mabsya Jurnal Manajemen Bisnis Syariah*, *3*(1), 44–59. DOI: 10.24090/mabsya.v3i1.4688

Utomo, S. B., Sekaryuni, R., Widarjono, A., Tohirin, A., & Sudarsono, H. (2021). Promoting Islamic financial ecosystem to improve halal industry performance in Indonesia: A demand and supply analysis. *Journal of Islamic Marketing*, *12*(5), 992–1011. DOI: 10.1108/JIMA-12-2019-0259

Uwai, K., Okuyama, Y., Nakano, H., Furukawa, K., Hiroshima, E., Azuma, H., Watanabe, M., Matsumoto, T., Tokiwa, M., & Takeshita, M. (2014). Biotransformation of organic compounds in vivo using larvae of beetles (*Allomyrina dichotoma*) as biocatalysts. *Biocatalysis and Agricultural Biotechnology*, *3*(4), 129–133. DOI: 10.1016/j.bcab.2014.09.005

Vafaei-Zadeh, A., Nikbin, D., Wong, S. L., & Hanifah, H. (2024). Investigating factors influencing AI customer service adoption: An integrated model of stimulus—organism—response (SOR) and task-technology fit (TTF) theory. *Asia Pacific Journal of Marketing and Logistics*.

Van Bruinessen, M. (1995). *Kitab Kuning Pesantren dan Tarekat: Tradisi-Tradisi Islam di Indonesia*. Mizan.

Vandeweyer, D., De Boeck, J., & Knapen, S. (2021). Food safety challenges in the use of edible insects for human consumption. *Journal of Food Safety*, *41*(3), e12854. DOI: 10.1111/jfs.12854

Vandeweyer, D., Lievens, B., & Campenhout, L. V. (2020). Microbiological safety of industrially reared insects for food: identification of bacterial endospores and targeted detection of foodborne viruses. https://doi.org/DOI: 10.1101/2020.04.22.055236

Vasudevan, H., & Aslan, I. (2021). Cosmetology advertising perspectives: Application of ethical theories during COVID-19 crisis. *Marketing and Management of Innovations*, *5*(4), 121–136. DOI: 10.21272/mmi.2021.4-10

Venkataraman, S. (2019). The distinctive domain of entrepreneurship research. In *Seminal ideas for the next twenty-five years of advances* (pp. 5–20). Emerald Publishing Limited. DOI: 10.1108/S1074-754020190000021009

Venkateswaran, N. (2023). AI-driven personalization in customer relationship management: Challenges and opportunities. *Journal of Theoretical and Applied Information Technology*, *101*(18), 7392–7399.

Very. (2025). Menteri Pariwisata Kunjungi Desa Wisata Pentingsari, Peraih Community Best Tourism dari ASEAN Tourism Award 2025. indonews.id, 12 Mei 2025. https://indonews.id/artikel/344004/Menteri-Pariwisata-Kunjungi-Desa-Wisata-Pentingsari-Peraih-Community-Best-Tourism-dari-ASEAN-Tourism-Award-2025

Vinzi, E. (2013). Editorial Partial Least Squares Structural Equation Modeling : Rigorous Applications. *Better Results and Higher Acceptance.*, *46*, 1–12. DOI: 10.1016/j.lrp.2013.01.001

Visschers, V. H., Wickli, N., & Siegrist, M. (2016). Sorting out food waste behaviour: A survey on the motivators and barriers of self-reported amounts of food waste in households. *Journal of Environmental Psychology*, *45*, 66–78. DOI: 10.1016/j.jenvp.2015.11.007

Vivekananda, S. (2012). *The Yoga Sutras of Patanjali*. CreateSpace Independent Publishing.

Voak, A. (2021). Fake: The Rise of Food Fraud in the Halal Supply Chain. [Halal Awareness Opinion Research and Initiative]. *Nusantara Halal Journal*, *2*(2), 82–88. DOI: 10.17977/um060.2021v2p082-088

Wahyuni, H. C., Rosid, M. A., Azara, R., & Voak, A. (2025). Blockchain technology design based on food safety and halal risk analysis in the beef supply chain with FMEA-FTA. *Journal of Engineering Research (Kuwait)*, *13*(2), 590–595. Advance online publication. DOI: 10.1016/j.jer.2024.02.002

Wajon, E., & Richter, J. (2019). *Students' Intention to Reduce Food Waste: An approach with an extended version of the Theory of Planned Behavior*. Uppsala University.

Wang, C., Ahmad, S. F., Ayassrah, A. Y. A. B. A., Awwad, E. M., Irshad, M., Ali, Y. A., Al-Razgan, M., Khan, Y., & Han, H. (2023). An empirical evaluation of technology acceptance model for Artificial Intelligence in E-commerce. *Heliyon*, *9*(8), e18349. DOI: 10.1016/j.heliyon.2023.e18349 PMID: 37520947

Wang, Y. (2024). Islamization of the Term " "(Qing Zhen): Its Analysis for Purity and Authenticity for Muslim in China. *Journal of Al-Tamaddun*, *19*(1), 273–295. DOI: 10.22452/JAT.vol19no1.20

Wibowo, W., Ariga, A., Azizah, S.N., Panggabean, N.A. and Irfaniah, N.R. (2025). Kampung Ramadhan Jogokariyan (KRJ): Peran Manajemen Masjid dalam Pariwisata Ramah Muslim dan Ekonomi Lokal. AKUA: Jurnal Akuntasi dan Keuangan, 4(2), pp.161–170. .DOI: 10.54259/akua.v4i2.4258

Wibowo, W., Choiri, A., Aminuddin, A., Emilda, P. and Salim, F. (2025). Sustainable Islamic tourism: Jogokariyan Ramadan Village as a sustainable religious and economic tourism destination (case study in Jogokariyan Ramadan Village). Ecopreneur: Jurnal Ekonomi dan Bisnis Islam, 6(1), pp.61–76. .DOI: 10.47453/ecopreneur.v6i1.3091

Wibowo, A., Muhammad, D. R. A., Lestari, E., & Karsidi, R. (2021). Community empowerment based on religious ecology leading to sustainable agricultural development (A case study of Isy Karima Islamic boarding school in Karanganyar, Central Java). *IOP Conference Series. Earth and Environmental Science*, *905*(1), 012035. DOI: 10.1088/1755-1315/905/1/012035

Widiyanti, E., Cahyadin, M., Santoso, A. I., Santoso, R. E., Widyamurti, N., & Ertimi, B. (2024). Synergy of Digital Literacy and E-Commerce in Boosting SME Performance. *EcceS. Economics Social and Development Studies*, *11*(1), 49–72.

Wijayanti, M., Giningroem, D. S. W. P., & Setyawati, N. W. (2023). Brand Fidelity Millennial Generation on Halal Cosmetic Brand Through Brand Experience and Brand Trust: The Role of Brand Love as Mediation. *Majalah Ilmiah Bijak*, *20*(1), 88–96. DOI: 10.31334/bijak.v20i1.3110

William, M., Mokoboki, H. K., Manyeula, F., Mabelebele, M., & Sebola, N. A. (2023). Carcass Characteristics And Meat Quality Of Weaned New Zealand Rabbits Supplemented With Moringa Oleifera Leaves Meal. *Italian Journal of Animal Science*, *22*(1), 463–471. DOI: 10.1080/1828051X.2023.2206416

Wilson, G., Johnson, O., & Brown, W. (2024). The Impact of Artificial Intelligence on Digital Marketing Strategies. *Journal of Digital Marketing*, *15*(3), 112–128. DOI: 10.20944/preprints202408.0276.v1

Wilson, J. A. J., & Grant, D. (2013). Islamic marketing – a challenger to the classical marketing canon? *Journal of Islamic Marketing*, *4*(1), 7–21. DOI: 10.1108/17590831311306327

Wilson, J. A. J., & Liu, J. (2010). Shaping the halal into a brand? *Journal of Islamic Marketing*, *1*(2), 107–123. DOI: 10.1108/17590831011055851

Wu, C. M. E., & Teng, C. C. (2022). Reducing food waste in buffet restaurants: A corporate management approach. *Foods*, *12*(1), 162. DOI: 10.3390/foods12010162 PMID: 36613378

Wulandari, S. R., & Hasriadi, . (2022). Online Marketing Strategy in a Sharia Economic Perspective. ETDC. *Indonesian Journal of Research and Educational Review*, *2*(1), 28–41. DOI: 10.51574/ijrer.v2i1.1166

Wu, S., Zhou, X., & Zhu, Q. (2023). Green credit and enterprise environmental and economic performance: The mediating role of eco-innovation. *Journal of Cleaner Production*, *382*, 135248. DOI: 10.1016/j.jclepro.2022.135248

Xu, Y., Geldsetzer, P., Manne-Goehler, J., Theilmann, M., Marcus, M. E., Zhumadilov, Z., Quesnel-Crooks, S., Mwalim, O., Moghaddam, S. S., Koolaji, S., Karki, K. B., Farzadfar, F., Yuanitasari, D., & Sardjono, A. (2023). Halal Regulation Challenges For Micro And Small Business Actors: A Socio-Legal Study In Kupang East Nusa Tenggara. *DIURNAL ACTA Journal Of Notary Law, 6*(2), 254–267. Https://Doi .Org/10.23920/ACTA.V6I2.1474

Yahaya, S. (2020). Intrinsic factors affecting the acceptance of muslim small entrepreneurs in kelantan towards ar-rahnu. *International Journal of Business and Society*, *21*(2), 507–520. DOI: 10.33736/ijbs.3268.2020

Yahaya, S., & Mohamad, S. S. (2019). Factors influence the acceptance of al-rahn among entrepreneurs. *Academy of Entrepreneurship Journal*, *25*(2), 1–6. DOI: 10.1080/85072152424

Yang, J., Chen, Y., Zhang, L., Zhou, S., You, L., & Song, J. (2025). Application of edible insects to food products: A review on the functionality, bioactivity and digestibility of insect proteins under high-pressure/ultrasound processing. *Food Chemistry*, *468*, 142469. DOI: 10.1016/j.foodchem.2024.142469 PMID: 39693885

Yasin, F., & Abdelkhair, F. (2024). *Celebrate Branding: Brand Experience and Brand Trust Mediated by Brand Awareness Farah Yasin Farah Abdelkhair.*

Yasin, R., Ariffin, Z. Z., Mohamed, H. A.-B., Zawawi, Z., Ghani, S. A., & Liaw, J. O. H. (2025). Islamic Values in Entrepreneurial Marketing Strategy. In *Dynamic Strategies for Entrepreneurial Marketing* (pp. 311–330). IGI Global Scientific Publishing. DOI: 10.4018/979-8-3693-3936-7.ch015

Yazici, G. N., & Ozer, M. S. (2021). Using edible insects in the production of cookies, biscuits, and crackers: A review. *Biology and Life Sciences Forum, 6*(1), 80.

Yin, J., & Qiu, X. (2021). AI technology and online purchase intention: Structural equation model based on perceived value. *Sustainability (Basel)*, *13*(10), 5671. DOI: 10.3390/su13105671

Yin, J., Qiu, X., & Wang, Y. (2025). The Impact of AI-Personalized Recommendations on Clicking Intentions: Evidence from Chinese E-Commerce. *Journal of Theoretical and Applied Electronic Commerce Research*, *20*(1), 21. DOI: 10.3390/jtaer20010021

Yin, R. K. (2018). *Case study research and applications: Design and methods* (6th ed.). SAGE Publications.

Yoo, B., & Donthu, N. (2001). Developing and validating a multidimensional consumer-based brand equity scale. *Journal of Business Research*, *52*(1), 1–14. DOI: 10.1016/S0148-2963(99)00098-3

Yoon, Y., & Uysal, M. (2005). Kajian Pengaruh Motivasi dan Kepuasan terhadap Loyalitas Destinasi: Sebuah Model Struktural. *Manajemen Pariwisata*, *26*(1), 45–56. DOI: 10.1016/j.tourman.2003.08.016

Yousef, W. (2018). A thesis submitted in partial fulfilment of the requirements for the degree of Doctor of Philosophy. *English, February*.

Yushaniza, Z., Yusoff, M., Ishak, M. K., & Alezabi, K. A. (2021). The Role of RFID in Green IoT: A Survey on Technologies, Challenges and A Way Forward. *Technology and Engineering Systems Journal*, *6*(1), 17–35.

Yusmazida, M. Y., Omar, M. K., Yusliza, M. Y., Samad, S., & Abdul Mokmin, K. (2025). Developing an Islamic structural capital model: Perspectives from SMEs. *Journal of Islamic Marketing*, *16*(11), 3413–3455. Advance online publication. DOI: 10.1108/JIMA-06-2024-0238

Zaelor, J., & Kitthawee, S. (2018). Growth response to population density in larval stage of darkling beetles (Coleoptera; Tenebrionidae) *Tenebrio molitor* and *Zophobas atratus*. *Agriculture and Natural Resources (Bangkok)*, *52*(6), 603–606. DOI: 10.1016/j.anres.2018.11.004

Zafar, M. B. (2025). *Halal purchasing decisions and consumer behavior : a multi method review*. DOI: 10.1108/JIMA-08-2024-0365

Zafar, M. B., Abu-Hussin, M. F., & Ali, H. (2024). Mapping the research on halal industry: A retrospective analysis. *Journal of Islamic Marketing*. Advance online publication. DOI: 10.1108/JIMA-08-2024-0348

Zafitriani, D. A., Khasanah, K., Abdurrahman, U. K., & Pekalongan, W. (2024). Legal Certainty In The Implementation Of Supervision Of Halal Certified Products In Indonesia. *El_Hisbah, 4*(1). Https://Doi.Org/10.28918/ELHISBAH.V4I1.7551

Zahro, U. C. (2024). *Building A Sharia Entrepreneurial Ecosystem Through Halal Value Chain for MSMEs*. JURNAL PENGABDIAN TEKNOLOGI TEPAT GUNA., DOI: 10.47942/jpttg.v5i3.1793

Zailani, S., Arrifin, Z., Wahid, N. A., Othman, R., & Fernando, Y. (2010). Halal traceability and halal tracking systems in strengthening halal food supply chain for food industry in Malaysia (A review). *Journal of Food Technology*, *8*(3), 74–81. DOI: 10.3923/jftech.2010.74.81

Zailani, S., Iranmanesh, M., Aziz, A. A., & Kanapathy, K. (2017). Halal logistics opportunities and challenges. *Journal of Islamic Marketing*, *8*(1), 127–139. DOI: 10.1108/JIMA-04-2015-0028

Zailani, S., Omar, A., & Kopong, S. (2011). Studi Eksploratif tentang Faktor-Faktor yang Mempengaruhi Ketidakpatuhan terhadap Standar Halal di Kalangan Pengusaha Hotel di Malaysia. *Manajemen Bisnis Internasional*, *5*(1). Advance online publication. DOI: 10.3923/ibm.2011.1.12

Zakaria, N. S., & Othman, A. (2023). *Pelestarian Agama (Hifz Al-Din) dalam Paket Wisata Syariah*. Jurnal Studi Islam Internasional Al-Qanatir.

Zakaria, Z., Majid, M. D. A., Ahmad, Z. A., Jusoh, Z., & Zakaria, N. (2018). Influence of Halal certification on customers' purchase intention. *Revue des Sciences Fondamentales et Appliquées*, *9*(5S), 772. DOI: 10.4314/jfas.v9i5s.55

Zaki, I., Widiastuti, T., Yudha, A. T. R. C., Wijayanti, I., & Mi'raj, D. A. (2020). Implementation of Islamic entrepreneurial culture in Islamic boarding schools. *International Journal of Innovation. Creativity and Change*, *11*(11), 452–469.

Zaki, I., Zusak, M. B. F., Mi'raj, D. A., & Hasib, F. F. (2022). Islamic community-based business cooperation and sustainable development goals: A case of pesantren community in Indonesia. *International Journal of Ethics and Systems*, *38*(4), 621–632. DOI: 10.1108/IJOES-12-2021-0218

Zaki, R. M., & Elseidi, R. I. (2024). *Religiusitas dan niat beli: perspektif kepribadian merek pakaian Islami*. Jurnal Pemașaran Islam., DOI: 10.1108/JIMA-09-2022-0257

Zamani-Farahani, H. & Eid, R. (2016). Muslim World: A Study of Tourism & Pilgrimage Among OIC Member States. Tourism Management Perspectives, vol. 19, part B, pp. 144–149, .DOI: 10.1016/j.tmp.2015.12.009

Zarkasyi, M. R., Kurniawan, D. A., Surya, F., & Anggara, A. (2022). Stakeholders Approach in Halal Tourism Development Strategy: A Case Study in Ponorogo District. *Jurnal Ilmiah Bidang Ilmu Ekonomi, 17*(2), 171–181. http://journal.umpo.ac.id/index.php/ekuilibrium

Zeeshan, A. (2021). Is Islamic Banking Another Marketing Gimmick? *International Journal of Business and Administrative Studies*, *7*(3), 42. DOI: 10.20469/ijbas.7.10004-3

Zehir, C., Şahin, A., Kitapçi, H., & Özçahin, M. (2011). The effects of brand communication and service quality in building brand loyalty through brand trust; the empirical research on global brands. *Procedia: Social and Behavioral Sciences*, *24*, 1218–1231. DOI: 10.1016/j.sbspro.2011.09.142

Zeybekci, N. (2025, 2025, May 16). Halal is also a tool for protecting economic interests. Retrieved from https://russia-islworld.ru/en/novosti/nihat-zeybekci-halal-is-also-a-tool-for-protecting-economic-interests-2025-05-16-49192/

Zhang, S., Peng, M. Y. P., Peng, Y., Zhang, Y., Ren, G., & Chen, C. C. (2020). Expressive Brand Relationship, Brand Love, and Brand Loyalty for Tablet PCs: Building a Sustainable Brand. *Frontiers in Psychology*, *11*(March), 1–10. DOI: 10.3389/fpsyg.2020.00231 PMID: 32210865

Zhang, Y., Zhang, J., & Chen, J. (2013). Critical success factors in IT service management implementation: People, process, and technology perspectives. *Proceedings of International Conference on Service Science, ICSS, April 2013*, 64–68. DOI: 10.1109/ICSS.2013.38

Zidni, A. R., Sholihin, M., Hanafi, S. M., & Maulana, A. I. (2022). *Pariwisata Halal: Tinjauan Literatur yang Sistematis*. https://journal2.uad.ac.id/index.php/ijiefb/article/view/6490

Zimu, F. (2023). Exploring the impact of cultural factors on consumer behavior in E-commerce: A cross-cultural analysis. *Journal of Digitainability* [DREAM]. *Realism & Mastery*, *2*(03), 31–36. DOI: 10.56982/dream.v2i03.90

Zreik, M. (2023). Harnessing Islamic entrepreneurship for the belt and road initiative: Opportunities, challenges, and future directions. In (pp. 119-135).

Zulaikhah, S., Wusko, A. U., & Kusumawati, A. (2023). Pengaruh Citra Destinasi dan Nilai Islam terhadap Nilai Persepsi dan Kepuasan (Survei pada Wisatawan Muslim Wisata Halal di Banyuwangi). *Jurnal Studi Administrasi Publik*, *8*(1). Advance online publication. DOI: 10.21776/ub.jpas.2023.008.01.6

Zulkifli, S. N., & Yusuf, S. N. S. (2023). Maqasid Syariah and Digital Transformation of Halal Supply Chain With Governance Elements. *Proceedings of the International Conference in Technology, Humanities and Management (ICTHM 2023)*, 12-13 June, 2023, Istanbul, Turkey, *131*, 103–115. DOI: 10.15405/epsbs.2023.11.9

Zulvianti, N., Aimon, H., & Abror, A. (2022). The Influence of Environmental and Non-Environmental Factors on Tourist Satisfaction in Halal Tourism Destinations in West Sumatra, Indonesia. *Sustainability (Basel)*, *14*(15), 9185. DOI: 10.3390/su14159185

Zunzunegui, I., Martín-García, J., Santamaría, Ó., & Poveda, J. (2024). Analysis of yellow mealworm (*Tenebrio molitor*) frass as a resource for a sustainable agriculture in the current context of insect farming industry growth. *Journal of Cleaner Production*, *460*, 142608. DOI: 10.1016/j.jclepro.2024.142608

Zuraidah, Z., & Aisyah, E. N. (2022). the Implementation of Islamic Business Ethical Theory in E-Commerce. Advances in Social Science, Education and Humanities Research. *Advances in Social Science, Education and Humanities Research*. Advance online publication. DOI: 10.2991/assehr.k.220206.021

About the Contributors

Ahmad Rafiki is currently as an Associate Professor in Faculty Economics and Business, the Dean of Faculty of Economics and Business and the Head of Islamic Management and Halal Industry Center at Universitas Medan Area, Indonesia. Previously he was an Assistant Professor in Department of Business Administration of University College of Bahrain. He obtained his Bachelor Degree in Business Administration with a major of Marketing from MARA University of Technology (UiTM) and Masters in Management from International Islamic University of Malaysia (IIUM). In March 2014, he completed his thesis for the award of Doctor of Philosophy from Islamic Science University of Malaysia (USIM). He is holding Certified Islamic Marketer (CIMA) from the International Islamic Marketing Association (IIMA). He actively engages with other consultation centers as the co-founders and members such as Islamic Management and Education Center, TAIF Digital Institute of Islamic Finance, and the Indonesian Association of Islamic Economist. He involves in some projects of consultancies on regional planning and development programs by Indonesian governments. Before joining the academic field, he has vast experiences in sales and marketing and business development positions in education sector with Malaysian companies, where he was in charged for the South East Asia sales territory. His research's interest is on the Islamic entrepreneurship, management, marketing and leadership. He has published many chapters of books/authored books and articles/papers related to the field of management, entrepreneurship, small and medium enterprises, leadership and halal industry by international publishers such as IBA-MacMillan, IGI Global, Emerald Publishing, Springer, IntechOpen, Routledge etc. He also became the editorial advisory board and reviewer particularly in reputable publishers of Emerald and Elsevier, and has presented academic papers in various international conference and seminars in several countries. He just won as the Outstanding Reviewer of Literati Awards 2020 by Emerald Publishing.

Hidayatul Ihsan is an Associate Professor and Head of the Accounting Department at Politeknik Negeri Padang, specializing in Islamic accounting, particularly waqf accounting and governance. He holds a Ph.D. and an M.Sc. in Accounting from the International Islamic University Malaysia and a Bachelor's degree from Andalas University, Indonesia. A Chartered Accountant, he is an active member of the Sharia Accountant Compartment at the Indonesian Institute of Chartered Accountants. Dr. Ihsan has contributed to waqf accounting and governance through his research, publications, and community engagement. He is the founder of the Padang State Polytechnic Waqf and an advisor at WaCIDS – Waqf Center for Indonesian Development & Studies. He also serves on the Working Group for Waqf Accounting Standards at the Indonesian Institute of Chartered Accountants and as a Supervisory Board Member of Dharma Andalas Waqf Institution. Previously, he was a member of the Indonesian Waqf Board for West Sumatra.

Azman Ab Rahman is a Professor at the Faculty of Shariah and Law, University of Islamic Sciences Malaysia (USIM) and also holds position as Director at Institute of Fatwa and Halal (IFFAH). He holds a Bachelor Degree from the University of al Al-Bayt, Mafraq, Jordan in the field of Fiqh and Usul. He obtained a Masters and Doctor of Philosophy from the International Islamic University of Malaysia (UIAM) in the field of Fiqh and Usul Fiqh. He has published more than 100 articles in indexed and non-indexed journals and also produced more than 50 academic books in the field of zakat and contemporary fiqh. He has led 50 research grants and member for more than 90 research projects including research grants awarded by USIM, Ministry of Education, other state agencies and private institutions. His outstanding outputs in research were evident from his receiving distinguished awards at national and international levels.

***

Mohamed Syazwan Ab Talib research and teaching focuses primarily on logistics and supply chain management with the inclusion of halal principles and Islamic distribution. His research also encompasses the halal management standard that centred on the association between halal standard implementation and business performance. Syazwan welcomes industry consultation, research collaboration, and academic coaching opportunities for industry professionals and fellow academics.

Hussein 'Azeemi Abdullah Thaidi is the Director of the Maslahah Centre for Social Finance and Well-being (MASLAHAH) at Universiti Sains Islam Malaysia. He also serves as a Shariah Committee Member at BNP Paribas Malaysia. Dr. Hussein earned his Ph.D from the University of Aberdeen, Scotland, where he focused on

Islamic microfinance and Maqasid Shariah. His academic and professional interests encompass Islamic banking and finance, Islamic social finance and Halal studies.

Shujahat Ali, holds a PhD in Management Sciences from the University of Science and Technology of China (USTC) in Hefei, a prestigious institution consistently ranked among the top 100 universities globally. Graduating from the School of Management, which is accredited by the renowned AACSB and AMBA, Dr. Ali has established a strong foundation in his field. During his time at USTC, he served as a graduate instructor, imparting knowledge and inspiring students in China. His commitment to societal betterment is reflected in his active participation in community development projects with non-governmental organizations. Currently an Assistant Professor, Dr. Ali also heads the Technology Incubation Center and Entrepreneurship Research Lab. His specialization in entrepreneurship innovation and SME finance is complemented by his expertise in business research methods, CSR, media, finance, and behavioral studies. As a researcher, Dr. Ali's work is instrumental in bridging theoretical knowledge with practical applications, fostering an environment of innovation and entrepreneurship.

Sevdie Alshiqi Bekteshi is an Assistant Professor at the University of Prishtina "Hasan Prishtina", specializing in Management and Informatics within the Faculty of Economics. She holds dual Doctor of Science degrees in Entrepreneurship and SME Management from the Regional Joint Doctoral Programme in Entrepreneurship and SME Management for Western Balkan Countries (DOCSMES) at St. Climent University Bitola, and a Doctor of Business Administration (DBA) from Université Côte d'Azur in Nice, France. With over 19 years of professional experience, Dr. Bekteshi serves as the co-owner and CEO of Business Kosova Center, focusing on teaching, economic development consultancy, and training in areas such as financial management, human resources, organizational development, and financial strategies for small and medium enterprises (SMEs). She is an accredited counselor and trainer under the Counseling and Training Scheme supported by Vaucher, an initiative of the Agency for Support of SMEs within the Ministry of Trade and Industry. In this capacity, she provides business consulting and training services for SMEs in Kosovo.

Syaza Azhari is currently a Senior Lecturer in the Industrial Chemical Technology Programme at the Faculty of Science, Universiti Sains Islam Malaysia (USIM). She obtained her Bachelor of Science in Chemistry from Universiti Teknologi Malaysia (UTM) in 2011, followed by a Doctor of Philosophy (Ph.D.) in Chemistry from the same institution in 2017. Her research interests lie in environmental chemistry and electrochemistry, with a focus on developing innovative and sustainable solutions to address environmental challenges.

Siti Nur Azizah is a lecturer in the Sharia Banking Program at the Faculty of Islamic Economics and Business, State Islamic University (UIN) Sunan Kalijaga Yogyakarta, Indonesia. Her research interests include Islamic economics, Islamic banking, the Halal industry, gender studies, and family economics.

Zahidah Borhan is a Business Administration degree holder with a strong passion for sustainability and waste management. This interest grew during her visit to South Korea after experiencing the country's efficient waste management system. This inspired her to investigate similar issues in Brunei as her final year research with an emphasis on consumer behaviour and household food waste. With a strong commitment to environmental responsibility, she aspires to make a significant impact by conducting research that encourages sustainable habits across various fields including but not limited to food waste.

Buyamin Buyamin, Associate Researcher at the Research Center for Public Policy, National Research and Innovation Agency, Indonesia, since 2021. Previously experienced in management functions at the Ministry of Transmigration of the Republic of Indonesia and also at the Ministry of Manpower of the Republic of Indonesia.

Wajahat Ali Ghulam is a doctoral researcher at the School of Management, University of Science and Technology of China (USTC). His research interests span the domains of halal entrepreneurship, sustainable business models, Islamic finance, and knowledge-based innovation systems. With a strong foundation in entrepreneurship and management sciences, he actively contributes to research that bridges ethical frameworks and business practices. Wajahat has participated in various international research collaborations and has published in peer-reviewed journals focused on sustainability, ethical entrepreneurship, and socio-economic development. He is committed to advancing scholarship that aligns with the United Nations Sustainable Development Goals (SDGs) and the principles of value-driven enterprise.

Halili Halili was born in Jember on April 25, 1993. He received intensive education at Nurul Qarnain Islamic Boarding School in Jember (2007–2011), and continued his studies at Salafiyah Syafiiyah Sukorejo Islamic Boarding School in Situbondo (2011–2018). He also studied at Ma'had Aly Li Ilma al-Fiqh wa Ushulih Sukorejo as a student of Marhalah Ula and Tsani (M1–M2) from 2011 to 2017. He completed his undergraduate degree in Islamic Guidance and Counseling (S.Sos.) at Institut Agama Islam Ibrahimy Sukorejo Situbondo in 2018, followed by a Master's degree in Islamic Economics (M.E.) at Universitas KH Achmad Shiddiq Jember (2019–2021). Currently, he is pursuing doctoral studies (PhD) in Islamic Studies at

Universitas KH Achmad Shiddiq Jember (since 2024). Presently, he works as a lecturer at Sekolah Tinggi Ilmu Syariah Nurul Qarnain Jember.

Zaenol Hasan was born in Bondowoso on October 26, 1993. He received intensive education at Nurul Qarnain Islamic Boarding School in Jember (2007–2011), and continued his studies at Salafiyah Syafiiyah Sukorejo Islamic Boarding School in Situbondo (2011–2018). He also studied at Ma'had Aly Li Ilma al-Fiqh wa Ushulih Sukorejo as a student of Marhalah Ula and Tsani (M1–M2) from 2011 to 2017. He completed his undergraduate degree in Economics (S.E.) at Institut Agama Islam Ibrahimy Sukorejo Situbondo in 2017, followed by a Master of Laws (M.H.) at Universitas Ibrahimy Sukorejo Situbondo (2017–2019). Currently, he is pursuing doctoral studies (PhD) in Islamic Studies at Universitas KH Achmad Shiddiq Jember (since 2024). At present, he works as a lecturer at Sekolah Tinggi Ilmu Syariah Nurul Qarnain Jember. He is an active member of the Association of Islamic Economic Law Study Programs and Lecturers in Indonesia (POSDHESI)

Andre Hasudungan Lubis serves as a lecturer in the Informatics Engineering program at the Faculty of Engineering, University of Medan, and holds the position of Head of the Informatics Engineering Laboratory at Medan Area University. He earned his Bachelor's degree in Information Technology from the Faculty of Computer Science and Information Technology at the University of North Sumatra in 2015 and later obtained a Master's degree in Communication and Information Technology from Universiti Malaysia Perlis in 2017. His research focuses on data science, multi-criteria decision-making, and topics related to social informatics. Additionally, he is pursuing a Ph.D. in Machine Learning, further expanding his expertise in the field. Through his academic and research contributions, Andre continues to play an active role in advancing technology, especially in utilization of artificial intelligence in marketing.

Syamila Mansor is a University Lecturer specializing in Food Science and Technology, with expertise in food labelling, regulations, halal science, food safety and quality, food processing, and product development. She holds a Ph.D. in Bioscience from the University of Nottingham, UK, a Master of Science from Drexel University, USA, and a Bachelor of Science (Hons) from Universiti Sains Islam Malaysia (USIM). Her work focuses on sustainable food innovations, including alternative protein and carotenoids sources, fruit seed utilization, and green solvents for antioxidant extraction, guided by Islamic principles and halalan thayyiban values.

Riza Fanny Meutia is a dedicated academic and researcher affiliated with Universitas Medan Area. She specializes in management and has published several studies on consumer behavior, brand image, and digital marketing. Her work includes articles in reputable international journals, highlighting her expertise in social media empowerment and business development. Riza is passionate about contributing to the understanding of marketing strategies among young consumers in Medan. She continues to pursue her academic and professional growth to make meaningful impacts in her field.

Hj. Hasan Al-Banna Mohamed is a Professor in Department of Management, Faculty of Management and Defence Studies, National Defence University of Malaysia (NDUM), Kuala Lumpur. He obtained his PhD from Malaya University (MU) in the Islamic Quality Management in 2015. In addition to the academic post, he experienced working as the Director for Division of Quality Assurance and Data Management, UPNM from 2010 until 2022. After that, he has been appointed as a Senior Director for the Project Management and Strategic Planning Division, in the Assistant Vice Chancellor office (Project Management and Strategic Development), NDUM and was promoted to Assistant Vice Chancellor (Project Management and Strategy Development) and after the organizational restructuring in 2025, he was appointed as Assistant Vice Chancellor (Data Management and Quality) at NDUM. His areas of expertise and research are in Islamic Management, Quality Management, Human Resource Development and HRM, Islamic Studies.

Mohd Zohdi Mohd Amin is an Associate Professor at the Faculty of Quran and Sunnah Studies (FPQS), Universiti Sains Islam Malaysia (USIM). He was born on 31 January 1974 in Pekan, Pahang, and obtained his Bachelor's degree in Usuluddin from Al al-Bayt University, Jordan (1999), his Master's degree in Quran and Sunnah Studies from Universiti Kebangsaan Malaysia (2002), and his PhD in Quran and Hadith Studies (2014). He has served at USIM since 1999, holding several key positions including Head of the Quran with Multimedia Program (2014–2016), Deputy Dean of Academic and Research (2016–2020), and currently Dean of FPQS since 2021. His expertise focuses on Hadith and Islamic psychospiritual studies, particularly in addressing issues such as drug abuse, gender dysphoria, Islamic healing, and wisdom-based da'wah approaches. He has led several major research projects funded under the Fundamental Research Grant Scheme (FRGS), including the development of psychospiritual therapy models based on the Quran and Hadith for drug rehabilitation and transgender recovery, as well as a holistic framework for community guidance centers grounded in psychospiritual therapy.

Mohd Mahyeddin Mohd Salleh is a university lecturer in the Shariah (Halal Industry) programme at the Faculty of Syariah and Law, Universiti Sains Islam Malaysia. He also serves as the Coordinator of the Research, Publication and Innovation Unit at the Institute of Fatwa and Halal (IFFAH), Universiti Sains Islam

Malaysia. Dr. Mahyeddin earned his Ph.D. in Shariah and Halal Laws from Universiti Putra Malaysia. His areas of expertise include Shariah and Halal Laws, Halal Issues and Fatwa, Islamic Consumerism and Veterinary Fiqh.

Ridan Muhtadi is a Lecturer in the Department of Islamic Economics, Faculty of Sharia, Institut Agama Islam Miftahul Ulum (IAIMU), Pamekasan, Indonesia. He has served as Chairperson of the Indonesian Cooperative Council (DEKOPIN) at the District Level for Pamekasan Regency since 2023–2025. Additionally, he is actively involved in several non-governmental organizations, including the Nahdlatul Ulama Economic Institution (LPNU) and the Indonesian Islamic Economics Society (MES). His research interests include Islamic economics, Islamic banking and finance, Islamic wealth management, and Islamic business management. He has authored several international journal articles and book chapters. He is currently pursuing a PhD at UIN Kiai Haji Ahmad Siddiq Jember in the Department of Islamic Studies, following completion of his Master's degree (MSc) in Islamic Economics at Universitas Airlangga, Indonesia.

Khairunnisa Musari is an Assistant Professor at Faculty of Islamic Economics and Business (FEBI) & Postgraduate Program, Kiai Haji Achmad Siddiq State Islamic University (UIN KHAS), Jember, Indonesia. She is a Secretary of the Indonesian Association of Islamic Economists (IAEI) for the Provincial Board of East Java and a member of the International Association for Islamic Economics (IAIE). Her research interests in sukuk, waqf, esham, fiscal & monetary policies, circular economy, halal logistics, sustainable finance, climate change, and Islamic microfinance & nanofinance. She has several book chapters with international reputable publishers such as IGI Global, Emerald Publishing Limited, World Scientific Publishing, Routledge, Springer, and Palgrave Macmillan. She has experience as a Senior Specialist for Islamic Finance of United Nations Development Programme (UNDP) Indonesia and was listed as one of the Top 300 Most Influential Women in Islamic Business & Finance 2019, 2020, 2021, WOMANi Significancica 2022, and WOMANi Academica 2023, 2024, by Cambridge-IFA.

A'wani Aziz, Nurdalila received her secondary education at SMK Jalan Bukit, Kajang, Selangor. She pursued her undergraduate studies at Universiti Selangor. From her Bachelor's degree, she advanced directly to the Doctor of Philosophy (PhD) level without the need to complete a Master's degree. Her PhD was conducted through research in the field of Systems Biology at Universiti Kebangsaan Malaysia (UKM). She is currently serving as a senior lecturer at Kolej PERMATA Insan (KPI) and as a Coordinator at the Institute of Fatwa and Halal (IFFAH), Universiti Sains Islam Malaysia (USIM).

Nur Shaliza Sapiai brings over two decades of expertise in the education sector, specializing in knowledge management.

Zulfia Hanum Alfi Syahr is a researcher at the Research Center for Public Policy of National Research and Innovation Agency since 2022 until now. The career as a researcher began from 2015 to 2021 at the Center for Research and Development of Law and Justice of the Law and Training and Judicial Agency of the Supreme Court of the Republic of Indonesia. With the research expertise is public management with focus on judicial management and public service management in government institutions.

Wahyu Wibowo is a graduate student in the Master's Program in Shariah Economics at UIN Sunan Kalijaga Yogyakarta. His academic interests include the Halal industry, Islamic philanthropy, and economic literacy. He received four DIKTI-funded PKM grants (2012–2014), three of which focused on community service—ranging from Jarimatika training to literary-mathematical education for orphans, one of which was selected as a national finalist. He also initiated an entrepreneurship project titled IBU SASTIKA (Innovative Mathematical Literature Book) that combines educational innovation with creative content.

Nazariyah Yahaya University Lecturer, Program Food Biotechnology, Faculty of Science and Technology, Universiti Sains Islam Malaysia. Nazariyah earned her Ph.D. in Plant Science from the University of Sheffield, United Kingdom. Since joining USIM, she has focused on plant-microbe interactions, functional food, future food, and halal science.

Zuhaira Muhammad Zain received her B.IT degree in Information Science from Universiti Kebangsaan Malaysia in 2000, an M.IT degree in Computer Science from Universiti Kebangsaan Malaysia in 2007, and a Ph.D. degree in Software Engineering from Universiti Putra Malaysia in 2013. She was a Programmer with Fujitsu System Business Malaysia Bhd. from 2000 to 2007. She works as Associate Professor at the College of Computer and Information Sciences, Princess Nourah bint Abdulrahman University, Riyadh, Saudi Arabia. Her research interests include software engineering, data mining, machine learning, deep learning, data analytics, software quality, and software evaluation.

Index

A

Artificial Intelligence 1, 2, 3, 5, 7, 9, 22, 23, 28, 32, 33, 39, 40, 41, 44, 45, 47, 53, 55, 58, 125, 241, 244, 278, 280, 310, 311, 312, 313, 315, 316, 317, 319, 320, 335

B

Behavioural Intentions 249, 255, 256, 257, 265, 318
brand love 249, 250, 251, 252, 253, 254, 255, 257, 259, 261, 262, 263, 264, 265, 266, 268, 269, 271, 272, 273, 274, 275
brand trust 254, 255, 257, 261, 263, 267, 269, 271, 274, 275
Bridging 22, 35, 36, 38, 45, 48, 49, 50, 51, 52, 53, 54, 55, 56, 95, 110, 196, 363
Business Ecosystem 109, 151, 163, 240, 303, 308, 365

C

Cold Chain Logistics 321, 322, 324, 326, 327, 328, 329, 330, 331, 333
Consumer Loyalty 265, 273, 277, 280, 281, 284, 285, 287, 289, 290, 291, 292, 293, 295, 305, 306, 307, 308, 309
CRM 277, 278, 279, 280, 281, 283, 284, 285, 287, 288, 289, 290, 291, 294, 295, 296, 304, 305, 306, 307, 308, 309, 310, 315

D

Digital Literacy 23, 277, 280, 290, 291, 292, 293, 306, 307, 308, 309, 311, 313, 315, 319
Digital Transformation 1, 2, 4, 9, 12, 15, 17, 19, 20, 22, 23, 25, 26, 28, 31, 37, 64, 120, 154, 162

E

Eco-Innovation 89, 90, 92, 93, 94, 95, 99, 100, 101, 102, 103, 104, 105, 106, 107, 111, 112, 114, 115, 117, 118, 119, 120, 122, 123, 125, 126
ECT 280, 285, 286, 288, 289, 290, 291, 292, 305, 307, 308, 309
Edible Insect 194, 216, 220, 221, 222

F

Fatwa and Halal 193, 218
Food Processing 71, 205, 208, 221
Food Safety 4, 33, 52, 75, 193, 209, 213, 214, 215, 221, 223, 267, 330, 333, 335, 370, 372, 373, 377, 379, 380, 381, 384, 385, 386
Food Waste 14, 125, 127, 128, 129, 130, 131, 132, 133, 134, 135, 136, 137, 139, 140, 141, 142, 143, 144, 145, 146, 147, 148, 149, 150, 204
Food Waste Reduction 129, 131, 141, 144, 149
Future Food 193, 196, 214, 215, 219

H

Halal branding 226, 252, 255, 265
Halal Business 40, 67, 95, 106, 112, 113, 114, 127, 157, 163, 277, 280, 284, 285, 294, 303, 307, 308, 309
Halal E-Commerce 9, 32, 225, 228, 229, 230, 231, 236, 237, 239, 243, 279, 294, 298
Halal Entrepreneurship 151, 152, 153, 155, 156, 157, 158, 159, 162, 163, 165, 166, 167, 168, 170, 172, 173, 174, 177, 178, 179, 181, 182, 187, 188, 189, 190, 231
halal fast food 249, 263, 266, 272
Halal Food 18, 25, 28, 29, 31, 32, 33, 44, 52, 58, 62, 63, 74, 84, 87, 92, 94, 96, 123, 127, 128, 129, 132, 133, 134, 136, 153, 155, 157, 158, 159, 160, 161, 164, 169, 170, 171, 172, 173, 180, 190, 194, 196, 197, 230, 241,

250, 251, 252, 254, 255, 261, 264, 267, 268, 269, 270, 273, 274, 294, 312, 316, 340, 341, 351, 356, 372, 379, 388, 389, 390
Halal Industry 1, 2, 3, 9, 12, 14, 19, 20, 22, 25, 26, 28, 33, 36, 37, 39, 40, 42, 45, 49, 50, 55, 56, 60, 61, 67, 69, 70, 71, 72, 73, 79, 83, 84, 85, 86, 87, 89, 90, 91, 92, 93, 94, 95, 96, 97, 99, 104, 105, 106, 108, 109, 110, 111, 113, 114, 115, 116, 117, 118, 119, 124, 125, 144, 160, 161, 165, 174, 177, 179, 180, 181, 195, 215, 216, 226, 227, 229, 230, 231, 238, 239, 242, 246, 250, 252, 268, 275, 278, 279, 280, 282, 285, 286, 288, 289, 291, 292, 294, 295, 308, 319, 331, 333, 336, 338, 361, 363, 365, 372, 374, 377, 379, 380, 383, 384, 385
Halal Information Systems 35, 36, 37, 38, 39, 40, 41, 43, 44, 45, 47, 48, 49, 50, 51, 52, 54, 55, 56
Halal marketing 175, 227, 228, 286, 315, 317
halal products 2, 5, 8, 9, 10, 11, 13, 14, 25, 32, 36, 39, 41, 43, 49, 50, 60, 65, 67, 69, 70, 71, 72, 73, 74, 75, 85, 87, 88, 90, 93, 97, 105, 106, 110, 118, 119, 144, 152, 155, 156, 157, 161, 162, 164, 170, 178, 187, 188, 215, 216, 228, 231, 243, 250, 252, 253, 267, 272, 282, 284, 296, 325, 328, 329, 351, 379, 381
Halal Travel 279, 337, 342, 343, 344, 350

I

Insect-Based Product 194, 196, 205
Insect Protein 193, 194, 195, 196, 197, 209, 210, 211, 212, 213, 214, 216, 219, 220, 221, 222
Islamic Business Ethics 29, 32, 62, 126, 227, 229, 230, 234, 242, 246, 268, 281, 282
Islamic Theories 37, 38, 39, 41, 45, 48, 49, 54, 55, 56, 57
Islamic Thought 60, 242

M

Maqā id al-Sharīʿah 226, 228, 229, 230, 232, 233, 235, 236, 237, 238, 240, 337, 339, 340, 341, 342, 343, 344, 350, 351, 352, 353, 354, 355, 357, 358, 359, 360, 378
Marketing Control Framework 225, 227, 232, 236, 237, 238, 239
Muslim-Friendly Tourism 337, 338, 339, 340, 341, 342, 344, 350, 352, 353, 354, 355, 356, 358, 359, 360

N

Non-Islamic context 177, 179

O

Operational Challenges 101, 321, 323, 326, 330

P

Pesantren 89, 90, 91, 92, 93, 94, 95, 97, 98, 99, 100, 101, 102, 103, 104, 105, 106, 107, 108, 109, 110, 111, 112, 113, 114, 115, 116, 117, 118, 119, 120, 121, 122, 123, 124, 125, 126

Q

Qingzhen 185, 186, 187, 188, 189, 190

R

Religious Tolerance 388

S

Shariah-Compliant Marketing 225, 226
SOR Framework 314
Supply Chain Integrity 6, 26, 28, 62, 128, 230, 231, 241, 384
Sustainable Halal Industry 70, 89, 91, 95, 97, 104, 105, 106, 111, 114, 118, 119, 229, 230

T

TAM 280, 285, 286, 289, 290, 291, 292, 304, 306, 307, 308, 309, 310, 311, 312, 314, 315, 316
Theory of Planned Behaviour 127, 131, 132, 134, 135, 136, 137, 142, 143, 264
Travel Intention 337, 350, 352, 356

W

Western Theories 35, 36, 37, 38, 42, 44, 45, 48, 49, 54, 55, 56, 57

www.ingramcontent.com/pod-product-compliance
Lightning Source LLC
LaVergne TN
LVHW061526290926
849162LV00004B/682